Oracle SQL Developer 2.1

Database design and development using this feature-rich, powerful, user-extensible interface

Sue Harper

BIRMINGHAM - MUMBAI

Oracle SQL Developer 2.1

First published: November 2009

Production Reference: 1171109

Published by Packt Publishing Ltd.
32 Lincoln Road
Olton
Birmingham, B27 6PA, UK.

ISBN 978-1-847196-26-2

www.packtpub.com

Cover Image by Sue Harper (sue.harper@oracle.com)

Credits

Author
Sue Harper

Reviewers
Barry McGillin
Michael Wickham
Dermot O'Neill
Joyce Scapicchio
Kris Rice
Raghvendra Saboo
Vadim Tropashko

Acquisition Editor
James Lumsden

Development Editor
Ved Prakash Jha

Technical Editor
Hithesh Uchil

Indexer
Monica Ajmera

Editorial Team Leader
Akshara Aware

Project Team Leader
Priya Mukherji

Project Coordinator
Leena Purkait

Proofreader
Joel T. Johnson

Graphics
Nilesh R. Mohite

Production Coordinator
Adline Swetha Jesuthas

Cover Work
Adline Swetha Jesuthas

About the Author

Sue Harper is a product manager for Oracle SQL Developer, SQL Developer Data Modeler, and SQL Developer Migrations working in the Database Development Tools group at Oracle. She has a BSc in Mathematics and Physics from the University of the Witwatersrand, Johannesburg, and a post graduate teaching diploma. It was this teaching qualification that opened the doors to working with Oracle products in South Africa, where Sue started as an instructor in 1992, teaching SQL, PL/SQL, and SQL Forms and Reports. Before long, she'd added Oracle Designer to her repertoire and soon left for the UK to join the Oracle Designer curriculum development team. Sue was a course writer and then an Oracle Designer product manager, traveling extensively, meeting customers, presenting at conferences, and running train-the-trainer classes. Later, she became a product manager for Oracle JDeveloper working with the database and modeling tools and helping the Oracle Designer community learn about the new tools, before moving to the Database Development Tools group.

Based at home, Sue works with her team scattered around the world and with customers. She runs web-based training sessions and writes supporting material for the products. She frequently attends and presents at conferences and has a number of blogs, which she contributes to sporadically.

Sue lives in West London, where she enjoys walking her dog in the extensive local parks. As a walker, her favorite stomping ground is the Drakensberg in South Africa. With the 'berg' too many miles away, any local hills will do. As a keen photographer, she now enjoys the long distance trails in the UK and is often out in the countryside with her camera.

Acknowledgement

I'd like to thank the people who have helped me complete this book. In particular Barry McGillin, who reviewed each chapter for technical errors, and Michael Wickham, who joined Barry, to add his technical insight when my writing became more sporadic and the chapters backed up! The editorial staff and publishing team at Packt who patiently accepted each new delay to the schedule, while gently reminding me of the ever-encroaching deadlines.

I'd like to thank my friends who patiently listened each time I said I couldn't go out, "because I was writing…" even those in different countries who were also on the receiving end of my tales that life had become seven-days SQL Developer!

I wasn't planning on writing a book. Working with the product, the team, and customers keeps me busy enough, but there seemed to be more demand for a source of answers to the many questions that bubble up to the surface from forums and events, that it seemed a good thing to do. Believe it or not, I enjoyed it. This would not have been possible without the support of my team, which I am very happy to be a part of. Despite the distances, we are in regular contact, whether chatting to team members in Ireland or Northern Ireland, India or Bulgaria, or in any of the various States of America. We know that we can pick up the phone or dash off a quick instant messenger note and have a chat or ask a question. In particular, I'd like to thank my manager, Kris Rice, and Mike Hichwa who runs the group. Without their guidance and support, the team wouldn't work the way it does, a rare gift when managing a remote and culturally disparate group. Kris in particular, who has his hands full helping me keep things in perspective and constantly tries to help me maintain the balance.

About the Reviewers

Barry McGillin is the development manager for Oracle SQL Developer and has been with Oracle over 15 years. He is married to Lisa with two children, Rebecca and Katie-Ellen. Barry holds an honors degree in Computing and Information Systems from the University of Ulster and lives in Omagh, Northern Ireland. He has worked across most business areas in Oracle, from product development support and consulting, specializing in core database technology, and database migration, before working with Sue Harper and Kris Rice on Oracle SQL Developer. Barry has worked on several books as a Reviewer and Technical Advisor over the years, culminating in this work with Sue.

I'd like to thank Sue for asking me to review this book. She has a passion for completeness and accuracy, which has helped us create better tools for our customers. I'd also like to thank my family, my wife Lisa for patience, love and support, and the tea and coffee. And lastly, my two little ladies, Rebecca and Katie-Ellen who constantly challenge us to answer the questions of life and force us to be better as a result of trying to.

Michael Wickham is the Global Technical Lead for SQL Developer at Oracle Technical Support. He has a Bachelors Degree and Masters Degree in Computer Science from Colorado Technical University, an Associates Degree in Electronics and an Associates Degree in Aviation.

Michael may be reached at `mwickham_1@comcast.net`

Other interests are Videography and Hydroponics.

I would like to thank Sue Harper who has authored this book. For the years of assistance that she has given me and for all she has done for the advancement of Oracle Tools such as Oracle Designer, SQL Developer, SQL Developer Data Modeler, and others.

Table of Contents

Preface

Oracle SQL Developer is a relatively new product included in the range of Oracle products. It was first introduced to the world in September 2005, by its code name Project Raptor. Raptor is a name many still cling to, despite being replaced very quickly with the full product name, Oracle SQL Developer (and referred to in the rest of the book as SQL Developer). The first production version was released in early 2006 and had many Oracle customers both skeptical and excited.

SQL Developer is a Graphical User Interface (GUI) for browsing and working with databases. Primarily developed for the Oracle database, it also provides a GUI for a selection of popular non-Oracle databases. As technology has evolved, many developers are looking for modern tools to assist them in daily tasks. A clean, easy to navigate interface is essential and many tools are judged on looks, performance, and functionality.

Initially billed as a light-weight, clean, easy to install GUI for the Oracle database, SQL Developer is gaining momentum in the market and broadening its scope in its offering.

The skeptics mentioned are ever concerned that Oracle is not really interested in the product, backing up this concern with the fact that SQL Developer is free. Disappointing as it is that "free" is equated with "poor quality", the last couple of years have considerably stilled many of these dissenting voices and the market using SQL Developer continues to increase. Time will tell.

What this book covers

The book is designed to allow you to dip into any chapter that is your current area of focus. Having said that, if you have never used SQL Developer before, are new to Oracle and SQL, or have never used a GUI tool before, we recommend that you read the introduction, which gets you started slowly. You can then work through the first few chapters in order. Once you have covered the first three chapters, you should be on your way.

As the chapters progress, while they do not necessarily get more complex, they do rely to some extent on existing knowledge. The latter portion of the book is not considered to be more complex, but instead focuses on areas used by specific target audiences, such as Oracle Application Express or migrating from non-Oracle databases.

We have loosely divided the book into the following three sections.

I: Getting started

The first few chapters introduce SQL Developer. Use them to get to know the layout of the product and the essential features it provides. For those new to Oracle, or application developers who spend the day using other development tools, these first few chapters may be the only chapters needed.

In *Chapter 1: Getting Started with Oracle SQL Developer*, we provide general information about SQL Developer, where you can find it, how to install it, and how to get started. Using a simple example, you quickly walk through the product, touching a variety of areas to get a feel for the navigation, the layout, and some of the features available. We introduce the environment, how to navigate and manage the interface, the database, and schemas used in this book. The chapter includes tips for customizing the environment to suit your preferences.

In *Chapter 2: Browsing and Editing Database Objects and Data*, you will create, edit, and update database objects, such as tables, views, sequences, and instance data (the data in those tables), using data grids. You'll also learn how to access and use the utilities, wizards, and dialogs, which SQL Developer provides, to work with data and database objects. Lastly, you will use SQL commands and scripts, accessing the code formatter and other assistants that separate a GUI tool from a command-line environment.

In *Chapter 3: Working with the SQL Worksheet*, you see that the SQL Worksheet provides a scratch pad for all SQL, PL/SQL, and SQL*Plus statements and commands. In this chapter, you learn to work with the SQL Worksheet and the commands it supports, how to use code insight, templates, snippets, and formatting code. You learn how to manage the environment and to work with multiple worksheets. We introduce the Query Builder and how to write, test, and run SQL queries using the Query Builder.

In *Chapter 4: The Power of SQL Reports*, you look at the variety of SQL reports provided by SQL Developer, why they are useful in daily tasks, and how to run and use them. You'll learn how to create your own reports, such as master-detail or drill-down reports, and share your user-defined reports.

II: Delving a little deeper

These chapters are intended for all developers, perhaps more focused on those of you who spend your days working with database objects and data. While not strictly advanced features, there are areas here that can be more involved, and knowledge of how the tool works will complement your existing knowledge of developing and working with code.

In *Chapter 5: Working with PL/SQL*, we start by reviewing various PL/SQL structures. This chapter covers creating, editing, compiling, and debugging PL/SQL code. You'll see how the various search tools work, and use code templates and snippets. You'll learn how to refactor PL/SQL code, and search using the Oracle Database 11g PL/Scope feature.

Chapter 6: SQL and PL/SQL Tuning Tools. Although not designed to teach you how to optimize your code, this chapter shows you the different utilities that SQL Developer provides to help you see problem areas and work at fixing them. Utilities include using Explain Plan, reviewing trace files, and auto trace.

In *Chapter 7: Managing Files*, you'll see that SQL Developer provides an integrated file navigator that allows you to browse the file system and open files from within the tool. This chapter introduces the file navigator and the features it supports. Working in conjunction with the file navigator, SQL Developer integrates with open source version control systems. This chapter discusses the alternatives and shows you how to place your code under version control and work within a team sharing code, by comparing and merging code.

In *Chapter 8: Importing, Exporting, and Working with Data*, you'll learn how SQL Developer provides a number of utilities for moving or copying both the data structures and the instance data between schemas and databases. This chapter introduces you to the schema copy, diff, and export wizards and related export and import utilities.

III: Focus areas

The last few chapters are focused on specific audiences. We don't specifically cover complex features, but there are aspects of some of these features that require knowledge beyond the scope of this book.

In *Chapter 9: Database Connections and JDBC Drivers*, we'll look at the various types of database connections available, how to set them up, and when to use them. We'll look at various authentication methods, such as LDAP, OS authentication or strong authentication methods like Kerberos, and compare Basic, TNS, and JDBC connections.

This chapter also looks at setting up the required JDBC drivers and creating connections to non-Oracle databases. The chapter closes with a section on managing your connections.

Chapter 10: Introducing SQL Developer Data Modeler. Whether you just want a diagram of how your tables connect, or you want to build an entity relationship diagram, transform that to a relational model, and generate the DDL script to create the objects in your database, the SQL Developer Data Modeler provides the tools you need. This chapter introduces some of the modeling utilities available in SQL Developer Data Modeler. You'll also learn about the integration points with SQL Developer and the Data Modeler Viewer in SQL Developer.

In *Chapter 11: Extending SQL Developer*, you'll see that SQL Developer is an extensible tool. This means you, as an end user of the tool, can add in your own features. These may be small, providing just a single input or output field, and only require XML and SQL knowledge, while others are more extensive and require Java skills. This chapter reviews the various ways you can extend SQL Developer using SQL and XML.

In *Chapter 12: Working with Application Express*, you'll see how SQL Developer connects to and provides utilities for interacting with Application Express (Oracle APEX). In this chapter, features you'll learn to use include setting up the environment to work with Oracle APEX, importing, browsing, and deploying applications. You'll also see how to tune and refactor SQL and PL/SQL code.

In *Chapter 13: Working with SQL Developer Migrations*, you'll understand how SQL Developer helps you connect to and browse non-Oracle or third-party databases. This chapter looks at preparing the SQL Developer environment, and browsing the supported third-party databases. The focus of the chapter is on migrating from a third-party database to Oracle, from setting up the repository, through the capture and conversion phases, and ending with data migration. You'll also learn to translate pieces of code, such as translating T-SQL to PL/SQL.

Standards and assumptions

Unless otherwise stated, the environment used in the examples and referred to throughout the book is Oracle Database 11g Release 1, installed on Microsoft Windows XP. We use the shipped Oracle sample schemas, in addition to using the **SYSTEM** and **SYS** users.

Oracle offers a free database, Oracle Express Edition 10g (XE), which you can download and use for many of the examples. Some of the discussion is related to new Oracle Database 11g functionality that is not available on any Oracle Database 10g release, including XE. In the case where the feature is Oracle Database 11g specific, the text will indicate this. However, the text does not list anomalies for each database version.

This book was written using and is based on Oracle SQL Developer 2.1. Screenshots and menu items all refer to SQL Developer 2.1 and were accurate at the time of writing, completed just prior to the production release of the software. Minor differences are inevitable due to changes in the later stages of product development prior to production. You can also use the book, and much of the content, as a guide for working with earlier releases of SQL Developer. Where they are significant, we make note of the differences in features that have changed from earlier releases.

Who this book is for

This book provides you with in-depth detail about all aspects of using SQL Developer to assist you in your day-to-day database tasks and activities. It will also make you more productive in some of the more mundane tasks, while providing you with an extensible environment to support your ongoing needs.

No attempt is made to teach Oracle, SQL, or PL/SQL, or to suggest best practices. However, if you are new to the environment, SQL Developer should ably assist you in getting familiar with the database, SQL, and PL/SQL. We'll show you how to create data models and extend existing data designs. We do not teach data modeling and design. Additionally, no part of the book is focused on using non-Oracle databases, except when browsing or importing objects from these for the purpose of migration.

If you have ever accessed an Oracle Database for information on any database objects you are working with, such as tables, constraints, data, or PL/SQL code, whether you are building applications, doing data analysis, or just working with database structures, then you can use SQL Developer for these tasks and this book might be for you! If you are adept with SQL and PL/SQL, know your way around the database, and you're a command-line user, you might be intrigued and we hope that you can dip into this book on an ad hoc basis to get you started and on the road to a "GUI life". We're aware that you'll never fully move from the command-line, but you may well find that using the utilities SQL Developer provides, frees up some of your time to build a few extensions, providing an interface for the utilities you almost certainly already have! For those of you familiar with any of the many GUI tools available today, this book can help you with the details and specifics that make SQL Developer popular.

In general, you'll get more out of the book if you know SQL, PL/SQL, and have a general familiarity with Oracle concepts. There is excellent Oracle Documentation available online, so you can access those if we move into an area that is new to you.

Conventions

In this book, you will find a number of styles of text that distinguish between different kinds of information. Here are some examples of these styles, and an explanation of their meaning.

Code words in text are shown as follows: " To see the value of the bind variable in the worksheet shown, enter the SQL*Plus `PRINT` command. For example, `PRINT DEPTNUM`."

A block of code is set as follows:

```
SELECT DEPARTMENT_NAME
FROM DEPARTMENTS WHERE DEPARTMENT_NAME = &DNAME;
```

When we wish to draw your attention to a particular part of a code block, the relevant lines or items are set in bold:

```
SELECT EMPLOYEE_ID,FIRST_NAME,LAST_NAME,EMAIL,DEPARTMENT_ID
FROM EMPLOYEES
WHERE department_id = :DEPARTMENT_ID
```

New terms and **important words** are shown in bold. Words that you see on the screen, in menus or dialog boxes for example, appear in the text like this: "Select the **Output SQL** option, and select the required language from the drop-down list".

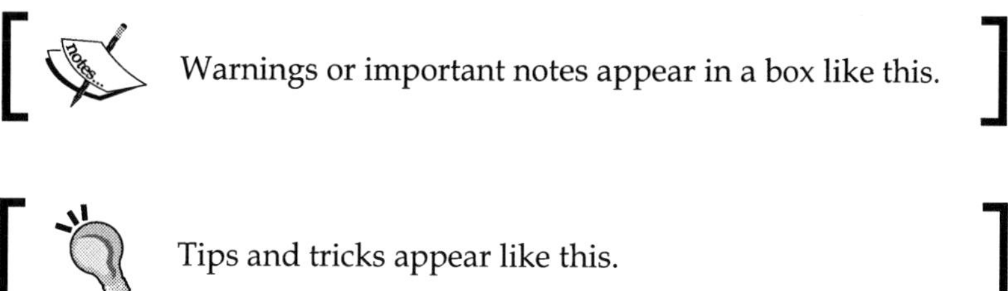

Reader feedback

Feedback from our readers is always welcome. Let us know what you think about this book—what you liked or may have disliked. Reader feedback is important for us to develop titles that you really get the most out of.

To send us general feedback, simply send an email to `feedback@packtpub.com`, and mention the book title via the subject of your message.

If there is a book that you need and would like to see us publish, please send us a note in the **SUGGEST A TITLE** form on `www.packtpub.com` or email `suggest@packtpub.com`.

If there is a topic that you have expertise in and you are interested in either writing or contributing to a book on, see our author guide on `www.packtpub.com/authors`.

Customer support

Now that you are the proud owner of a Packt book, we have a number of things to help you to get the most from your purchase.

Downloading the example code for the book

Visit `http://www.packtpub.com/files/code/6262_Code.zip` to directly download the example code.

Errata

Although we have taken every care to ensure the accuracy of our content, mistakes do happen. If you find a mistake in one of our books—maybe a mistake in the text or the code—we would be grateful if you would report this to us. By doing so, you can save other readers from frustration, and help us to improve subsequent versions of this book. If you find any errata, please report them by visiting `http://www.packtpub.com/support`, selecting your book, clicking on the **let us know** link, and entering the details of your errata. Once your errata are verified, your submission will be accepted and the errata added to any list of existing errata. Any existing errata can be viewed by selecting your title from `http://www.packtpub.com/support`.

Piracy

Piracy of copyright material on the Internet is an ongoing problem across all media. At Packt, we take the protection of our copyright and licenses very seriously. If you come across any illegal copies of our works, in any form, on the Internet, please provide us with the location address or web site name immediately so that we can pursue a remedy.

Please contact us at `copyright@packtpub.com` with a link to the suspected pirated material.

We appreciate your help in protecting our authors, and our ability to bring you valuable content.

Questions

You can contact us at `questions@packtpub.com` if you are having a problem with any aspect of the book, and we will do our best to address it.

1
Getting Started with SQL Developer

This book is divided into chapters that focus on the different areas or functionality in SQL Developer. The progression through the chapters is from the more frequently used features to those less frequently used. This initial chapter is all about preparing your environment, installation, and getting started.

SQL Developer is easy to set up and use, so there is very little setup required to follow the examples in this book. The best way to learn is by practice, and for that you'll need a computer with access to an Oracle database and SQL Developer. This chapter, and indeed the rest of the book, assumes you have a computer with Microsoft Windows, Linux, or Mac OS X installed, and that you have access to an Oracle database. It focuses on the alternative installations available for SQL Developer, where to find the product, and how to install it. Once your environment is set up, you can follow a quick product walk-through to familiarize yourself with the landscape. You'll create a few connections, touch on the various areas available (such as the SQL Worksheet and Reports navigator), and learn about the control of the windows and general product layout.

Preparing your environment

Preparing your environment depends on a few factors, including the platform you are working on and whether you have an early edition of SQL Developer previously installed. First, you need to locate the software, download, and install it.

Finding and downloading the software

SQL Developer is available through a variety of sources as both a standalone download and as part of the Oracle Database and Oracle JDeveloper installations.

SQL Developer is a free product, and you can download it from the Oracle Technology Network, `http://www.oracle.com/technology/products/database/sql_developer`. Use this link to reach the download for the latest standalone production release. It also includes details of the release and is regularly updated with news of preview releases and new articles. While SQL Developer is free to download and use, you are required to read and agree to the license before you can proceed with the download. The product also falls under Oracle Support contracts, if you have a Support contract for the database, which means that you can log Oracle Support tickets.

Downloading and installing the Java Development Kit

SQL Developer requires the **Java** SE **Development Kit** (**JDK**); this includes the **Java Runtime Environment** (**JRE**) and other tools, which are used by SQL Developer utilities such as the PL/SL Debugger.

For Microsoft Windows, you can download and install SQL Developer with the JDK already installed. This means you'll download and unzip the product and will be ready to start, as there are no extra steps required. For the other operating systems, you'll need to download the JDK and direct SQL Developer to the path yourself. Indeed, as many other products require a JDK to be installed, you may already have one on your system. In this case, just direct the product to use an existing JDK installation. For Microsoft Windows, ensure you download SQL Developer without the JDK to make use of an existing JDK installation.

The SQL Developer download site offers a selection of download choices:

- Microsoft Windows (with or without the JDK)
- Linux (without the JDK)
- Mac OS X (without the JDK)

In each case, make your selection and download the required file.

The download sites for the JDK are as follows:

- For Microsoft Windows and Linux:

  `http://java.sun.com/javase/downloads/index.jsp`

- For Mac OS X:

  `http://developer.apple.com/java/download/`

SQL Developer is shipped with the minimum JDK required. You can download and use the latest updates to the JDK. You should be aware that some updates to the JDK are not supported. This detail is posted on the SQL Developer Downloads page for each release. Starting from SQL Developer 2.1, JDK 1.6 is the minimum JDK supported.

Once you have installed the JDK, you can start SQL Developer.

Installing and starting SQL Developer

SQL Developer does not use an installer. All you need to do is unzip the given file into an empty folder, locate, and run the executable.

Do not unzip SQL Developer into an `$Oracle_Home` folder or an existing SQL Developer install.

Unzipping the file creates an `sqldeveloper` folder, which includes a selection of sub-folders and files, including the `sqldeveloper.exe` executable.

If your download does not include the JDK, then you'll be prompted for the full path of the `java.exe`. Browse to the location of the file and select it. The path should include the full path and executable (for example, `C:\Program Files\Java\jdk1.6.0_13\bin\java.exe`):

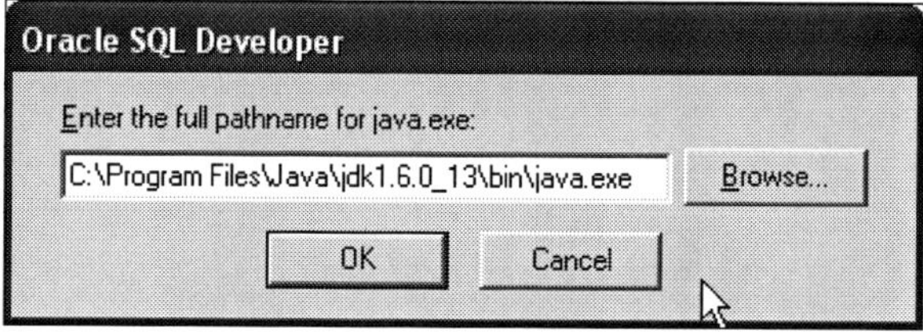

Working with different platforms

Whether you are accessing SQL Developer as part of the Oracle Database 11g installation or as a stand-alone install, there is a selection of executables available to you. These are either platform specific or provide additional detail while running the product.

Microsoft Windows

The first executable you'll find is in the root folder `\sqldeveloper`. This is the executable more generally used. If you navigate down to `\sqldeveloper\bin`, there are two additional executables, `sqldeveloper.exe` and `sqldeveloperW.exe`. The latter is the same as the executable in the root folder. Use either of these for running SQL Developer.

The additional executable is often used for debugging purposes. Use `\sqldeveloper\bin\sqldeveloper.exe` to invoke SQL Developer and a separate console window which displays additional Java messages. You can use these messages when encountering errors in the product and if you want to log an issue with Oracle Support.

Oracle SQL Developer
Three steps to getting started on Microsoft Windows:

Download: Download the full file, with JDK, from the Oracle Technology Network web site.

Unzip: Unzip the file to an empty directory.

Double-click: Double-click on the `\sqldeveloper\sqldeveloper.exe` file.

Alternative platforms

Microsoft Windows is the predominant platform used by SQL Developer users. There is a steadily growing audience for Linux and Max OS X. As neither of these platform downloads include the JDK, you need to first access, download, and install the JDK. On starting either Linux or the Mac OS, you'll be prompted for the full path of the JDK as described.

Mac OS X

Download the file specific to Mac OS X and double-click to unzip the file. This creates an icon for SQL Developer on your desktop. Double-click to run the application.

Linux

Use the Linux rpm command to install SQL Developer. For example, your command might look like this:

```
rpm -Uhv sqldeveloper-1.5.54.40-1.noarch.rpm
```

In the same way that unzip creates an sqldeveloper folder, with sub-folders and files, the rpm command creates an sqldeveloper folder, complete with files and sub-folders. Switch to this new folder and run the sqldeveloper.sh executable.

Migrating settings from a previous release

On the initial startup of any release of SQL Developer, you may be asked one or two questions. The first is the location of the Java executable of the JDK as discussed. If you have installed the full release with the JDK, this question is skipped. The second question is if you want to migrate any preferences from a previous release. Regardless of whether this is the first SQL Developer install on the machine or not, the first time you invoke SQL Developer, you are offered the choice of migrating your settings. You can migrate settings of any release from SQL Developer 1.5 and above. By default, the utility looks for the latest previous installation of the software.

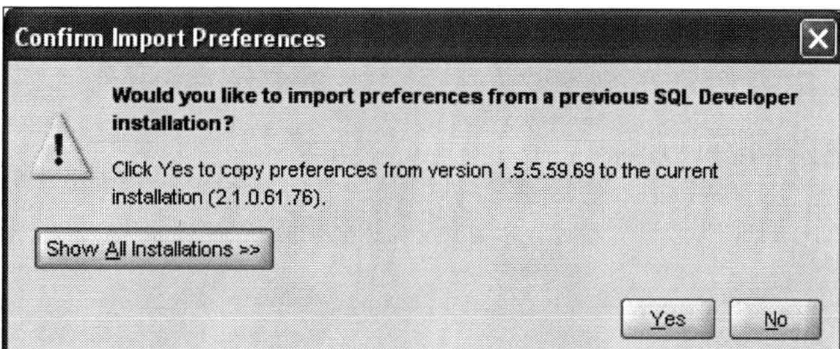

If you want to migrate from a different installation, select the **Show All Installations** button (seen above). This displays a list of all SQL Developer installations that have the system folder in the Documents and Settings system folder (for example, C:\Documents and Settings\<your_user>\Application Data\SQL Developer\system1.5.1.54.40) and includes releases from SQL Developer 1.5 and above. For releases prior to SQL Developer 1.5, the system folder was created within the SQL Developer install (for example, D:\SQLDeveloper\Builds\1.2.1\1.2.1.3213\sqldeveloper\sqldeveloper\system).

Maintaining your environment

Once you have SQL Developer installed, it is helpful to know about the environmental settings and some of the files that are created when you start the product. Knowing about the version you have installed is important if only to be able to identify this when asking questions on the forum, or when contacting Oracle Support.

Verifying the current release

To verify the SQL Developer release you have, select the **Help | About** menu once you start SQL Developer or JDeveloper. In the dialog invoked, select the **Extensions** tab and find the Oracle SQL Developer extension, as shown in the next screenshot. This will match the build number on the download site if you have the latest release. The screenshot shows a number of the extensions that make up SQL Developer. If your dialog does not show the **Version** or **Status** columns, you can select the column headers to resize the visible columns and bring the others into focus.

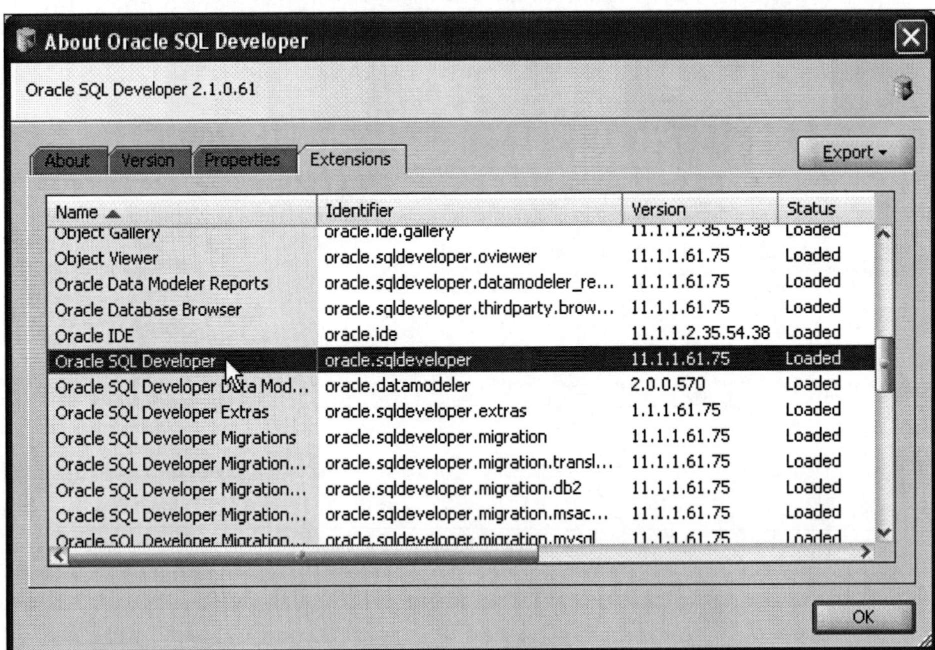

Using Check for Updates

SQL Developer offers a built-in patching and extensions utility, known as **Check for Updates**. Check for Updates is used to release:

- SQL Developer extensions
- General Oracle extensions
- Minor patches
- Third-party tools required by SQL Developer, such as the non-Oracle database drivers
- Third-party extensions

You can control whether Check for Updates warns you about new updates using the **Tools | Preferences** menu. Select **Extensions** and then select **Automatically Check for Updates**. For SQL Developer extensions, if you already have SQL Developer installed and you're not secured by a firewall, you'll be alerted about new updates. You need not use the utility to get the updates, but you'll be aware of the latest release from the alert. For all other extensions, you need to start **Check for Updates** to see what's available. To do this, select **Help | Check for Updates**. In either situation, just follow the dialog to find the updates you require.

You can initially elect to see just the third-party updates, or all updates available, by selecting all options, as shown in the following screenshot:

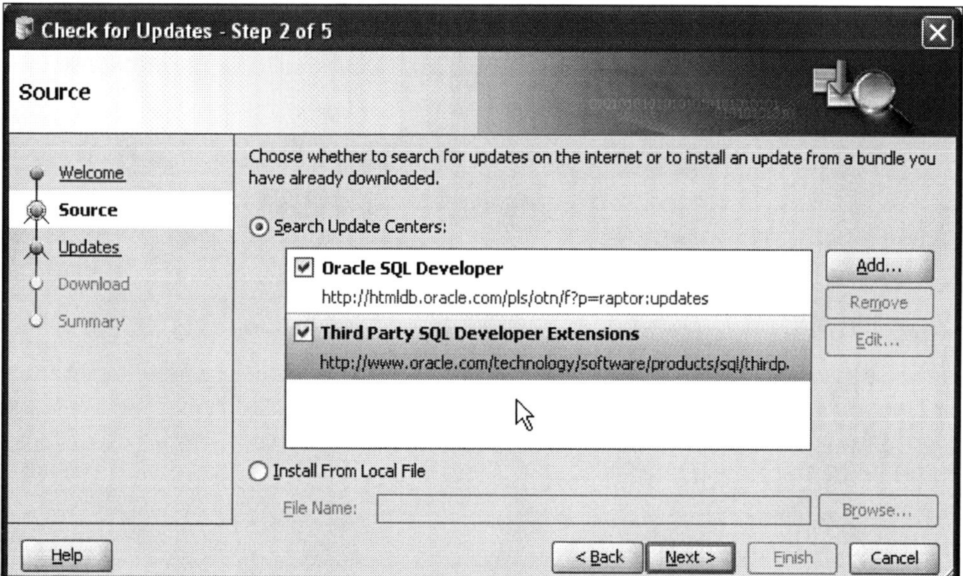

The database drivers for some of the non-Oracle databases are located in **Third Party SQL Developer Extensions**. The Third Party update center also includes a selection of customer developed SQL Developer extensions. The customer extensions are developed, supported, and updated by the customer involved, and are not tested, certified, or supported by Oracle.

As with all software downloads from the Internet, you are required to read and accept the license agreements. The **Check for Updates** utility directs you to the appropriate licenses, before downloading the software. If the updates are from Oracle, you will need to provide your Oracle Technology Network sign-on details.

Check for Updates is only used to apply patches to your install. Starting with SQL Developer 1.5.1, the team released patches which are applied to upgrade the product in place. These patches fixed one or two bugs and did not constitute a new download, or even a full install. For all other releases, you need to do a full install as described earlier.

Managing the system folder and other files

SQL Developer maintains a series of files as you work with the product. These files are created and stored in the `\Documents and Settings\<your_user>\Application Data\SQL Developer` folder. On Linux, these files are all stored in a folder `~/.sqldeveloper/`.

Deleting this folder is equivalent to returning a SQL Developer installation to its factory settings. The files at this highest level are:

- `CodeTemplate.xml`—created as you add your own user defined code templates
- `UserReports.xml`—created as you add your own user defined reports
- `SqlHistory.xml`—created as you execute SQL and PL/SQL commands in the SQL Worksheet
- `UserSnippets.xml`—created as you add your own snippets

These files are used by each of the SQL Developer installations you have. For example, you may elect to have the latest installation in addition to a number of earlier releases. Having several different releases of SQL Developer on one machine is acceptable, as the installations have no impact on each other, except that they do share these files.

Once you have started SQL Developer, a folder with sub-folders and files is created in the `\Documents and Settings\<your_user>\Application Data\SQL Developer` folder. The top-level folder is labeled `systemx.x.x.x.x` (for example `system1.5.0.54.40`). The `systemx.x.x.x.x` folder contains all of the other preferences and the settings that pertain to the specific release in use. In this case, deleting the system folder is almost equivalent to resetting SQL Developer to its factory settings, except that any user defined reports, SQL history, and code templates are not lost.

Sharing preferences

Preferences are set for your local environment and are therefore not shared globally between teams. However, you can export the SQL Formatter preferences set. This allows you to share the settings between team members and ensure that you all code to the same settings. To export your SQL Formatter settings, select **Tools | Preferences** and expand the **Database** node in the tree. Select **SQL Formatter**, you can now export or import previous saved settings.

Alternative installations of SQL Developer

We have been discussing the installation and management of the independent release of SQL Developer available on the Oracle Technology Network. SQL Developer is also available as part of the Oracle Database and Oracle JDeveloper installations.

Oracle JDeveloper

Most of SQL Developer is integrated into Oracle JDeveloper, which means you need to install JDeveloper to access and use the SQL Developer components. Having SQL Developer as part of JDeveloper means that, if you are building Java applications and working with the Fusion Middleware platform, you can access and work with the Oracle Database without an additional install of SQL Developer. JDeveloper does not consume all of the extensions for SQL Developer (for example, extensions like Migrations and Versioning are not included).

Oracle JDeveloper 11g includes SQL Developer 1.5.6.

Oracle Database 11g

SQL Developer is also shipped with the Oracle Database. Initially, Oracle Database 11g Release 1. SQL Developer is installed by default when you install the database. Once the installation is complete, locate the sqldeveloper directory (for example, `\product\11.1.0\db_1\sqldeveloper\sqldeveloper.exe`) to start SQL Developer.

Be aware that Oracle database releases are less frequent than those of SQL Developer, which, by its nature and size, allows for more frequent updates. This means the version of SQL Developer shipped with the database may not be the most current release. Oracle Database 11g Release 2 is shipped with SQL Developer 1.5.5. All examples in this text are using SQL Developer 2.1. You may also update your database version less frequently than a client tool.

To upgrade the SQL Developer installation in Oracle Database 11g Release 1, you should do a full new install. As with other installs, create a new folder and unzip the latest download.

Oracle Database 11g Release 1 ships with SQL Developer 1.1.3
Oracle Database 11g Release 2 ships with SQL Developer 1.5.5

Troubleshooting

It seems ominous to provide a section on troubleshooting at the start of a book! If you accept that software can get in a tangle sometimes, either if you use the product as it's not designed, or perhaps include extensions that you'd prefer not to have and the product is no longer behaving as expected, then a few hints on how to escape that tangle can be useful.

Removing extensions

If you have created your own extensions, or have downloaded and installed other extensions that you no longer require, then invoke the preferences, using the menu **Tools | Preferences** and select **Extensions** from the tree. Here you see that SQL Developer includes a number of default extensions, such as the Oracle TimesTen extension. In addition, any extension that you have included is listed here. You can deselect extensions here and the product will no longer access them. This does not delete the files installed for the extension. You will need to manually delete any files downloaded for that to happen. However, it does mean that you can restart the product and see if the extension is the root of the problem.

Resetting shortcut keys

Some users find that their keyboard shortcuts no longer work as expected. In this circumstance, you can select the menu **Tools | Preferences,** and then select **Shortcut Keys** from the tree. Click on the **More Actions** drop-down list and select **Load Keyboard Scheme...**, as shown in the following screenshot. Select **Default** from the dialog to reset the keyboard accelerators to the shipped settings. This also replaces any settings you have added.

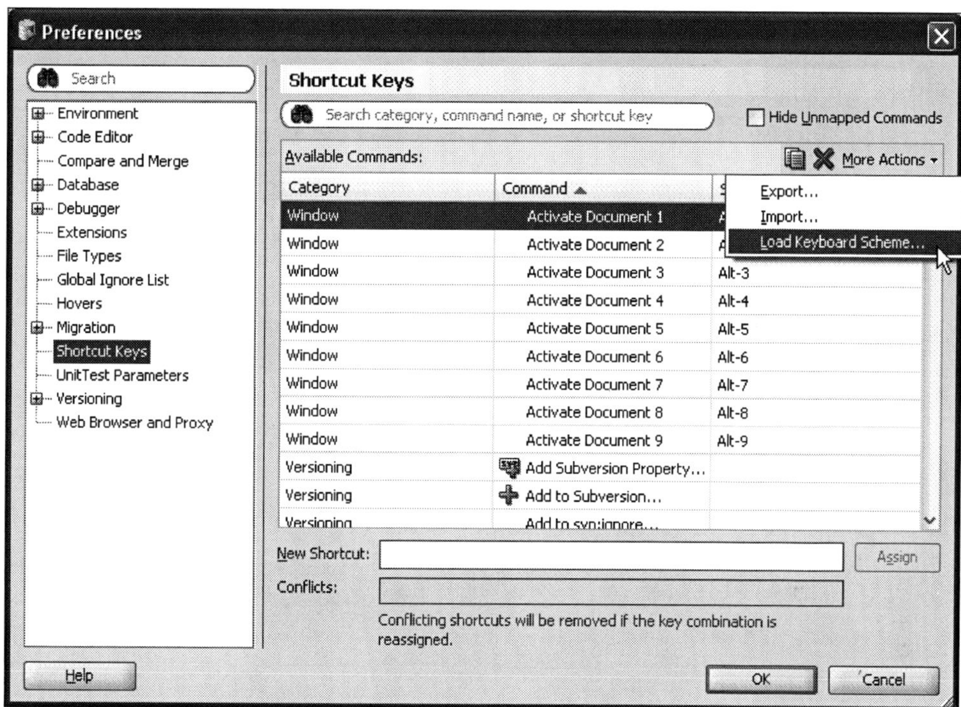

In releases prior to SQL Developer 2.1, the **Shortcut Keys** are called **Accelerators**. In these releases, to reset the keys, select **Load Preset**.

Reset the environment, do not reinstall the product

When things go wrong, users sometimes resort to deleting and reinstalling a product. This may even require downloading the files again. This is time consuming, and in the case of SQL Developer, not necessary. Assuming you have not edited any of the `.jar` files (it's been known to happen and not legally permitted), you can reset the product to the shipped factory settings by deleting the system folder. Before you delete the system folder, export your connections and shut down SQL Developer.

Export Connections: To export your connections, select **Connections**, right-click and select **Export Connections**. Save the file to a new location.

When troubleshooting, deleting the system folder is useful. However, by deleting this folder you are also deleting all of the changes made to the preferences, your connections, and any layout changes you have made. Therefore, it is recommended that you delete the folder as a last resort, and not as a standard approach to troubleshooting.

Reset to factory settings

For Microsoft Windows, delete the `\Documents and Settings\<your_user>\Application Data\SQL Developer` folder to reset SQL Developer to the shipped factory settings.

For Linux, remove the `~.sqldeveloper` folder and on the Mac, remove the `~/Library/Application Support/SQL Developer` folder.

In addition to deleting all of the preferences set and connections created, this action **also** deletes user-defined reports, your SQL history, and any code templates and snippets you have created. In general, delete the lower level system folder for a less drastic reset.

A quick overview

Let's start with a walk-through of the product. This book is all about SQL Developer, using the product, and getting to know it. You may well ask yourself why there is a need for a book if we can walk through the product in twenty minutes or less. By spending a little time dipping into a number of areas of the product, you can start laying down a map of how the pieces connect and provide a base that you can drill down into later.

Sample schemas

To follow the examples in the book, you need access to SYSTEM and the shipped sample schemas, **HR**, **OE**, **SH**, **PM**, and **IX** available in Oracle Database 9*i*, 10*g*, or 11*g*. Specifically, this book uses the sample schemas shipped with Oracle Database 11*g*.

There are two ways to install the sample schema. The first way is when you install the database. You can elect to have the sample schema installed at that point.

Second, if you have not installed these, then you can locate the sample schema in the `$ORACLE_HOME/demo/schema` folder and follow the instructions on installing them using the Oracle online documentation. Not all of these schemas are available for Oracle Express Edition. In this chapter, we use SYSTEM to verify the HR schema is unlocked, and then we use the HR sample schema, which is available in Oracle Express Edition.

Creating your first connection

To complete this quick walk-through, you need to know the username and password of the SYSTEM user. You also need to know the location of the database, whether this is the machine name or the IP address, and the database SID.

To begin, start SQL Developer. The very first time you start SQL Developer, you'll be asked if you want to migrate from a previous version. Select **No** and allow the tool to start up.

The first thing you need to do after you have started SQL Developer for the first time is to create your initial connections.

Create a connection for SYSTEM:

1. Select **Connections**, right-click and select **New Connection**. This invokes the **New Database Connection** dialog. You can edit and control all of the connection details using this dialog.
2. Complete the details, as seen in the following screenshot, relevant to your environment.
3. Click on **Test** to ensure you have the connection details correct and click on **Connect**.

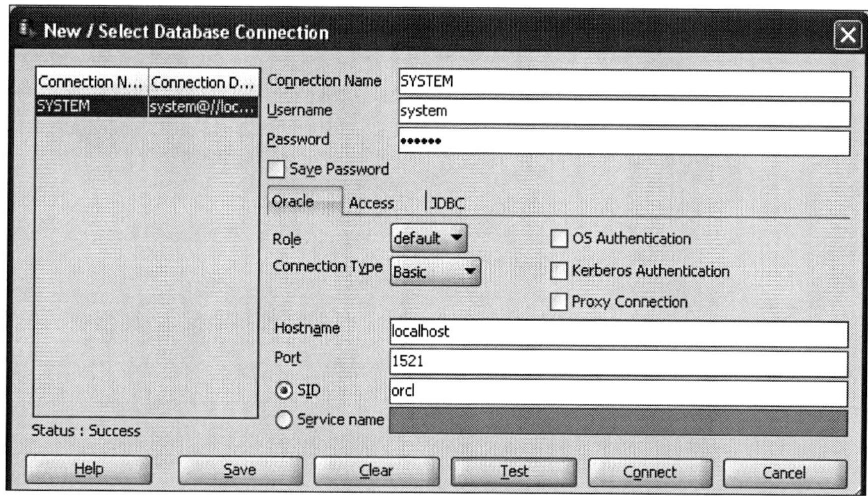

You are now connected as SYSTEM. Use this connection to verify your other users, by continuing as follows:

1. Select the new connection you have created, expand the node, and scroll down to **Other Users**.
2. Expand **Other Users** and find the user **HR**. Right-click and select **Edit User**. Verify that the account for HR is unlocked and the Password has not expired, that is, the properties **Account is Locked** and **Password Expired** are deselected. If either of these is selected, deselect them. You can change the password for HR at this point too. It's good practice to modify the passwords of the shipped sample schemas once you have unlocked them.

Now you are really ready to begin!

1. Once again, select **Connections**, right-click and select **New Connection**.
2. Give the connection a name (for example, **HR_11g**).
3. Provide the **Username** (**HR**) and a **Password**. If you are working on Oracle Database 11g, be aware that passwords are now case sensitive.
4. Select the **Save Password** checkbox. This makes life easy while you are working with SQL Developer. Passwords are stored in an encrypted file. However, you should always be aware of saving passwords and possible security implications this may have.
5. Use the **Basic** connection. This requires no more detail than the location of the database and the **SID**, details you have.
6. Click on **Test** to test the connection.
7. Click on **Connect**.

Using basic commands in the SQL Worksheet

As soon as you connect to a user, SQL Developer opens an SQL Worksheet. You may have started working with Oracle using the SQL*Plus command line, or even the GUI window. Either way, you'd start with a selection of SQL*Plus and SQL commands.

Enter the following into the SQL Worksheet:

```
DESC DEPARTMENTS
SELECT * FROM DEPARTMENTS;
```

Press the *F5* key (or use the **Run Script** button).

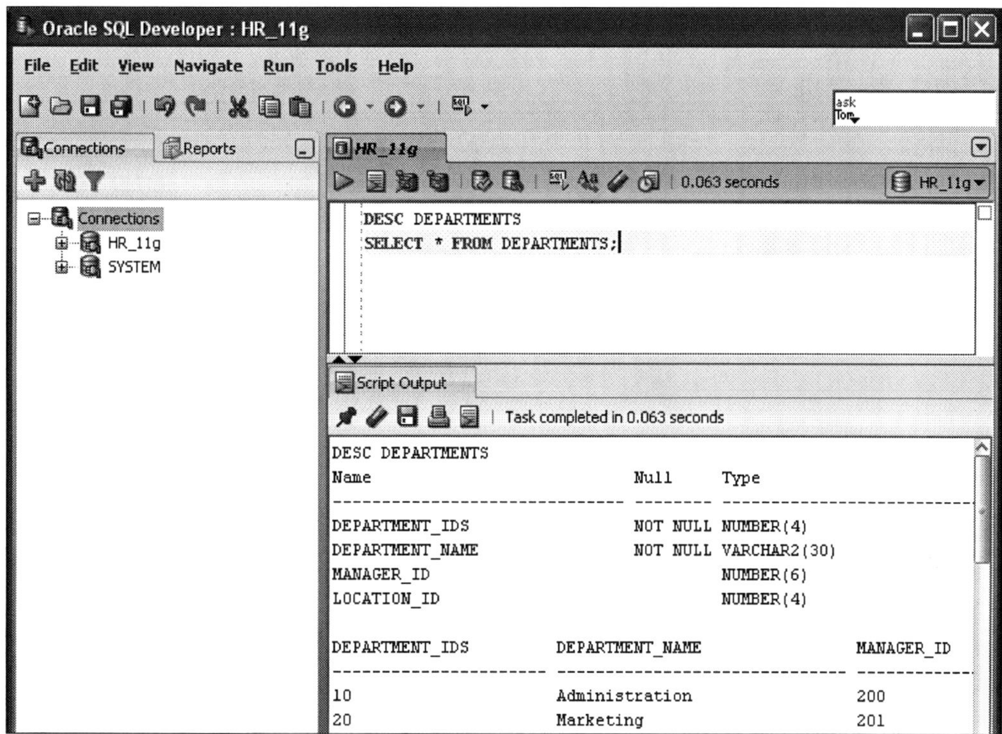

The output of both commands appears in the **Script Output** tab, which appears below the SQL Worksheet (as seen in the previous screenshot). Both commands are handled by a few simple clicks of the mouse in SQL Developer.

Select and expand the **HR_11g** connection in the **Connections** navigator. Expand the **Tables** node and select **DEPARTMENTS**.

The **DEPARTMENTS** tab now opens, displaying a list of the column names and details. These are the same details as given by the `DESC` (describe) SQL*Plus command that you entered in the SQL Worksheet. It also provides additional detail, such as the Primary Key and column comments.

Select the **Data** tab and notice that you now see the output from your second command. These two tabs are included with a number of other tabs, each with additional details about the **DEPARTMENTS** table. You would need to write a number of SQL queries in order to get the additional detail from the data dictionary if you were working in SQL*Plus.

Select the **EMPLOYEES** table. Notice that the new table, **EMPLOYEES**, immediately replaces the previous **DEPARTMENTS** table with its details. Select the **Triggers** tab, and select one of the triggers. The trigger and related trigger detail is displayed in a master-detail window:

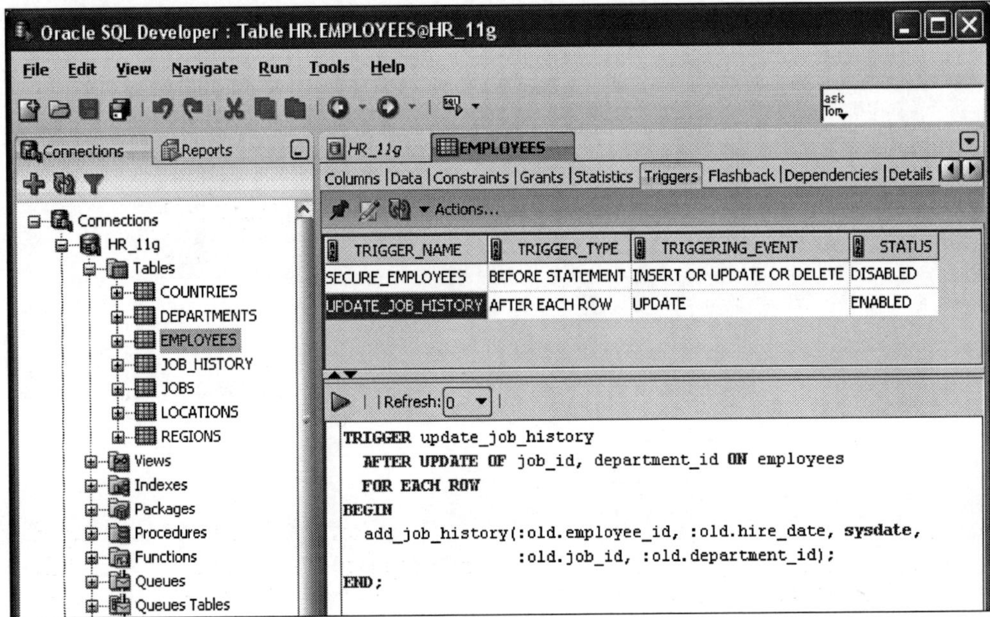

Browsing and updating data

Return to the **EMPLOYEES** data by again selecting the **Data** tab. The data grid that is displayed provides a variety of options. To get started with the data grid, double-click on an item or field, such as the name of one of the employees, and change it. Tab out of the field and notice that the change is applied to the data grid and an asterisk (*) flags the record. **Commit** and **Rollback** buttons are available to send the change to the database, or to undo your action. Roll back the changes.

Once again you get feedback, this time in the **Data Editor** log, as shown in the following screenshot:

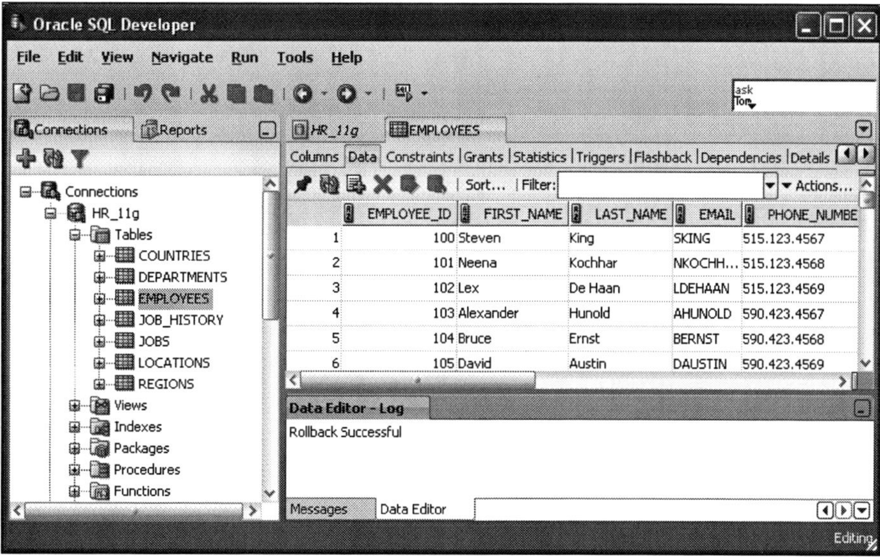

Running reports

Select the **Reports** navigator and expand the **Data Dictionary Reports** node. Expand the **Table** node and review the available reports. Expand **Constraints** and select the **Unique Constraints** report. As you select the report, a dialog displays requesting the Connection name. Select the connection you created, **HR_11g**, and click on **OK**. An **Enter Bind Values** dialog now appears, requesting the table name as an input parameter. Click on **Apply** to accept the default, which in this case, means all tables:

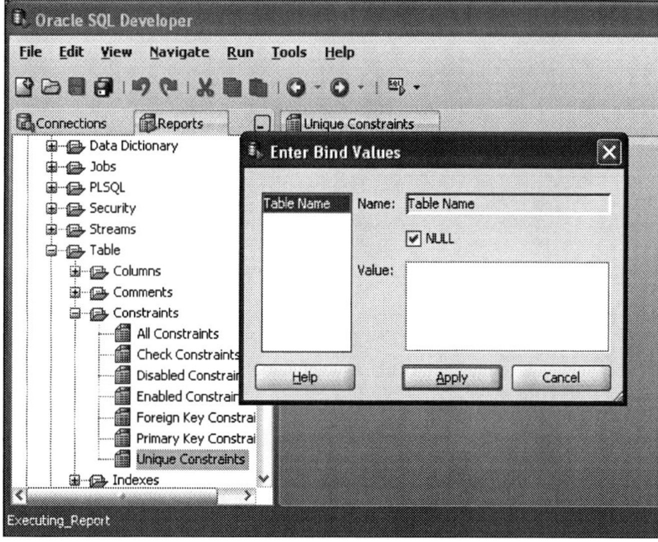

Run the same report for any user by selecting the **Connections** drop-down list on the right-hand side.

Navigating around SQL Developer

SQL Developer has a selection of windows, navigators, and tabs. On start-up, you are presented with the main navigator toolbars and menus:

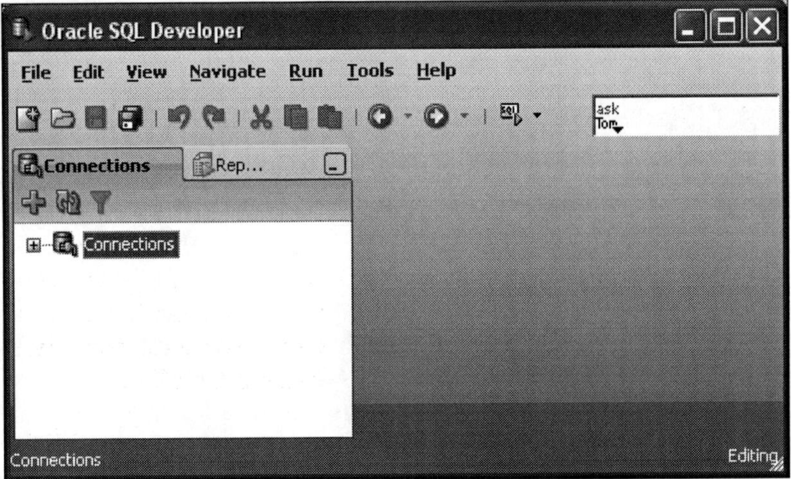

The two main navigators: **Connections** and **Reports**, are presented in a tabbed window. These and other navigators, such as the **Versioning Navigator**, are available through the main **View** menu. You can also open windows such as **Snippets**, **Recent Objects**, and **Find DB Objects** using the **View** menu.

Any navigators that you open during a session, and that are still open when you close the product, are automatically opened when you restart the product.

Managing SQL Developer windows

With the exception of the SQL Worksheet and its associated tabs, all of the main tabbed dialogs can be minimized or maximized and accessed while docked or undocked. These menu controls are available through context menus in the tabs:

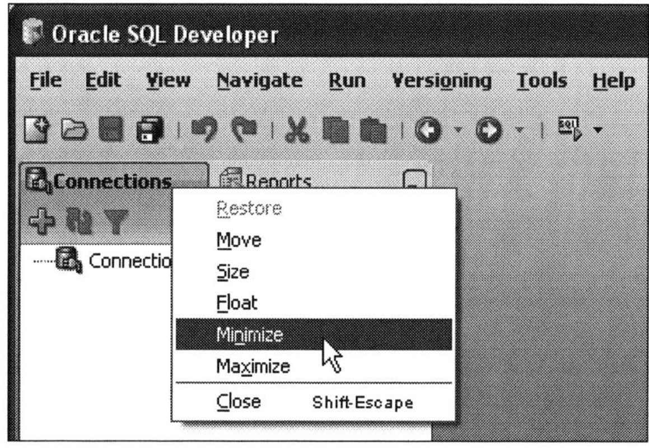

You can rearrange tabbed windows by selecting and dragging the tab into place. Once any window is minimized, roll your mouse over the minimized tab to display a floating window that stays active while your mouse lies over it and rolls back into place when you move off. This is very useful when working with temporary windows such as **Snippets** and **Find DB Object**. The following screenshot shows the floating window for the **Snippets** dialog. If you roll the mouse over the area, you can work in the window (for example, navigating about until you have located the snippet of code you are after, and then drag the code onto the worksheet). The window will minimize out of the way once you have moved off it.

You can undock the floating window, move it off to one side, and keep it undocked while you work with the SQL Worksheet. In a dual-monitor setup, you can drag the floating window onto one monitor, while working with the SQL Worksheet on the other monitor.

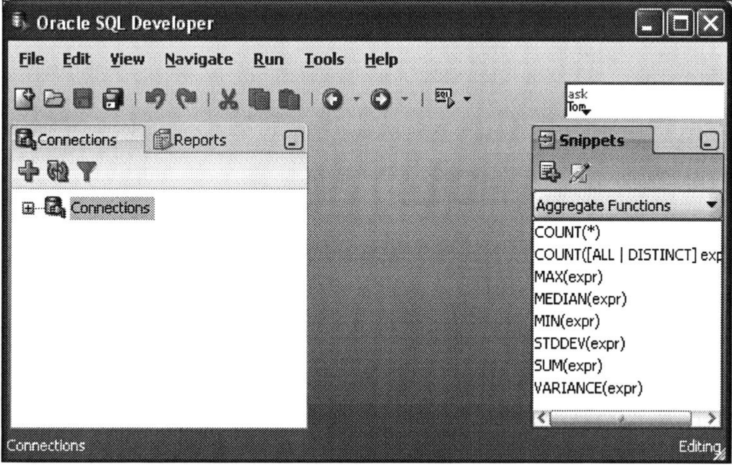

Tiling windows

Once you start working with connections, you have more windows and tabs to deal with, especially if you have more than one connection created. Select the **HR_11g** connection created in the previous section, expand the connection and **Tables** node, and select **EMPLOYEES**. In the table definition window, select the pin button, as shown below, to freeze the view.

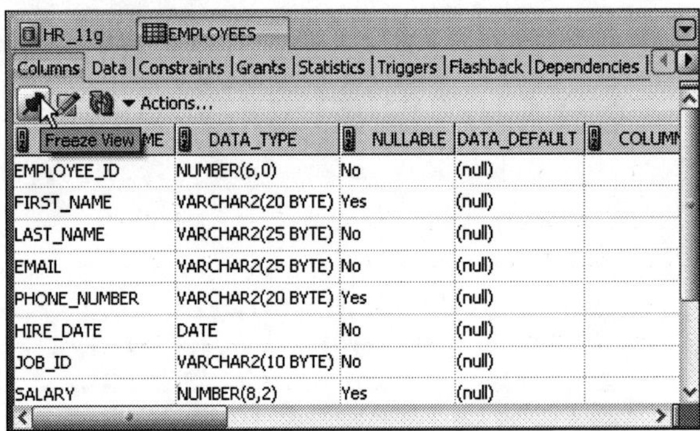

Now, select the **DEPARTMENTS** table. A second table definition window opens to display the details from the new table. Select the **DEPARTMENTS** tab and drag it down to the lower portion of the screen. Notice the shape of the dragged object change as you drag it slightly to the left, to the center, and the lower portion of the window. Each of the shapes represents a different layout position. Release the mouse to secure the new position. The screenshots, which follow, display two of the available positions:

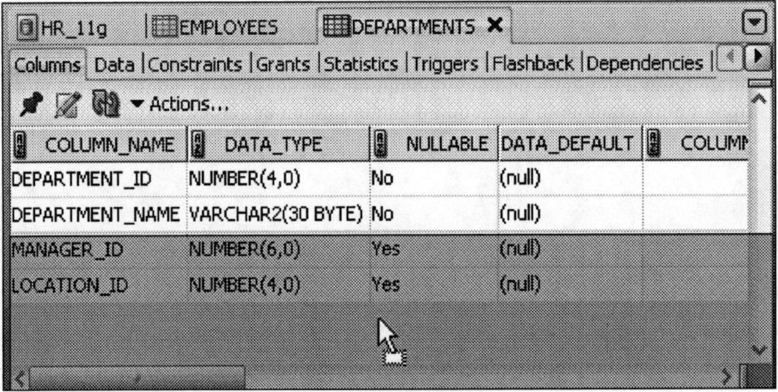

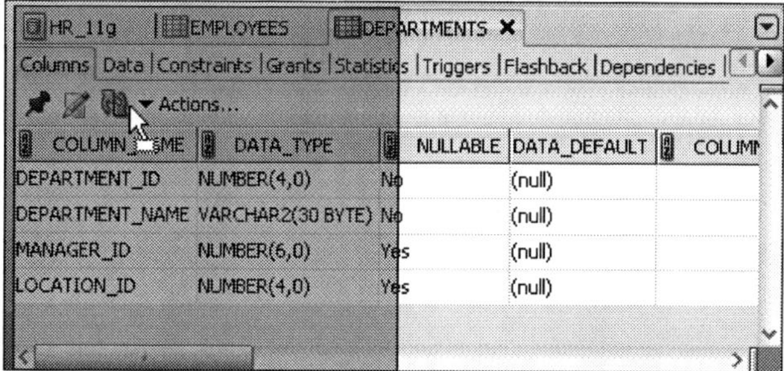

Splitting documents

When you tile windows, you can compare the details of two tables. However, as each table has a selection of tabs, it's useful to be able to review details in the tabs without having to switch back and forth between tabs. As is true for other layout features, you can split the document using a menu, or by drag-and-drop. Each of the object definitions tabbed displays has a drag bar on the top and bottom right that you can select and drag to split the window horizontally, or vertically:

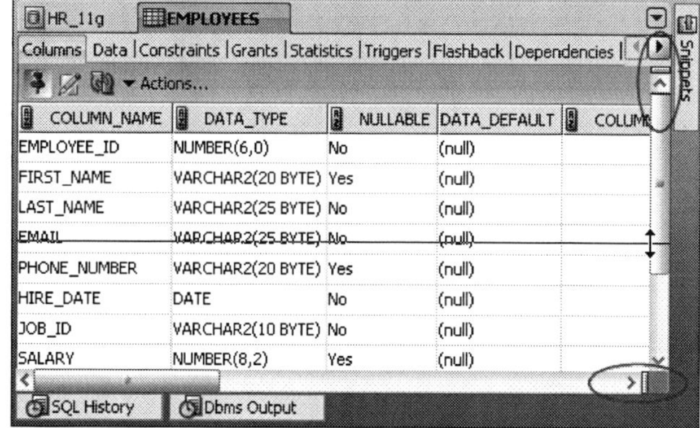

Maximizing detail

Almost all of the tabs in SQL Developer will maximize when double-clicked. There are a few that do not follow this rule, such as the tabs related to the SQL Worksheet. In general, this works for top-level tabs, which is any tab you can undock and move about, and not for secondary tabs. To maximize a tab, double-click on the tab. A second double-click will reverse the process.

[Double-click on the tab to maximize a top-level tab. Double-click again to revert to the previous layout.]

Resetting the window layout

If you move your windows about a great deal, you may find that you want to get things back to the default settings.

The example in the following screenshot displays the standard docked **Connections** and **Reports** windows to the left. We have also opened the **Versioning Navigator**, which by default docks below the connections. We have also docked the **Snippets** window to the right. These windows fill the columns to the left and right, leaving a central window for the editors and log files.

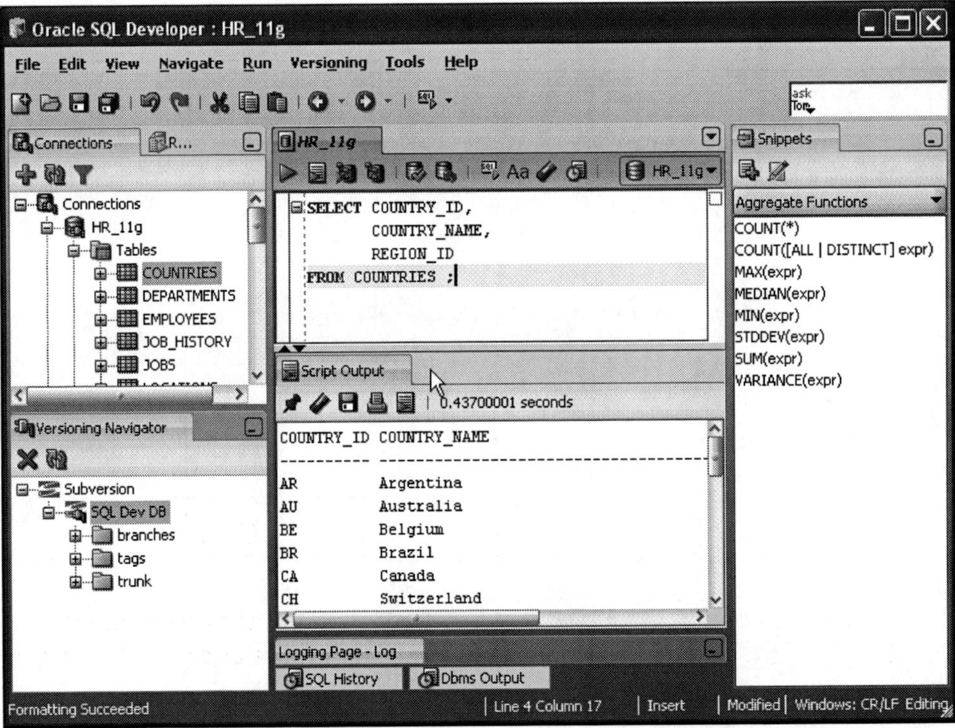

The layout is controlled by the window layout set in the preferences. Select **Tools | Preferences**, under the **Environment** node in the tree select **Dockable Windows.** The default layout, and the one that matches the example in the previous screenshot, is shown in the following screenshot:

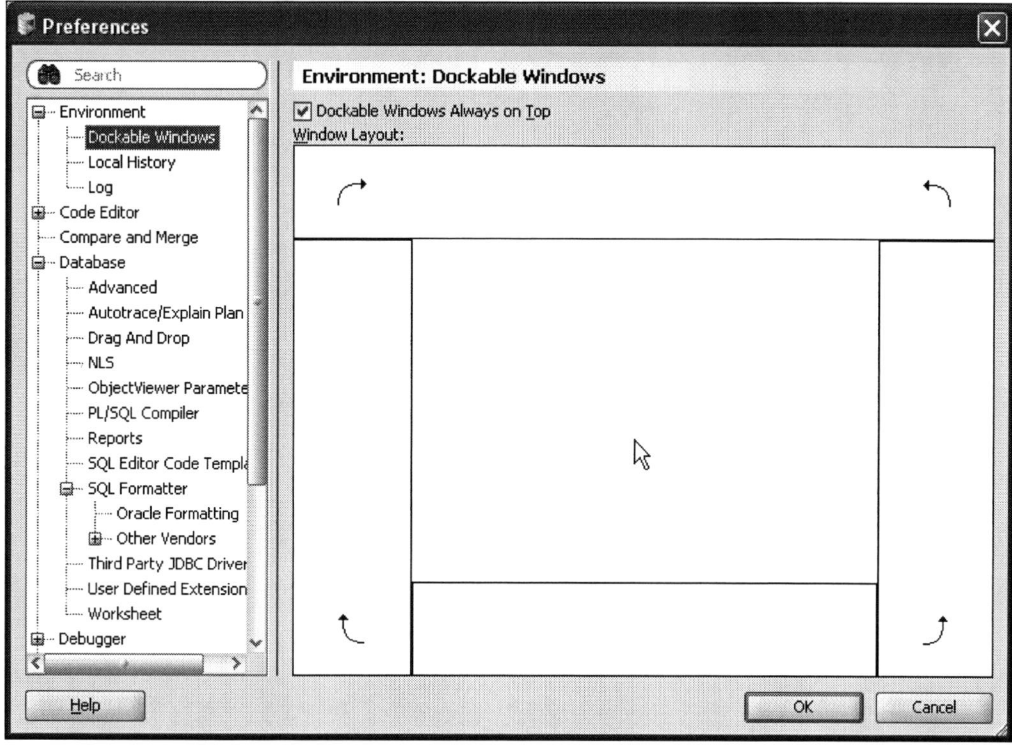

Each of the little curved arrows on the diagram is clickable, and as such controls the positioning of the windows. Clicking on the arrow extends or contracts the area taken up by the docked window.

In our example, and in the default SQL Developer environment, there is no full-docked window across the top of the screen. However, if you drag a window into the docked position below the main tool bar, it would stretch across the screen, as shown in the following screenshot:

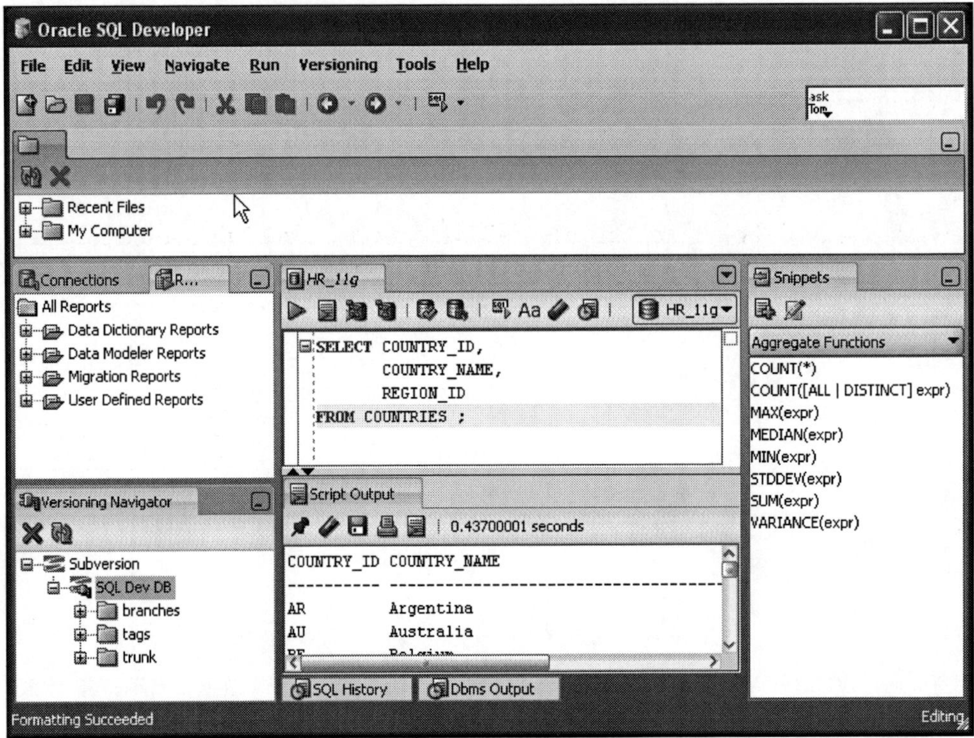

If you find your windows are in a muddle, first verify that the **Dockable Windows** layout is what you want, and then drag the various dockable windows back into place. Some suggestions on the SQL Developer forum are to remove the system folder (it works, but that's an extreme solution).

Finding more help

SQL Developer has a site on the Oracle Technology Network, `http://www.oracle.com/technology/products/database/sql_developer/index.html`. This provides links to current and past magazine articles, white papers, and team blogs. It also has links to brief product demonstrations and longer hands-on exercises.

There is an active user forum on OTN, `http://forums.oracle.com/forums/forum.jspa?forumID=260`, which is monitored by the development team and end users.

The SQL Developer Exchange, `http://sqldeveloper.oracle.com`, is a site where anyone using SQL Developer can log feature requests and vote on other requests already posted. In addition to posting feature requests, the site hosts reports and code snippets.

Summary

You've started and should now have SQL Developer installed. You should have a few connections created and an initial idea of how to navigate around the product. You are now set to learn a lot more about SQL Developer. From here you can dip into different chapters, focusing on the areas you're most interested in.

In the next chapter, we'll show you how to browse different types of objects, and use SQL Developer to look at them in greater detail. We'll review the different editors and dialogs available and how you can manage what you see using preferences. We'll also show you the different ways you can create objects and how to manipulate the data.

2

Browsing and Editing Database Objects and Data

Those developers, who access the Oracle database regularly, typically spend the bulk of their time querying, creating, and updating database objects and data. There are those who only need to browse the objects and see how they relate to each other, while others create and update the objects, and many only query and manipulate the data. SQL Developer provides an intuitive user interface that supports all of these activities, which makes accessing and updating database objects and data a point-and-click activity. In this chapter, we look at the broad choices offered by SQL Developer, by reviewing the available browsing, creating, and updating features.

Browsing objects

Whether you are about to embark on new development, modify existing objects, or just want to see what's in your database, you are likely going to start by browsing the schema or schemas you have access to. Technically, you are querying the Oracle database, and so many of the actions in this chapter, such as using a menu to drop a table, or a dialog to create a new table with columns and constraints, can be done by writing the SQL in the SQL Worksheet or SQL*Plus. By using the functionality the tool provides, you can quickly complete a multitude of tasks. In SQL Developer, you use the **Connections** navigator to browse (or query) the database objects. To follow the examples in this section, you need to create database connections for the sample schemas **HR** and **OE**. You will also need access to **SYSTEM**, or a user capable of granting privileges to other users.

Working with the Connections navigator

Objects are grouped into nodes in the **Connections** navigator to reflect their types. They are ordered by *most commonly* used with **Tables, Views**, and **Indexes**, at the top of the list. You can refer to the following screenshot to see the grouping, order, and some of the currently available types displayed in the **Connections** navigator. The selection of browsable object types available increases with each release as the SQL Developer team adds support for more features. For example, **Queues** and **Queues Tables** were introduced in Oracle SQL Developer 1.5, and **Jobs** were added in SQL Developer 2.1.

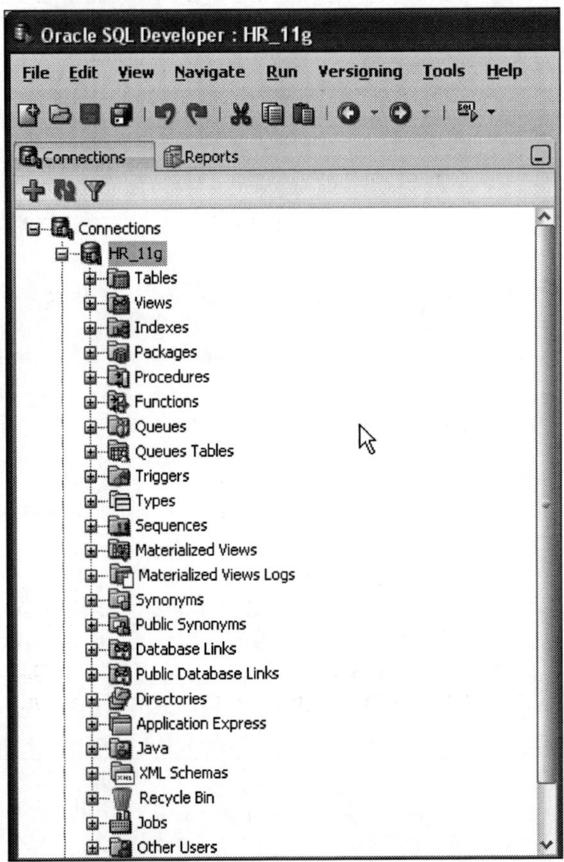

Opening connections

To open a connection in the navigator:

1. Double-click the connection.
2. Expand the node.
3. Select **Connect** from the context menu.

The first time you connect to a database schema, whether you open an existing connection or click on **Connect** in the **New Database Connections** dialog, SQL Developer automatically expands the connection in the **Connections** navigator and opens a SQL Worksheet. This automatic opening of the SQL Worksheet is controlled by a preference: **Open a Worksheet on connect**. Select **Tools | Preferences**, expand the **Database** node and select **Worksheet.**

Reconnecting users

When doing administrative work with users, it can help to disconnect the user you are working with before making the changes, and reconnect them afterwards. Some actions, such as dropping users or renaming connections, will not be possible without first disconnecting the connection.

Database schema or user?

The Oracle Concepts Guide states,

"*A schema is a collection of database objects. A schema is owned by a database user and has the same name as that user.*"

Throughout the text, we use schema and user interchangeably. For the most part, we refer to the OE and HR schemas, meaning the collection of database objects. When closely or directly related to an activity we use "user", as the code does this. For example, `DROP user HR cascade;` a piece of code that drops all of the objects in the schema and the user itself.

Working with objects

To work with any object, select and expand the node. The most common node you'll work with is the **Tables** node. This displays all of the tables the user owns (all of the tables in the schema). Each of the object nodes is identified by an icon, and the **Tables** node highlights some of the main table types using these icons. Not all are singled out, but the more commonly used ones are. If you expand the HR **Tables** node, the **COUNTRIES** table, which in the sample is an index-organized table, is identified by the slightly different table icon used. Partitioned tables are also distinguished from regular, simple tables using icons. The following screenshot displays the index organized, regular, external, partitioned, and temporary icons:

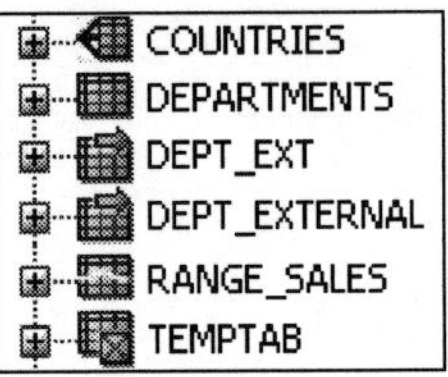

Filtering objects

Using the HR and OE schemas is useful for illustrating various features within SQL Developer. They do not reflect reality, where you'd typically be working with many more objects or sets of objects, within a schema or across schemas, and the mere act of expanding a node exposes a long and possibly unworkable list of objects. SQL Developer provides filtering for each object type, which allows you to control the display of objects.

To use the filter, select an object node, such as **Tables**, and select **Apply Filter...** from the context menu.

Depending on the object node selected, the choice of filter criteria varies. An important feature to note is the **Include Synonyms** checkbox, available for tables and views. All object nodes will only display those objects that belong to the schema. If one schema has access to the objects in another schema, you can create synonyms for those objects and, using the filter, have them display in the object node. Without the filter, you need to use the **Other Users** node to see the objects in another schema.

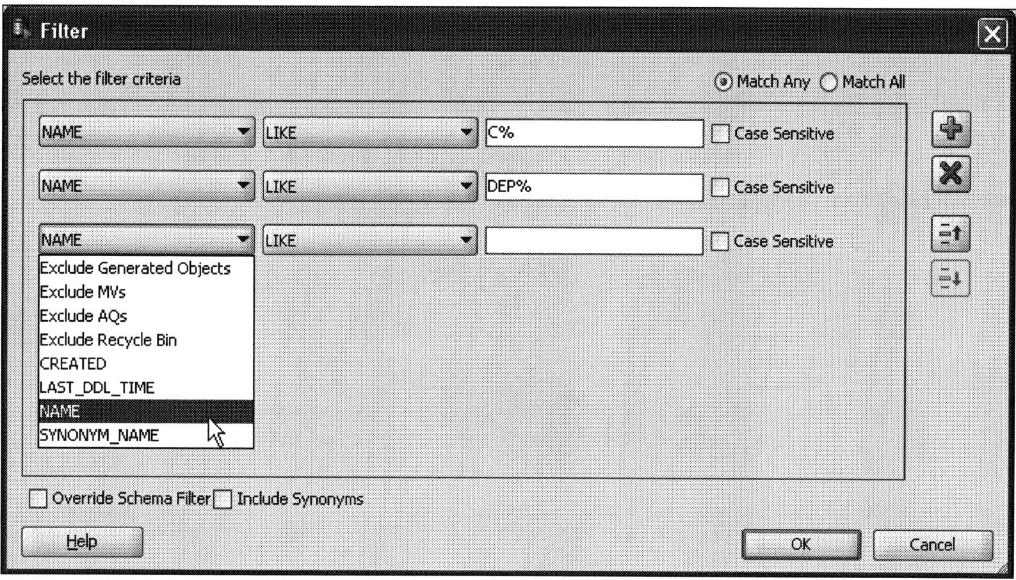

In the previous screenshot, the **Filter** dialog is for tables. For all object filters, you can add multiple selections as shown and select the options:

- Match Any
- Match All

The filter criteria provides lists of choices. In the first for the column, values such as `CREATED` and `LAST_DDL_TIME`, and for the operator, values such as `LIKE` or `<>`. Prior to SQL Developer 2.1, the column drop-down list displayed only four choices. These four choices have since been expanded to provide greater control of the objects displayed.

In SQL Developer 2.1, the underlying query no longer includes the restrictions defined in earlier releases. For example, there is no longer the restriction `ALL_OBJECTS.GENERATED = 'N'`, which means that your list of tables also includes generated tables. If you tend not to work with these objects, then applying only that filter is worthwhile.

Schema level filtering

To avoid needing to apply a schema at the level of each object type in the browser, you can set a schema filter. This is particularly useful if you enforce a naming standard that requires all objects to have a prefix or suffix to designate the application or schema with which they are associated. Select **Apply Filter...** from the database connection for the schema to invoke the dialog:

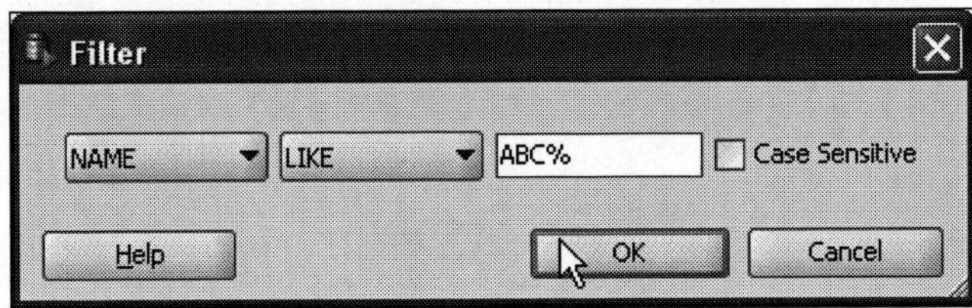

You can override the schema level filter using a filter at the object type level. The object filter dialog includes an **Override Schema Filter** option.

Display editors

Once you have expanded an object type node in the **Connections** navigator, selecting any object in that node opens a window of tabs, called *display editors*, which define the object. Each editor displays a data grid of details describing the selected object. These are based on queries against the data dictionary and you can get the same results by writing the SQL yourself.

The number and types of editors displayed will vary depending on the object or database that you are connected to. If you are connected to Oracle Database 11g, then an additional **Flashback** editor displays with the other table display editors.

The **Partitions** tab is permanently displayed from SQL Developer 2.1.

General display editors

Instead of itemizing each of the object types and the different collections of display editors, we'll use the **Tables** node to review some of the display editor details.

Using the **HR** connection, select **EMPLOYEES** in the **Tables** node to see the general display editors:

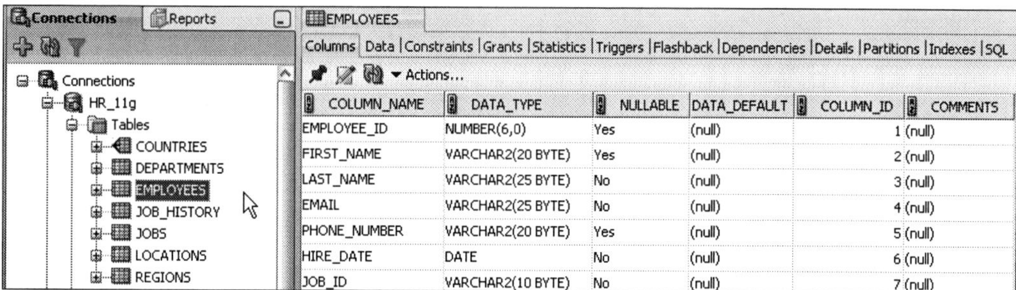

The **Columns** editor displays all of the column detail, including column comments. To get a feel for queries that run behind the editors, run the following query in the SQL Worksheet:

```
SELECT COLUMN_NAME,DATA_TYPE
FROM ALL_TAB_COLUMNS
WHERE TABLE_NAME ='EMPLOYEES'
AND OWNER = 'HR';
```

The output from the query matches the first two columns of the **Columns** display editor (this is a simplified example). If you need to find out more information about any object in the database, without a GUI tool, you need to start by querying the data dictionary to determine which tables hold the metadata about your objects. From there, you must decide what detail you need from these tables, in our example it was the single `ALL_TAB_COLUMNS` table, and then write the join clause to query all of the selected tables.

There is a set of editors for each of the object types. For tables, these include **Constraints, Grants, Statistics, Triggers,** and **Partitions**. The data in each data grid is a result of a query joining a number of data dictionary tables. SQL Developer provides a framework for you to create and add your own display editors. You can do this with user extensions, which are discussed in the chapter on *Extending SQL Developer*.

Some of the editors display master-detail output. To see the detail result set you need to select an individual record in the master result set. The following screenshot shows the **EMP_NAME_IX** for the **EMPLOYEES** table. By selecting the index, you can quickly see that this index is made up of two columns:

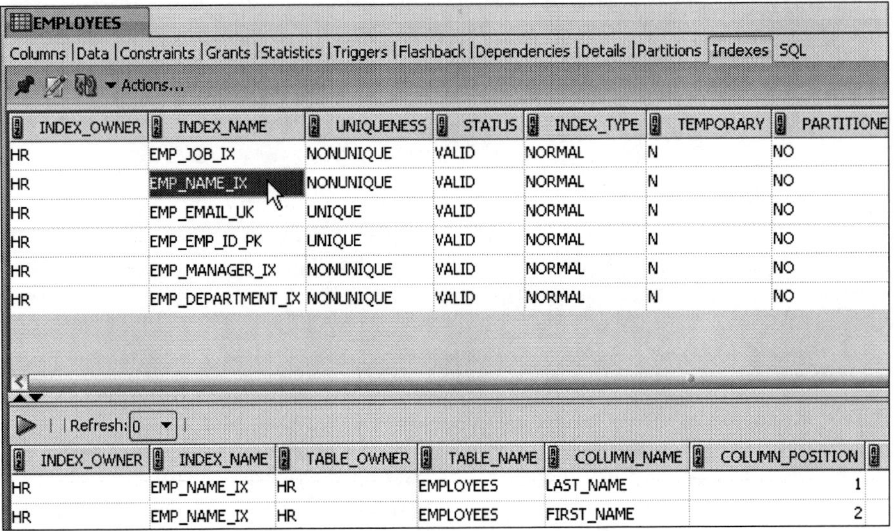

To create the index using SQL, use the following query:

```
CREATE INDEX "EMP_NAME_IX" ON "EMPLOYEES" ("LAST_NAME", "FIRST_NAME");
```

Working with the display editors

Each new object selected in the navigator replaces the last, regardless of object type or connection, unless you click on the **Freeze View** pin button ( ) on the object display. This locks the window and a new window opens with a new set of editors.

To see this feature in action, expand the HR **Tables** node. Select the **EMPLOYEES** table and note the set of display editors. Now select the **DEPARTMENTS** table, and note that it replaces the details of the **EMPLOYEES** table. Expand the **Sequences** node and click through each of the sequences available. These now replace the tables which were previously displayed. This replacing feature is very useful as it saves screen real estate, and keeps the screen and work area uncluttered. However, it is also very useful to be able to compare two sets of data, side by side. Therefore, by selecting the **Freeze View** pin, each new object selected opens in a new window and you can then tile the windows.

Freezing the Object Viewer

You can control whether each new object select opens a new set of editors. Select **Tools | Preferences**, in the tree display, expand **Database**. Next, click on **ObjectViewer** and select **Automatically Freeze Object Viewer Windows.**

SQL Developer automatically opens the display editors as you click on the object, or if you navigate down through the objects using the keyboard. You can control this by changing the default **Open Object on Single Click** behavior. Select **Tools | Preferences**, in the tree displayed, expand **Database**, select **ObjectViewer** and deselect **Open Object on Single Click.**

Using the SQL display editor

The **SQL** editor is displayed at the end of the set of shipped display editors and is available for most object types (any editors you create are added after the **SQL** editor). The **SQL** editor displays the query required to recreate the object selected. When you select the **SQL** editor, SQL Developer uses the package `DBMS_METADATA` to query the database and return the SQL required for recreating the object selected. So, clicking on the editor with a table selected displays the SQL (DDL) for that table.

Select the **COUNTRIES** table in the **Connections** navigator. The default display provides the full `CREATE TABLE` SQL in a single statement as shown in the following screenshot:

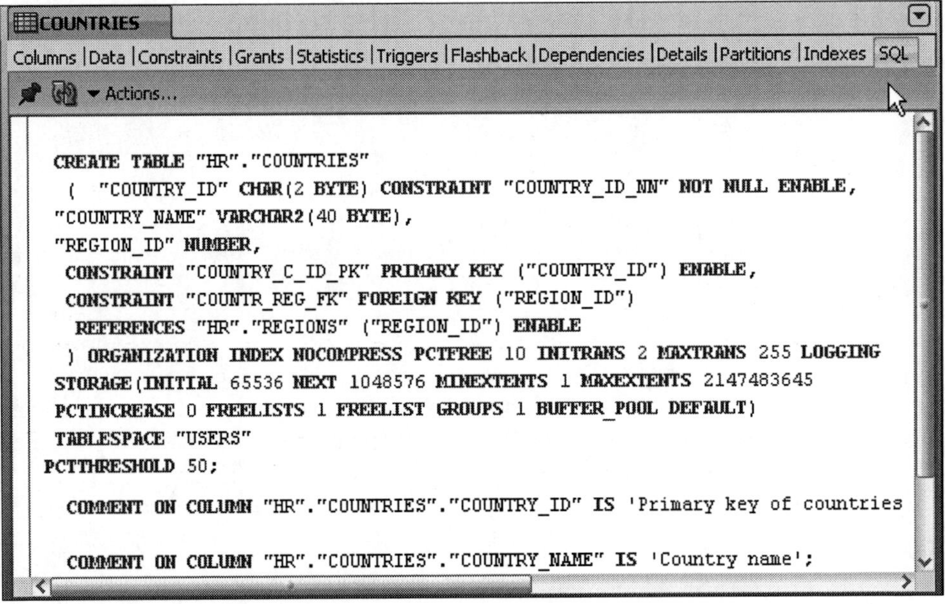

You can control the SQL output for tables by adjusting the parameters passed to the `DBMS_METADATA` package. This is done by using the SQL Developer preferences in the **Tools | Preferences** dialog, and by setting **Database | ObjectViewer** options. To illustrate this, deselect **Show Schema, Show Storage**, and select **Show Constraints as Alter** and then click on **OK**:

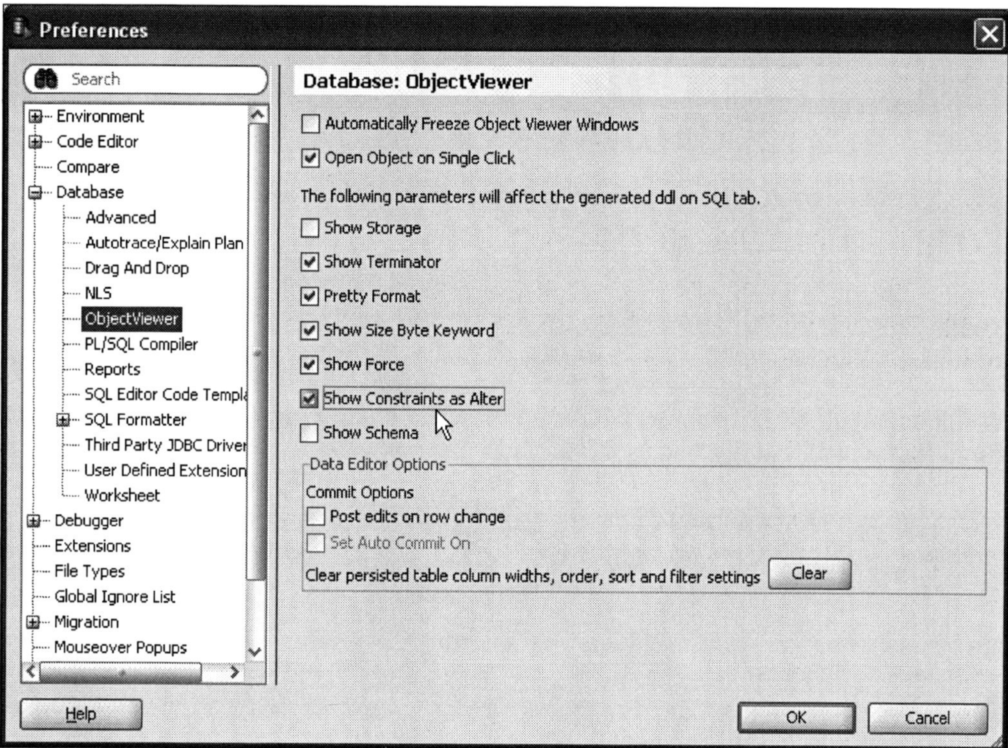

Refresh the SQL editor to display the updated output. Notice how the schema prefix "HR" is no longer displayed and the storage specifics are now excluded. This makes it a very useful script to reuse on other databases, or for other schemas. You may also like to create the tables with no constraints, add data, and then apply the constraints subsequently:

COUNTRIES

Columns | Data | Constraints | Grants | Statistics | Triggers | Flashback | Dependencies | Details | Partitions | Indexes | SQL

Actions...

```
CREATE TABLE "COUNTRIES"
 (  "COUNTRY_ID" CHAR(2 BYTE) CONSTRAINT "COUNTRY_ID_NN" NOT NULL ENABLE,
"COUNTRY_NAME" VARCHAR2(40 BYTE),
"REGION_ID" NUMBER,
 CONSTRAINT "COUNTRY_C_ID_PK" PRIMARY KEY ("COUNTRY_ID") ENABLE
 ) ORGANIZATION INDEX NOCOMPRESS ;
ALTER TABLE "COUNTRIES" ADD CONSTRAINT "COUNTR_REG_FK" FOREIGN KEY ("REGION_ID
  REFERENCES "REGIONS" ("REGION_ID") ENABLE;
```

The **Database | ObjectViewer** preferences that you set are used to format the SQL display editor code. These preferences also format the SQL created by the **Export DDL** context menu for the table.

Working with the data grids

The contents of each display editor are displayed in data grids, which typically have three or more columns of data within the grid. A few are two column name-value pair data grids, such as the **Details** editor. The data in these grids is not editable and merely reflects the details about the object or structure selected. There are two exceptions. The first exception is the **Data** editor included with the set of display editors for certain objects, such as tables and views. The **Data** editor displays the *instance* data for a table and, depending on the object, this data can be edited and the changes can be committed to the database. The second exception is new to SQL Developer 2.1. This is the **Code** editor for PL/SQL objects, where you are placed into a PL/SQL editor when you select the object.

Data grids throughout SQL Developer have context menus on the column's headings and the data grid itself. You can control the layout and what data is displayed by using these two context menus. For the remaining portion of this section we'll review the various options on these context menus.

Controlling the column display

The easiest way to control the column order displayed in the data grid is to use drag-and-drop. Select the column header and drag it to a new position. Alternatively, you can select **Columns...** from the context menu on the column heading as shown in the following screenshot:

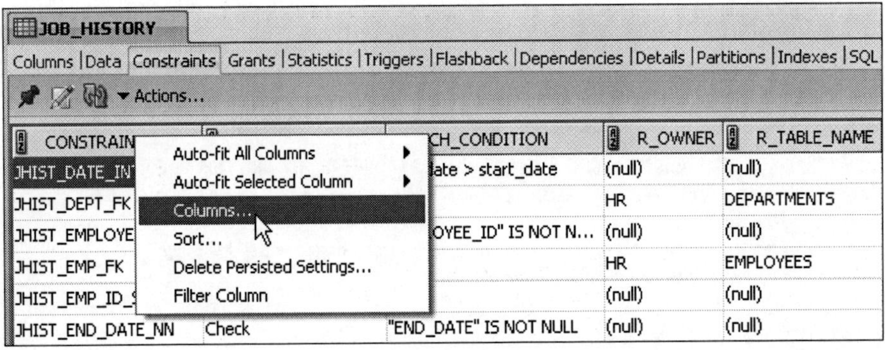

This invokes the **Manage Columns** dialog, which supports reordering of columns. The same dialog also supports the ability to selectively hide and show columns. Regardless of how you reorder or change the display of columns, the new column order remains in place when you close and reopen the display editor, as well as if you close SQL Developer. Along with the other display settings, this value is persisted until you actively change the setting or clear the settings by selecting **Delete Persisted Settings...** from the same context menu displayed in the earlier screenshot.

The column headings also provide a context menu to **Auto-Fit** selections. This allows you to resize the column based on the header or the contents of the column. There is also a **Best Fit** option, which uses a combination of these. Using *Ctrl* or *Shift+select*, you can select multiple columns and apply these conditions to all of the columns. An additional **Fit Screen** option is available to ensure all of the columns fit within the extent of the display area.

> **Clearing object display settings**
>
> You can clear all of the persisted display settings, including column widths and order using a preference. Select **Tools | Preferences.** Expand **Database** in the tree and select **ObjectViewer**. Click on **Clear**.

Sorting the data

With the exception of the two column name-value pair displays, you can sort the records displayed by double-clicking on most of the column headings. This is true for all of the data grids throughout SQL Developer. Columns that allow for sorting display this icon to the left of the column header. You can also perform multiple column sorts by selecting **Sort...** from the column header context menu. The following screenshot displays the detail of placing two sort settings on the data grid:

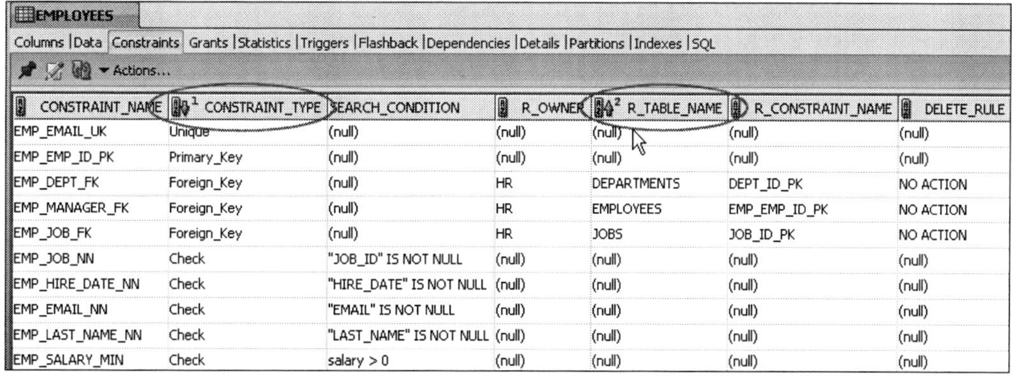

CONSTRAINT_NAME	CONSTRAINT_TYPE	SEARCH_CONDITION	R_OWNER	R_TABLE_NAME	R_CONSTRAINT_NAME	DELETE_RULE
EMP_EMAIL_UK	Unique	(null)	(null)	(null)	(null)	(null)
EMP_EMP_ID_PK	Primary_Key	(null)	(null)	(null)	(null)	(null)
EMP_DEPT_FK	Foreign_Key	(null)	HR	DEPARTMENTS	DEPT_ID_PK	NO ACTION
EMP_MANAGER_FK	Foreign_Key	(null)	HR	EMPLOYEES	EMP_EMP_ID_PK	NO ACTION
EMP_JOB_FK	Foreign_Key	(null)	HR	JOBS	JOB_ID_PK	NO ACTION
EMP_JOB_NN	Check	"JOB_ID" IS NOT NULL	(null)	(null)	(null)	(null)
EMP_HIRE_DATE_NN	Check	"HIRE_DATE" IS NOT NULL	(null)	(null)	(null)	(null)
EMP_EMAIL_NN	Check	"EMAIL" IS NOT NULL	(null)	(null)	(null)	(null)
EMP_LAST_NAME_NN	Check	"LAST_NAME" IS NOT NULL	(null)	(null)	(null)	(null)
EMP_SALARY_MIN	Check	salary > 0	(null)	(null)	(null)	(null)

Filtering columns

SQL Developer 2.1 introduced column filters, which are like a `WHERE` clause for the display editors. Click on the column header, or select **Filter Column** from the context menu on the column header. Either action opens a floating menu of choices to restrict the column:

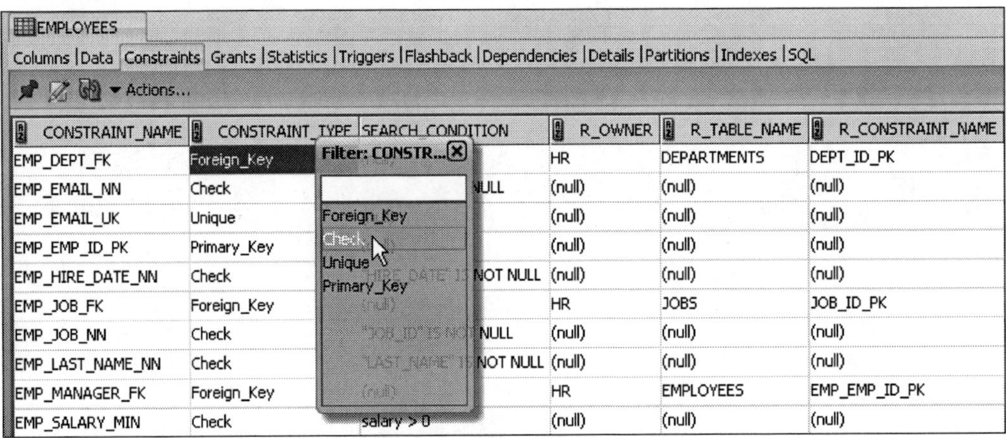

Filtered columns display a filtered symbol. To clear these column filters, invoke the filter menu again and select **All...**, or select **Remove All Filters** from the columns context menu.

Navigating the grid

Navigating the data grid is done using the mouse to click through records, or dragging the scroll bar down through sets of records. You can even use the *Page Up* and *Page Down* keys on the keyboard to skip through larger sets of records.

Two additional key combinations, useful for large sets of data, are *Ctrl+Page Down* to get you to the last record and *Ctrl+Page Up* to get you back to the start of the records.

More data grid context menus

Let's move down to the context menu available on the data grids. These are available throughout SQL Developer, wherever a data grid is displayed, and tend to vary slightly. For example, the reports data grids have an additional navigation menu and the updateable data grids have an additional option for duplicating rows. In the next section, we'll consider a few of the options available.

Highlighting data

The **Filter/Highlight** option is available for most data grids. In the following screenshot, we have used one of the data dictionary reports, which has a larger set of data available. The report here is the **All Objects** report under **Data Dictionary Reports | All Objects.**

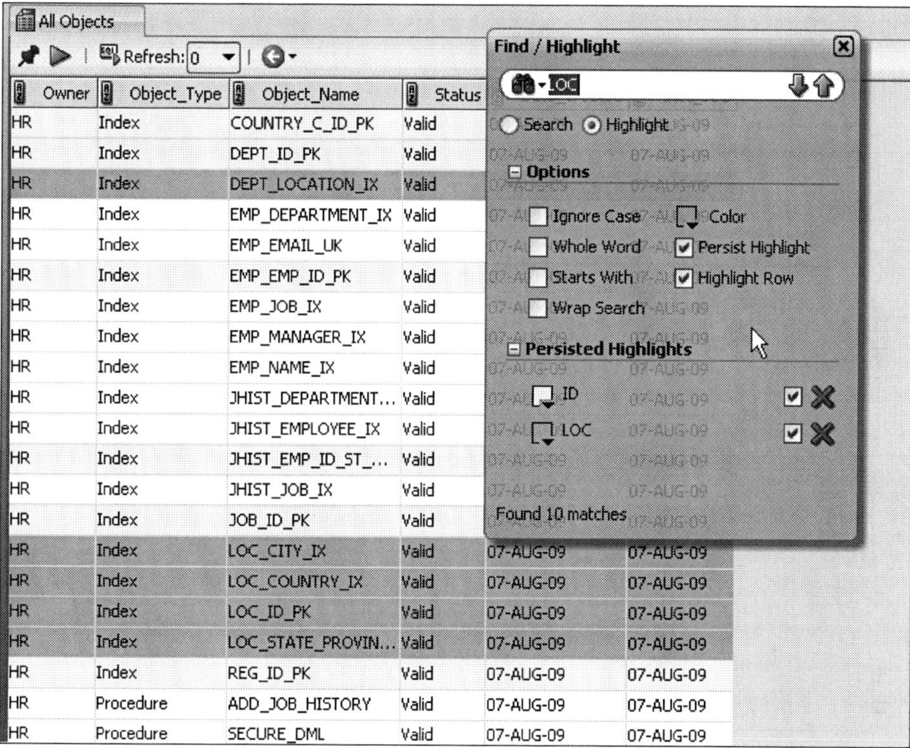

The **Find/Highlight** dialog allows you to search for a string in any cell in the grid or in a particular column in the grid. Use the drop-down list to the left-hand side of the search field to select the column for the search. The default is all columns.

The **Highlight** option is illustrated in the previous screenshot. Here, we applied two searches and highlighted each independently. The persisted searches are tracked in the dialog. If these are not visible, expand the floating window. These highlights persist when you close the dialog, or indeed if you close the report or data grid. Remove the persistent highlights using the same window.

Count Rows and the Single Record View

The context menu on any data grid includes:

- Single Record View
- Count Rows

While these are useful on any data grid, they are more useful for data grids where the number of columns displayed is unwieldy, or the number of records displayed is extensive.

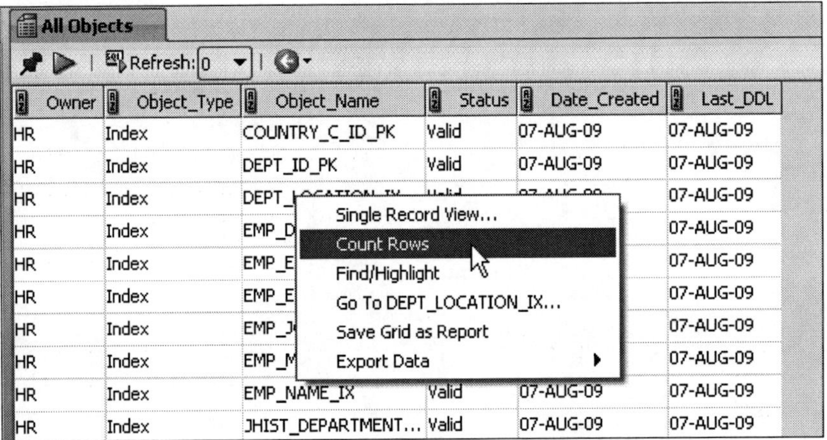

The **Single Record View...** switches the display of a single record to a form layout. This allows you to see the contents of the cells more clearly as you are now able to scroll down through the column heading, and not across the page.

Save Grid as Report

The **Save Grid as Report** option is a useful addition to SQL Developer 2.1. This data grid context menu option writes the SQL query, which produced the grid, to the **Create Report** dialog. This allows you to see and review all of the SQL queries that make up any data grids within the product and create a new user defined report, based on the query. For more information on working with reports, refer to the chapter on *The Power of SQL Reports*.

Working with Updating Data Grids

The **Data** and **Flashback** editors are slightly different to the read-only display editors in that they are related to instance data. The **Data** editor displays the table data in a grid. You can update, delete, or insert new data using the grid. The **Flashback** editor also displays the data in the table, and focuses on the changes made to the data.

In the next section, we'll look at the **Data** editor and focus on the different features available when working with this updatable data grid. To invoke an updatable data grid, select any table in the **Connections** navigator, and click on the **Data** editor.

Sorting and filtering data

Like the previously discussed data grids, the **Data** editor data grid has two sort options. The first option is on the column heading, where only one sort applies at a time and each sort replaces the last. The second option allows you to sort on multiple columns. To sort columns on multiple criteria, select the **Sort...** option just above the data grid. This allows you to sort on a selection of columns, which can be sorted in ascending or descending order.

Filters are restrictions on the displayed data. When you add a filter to the data grid, you are in effect adding a `WHERE` clause to the select statement. An example of adding a filter to the **COUNTRIES** data grid is `COUNTRY_NAME LIKE 'A%' OR COUNTRY_NAME LIKE 'C%'`. Each time you invoke the **Data** editor for a table, the full set of data is returned, that is, without any filters applied. However, any previous filters on the table are stored and you can invoke them from the **Filter** drop-down list.

The following screenshot displays the **EMPLOYEES** table with a multiple column sort applied, as indicated by the bold **Sort...** option. The **Filter** drop-down list indicates a selection of previous filters for the table:

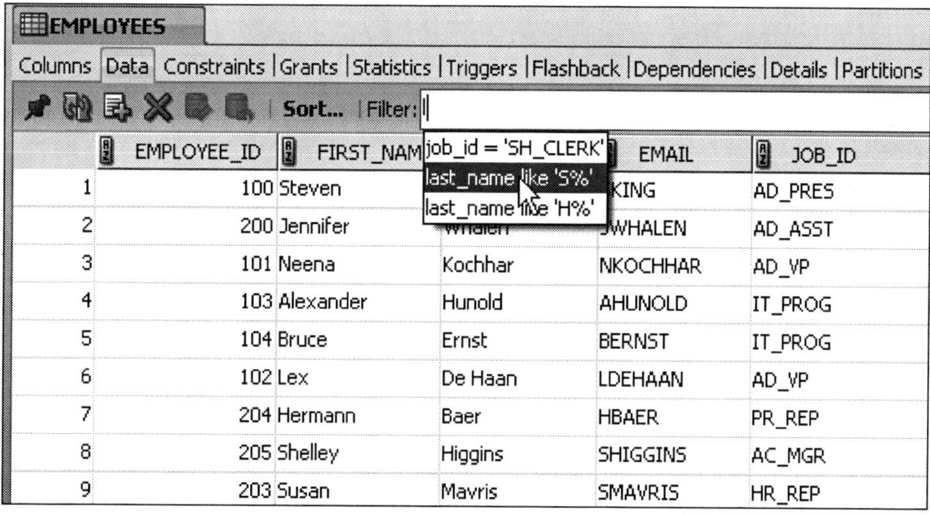

To invoke the drop-down list, place the cursor in the filter field and start typing or use the down arrow.

Updating data

To update any data item in the grid, select the item and start typing. As soon as you are in edit-mode, the **Edit Value** dialog button displays. Clicking on this button invokes an edit dialog, which is useful for larger text fields such as comments:

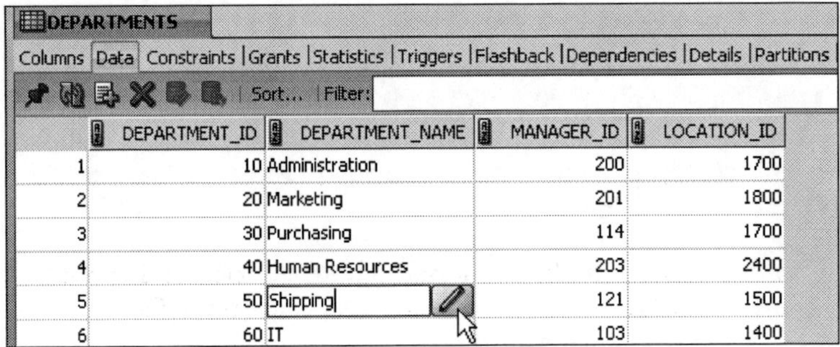

Working with LOBS in the data grid

For LOB columns, the value stored is not displayed in the data grid. Instead, the word (BLOB) displays. To see the value, such as the image stored, you can edit the value by selecting the **Edit Value** dialog button. In the following example, the image is stored in the database. To view the image select the **Image** checkbox. To use the data grid to add an image, or file to the database, click on **Load** and select the file. This is not saved to the database until you have committed the changes. Click on **OK** to close the dialog and then click on the **Commit Changes** button. You can now view the image or file by once again clicking on the **(BLOB)** field:

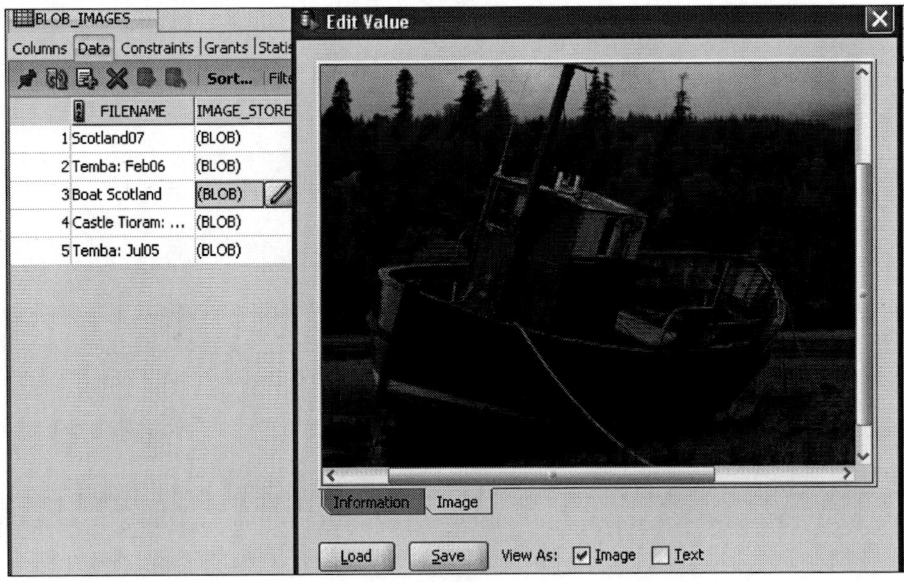

Using flashback

The **Flashback** display editor is displayed when you are connected to an Oracle Database 11*g*. To see the **Flashback** feature in action, select the **Data** editor for one of the HR tables, such as **DEPARTMENTS**. Modify a record and **Commit** the changes. Now, select the **Flashback** display editor. You should see **Update** in the **Operation** column. If it is not immediately apparent, double-click on the **Operation** column to sort the data. Select the updated record. The updated record is displayed in the **Data** editor below the records. Select the **Undo SQL** tab to view the query required to reinstate the original's record. The **Undo SQL** tab shows the SQL needed to restore the state for the whole transaction.

To review the **Undo SQL** syntax in the **Flashback** editor, grant the schema the `SELECT ANY TRANSACTION` system privilege (for example, `GRANT SELECT ANY TRANSACTION TO HR;`).

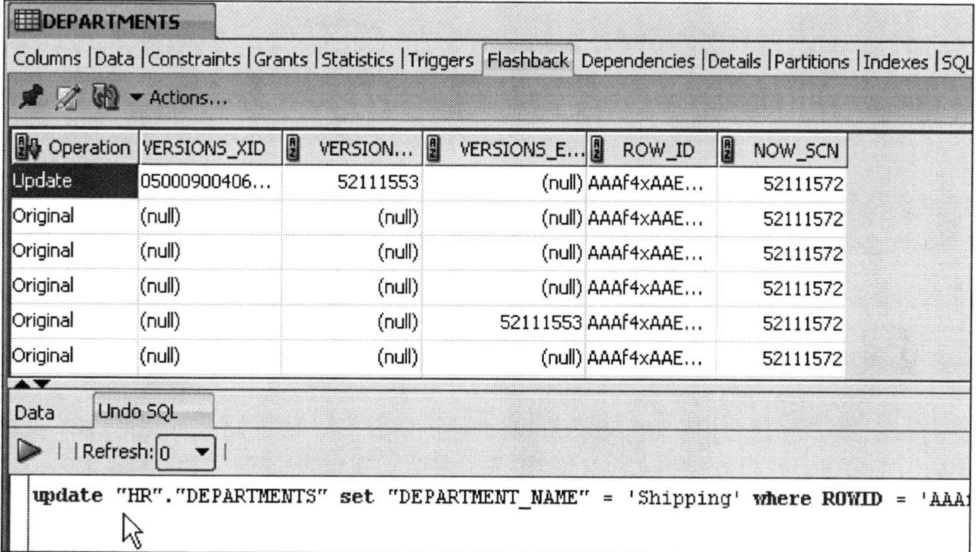

Reviewing other database object nodes

As you select each of the other database objects, you'll notice that the set of display editors varies considerably.

It would be tedious to single out each of the object nodes and describe them here. The display editors and data grids behave the same for each of them. In this next section, we review the nodes where the behavior or interaction is slightly different and worth noting.

Working with PL/SQL objects

Triggers, functions, procedures, and packages all have their own separate nodes in the **Connections** navigator. Prior to SQL Developer 2.1, a single-click on any object in these PL/SQL nodes behaved as for all other database objects, that is, a set of defining display editors opens. In order to edit a PL/SQL object, you needed to select the **Edit...** menu item, or click on the **Edit** button. Historically, conforming to that standard served only to confuse users wanting to open and edit PL/SQL code.

SQL Developer 2.1 changed this behavior by opening a single set of editors, with the first being the editable PL/SQL code:

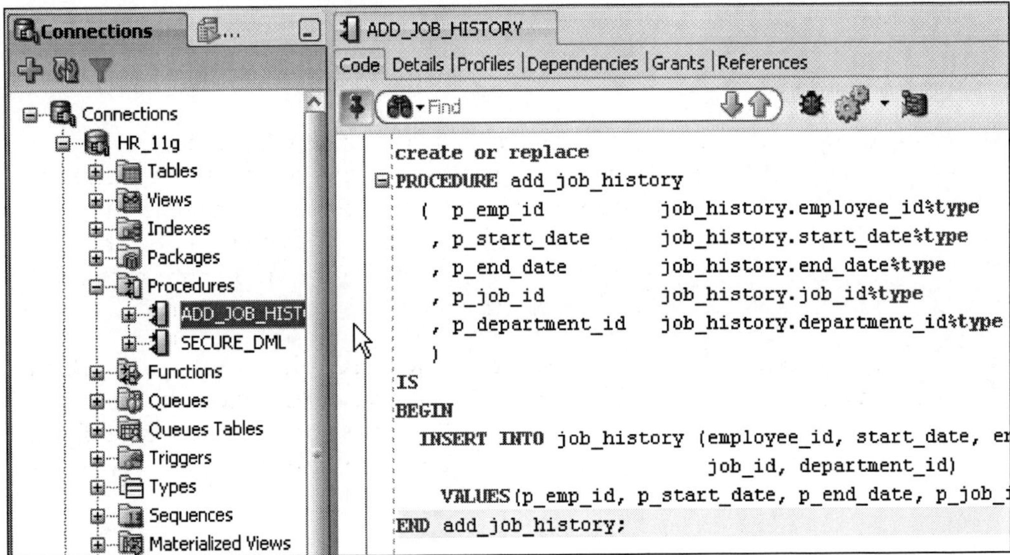

In the screenshot just displayed, the initial **Code** editor is the editable PL/SQL code editor. This **Code** editor is included in the set of display editors for the selected procedure. This differs from earlier product releases, where the code editor was a separate window.

> Unlike with other database objects, each new selected PL/SQL object opens a new window. In other words, the windows are automatically pinned for the PL/SQL windows. For more information, see the chapter on *Working with PL/SQL*.

Accessing objects you don't own

Very often, you may have the connection details for one schema that has access to objects in another schema. One of the most frequently asked questions on the SQL Developer forum is about viewing objects that the schema does not own.

Other users

As discussed, the objects under your connection are objects created or owned by the schema defined in the connection. To view any other objects that your connection (schema) has access to, use the **Other Users** node. When you expand **Other Users**, for your current connection, you are executing the equivalent SQL query `SELECT * FROM ALL_USERS;`. This query returns all of the users in the current database. However, it does not mean that you have access to the objects in each of those schemas.

To review the objects the HR schema has access to, expand the **Other Users** node for the HR connection. Select and expand the user OE, and then expand the **Tables** node. You should see the selection of OE tables displayed. Not only does HR have access to these objects, the HR schema can query the data. You can select each table and display the set of editors available. HR is not a privileged user, but is granted the `SELECT ANY TABLE` system privilege.

The user SCOTT/TIGER is another of the Oracle database shipped schemas. SCOTT was the original sample user and is not a privileged user. If you have access to SCOTT, create a new database connection for SCOTT and repeat the exercise. If you expand the OE or HR tables nodes under SCOTT's **Other Users** node, the nodes are empty. SCOTT does not have access to these objects.

Synonyms and filters

You can expand and work with objects you have access to in the **Other Users** node. You can also create synonyms for these objects and then, using **Filters**, display the objects within each respective object type node in your connection.

Consider the following example. The HR schema has access to query the OE's **CUSTOMERS** table. HR can query the table, using `SELECT * from OE.CUSTOMERS;`. Now, create a synonym using, `CREATE SYNONYM CUSTOMERS FOR OE.CUSTOMERS;`. This means the HR schema can write the queries without having to refer to the OE schema.

In SQL Developer, the synonym definition appears in the **Synonyms** node. The **CUSTOMERS** object will appear in the **Tables** node by setting the **Include Synonyms** option in the **Filter** dialog.

In the following screenshot, the tooltip shows that the **CUSTOMERS** table belongs to OE. The **Tables** node is also marked as **Filtered**:

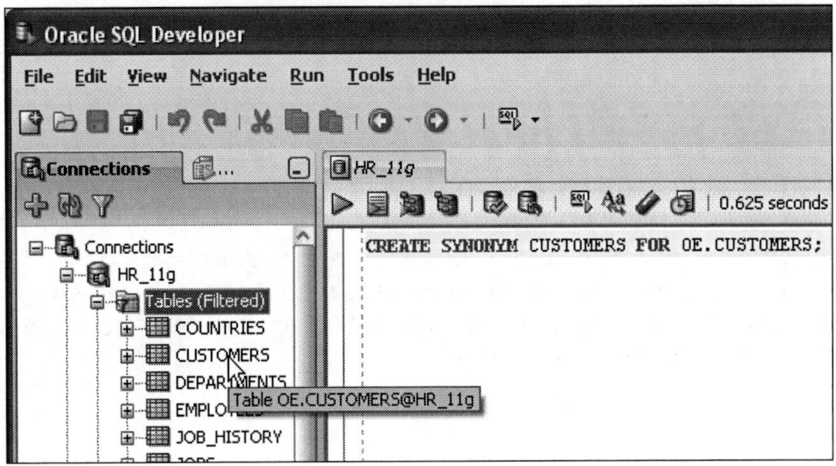

Recycle Bin

The **Recycle Bin** was introduced to Oracle databases in Oracle Database 10g. SQL Developer displays the contents of the Recycle Bin in the **Recycle Bin** node. For supported databases, the Recycle Bin provides a listing of all objects deleted from the schema. The information displayed about dropped objects, includes the date the object was created and dropped, and whether the object can be **undropped** (reinstated) or purged. SQL Developer displays the original name of the object in the **Connections** navigator for ease of use. However, once dropped, the object has a new name. This allows you to drop objects and create new ones without the dropped object name blocking the action. In SQL Developer, displaying the old name makes it easier to decide what object you are dealing with, unless of course you repeatedly recreate and dropped the object.

Creating and updating database objects

In the first section of the chapter, we looked at browsing objects and data in the database. You may, if you are an application developer and working with a completed database design, spend most of your time doing just that. It is more likely though, that you'll need to make changes such as adding or modifying structures and data. SQL Developer provides the dialogs to assist you.

Creating new objects

In the same way that you can write SQL queries to extract information about the objects you have access to, you can write the SQL **Data Definition Language** (**DDL**) to create, edit, and modify these objects. Almost all of the object nodes in the **Connections** navigator provide a context menu to create a new object. To invoke a dialog that creates any new object, select the object in the navigator and invoke the context menu.

Once again, instead of reviewing each of the Create dialogs available in SQL Developer, we'll look at a few of the more common ones, show off some of the features, and then single out a few.

With the exception of **Packages** and **Types**, each Create dialog has at least two tabs. One of these is the **DDL** tab which displays the DDL syntax that will be executed, based on the detail provided on the preceding tabs. The details needed to populate the code in the **DDL** tab vary considerably, from the more involved trigger dialog to the straightforward synonym dialog.

Creating tables

The tables and views Create dialogs offer a choice of layout. The initial dialog displayed is the same as all of the other create dialogs, offering two tabs. The first of these tabs is for the input required to assemble the DDL to be executed, which is displayed in the second of the two tabs.

The DDL to create tables and views can get quite involved, so you have a second option in these dialogs. Select **Advanced** on the initial **Create Table** dialog to switch the display. You can switch back and forth with no loss of detail. While referred to as the advanced dialog, this is arguably the easier dialog to work with, as the Create DDL is broken down into components. Here, you can address all of the aspects of creating the table. Once you have selected **Advanced** for either tables or views, this layout will be displayed for each new table or view, until you reset the choice. In the **Advanced** dialog, the DDL is a node in the tree and no longer displays in a separate tab.

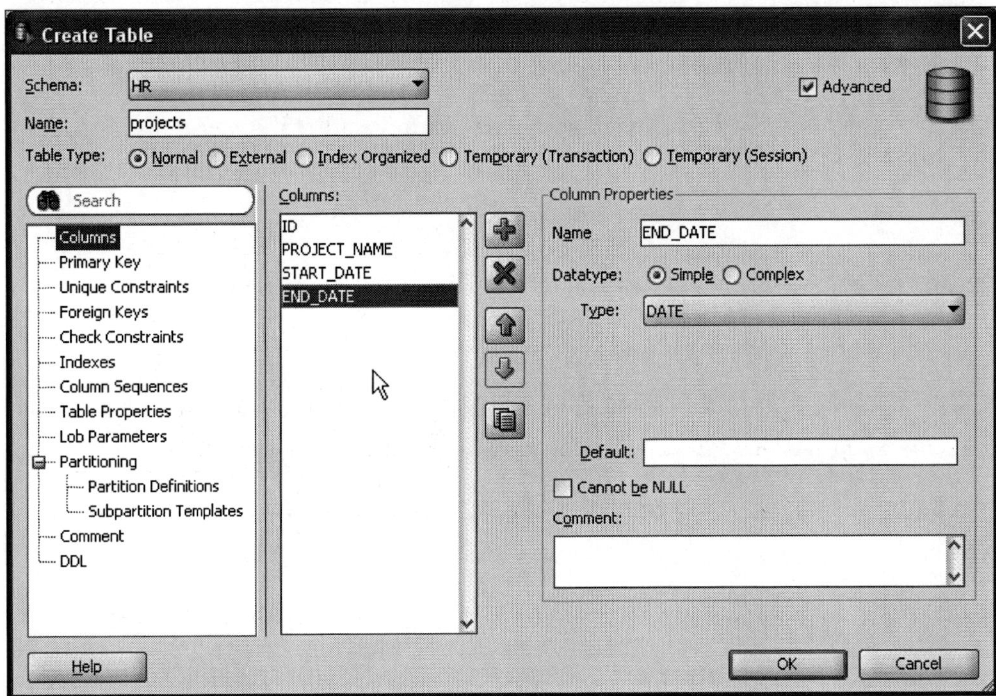

Early decisions

Using the previous screenshot displayed; there are various points to consider. The first is that the set of properties displayed varies, depending on the **Table Type** setting. You can set the **Table Type** setting after you have added many of the properties. However, it is advisable to set this property first as you are then directed to add type-appropriate details. While using the dialog, you can check whether verifying the DDL is as you expect, by selecting DDL in the tree. It is important to make the **Table Type** decision when creating the table, as this cannot be modified after the table has been created. For example, the table is either **Normal** or **Temporary**, you can't subsequently decide to make a **Normal** table **Temporary**. Another decision to make as you create the table is about partitioning. Again, once the table is created without partitions, you can't return to it later and add partitions.

You can modify tables after they are created in many ways, and possibly the most common is to add columns. Here too, it is important to remember that columns added to an existing table are added at the end, after the existing columns. The best time to handle column order is on creation. This **Create Table** dialog allows you to switch the column order. While not attempting to teach best practice here, it is best to keep the **Not Null** columns up at the top, and the less important columns, which may stay empty for the most part, at the end. To review all of the column detail, it may be useful to switch back to the **Create Table** grid layout. Using this layout, you can ascertain whether the mandatory columns are at the top of the list, or even verify that you have the data types correct. The grid layout is shown in the following screenshot:

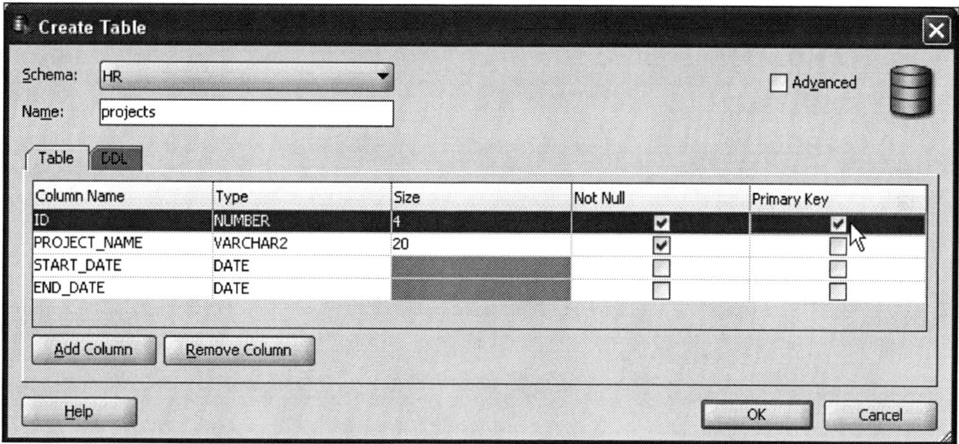

Adding constraints

You can add or modify constraints at any point, so it is not critical to do so at the point of creating the table. Certain keys, such as the Primary Key, and possibly even the Foreign Key, may be known and so it is easy enough to add them while in the dialog.

To add any of the constraint types while creating the table you need to select **Advanced** in the **Create Table** dialog. Select the appropriate node in the tree, and complete the details as required. We'll review adding a Foreign Key to the **projects** table example shown earlier. To add a Foreign Key constraint:

1. Switch to **Advanced** in the **Create Table** dialog.
2. Select the **Foreign Keys** node in the tree.
3. Click on **Add**. This enables the various drop-down lists available in the dialog and pre-populates the fields.
4. Select the reference schema. Note you do not need to select a table within the current schema.

5. Select the **Referenced Table** and **Referenced Constraint** from the lists available.
6. Set the associated columns for the Foreign Key.
7. You can deselect **Enabled** to create the constraint, but leave it disabled initially.

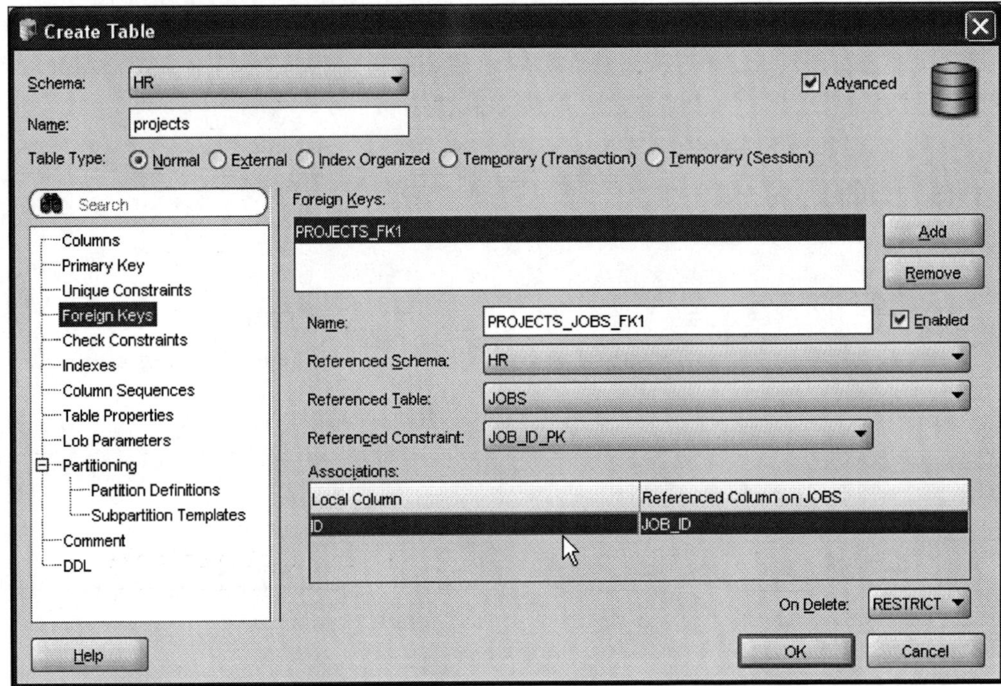

Creating column sequences

For some tables, users define a surrogate key for the Primary Key. As you are not using a real value for the data, you can populate this key using a sequence. In this case, you need to create a sequence and a trigger that fires each time you add a new record. This fetches the next value from the sequence and populates the record. You may have a general sequence that is used for all tables, or you may create a new sequence for each table. Either way, SQL Developer provides assistance when creating a table, for creating the sequence and trigger. Like constraints, this is something that can be done after you have created the table. However, in this case, you need to add the code manually or use another SQL Developer utility, as the option is not available in the table editor once the table has been created.

To add a sequence and trigger to populate a column, select **Column Sequences** in the tree. Select the required column and decide whether you are going to use an existing sequence or create a new one:

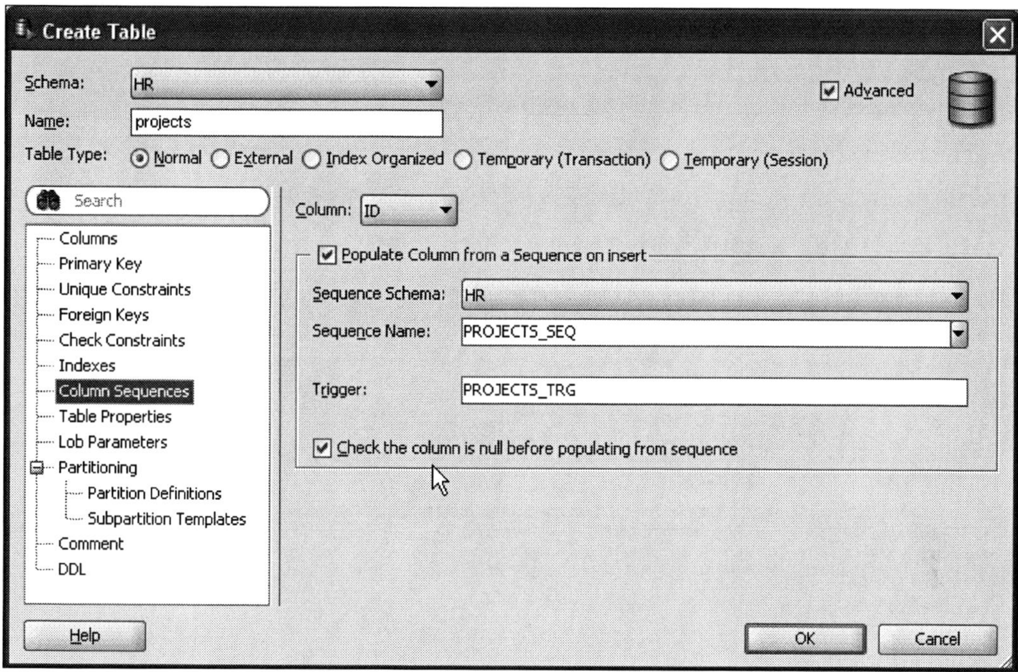

Additional properties

The advanced dialog provides you with panels for creating partitioned tables, setting up storage parameters for LOB columns, and general storage options.

Storage

You can set up storage parameters while creating the table using SQL Developer. To add general table storage options, select **Table Properties**. For LOB specific storage options, select the **Lob Parameters** node in the tree.

Partitions

Setting up partition requirements for a table must be done when you create the table. A table is either partitioned or not. This is not something you can switch on or off. SQL Developer provides you with the framework to create Range, Hash, or List partitions. If you elect to partition by Range, you can create further subpartitions. Once defined, you can specify storage and LOB storage properties.

Creating views

The **Create View** dialog also provides an **Advanced** dialog option. When creating views, you have a choice of three approaches:

- Write the **SQL Query**
- Use the **Quick-pick objects**
- Build up the query using elements in the dialog

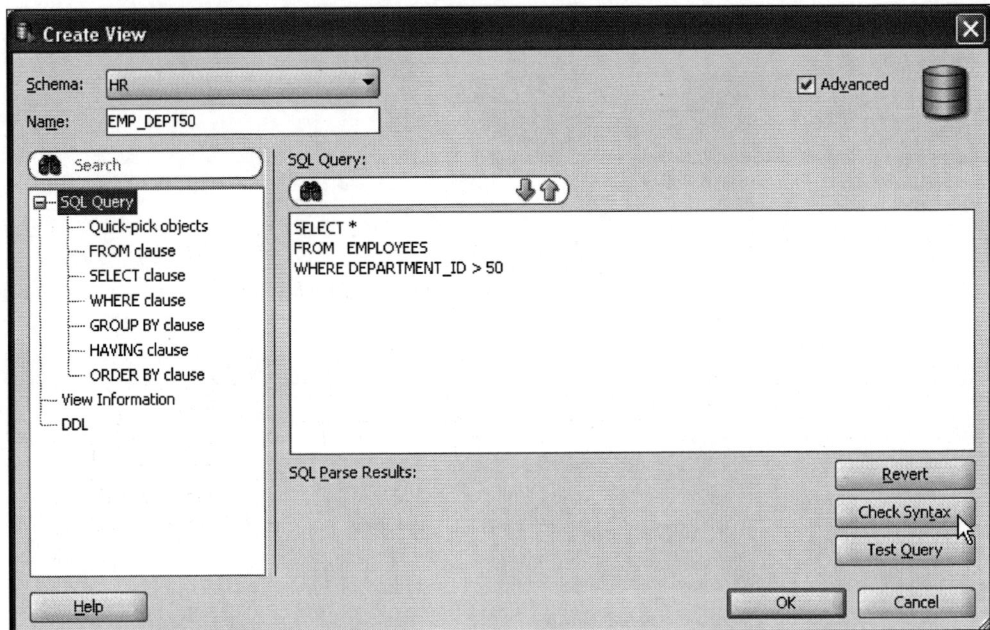

Writing the SQL query

You have a free text box to write the full syntax for the view (as seen in the previous screenshot). There is a **Check Syntax** button to verify the syntax and a **Test Query** button that executes the SQL to verify the validity.

For less complex queries, the syntax is parsed and the various other nodes, except the Quick-pick objects, are populated. In the simple example that we have just seen, once you have tested the SQL, the **EMPLOYEES** table is parsed out into the **FROM clause** node.

Using the Quick-pick objects

The **Quick-pick objects** node is useful when you are creating a view that joins a number of tables together. Select the tables based on the joins, and then the columns from the various tables, all in one step.

The first stage of the Quick-pick node is to query the objects available to you. You can either click on the **Query** button, or select the **Auto-Query** checkbox. Either way, you need to populate the **Available** section. Let's assume we want to create a view based on the **EMPLOYEES, DEPARTMENTS**, and **LOCATIONS** tables in the HR schema. We know that an employee works in a department, and that each department is in a location. Proceed as follows:

1. Starting with **EMPLOYEES**, expand the node to expose the Foreign Key, **EMP_DEPT_FK**.
2. Expand the **EMP_DEPT_FK** to expose the location Foreign Key, **DEPT_LOC_FK**.
3. Expand the **LOCATIONS** table.
4. Now, select a column from each table, and shuttle them over to the **Selected** section as shown in the following screenshot:

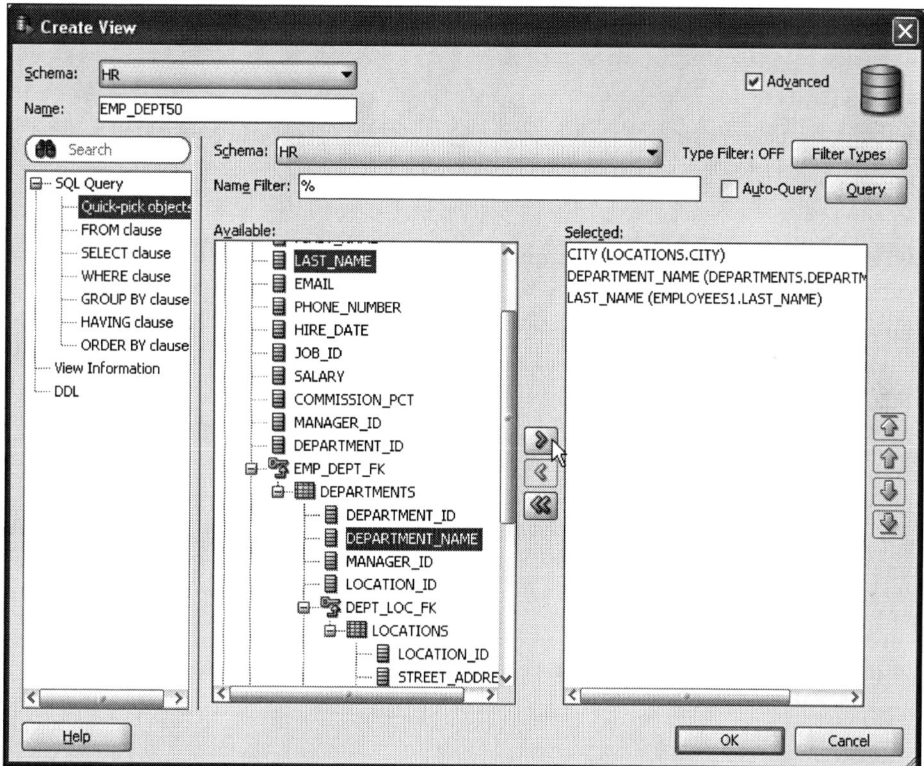

Once you have mastered the Quick-pick utility, you will find it provides a great start when creating views.

Now, select the **From clause** node in the tree. Notice that the joins are already listed and created. If you want to modify the joins even more, select each term **JOIN** in turn, and click on the **Edit** button. Using the **Edit Join** dialog (shown in the following screenshot), you can adjust the join syntax used in the view:

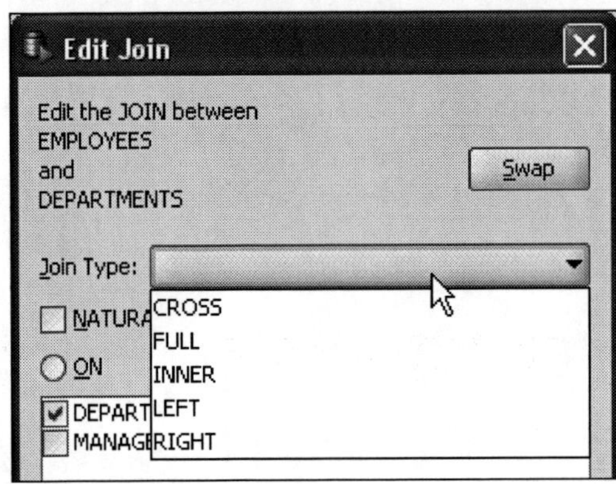

As you step down through each of the additional nodes in the tree, you can review the elements in the query already populated from the Quick-pick list and add further elements.

In the **SELECT clause**, you can start adding items by clicking the **+** button, which creates an empty field. To populate this, type the detail into the **Expression** field, provide an alias, and then click **Validate** to push the new item into the **<empty>** item above this. Alternatively, expand the **Expression Palette**, select, and double-click to shuttle the items to the **Expression** field. If you want to apply a function to the item, select the function for the lower list and, as before, **Validate** will validate and then populate the selected list. In the following screenshot, we want to add the **POSTAL_CODE**:

1. Click the green **+** to add a new item to the **SELECT List.**
2. Expand the **LOCATIONS** node in the **Expressions Palette.**
3. Select **POSTAL_CODE** and shuttle it to the **Expression** field on the left-hand side.
4. Click on **Validate** to add the new item.

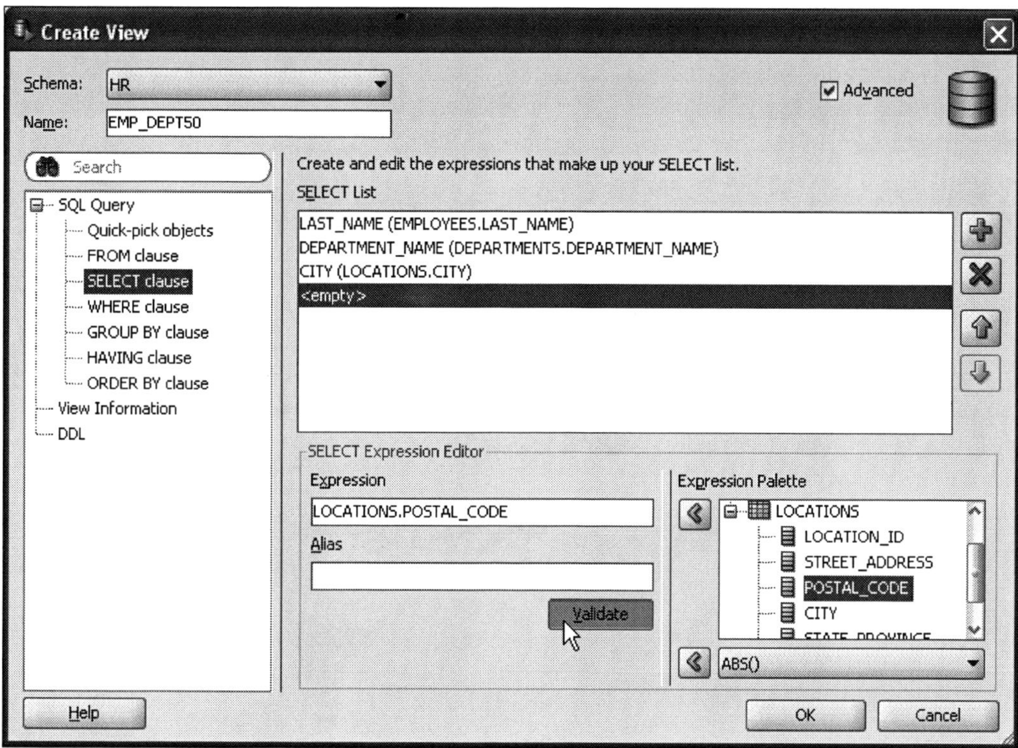

You can continue working through the view elements in the tree and add further detail, building up the view. Check any final view information and review the DDL. Click on **OK** to create the view.

Building the query using elements in the tree

The third option starts with the **FROM clause**, not using Quick-pick objects at all. This provides the same Auto-Query facility and the same tree for expanding. You can elect to shuttle individual tables across to the **Selected** section, you then need to create the joins. You can expose the tree and then shuttle the tables across as part of the tree, this will automatically create the joins.

Having started with the **FROM clause** section of the tree, you must then proceed to the **SELECT clause** and populate each of the items that you require, in the select list as described above.

Reviewing a few specific objects

We'll now consider a few additional database objects, which differ from the others in the tree.

Creating new users

To create new users, select the **Other Users** node for any privileged user, such as System, or any other user who has the Create User System Privilege.

The **Create User** dialog (as shown in the following screenshot) has a series of tabs for user details, including Tablespace settings, **Roles**, and **System Privileges**. This dialog also has an **SQL** tab, and when you click on **Apply**, the results of the execute SQL are displayed. While the `CREATE USER` statements are not complex, having a dialog that provides a complete listing of roles and privileges available for a user, means that you can quickly create new users.

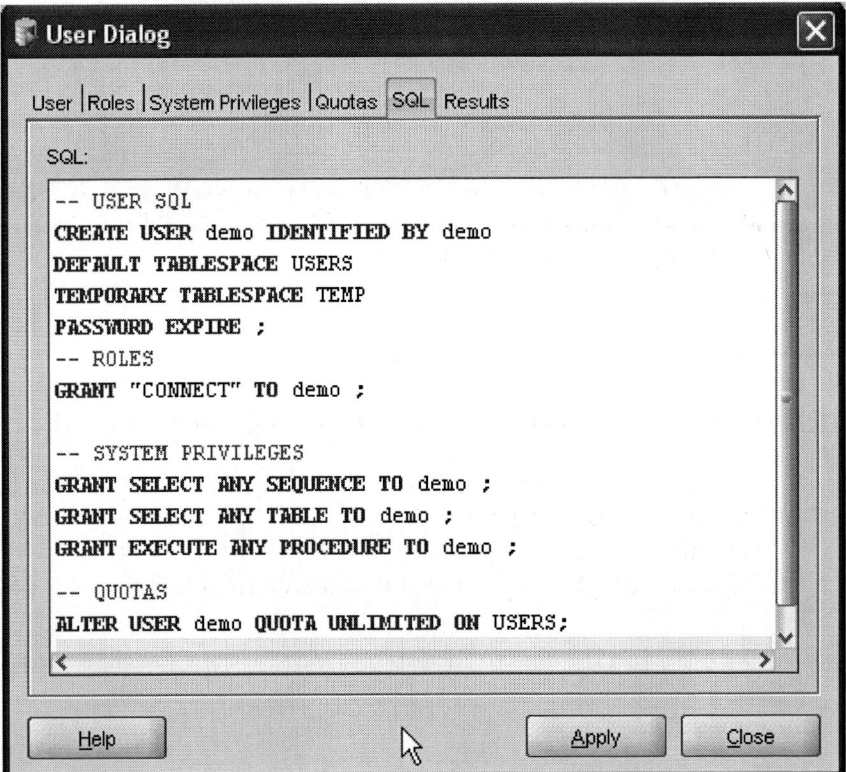

Setting the privilege to create new objects

You only have access to the create dialogs if you have the System Privilege to create the object. To see this in action, expand the **Other Users** node for the SYSTEM connection, select HR, invoke the context menu, and select **Edit User.** Under **System Privileges**, deselect **CREATE PROCEDURE**. Click on **Apply** and **Close**. Return to the top-level **Connections** navigator and expand your HR connection. Select the **Procedures** node and invoke the context menu. Note that the option to create a new object is now unavailable. If the user HR was connected when you changed the privilege, you need to disconnect and reconnect to activate the new privilege status (be sure to set the privilege back when you are done).

Editing objects: Putting context menus to work

Each object in the **Connections** navigator has a context menu associated with it. Each context menu invokes a dialog that supports SQL commands that range from a single, simple command (such as `DROP TABLE HR.COUNTRIES`) to a collection of basic and complex commands. Throughout the chapter, we have stated that any of the activities we're performing uses a UI as an interface for the underlying SQL command. Certainly, typing the drop table command is faster than selecting the items and invoking the dialog, assuming of course that you know the syntax. In this section, we'll briefly single out a few of these context menus.

Editing objects

Each of the Create dialogs has a matching Edit dialog. Most of the Edit dialogs directly match the object's Create dialog. If you invoke any Edit dialog, the **DDL** tab or node is initially empty, as it was when you first invoked the Create dialog. As soon as you change any of the properties, the **DDL** tab or node is populated with the SQL to reflect the changes. For many objects, such as triggers or views, editing the object results in a `Create` or `Replace...` command. For other objects, such as **Sequences** or **Tables**, editing the objects results in an `Alter...` command.

Consider the **Edit Table** dialog as shown in the following screenshot. The dialog is in the form of the advanced **Create** table dialog. Notice that you can no longer switch the table type, nor create partitions. While you can certainly add or delete columns, you cannot reorder them (unless you drop and recreate them). You'll find that other database rules, such as reducing the column width, are also enforced if the column already contains data.

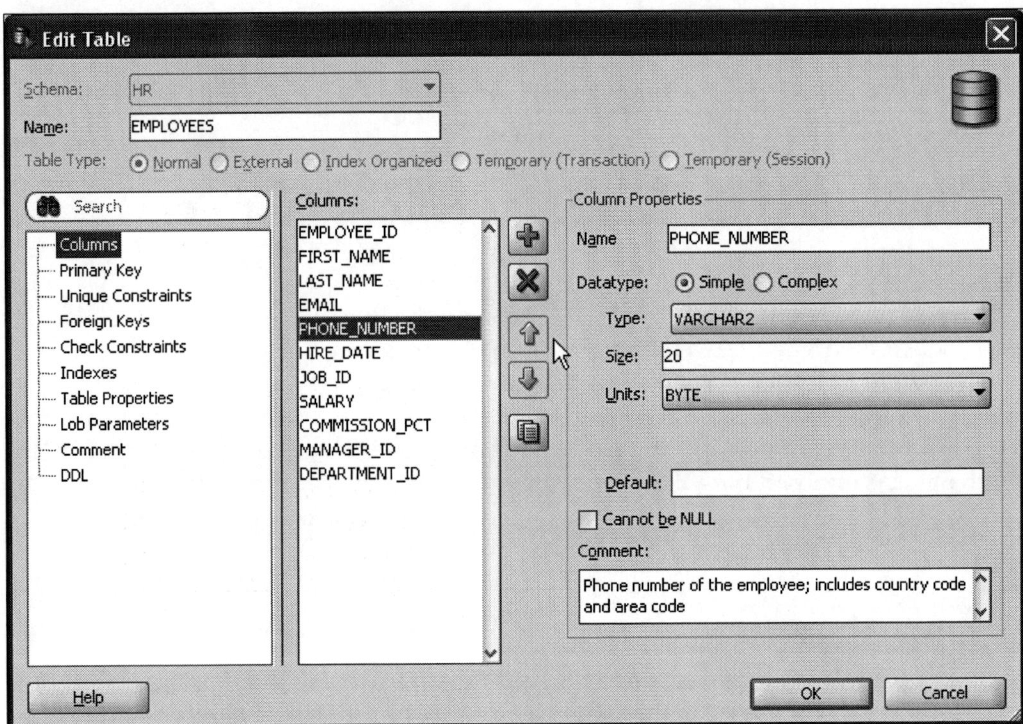

The Create and Edit table **Advanced** dialog includes a **Copy Columns** button. Use this to copy a selection of columns to another table.

Diving into context menus

Each object has an associated context menu, supporting many of the SQL statements associated with the object. For example, constraints can be created, renamed, or dropped, and disabled or enabled. Not only that, but you can also disable all constraints for a table or disable a single constraint. You can disable or enable all related Foreign Keys. These commands are available through a set of context menus of the **Tables** node:

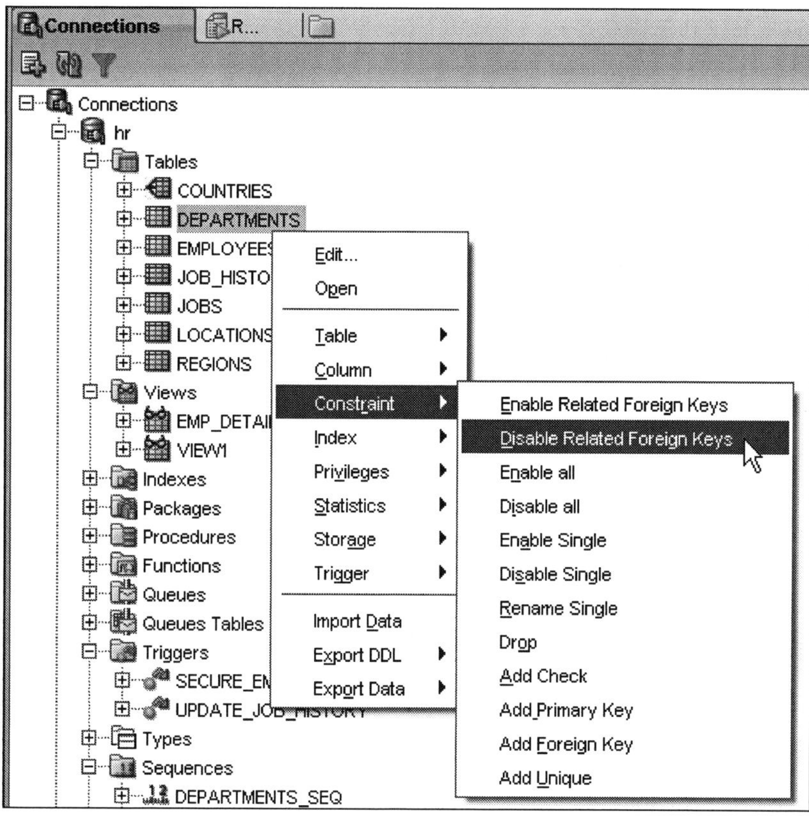

Using context menus as utilities

Some context menus invoke dialogs that go further than creating a single DDL command. They perform a series of actions, which we think of utilities. You have already seen a context menu that performs a number of DDL commands in the **Create Table** dialog, where you can populate the detail for the columns, the constraints, and add a new sequence and trigger. The resulting **DDL** tab displays a number of SQL commands, which are executed consecutively. Another dialog that can produce a long list of individual commands is the **Create / Edit User** dialog.

We'll now review two context menus which invoke dialogs that produce a number of SQL commands. As we review these menus, consider the kinds of SQL activities that you repeat. You can create your own context menus like these using user extensions to capture that activity. This is discussed in more detail in the chapter on *Extending SQL Developer*.

Normalizing data

You may, from time-to-time, work with spreadsheets of data. Some companies or teams have many spreadsheets that are passed around, containing valuable data. As the team grows, or someone realizes the data would be more valuably placed in a database, the detail in the spreadsheet is pulled into the database into a single table. This is no way to do database design, but it probably happens more often than it should. As soon as the data is displayed in a sortable grid, duplicate values become more apparent. The process of normalizing tables, with data in them, involves a few steps. Consider the following set of data (the script to create the **BIGEMP** table is available in the code bundle available on the Packt web site).

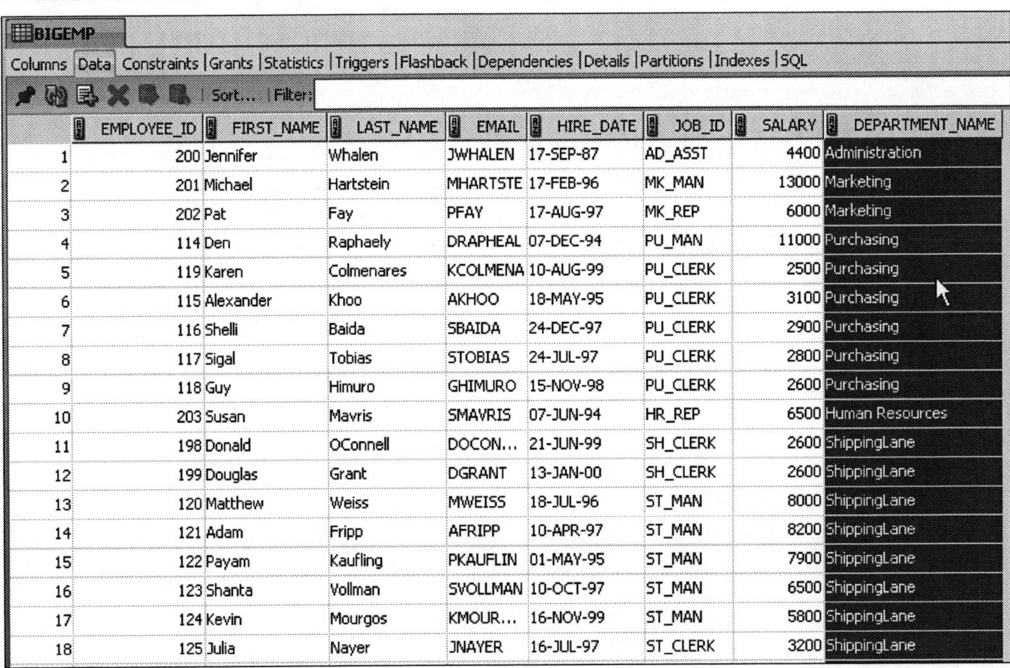

	EMPLOYEE_ID	FIRST_NAME	LAST_NAME	EMAIL	HIRE_DATE	JOB_ID	SALARY	DEPARTMENT_NAME
1	200	Jennifer	Whalen	JWHALEN	17-SEP-87	AD_ASST	4400	Administration
2	201	Michael	Hartstein	MHARTSTE	17-FEB-96	MK_MAN	13000	Marketing
3	202	Pat	Fay	PFAY	17-AUG-97	MK_REP	6000	Marketing
4	114	Den	Raphaely	DRAPHEAL	07-DEC-94	PU_MAN	11000	Purchasing
5	119	Karen	Colmenares	KCOLMENA	10-AUG-99	PU_CLERK	2500	Purchasing
6	115	Alexander	Khoo	AKHOO	18-MAY-95	PU_CLERK	3100	Purchasing
7	116	Shelli	Baida	SBAIDA	24-DEC-97	PU_CLERK	2900	Purchasing
8	117	Sigal	Tobias	STOBIAS	24-JUL-97	PU_CLERK	2800	Purchasing
9	118	Guy	Himuro	GHIMURO	15-NOV-98	PU_CLERK	2600	Purchasing
10	203	Susan	Mavris	SMAVRIS	07-JUN-94	HR_REP	6500	Human Resources
11	198	Donald	OConnell	DOCON...	21-JUN-99	SH_CLERK	2600	ShippingLane
12	199	Douglas	Grant	DGRANT	13-JAN-00	SH_CLERK	2600	ShippingLane
13	120	Matthew	Weiss	MWEISS	18-JUL-96	ST_MAN	8000	ShippingLane
14	121	Adam	Fripp	AFRIPP	10-APR-97	ST_MAN	8200	ShippingLane
15	122	Payam	Kaufling	PKAUFLIN	01-MAY-95	ST_MAN	7900	ShippingLane
16	123	Shanta	Vollman	SVOLLMAN	10-OCT-97	ST_MAN	6500	ShippingLane
17	124	Kevin	Mourgos	KMOUR...	16-NOV-99	ST_MAN	5800	ShippingLane
18	125	Julia	Nayer	JNAYER	16-JUL-97	ST_CLERK	3200	ShippingLane

Notice the duplicate **DEPARTMENT_NAME** values displayed. This detail should be in a separate **BIGDEPT** table. Normalizing the **BIGEMP** table means that we need to create a new table for the department's detail. The new table should have a Primary Key that is populated as we move the department name records across. It also needs a Foreign Key that links the tables.

SQL Developer handles all this detail in a single dialog. Select the table, and click on the **Column | Normalize** item in the context menu. Populate the fields with the details to create the new table. Include, the column that will be moved, the new sequence, and the trigger that fires to populate the Primary Key column. The following screenshot shows the initial dialog:

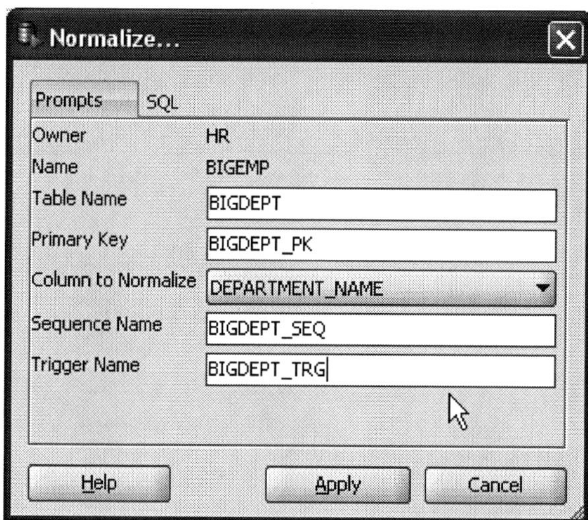

The **SQL** tab includes the set of SQL DDL statements wrapped in PL/SQL block:

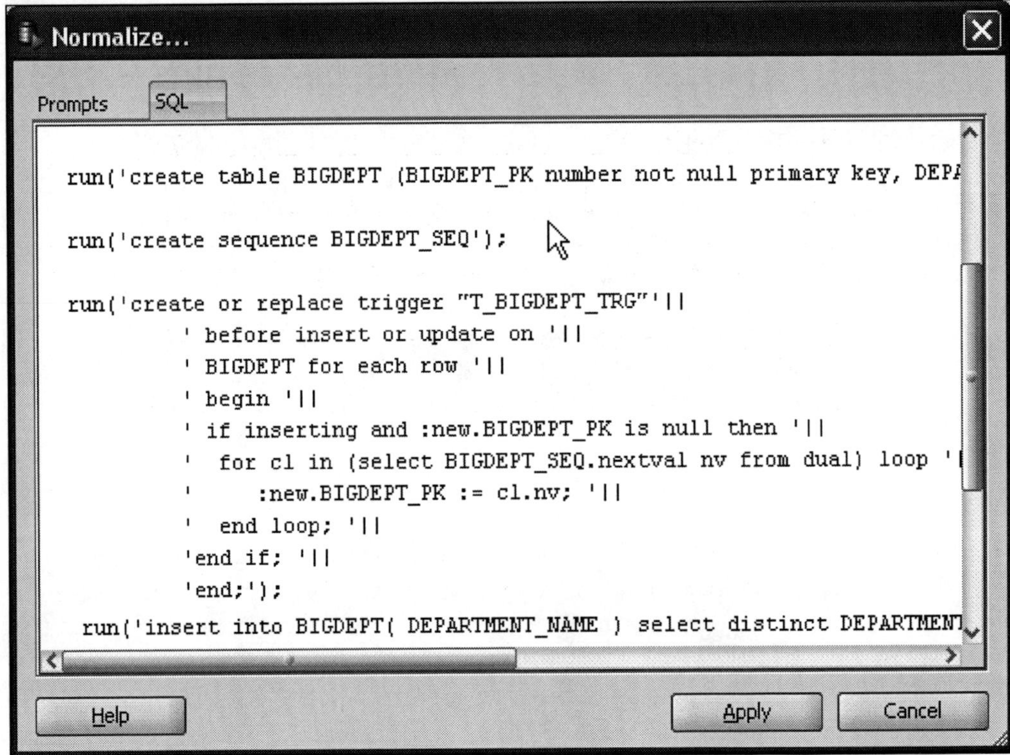

Triggers and sequences

In the same way as there are multiple options for constraints, there are a variety of context sensitive commands for triggers including enabling, disabling, creating, and dropping. The list of context menu items for a trigger also includes **Create (PK From Sequence)**.

This follows the same concept as described earlier when creating tables. As mentioned, you can create a sequence and trigger to populate the PK value from the sequence, at the time of creating a table. SQL Developer provides you with the context menu to do this after the table has been created. In this situation, the sequence should already exist.

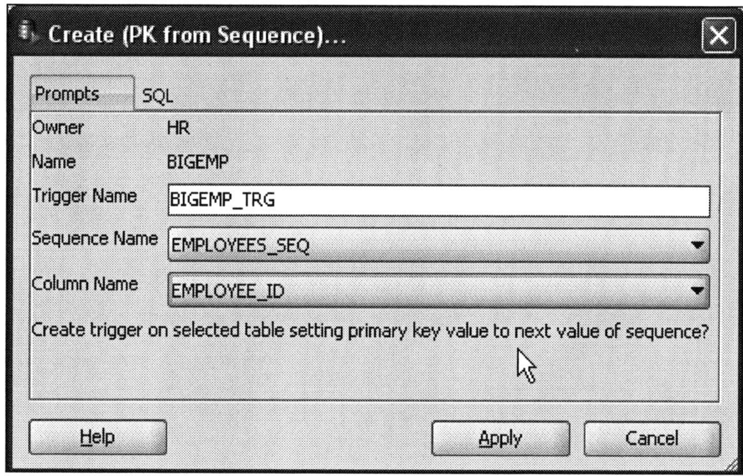

Summary

In this chapter, we have reviewed a variety of display editors and dialogs. Starting out by browsing objects that we have access to, we progressed through the Create and Edit dialogs, singling out certain dialogs on the way to illustrate notable points and features.

We have said that all of the activities completed here can be accomplished by writing SQL. In the next chapter, we look at the SQL Worksheet and the variety of features that are available to assist you when writing SQL and PL/SQL statements.

3
Working with the SQL Worksheet

The SQL Worksheet provides a scratch pad for all SQL, PL/SQL, and SQL*Plus statements and commands. You can run individual statements or a collection of commands. You can also run scripts and execute PL/SQL. In essence, doing all you might do in a command-line interface like SQL*Plus. The SQL Worksheet provides more, in that it offers code templates, provides code snippets, assists with code insight and completion, and maintains a history of commands. In this chapter, we look at these and other features offered in the SQL Worksheet and how to use them. We will use SQL and SQL*Plus commands to illustrate features, using PL/SQL only where needed specifically for a feature. All aspects of PL/SQL are addressed in the chapter on *Working with PL/SQL*.

Introducing the SQL Worksheet

The SQL Worksheet is an independent working environment in SQL Developer that you can use to interact with the database, much as you would using a command line or SQL*Plus. Before we look at the features in the worksheet, we'll look at the worksheet environment, how to invoke it, and the preferences that control it.

It is important to be aware of the user that is connected to the database. In SQL*Plus, if you are connected as one user and want to query details for another user, you might:

- Open a new SQL*Plus connection
- Change the currently connected user
- Query details in another schema by prefixing the object names with the new schema name (for example, while connected as OE, query an HR table using `SELECT * FROM HR.EMPLOYEES;`)

These alternatives are also true for the SQL Developer SQL Worksheet. By 'independent' we mean that objects created in the *worksheet* are not automatically reflected in the **Connections** navigator. If you execute a DDL command to create a table, you need to refresh the **Tables** node in the navigator to reflect this addition. There is, however, a close tie between the two, as you can drag a table from the **Connections** navigator onto the worksheet to create a SQL statement.

Controlling the environment

There are a number of preferences that control the general behavior of worksheets and database interactions. These preferences are in the **Preferences** dialog, under **Database | Worksheet** and include:

- Opening a worksheet on connect—selected by default, this preference determines that as soon as you invoke a database connection, the SQL Worksheet automatically opens.
- Automatically committing statements in the worksheet—this **Autocommit in SQL Worksheet** option should be used cautiously, as all records will be automatically committed as you exit the worksheet.
- Closing worksheet on disconnect—there is also an option to close all worksheets on disconnect. This feature is off by default, as requested by many users who leave their working environments either overnight, or to attend to other work. If the database connection times out while they're away, merely reconnecting the user allows them to continue from their last point of activity. You may find that closing all open worksheets on disconnect is preferable.
- Setting a default location for scripts that you run—this is an important setting when running files that call other files.

Controlling the SQL Worksheet

To set SQL Worksheet properties, such as opening a worksheet on connect, controlling auto-commit, and disconnection, use the **Database | Worksheet** preferences in the **Tools | Preferences** dialog.

Two additional environmental features to bear in mind are the following:

- Maximizing and minimizing windows—double-clicking on the tab of most windows in SQL Developer will maximize that window. A second double-click returns the layout to the previous state. This is useful when you only want to work with one or more worksheets and have no need to interact with other navigators.
- Sending update to the **Connections** navigator—any DDL commands issued in the SQL Worksheet, such as `DROP` or `CREATE TABLE`..., are not reflected in the **Connections** navigator until the connection is refreshed. This saves the navigator from constantly polling the database for updates. To refresh a connection, select the object node required, and click on **Refresh.**

Opening SQL Worksheets

To open a new SQL Worksheet, select the connection in the **Connections** navigator, and while using the context menu, select **Open SQL Worksheet**. Alternatively, use the button in the main toolbar, as shown in the following screenshot. This uses the currently highlighted connection from the **Connections** navigator to populate the first value in the list of available connections:

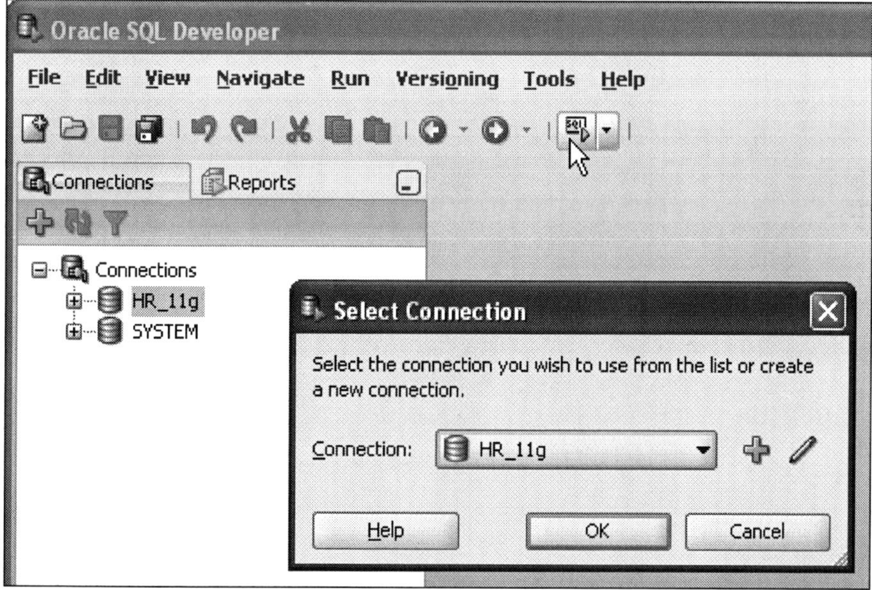

Working with multiple worksheets

SQL Developer allows you to open multiple SQL Worksheets for the same connection. To open another connection, follow any of the directions for opening a SQL Worksheet. The newly opened worksheets are sequentially named ~1, ~2, and so on. So, if your first connection is **HR**, then the subsequent worksheets are **HR~1**, **HR~2**, and so on. Because you can tile worksheets, this is very useful when you want to compare scripts and the output.

These are known as *shared worksheets* and use the same connection and session. This is the essence of SQL Developer. Throughout the tool, all objects, navigators, worksheets, and searches, share the same connection and session.

To open a new unshared worksheet with a new, *separate*, session, use the key sequence *Ctrl+Shift+N*. This allows you to work against the same schema, but within two separate sessions, and is typically used for long running queries. In SQL Developer 2.1, you can also invoke an unshared worksheet using the **Unshared SQL Worksheet** button on an open worksheet, as shown in the following screenshot. Unshared worksheets are labeled using __1, __2, and so on. The following screenshot shows two shared and one unshared worksheet open for **HR_11g**:

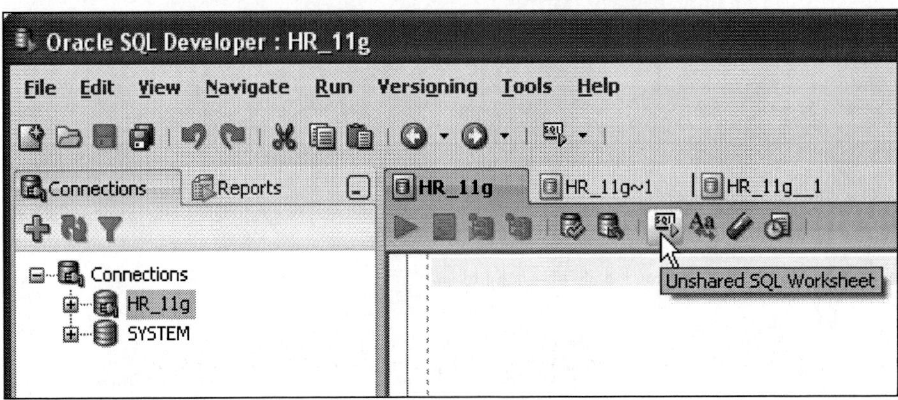

New worksheets are, by default, shared worksheets. You need to explicitly open unshared worksheets.

Switching connections

At any point you can switch the currently connected user on the SQL Worksheet to another user by using the drop-down list of all connections. The same drop-down list is used in a variety of places in SQL Developer, allowing you to switch users and run scripts or reports for other connections. The drop-down list is also useful if you lose or close your connection. Simply select the required user from the drop-down list to reinstate the connection:

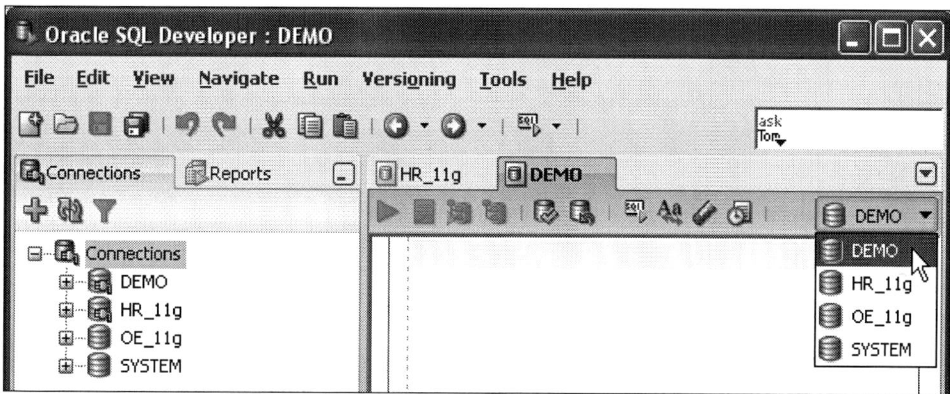

Getting started

Once you have a worksheet open, you are ready to start. Simply start typing commands. The worksheet also supports the ability to drag-and-drop elements from the **Connections** navigator onto the worksheet. These commands, and drag-and-drop features, are discussed in the next section.

Writing and executing commands

In this section, we will review the variety of commands you can enter in the SQL Worksheet and how to execute them. We'll start by looking at the SQL*Plus support within the worksheet and then move onto SQL commands. You'll see as we work that we use SQL*Plus, SQL, and PL/SQL commands or statements, and generally that's how you work with them in daily practice.

Writing your first statements

Immediately above the worksheet is a set of buttons. The first, **Run Statement** or *F9*, is generally for executing single statements, while the second, **Run Script** or *F5*, is for running scripts, single or multiple statements, and a blend of SQL, SQL*Plus, and PL/SQL commands.

Using an open SQL Worksheet for your HR connection, enter the following statements:

```
SELECT * FROM EMPLOYEES;
SELECT * FROM DEPARTMENTS;
SELECT * FROM COUNTRIES;
```

With the cursor on one line of code, press *F9* first and then the *F5* key. Notice that the *F9* key shows a set of results in a data grid for selected query, under the **Query Result** tab. The *F5* key displays the set of results for all of the queries, under the **Script Output** tab, and the display is similar to the output in SQL*Plus:

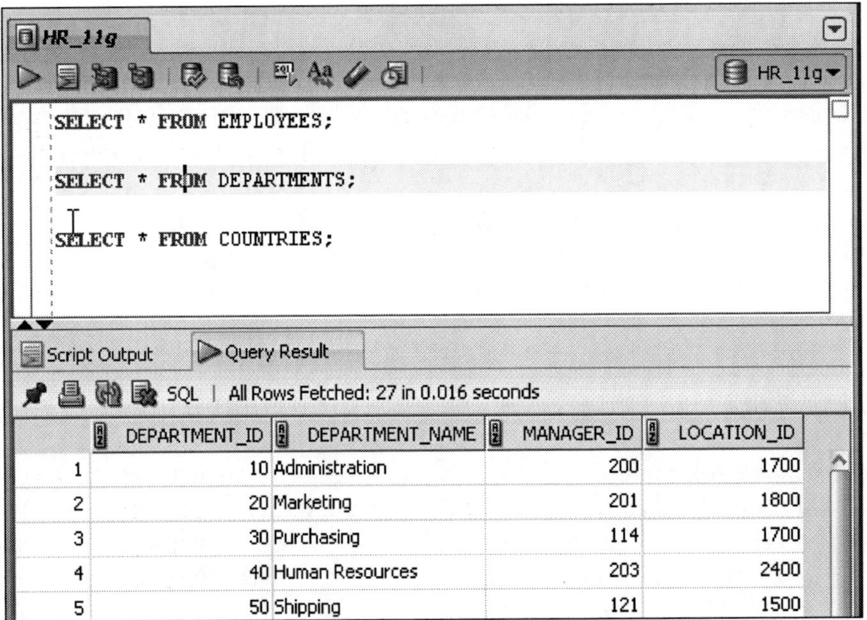

[To clear text from the SQL Worksheet or text output screens, use the Clear button.]

Running statements

The **Run Statement** or *F9*, command executes individual statements, sending the output sent to a data grid, much like the data grid you see when selecting a table in the **Connections** navigator, but without the same update capabilities. Due to the output style, the **Run Statement** is typically used, and recommended for SQL commands only. If you use *F9* for SQL*Plus commands, the results for certain commands, such as `DESCRIBE`, are sent to the **Statement Output** window, while others, such as `CONNECT`, are ignored.

Prior to SQL Developer 2.1, *F9* only worked on a single SQL statement, either the currently highlighted SQL or the last in a set of SQL statements. Now you are able to select and execute a number of SQL statements using the *F9* key. They are still executed as individual statements and are executed sequentially. In the case of multiple queries, the output of each statement is sent to a new and separate data grid.

Select all three of the statements in the previous example and press *F9*. The output is shown in the following image:

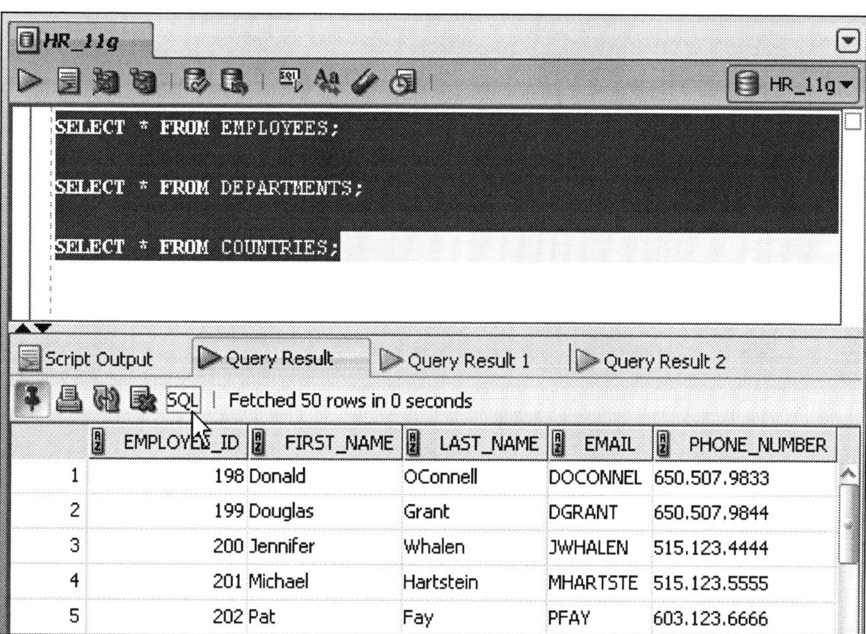

The advantage of this is that you can compare the output from each query in the separate data grids. In addition, for long running queries, you can continue to work with the connection and open new worksheets or do other activities, and leave the query to run untroubled in the background.

Because you can select and run any number of queries using *F9*, you can potentially open an unlimited number of new windows for each data grid.

If you hold the mouse over the tab title, the query for the grid is displayed directly above the grid. This allows you to easily see which query produced the data displayed below. If the query is short, then the rollover might be sufficient. In addition to this, there is a **SQL** button in the toolbar above the grid. Click on this to see the query in a popup window.

Run Statement (*F9*) executes one statement at a time. Selecting multiple statements, and then the **Run Statement,** sends the results to separate data grids. Do not be tempted to run SQL scripts using *F9*, as some SQL*Plus commands, such as `Connect`, are ignored.

Run script

Run Script or *F5*, executes all of the statements or commands in the worksheet, unless you highlight one single statement and run that as a single command. To highlight a single command for execution, place the cursor in the line of the statement and double-click. This highlights the complete statement and enables you to execute only that statement. At any point, if you highlight only part of a statement, *F5* will attempt to run just the highlighted code and may potentially fail.

The following screenshot shows an example of the **Script Output** using a selected single command:

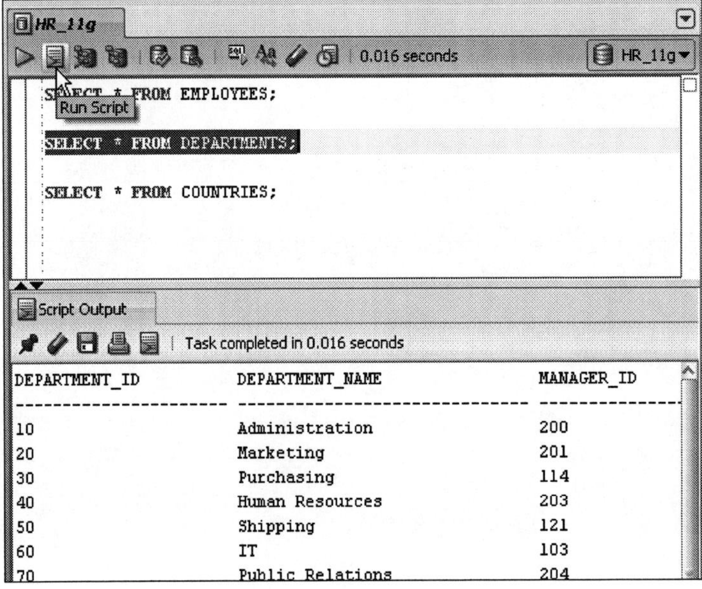

Using SQL*Plus commands

SQL*Plus is a command-line tool that is installed with every Oracle database and provides an environment for querying the database and running SQL and PL/SQL commands and scripts. SQL*Plus commands fall into broad categories, such as executing commands, defining objects, and controlling the environment. Many of the latter are related to formatting the output. This means that while some commands are still valuable in SQL Developer, there are many that are not required.

In this section, we'll look at a number of the more commonly used supported commands, and at some of those not supported. A full list of supported SQL*Plus commands is maintained at the SQL Developer site on the Oracle Technology Network (`http://otn.oracle.com/sqldeveloper`).

Supporting SQL*Plus

Each release of SQL Developer increases the list of supported SQL*Plus commands, with `DESCRIBE`, `DEFINE`, `CONNECT`, and `EXIT` being among the list of initially supported commands, and commands like `SPOOL` and `VARIABLE` added later.

Clear the worksheet and enter the following:

```
SPOOL C:\WORKING\DEPTS.SQL
/* This is a piece of code to show the SQL*PLUS commands used in SQL
Developer */

SET FEEDBACK ON
SET ECHO ON

DEFINE DEPTNUM = 100
DESC DEPARTMENTS

SELECT * FROM DEPARTMENTS
WHERE DEPARTMENT_ID < &DEPTNUM
OR DEPARTMENT_NAME LIKE '&&DNAME';

SELECT * FROM DEPARTMENTS
WHERE DEPARTMENT_NAME LIKE '&&DNAME';

UNDEFINE DNAME
SPOOL OFF
```

The code is a combination of SQL and SQL*Plus commands. In this example, not only is the output sent to screen, but the commands and the resulting output are also sent to a file, by using the `SPOOL` command. This example includes substitution variables, using the `DEFINE` command to setup the substitution variable ahead of execution time. SQL Developer supports `&&` for substitution variables, so you can reuse the initial value throughout the script.

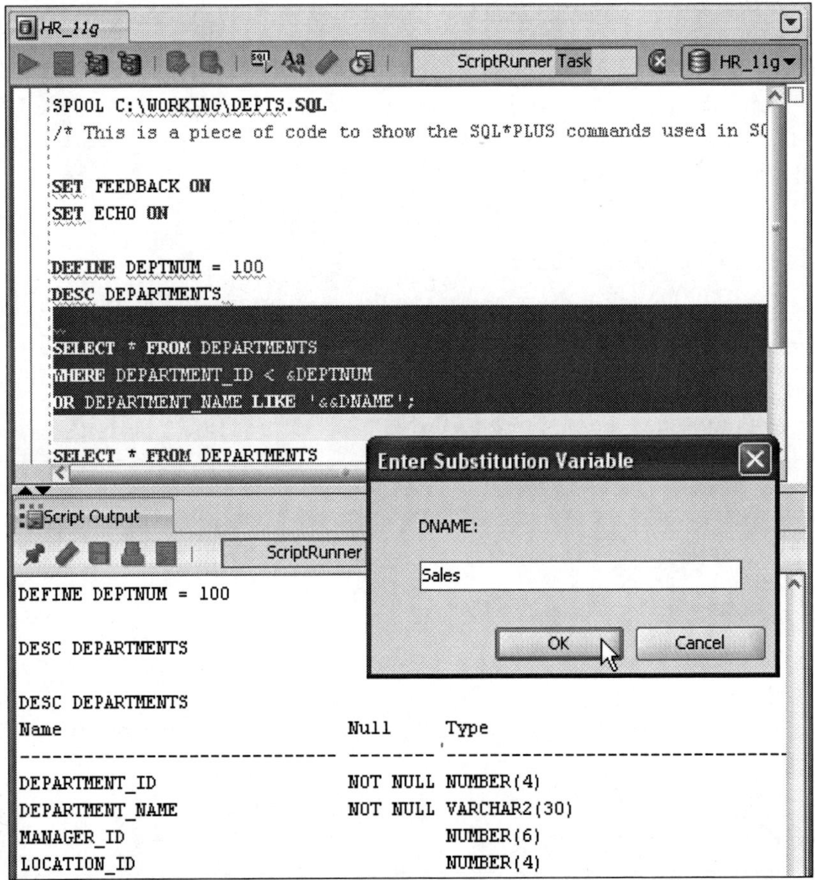

In the previous screenshot, the script has defined `DEPTNUM`, but not `DNAME` and you're therefore prompted for the second value. You can see the point of execution in the script, by the highlighted section.

Using the above example as a starting point, we'll investigate some of the SQL*Plus commands useful in SQL Developer.

Bind variables

A bind variable is a placeholder for an input value in a SQL query. So, `:DEPTNUM` in the following example is a bind variable:

```
SELECT * FROM DEPARTMENTS WHERE DEPARTMENT_ID < :DEPTNUM;
```

The SQL Worksheet supports the use of bind variables and you should use these instead of the (`&`, `&&`) substitution variables. We will change the script that we saw previously where we defined and accessed `DEPTNUM` and use a bind variable as follows:

```
VARIABLE DEPTNUM NUMBER
EXECUTE :DEPTNUM := 100
SELECT * FROM DEPARTMENTS
WHERE DEPARTMENT_ID < :DEPTNUM;
```

When using bind variables, you need to declare the variable using the `VARIABLE` command, and then reference the variable using PL/SQL to assign a value to the variable. In the SQL Worksheet you can use `EXECUTE` to do this. The next screenshot shows both the commands and output. Notice the **anonymous block completed** statement:

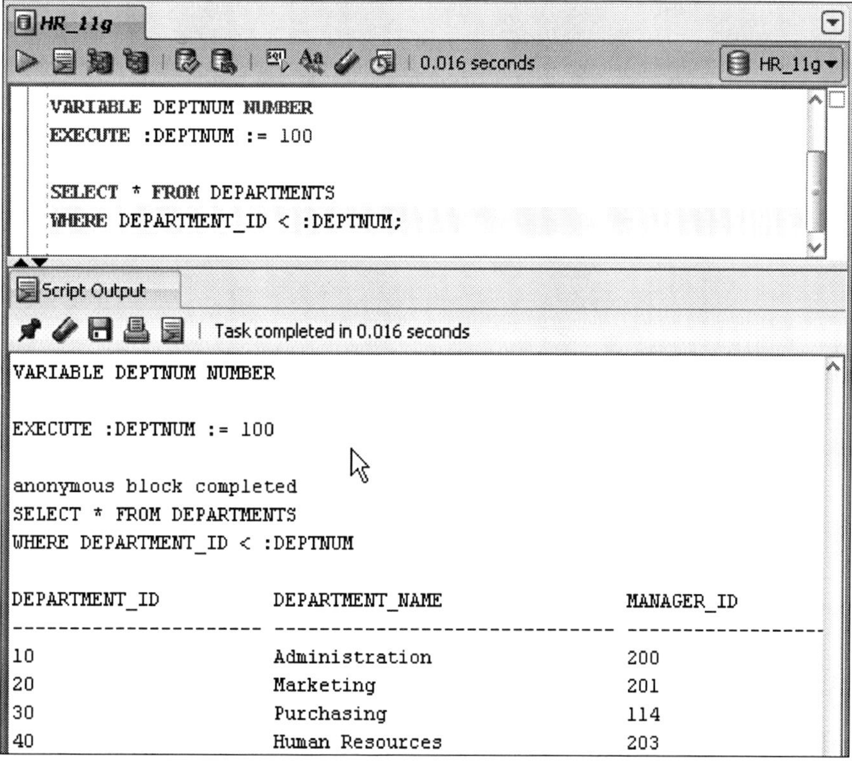

To see the value of the bind variable in the worksheet shown, enter the SQL*Plus `PRINT` command. For example, `PRINT DEPTNUM`.

The advantage of using bind variables

Bind variables are recommended over substitution variables for security and performance reasons. Without getting too deep into the technicalities of either, both are very important issues when running ad hoc queries against a database or building applications.

Bind variables and performance

Briefly, from a performance perspective, in order to return the results of a query, the Oracle database compiles and prepares a query execution plan, which uses a certain amount of resources. Before executing each query, Oracle first checks to see if the exact statement has been parsed and previously executed. If it has, the query execution plan is reused, thus reducing the amount of resources used. By using bind variables, the queries are seen as an exact match each time they're executed, and so compiled once and reused, thus using fewer resources.

Security and bind variables

The security issue is all about the SQL Injection, a significant topic not appropriate for this book, but one that we encourage you to learn more about. To illustrate SQL Injection using the queries we're working with, consider the query:

```
SELECT DEPARTMENT_NAME
FROM DEPARTMENTS WHERE DEPARTMENT_NAME = &DNAME;
```

Execute the command, and replace the **DNAME** value when prompted with `'TEST' UNION SELECT JOB_TITLE FROM JOBS` as shown in the following screenshot:

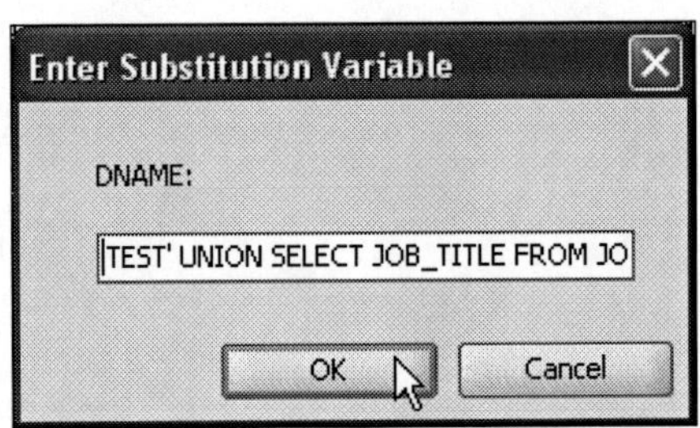

The resulting data set has no records from the DEPARTMENTS table, but instead has a listing of job titles. This is an overly simplified example, but an illustration of the point that you can "inject" additional pieces of code where least expected. It is recommended that you develop the habit of using bind variables, because you can't inject SQL in the same way.

Running scripts

Possibly, one of the most commonly used group of SQL*Plus commands are those that run scripts: @, @@, and start.

As with SQL*Plus, if you use @ or start to run a single SQL script file, you can either enter the full path (for example @D:\working\demobld.sql), or you can set the path in the **Preferences** dialog:

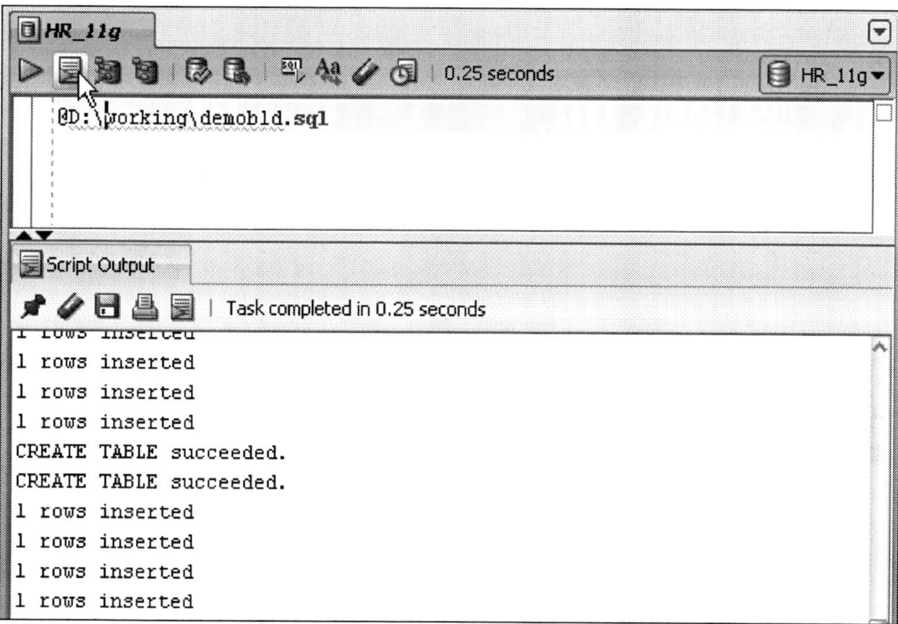

You need to use @@ when running one script that calls a second or third script. In this case, it is necessary to set the path for the top-level file.

For either, set the path using the **Database | Worksheet** preference. Press *F5* to run the script.

Set the default path for executing SQL scripts

To set the default path for scripts, invoke the **Preferences** dialog and set the path under **Database | Worksheet**. Click on **Browse** to locate or enter the path.

Reviewing unsupported SQL*Plus commands

Feedback from the user community indicates that they will only be completely happy when all SQL*Plus commands are supported in SQL Developer. This is not necessarily a practical request. Consider the SQL*Plus command **C[hange]**. This command helps you change a character, or characters, in the midst of a piece of text previously written. Due to the nature of a command line tool, where you can't access the previously written text, this is a valuable command and saves you from having to retype many lines of code. However, this is not necessary in a GUI, where you merely click on the text, select, and replace the text as required.

Less obvious examples are formatting commands typically used to create formatted reports. SQL*Plus commands like **Ti[tle]** and **Col[umn]** are not supported. Here, the argument for not supporting them is that you can output the results to the data grid, where a simple click-and-drag allows you to more easily see the data, or you can create a SQL Developer report for printing to various formats. By implication, these SQL* Plus commands are no longer appropriate. Even so, there are still a few commands that may need to be added to the list of supported commands.

Working with SQL

In this section, we'll focus on SQL commands and include a number of code editing and formatting features.

Dragging and dropping tables to create queries

Initially, the first gesture to use when creating SQL queries is to drag tables from the **Connections** navigator to the worksheet. You can select and drag a number of tables onto the SQL Worksheet work surface. Use *Ctrl+click* or *Shift+click* to select multiple items. The next screenshot shows a selection of tables, with the mouse indicating the area where they'll be dropped on the work surface:

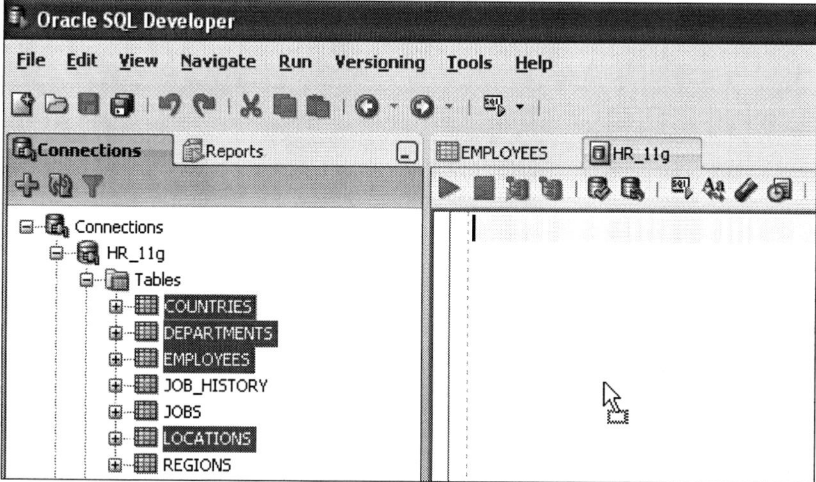

You are prompted to select the type of statement you want to create by the following dialog:

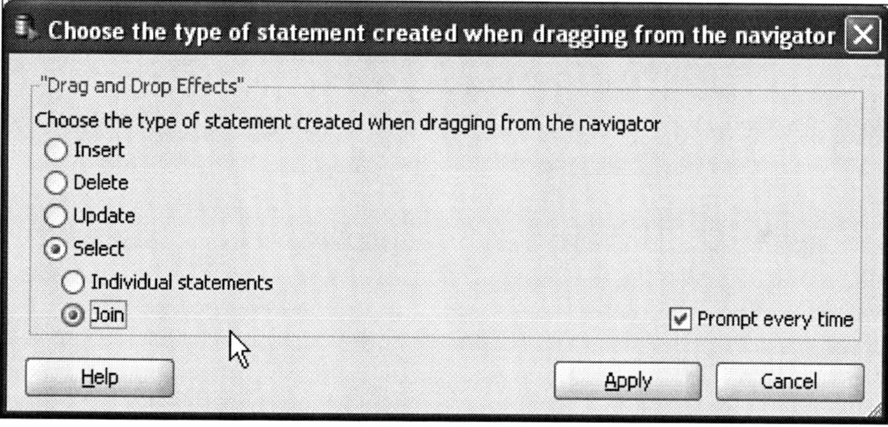

The default selection is that a separate statement is created for each table dragged onto the worksheet. You can control the appearance of the dialog, and the default drag-and-drop behavior, by using preferences. Open the **Preferences** dialog and select the **Database | Drag And Drop** node in the tree:

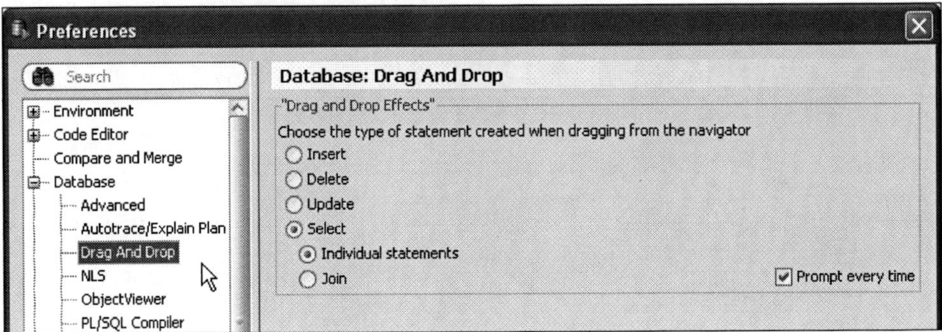

Notice in the dialog, that you can elect to be prompted each time you drag tables onto the worksheet. You can also choose whether you want insert, update, delete, or select statements to be created.

Changing the SQL Worksheet drag-and-drop behavior

To control the drag-and-drop behavior on the SQL Worksheet, use the **Database | Drag And Drop** preferences.

In releases prior to SQL Developer 2.1, these are grouped with the **Database | Worksheet** preferences in the dialog.

Formatting code

Having created a few SQL statements on the worksheet, it's worth looking at the code formatting options available.

Consider the following piece of code:

```
SELECT D.DEPARTMENT_NAME, E.EMPLOYEE_ID, E.FIRST_NAME, E.LAST_NAME,
E.EMAIL, E.HIRE_DATE, E.JOB_ID, E.SALARY, E.MANAGER_ID, L.LOCATION_ID,
C.COUNTRY_ID, C.COUNTRY_NAME, L.STREET_ADDRESS, L.POSTAL_CODE, L.CITY,
L.STATE_PROVINCE, L.COUNTRY_ID
FROM DEPARTMENTS D, LOCATIONS L, EMPLOYEES E, COUNTRIES C WHERE
L.LOCATION_ID = D.LOCATION_ID AND E.EMPLOYEE_ID = D.MANAGER_ID AND
D.DEPARTMENT_ID = E.DEPARTMENT_ID AND C.COUNTRY_ID = L.COUNTRY_ID;
```

Right-click on the code and select **Format** from the context menu:

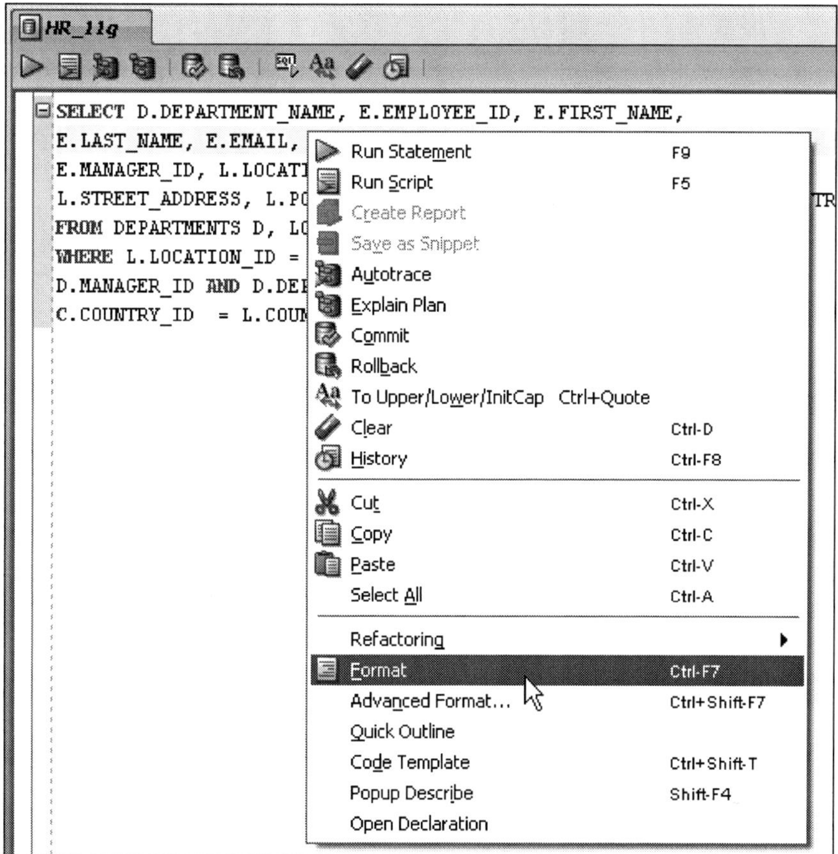

To modify code-formatting options, select the **Database | SQL Formatter** node in the **Preferences** dialog. The Formatter has been modified in SQL Developer 2.1 to support greater granularity and control of formatting options. As such, there are two nodes in the **SQL Formatter** tree:

- Oracle Formatting
- Other Vendors

This allows you to set different format rules depending on the vendor code you want to format. We will now take a look at the **Oracle Formatting**:

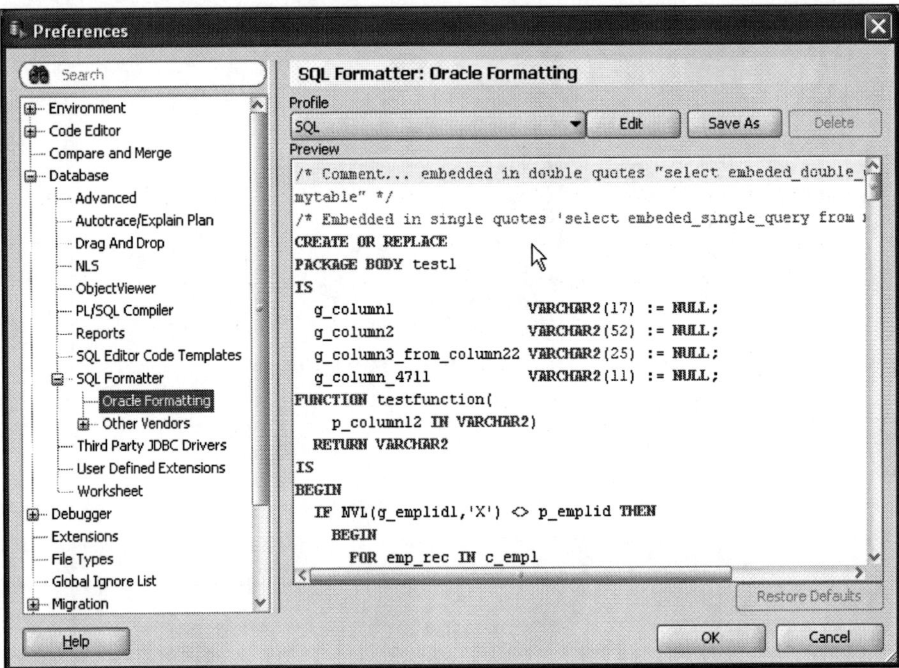

To start updating preferences, click on **Edit**. The new Oracle formatter window allows you to change and see the impact of the various settings using a piece of sample code. In the following example, we have chosen not to align on the keyword AS, but to align on commas. The changes are reflected in the sample code:

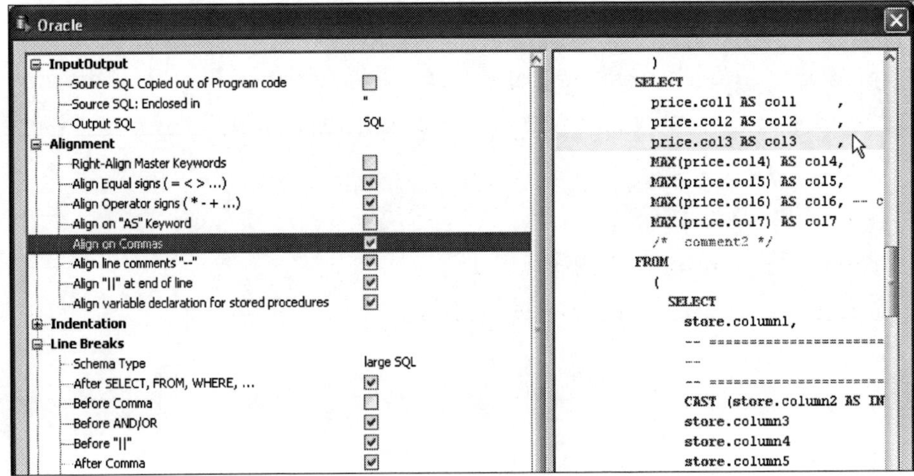

It's worth experimenting with different combinations to see which output best suits your needs or company standards. Using the piece of code provided, we set the options:

- Four commas per line
- Align on equals
- Line break after `SELECT`, `FROM`, and `WHERE`

The results in reformatting the selected code are shown in the following screenshot:

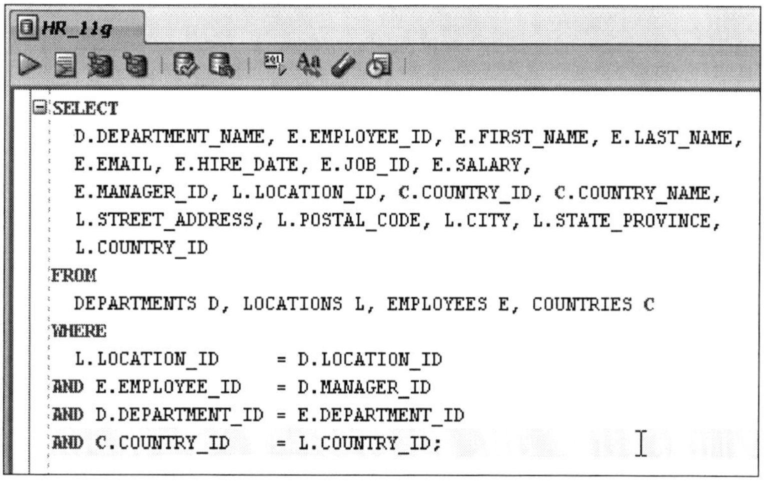

HR_11g

```
SELECT
  D.DEPARTMENT_NAME, E.EMPLOYEE_ID, E.FIRST_NAME, E.LAST_NAME,
  E.EMAIL, E.HIRE_DATE, E.JOB_ID, E.SALARY,
  E.MANAGER_ID, L.LOCATION_ID, C.COUNTRY_ID, C.COUNTRY_NAME,
  L.STREET_ADDRESS, L.POSTAL_CODE, L.CITY, L.STATE_PROVINCE,
  L.COUNTRY_ID
FROM
  DEPARTMENTS D, LOCATIONS L, EMPLOYEES E, COUNTRIES C
WHERE
  L.LOCATION_ID     = D.LOCATION_ID
AND E.EMPLOYEE_ID   = D.MANAGER_ID
AND D.DEPARTMENT_ID = E.DEPARTMENT_ID
AND C.COUNTRY_ID    = L.COUNTRY_ID;
```

Managing the case

SQL Developer allows you to manage the case of the code while you are typing. Using *Ctrl+Quote*, you can change the case, cycling through from upper to lower and mixed cases. The options are as follows:

- None—maintain case unchanged
- Initcap—capitalize the initial letter of each words you type
- Upper—switch the code you're typing to uppercase
- Lower—switch the code you're typing to lowercase
- Upper Keyword—set the keywords to uppercase
- Lower Keyword Upper ID—set the keywords to lowercase

To switch the case, select the code and either use the key combination or the button on the SQL Worksheet. A record of the case setting is maintained in the lower left-hand corner of the SQL Developer window, in the status bar, and is applied to the code as you type, switching to the choice set as you complete a line of code:

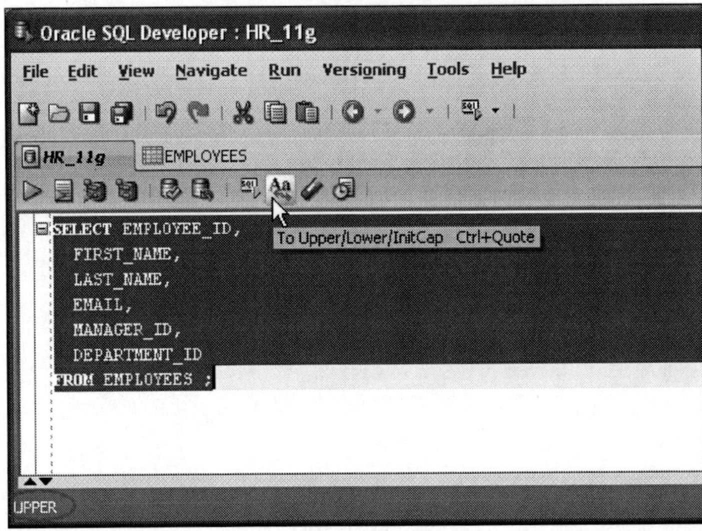

Formatting SQL for use in other languages

For developers who want to embed their SQL in Java or other languages, the Oracle formatter provides an option to do this. Select the **Output SQL** option, and select the required language from the drop-down list. In the following screenshot, the reformatted sample code is displayed for the **Java String** chosen:

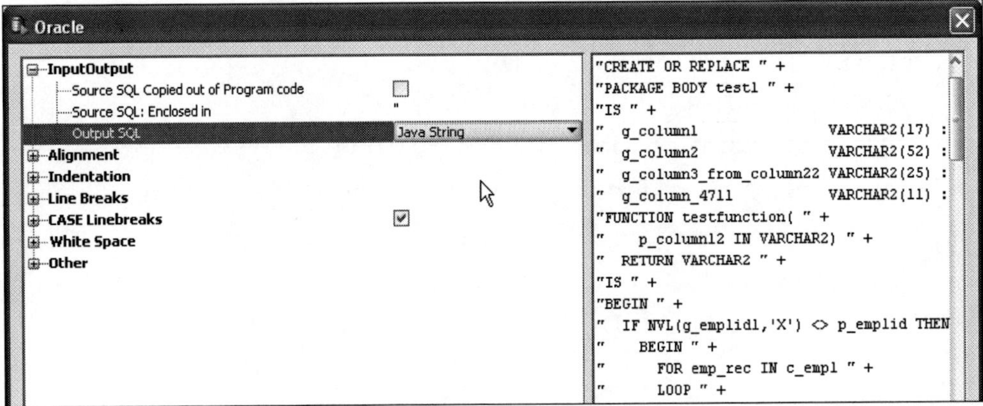

Working with code completion insight

Writing SQL statements from scratch requires some knowledge of your tables and columns. In SQL Developer, you can click on each table you have access to and the display editors show all of the detail you need. However, this is time consuming and cumbersome. Being prompted with detail can be very helpful. SQL Developer provides a code completion insight feature, which is often simply referred to as code insight.

If you start typing `SELECT * FROM` in the worksheet, you are prompted with a list of tables that you have access to, as shown in the following screenshot. You can start typing the table name and the list is reduced until your table is in the shortened list, or you can scroll to the required table:

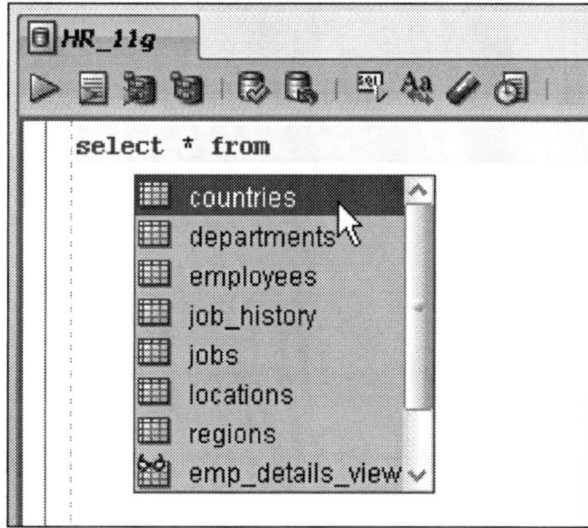

If you use the toolbar to scroll down through the pop-up list, you'll notice that the list of tables is short; since not all tables that HR has access to are displayed.

Consider the following query:

```
SELECT * FROM DICTIONARY;
```

This is a very often-queried table and, as HR can run this query, you might expect it to be on the initial drop-down list. Having access to all possible tables and objects would make the list unmanageable. The SQL Developer code insight is *intelligent*, initially displaying only tables and views that you own. If you start typing `select * from dic`, you'll get the result shown in the following screenshot:

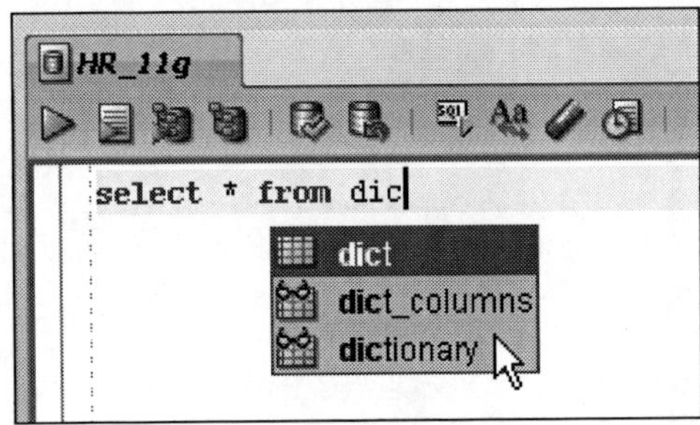

Notice that the code insight matches the case you type. The list of objects displayed varies as you start typing and as the code insight narrows down your search, including objects you have access to in other schemas.

[If the code insight does not appear, use *Ctrl+Space*.]

Controlling code completion insight in the SQL Worksheet

There are occasions when you might not want the code insight support:

- If you have a large number of objects in your schema
- If you know your schema well enough not to need the code insight assistance
- If you are working over a LAN where performance is poor

In these situations, we recommend that you adjust or switch off code insight.

[To control code insight, select **Code Editor | Completion Insight** in the **Preferences** dialog.]

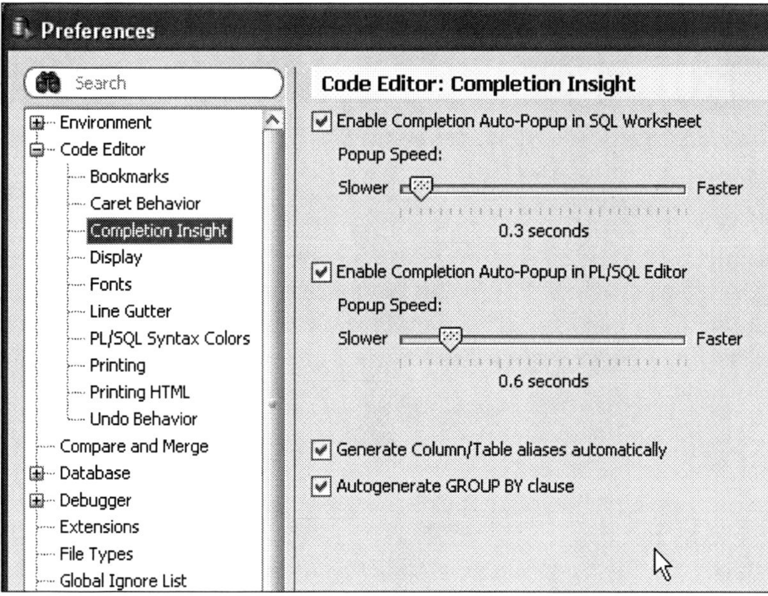

If you select the preference to automatically generate column and table aliases, the code insight will add the join clauses to the completion insight list. This is useful when you start to build the `WHERE` clause:

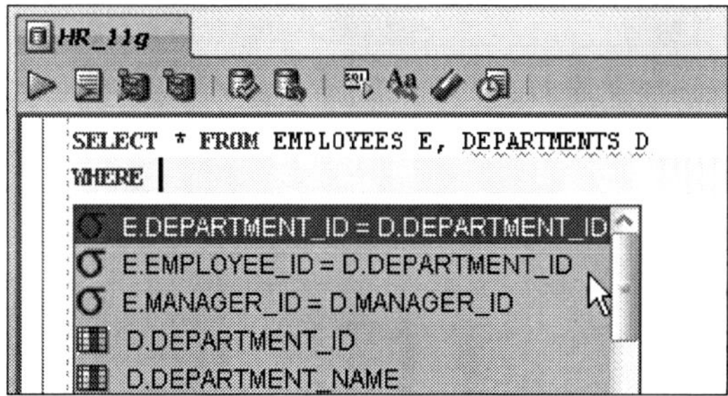

The code insight drop-down list follows the case of the text in the typed code. In the example just shown, the code was entered in uppercase, and the insight followed suit. Had the code been entered in lowercase, the insight options would have been displayed in lowercase.

[If you are not using code insight, you can use *Shift+F4* on any selected object to describe the object.]

Including code snippets

SQL Developer includes a code **Snippets** window. The **Snippets** window provides a quick reference to pieces of code and the syntax. To invoke the **Snippets** window, select the **View | Snippets** menu. You can now scroll through the various categories available and drag pieces of code onto the worksheet.

The pieces of code are grouped into categories, such as **Character, Date/Time**, and **Conversion** functions. While we often know the more commonly used functions, some of the less frequently used ones can have us reaching for the documentation. Therefore, having them so close to hand makes writing code easier. The categories also include **PL/SQL Programming Techniques** and **Optimizer Hints**, all handy pieces of code to reuse.

Managing the Snippets window

If you use the **Snippets** window frequently, you can drag the window into a permanent window position, or have it float in a convenient place. In releases prior to SQL Developer 2.1, the **Snippets** window was available by default, docked, and minimized to the right-hand side. This is a convenient way of working because you can work with the window when needed, but don't have the overhead of opening and closing it, nor do you lose real estate to a window you might not use all of the time. With the window minimized, just roll the mouse over the snippets area and the window pops up, allowing you to navigate and select the required code. Once you drag the code into position, the window rolls back closed. This is illustrated in the following screenshot:

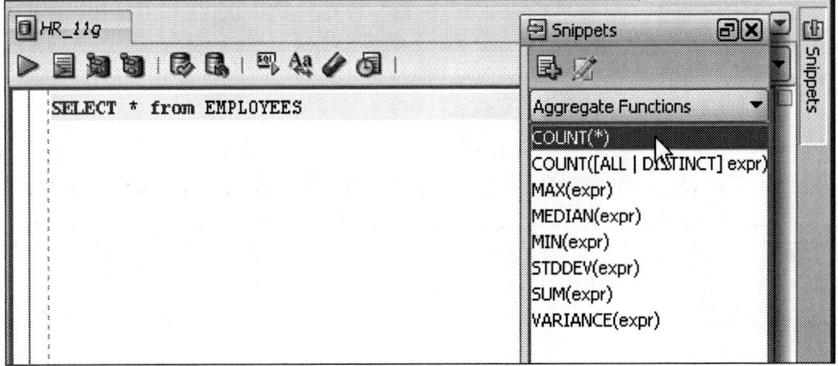

Adding code snippets

Code snippets are editable, meaning that you can add new categories, or update existing categories with additional pieces of code. Adding pieces of code to an existing category, or adding a new category, can be done in two ways:

- Enter the code in the SQL Worksheet and use the **Save Snippets** context menu for the selected code
- Using the **Add Snippet** button on the **Snippets** window

Both of these approaches invoke the dialog shown in the following screenshot:

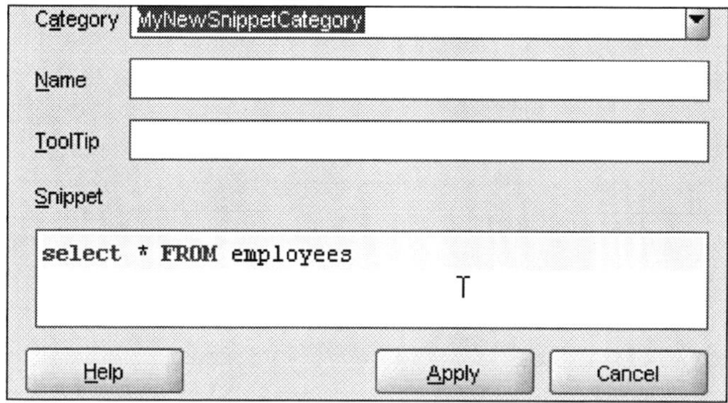

To create a new category, just type the new category name in the **Category** field. To add the new snippet to an existing category, select the category from the **Category** drop-down list.

Creating code templates

Code templates were introduced in SQL Developer 1.5 and are slightly different to the snippets described above. A small example list of predefined code templates ship with the product and you use them using a key combination in the worksheet.

To set up your code template, invoke the **Preferences** dialog and select **Database | SQL Editor Code Templates**.

The dialog displays two columns, the **Id** and **Template**. The **Template** holds the complete piece of code, while the **Id** is used in SQL Developer 1.5.x as the string or letter combination you type in the SQL Worksheet. This is no longer used in SQL Developer 2.1.

Enter the following example:

Id: `NoData`

Template

```
EXCEPTION
   WHEN NO_DATA_FOUND THEN
      DBMS_OUTPUT.PUT_LINE ('The query did not return a result set');
```

Click on **OK** and return to the SQL Worksheet. In SQL Developer 1.5.x, type the Id **NoData** followed by the keystroke *Ctrl+Shift+T*, which replaces the typed string with the full piece of code. In SQL Developer 2.1, simply start typing the code from the template, and the full code is displayed in the code insight drop list. Select the code to add it to the SQL Worksheet.

The advantages of the code templates are that you can build up a set of frequently used chunks of code to improve reusability and save time. You can also use these to standardize pieces of text used by the full development team.

Using the File navigator

SQL Developer 1.5 introduced the **Files** navigator. This integration of the Explorer with SQL Developer means that you can search for files and open them from within the product. To work with the **Files** navigator, select **View | Files.** The following screenshot shows a list of directories and files:

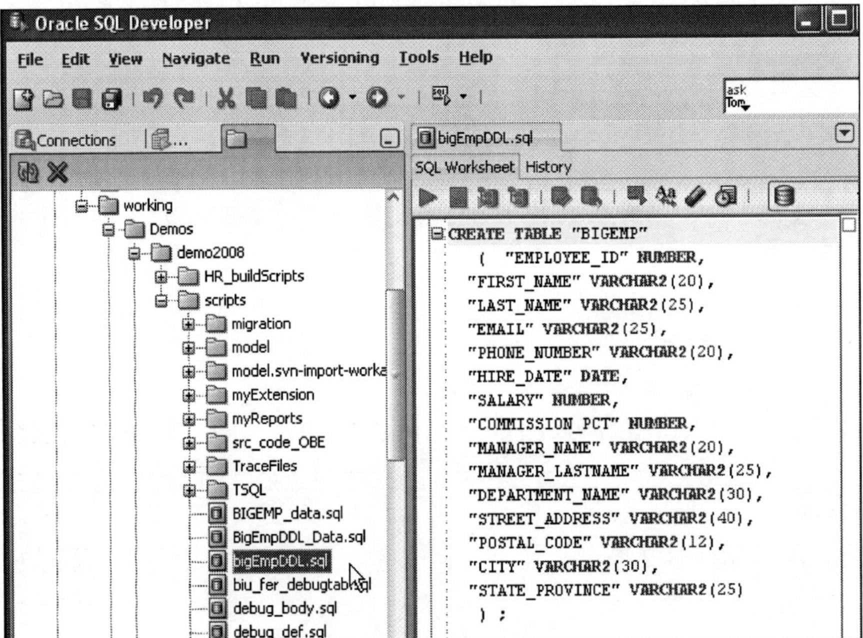

To open a file in SQL Developer, double-click on the file. For files recognized by SQL Developer, such as `.sql` or `.pks`, either an SQL Worksheet or PL/SQL Editor is opened. In the example shown, the **Run Statement** and **Run Script** commands are shown, but not available. This is because the drop-down list showing the connection is not populated. You can either use the drop-down list to select the connection you wish to run the file against, or you can just select *F5* (or *F9*) to run the script, which will first prompt you for a connection before running the file.

Opening files

Alternative ways to open files in SQL Developer are from the main **File** and **Navigate** menus. The former opens a file browser dialog and allows you to browse to the location. SQL Developer recalls the recently used directories and lists them in the panel on the left:

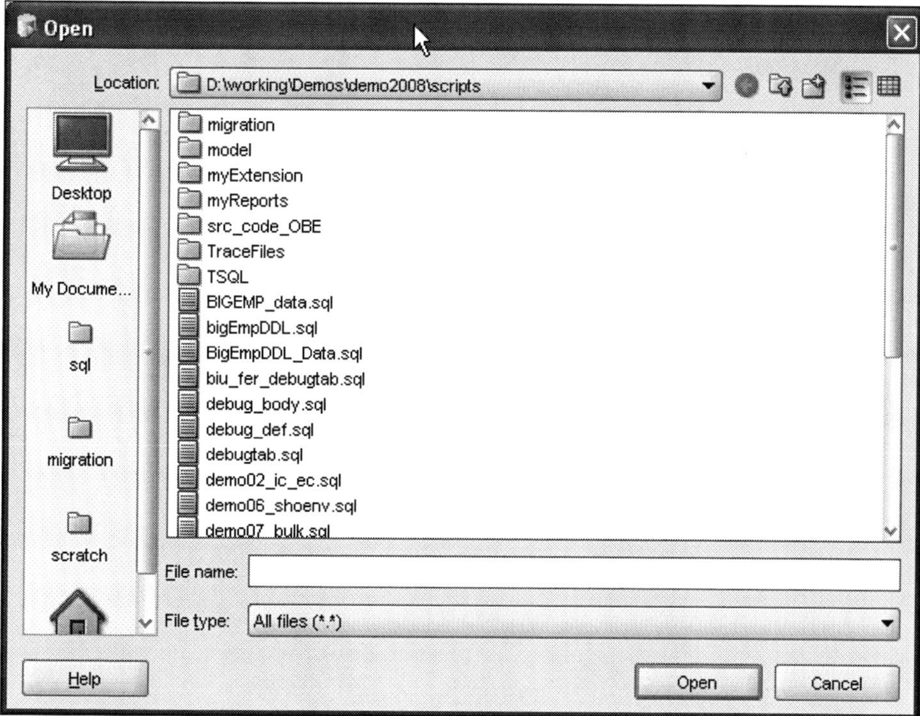

While you cannot set the default location for opening files, SQL Developer does recall the location of the previously opened file.

The alternative approach for opening files is to use **Navigate | Go to Recent Files...**

Using extra features in the worksheet

There are a number of additional windows associated with the SQL Worksheet. These include the:

- SQL History
- Dbms Output
- OWA Output

In SQL Developer 2.1, these are all now dockable windows, which are closed by default on start-up. Each can be docked, closed, or tiled in the same way you would for any of the other windows in SQL Developer. The advantage of this is you can conveniently float them out of the way, if you have enough screen real estate, and use them in conjunction with the SQL Worksheet. To open any of these windows, select them from the main **View** menu. The following screenshot shows all three windows docked below the **Script Output** window:

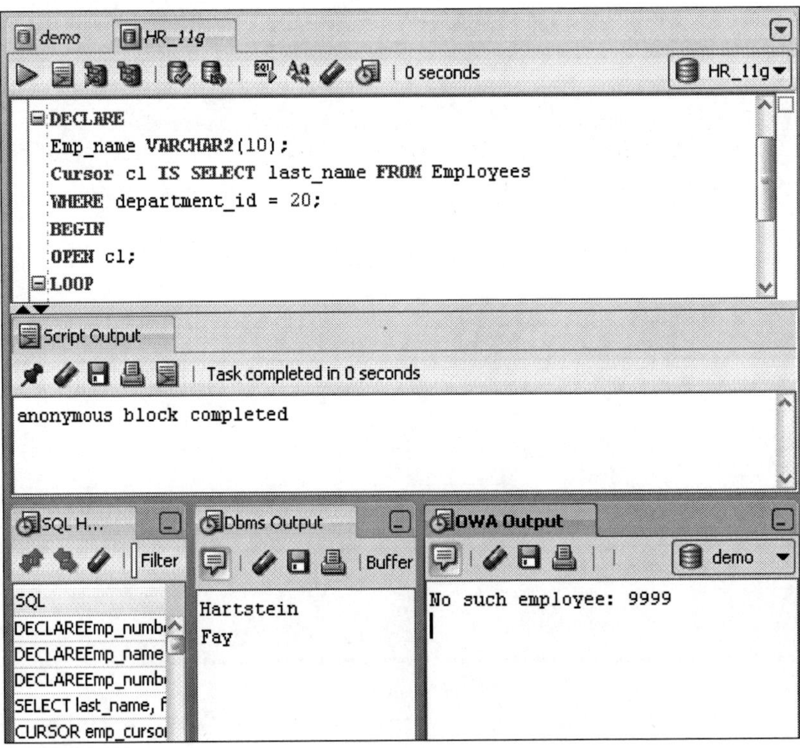

SQL History

The SQL History stores all recently used commands. This allows you to quickly and easily recall them for reuse. Initially, only the commands issued by the single **Run Statement** command were captured and sorted. Releases from SQL Developer 1.5 started to capture the syntax from both the **Run Statement** and **Run Script** commands. **Run Script** does not save all of the commands in a file (if a file is executed), instead, it only records the commands for running the file. Also, all of the commands are saved to the History, SQL, PL/SQL, and SQL *Plus, whether correct or not.

The **SQL History** file is created when you first start SQL Developer and is saved in the `C:\Documents and Settings\<YourUser>\Application Data\SQL Developer` folder.

You can use various operations on your history file, including:

- **Clear**—deletes all of the selected entries
- **Sort**—click the column header to sort the entries based on time, number of executions, or syntax
- **Replace or append**—either to replace the current statements with the statement selected in the history, or you can append the new statement to the contents of the worksheet

The history tracks the statement, time stamp of last execution, and the number of times a statement is executed:

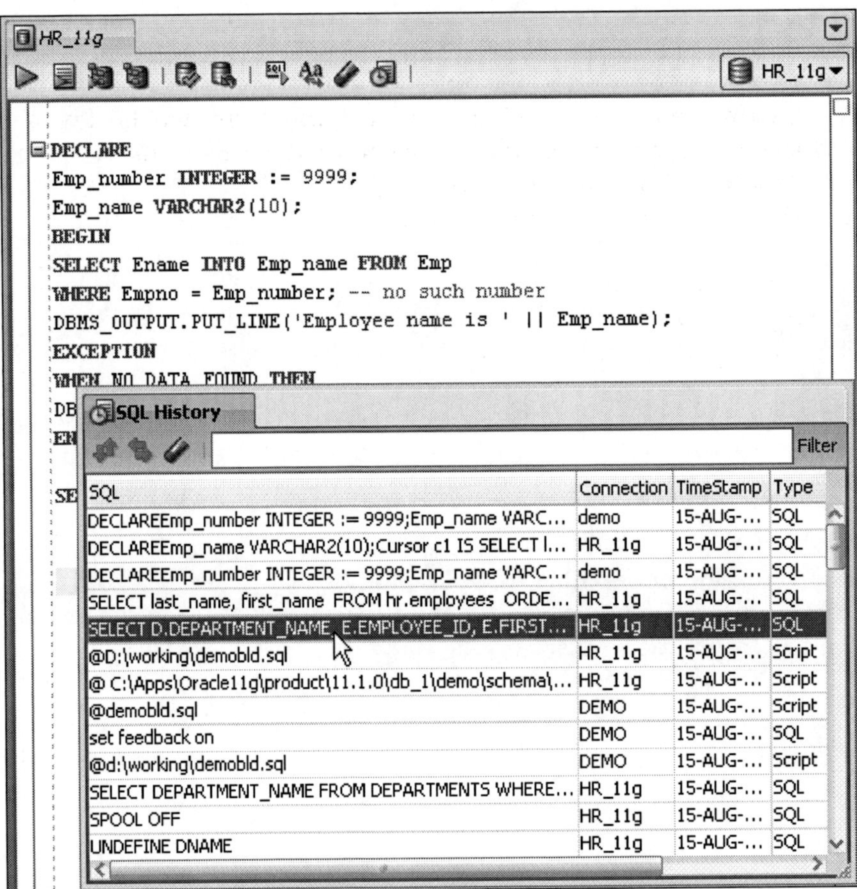

In the previous screenshot, the **SQL History** is undocked and floating. Double-clicking on the selected entry will insert the selected code into the worksheet at the cursor location.

> The **SQL History** limit is set to 100 by default. You can change this limit using a preferences in the **Database | Worksheet** node in the **Preferences** dialog.

DBMS Output

If you execute any PL/SQL in a worksheet that contains `DBMS_OUTPUT` commands, whether an anonymous block or a compiled procedure, the output is sent to the **Dbms Output** window. Prior to SQL Developer 2.1, you needed to alternate between the **Script Output** tab and the **Dbms Output** tab. This window is now a dockable window and, as shown in the following screenshot, can be made to float near the SQL Worksheet. Initially, you need to select a connection to listen for the output. Click the **Add new Dbms Output tab** button to open a tab for the connection. This also runs the `set serveroutput on` command.

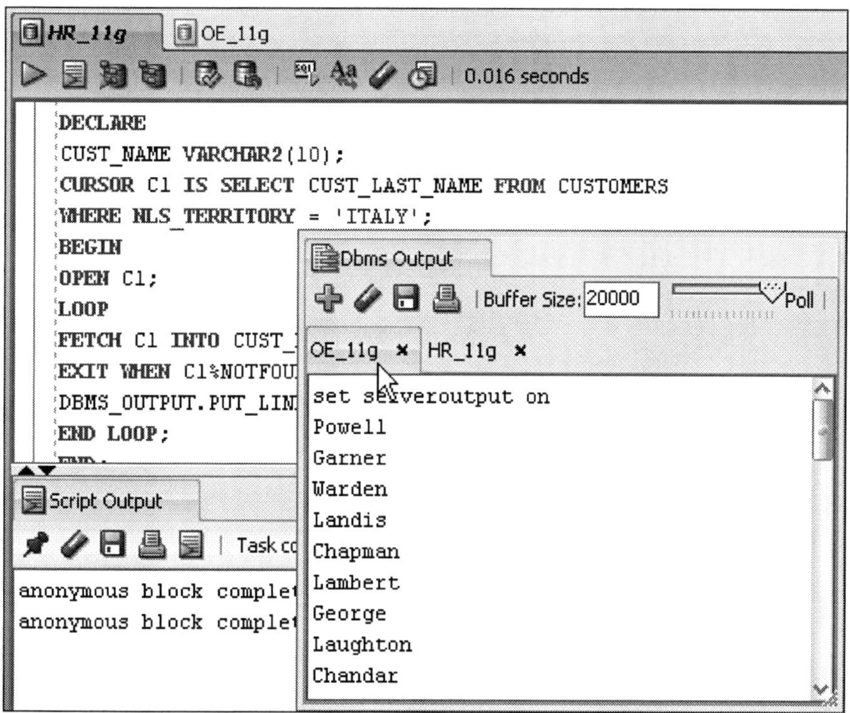

If you switch to another schema to execute PL/SQL for the new schema, the **Dbms Output** window is not affected. To see the output from this new user, you need to click the **Add new Dbms Output tab** button to open a tab for the new schema's connection.

In the example, PL/SQL was executed for both the HR and OE schemas. In both cases, the output was sent to the **Dbms Output** window. To see the results, select the appropriate schema using the connection tabs.

OWA Output

In the same way that the package DBMS_OUTPUT can send the output to screen, SQL Developer supports the ability to output details to screen for the packages that form part of the web PL/SQL toolkit, using the **OWA Output** window. The OWA package, and related procedures and functions, are primarily used for creating PL/SQL web pages. The **OWA Output** tab is now also a dockable window and behaves in the same way as the **Dbms Output** window, allowing you to switch between users to review the detail for different commands. The example shown in the following screenshot, has just replaced the DBMS_OUTPUT command with the HTP.PRINT command to serve as an illustration:

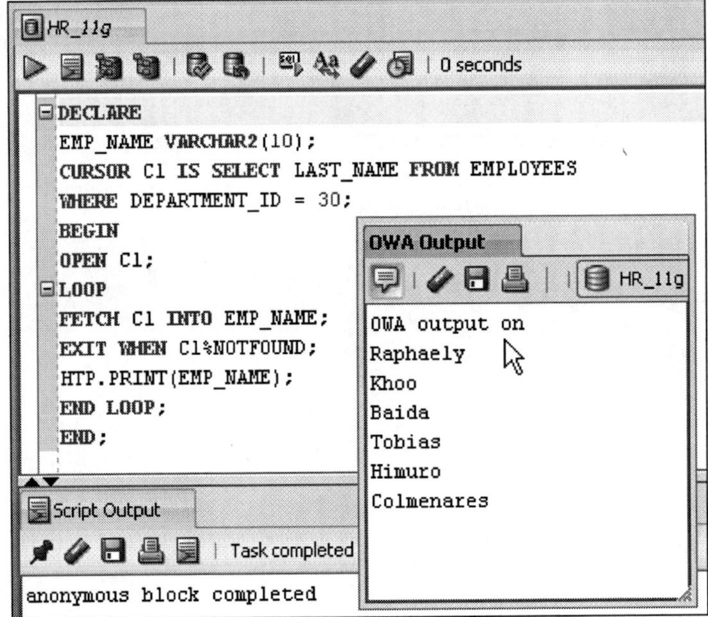

Using the Query Builder

SQL Developer provides a visual **Query Builder** to help you create queries. A visual **Query Builder** is useful when you are building complex queries based on a number of tables. It is also useful for users who are new to Oracle and SQL and are not familiar with writing SQL queries.

The **Query Builder** allows you to select any table or view you have permission to access. The schemas are all displayed in the drop-down list in the top left-hand corner. The initial user displayed is the current connection. Select one or more tables and drag them onto the work surface. You can rearrange the tables to suit your needs.

You can spend time moving back and forth between the editors, reviewing the query results, and fine-tuning the selection criteria. As soon as you select the **Apply** button, the query is written to the SQL Worksheet and the **Query Builder** is closed.

To invoke the **Query Builder**, use the context menu on the SQL Worksheet, or PL/SQL editor for your database connection. The following screenshot shows the Query Builder being invoked from the SQL Worksheet:

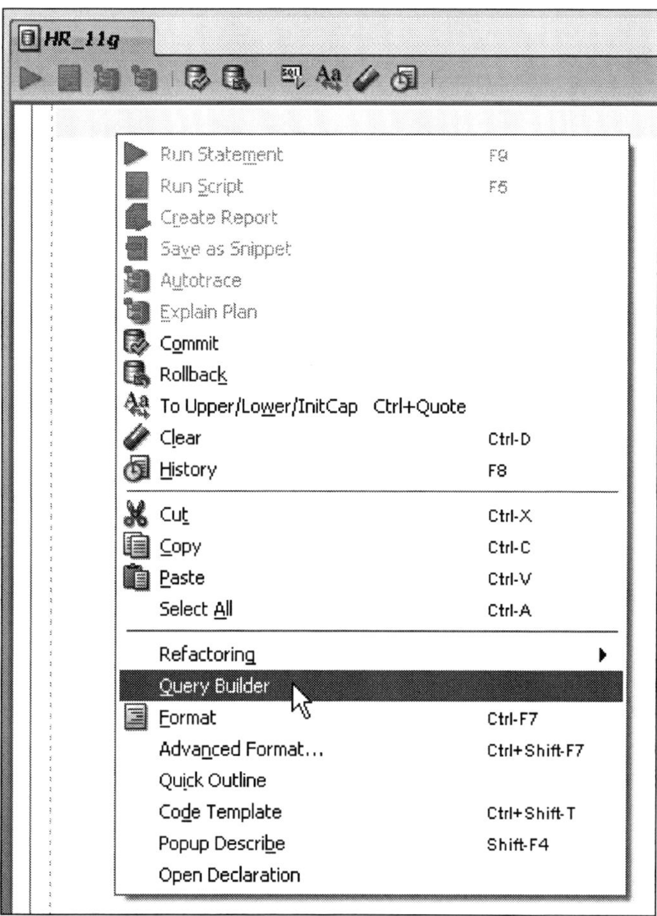

Building an SQL query

For the remainder of this chapter, we will build up a query using the **Query Builder**, and then save that query to the SQL Worksheet and run it. The **Query Builder** is not re-entrant, so don't close the window until you're sure the query is what you want. You can test the query outcome in the window and tab back and forth within the window before closing it.

Selecting the tables, column, and joins

For the example, we want to know the employee names and their departments for employees based in Seattle, San Francisco, or in the United Kingdom. To build this query, invoke the **Query Builder** and ensure that HR is displayed in the top left-hand side drop-down list. Select and drag **EMPLOYEES** onto the canvas:

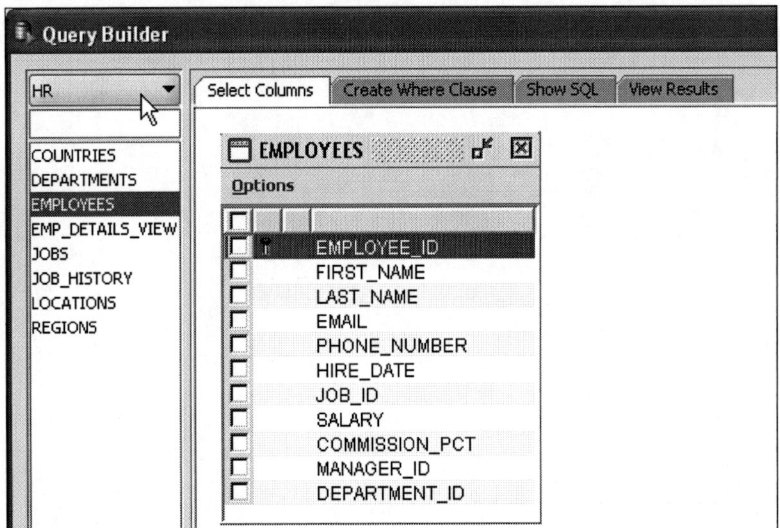

Select the **DEPARTMENTS**, **LOCATIONS**, and **COUNTRIES** tables and drag them onto the canvas. If relationships exist between the tables, they should appear on the canvas linking the tables, if not, then you can create the joins. In this example, there are Foreign Keys between the tables, so there is no need.

> To create joins between two tables in the **Query Builder**, select the required column in the first table and drag a line to the required column in the second table and then release. A solid line links the two tables. This is typically the Foreign Key relationship, but it does not need to be.

Before you display any results, you need to select at least one column from each table for the table to be included in the query. This is not true for `SELECT` statements, but for the **Query Builder**, you should follow this rule. You can remove columns from the `SELECT` clause later.

Place a check in each of the following: `LAST_NAME`, `DEPARTMENT_NAME`, `COUNTRY_NAME`, and `CITY`, as shown in the following example. Notice that, as you select items in each table, the line joining the tables switches to bold, to show it is enabled and will be included in the query:

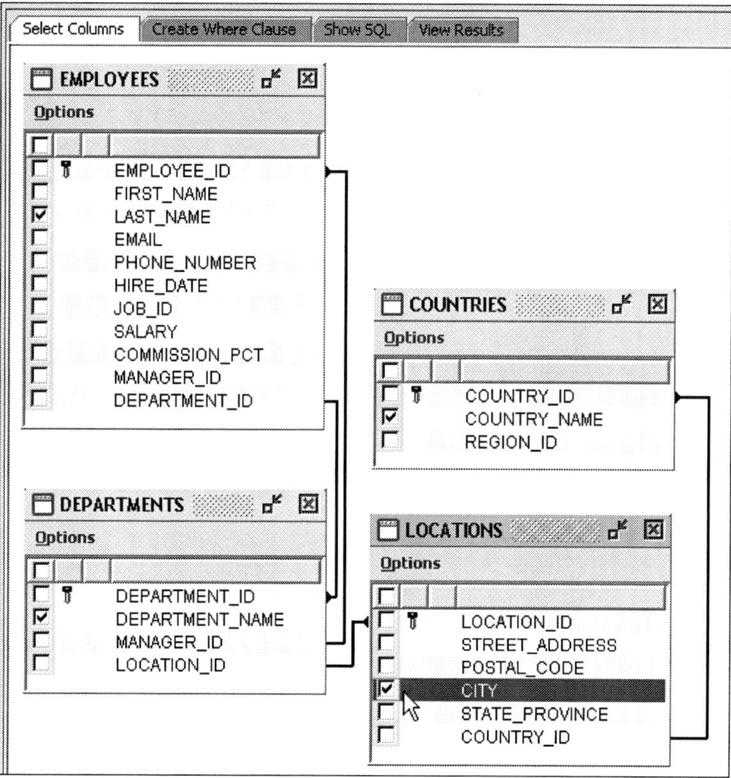

Viewing the Results

Select the **View Results** tab and click on the green **Run Report** arrow to run the query. The data grid here behaves as other data grids do. You can drag columns to reorder the sequence, double-click on the column headings to sort the data, and even use the query for the grid to create a new report. None of these affects the SQL query you are building. To permanently affect the order of columns you need to either edit the query in the SQL Worksheet, or reselect the columns in the **Select Columns** editor.

Adding the WHERE clause

To restrict the records returned, select the **Create Where Clause** editor. The detail you add here is actually added to any existing join clauses which are the starting point for the `WHERE` clause. If you have a single table, or no join clause, then you'd create the full `WHERE` clause at this point.

Once again, this is a visual construct that can be of great help when constructing complex `WHERE` clauses. Consider the following query:

```
SELECT * FROM LOCATIONS
WHERE CITY = 'Seattle';
```

The part of the query that you now need to build is that section of the `WHERE` clause that restricts the records. For our example, we want the names of the employees who work in Seattle, San Francisco, or in the United Kingdom.

Create `COUNTRIES.COUNTRY_NAME = United Kingdom` using the three drop-down lists available. Match the case and don't include any quotes. You can return to the **View Results** editor each time to re-run your query and verify that the results are starting to behave as required.

Select the ":" to the left of the column-name drop-down list and invoke the context menu. Click on **Insert OR**:

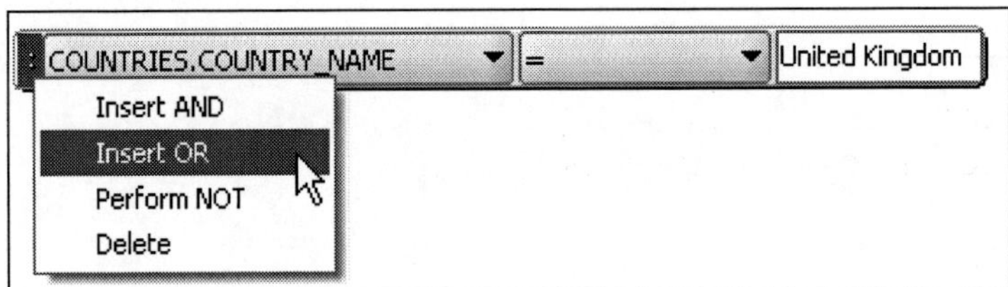

You immediately see a new branch display and you can select new criteria. Add `LOCATIONS.CITY = Seattle`. Now, select the ":" next to the `LOCATIONS.CITY` column and invoke the context menu. Select **Insert OR** and add an entry for `LOCATIONS.CITY contains San Francisco`. The visual `WHERE` clause should start to look like the following screenshot:

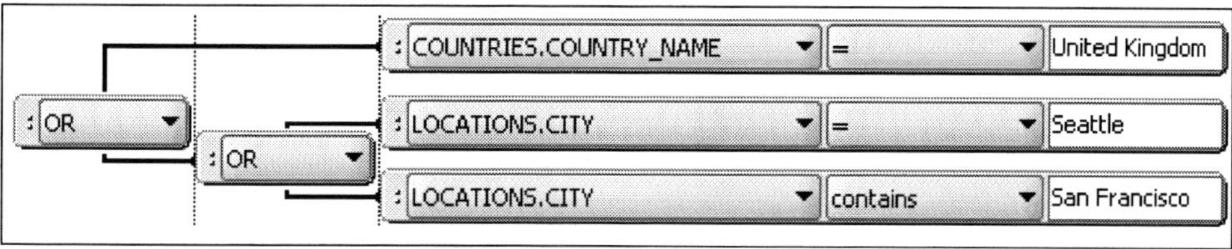

You can see how even straightforward queries can grow complex, and a tree structure can be of great benefit to both users starting out, or those wanting to build up a longer query made up of a number of tables and columns with many factors in the `WHERE` clause.

Returning to the SQL Worksheet

The final stage of the process is to take the query to the SQL Worksheet. Select **View Results** once more to verify the query is as you're expecting. The Query Builder is not re-entrant, so any queries you build with these releases should be verified before proceeding to the SQL Worksheet or you will need to start all over again.

You can select the **Apply** button on any of the **Query Builder** editors. This will write the query to the SQL Worksheet. As the query is not formatted, invoke the context menu and select **Format**.

While the layout will depend on your formatting choices set, your code should look similar to the following:

```
SELECT
  "HR"."EMPLOYEES"."LAST_NAME",
  "HR"."DEPARTMENTS"."DEPARTMENT_NAME",
  "HR". "LOCATIONS"."CITY",
  "HR"."COUNTRIES"."COUNTRY_NAME"
FROM
  "HR"."EMPLOYEES",
  "HR"."DEPARTMENTS",
  "HR"."LOCATIONS",
  "HR"."COUNTRIES"
WHERE ("HR"."EMPLOYEES"."DEPARTMENT_ID" =
       "HR"."DEPARTMENTS"."DEPARTMENT_ID")
```

```
AND ("HR"."DEPARTMENTS"."MANAGER_ID"  = "HR"."EMPLOYEES"."EMPLOYEE_ID")
AND ("HR"."DEPARTMENTS"."LOCATION_ID" = "HR"."LOCATIONS"."LOCATION_ID")
AND ("HR"."LOCATIONS"."COUNTRY_ID"     = "HR"."COUNTRIES"."COUNTRY_ID")
AND (("HR"."COUNTRIES"."COUNTRY_NAME" = 'United Kingdom')
OR (("HR"."LOCATIONS"."CITY"           = 'Seattle')
OR ("HR"."LOCATIONS"."CITY" LIKE '%San Francisco%')))
```

You can run, edit, and save the query. Many use these queries as the basis for reports.

[The **Query Builder** menu is on the context menu for the SQL Worksheet and the PL/SQL Code Editor.]

Summary

In this chapter, we reviewed the SQL Worksheet and all of the features it supports. From the Query Builder, which assists you in building queries, to drag-and-drop queries that can join multiple tables to writing the SQL syntax from scratch, the SQL Worksheet has features to assist in your daily tasks.

In the next chapter, we will introduce all of the shipped SQL Developer reports and show you how to create and run your own. You do not need to have completed this chapter to complete the chapter on reports. However, having an understanding of building SQL scripts will be useful.

4
The Power of SQL Reports

In addition to browsing objects and writing your own ad hoc queries against the database, Oracle SQL Developer has a separate Reports navigator, with a set of predefined SQL queries known as reports. The main focus is the set of predefined data dictionary reports which range from providing basic details about your database, to database administration, security, and quality assurance. Having these predefined reports means that you can quickly run a variety of SQL queries to analyze and assess the health and status of your database, saving you from needing to write the queries yourself.

The Reports navigator provides shipped reports for reviewing the results of any non-Oracle database migrations that have been run, the details of any Data Modeler designs that have been exported, and any available Oracle Application Express applications. The output of any of these reports is controlled by the database connection used when executing a report.

You can extend the set of shipped, predefined reports by adding your own local or shared reports. When creating your own reports, not only can you add to the existing data dictionary reports, but you can also build up a set of reports to review and analyze the instance data in any applications under development.

In this chapter, we review the full Reports navigator, and you will learn more about the shipped reports and how to run them. We'll look briefly at the Migration, Oracle APEX, and Data Modeler reports. These are also covered in the chapters on each of those topics. We'll review the various report styles available, and show how you can make use of these different styles when creating your own reports.

Introducing SQL Developer reports

Whether you are a DBA or an application developer, running SQL queries against the data dictionary is a useful source of information. It provides you with the details about the objects various schemas own, the health of a system, and the integrity of the data in applications. If you work with the Oracle database regularly, you almost certainly already have a set of queries that you frequently run. For example, you might have a query to determine the tables that have no Primary Keys or, if you are a DBA, a query to find out the currently connected sessions. Over the years, you may gather these queries in a file and have them on hand, no matter what project you are working on, and they can play a significant role in your daily tasks.

SQL Developer has a categorized group of these SQL queries (reports) and also provides the tools to create and save your essential queries as reports.

In this first section, we'll discuss the Reports navigator in general, how to run and use the reports, and any errors you might encounter.

To run any report in SQL Developer you need a connection to the database. If you have just started working with SQL Developer, refer to the chapter on *Database Connections and JDBC Drivers* for more details.

Who can run reports?

Anyone can run or create reports in SQL Developer, from the least to the most privileged user. What you see depends on your security access, which is true throughout SQL Developer. It is not the product that enforces security, but the database itself. So, if you are presented with an error when running a report, consider the privileges you have and whether you'd be able to run this query in any other environment or circumstances, such as in SQL*Plus or the SQL Worksheet. Invariably, the error message displayed does explain the problem at hand and more often than not, it is a security level access issue.

When do you use reports?

You can use reports on a daily basis throughout a project, to track details about your system. Reports provide high-level detail about your database and can be used to drill down to the finest detail. The following screenshot shows the broad categories of the shipped reports available:

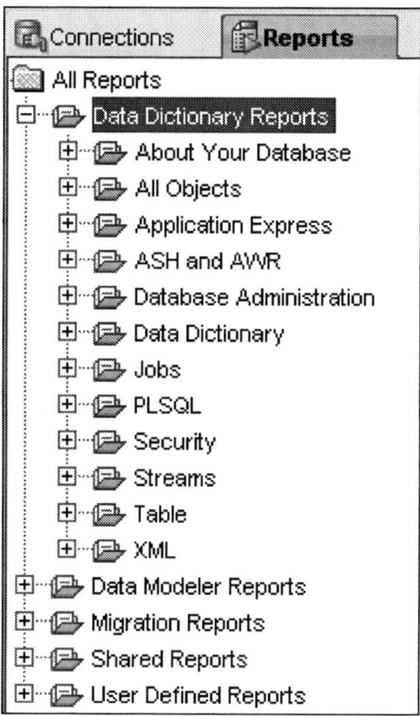

Use the shipped reports to determine the details about your system, which includes:

- Finding the version and parameters details of the database that you are connected to
- Learning more about the data dictionary
- Reviewing the tables and related details for a particular schema
- Finding the objects in a schema
- Reviewing the valid and invalid PL/SQL in a system
- Searching for PL/SQL text

Running a report

To run a report, expand any of the nodes in the **Reports** navigator and select the report. The first time you select a report, the **Select Connection** dialog is invoked, to offer a choice of connections, as shown in the following screenshot:

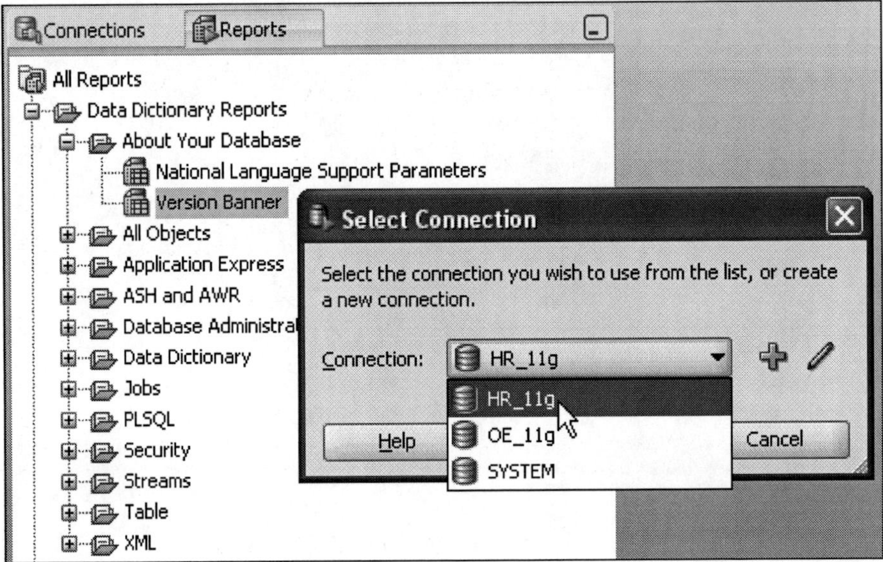

Using bind variables

Some reports are parameter-driven. Therefore, you are prompted for the bind variable, or input values, as you run the report. The default value is null, to return all records. Just start typing to enter an input parameter. This will automatically deselect the **NULL** checkbox:

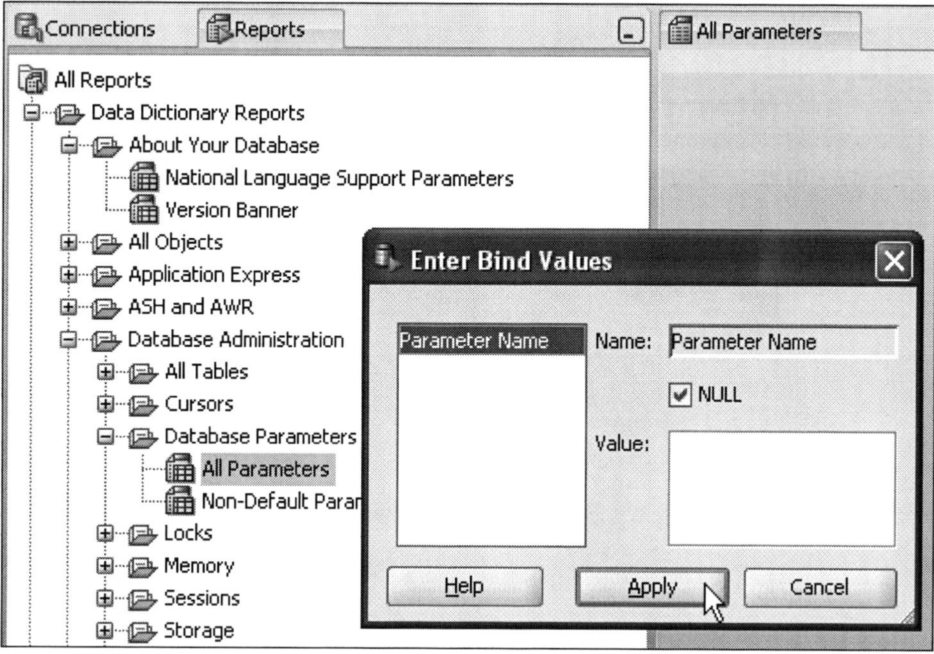

Privileges required for running reports

Most users can successfully run most of the shipped reports, needing only the database connection to start. Even users with the most limited connection privileges can run many of the reports, such as those in the **About Your Database** category. However, they will have limited or no access to the reports in the **Database Administration** category, as SYSTEM or DBA privileges are required to run these.

If you do not have access to the underlying tables being queried, you get the standard Oracle error message, **"table or view does not exist"**. This is a common security access error message and you will need to switch to another, more privileged, user to run the report:

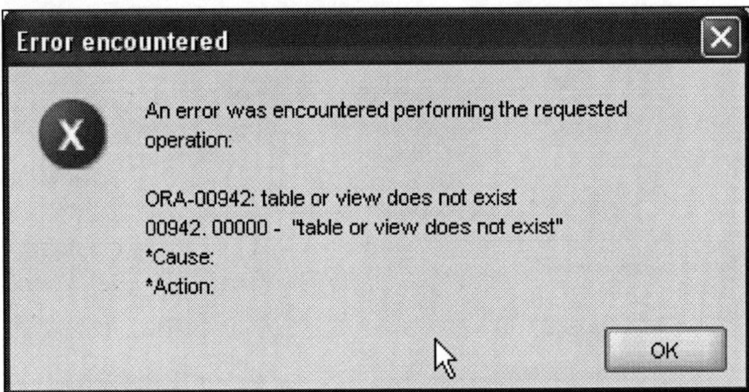

In the same way, you also need access to the underlying tables in a project to run user defined reports, where you might create a report for the instance data.

Instance data, in this context, is the data in the application. In our examples, the instance data is the data in the HR and OE tables.

Switching users

You can run the same report for any number of users. This is useful when you want to compare data between users or across databases. For example, if you regularly connect to different databases, you might want to verify the details of each version of the database for a database connection. You can do this using the **Version Banner** report under the **About Your Database** node. Having ascertained the version for the first connection, switch connections, and then run the report again.

Switching between users

Use the Connections drop-down list on the right-hand side to rerun a report for a different database connection.

Browsing shipped reports

SQL Developer ships with a set of reports that you can run for various connections or copy and repurpose. Due to the large number of shipped reports, it's neither practical nor useful to discuss each report here. In the next section, we'll consider a *few* of the top reports we like to use. While everyone will have their own set of important reports, by highlighting a few of the different reports and report categories provided, you can see the types of reports available, and then either look for others or create your own.

Running data dictionary reports

The first major category of reports shipped with SQL Developer is the **Data Dictionary Reports** node. These are, by definition, about the data dictionary, and therefore do not include any instance data reports, which you can define in the **User Defined Reports** section.

Getting to know the data dictionary

Once you have learned to write a select statement, getting to know the data dictionary is an important and useful progression to make. This is the data dictionary that holds the metadata about your database. Knowing how to query the data dictionary means you can determine which dictionary view holds the information about the tables, columns, constraints, and privileges you can access. Therefore, you can find details about the project or the application that you are working on. As mentioned earlier, many people who are familiar with the data dictionary have SQL scripts and queries, which they frequently run. This is exactly what the shipped reports provide.

We have said that SQL Developer provides a long list of reports that query the data dictionary, but these do not cover every possibility. Starting with the two reports under the **Data Dictionary** node will help you become familiar with this environment:

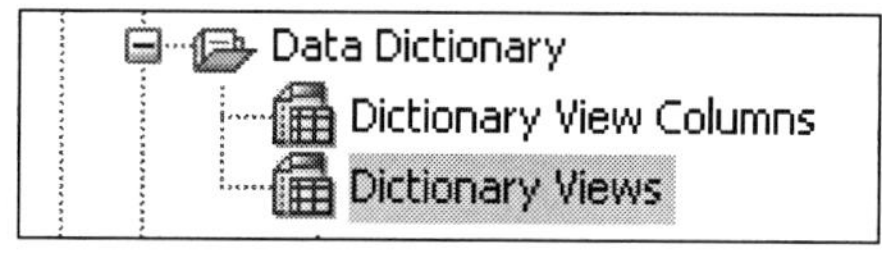

If the reports SQL Developer provides are sufficient for all your query purposes, then you may never use them. However, if you want to know something about your database, that is not available through any report provided, then you can start with these two dictionary views and build a query based on your findings.

For example, SQL Developer does not provide any reports on dimensions. If you want to learn about any dimensions you have, you can write an SQL query, but you first need to know which dictionary views to query. This is where the **Data Dictionary | Dictionary Views** report can help. Select the report and run it. Provide the bind variable input parameter "dimension" when prompted. You do not need to add any wild cards (%), as the report does that for you.

The report returns the set of records that relate to dimensions, listing the view names and the descriptions about the views. Once you have determined which view to use, use the **Data Dictionary | Dictionary View Columns** report (as shown in the following screenshot) to determine the columns in the view. You can now use the detail to write the query in the SQL Worksheet.

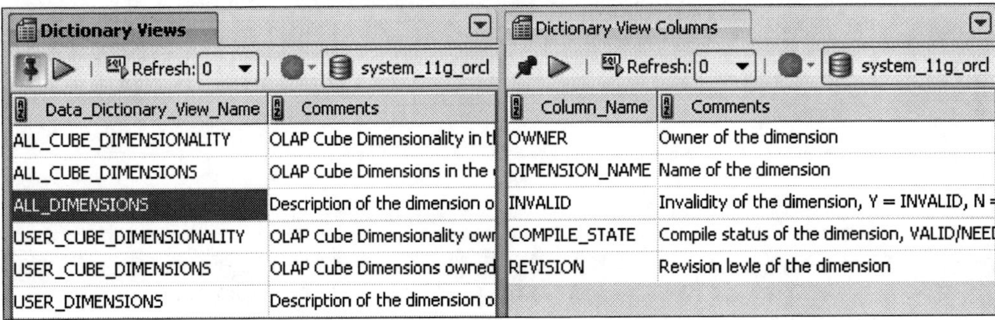

Both reports are shown in the previous screenshot, illustrating the detail you now need to be able to write your own query.

About the database

If you work with a number of different databases, then there are a few reports that are very useful for determining the version of the database you're connected to and which database parameters are set. These reports fall under two categories:

- **About Your Database**
- **Database Parameters**—found in the **Database Administration** section

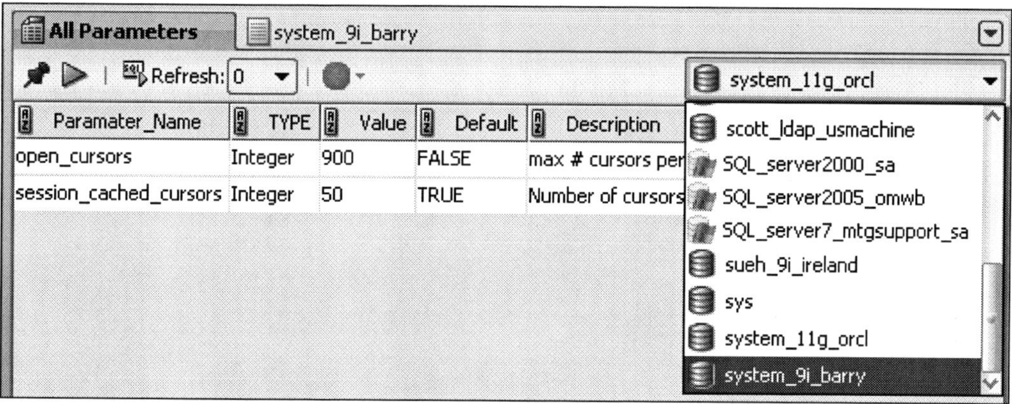

In the example that we have just seen, the **All Parameters** report has been run, with a bind variable of "cursors", to list all of the parameters relating to cursors. By using the connections drop-down list to the right-hand side, you can switch between database connections and compare these cursor parameters between databases.

Reviewing Privileges and Security reports

SQL Developer provides a number of reports that are related to security issues, including **Auditing** and **Encryption** reports. If you are new to the database, and getting to know your environment, the group of security related reports you are more likely to run frequently are in the **Grants and Privileges** folder. If you are unable to access certain objects, or find you have no ability to create, edit, or update objects, then reviewing the **Role Privileges** and **System Privileges** reports is a good place to start.

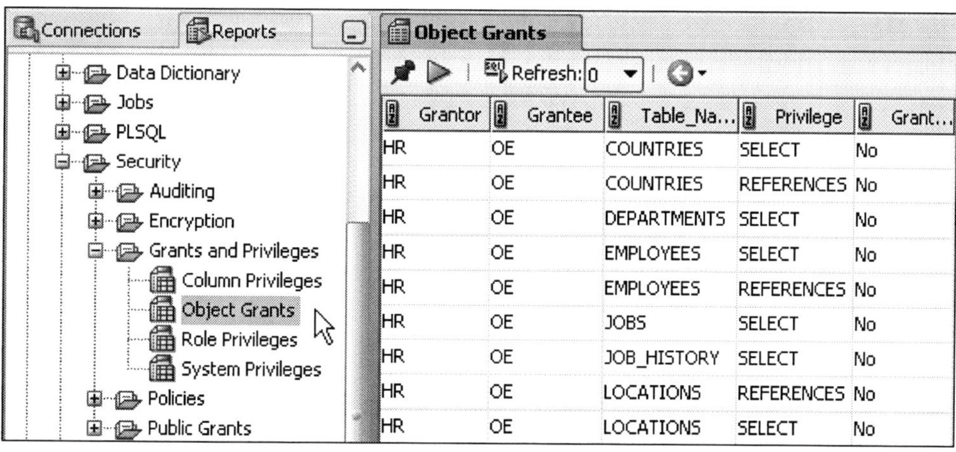

In the example shown in the previous screenshot, we have selected the **Object Grants** report for **HR**. Here, we see that the **OE** schema has **SELECT** and **REFERENCES** access to some of the **HR** tables.

Assisting with quality assurance

The selection of **Quality Assurance** reports in the **Table** node is useful when working on a project or application development. This is not a comprehensive list (as shown in the following screenshot), but a good indication of the type of reports you might create to keep a check of the status of an application:

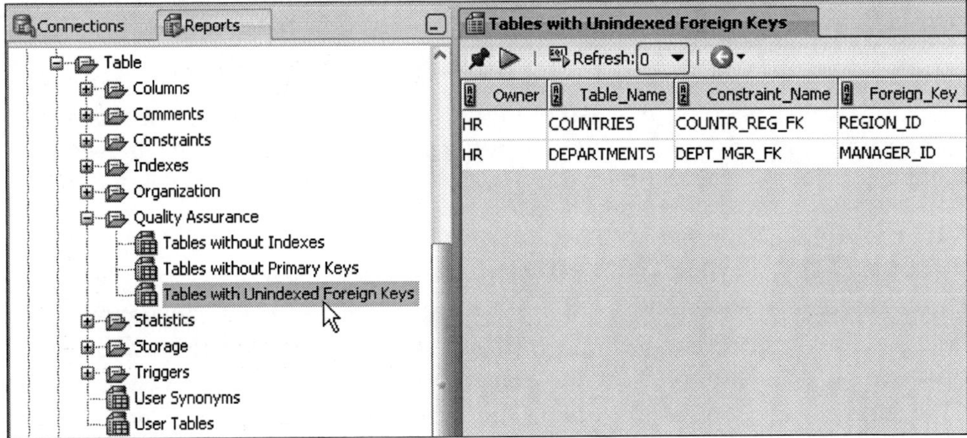

It's also worth noting that these are just reports and not suggestions of best practice. While it is advisable to have indexes on your tables, there may be a good reason why some tables are not indexed. For example, if you were adding bulk sets of data, you would want to add the indexes after the fact. Having the report indicates where there are gaps. You'll need to make the decisions based on the results.

Using the PL/SQL reports

There are a few reports in the **PLSQL** node. Possibly, the most useful is the **Search Source Code** report. SQL Developer provides a number of search facilities, not just in the reports area, which help you find:

- Parameters in PL/SQL code
- Objects in a schema
- Words and text in the current editor

If you use a command line tool, such as SQL*Plus to access the database, then you need to write an SQL query to search for specific strings in SQL or PL/SQL code. The **PLSQL | Search Source Code** report allows you to look for either the PL/SQL object by name, or you can look for a string or piece of text in the code, as shown in the following screenshot:

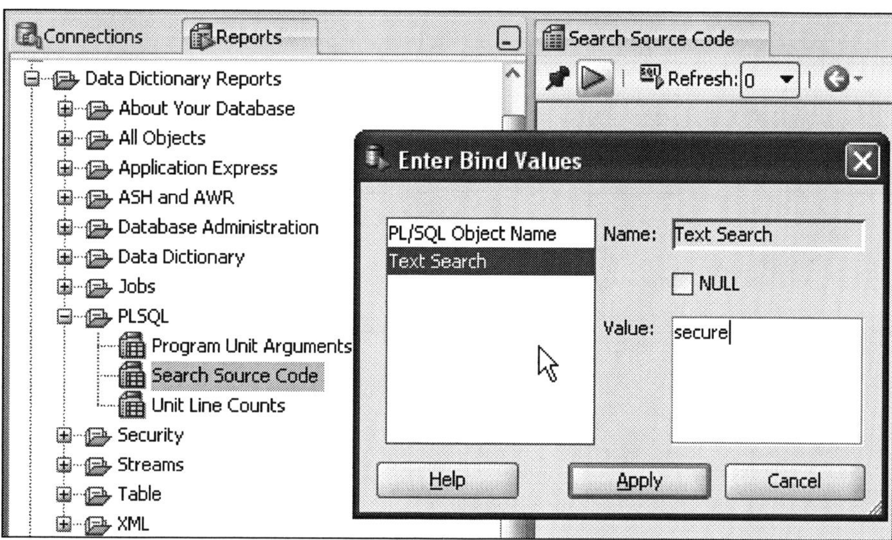

Once you have found the source code, you can move to the code by using the context menu on the object name, or by double-clicking on the object name.

Running ASH and AWR reports

There are a growing number of Oracle **Active Session History** (**ASH**) and **Automatic Workload Repository** (**AWR**) reports provided by SQL Developer. First introduced in SQL Developer 1.5, more reports were added in SQL Developer 1.5.3. AWR captures workload-related performance data at user and system levels. ASH provides the history of the activities in recent active sessions. The report below is a chart of **Daily ASH Statistics**:

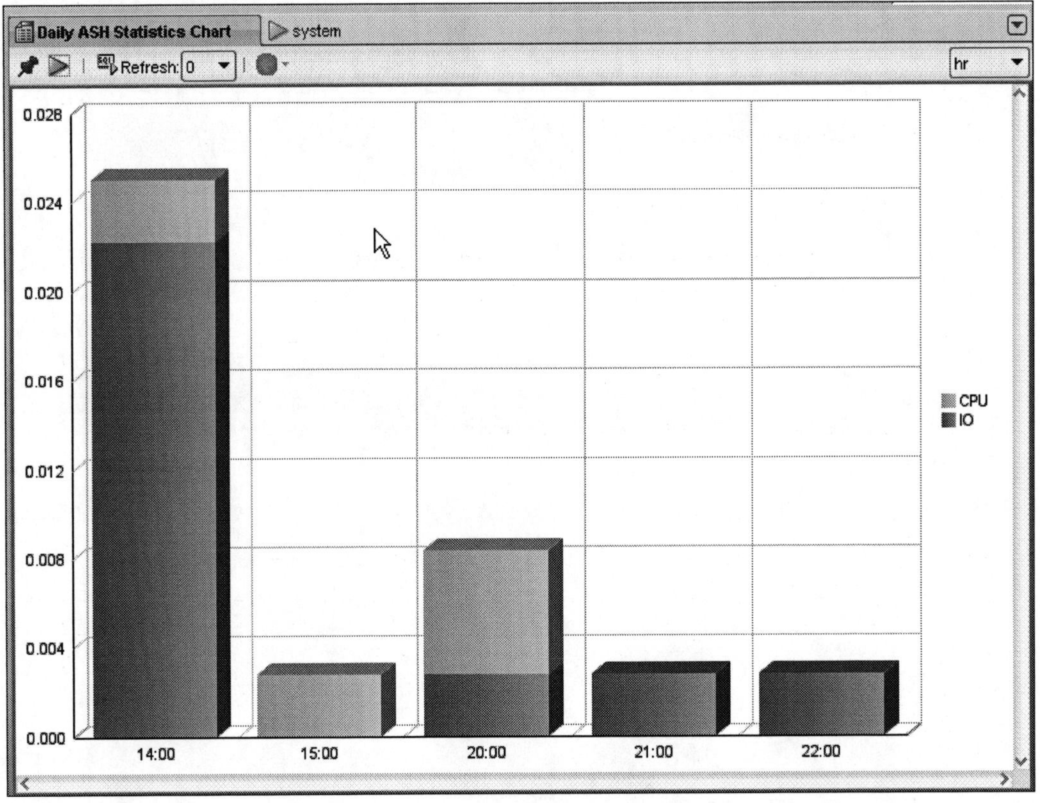

These reports are database specific and require the **Oracle Diagnostics Pack** to be licensed for the databases that you run the reports against. You are warned before you run these reports that the underlying reports require the license.

Other categories

There are separate chapters on *Working with SQL Developer Migrations, Working with Application Express*, and *Introducing SQL Developer Data Modeler*. However, it is fitting to briefly mention the availability of the reports here.

Migration reports

SQL Developer provides a selection of reports that are useful if you are involved in migrations from non-Oracle databases. As for other reports, if you do not have access to the underlying structures, the reports will deny you access. You'd typically run these reports as the migrations repository owner, or as a migrations user with similar privileges.

Application Express reports

SQL Developer provides a selection of Application Express reports. These are listed in the **Application Express** node under **Data Dictionary Reports**. These reports provide details about applications you have access to. The **Applications** and **Pages** reports provide the same details that are available in the **Connection** navigator. For more information on this and all Application Express support in SQL Developer, see the chapter on *Working with Application Express*.

Data Modeler reports

A new category of reports was added in SQL Developer 2.1. This is the **Data Modeler Reports** node. The tables that these reports run against are first created and populated when you export your design from Oracle SQL Developer Data Modeler. Subsequent records are added each time you export a design in the Data Modeler. The reporting repository and the Data Modeler are discussed in the chapter on *Introducing SQL Developer Data Modeler*.

Running reports from other menus

Initially, all reports were only listed under the **Reports** navigator. However, starting from SQL Developer 1.5, a few reports were added to context menus (having been requested so frequently in various forums). A report available from a top-level menu saves having to navigate to the report in the correct category. These reports are **Monitor Sessions** and **Monitor SQL**, which are both available on the main **Tools** menu, and the **Manage Database** report, available in the **Connections** main context menu. We'll now review each of these reports.

Monitor sessions

The **Monitor Sessions** report displays the connected SQL Developer sessions and is available:

- In the **Sessions** category in the **Database Administration** section
- On the main **Tools** menu

The context menu for the report includes two additional items, **Trace Session** and **Kill Session** (as shown in the following screenshot). If you run this report as SYSTEM or a DBA, you can terminate these SQL Developer sessions using the menu. This is particularly useful if a session has not terminated in a clean manner and needs to specifically be terminated.

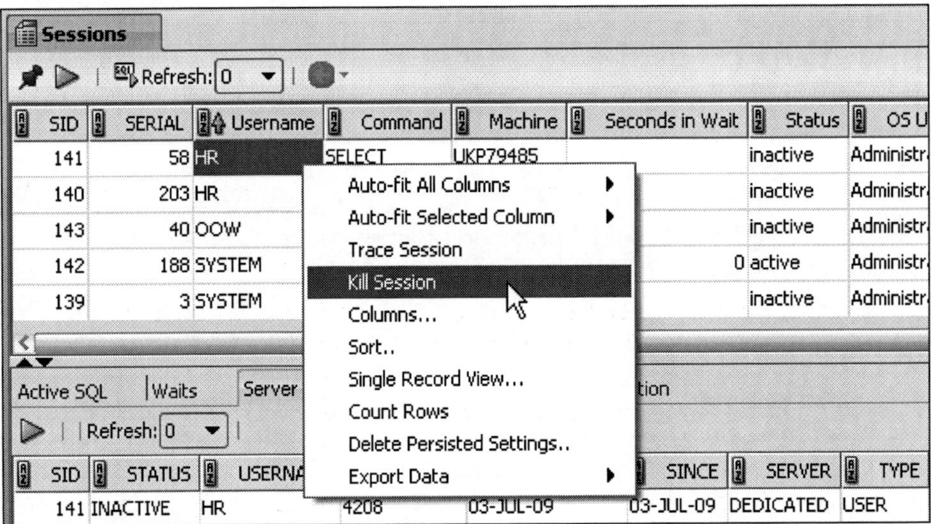

Managing the database

You can run the **Manage Database** report using the context menu for any connection in the **Connections** navigator. This report displays the tablespaces and the associated details. If you run the report as SYS, you can also shutdown the database from this report as the report provides an additional **Shutdown** button:

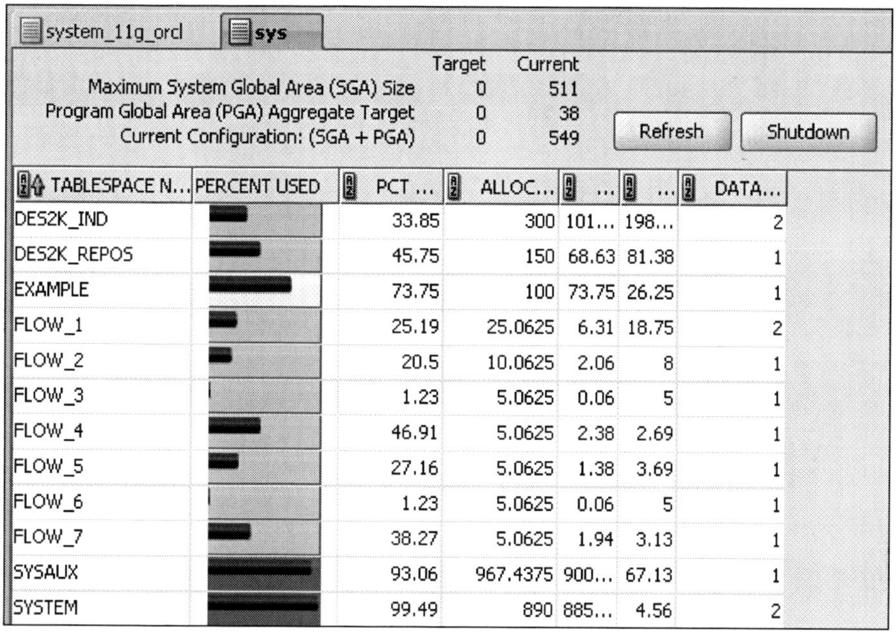

system_11g_orcl | sys

	Target	Current
Maximum System Global Area (SGA) Size	0	511
Program Global Area (PGA) Aggregate Target	0	38
Current Configuration: (SGA + PGA)	0	549

Refresh Shutdown

TABLESPACE N...	PERCENT USED	PCT ...	ALLOC...	...	...	DATA...
DES2K_IND		33.85	300	101...	198...	2
DES2K_REPOS		45.75	150	68.63	81.38	1
EXAMPLE		73.75	100	73.75	26.25	1
FLOW_1		25.19	25.0625	6.31	18.75	2
FLOW_2		20.5	10.0625	2.06	8	1
FLOW_3		1.23	5.0625	0.06	5	1
FLOW_4		46.91	5.0625	2.38	2.69	1
FLOW_5		27.16	5.0625	1.38	3.69	1
FLOW_6		1.23	5.0625	0.06	5	1
FLOW_7		38.27	5.0625	1.94	3.13	1
SYSAUX		93.06	967.4375	900...	67.13	1
SYSTEM		99.49	890	885...	4.56	2

Real-time SQL monitoring

Oracle Database 11g introduced real-time SQL monitoring, a feature now also exposed in SQL Developer 1.5.3 and subsequent releases. Tuning is often considered the domain of DBAs, and this feature is typically used for monitoring performance and finding problem areas (for example, what point a query has reached in the explain plan and where the time is being spent). Having a report that you can easily run, brings tuning closer to the developer. Real-time SQL monitoring is useful for long running queries and comes into play by default when:

- `STATISTICS_LEVEL` initialization parameter is set to `ALL` or `TYPICAL` (the default value)
- SQL statements that consume more than five seconds
- SQL queries run in parallel

In SQL Developer, the report is **Monitor SQL** under the **Tools** menu. When you run it, it displays a grid of all monitored statements.

In the following example, we used the shipped reports, **All Objects | Object Count by Type**. You can write your own long running query or do the same. Once the report has started running, switch to or invoke the **Monitor SQL** report. A data grid of records is displayed, as shown in the following screenshot:

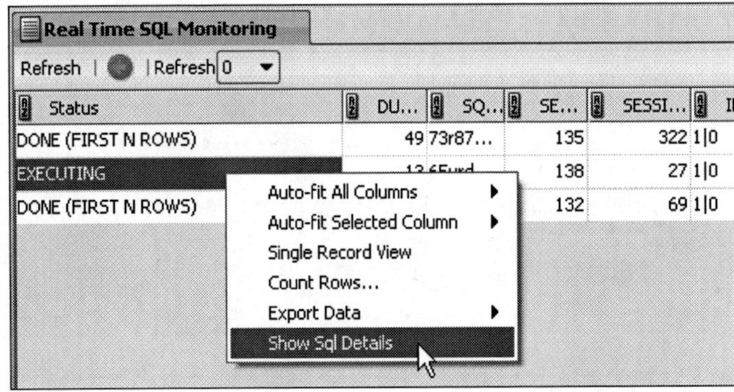

We have run a number of reports and so have a record for each of the queries that fit the above criteria. To see the report detail, invoke the context menu and select **Show Sql Details**:

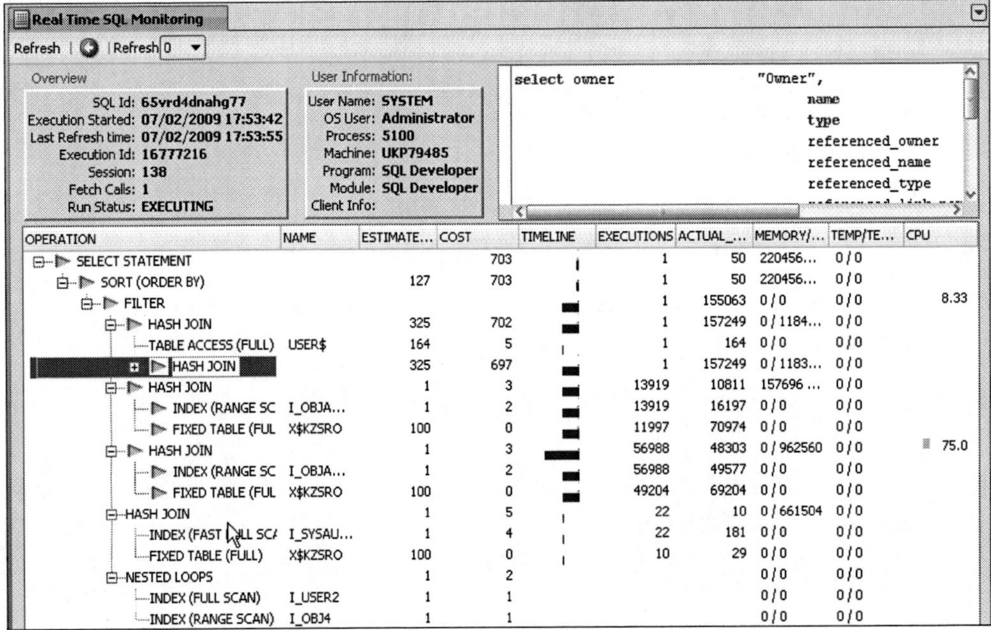

This query is still in progress, so the statements with the green arrows are still executing.

[The real-time SQL monitoring feature is part of the Oracle Tuning Pack, an Oracle Database 11g Cost Option, and as such, you are warned of this detail when you invoke the report.]

Creating your own reports

You can create any of the reports described above under **User Defined Reports**, either by copying them and then making modifications, or by starting from scratch. Defining your own reports also means that you can query instance data in your application or project. If you run certain queries regularly, they are well suited to being stored as reports.

User defined report styles include basic tabular reports, charting, and master-detail reports. In this section, we use the HR sample schema to demonstrate how to build your own reports. You can use the techniques described to build more complex reports.

Getting started

The first time you use the SQL Developer **Reports** navigator, the **User Defined Reports** folder is available and initially empty. You can populate the folder using a number of approaches:

- Importing existing reports previously created
- Copying a report
- Creating a report from scratch

Regardless of the approach used, it is advisable to categorize your reports. You can do this by using folders.

Creating folders

Storing reports in folders serves a number of purposes in SQL Developer. Folders help you categorize reports that belong to a particular project or have a similar theme. This in turn helps you quickly find a category of reports, whether instance data or data dictionary reports. In addition, having folders of reports means that you can export, and therefore later import, the folders for reuse and sharing. Create nested folders to further organize your reports.

To create a folder, select the **User Defined Reports** node in the **Reports** navigator and select **Add Folder** from the context menu:

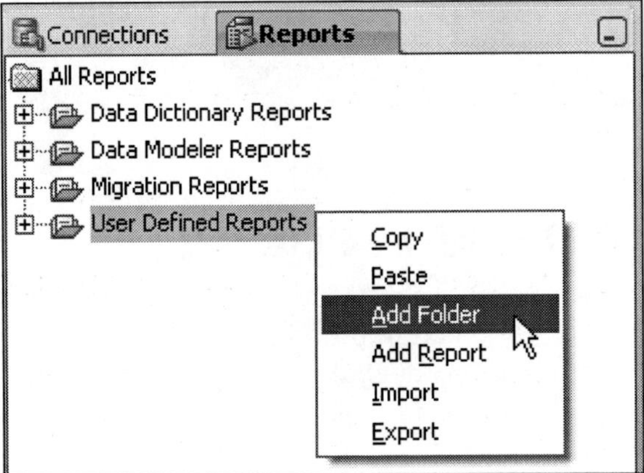

This invokes a simple dialog as shown in the following screenshot, which you can then populate with the details about the folder. This folder dialog only requires the **Name** field to be filled. However, if you provide more detail, it is useful for sharing reports later.

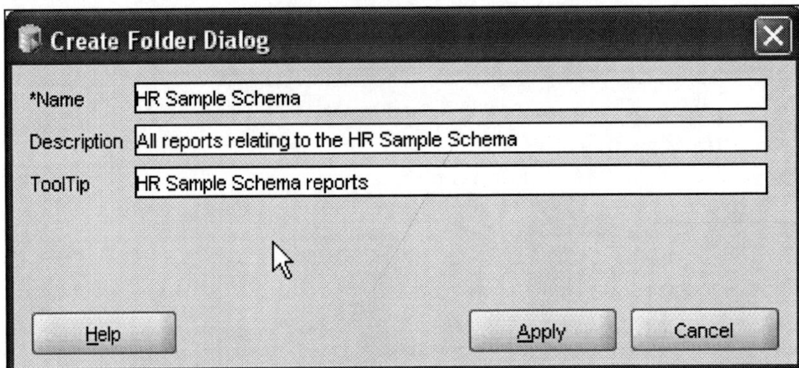

Storing reports

As soon as you have created an initial folder or report, a new UserReports.xml file is created in the C:\Documents and Settings\<user>\Application Data\SQL Developer folder.

Notice that the file is stored at the highest level of the SQL Developer folder, (it is not associated with a particular installation of SQL Developer). So, if you upgrade to a later release, you can run and edit the reports you have previously defined. This is true for all reports created in SQL Developer Release 1.1 and above. Reports created in SQL Developer 1.0 can be read, but not updated in later releases. It also means that you can have different versions of SQL Developer installed. They will all access the same user-defined reports file.

The other change to be aware of is that reports created prior to SQL Developer 1.5 were created in the UserReports.xml and stored in the C:\Documents and Settings\<user>\.sqldeveloper folder. In SQL Developer 1.5, this location was changed to the Application Data folder as described.

The initial code created, using the folder example above, looks like this:

```
<?xml version="1.0" encoding="UTF-8" ?><displays><folder>
  <name><![CDATA[HR Sample Schema]]></name>
  <tooltip><![CDATA[HR Sample Schema reports]]></tooltip>
  <description><![CDATA[All reports relating to the HR Sample
                Schema]]></description>
   </folder>
</displays>
```

This is the file that your new reports are added to and is the file that you share with other users. We'll discuss sharing reports later.

As soon as you add reports to a folder or edit reports in the folder, the folder is rendered in italics. Saving the new updates, using the **Save All** ( ) button updates the folder definition and updates the UserReports.xml file.

Creating general reports

To create a report, select the **User Defined Reports** node, or a subfolder under the node, and invoke the **Create Report** dialog using **Add Report** from the context menu. The initial dialog is the same for all reports. At this point, you can enter all of the details about the report, including the **SQL** that defines the report, as shown in the following screenshot:

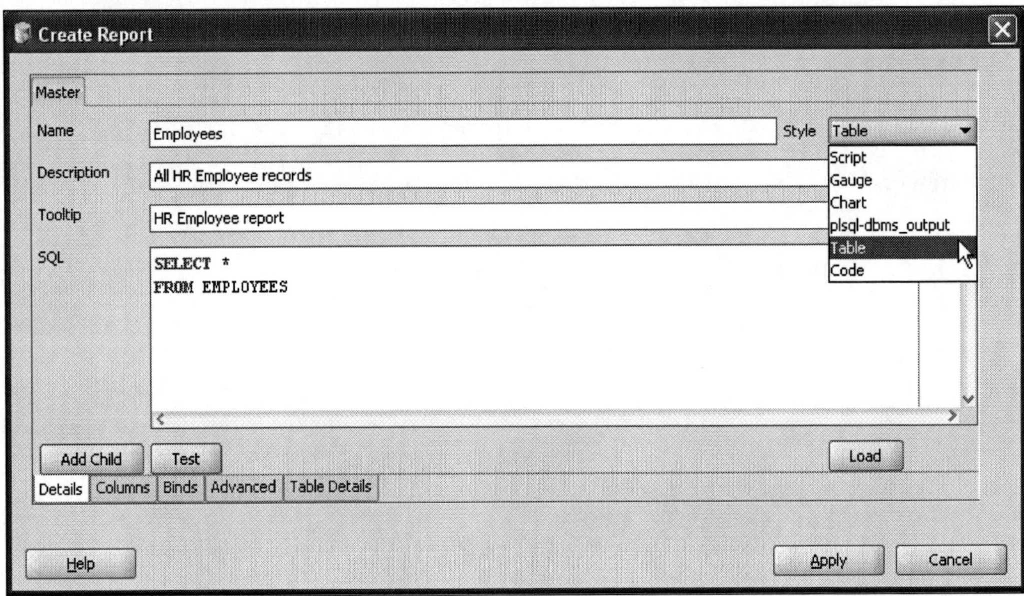

In the example that we have just seen, notice the report **Style** drop-down list. This allows you to control the visual output of the report (for example, a table or chart).

The **Test** button allows you to test the SQL script for validity and so it's often easiest to leave the report style unchanged. The default **Style** is **Table**. Test the SQL and then change the style as required.

Use the SQL Worksheet when creating the SQL

For all reports, it's easiest to create and test the SQL in the SQL Worksheet. You can take advantage of the code insight and other SQL Worksheet features, while developing the SQL script, and then copy and paste it into the report. In SQL Developer 2.1, you can highlight the SQL in the SQL Worksheet, invoke the context menu and select **Create Report**. This will open the **Create Report** dialog with the selected SQL text included.

Building general tabular reports

This is the most common form of reporting used and, with the exception of the few charts provided, all shipped reports follow this style. Tabular reports are also used in drill-down and master-detail reports. Regardless of the report you're about to create, you need to start with the initial SQL query. Consider the following query:

```
SELECT B.DEPARTMENT_ID,
   B.DEPARTMENT_NAME,
   A.FIRST_NAME,
   A.LAST_NAME,
   A.PHONE_NUMBER,
   A.HIRE_DATE,
   A.SALARY,
   C.JOB_TITLE
FROM HR.DEPARTMENTS B,
   HR.EMPLOYEES A,
   HR.JOBS C
WHERE A.EMPLOYEE_ID = B.MANAGER_ID
AND B.DEPARTMENT_ID = A.DEPARTMENT_ID
AND C.JOB_ID        = A.JOB_ID;
```

When this query is used in a tabular report, the output appears as shown in the following screenshot:

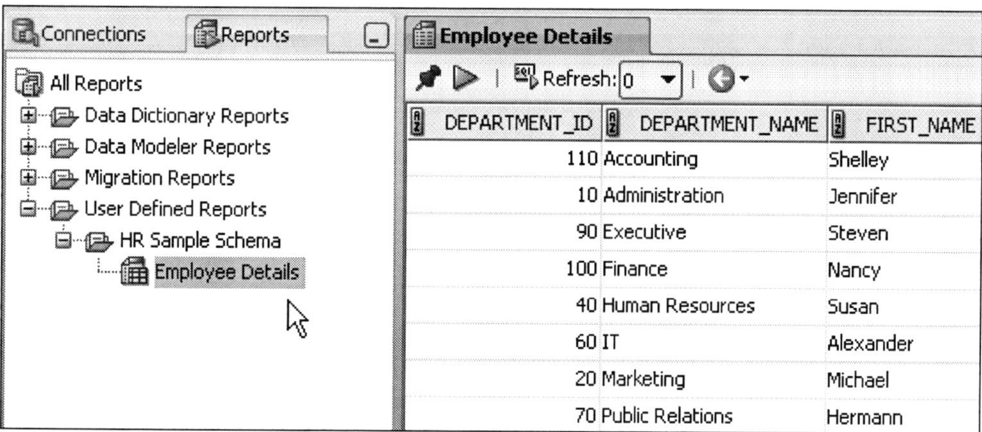

Adding bind variables

If you work with large sets of data, restricting the records returned by using a `WHERE` clause makes the result set more manageable. By writing the query to support input values, or a bind variable, means that you can re-run the query using different values. This kind of query makes a good report, because you can pass in values to restrict the result set.

It is important to know that when writing a query with bind variables, unless otherwise handled, the data is stored in the database in uppercase. If you have data in mixed case in the database, you'll need to code for that.

For example, you can add `AND C.JOB_TITLE LIKE :JOB_NAME` to the previous query. This is fine, except you need to know what you are searching for and that in this case, that Job Titles is stored as mixed case. So, entering "sales" or "manager" would not return any records. In this example, it's safer to enter the code `AND UPPER (C.JOB_TITLE) LIKE UPPER (:JOB_NAME)` and then the user does not need to know the composition of the data.

Once you have set up the binds in your report, you can run the report and will be prompted for the value, which you can add as shown in the following screenshot:

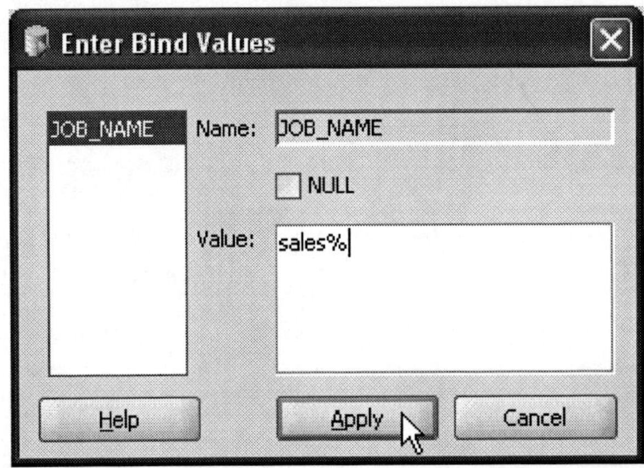

The **Create Report** dialog also provides the opportunity to add more meaningful detail to the binds in your reports.

Below the **SQL** script region is a set of tabs, one of which is the **Binds** tab, as shown in the following screenshot. Using this allows you to add more detail to the bind variables declared, which is useful, and especially true if you pass a number of parameters.

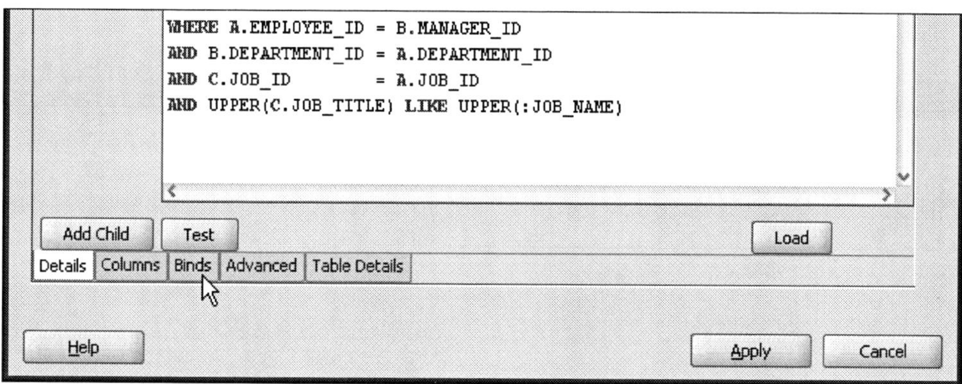

In the example shown in the following screenshot, we have provided a **Default** search value, a **Prompt**, and **ToolTip**. All of these provide added information to other users running the report.

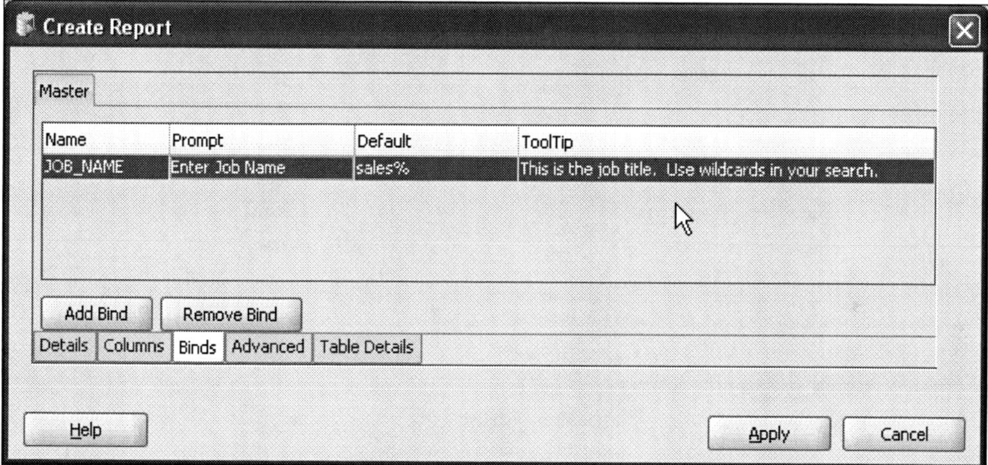

To invoke the **Create Report** dialog after it has been closed, select **Edit Report** from the context menu while highlighting the report.

Drilling down through reports

You can create a report that steps from one report to the next. You can also navigate to the definition of an object. Therefore, a report that returns a list of tables has an additional context menu that you can use to navigate to the table in question. The shipped reports also support drill-down reports. Consider the **All Constraints** report in the **Tables | Constraints** node. In addition to returning the Constraint details, the report displays a list of tables. Here, the context menu displays an extra menu option to navigate to the table in question:

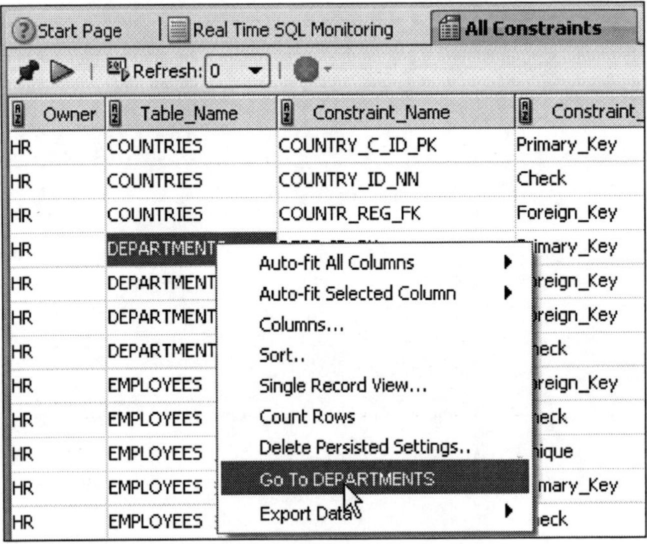

Creating a drill-down report

To create a drill-down report, create the initial master report, as you do for any other tabular report. By way of an example, we'll create a master or top-level report using the same query used before:

```
SELECT DEPARTMENT_ID,
       DEPARTMENT_NAME,
       LOCATION_ID
FROM DEPARTMENTS
```

Create a second report, using a query that will provide the results of the detail records, (following the drill-down action from the first):

```
SELECT EMPLOYEE_ID,FIRST_NAME,LAST_NAME,EMAIL,DEPARTMENT_ID
FROM EMPLOYEES
WHERE department_id = :DEPARTMENT_ID
```

Give the report a descriptive name (for example, Employee Details) you'll need to access this later. Notice for this report we included a bind variable. Therefore, the report either requires a value to be entered using the **Bind Variable** dialog, or has a value passed from the top-level, or master report.

Now, return to the top-level report and select the **Advanced** tab.

Select **Add Report** and enter the **Name** of the detail report. This is the value that is displayed in the context menu. In the **Report** field, there is a drop-down list of all reports available, whether shipped or user-defined. Find and select the detail report you created as shown in the following screenshot. Clicking on **Apply** saves the changes and runs the report.

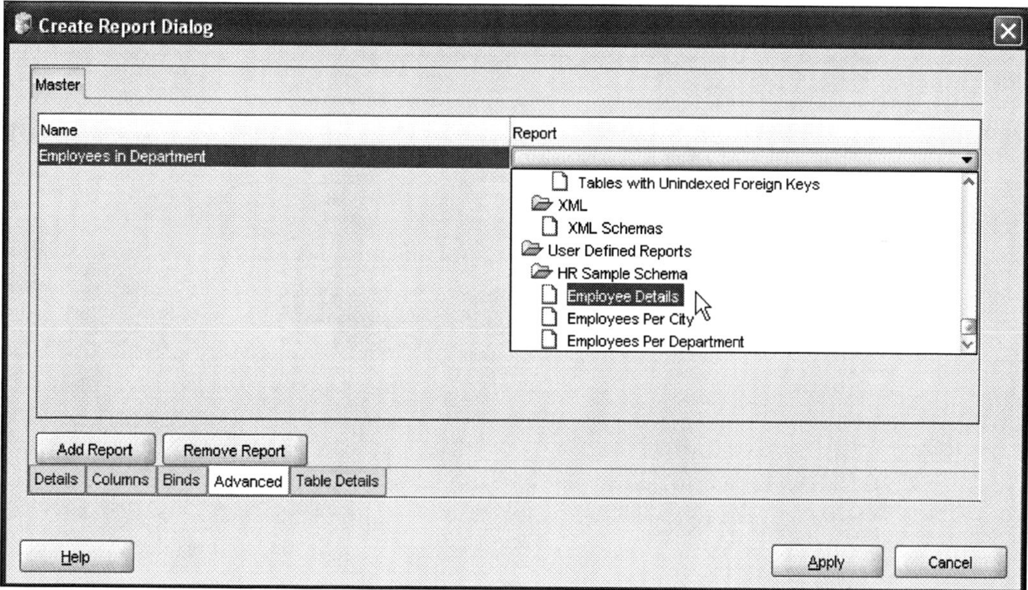

Running the top-level report is no different from any other tabular report. The context menu now displays an addition menu called **Reports**. All of the reports that you can navigate to from this report are displayed in the sub-menu. In the following example, the value that you have selected is passed to the called detail report as a bind parameter:

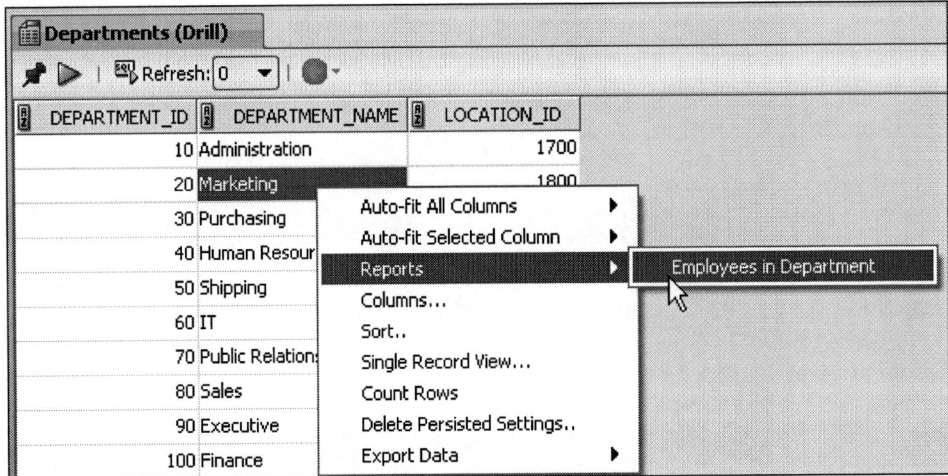

When drilling down through reports, a new button becomes available to allow you to traverse back up through the reports, as shown in the following screenshot:

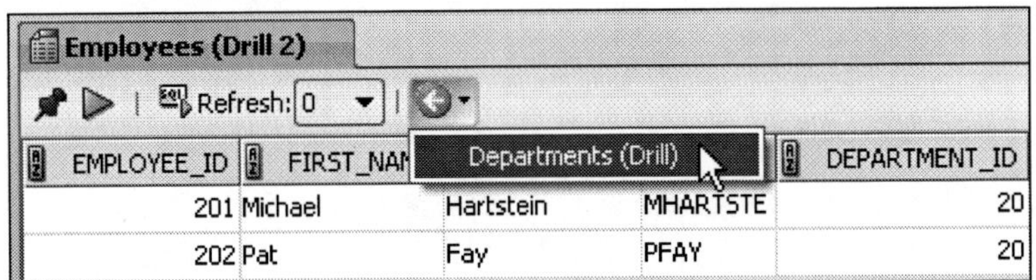

Case sensitive bind variables

Bind variable values are case sensitive. For bind variables that access a column name in the database, use the case of the column, as it is stored. The default is uppercase.

Master-detail reports

Master-detail reports are useful for reviewing related data on a single screen. Initially, when you run a master-detail report, only the master records are displayed. Once you select one of the master records, the details for that master are displayed. Consider one of the shipped **Data Dictionary** reports, **Active Sessions**, shown in the following screenshot (this can be found under **Database Administration | Sessions**). The report has a number of sibling details that are displayed in a set of tabs below the master record:

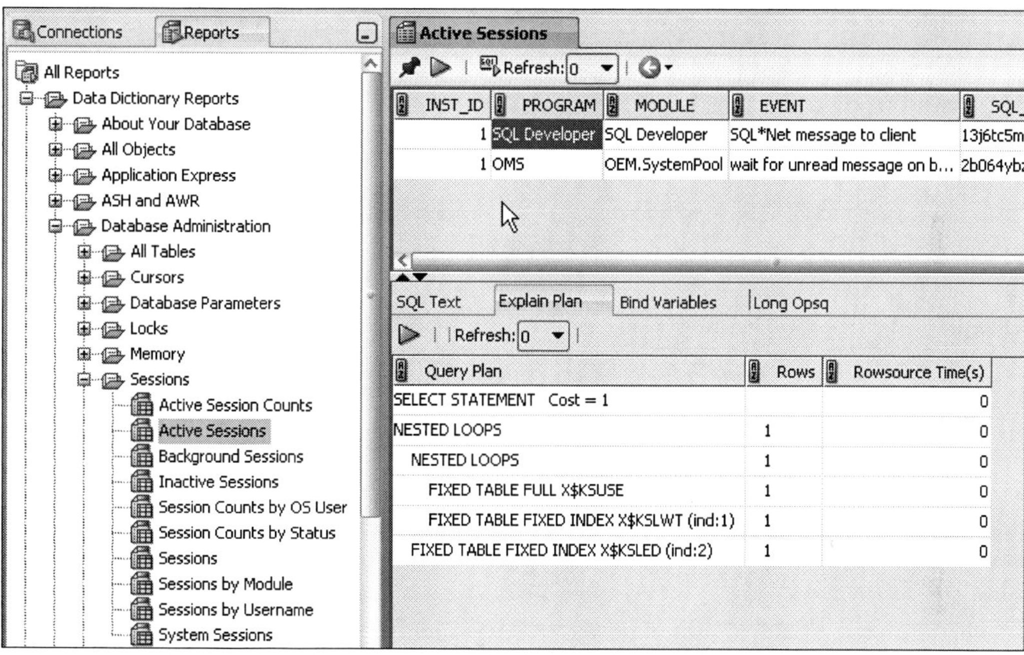

Creating master-detail reports

Initially, you create a regular tabular report, as the master report. In the following example, we use the same query as before:

```
SELECT DEPARTMENT_ID,
       DEPARTMENT_NAME,
       LOCATION_ID
FROM DEPARTMENTS
```

You can create, test, and even run the report as you would in any tabular report. This will ensure the master records and reports are correct. In the example shown in the following screenshot, we have run the **Report Test**:

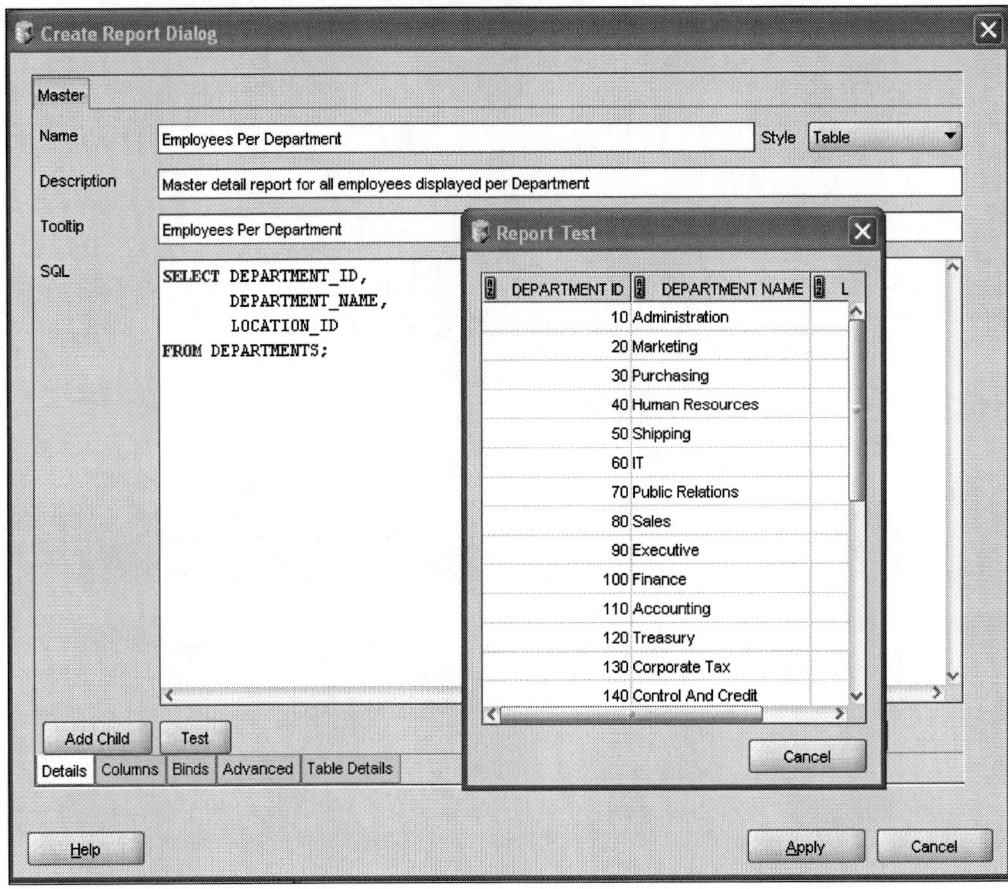

To add the detail, click on the **Add Child** button on the main report. This invokes a new panel in the dialog and allows you to add the detail records:

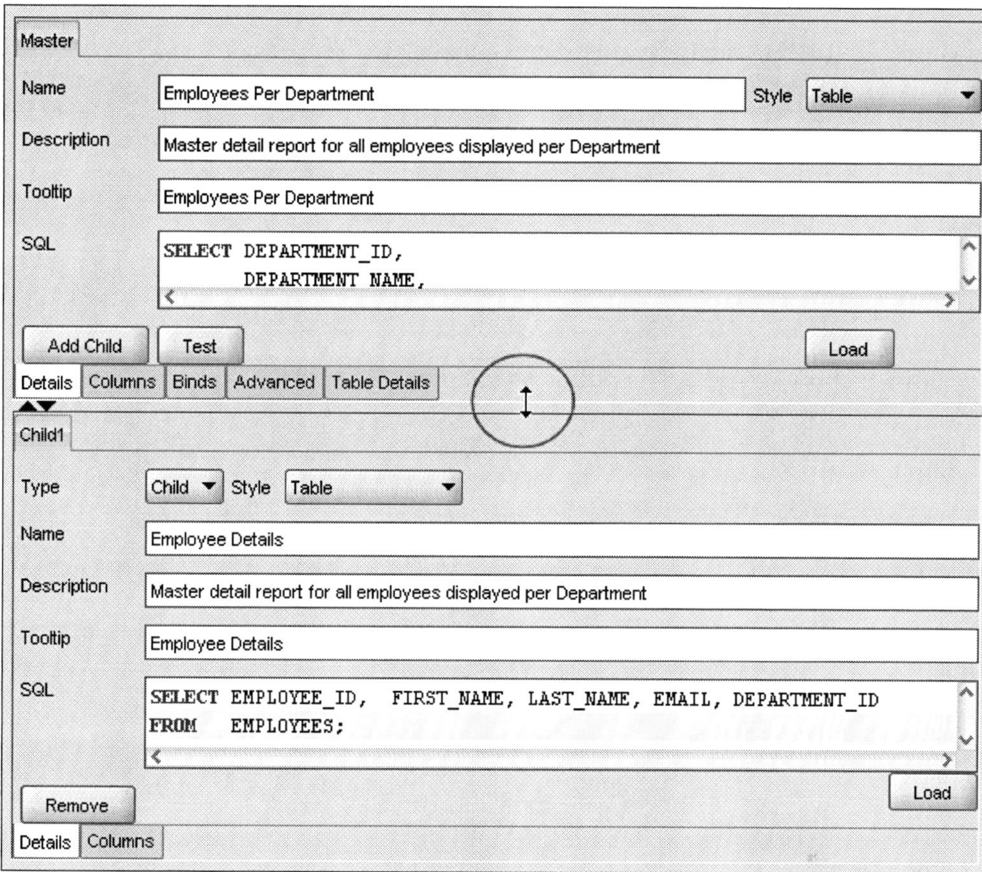

The example in the screenshot above, displays the full set of employees for any record in the master report. In order to have a meaningful set of records for each department, you need to link the master to the detail. For example:

```
SELECT EMPLOYEE_ID,FIRST_NAME,LAST_NAME,EMAIL,DEPARTMENT_ID
FROM   EMPLOYEES
WHERE  department_id = :DEPARTMENT_ID
```

Two key elements here are first that the `department_id` bind variable is in upper case (or the case of the column name in the database), as the report is looking for this "variable" in the database, and second that you have the join value in the master report.

Working with the master-detail report dialog

To work with either the master or detail portion of the report, use the ▲▼ button to switch between the panels. This is particularly useful if you do not have the real estate to spare on the screen. You can also use the drag bar between the master and detail sections of the dialog to resize the area you are working in.

Once you have created the report, you can tab through the master records to display each set of related detail records.

Notice that it is the name of the report that displays in the master and detail tabs:

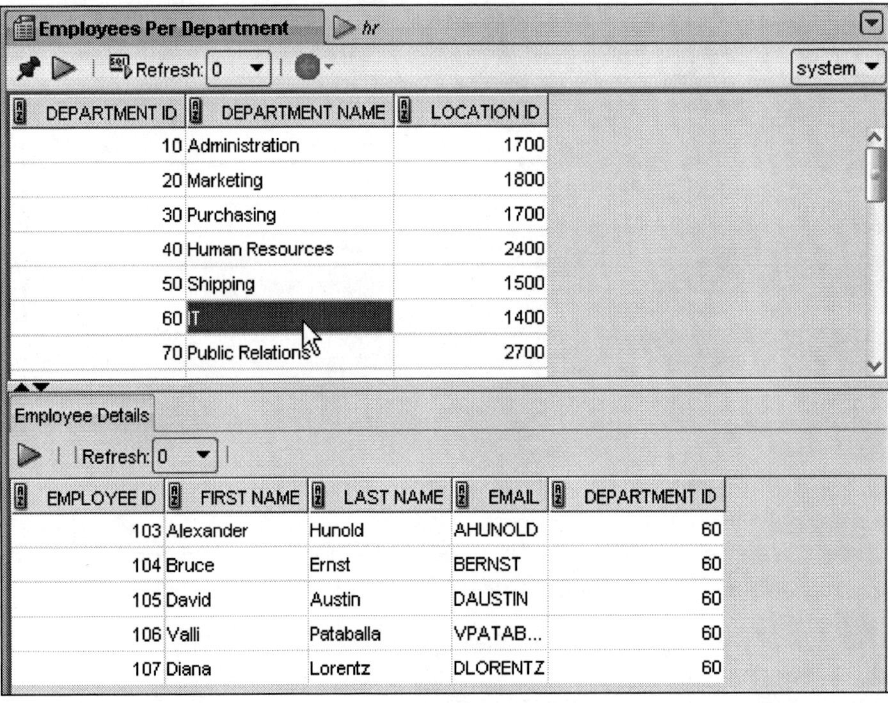

Creating sibling details

Having created a single detail report for the master report, you can continue to create further sibling detail reports. Using the **Create Report** dialog, click on **Add Child**. Make sure that the connecting bind variable you use in each detail report is also selected in the master query.

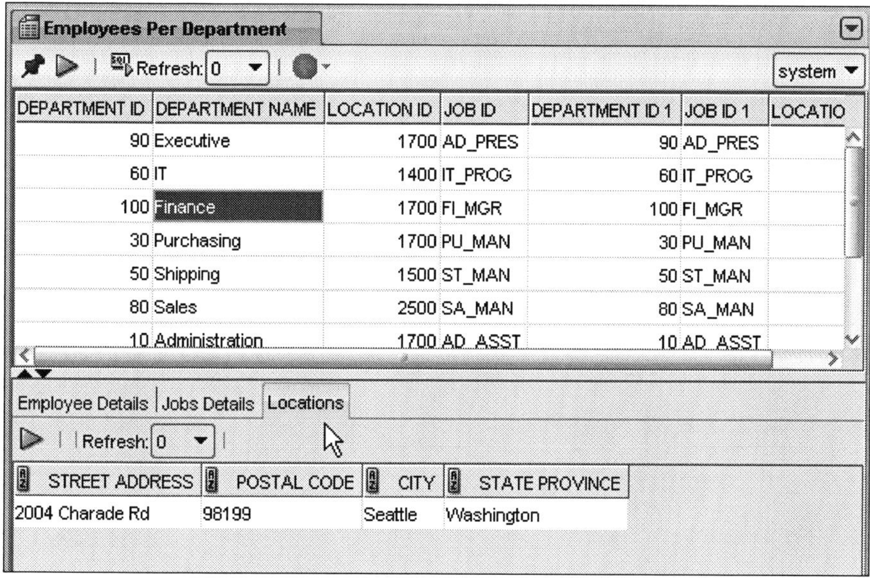

SQL Developer 2.1 allows you to control the display of columns in data grids. This is useful for master-detail reports where the columns needed for the join clutter the final report. Invoke the context menu for the columns header for the report output and select **Columns...**. Use the dialog to show, hide, and reorder the columns.

Adding charts

You can create reports and display them as charts instead of as a tabular output. The basic premise of a chart is that you need values for the x- and y- axis and the central value. Therefore, a report query is structured as follows:

```
SELECT <group>,<series>,<value>
FROM <table(s)>
```

The query `SELECT DEPARTMENT_ID, LAST_NAME, SALARY FROM EMPLOYEES` is an easy example to start with.

Once you have entered the query, switch the display style to **Chart** and select the **Chart Details** tab:

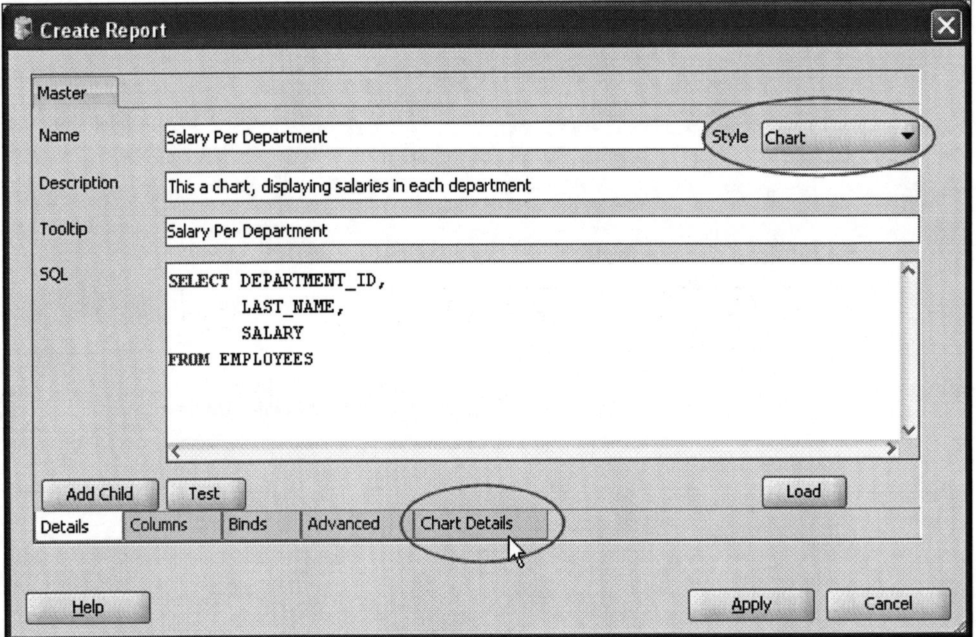

The **Chart Details** tab provides you with more control of the style of chart you are going to display. The choices of chart styles are:

- Pie
- Bar Stacked (vertical or horizontal)
- Bar Cluster (vertical or horizontal)

The number of records returned should drive the choice of the chart style you make. For example, the **PIE_MULTI** choice for **Chart Type** produces a pie chart for each record, and is therefore better suited to fewer records or to a query different from the one displayed above.

There are a number of other settings, which you can adjust, that control the appearance of the final chart. In the example we are using, the Legend has been switched off as this displays each **LAST_NAME** and makes the report very busy:

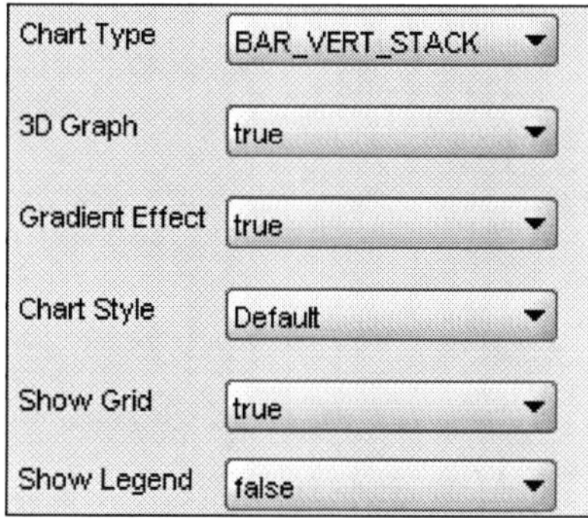

The final output for the chart is shown in the following screenshot:

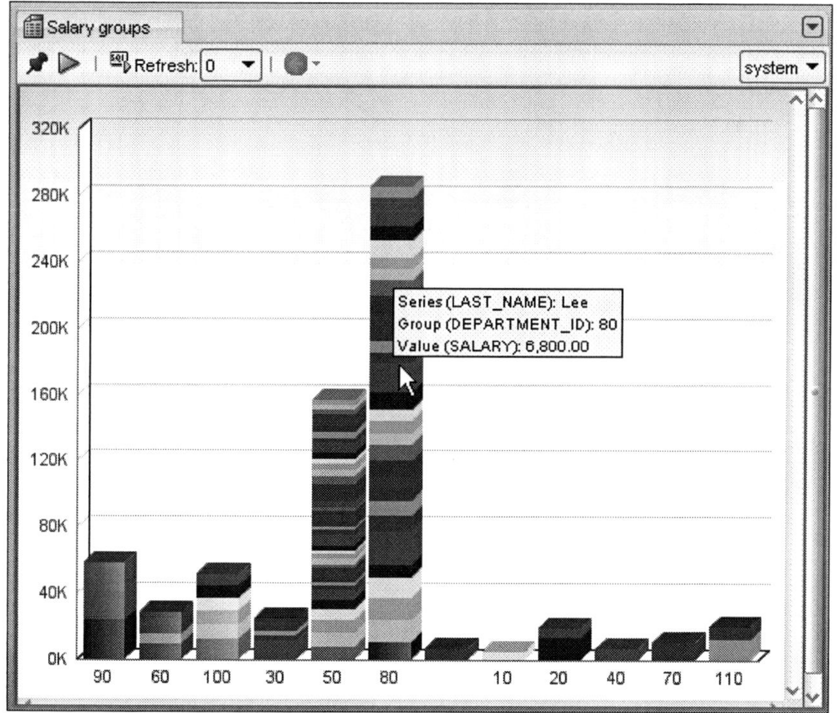

Notice that as you roll the mouse pointer on the various regions in the chart, the values are displayed.

You can now incorporate these charts as details in a master-detail report.

Building other graphical reports

SQL Developer offers a limited choice of graphical reports. The product is not a graphical reporting tool, so while these reports may seem limited, they do provide a visual report of the data being queried.

Creating pie chart reports

The pie chart is an option in the display setting for a regular chart. In the previous example, we have illustrated the bar chart. For the pie chart report, use the following query:

```
SELECT DEPARTMENT_ID, LAST_NAME,SALARY
FROM EMPLOYEES
WHERE DEPARTMENT_ID = :DEPT_ID
```

Set the report **Style** to **Chart,** and set the **Chart Type** to **PIE_MULTI**. In this example, it is important to consider the query and the number of records returned. We could use the same query for all of the departments in the bar chart, but that would display a small, possibly unreadable pie chart for each department. Restricting the records to each department, as shown in the following screenshot, provides a readable and useful pie chart:

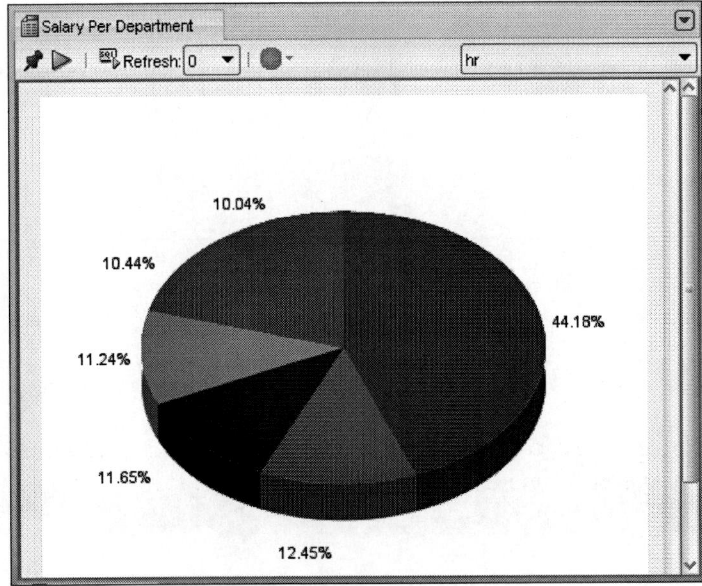

If the result of your query produces two pie charts, labeled Group A and Group B, then there has been an error in your query and SQL Developer is unable to render the chart. Verify your query has the correct structure as described at the start of the charts section.

Using gauges in reporting

SQL Developer provides a simple gauge report. An example of the gauge report is the **Manage Database** report, discussed earlier. The syntax for the gauge is:

```
SELECT <value-column>, <min>, <max>, <low>, <high>
FROM <table-name>
```

Create the report as you would any other user-defined report, and switch the report **Style** to **Gauge**. Once you have switched, the **Gauge Details** tab is displayed. Select this to control some of the gauge values. If you set **Query Based** to true, then you must control the **Min** and **Max**, **Low** and **High** values using your query. By setting **Query Based** to false, you can set the values in the dialog.

You don't have more control than this in a **Gauge** report, so you have no control over the default colors or values displayed:

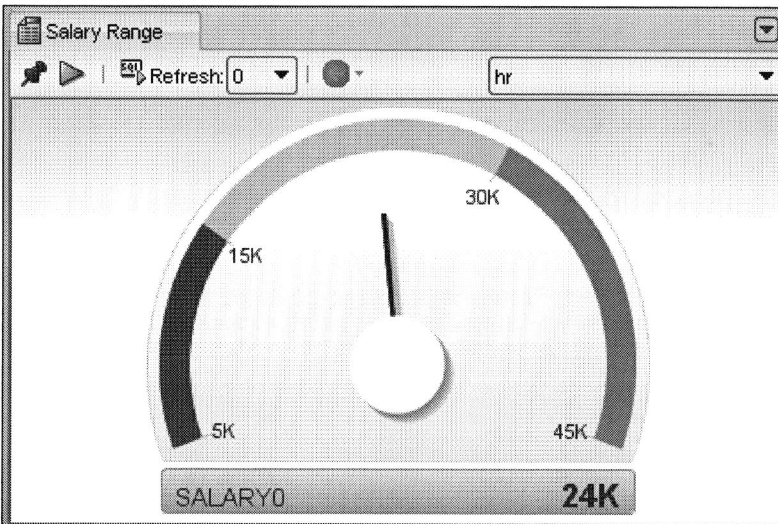

The syntax for the gauge can also be used in the SQL Worksheet. In this case, the gauge is displayed as a meter, as it is in the **Manage Database** report.

Other reports styles

SQL Developer also has a variety of additional report styles. In this section, we'll review each briefly, using small pieces of code to illustrate the point.

Using the Script style report

The Script style report runs the code as for other reports, but more specifically will run an executable style report. So you can, for example, include the text `@d:\working\demobld` in the **SQL** text region. By setting the report **Style** to **Script**, you will be able to run the report for any user. Be warned! In this example, `demobld.sql` drops and recreates a few demonstration tables including EMP and DEPT. If you add a script like this into a report, you'll need to be quite aware of where the report will be run and the contents of the file to be run.

`demobld.sql` is a script that can be found at `http://www.oracle.com/technology/sample_code/tech/sql_plus/htdocs/demobld.html`.

The **Script** style is also useful for formatting report text. Many reports consist of SQL or PL/SQL code or text, stored in the data dictionary. The code is displayed as unformatted text stored in records. You can see this if you run the **Search Source Code** report, which is in the **PLSQL** reports group. If we create a simplified version of that report in the **User Defined Reports** section using the query `SELECT TEXT FROM USER_SOURCE WHERE NAME = 'ADD_DEPT'`, and create a standard tabular report, the output displays as shown in the following screenshot:

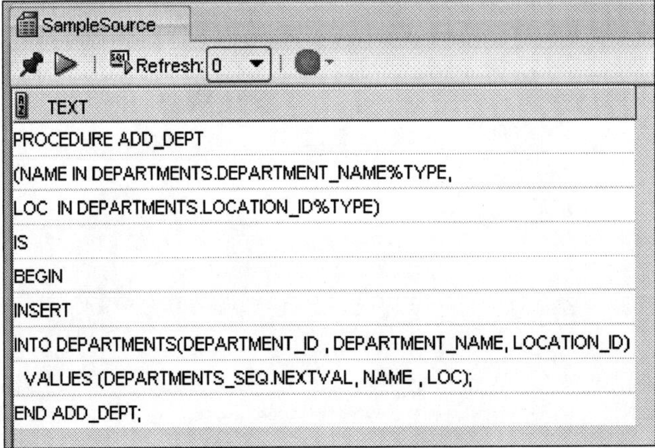

By changing the report **Style** to **Script**, you can change the formatting for each of the displayed records. The formatting does not change the lines used, but adds color coding for reserved words and variables, as shown in the following screenshot:

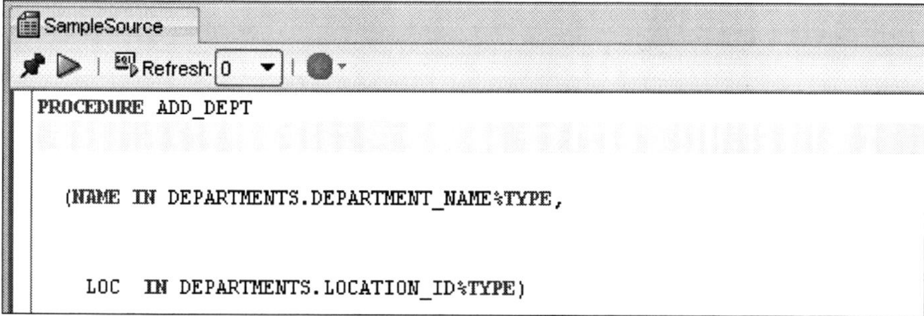

Using PL/SQL in a report

You can create a report using PL/SQL. This is designed to output information from dbms_output, so you can create an anonymous block to produce a report, formatting the output using HTML tags as shown in the following screenshot:

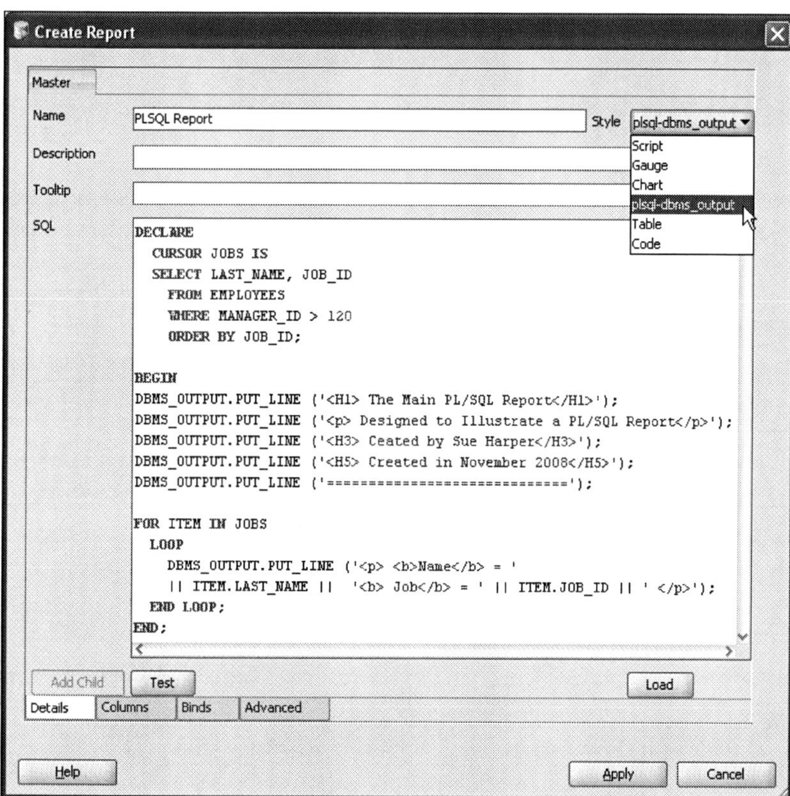

The output from the previous report is as follows:

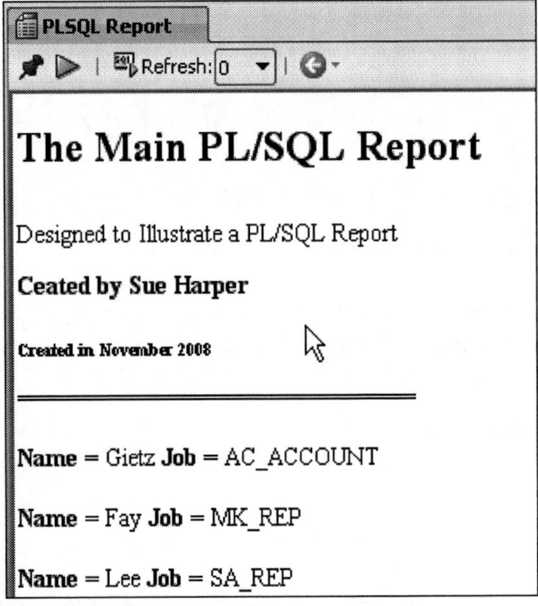

Sharing reports

Reports are a great vehicle for sharing knowledge about the database, through the detail in the dictionary tables and about instance detail of your project. Good reports should be shared in a team.

Copying and reusing reports

You can learn a great deal about creating your own reports by copying the shipped reports.

Initially, run the report to see if the output is what you require. You can then copy the report to the SQL Worksheet by clicking the **Run Report in SQL Worksheet** button at the top of the report:

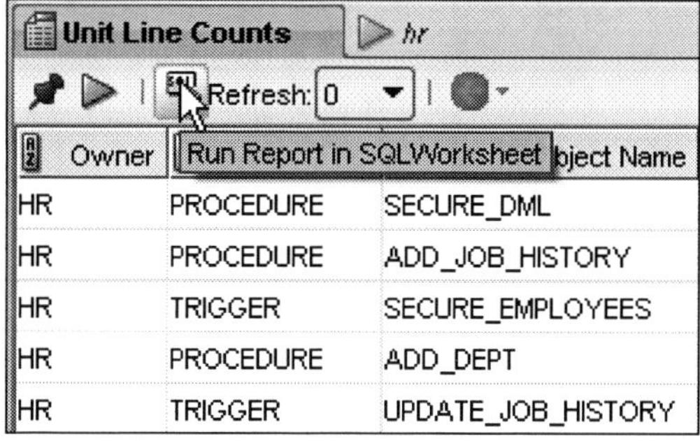

Once in the SQL Worksheet, you can edit and modify the SQL query to suit your requirements, running the report each time to verify the output is as required. Once you are happy, you can create a new report with the query.

Alternatively, you can just copy and paste a report directly, and then edit the newly created report.

Copy and reuse reports

Use the **Copy** context menu for any selected shipped report, and paste into **User Defined Reports** at the highest level or into a folder.

Importing and exporting

Once you have a selection of reports created, you can export and save or share the reports. To export a report, or folder of reports, select **Export** from the context menu. You can export:

- The highest level of **User Defined Reports**
- A folder and sub-folders
- Individual reports

If you have created folders to categorize reports, then these folders are ideal to export:

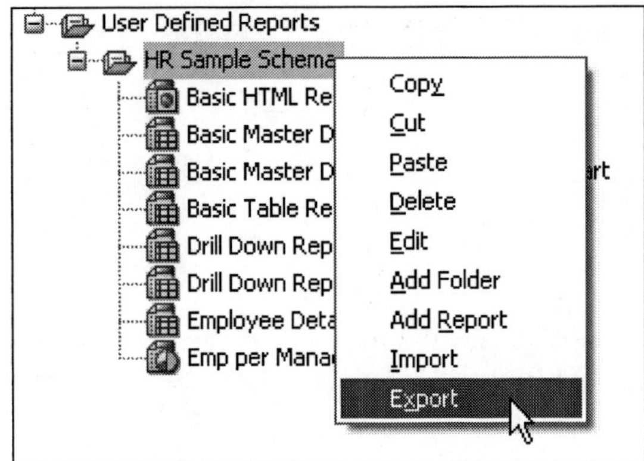

In the same way that you can export folders of reports or individual reports, you can import reports and folders of reports from other users. Any reports that you import are added to your personal `UserReports.xml` file, and as such can be edited and deleted as you choose.

Sharing reports through user defined extensions

If you create a selection of reports that you want to share among team members, but which should be shared as read-only reports, you can include these in a separate **Shared Reports** node. These reports are not editable, much like the shipped reports, although they can be copied and added to the **User Defined** reports section and edited at that point.

To share reports, you need first to export a set of reports. Once you have the new XML file or reports, place it on a shared server that is available for all users who need access. Open the **Preferences** dialog from the **Tools** menu, expand the **Database** node in the tree on the left, and select the **User Defined Extensions**. Here, you can add the reports by browsing to the location of the report. The location should include the XML file name. Set the **Type** to **REPORT**:

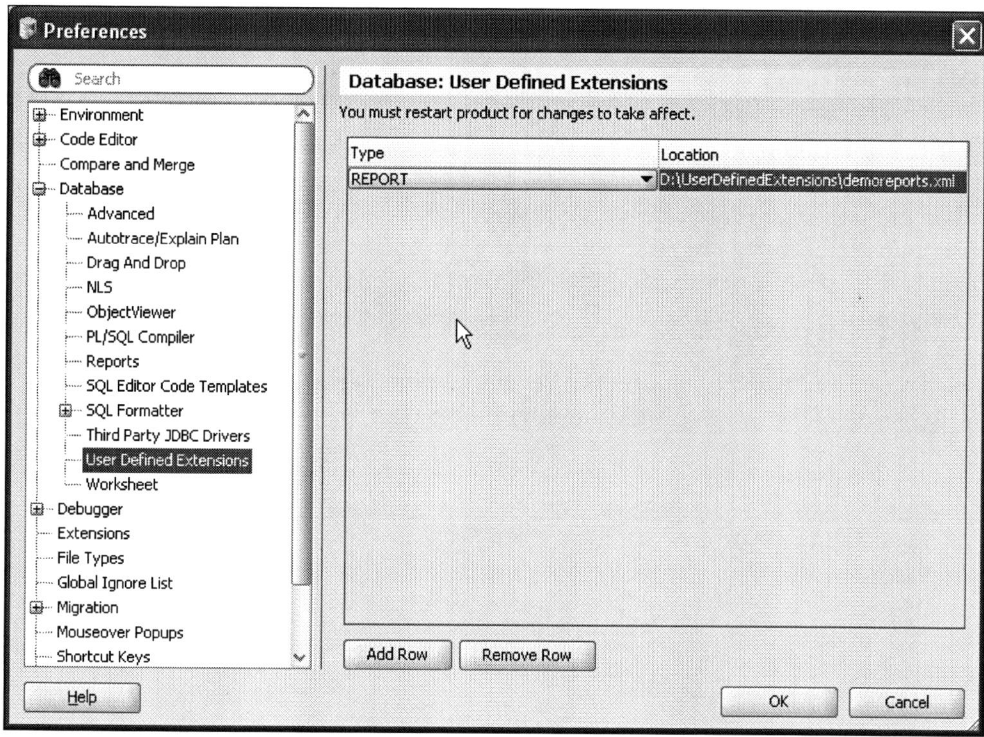

Once you have completed this step, you need to restart SQL Developer for the new extension type to be included. Once reopened, the new **Shared Reports** node displays in the top-level list of folders:

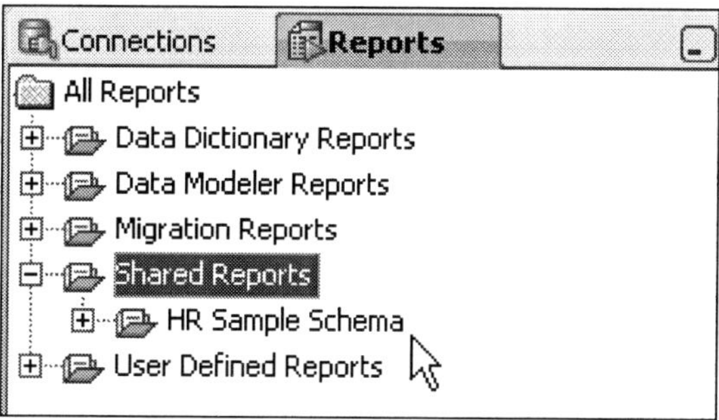

Save shared reports on a web server

You can save the report's XML file on a web server. If the file is stored on a web server, use the full URL for the location of the file in the **User Defined Extensions** settings.

Summary

SQL Developer provides the ability to create and save SQL queries as reports. You can create your own reports using various reports styles, including graphs or master-detail reports, with sibling detail reports. In addition to being able to create your own reports, SQL Developer supplies a set of shipped reports that access the data dictionary and provide you with an easy start to assessing the status of your application. In this chapter, you saw that by using these SQL reports, you can determine the general health and status of all of the database aspects of the systems you are working with, including the general health of the database, the database objects, and instance data in the application. Using SQL Developer, you can build your own reports, and export them to be shared with colleagues by sharing the exported XML file, or through the user defined extension mechanism.

In the next chapter, we'll look at how SQL Developer supports working with PL/SQL. You'll see how the tool can support you when creating and editing PL/SQL, and how to compile and debug PL/SQL packages, procedures, and functions.

5
Working with PL/SQL

Unique to the Oracle database, PL/SQL code forms the core of many Oracle database applications. Whether a database centric application, or one using open source technologies, if the Oracle database underpins the application, PL/SQL code is almost certainly present and is stored in the database or sent in blocks of code to the database for execution. PL/SQL is a language extension to SQL, offering a procedural language structure in the Oracle Database, which is required for more complex application development. SQL Developer supports PL/SQL development by allowing you to work with text files or develop and test code directly against the database. In this section, we will review this support and show you how to create, compile, and debug PL/SQL and look at a number of useful features available to facilitate writing PL/SQL. This chapter is not about teaching PL/SQL or best practice programming techniques. Instead, the examples used here serve to illustrate how the tool might be used and are based on the many coding examples available in the Oracle documentation.

Creating PL/SQL code

You can use either the SQL Worksheet, or the PL/SQL Editor, to create and edit your PL/SQL code. You can think of the SQL Worksheet as a free format text editor where you can create anonymous PL/SQL blocks or more formal structured program units, such as procedures. Using the PL/SQL Editor, you can edit program units already in the database. In either case, SQL Developer provides you with a set of tools to help you create, edit, refactor, and debug your code. Coding assistants, such as code insight, code templates, or code snippets, are available in both the SQL Worksheet and the PL/SQL Code editors. However, feedback on errors is only available in the PL/SQL Code editor. We'll start the section by reviewing some of the code editing options available by initially working in the SQL Worksheet with anonymous PL/SQL blocks.

Writing PL/SQL in the SQL Worksheet

The SQL Worksheet is an excellent scratch pad for working with SQL, SQL*Plus, and PL/SQL, and combinations of these. When starting to develop a new program unit, having access to pieces of previously written code is useful. Time-saving code completion means less typing or the need to remember the correct spelling of object names or columns in tables.

Using code insight

SQL Developer provides a facility called code insight that displays in a popup list of possible choices for the next value or statement in the code. Consider the following code:

```
DECLARE
  BONUS NUMBER;
  SAL NUMBER;
  COMM NUMBER;
  EMP_NAME VARCHAR2 (20);
BEGIN
  SELECT LAST_NAME, SALARY, COMMISSION_PCT
  INTO EMP_NAME, SAL, COMM
  FROM EMPLOYEES
  WHERE EMPLOYEE_ID = 157;
  BONUS := (SAL * 0.10) + (COMM * 0.15);
  DBMS_OUTPUT.PUT_LINE('EMPLOYEE '|| EMP_NAME || ' EARNS A NEW BONUS
OF ' || BONUS );
END;
```

If you use the SQL Worksheet and start entering that code, a short list of values is displayed soon after you have typed `BONUS`, as shown in the following screenshot:

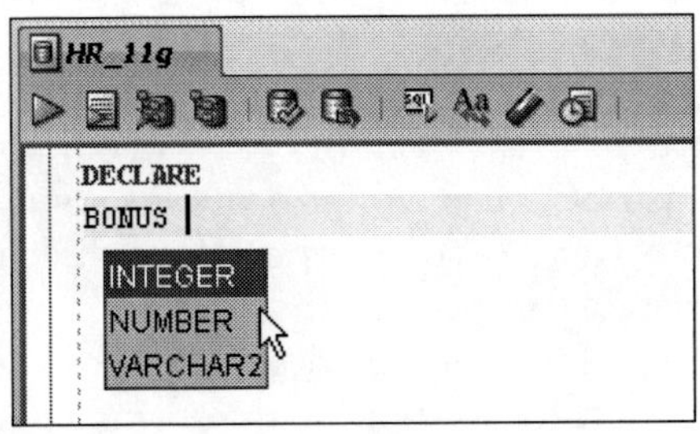

You can tab down, select `NUMBER`, and you're done. You can also type **N** and the list changes, in general revealing more possible options, thus revealing that the initial selection contained a shortened list of the most commonly used choices (in this case displaying only **NUMBER**).

You can also choose to type any other letter and change the list of choices altogether. The list of choices here includes schema names, tables, columns, variable declarations, and procedure or function calls. Once declared, the variables `BONUS`, `SAL`, and `COMM`, in our example are available for use in the anonymous block. So, as you type, these are made available through the same drop-down list mechanism as before.

Each selection from the list reduces and changes the next list displayed. For example, take a package with procedures included. If you start typing the package name, the code insight feature provides a list of all packages with those initial letters. Once you have the package entered, typing the "**.**" invokes the list of public procedures and functions available within the package. In the example that follows, the package and procedure are already in place and the code insight now reveals the parameters and data types required for input:

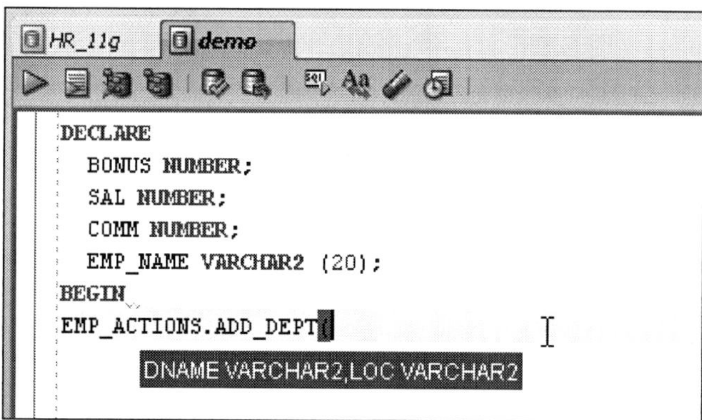

For more detail on controlling or switching off code insight, see the earlier chapter on *Working with the SQL Worksheet*.

Using code snippets and code templates

Code snippets are useful as they provide the framework for larger or smaller chunks of code. There are PL/SQL snippets under the category **PL/SQL Programming Techniques**, in the **Snippets** window (shown in the following screenshot), which provide a useful selection of PL/SQL constructs.

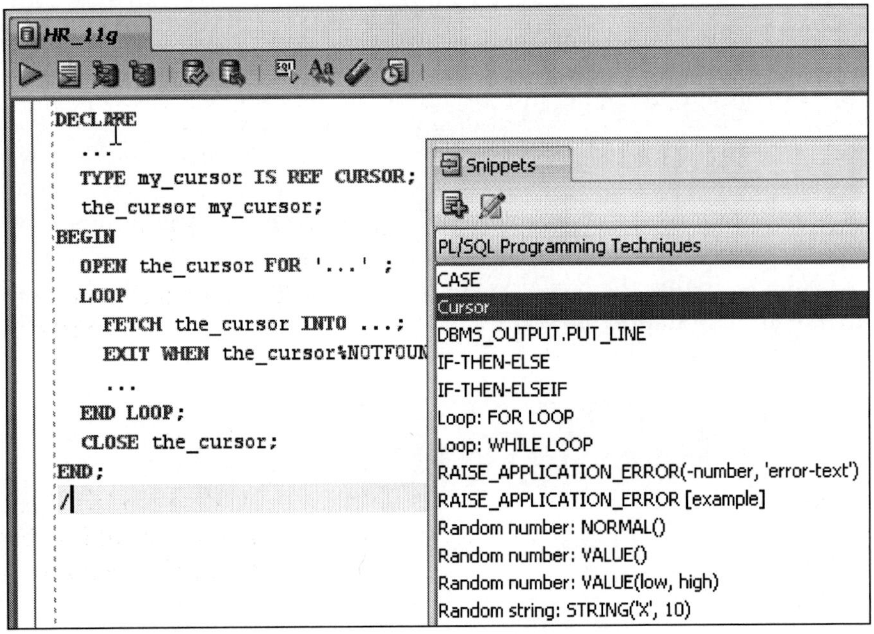

HR_11g

```
DECLARE
  ...
  TYPE my_cursor IS REF CURSOR;
  the_cursor my_cursor;
BEGIN
  OPEN the_cursor FOR '...' ;
  LOOP
    FETCH the_cursor INTO ...;
    EXIT WHEN the_cursor%NOTFOUN
    ...
  END LOOP;
  CLOSE the_cursor;
END;
/
```

Snippets

PL/SQL Programming Techniques

- CASE
- Cursor
- DBMS_OUTPUT.PUT_LINE
- IF-THEN-ELSE
- IF-THEN-ELSEIF
- Loop: FOR LOOP
- Loop: WHILE LOOP
- RAISE_APPLICATION_ERROR(-number, 'error-text')
- RAISE_APPLICATION_ERROR [example]
- Random number: NORMAL()
- Random number: VALUE()
- Random number: VALUE(low, high)
- Random string: STRING('X', 10)

In the example above, both the **Snippets** window and the resulting code skeleton, created here by dragging the **Cursor** snippet onto the SQL Worksheet, are shown. You can extend the selection of snippets provided by adding your own.

Code templates are very similar in concept, except that SQL Developer only provides a few default code templates. Instead, you have a blank canvas in which to add your own. You invoke code templates by entering the first few letters of the template, which displays the code using code insight. Code templates are useful for frequently used chunks of complete code, such as exception handlers.

> Creating, editing, and updating code snippets and code templates are discussed in greater detail in the chapter on *Working with the SQL Worksheet*. They are included here for completeness and as a reminder that these features are available in the SQL Worksheet and **Code** editor and that they are very useful when editing PL/SQL code.

Creating and compiling PL/SQL program units

SQL Developer supports creating, editing, and debugging PL/SQL program units. **Triggers**, **Functions**, **Procedures**, and **Packages** are listed in the **Connections** navigator, and you can view the details of these by selecting and clicking on each to open the display editors. In this section, we'll look at each of these constructs in turn and at the dialogs and utilities associated with them.

Working with triggers

Oracle database triggers fire when you manipulate or update data, update database objects (such as dropping a table), or on certain database events (such as logging on). SQL Developer provides a number of utilities and dialogs to simplify creating and working with triggers.

Using the Create Trigger dialog

You can use the SQL Developer worksheet to write the PL/SQL code for the complete database trigger, without having the formal or, if you know the trigger structure very well, perhaps confining restrictions of a dialog. However, if you are a bit unfamiliar with creating triggers, then the **Create Trigger** dialog can be really useful by providing the structure for the DML event clause and any condition details.

Consider the following example:

```
CREATE OR REPLACE
TRIGGER TRACK_SALARY_HISTORY
BEFORE INSERT OR UPDATE OF SALARY ON EMPLOYEES
FOR EACH ROW
WHEN (NEW.EMPLOYEE_ID >0)
DECLARE SAL_DIFF NUMBER;
```

```
BEGIN
  SAL_DIFF := :NEW.SALARY - :OLD.SALARY;
  INSERT INTO SALARY_HISTORY (EMP_ID, NEW_SAL, OLD_SAL, INCREASE,
UPDATED_ON)
  VALUES (:NEW.EMPLOYEE_ID,:NEW.SALARY, :OLD.SALARY, SAL_DIFF,
SYSDATE);
END;
```

By providing checklists, radio groups, and drop-down lists, the dialog shown below helps you create most of the structure of the trigger:

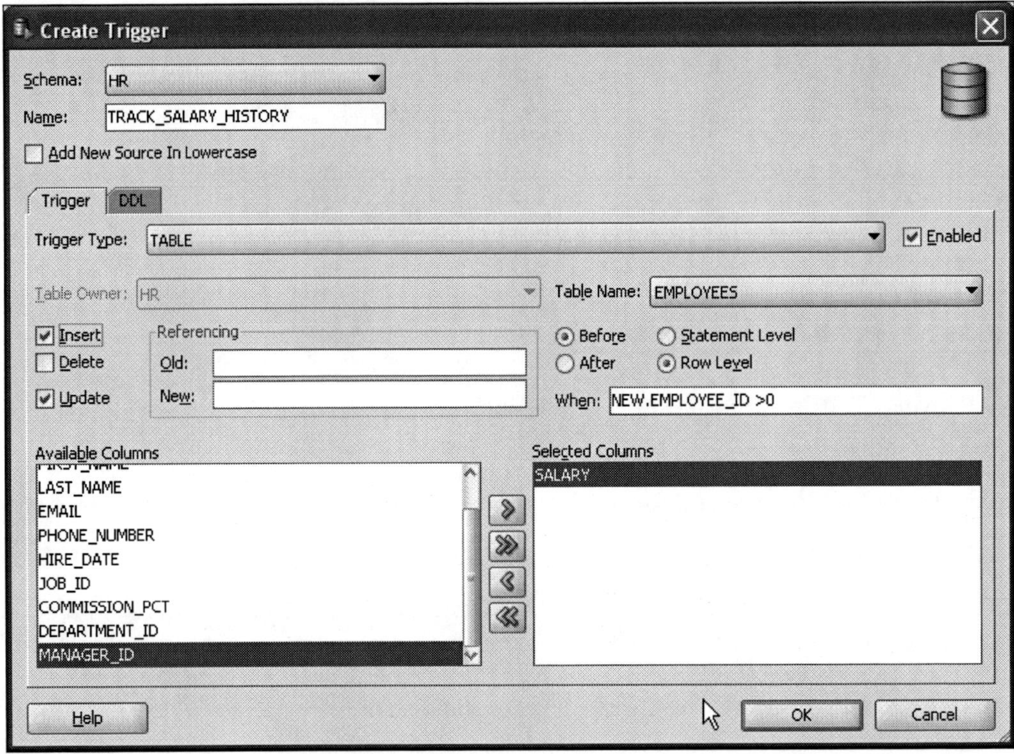

Once you have completed the dialog, all that is left for you to add are any variable declarations and the body of the PL/SQL block.

The **Create Trigger** dialog also has the advantage of setting a context, so that certain sections of the dialog are only editable for set conditions. For example, if you are creating a trigger that fires before or after `INSERT` or `DELETE`, then it is not relevant to select specific columns since these actions affect the entire record. However, you may want a trigger to fire on `UPDATE` of a specific column. In this case, when you select the **Update** option, the **Selected** and **Available Columns** fields are enabled. It is also not relevant to add a **When** clause to a **Statement Level** trigger, so this item is only enabled for **Row Level** triggers.

Once you have completed the details in the **Trigger** tab of the dialog, you can select the **DDL** tab to review the code that will be executed, and then click on **OK** to create the trigger. You need to add the PL/SQL trigger body and any additional declarations required, and then compile the code. For this example, before you can compile the code, you need the `SALARY_HISTORY` table. To compile the code select the **Compile** button:

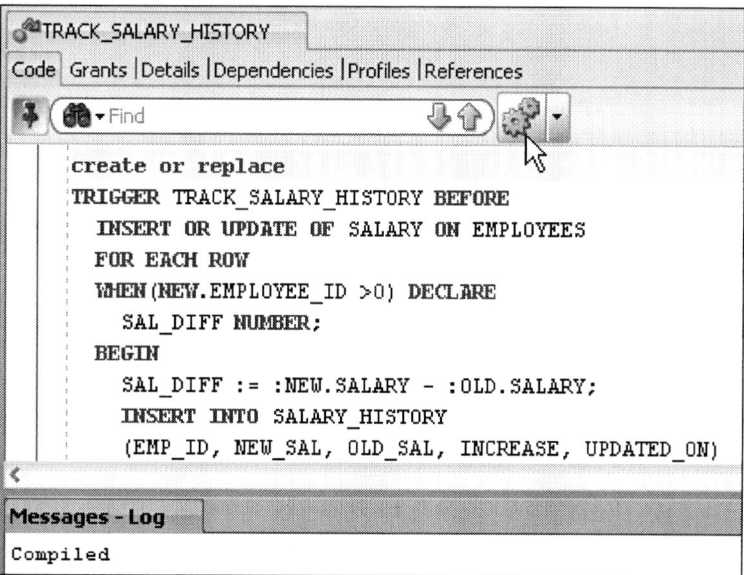

Once a trigger has been compiled, you can test the code by performing the various operations that cause it to fire. In this case, it should fire on inserting a new record, but not on delete. It should fire when updating the salary, but not for updating any other column values. In each case, the auditing table, `SALARY_HISTORY` table is updated.

Creating INSTEAD OF triggers

The **Create Trigger** dialog supports creating advanced triggers, which are fired not only on table insert, update, and delete events, but also on these events for views. If a view is updateable, it means that you can update the underlying table, or tables, by executing insert, update, or delete statements against the view. In general, complex views are not updateable, meaning that you can't use DML statements directly against the view to update the underlying table or tables. In this case, you can use `INSTEAD OF` triggers. When using the **Create Trigger** dialog, switching the trigger type from **TABLE** to **VIEW** causes the dialog to change to support the `INSTEAD OF` trigger.

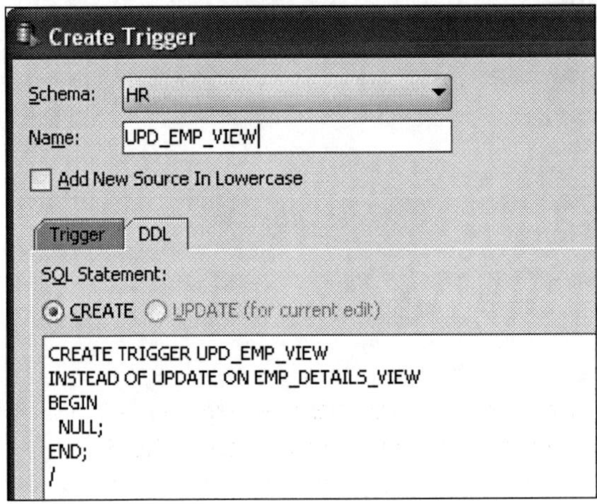

In the previous screenshot, the trigger type of **VIEW** was selected, producing the skeleton shown. Once created, `INSTEAD OF` triggers are listed with other triggers in the **Triggers** node and can also be found in the triggers display for the views they are associated with.

Creating system triggers on the database or schema

In addition to creating the trigger code for updates to tables and views, the **Create Trigger** dialog also supports creating triggers on the database or on schemas. When using the **Create Trigger** dialog to create system triggers, switch the **Trigger Type** to **DATABASE** or **SCHEMA**. The switch changes the dialog and you are given a listing of the available system events on which the trigger will fire:

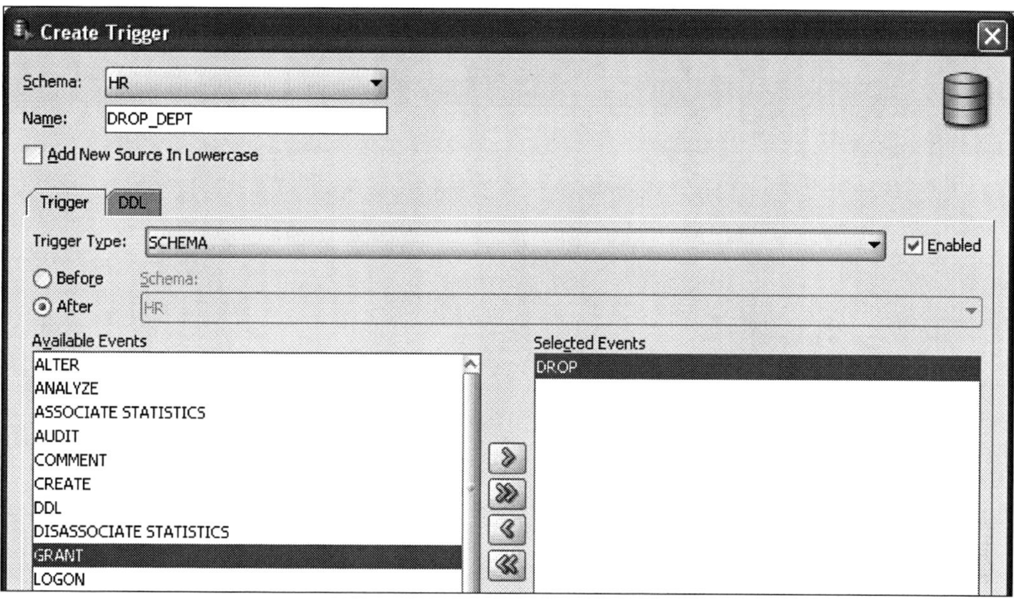

Viewing trigger details

You can find all of the trigger details under the **Triggers** node in the **Connections** navigator. As is also true for all of the other objects in the **Connections** navigator, when you select the trigger, a set of display editors is invoked. In SQL Developer 2.1, the set of display editors includes the updateable **Code** editor:

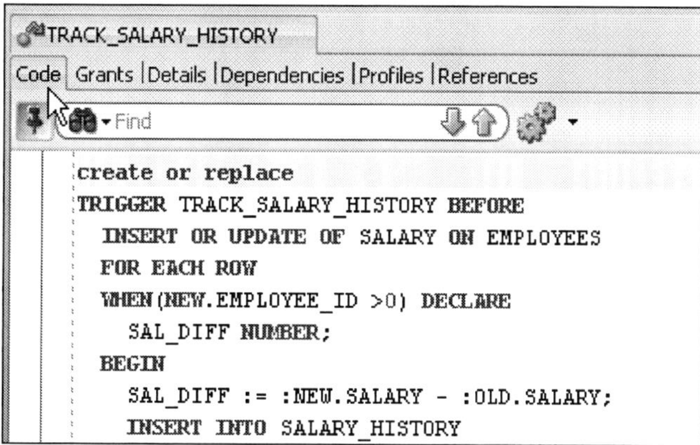

Alternatively, you can select the specified table or view in the navigator, in this example, the **EMPLOYEES** table, and click on the **Triggers** display editor. This lists all of the triggers associated with the table. By selecting any of the listed triggers, you can see the associated code. In addition, this shows a listing of all of the triggers that will fire, depending on circumstances, for this table. You can also see at a glance what the various triggering events are and the status of each of the triggers:

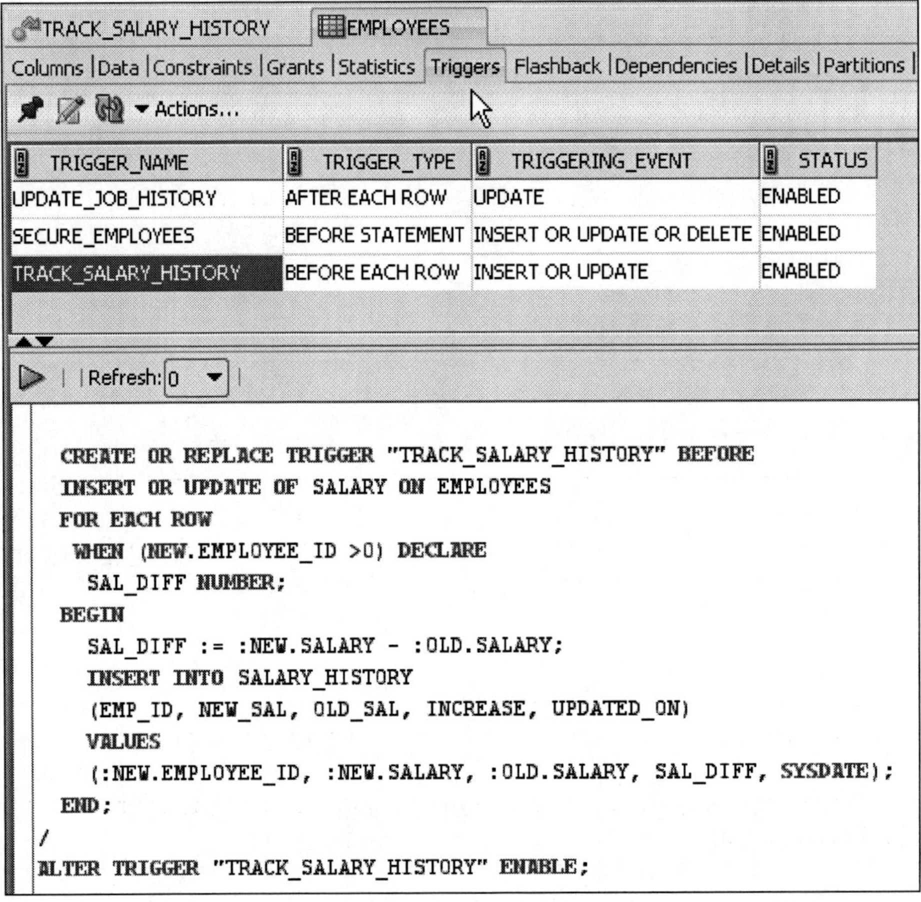

Controlling triggers

SQL Developer provides a number of context sensitive menus which provide a quick route to enabling, disabling, and compiling triggers. Select any trigger in the navigator and invoke the context menu as shown in the following screenshot:

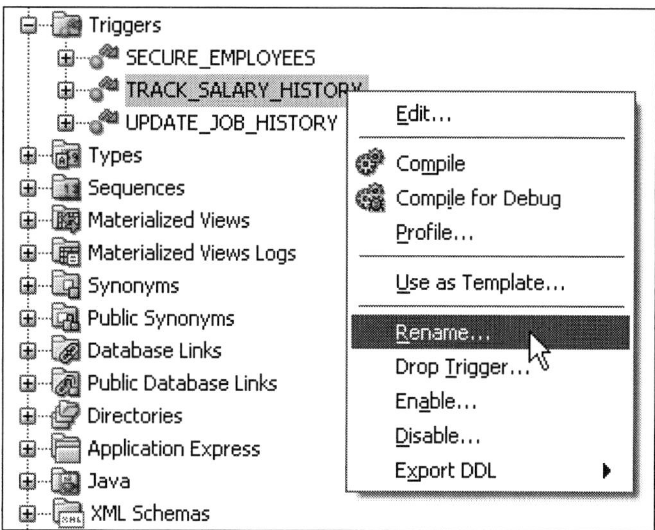

You can also apply global updates to triggers by invoking the context menu selection for tables. This displays a trigger menu that includes **Enable All** and **Disable All** options.

Adding triggers that populate columns

For some tables, the Primary Key may be derived from a value drawn from a sequence, and is inserted using a trigger that fires for each new record inserted. You can do this manually by creating the sequence and the trigger, or you can use SQL Developer to:

- Create the sequence and trigger when you initially create the table
- Create the trigger using an existing sequence after the table has been created

If you want to create the sequence and trigger at the time when the table is created, you need to switch to the **Advanced Create Table** dialog. The **Create Table** dialog includes an additional node in the tree called **Column Sequences**. This is only available when creating a table and not subsequently available when editing the table (the reason for this is that a sequence has no relationship with a trigger or table, it is only accessed as a result of code being fired in the trigger). The following screenshot displays a choice of using an existing sequence or having an additional new sequence created:

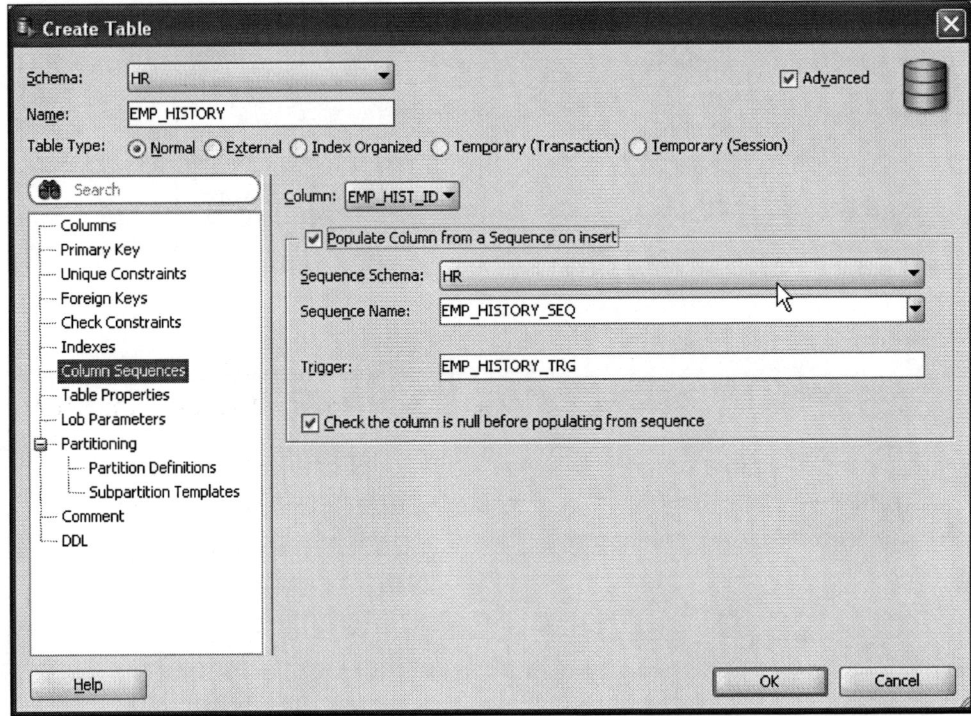

Once the table has been created, you can edit the sequence, trigger, and table independently, each object in its own dialog.

If you elect to add a trigger to populate the Primary Key from a sequence after a table has been created, you can use the context menu option to do so. In this case, you need to ensure there is an existing sequence for the purpose. Invoke the context menu and select **Trigger | Create (PK from Sequence)...**.

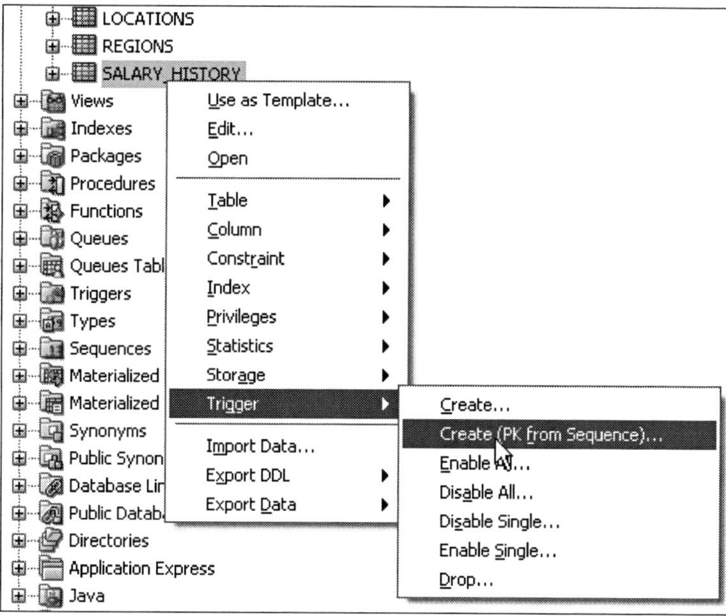

The menu item name is something of a misnomer as you can use this technique to populate any Unique Key on insert of new records. However, it's most commonly if not exclusively used for the Primary Key.

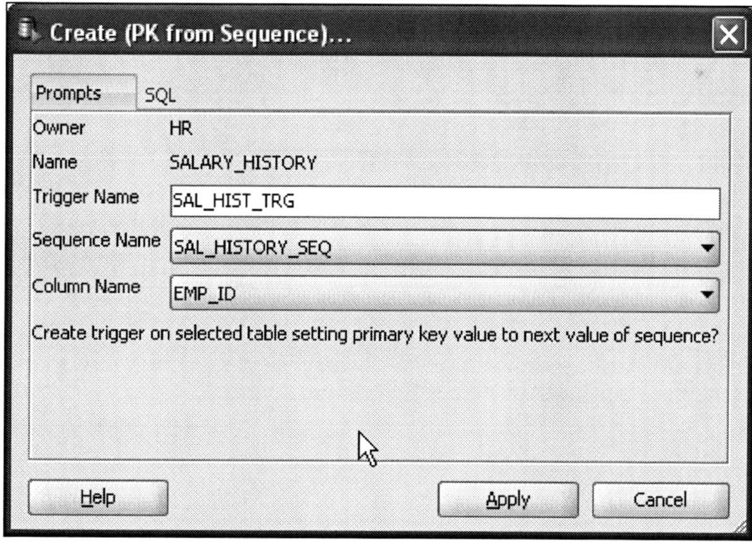

Adding functions or procedures

You can create functions or procedures using the **Create New Function** or **Create New Procedure** dialogs, or by using the SQL Worksheet. The dialogs for creating functions and procedures are very basic, providing only the structure for naming and adding parameters. For functions, a default `RETURN` parameter is also defined:

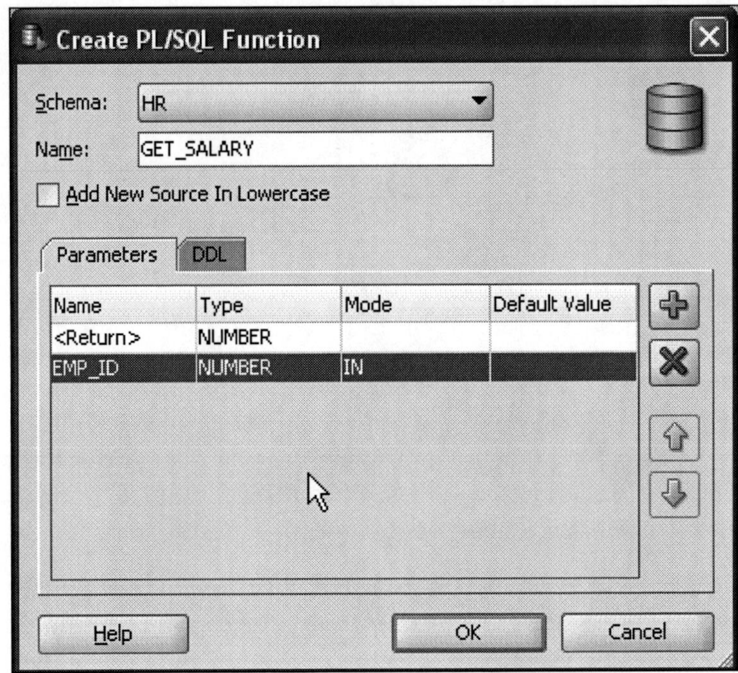

The main content, the body, still needs to be written, but the dialog creates the framework, making it easier to get started. If you have no input parameters and only the return value, you can do this as easily in the SQL Worksheet by just typing the text. The advantage of using the dialog is that the skeleton code is opened in the PL/SQL code editor and you can get the immediate added benefit of the compiler messages. In the examples that follow, we use functions to illustrate the point, but the detail is pertinent to procedures too. For the most part, we'll refer to sub-programs to include both functions and procedures.

Consider the following piece of code:

```
CREATE OR REPLACE
FUNCTION GET_SALARY (EMP_ID NUMBER) RETURN NUMBER IS
  CURR_SAL NUMBER;
BEGIN
  SELECT SALARY INTO CURR_SAL FROM EMPLOYEES
      WHERE EMPLOYEE_ID = EMP_ID;
  RETURN CURR_SAL;
END GET_SALARY;
```

Whether you used the SQL Worksheet or the Create Function dialog, once you have created the skeleton, open it in the PL/SQL code editor. If you have used the SQL Worksheet, once you execute the code to create the function, **Refresh** the **Functions** node in the navigator and click on the name of the new function. By way of example, enter the following piece of code in the SQL Worksheet, and press *F5* to run the code:

```
CREATE OR REPLACE
FUNCTION GET_SALARY(EMP_ID NUMBER)
  RETURN NUMBER
  AS
  BEGIN
    RETURN NULL;
END GET_SALARY;
```

To invoke the code editor (shown in the following screenshot), click on the function name in the navigator and select **Code**.

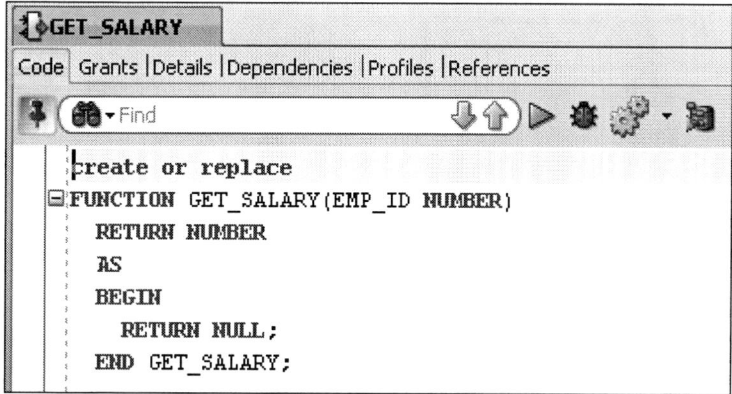

To review the details of a procedure or function, click on the object name to open the set of display editors. Prior to SQL Developer 2.1, a double-click opened a set of display editors to define the procedure as well as a second separate editor to edit the code. These are now grouped together with a single code editor, and opened on a single-click. This allows users to edit the code and review other aspects of the sub-program in the same set of tab editors.

Editing program units

You can of course continue to work in the SQL Worksheet and create the complete sub-program. However, when you run the code, the only feedback you are provided with is "Compiled" or "Compiled with Errors". Working in the PL/SQL code editor brings the advantage of unobtrusively highlighting the errors as they appear. If you add or omit a ';' this is shown in the code, in the same way as spelling errors display as you type when using some word processing programs.

In both the SQL Worksheet and the **Code** editor, you can rely on the code insight to prompt you for expressions, columns, and table names. Once you have defined parameters and variables in the program unit, they also appear in the code insight drop-down lists. In the example shown in the following screenshot, we have defined `CURR_SALE`, which is now available for use in the function:

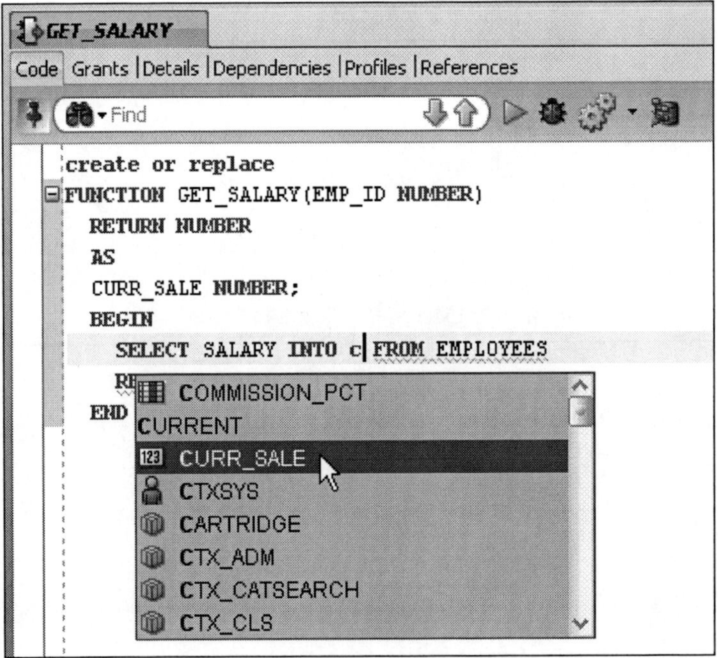

With the sample of code provided, you can complete and then, using the **Compile** button, compile the code. We will discuss errors and how to handle them in the next section.

Working with errors

The **Connections** navigator displays all packages, procedures, and functions the user owns, including those that are currently compiled with errors. A red cross overlaying the object icon indicates the object is compiled with errors. In the following screenshot, the procedure **EMP_LIST** has errors, while **ADD_JOB_HISTORY** has none. Errors may be syntactical, or might have errors if dependencies have been removed (for example, if a table that the function relies on has been dropped).

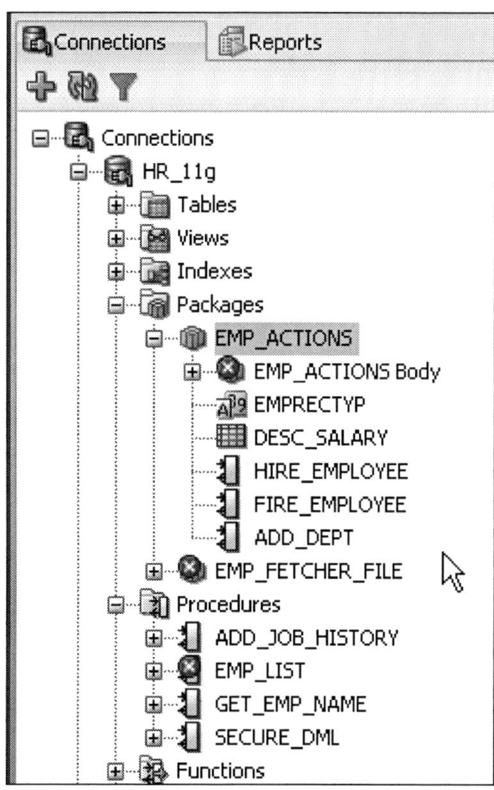

The other area to look for compile-time errors is in the editor itself. Once you have compiled a program, the errors are marked:

- Within the code, using a line under the code.
- In the right-hand margin. You can see each message by rolling the mouse over the point in the margin.
- In the messages log window, displaying all of the errors and warnings, up to a maximum of 20 messages.

In the following screenshot, we have shown all three elements:

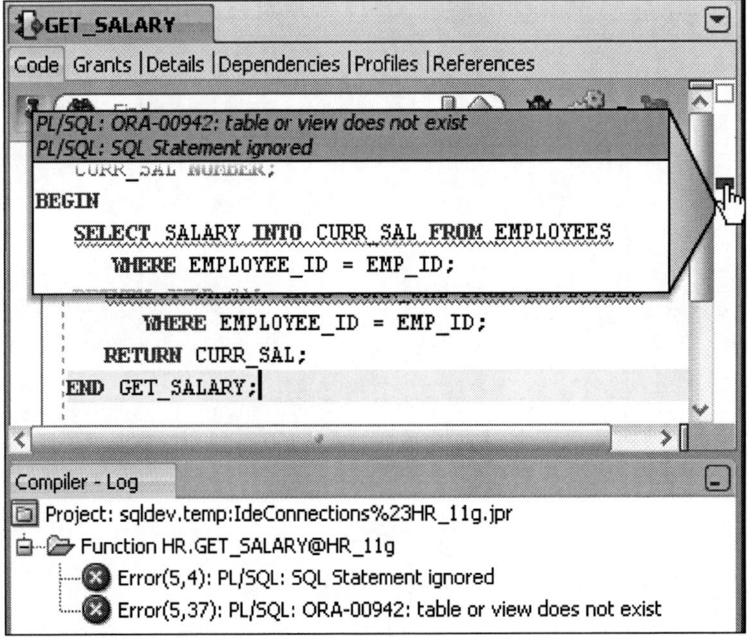

There is a database hard limit of 20 messages displayed in the log window, including both warnings and errors. If you have 20 warnings before the first error is encountered, you will not see the error messages. Oracle Database 11g Release 2 has changed this to 20 errors and unlimited warnings.

Handling multiple error messages

You can control the type of PL/SQL warning messages that are displayed using **Preferences**. Select **Database | PL/SQL Compiler**. The settings control whether the types of warnings are displayed or suppressed, and whether they are treated as errors.

Testing and executing program units

Once you have successfully compiled any program unit, you can run it from the code editor. When running functions or procedures in a command-line environment, you may need to create an anonymous block to call or execute them. SQL Developer provides this facility automatically:

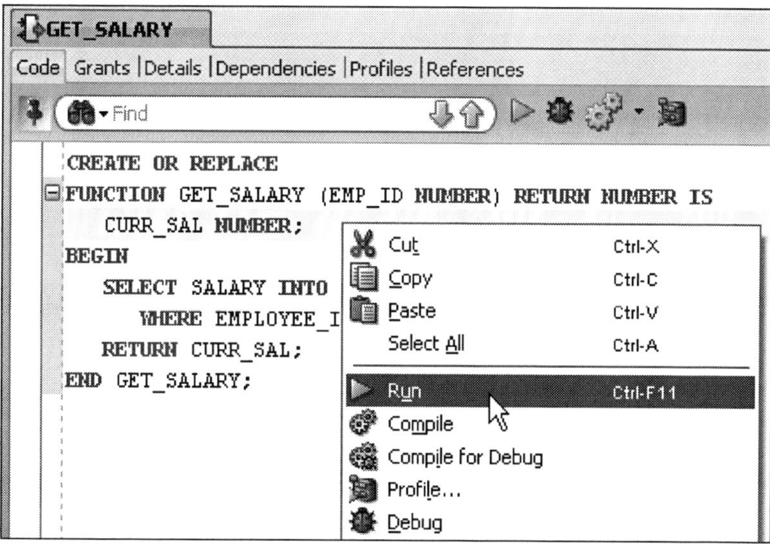

Selecting *Ctrl+F11* to run the function invokes a new dialog where you can provide the required parameters. It also provides the facility to display the return value, using `DBMS_OUTPUT`. This anonymous block is editable, and so you can modify and save the code should you choose. As the program unit is invariably going to be used elsewhere, the default mechanism is suitable to use for testing purposes. However, if you find yourself modifying the block for a particular procedure, then being able to recall the code you want later is useful. In the following screenshot, we have provided an employee ID and replaced the output string, `v_Return`, with one of our own:

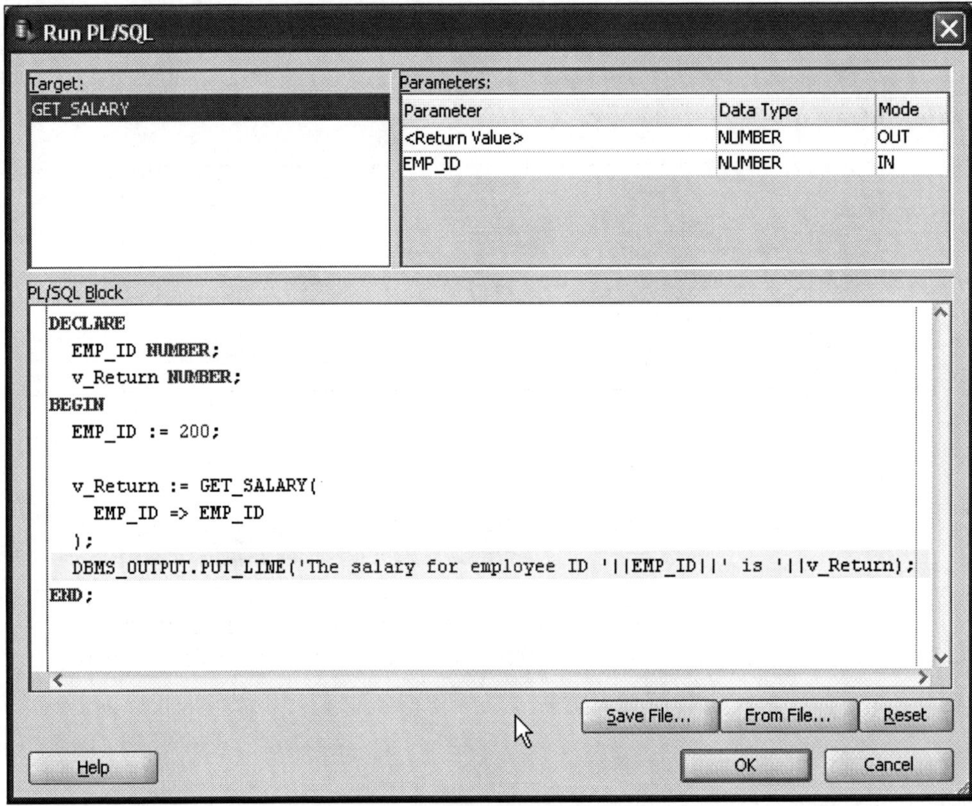

On completion, any output is sent to the **Log** window as shown in the following screenshot:

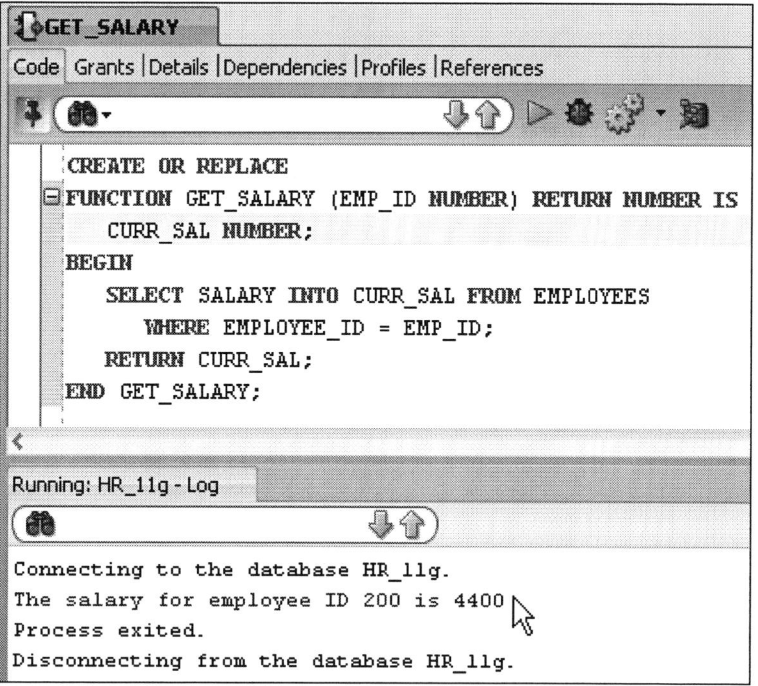

Creating packages

Creating packages requires a specification and body to be created. In this case, the new dialog for the package specification only serves to provide the skeleton, requiring only a name as an input value. Once you click on **OK**, the package specification opens in the PL/SQL **Code** editor and you need to enter all of the required declarations. The following screenshot shows the very basic skeleton created by the **Create PL/SQL Package** dialog:

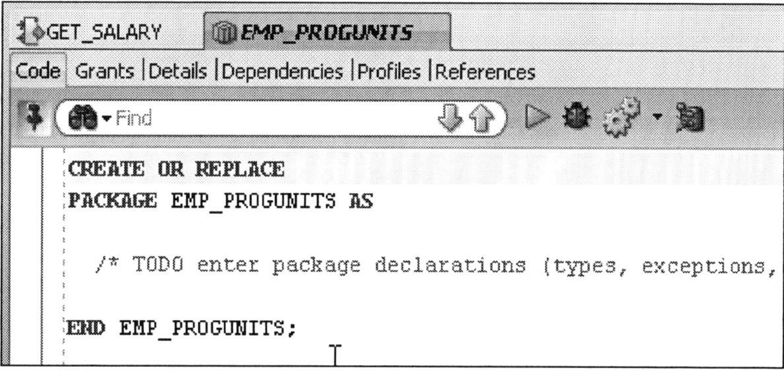

To complete the specification, you need to manually enter the code, such as declaring the public variables, procedures, and functions as needed. We added the following highlighted code to the example:

```
CREATE OR REPLACE
PACKAGE EMP_PROGUNITS AS
 TYPE EMPRECTYP IS
    RECORD (EMP_ID INT, SALARY REAL);
    CURSOR DESC_SALARY
       RETURN EMPRECTYP;
 PROCEDURE HIRE_EMPLOYEE
    (LAST_NAME VARCHAR2, JOB_ID VARCHAR2,
    MANAGER_ID NUMBER, SALARY NUMBER,
    DEPARTMENT_ID NUMBER);
 PROCEDURE FIRE_EMPLOYEE (EMP_ID NUMBER);
 PROCEDURE ADD_DEPT
    (DEPARTMENT_NAME IN DEPARTMENTS.DEPARTMENT_NAME%TYPE,
    LOCATION_ID IN DEPARTMENTS.LOCATION_ID%TYPE);
END EMP_PROGUNITS;
```

Creating the body

Once you have provided all of the package declarations, using the **Code** editor, you can use the new package body dialog to create the skeleton. Of all the PL/SQL Create dialogs, this is the most useful. It provides skeletons in the package body for each of the procedures or functions declared in the package specification.

To automatically create the body, select the package specification, invoke the context menu, and select **Create Body...** to invoke the new package body dialog:

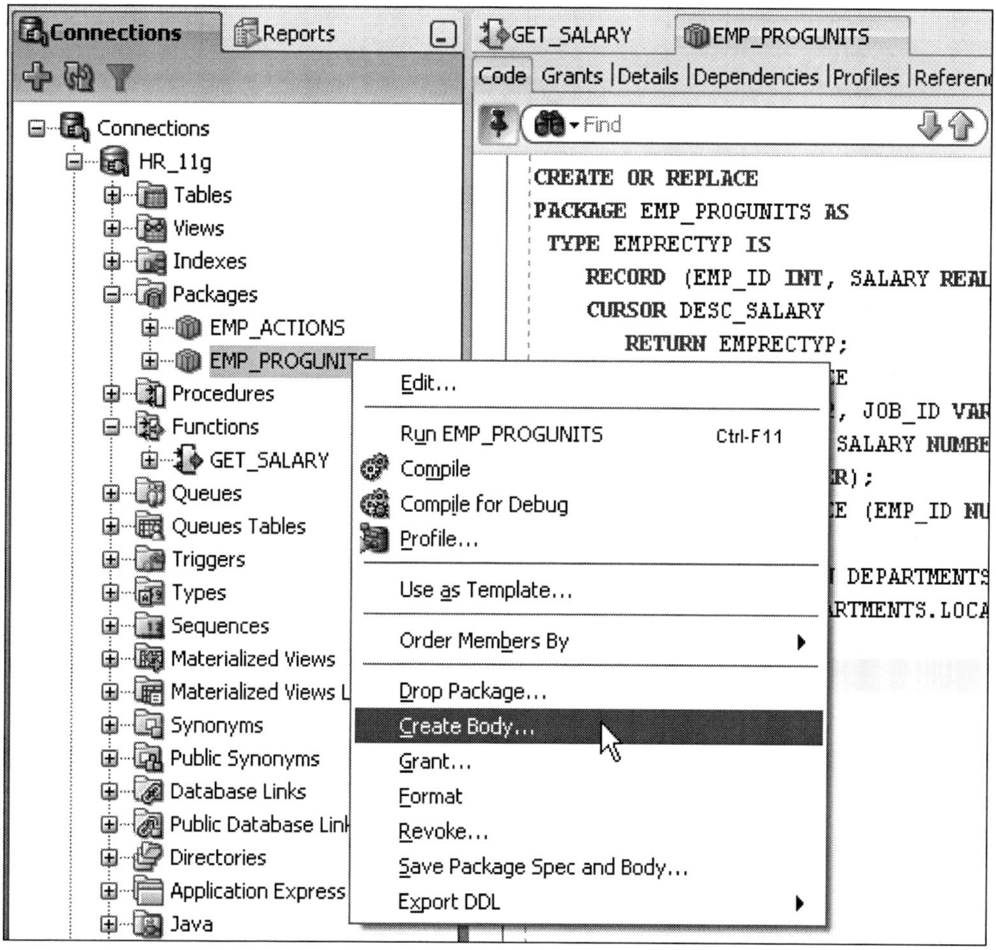

Creating a package body

Save time setting up the package body by defining all of the procedure and function declarations in the package specification, and then using the **Create Body** context menu to automatically create a skeleton of procedures and functions.

The following screenshot shows an initial skeleton created by the **Create Body** menu:

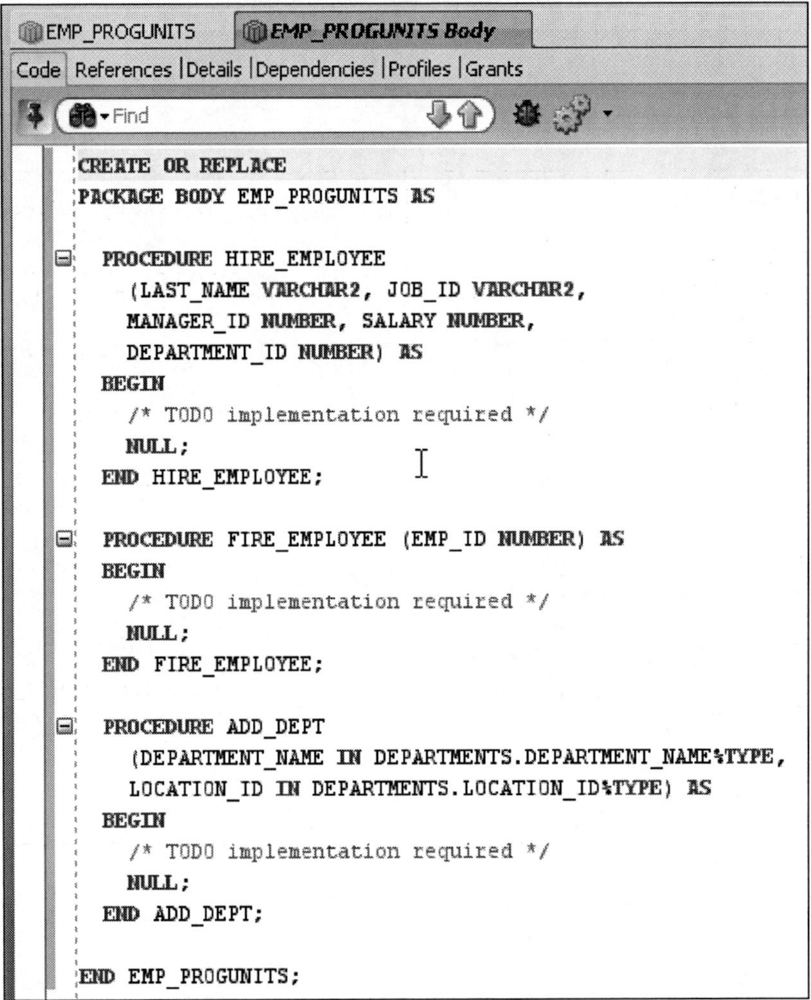

Reviewing a package

Once you have created the package specification and body, you can review the structure in the **Connections** navigator.

Select and expand the **Packages** node, and expand either or both the specification and body. The navigator lists the specification and body declarations. For large packages, it is sometimes easier to list these declarations alphabetically. However, the default setting is to list them as they're declared in the specification. The following example shows the menu to switch the order of the declarations in the **Connections** navigator:

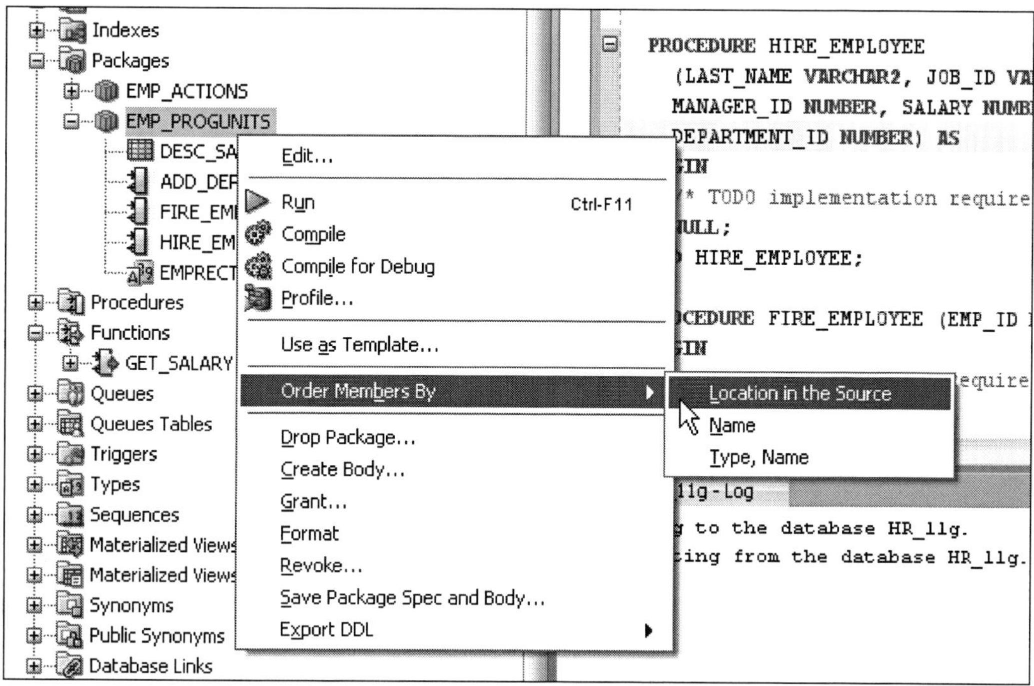

Testing packages

In order to run and test a procedure or function that is part of a package, you need to select the *package specification* and run it. The **Run PL/SQL** dialog that is invoked lists all of the procedures and functions in the package, along with all the related parameters. Select the program unit you want to test, as shown in the following screenshot. This displays the appropriate anonymous block and related input parameters. Provide the detail as you would for any procedure or function and click on **OK** to run:

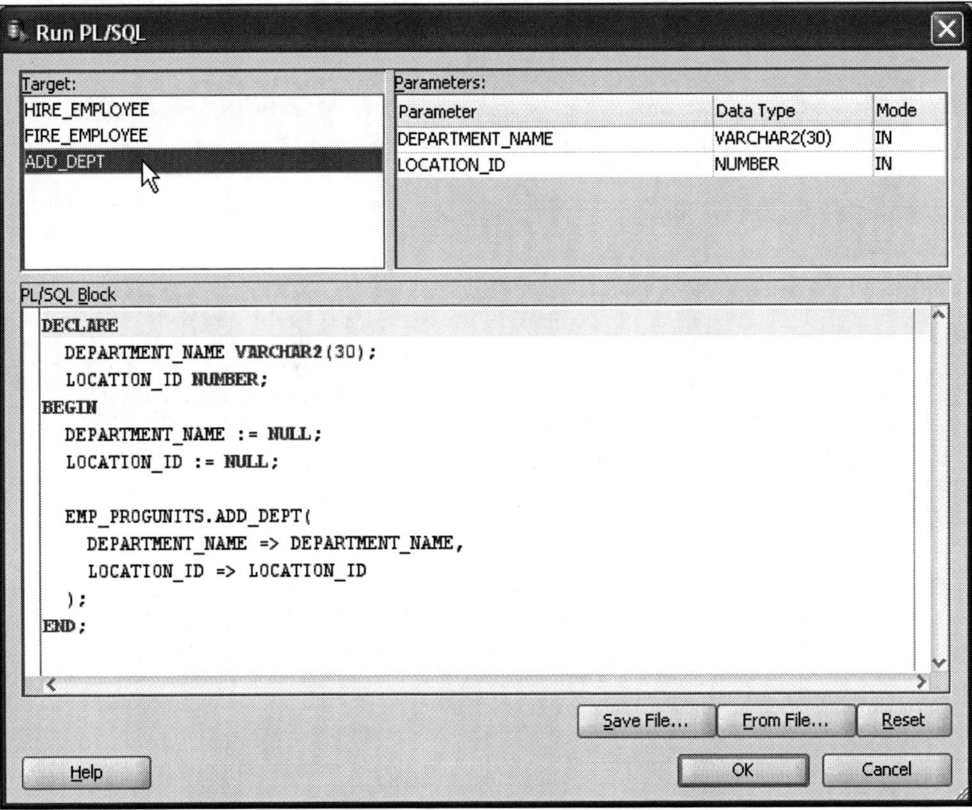

Editing code

The utilities discussed in this section can once again be used in either the SQL Worksheet or the **Code** editor. While all are not necessarily confined to PL/SQL, such as the **Find DB Object** search utility, it is useful to discuss them here.

Refactoring code

Refactoring code is the process of redesigning the code to restructure it or improve the performance, without impacting the resulting behavior. SQL Developer 2.1 supports a number of refactoring options, which include:

- Surrounding the code with the following PL/SQL constructs
    - FOR loop
    - WHILE loop
    - PL/SQL block
- Extracting a procedure
- Renaming a local variable

Some of these can assist you while writing your code, such as **Surround with...**, and so are as much about being productive as they are about refactoring. One feature that is useful when refactoring is **Extract Procedure...**.

When you are creating PL/SQL code, it is often recommended that you create chunks of code that you can call from another program unit. This introduces reusability and readability to your code. In particular, it is recommended that you keep the lines of code in your triggers to a minimum, calling procedures from the trigger, instead of writing the full text in the trigger itself. Often, at the time of writing, you don't see the need for this chunking, nor does it seem to be necessary. However, as the code grows and becomes possibly less manageable, it is advisable to return to the code and rework or refactor it.

Consider the trigger, which is part of the HR schema, below:

```
CREATE OR REPLACE TRIGGER SECURE_EMPLOYEES
  BEFORE INSERT OR UPDATE OR DELETE ON EMPLOYEES
BEGIN
  IF TO_CHAR (SYSDATE,'HH24:MI') NOT BETWEEN '08:00' AND '18:00'
  OR TO_CHAR (SYSDATE, 'DY') IN ('SAT', 'SUN') THEN
  RAISE_APPLICATION_ERROR (-20205, 'YOU MAY ONLY MAKE CHANGES DURING
NORMAL OFFICE HOURS');
  END IF;
END SECURE_EMPLOYEES;
```

This is not a large piece of code in the body of the trigger. We'll use it to illustrate the refactoring capabilities in SQL Developer. Select and highlight the code that can stand alone as a procedure, invoke the context menu, and select **Refactoring | Extract Procedure...**:

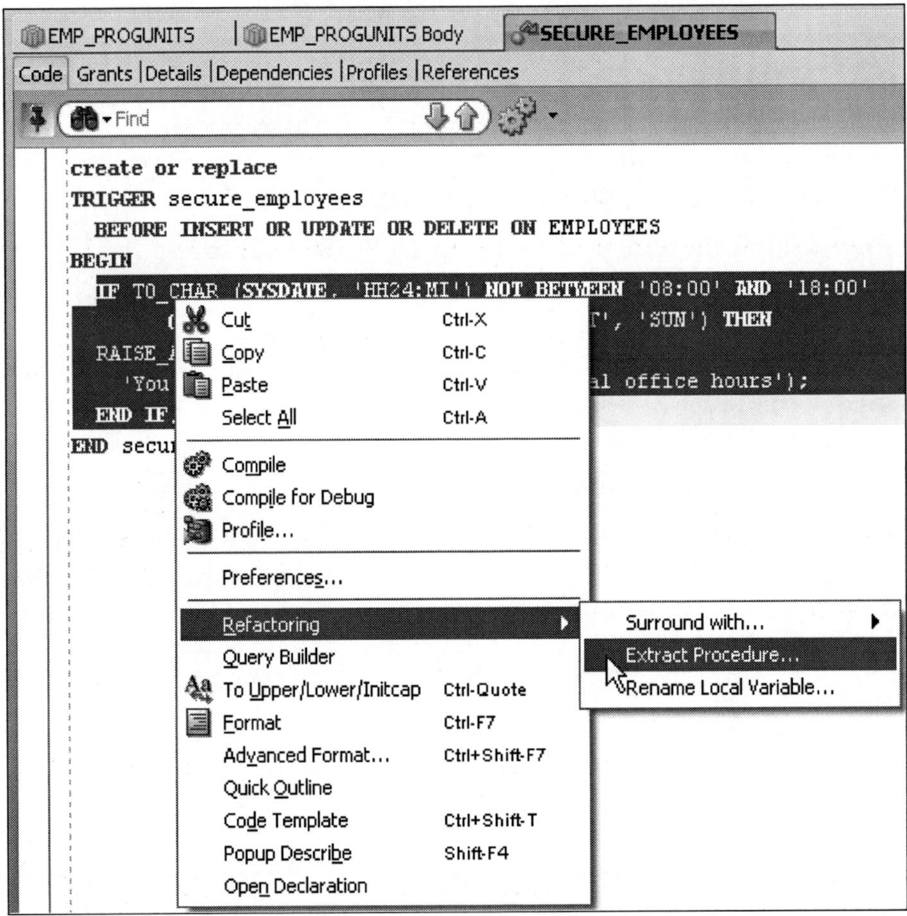

If you have selected an incomplete piece of code, an error message will display stating that you have not selected a complete set of PL/SQL statements. If the code is acceptable, you are shown a dialog where you can provide the name of your new procedure:

Once you have provided a name for the new procedure, a new editable screen is displayed (shown in the following screenshot), allowing you to modify the procedure before you accept the code. You can of course just accept the code straightaway and make any additional modifications in the code editor. However, the intermediate code window allows you review the code before accepting the changes. This is particularly useful if you've selected too much or too little code to refactor. Until you have accepted the dialog, the underlying trigger or procedure is not affected.

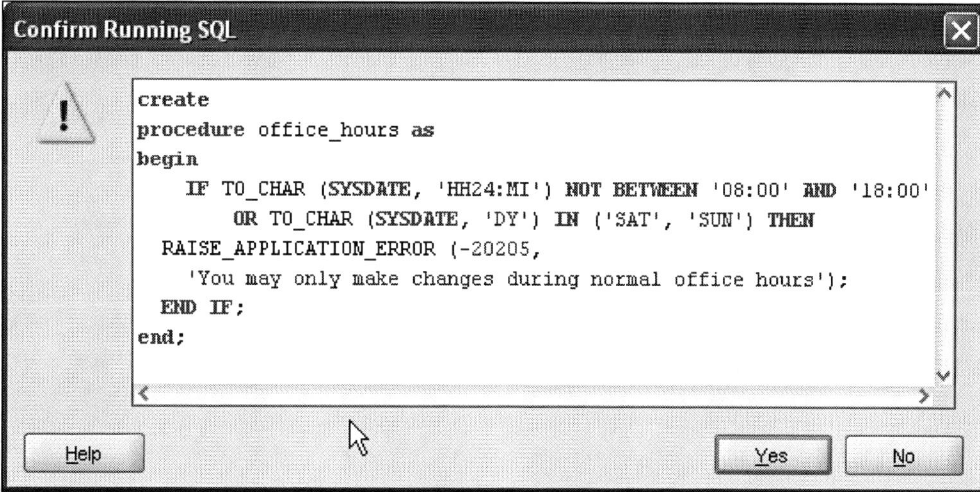

Once you have accepted the new procedure, the refactored trigger now includes the call to the new procedure, replacing the chunk of code, and the new procedure joins the others in the list of available procedures in the **Connections** navigator:

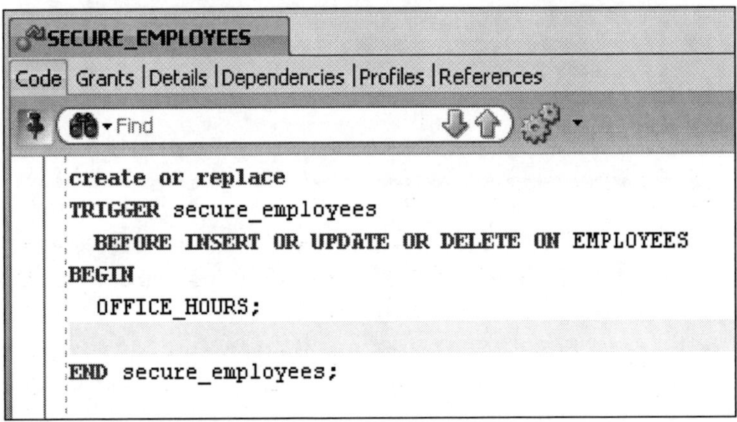

Searching for code

SQL Developer provides a number of utilities to search for strings of text. For searching for strings within a piece of code, use the menu choice **Find** or **Replace**. There are also **Incremental Find Forward** and **Incremental Find Backward** for searching for strings. Often, developers want to search for tables within a schema or across schemas or for PL/SQL declarations. The **Find DB Object** mechanism provides this facility.

Finding DB Object

You can use the **Find DB Object** feature, on the **View** menu, to look for object types like tables, views, and procedures in all databases supported by SQL Developer. In SQL Developer 2.1, the **Find DB Object** and **Extended Search** have been incorporated into a single search dialog. Therefore, you are able to search for objects and to drill down and search for variable declarations and references. To search for variable declarations, you need to be connected to Oracle Database 11g, as this search mechanism takes advantage of the PL/Scope facility that was introduced in Oracle Database 11g.

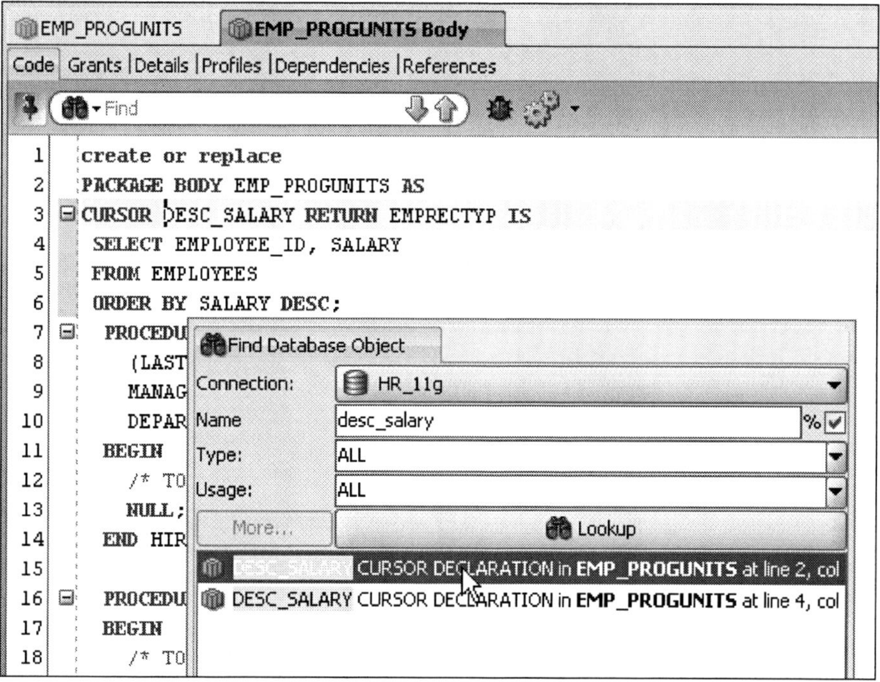

If you have access to Oracle Database 11g, then you can click the **More...** button on the **Find Database Object** dialog (shown in the previous screenshot). This extends the dialog to include **Type** and **Usage** options, which allow you to drill into the PL/SQL code units. Once you complete the search, select the required return links and the program unit is invoked in the **Code** editor in the background, with the cursor highlighting the point of reference.

Debugging PL/SQL

Once your PL/SQL code has successfully compiled, it is important to review it to make sure it does what is required and that it performs well. You can consider a number of approaches when tuning and testing code. These approaches include:

- Debugging—run the code and add break points to stop and inspect areas of concern.
- SQL performance—use Explain Plan results to review the performance.
- PL/SQL performance—use the PL/SQL Hierarchical Profiler to identify bottlenecks.
- Unit testing—review edge cases and general function testing. Does the code do what you intended it to do?

In this section, we'll review the debugger. In the next chapter, we'll look at the Explain Plan and Hierarchical Profiler.

Debugging PL/SQL code

SQL and PL/SQL code may execute cleanly, and even produce an output. PL/SQL code may compile and produce results, but this is part of the task. Does it do what you are expecting it to do? Are the results accurate? Does it behave as expected for high and low values, odd dates or names? Does it behave the same way when it's called from within a program as it does when tested in isolation? Does it perform as well for massive sets of data as it does for a small test case? All of these are aspects to consider when testing code, and many can been tracked by debugging the code.

Using the debugging mechanism in SQL Developer

Once again, you need a piece of compiled, working code. For this exercise, we will use the following piece of code:

```
PROCEDURE EMP_DEPTS
  (P_MAXROWS VARCHAR2)
AS
CURSOR EMPDEPT_CURSOR IS
SELECT D.DEPARTMENT_NAME, E.LAST_NAME, J.JOB_TITLE
FROM DEPARTMENTS D, EMPLOYEES E, JOBS J
WHERE D.DEPARTMENT_ID = E.DEPARTMENT_ID
  AND E.JOB_ID = J.JOB_ID;
EMP_RECORD EMPDEPT_CURSOR % ROWTYPE;
TYPE EMP_TAB_TYPE IS TABLE OF EMPDEPT_CURSOR % ROWTYPE INDEX BY
BINARY_INTEGER;
EMP_TAB EMP_TAB_TYPE;
I NUMBER := 1;
BEGIN
  OPEN EMPDEPT_CURSOR;
  FETCH EMPDEPT_CURSOR
  INTO EMP_RECORD;
  EMP_TAB(I) := EMP_RECORD;
```

```
    WHILE((EMPDEPT_CURSOR % FOUND) AND(I <= P_MAXROWS))
     LOOP I := I + 1;
     FETCH EMPDEPT_CURSOR
      INTO EMP_RECORD;
      EMP_TAB(I) := EMP_RECORD;
     END LOOP;
  CLOSE EMPDEPT_CURSOR; FOR J IN REVERSE 1 .. I
    LOOP DBMS_OUTPUT.PUT_LINE('THE EMPLOYEE '|| EMP_TAB(J).LAST_NAME ||
  ' WORKS IN DEPARTMENT '|| EMP_TAB(J).DEPARTMENT_NAME);
    END LOOP;
 END;
```

Before you can debug code, you need to have the following privileges:

- `EXECUTE` and `DEBUG`—you need to be able to execute the required procedure
- `DEBUG CONNECT SESSION`—to be able to debug procedures you execute in the session

Note, when granting the system privilege `DEBUG ANY PROCEDURE`, you are granting access to debug any procedure that you have execute privilege for and has been compiled for debug.

Using the Oracle debugging packages

Oracle provides two packages for debugging PL/SQL code. The first, `DBMS_DEBUG`, was introduced in Oracle 8*i* and is not used by newer IDEs. The second, `DBMS_DEBUG_JWP`, was introduced in Oracle 9*i* Release 2, and is used in SQL Developer when debugging sub-programs.

Debugging

When preparing to debug any code, you need to set at least one break point, and then you should select **Compile for Debug**. In the following screenshot, the breakpoint is set at the opening of the cursor, and the **Compile for Debug** option is shown in the drop-down list:

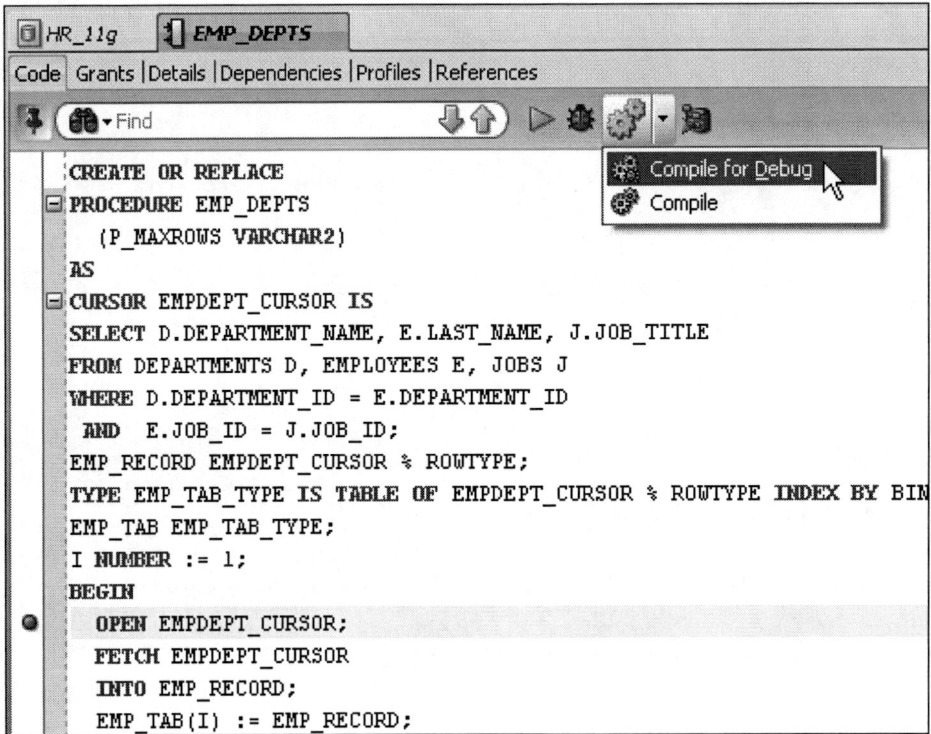

Instead of using the drop-down list to select the **Compile** or **Compile for Debug** options, just click the Compile button. This compiles the PL/SQL code using the optimization level set in the **Preferences**. Select **Database | PL/SQL Compiler**. By setting the **Optimization Level** preference to **0** or **1** the PL/SQL is compiled with debugging information.

Any PL/SQL code that has been compiled for debugging will show the little green bug overlaying the regular icon in the **Connections** navigator. The next screenshot shows the `EMP_DEPTS` procedure and the `GET_SALARY` function have both been compiled for debug:

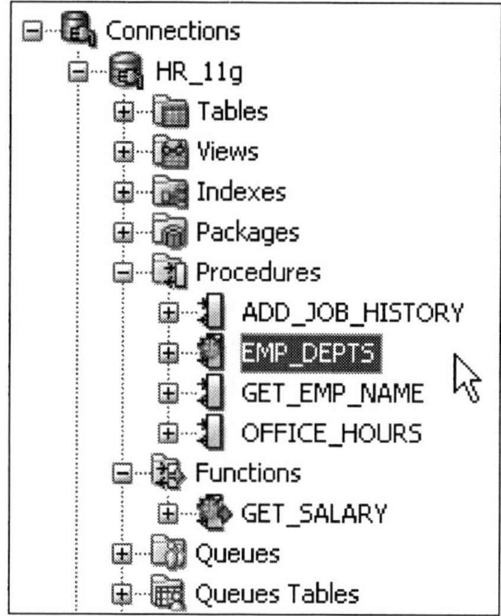

Compile for debug

Once you have completed a debugging session, be sure to compile again afterwards to remove any debug compiler directives. While negligible, omitting this step can have a performance impact on the PL/SQL program.

You are now ready to debug. To debug, click the **Debug** button in the toolbar. SQL Developer then sets the sessions to a debug session and issues the command `DBMS_DEBUG_JDWP.CONNECT_TCP (hostname, port);` and sets up the debug windows as shown in the following screenshot:

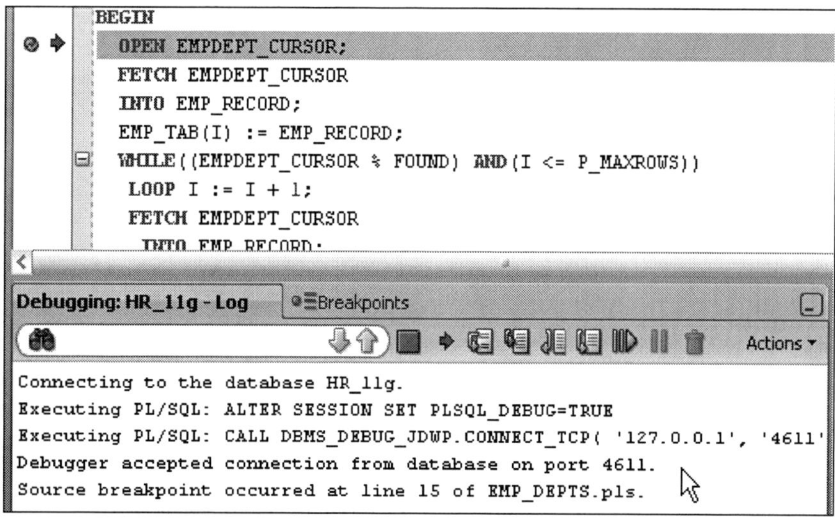

This connects you to a debugger session in the database. In some instances, the port selected is not open, due to firewall or other restrictions. In this case, you can have SQL Developer prompt you for the port. To set this option, open the **Preferences** dialog, and select the **Debugger** node. You can also specify the port range available for SQL Developer to use. These options mean that you can have more control over the ports used.

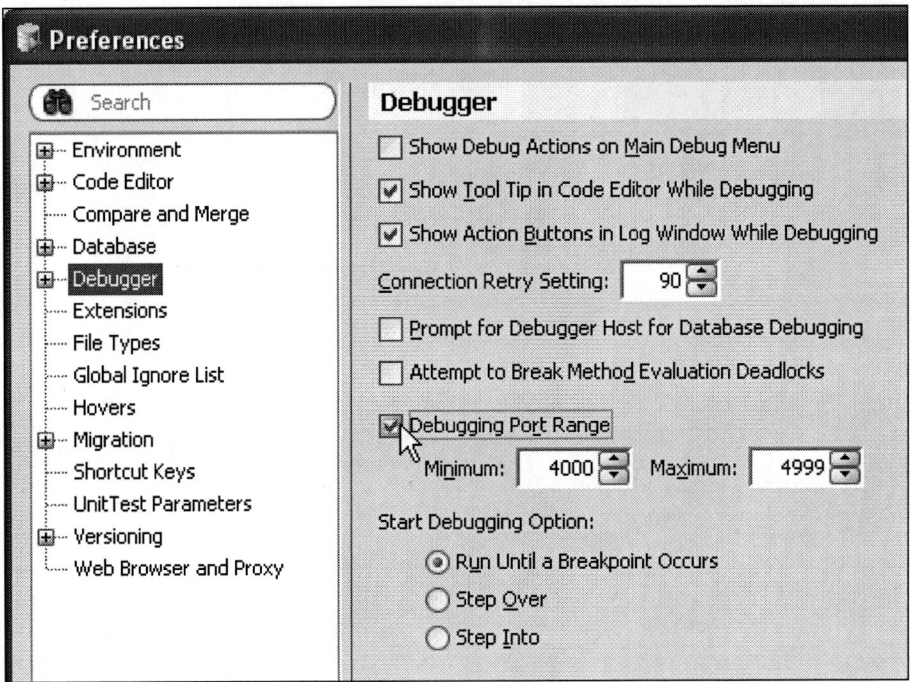

Navigating through the code

The PL/SQL debugger provides a selection of buttons (or menu items) to step through individual lines of code, or to step over blocks of code. You can step through or over procedures, navigating to the point of contention or the area you wish to inspect.

Once you start stepping into the code, you can track the data as it changes. The data is displayed in a second set of tabbed dialogs. In this example, we are looping through a set of records in order for you to see how each of the windows behaves. As you start stepping into the code, the **Data** tab starts to display the values:

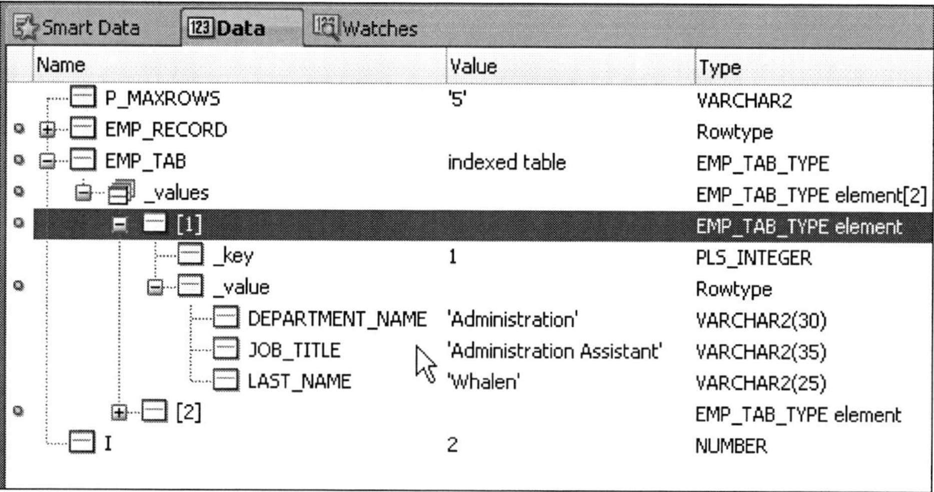

This **Data** tab continues to collect all of the variables as you continue to step through the code. Even if you step over and skip blocks of code, all of the code is executed and the results are gathered here.

The **Smart Data** tab keeps track of the same detail, but only the values immediately related to the area you are working in. This is more useful in a large procedure than in a small one like the example shown.

The context menu provides you with a set of options while debugging.
These include:

- **Run to Cursor**—allows you to start debugging and then to quickly move to another part of the code. The code in-between is quickly executed and you can continue debugging.
- **Watch**—allows you to watch an expression or code while you are debugging.
- **Inspect**—allows you to watch values as you debug.

In the following screenshot, the current execution point is at the start of the `WHILE` loop. If the loop is required to loop multiple times, you can skip that and have the code execute to a point further down in the code, in this case after the cursor has been completed and closed:

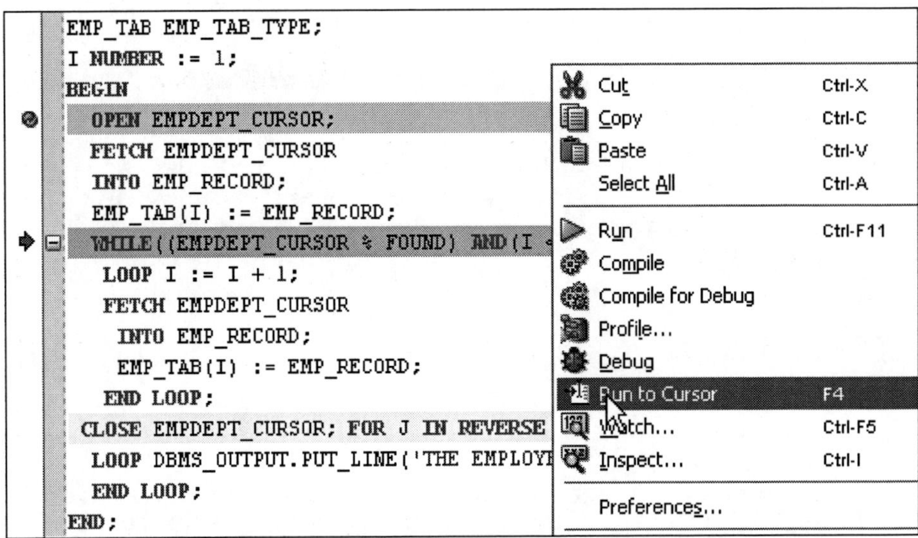

The **Watch** and **Inspect** options remain set up if you stop and restart the debug session. This allows you to stop, change the input values, and start debugging and these will change according to the new parameters. You do not need to set up watch or inspector values each time you debug the procedure. The values appear in dockable windows, so you can dock or float them near the code as required:

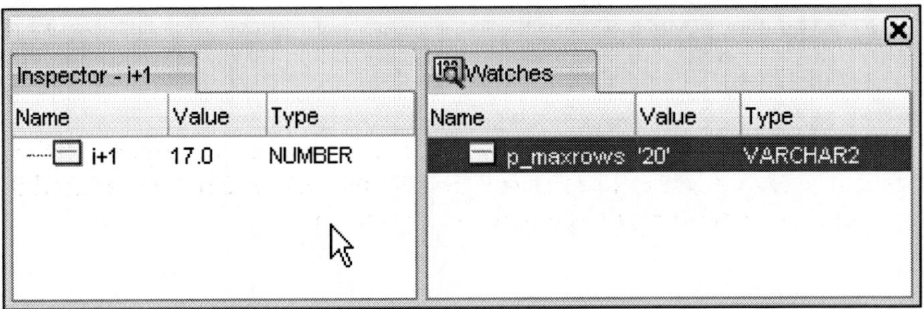

You can modify values that you are watching. In the following example, 'i' is the counter that we're using in the loop. You can modify this value to skip over chunks of the loop, and then continue from a particular point.

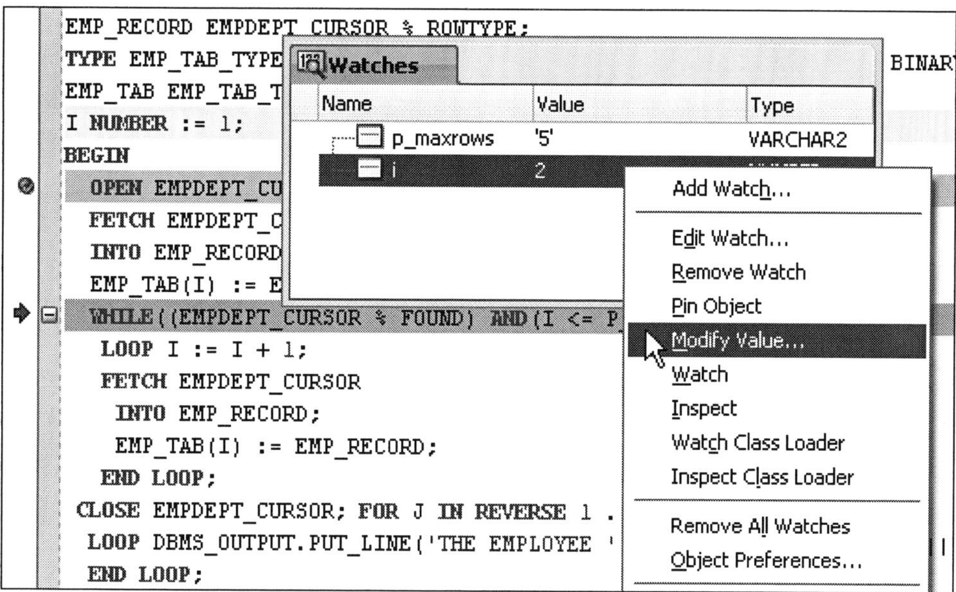

Modifying values in the middle of the code can be useful, as you might want to test how the program reacts in certain circumstances. For example, before the millennium, testers may have wanted to see how code behaved, or output changed once the date switched over to the year 2000.

Remote debugging

You can debug any sub-program that you have `EXECUTE` and `DEBUG` access to, as previously mentioned. So, even if a database procedure is being called or accessed from within an application, you can debug it using SQL Developer. However, some of the problems appear when a procedure is being called, so you need to debug it in place. This is called remote debugging.

The easiest way to illustrate remote debugging is to use SQL Developer together with another client application, in this case SQL*Plus. Once we have prepared the scene, we can then expand that to consider other scenarios.

Preparing for remote debugging

Regardless of where the sub-program resides, if you are going to use SQL Developer to debug the code, you need to start by preparing SQL Developer. You do this by selecting the connection that will be used to debug the code and selecting **Remote Debug...** from the context menu:

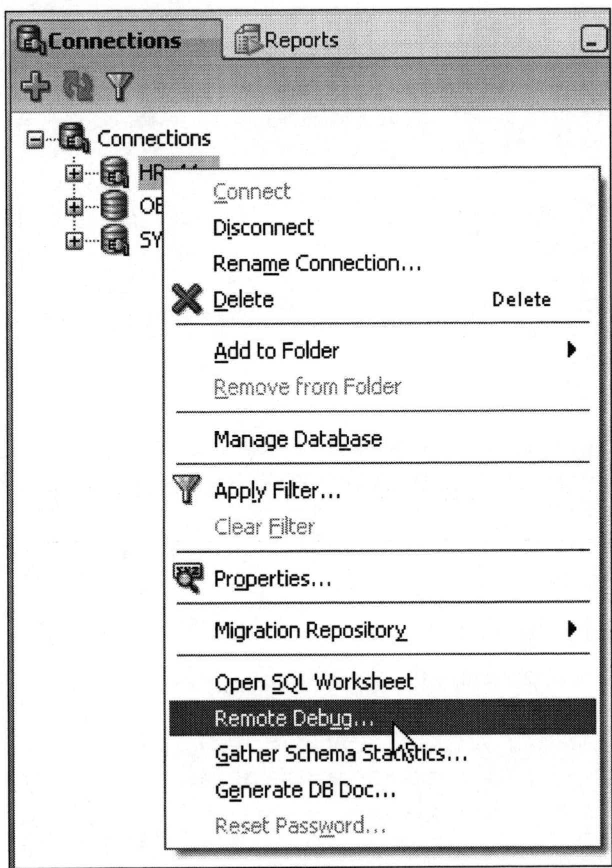

As soon as you select the **Remote Debug...** option, you are prompted for the port and IP address of the machine running SQL Developer.

You can set the range of ports using in the **Tools | Preferences** dialog, using the **Debugging Port Range** under the **Debugger** preferences.

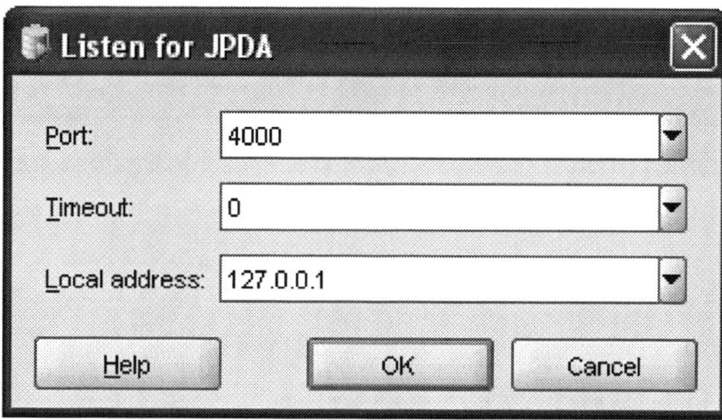

This prepares SQL Developer for the connection to the debugger and opens the process. Once done, you need to prepare the remote site. In the same way that SQL Developer executes `DBMS_DEBUG_JDWP.CONNECT_TCP` (the procedure to connect to the debugger) you need to execute this in the remote site. In this example, we need to use the procedure call:

```
EXECUTE DBMS_DEBUG_JDWP.CONNECT_TCP ('127.0.0.1', 4000);
```

Now, execute the procedure you are going to debug. In the following screenshot, the debug package has been executed and the procedure to be debugged has been called:

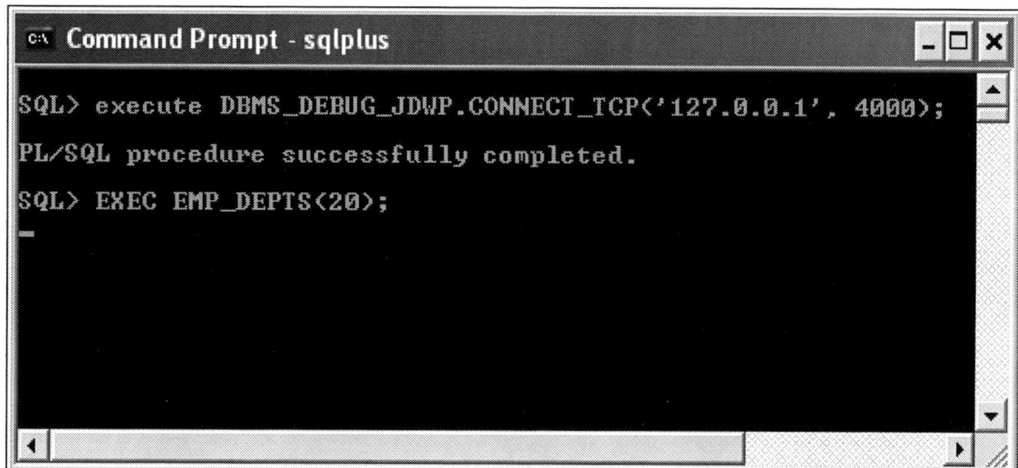

> Instead of executing the `DBMS_DEBUG_JDWP` command, you can set an environment variable before running your application. For example, using the same parameters as shown above, use:
>
> ```
> SET ORA_DEBUG_JDWP=host=127.0.0.1;port=4000
> ```

At this point, control is passed back to SQL Developer and the rest of the execution is exactly as is described for local debugging. Once complete, the control is passed back to the calling program, in this case SQL*Plus.

If you had issued a `SET SERVEROUTPUT ON` command before executing the procedure, the output appears on screen as shown:

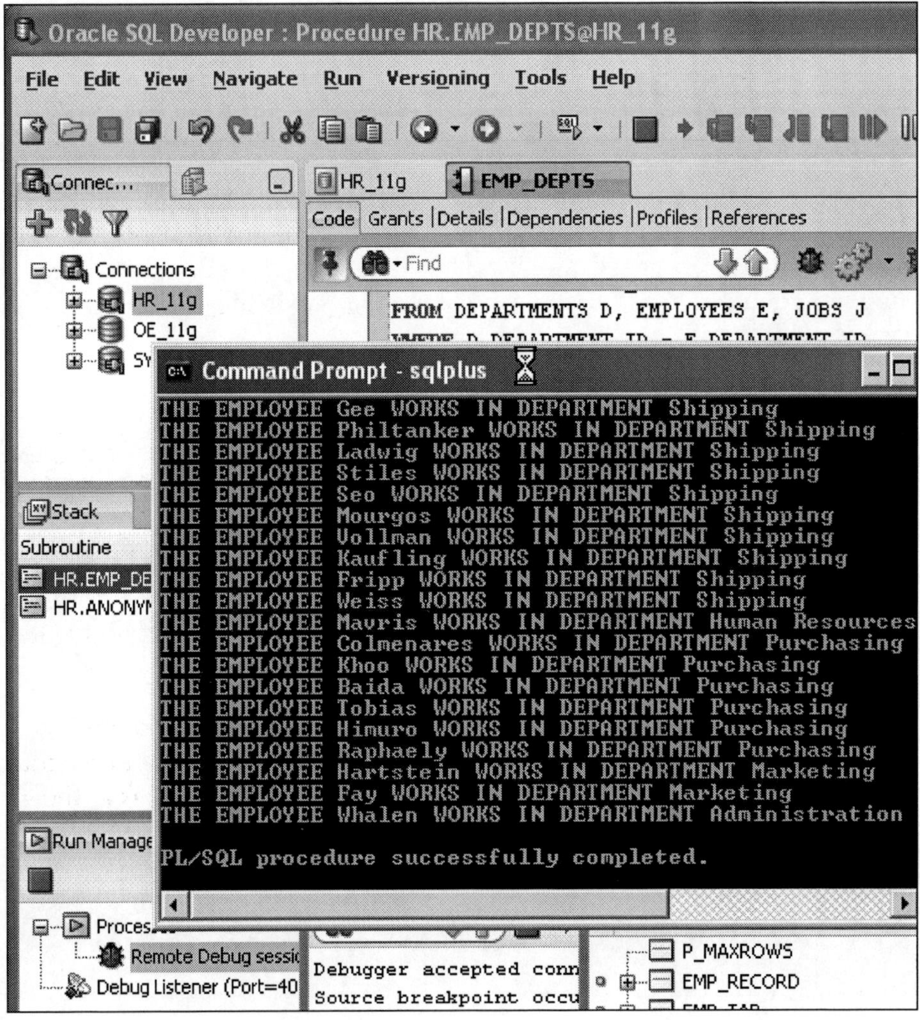

Remote debugging with Application Express

The process previously described is the same when debugging PL/SQL code in Oracle APEX. You can use SQL Developer to browse to and compile the PL/SQL code being called in Oracle APEX. If you are debugging, you need to select **Compile for Debug** and include a breakpoint.

In this case, you need to include the `DBMS_DEBUG_JDWP.CONNECT_TCP ('127.0.0.1', 4000);` call in Oracle APEX. For releases prior to Oracle APEX 3.1.1, you need to edit the procedure in Oracle APEX to include this call, but from Oracle APEX 3.1.1, if you change the YES/NO debugging parameter to `REMOTE`, this will execute the `CONNECT_TCP` call. For example, in the following Oracle APEX URL, change the `NO` to `REMOTE`:

```
http://127.0.0.1:8080/apex/f?p=101:12:1695620006850010::NO:::
```

As soon as the `CONNECT_TCP` has been set up and you invoke the desired procedure, the control passes back to SQL Developer and you can debug the code as before.

Summary

SQL Developer supports creating, editing, and compiling PL/SQL code. The SQL and PL/SQL parsing capabilities provided by the tool mean that additional utilities, such as code insight and completion, can be an invaluable resource to developers working with many objects to hand. Utilities as simple as a small dialog, save time by providing frameworks of code, while code templates and code snippets mean that frequently used code is not far out of reach. Using the utilities provided, and adding your own code to them, can be an invaluable coding resource.

In the next chapter, we'll show you the different utilities that SQL Developer provides to help you find and tune problem areas in our code. The utilities include invoking an explain plan, reviewing trace files, and autotrace. We'll look at the top SQL reports and dig into PL/SQL profiles using the hierarchical profiler.

6 SQL and PL/SQL Tuning Tools

SQL Developer is marketed as a tool for database developers who spend the bulk of their daily tasks writing and working with SQL and PL/SQL code, while Oracle Enterprise Manager is the tool of choice for the Database Administrator. Often seen as the domain of the DBA, "tuning" is a vast topic and ranges from tuning the database, right down to tuning SQL statements. It is the area of writing and tuning SQL statements that we'll be looking at in this chapter. While it is true that the DBA can focus on tuning the database server, and does indeed also tune SQL statements, developers should not write code and then "throw it over the wall" for the DBA to tune. Anyone who writes SQL or PL/SQL should be aware of the performance implications of the code they're writing. SQL Developer provides easy-to-use tools that can highlight areas of poor performance or where time is being spent on the server. In this chapter, we'll look at a few of the database utilities exposed in SQL Developer which will help developers investigate their code, such as using the Explain Plan and Autotrace features in the SQL Worksheet. We'll also look at reviewing trace files, monitoring SQL and at the SQL Reports provided to trace long running queries. The chapter does not teach any tuning techniques, and the examples used are designed to illustrate a feature in the tool and do not suggest best practices. There are many books available on tuning and Oracle's online documentation addresses tuning, in a number of the books in the documentation library, which also includes a complete Performance Tuning Guide.

Support for tuning code in the SQL Worksheet

As mentioned, tuning encompasses a full range of subjects, including tuning the database and tuning SQL statements. In SQL Developer, we only look at the latter, focusing on SQL and PL/SQL statements. When writing SQL, it is important to bear in mind that every query written and executed uses system resources. When tuning code, the main concern is to reduce the impact of the execution of the code on the system, effectively reducing the workload. Oracle prepares and compiles an execution plan for all of the DML statements executed. This execution plan shows the SQL optimizer's query execution path and is reused if a query is an exact match to a previously executed query. Oracle provides a number of utilities to read and review these execution plans.

In this first section, we'll look at the queries written and executed in the SQL Worksheet and how you can use the SQL Developer tools provided to examine the code written.

Working with EXPLAIN PLAN

Oracle puts together a sequence of operations, called an execution plan, required to run SQL statements. Working specifically with DML statements `SELECT`, `INSERT`, `UPDATE`, and `DELETE`, the `EXPLAIN PLAN` statement displays the execution plans prepared by the optimizer and inserts rows into a global temporary table called the `PLAN_TABLE`. If you use SQL*Plus, you need to write queries to display the execution plans in the `PLAN_TABLE` . However, if you use SQL Developer, you need only use the **Explain Plan** button to output the execution plan report below your query.

If you are new to these execution plans, then write a few basic queries and see the impact changing the query has on the output. In the first screenshot, we have used a simple `SELECT` statement, `SELECT * FROM EMPLOYEES;`. Click on the **Explain Plan** button, or press *F10,* to show the results. Notice that this is a full table scan, which makes sense as you have selected all columns and all rows from the table:

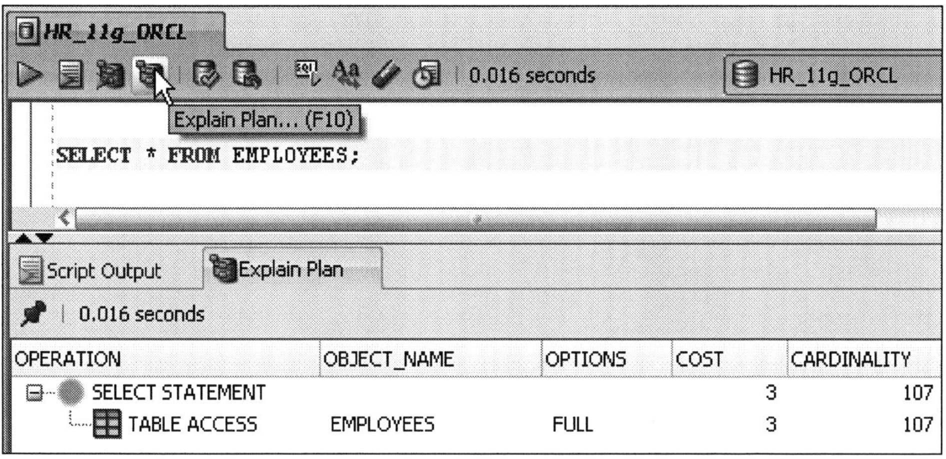

A full table scan has a high impact on resources, and is not advisable for large tables. More often than not, we want to look at a restricted set of records, and so we need to learn to write queries that restrict the records returned. A simple `WHERE` clause restricts records, but even that can be written more efficiently depending on the search conditions provided. If we restrict the query as shown in the next query, the **Explain Plan** output differs considerably:

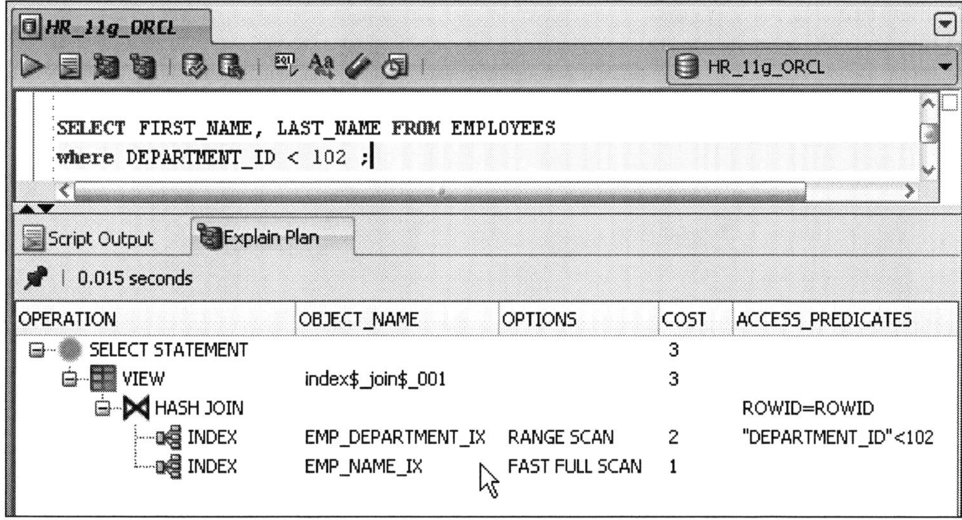

In this case, you see the indexes are now being used and that the index on the `DEPARTMENT_ID` column is used in a range scan.

Controlling the Explain Plan output

SQL Developer provides options for controlling what is displayed in the **Explain Plan** output. In the previous screenshot, the predicate detail is shown in its own column, but on switching the preference and selecting the **Predicates** option, the detail is included in the tree as shown in the following screenshot:

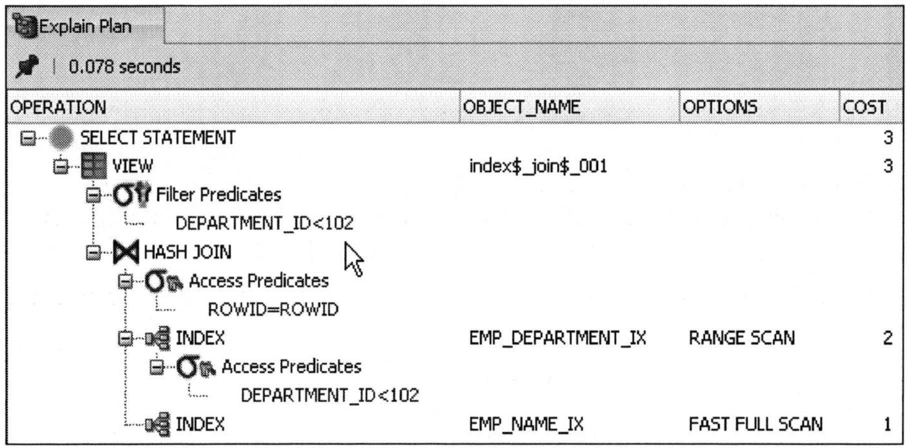

To control the detail in the **Explain Plan** report, use the **Tools | Preferences** menu to invoke the **Preferences** dialog, and then select **Database | Autotrace/Explain Plan** and select or deselect the settings as required:

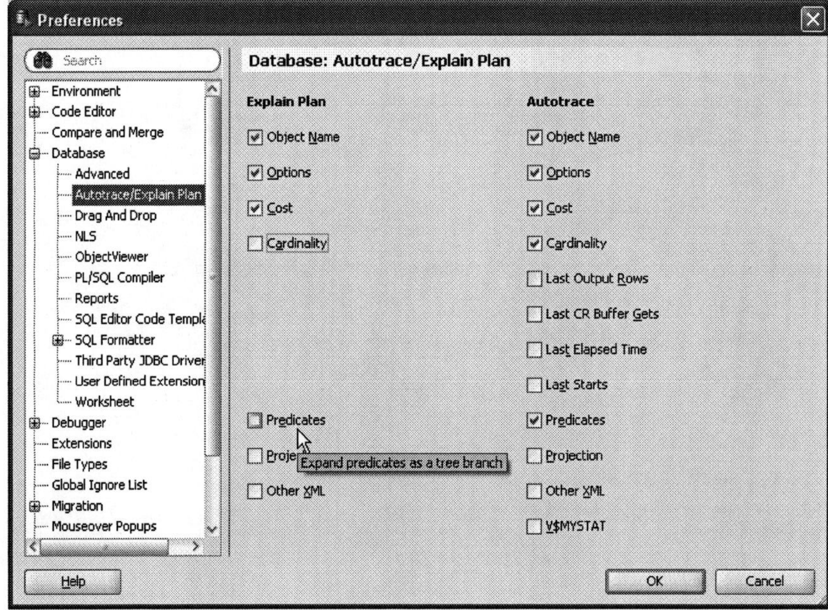

Execution plan details

Depending on which preferences you have selected, the **Explain Plan** report in SQL Developer displays the following detail:

- **Operation**—this part of the execution plan tree is always displayed and lists the method of access being used. This includes table access, or sort operations, and includes the join methods if used in the statement.
- **Object Name**—this includes the tables referenced in the statement.
- **Options**—this is the access method used, whether it's a full or range scan for example.
- **Cost**—this is used to optimize the query and is the relative cost of the operation based on a number of factors, such as initialization parameters, bind variable types if used, or statistics, if calculated for the tables.
- **Predicates**—this lists the predicates used in the query and by the statement.

To illustrate the variation in operations displayed in the output, we have created a partitioned table, such as the `CUSTOMERS_PART` partitioned table:

```
CREATE TABLE CUSTOMERS_PART
 (CUSTOMER_ID NUMBER(6,0),
   CUST_FIRST_NAME VARCHAR2(20 BYTE),
   CUST_LAST_NAME VARCHAR2(20 BYTE),
   NLS_TERRITORY VARCHAR2(30 BYTE),
   CREDIT_LIMIT NUMBER(9,2)
  )
 PARTITION BY RANGE (CREDIT_LIMIT)
 SUBPARTITION BY LIST (NLS_TERRITORY)
 SUBPARTITION TEMPLATE (
 SUBPARTITION EAST VALUES ('CHINA','JAPAN','INDIA', 'THAILAND'),
 SUBPARTITION WEST VALUES ('AMERICA', 'GERMANY', 'ITALY',
'SWITZERLAND'),
 SUBPARTITION OTHER VALUES (DEFAULT))
 (PARTITION P1 VALUES LESS THAN (1000),
  PARTITION P2 VALUES LESS THAN (2500),
  PARTITION P3 VALUES LESS THAN (MAXVALUE));
```

We have written a basic `SELECT` statement and included an `ORDER BY` clause:

```
SELECT CUSTOMER_ID, CUST_LAST_NAME, CREDIT_LIMIT
FROM CUSTOMERS_PART
ORDER BY CUSTOMER_ID;
```

The resulting **Explain Plan** report is shown in the following screenshot:

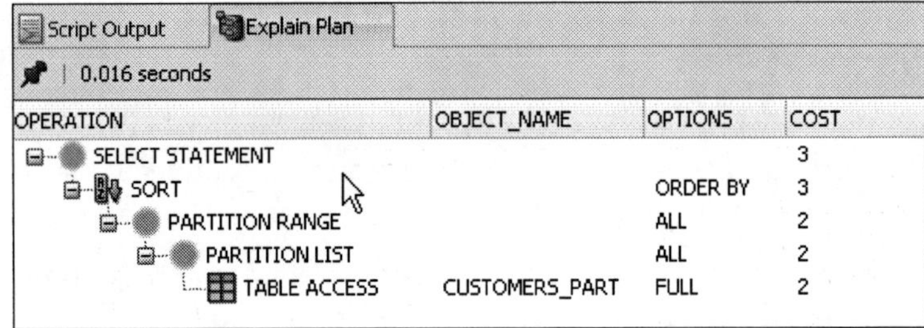

The next example takes the same query we used earlier and expands it to include two tables, adding the predicates to join and restrict the query. The impact of adding these is shown in the following screenshot:

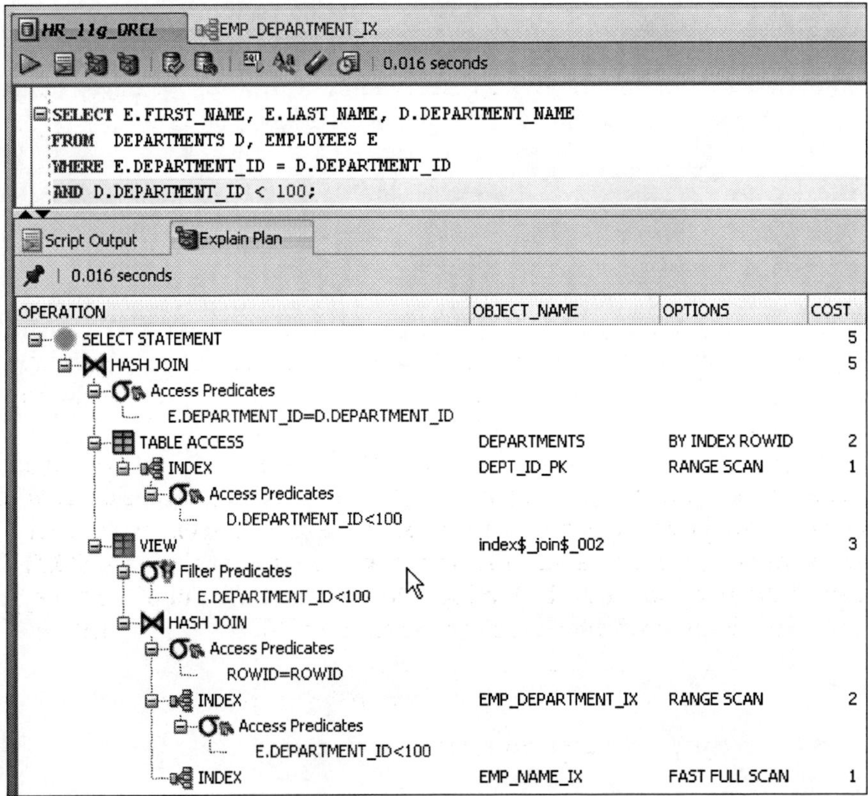

These few examples serve to illustrate the broad topic that encompasses tuning SQL statements. If you are new to the subject, then change a few entries in the basic statements, such as changing the predicates in the `WHERE` clause, and observe the difference.

Something as seemingly innocent as changing the last line of the above query to `AND D.DEPARTMENT_ID = 100;` results in the following output:

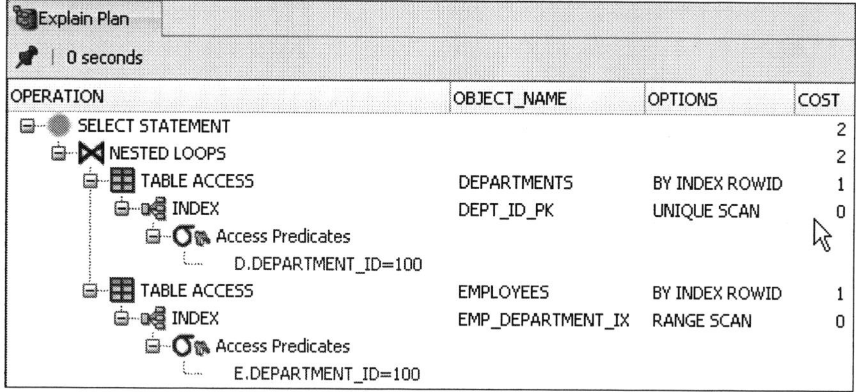

Notice the significant impact of the small change on the access and the cost. SQL execution plan is only as good as its cost estimate. In the next section we'll describe a utility that allows you to compare the cost with real execution performance statistics.

Using Autotrace

Oracle's Autotrace facility is useful for monitoring and tuning the performance of successful SQL DML statements `SELECT`, `INSERT`, `UPDATE`, and `DELETE`. Autotrace uses the `V$SQL_PLAN` view to display the execution plan and the `V$SQL_PLAN_STATISTICS` view to provide the execution statistics for each operation in the plan.You need access to `V$MYSTAT` and have the `PLUSTRACE` role granted to you (a user with DBA privileges can grant this role to you). In an environment like SQL*Plus, you need to set the `AUTOTRACE` system variable, and set up a `PLAN_TABLE`. Using SQL Developer, the tool detects whether you have the correct privileges. In the following example, we have connected as the sample schema SCOTT. A user with very few privileges, SCOTT can use the **Explain Plan** option in SQL Developer to review the output of the `PLAN_TABLE`, but is given the following warning when trying to access the Autotrace facility:

In addition to the output of the Explain Plan, Autotrace also provides a set of statistics that log the system resources needed for your SQL statement.

If we use the same query used against the `CUSTOMERS_PART` table that was created earlier, and select the **Autotrace** (*F6*) option, then you'll see the additional statistics output displayed below the query and Explain Plan:

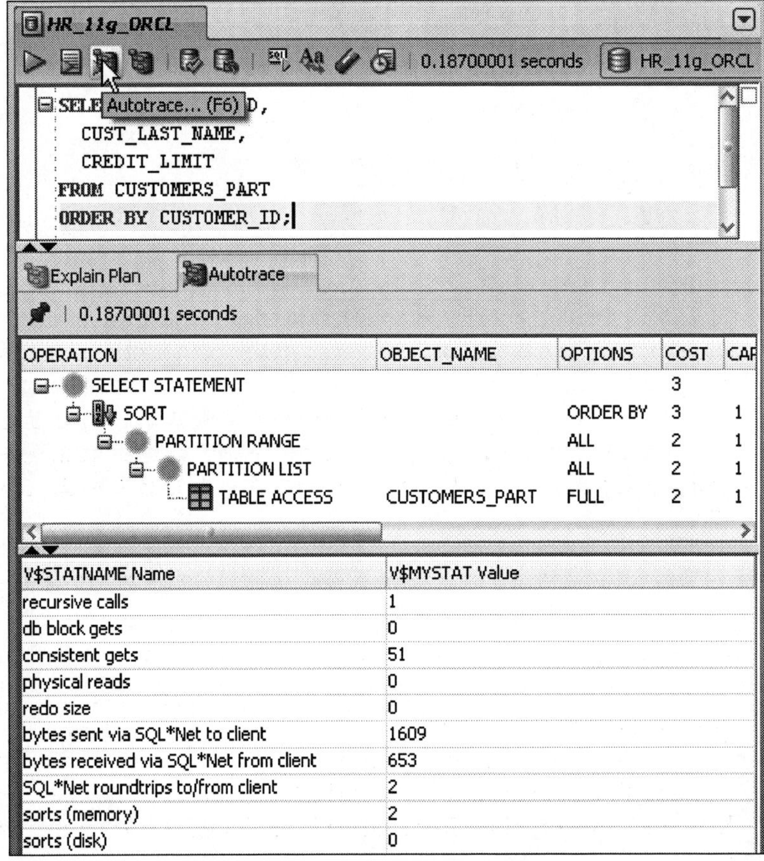

In the same way that you can control the content displayed for the Explain Plan output, you can control the content displayed when using Autotrace in SQL Developer. Select the **Tools | Preferences** menu to invoke the **Preferences** dialog as before. Select **Database | Autotrace/Explain Plan** and select the options.

Check the **V$MYSTAT** preference in the **Database | Autotrace/Explain Plan** section of the **Preferences** dialog to display the statement execution statistics.

To learn more about interpreting the details in the Autotrace output, see the *Performance Tuning Guide*, which is part of the Oracle Documentation.

Additional performance tuning tools

In the previous section, we looked at SQL statements and at how using the Explain Plan output can assist you when you are learning to write queries that perform better. It is good to try to write sound queries from the outset, but more often than not, what happens is that users come back to the developers complaining about performance. In this case, there is no sense in starting to wade through all of the code in the application, instead you need to determine which queries have the greatest impact on the system, such as the top running SQL statements. Once you have determined where the offending code is, you can review the execution plans for each of these and then work at reducing the impact these have on the system by improving the statements.

Using SQL reports

SQL Developer provides a number of packaged reports that you can use when tuning your queries. You can start by looking at **Data Dictionary Reports | Table | Statistics**. These are simple reports, which report when the table was last analyzed and at the number of rows per table. In the following example, the new `CUSTOMERS_PART` table has been analyzed and the row count of each of the tables in the schema is displayed. Knowing which are the smaller tables in a system is useful when writing queries that join multiple tables.

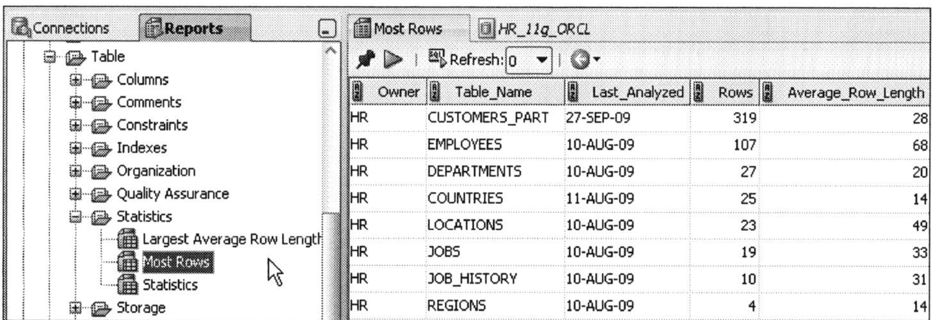

Running the Top SQL reports

In the packaged reports are six reports that look at the top SQL statements executed in the system. These include all of the SQL statements that are being executed and can be quite daunting when you first run the report. You'll find these reports in **Data Dictionary Reports | Database Administration | Top SQL**. If you select **Top SQL by CPU**, the output may look a little like the one we have illustrated in the following screenshot:

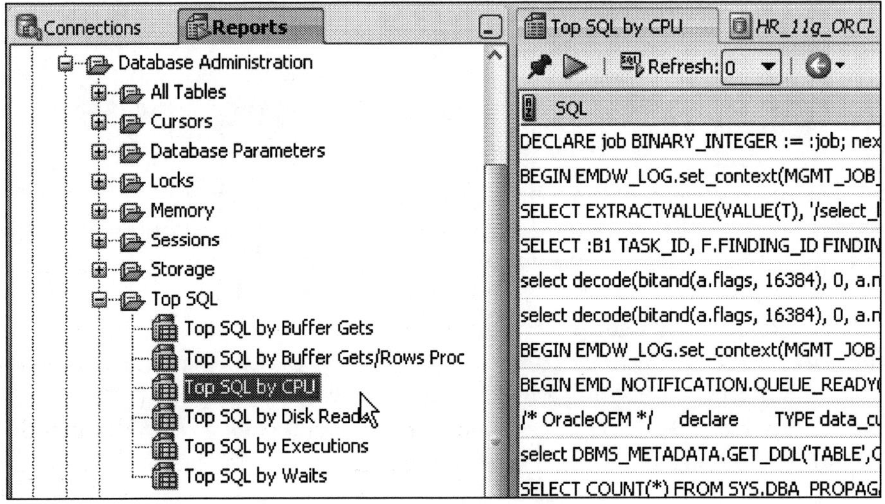

This report contains a lot of detail, and so reorganizing it to display what suits you can help when using the report to determine the top SQL queries affecting you.

To reorganize the report, right-click on the SQL column heading and select **Columns...** from the context menu:

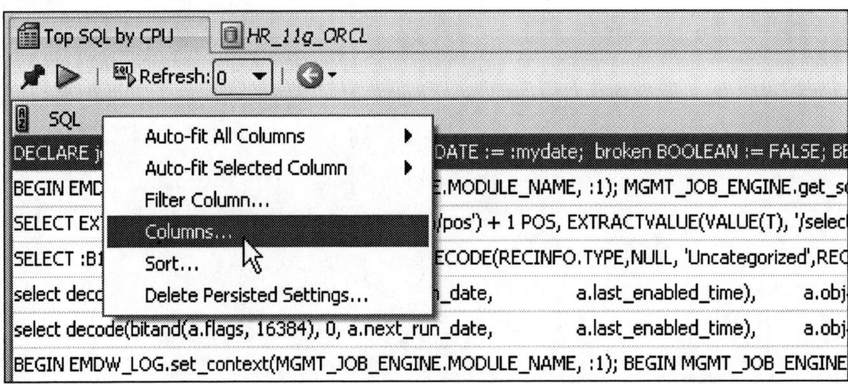

This invokes a dialog which you can use to manage the display of the columns in the report, or any data grid. If you are working with a particular application, then shuttle the **Module** column to the first position as shown:

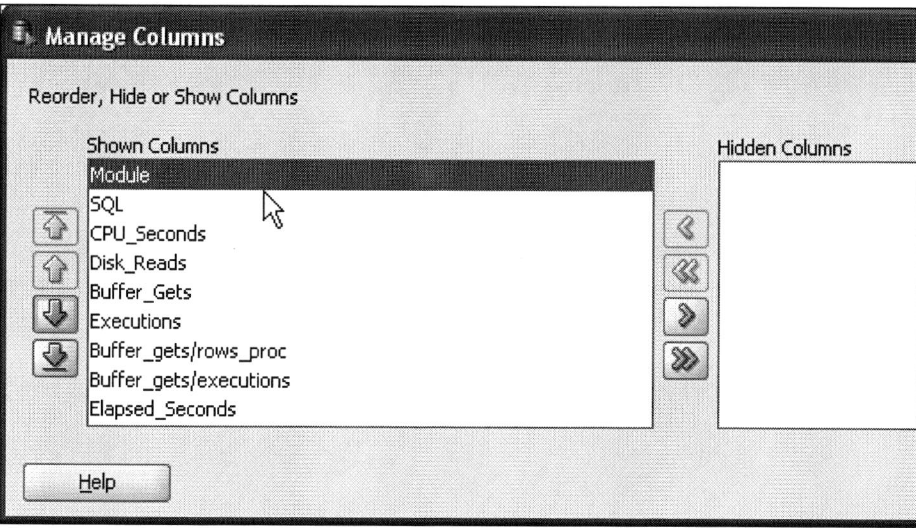

Click on **OK** to accept the changes and close the report. You can now double-click on the column heading to sort the output per module. This groups all of the top queries by module, and you can focus on the module or application you are working with. At this stage, it is also useful to restrict the report to the module you are working on, such as your application. To restrict the list of modules, select the column heading and invoke the filter:

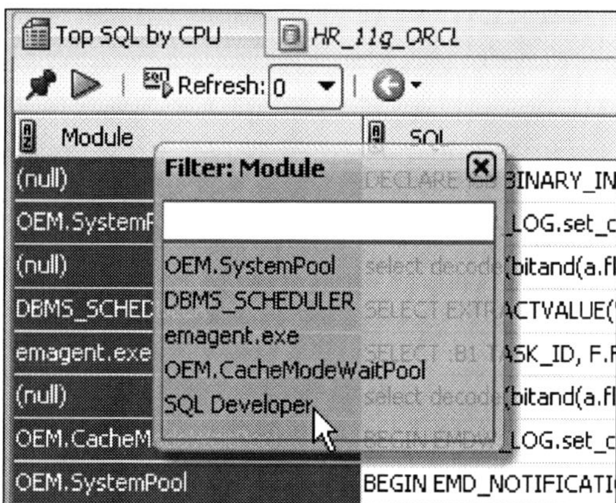

As shown in the previous screenshot, you can track the queries run by an application, such as SQL Developer or Oracle Enterprise Manager. It is more useful to track the queries in the applications which you can control. For example, you might be tuning an Oracle APEX application.

In the following screenshot, we have filtered the modules display to only the Oracle APEX Application 101. Once filtered, we can now look at sorting the remaining columns and reviewing the queries:

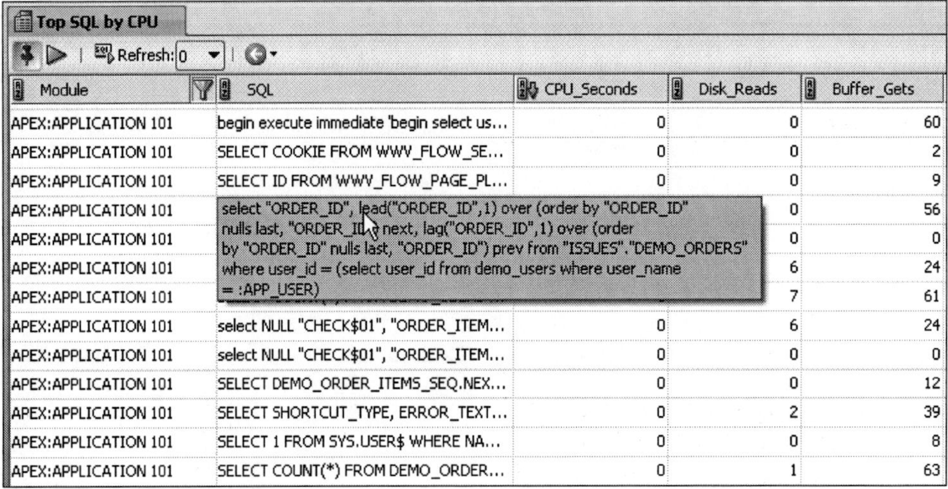

Module	SQL	CPU_Seconds	Disk_Reads	Buffer_Gets
APEX:APPLICATION 101	begin execute immediate 'begin select us...	0	0	60
APEX:APPLICATION 101	SELECT COOKIE FROM WWV_FLOW_SE...	0	0	2
APEX:APPLICATION 101	SELECT ID FROM WWV_FLOW_PAGE_PL...	0	0	9
APEX:APPLICATION 101			0	56
APEX:APPLICATION 101			0	0
APEX:APPLICATION 101			6	24
APEX:APPLICATION 101			7	61
APEX:APPLICATION 101	select NULL "CHECK$01", "ORDER_ITEM...	0	6	24
APEX:APPLICATION 101	select NULL "CHECK$01", "ORDER_ITEM...	0	0	0
APEX:APPLICATION 101	SELECT DEMO_ORDER_ITEMS_SEQ.NEX...	0	0	12
APEX:APPLICATION 101	SELECT SHORTCUT_TYPE, ERROR_TEXT...	0	2	39
APEX:APPLICATION 101	SELECT 1 FROM SYS.USER$ WHERE NA...	0	0	8
APEX:APPLICATION 101	SELECT COUNT(*) FROM DEMO_ORDER...	0	1	63

Hover the mouse pointer over the SQL statements to display the full query.

For further detail about how to interpret the detail in the Top SQL report, see the *Performance and Tuning Guide* in the online Oracle documentation.

SQL Developer also provides a selection of ASH (Automated Session History) and AWR (Automatic Workload Repository) reports. Statistical details useful for diagnosing performance issues are stored in the AWR and the **Automatic Database Diagnostic Monitor** (**ADDM**) analyzes this data. To review the SQL Developer reports, select **Data Dictionary Reports | ASH and AWR**:

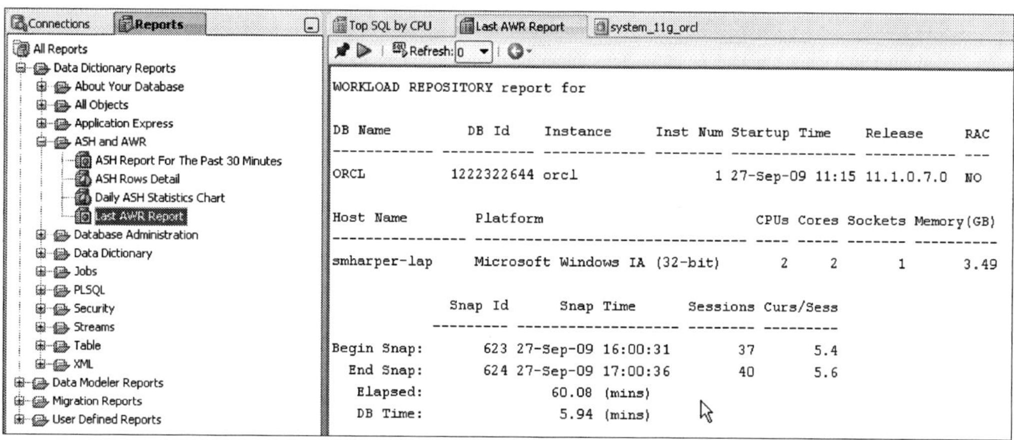

ASH, AWR, and ADDM are part of the Oracle Diagnostic Pack, an Oracle Database 11g Cost Option, and as such are an additional cost.

Monitoring your environment

Oracle Database 11g provides a feature that allows you to monitor the performance of your SQL statements while they are executing. Particularly useful for long running queries, this real-time SQL monitoring feature is exposed in SQL Developer through the **Tools | Monitor SQL...** menu.

Real-time SQL monitoring is part of the Oracle Tuning Pack, an Oracle Database 11g Cost Option.

If you have the database initialization parameter `STATISTICS_LEVEL` set to `ALL` or `TYPICAL`, then SQL monitoring starts automatically when a query consumes more than five seconds, or for queries that are executed in parallel. You can also include `/*+MONITOR*/` in your SQL queries to force SQL monitoring. Once you have a query running, select **Tools | Monitor SQL...**.

Once you have long running queries in the **Real Time SQL Monitoring** window, select the query you want to review, and invoke **Show Sql Details** from the menu:

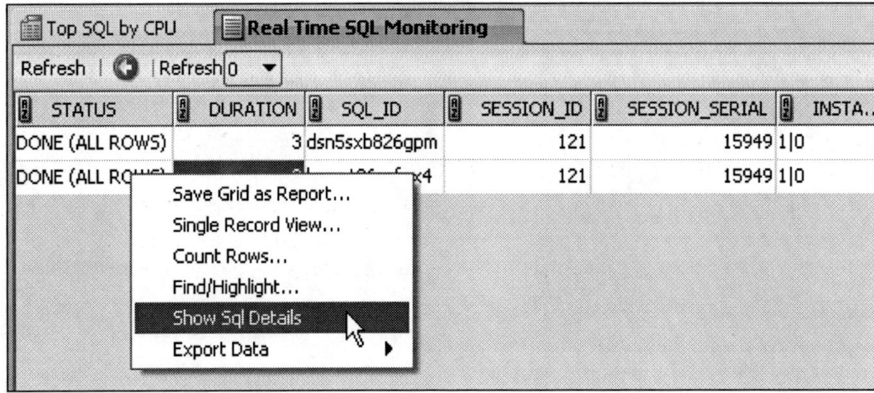

The report output includes details about the operations used, and the name of the objects accessed, like those you have seen in the Explain Plan. In addition, there are columns with estimated and actual rows accessed, and you can see the full SQL query:

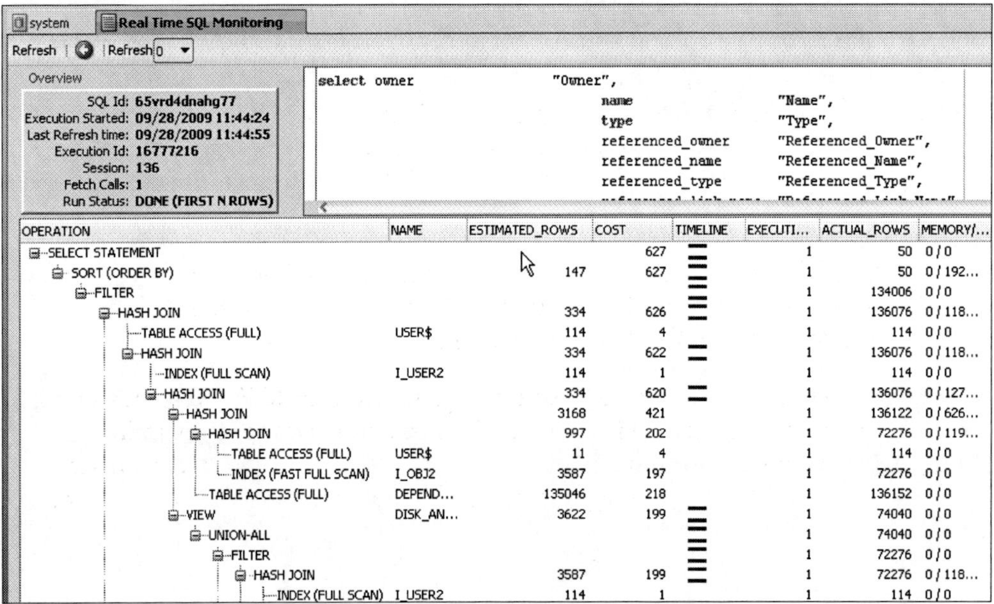

You can access and view the report while the query is running, with the time lines changing as the report runs and completes.

Inspecting SQL trace files

Oracle has a few tools that help you monitor applications while they run, such as the performance diagnostic tools SQL Trace and TKPROF. These, together with Explain Plan, provide a useful set of tools for monitoring, and then determining, areas of resource overload that can impact the performance in an application.

SQL Developer provides a session report which allows you to track the various sessions running on the server. You can also use this report to trace the session. To invoke the report, select **Tools | Monitor Sessions...** Once the report is running, right-click to invoke the context menu and select **Trace Session** (as shown in the following screenshot). You need to run the report as SYSTEM, or have been granted privilege to the `DBMS_MONITOR` package. This tracing is terminated when you disconnect the connection, terminating the session.

SQL Trace gathers performance statistics for all SQL statements executed in a session. Therefore, you should enable SQL Trace for a session with care as this can have an impact on performance itself.

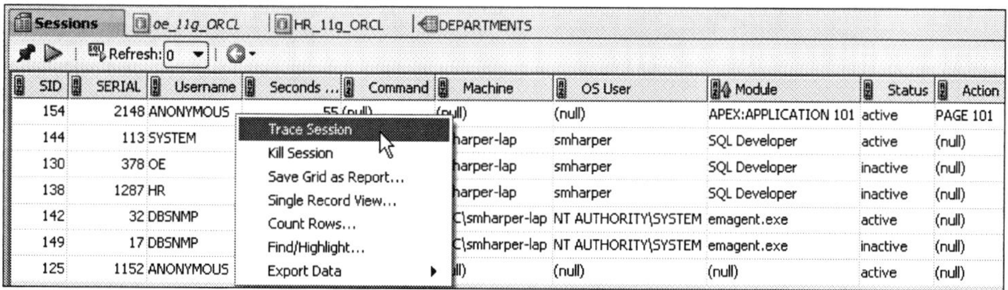

This trace file is written to the location of all your trace files. For example, using Oracle 11g with a default installation on Microsoft Windows, the files are written to `[ORACLE_HOME]\diag\rdbms\orcl\orcl\trace`.

In general, once you have the trace file, you need to use TKPROF to format the file, making it easier to read and interpret. SQL Developer provides a similar facility, by allowing you to open the trace file in the GUI. Once you have a trace file, open it in SQL Developer by simply dragging it onto the SQL Developer work surface as shown:

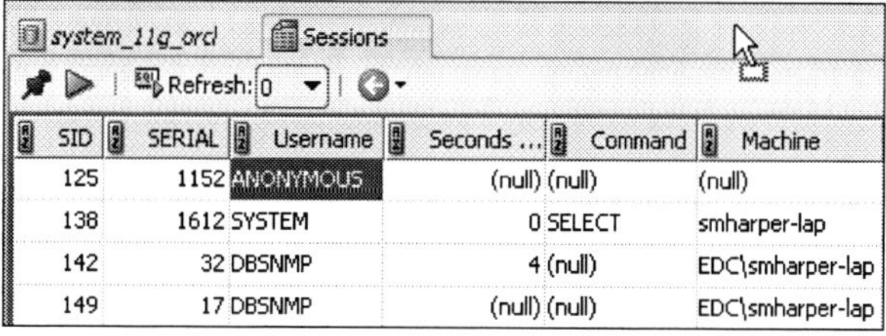

This opens a graphical layout of the trace files and allows you to view the contents:

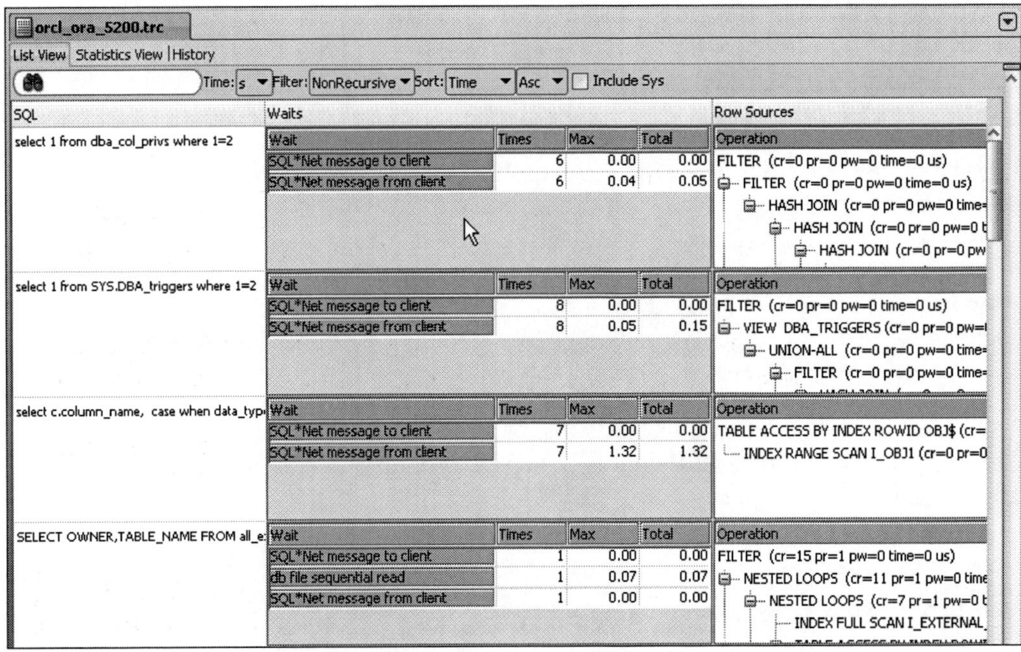

SQL Developer provides drop-down lists that let you sort the data returned based on values such as Time, CPU, Query, and Rows, or you can switch from the **List View**, previously shown, to the **Statistics View** as shown in the following screenshot:

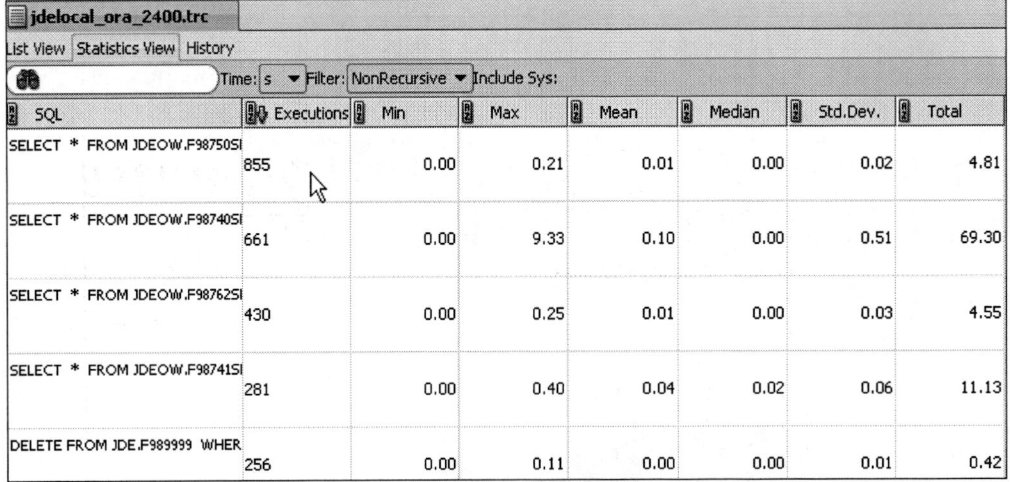

For further detail about SQL Trace and TKPROF, and interpreting the output of these files, see the *Performance and Tuning Guide* in the online Oracle documentation.

Profiling PL/SQL

Oracle Database 11*g* introduced the PL/SQL Hierarchical Profiler which records not only the time spent in each sub program, but also (arguably, more useful) the number of calls to the subprogram.

The detail is stored in a set of database tables, which you can run custom reports against to retrieve. The package `DBMS_HPROF` provides procedures that start and stop the hierarchical profiler data collection. Instead of managing this process manually and from a command line, SQL Developer provides the tools to create these tables, set up the environment, and a set of reports for you to review the output.

The PL/SQL Hierarchical Profiler was introduced in Oracle Database 11*g*. Integration with SQL Developer was introduced in release 1.5, and is only available in the user interface when accessing Oracle Database 11g Release 1 and above.

Getting started

To run the profiler, once you have a compiled subprogram, invoke the PL/SQL code editor for the selected code:

```
create or replace
PROCEDURE EMP_LIST(
    pMaxRows IN NUMBER )
AS
  CURSOR emp_cursor
  IS
    SELECT l.state_province,
      l.country_id,
      d.department_name,
      e.last_name,
      j.job_title,
      e.salary,
```

The same window that you see when running any procedure or function, displaying an anonymous PL/SQL block, is opened. The only difference here is the dialog is called **Profile PL/SQL**. To continue the process, provide any input parameters required and accept the dialog.

The first time you access the profile, you'll be prompted to set up the environment. Otherwise, the code completes and updates the hierarchical profiler tables.

Preparing the environment

You can either allow SQL Developer to setup the environment, or you can prepare it separately, using the SQL Worksheet or SQL*Plus. If the tables have been set up, and `DBMS_HPROF` package has been previously called, you can see the results in the **Profiles** tab in SQL Developer. In the following example, the tables have not been set up and the **Profiles** tab displays a warning:

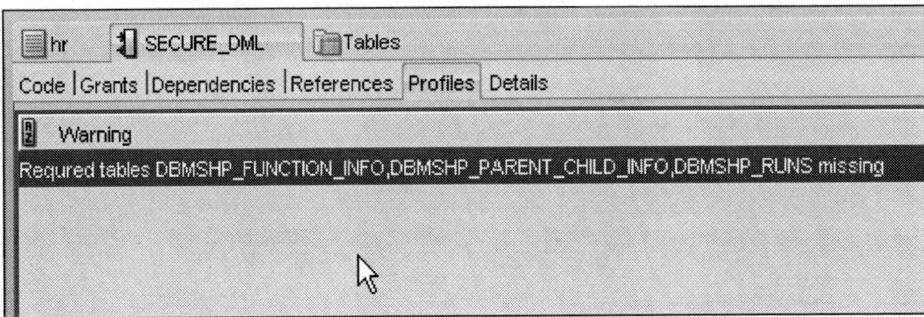

Whether you are using SQL Developer or not, there are a few elements that you need to execute, and as such need the following additional privileges before you can proceed:

- `EXECUTE`—on the `DBMS_HPROF` package.
- `CREATE DIRECTORY`
- `WRITE`—on the directory. This is used when the `DBMS_HPROF.START_PROFILING` procedure is called.

The first time you run the Hierarchical Profiler in SQL Developer, you are prompted for details and a dialog displaying the SQL that is about to be executed. You can accept the dialog to execute the code, or copy and execute this independently.

As you start, you are prompted for a log profiler directory as follows:

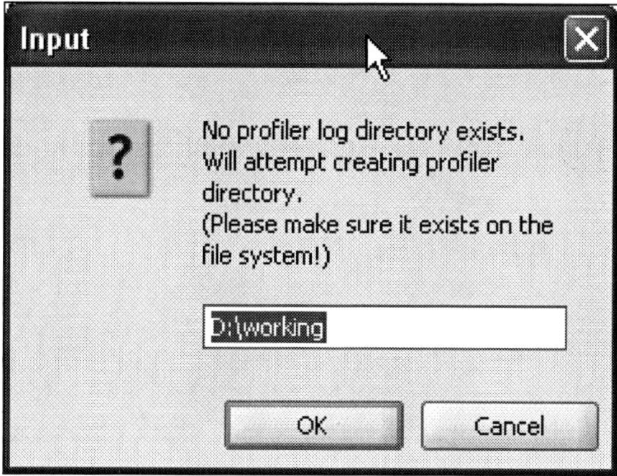

Be sure to note the directory and modify it as required, before you accept the dialog. The next dialog shows the code that is about to be executed to prepare the environment:

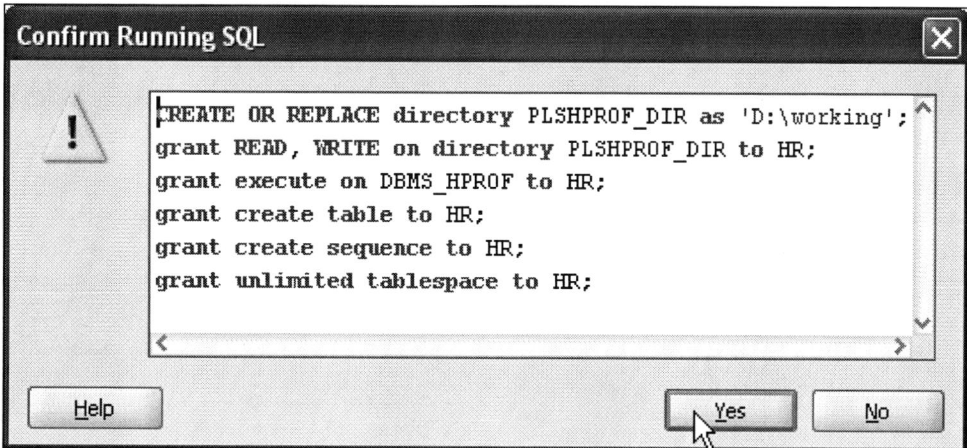

Once you accept this dialog, you are prompted for the **SYS** password to execute the procedure. This is then followed by an additional dialog if the hierarchical tables have not been created. These tables are then created in the default schema for the user specified. In the following example, the profiler tables are created in the HR schema:

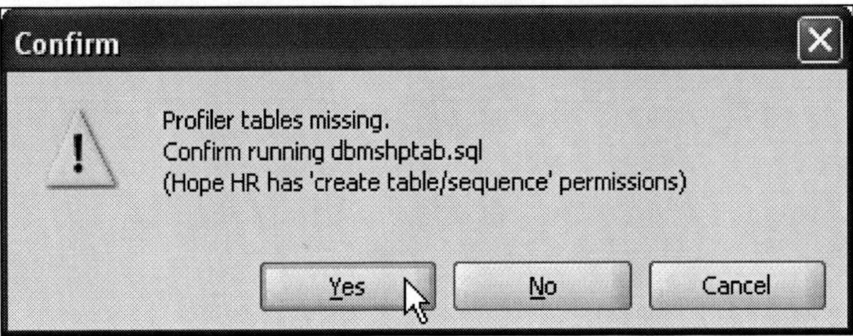

Reviewing the output

Once you have set up the tables and access, you can profile the code reviewing the changes in the results depending on external environmental conditions or parameters passed. In the following example, the same procedure has been profiled a number of times. The **Total Elapsed Time** results vary, and so it's at this stage that you want to review the details to see what has caused the changes. Notice specifically that the last two entries are run on the same day, with the timing so close, they must have been run one after the other:

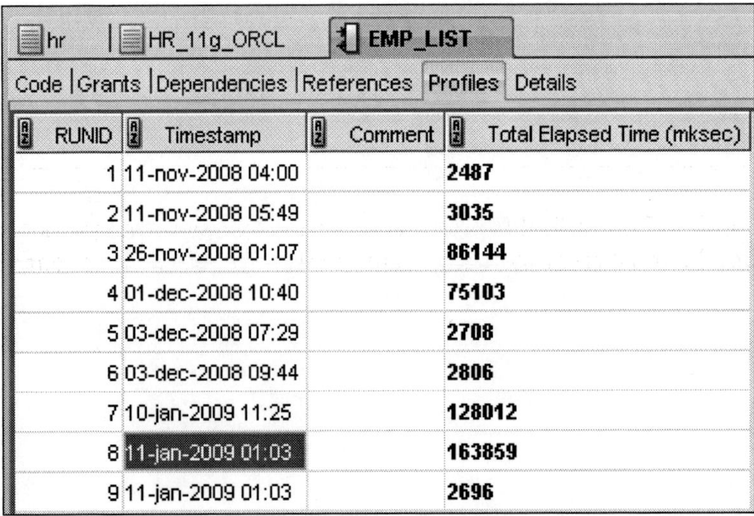

RUNID	Timestamp	Comment	Total Elapsed Time (mksec)
1	11-nov-2008 04:00		2487
2	11-nov-2008 05:49		3035
3	26-nov-2008 01:07		86144
4	01-dec-2008 10:40		75103
5	03-dec-2008 07:29		2708
6	03-dec-2008 09:44		2806
7	10-jan-2009 11:25		128012
8	11-jan-2009 01:03		163859
9	11-jan-2009 01:03		2696

To review the details, select each of the records, and a set of details records are displayed as shown in the following screenshot:

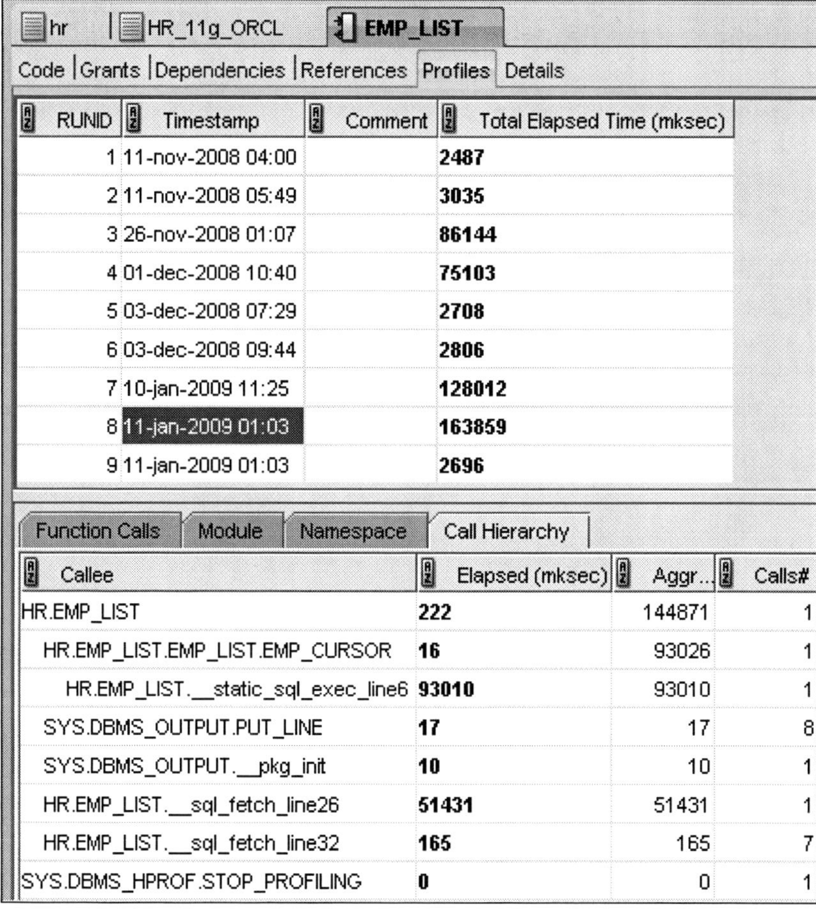

RUNID	Timestamp	Comment	Total Elapsed Time (mksec)
1	11-nov-2008 04:00		2487
2	11-nov-2008 05:49		3035
3	26-nov-2008 01:07		86144
4	01-dec-2008 10:40		75103
5	03-dec-2008 07:29		2708
6	03-dec-2008 09:44		2806
7	10-jan-2009 11:25		128012
8	11-jan-2009 01:03		163859
9	11-jan-2009 01:03		2696

Callee	Elapsed (mksec)	Aggr...	Calls#
HR.EMP_LIST	222	144871	1
HR.EMP_LIST.EMP_LIST.EMP_CURSOR	16	93026	1
HR.EMP_LIST.__static_sql_exec_line6	93010	93010	1
SYS.DBMS_OUTPUT.PUT_LINE	17	17	8
SYS.DBMS_OUTPUT.__pkg_init	10	10	1
HR.EMP_LIST.__sql_fetch_line26	51431	51431	1
HR.EMP_LIST.__sql_fetch_line32	165	165	7
SYS.DBMS_HPROF.STOP_PROFILING	0	0	1

Using the PL/SQL Hierarchical Profiler, you can determine which parts of the code are consuming the most resource and where the most time is being spent.

Summary

In this chapter, we looked at the different features provided by SQL Developer that support tuning SQL statements. While working with the SQL Worksheet, writing ad hoc queries, or preparing queries for an application, you can use the Explain Plan and Autotrace features to determine the execution plans for queries you have written, and whether they are performing efficiently. Other tools provided by Oracle and exposed in SQL Developer are reports for finding the top SQL running on the server, and for monitoring your server in general, you can use the tracing and monitoring tools.

In the next chapter, we'll look at how to manage files. We'll introduce the integrated file navigator and the file history. This will be followed with a review of how SQL Developer acts as a client to open source version control systems. You'll learn how to place your code under version control and work within a team sharing code, by comparing and merging code.

7
Managing Files

Source code control is important in any development environment, whether you are working on your own or with other users in a team accessing the same files. Sometimes called source code management or version control, source code control provides a revision history of the code you are working on and the ability to compare changes and merge documents. There are a number of open source version control systems available and Oracle SQL Developer provides tight integration with two of them, **Concurrent Versions System** (**CVS**) and **Subversion** (**SVN**). In this chapter, we'll look at this integration, focusing specifically on Subversion. We'll look at browsing files in the file system from within SQL Developer, in addition to working with your versioning repository in SQL Developer, by importing files into the repository and checking them out, modifying them, and checking them back in.

Introducing source code control

We almost all use some form of file management when we're working, whether this is just renaming a file to save it as a backup copy, or using a well-defined directory structure or naming system. More sophisticated version control management systems allow you to manage the changes in your files or documents. This file management becomes more important when multiple users access the same files and is essential as users who share files are often working in different locations and different time zones.

Overview

With multiple users accessing the same files, you need a central location for storing the shared files. In many version control systems, files are stored in a repository held on a shared server, with each user checking out the files they need to work on. Once complete, these files are checked in. If another user tries to check in at the same, with their own updated files, the version control system will request a compare and merge before updating the repository. In this first section we introduce some key concepts and review the tools SQL Developer has access to.

Ways of working

Each version control system has methods of working and most companies have a set of defined procedures in place when teams create, edit, and update files. Some teams will insist that when you check in and merge files, you ensure that your updates do not adversely affect anyone else who may subsequently use or update associated files. In other words, once you have checked in all of your files, you may need to run a set of sanity tests to ensure the new files have integrated correctly. This type of team awareness is particularly relevant for more distributed teams. For example, one developer might check in code and update the system before leaving for home. This would be the start of the day for someone in another geographical location, who will pick up the changes made before starting work and will no doubt not be pleased if they need to start with broken or incomplete changes.

The repository is the point of truth

For repository-based systems, most users consider the repository as the point of truth. This is where the up-to-date files are stored. To include any file in a project it must initially be added to the repository. After the initial import, the file is checked out, updated, and then returned to the repository. In some systems, other users can also check out and update the same file. If the administrator allows this, in these situations, the users need to manage the conflicts.

In some cases, you can use *reserved checkouts*, which locks files that you check out. This locking prevents other users from taking a copy of the file, or if they are able to take a copy, may not check it back in until you have checked in your file. They are then required to merge any changes. Each of these scenarios is possible with most version control systems and will depend on the approach you specify.

SQL Developer integration

SQL Developer provides out-of-the-box integrated support for Subversion (SVN). Prior to SQL Developer 2.1, Concurrent Versions System (CVS) was also automatically installed. This is now available through the **Check for Updates** utility. Once added, the support is integrated in the same way as it is for Subversion. Support for additional tools like Perforce will also use this mechanism.

You can also add links to invoke other version control systems and pass parameters to them, as you would using the command line, by using the support SQL Developer provides for adding all external tools. This is not tight integration, but does allow you to invoke alternative version control tools. The integrated version control tools have been briefly introduced in the sections that follow.

Subversion (SVN)

SQL Developer integration with Subversion supports the ability to import files into the repository to bring them under version control, check out the files, edit, and commit the changes back to the repository. If other users have updated the files in the repository, you can update the working copy to pick up the changes made.

Subversion supports atomic commits, which means that no part of the commit is complete until the entire commit is complete. You'll also notice that revision numbers are increased after a commit and are not on a file-by-file basis.

Concurrent Versions System (CVS)

Once installed, the integrated support for CVS means you can work seamlessly with the CVS repository. This allows you to check out files, edit, and check them back in, using the menus provided from within SQL Developer.

Other version control systems

An additional extension for Perforce is also available for download from the Oracle Technology Network. This is not available as part of the SQL Developer install. Instead, you need to use the SQL Developer **Check for Updates** utility to include the extension. Once included, you can use it in the same way as the others.

For other version control systems, such as **IBM Rational ClearCase**, you can use SQL Developer's **External Tools** dialog to add a menu to invoke the product from within SQL Developer. Using this approach, you can pass any parameters you use in the command-line interface to the product, from within SQL Developer.

In the following screenshot, both **CVS** and **Perforce** have been added using **Check for Updates**. As you add the extensions for these additional tools, so the main **Versioning** menu expands to reveal the options for the new tools:

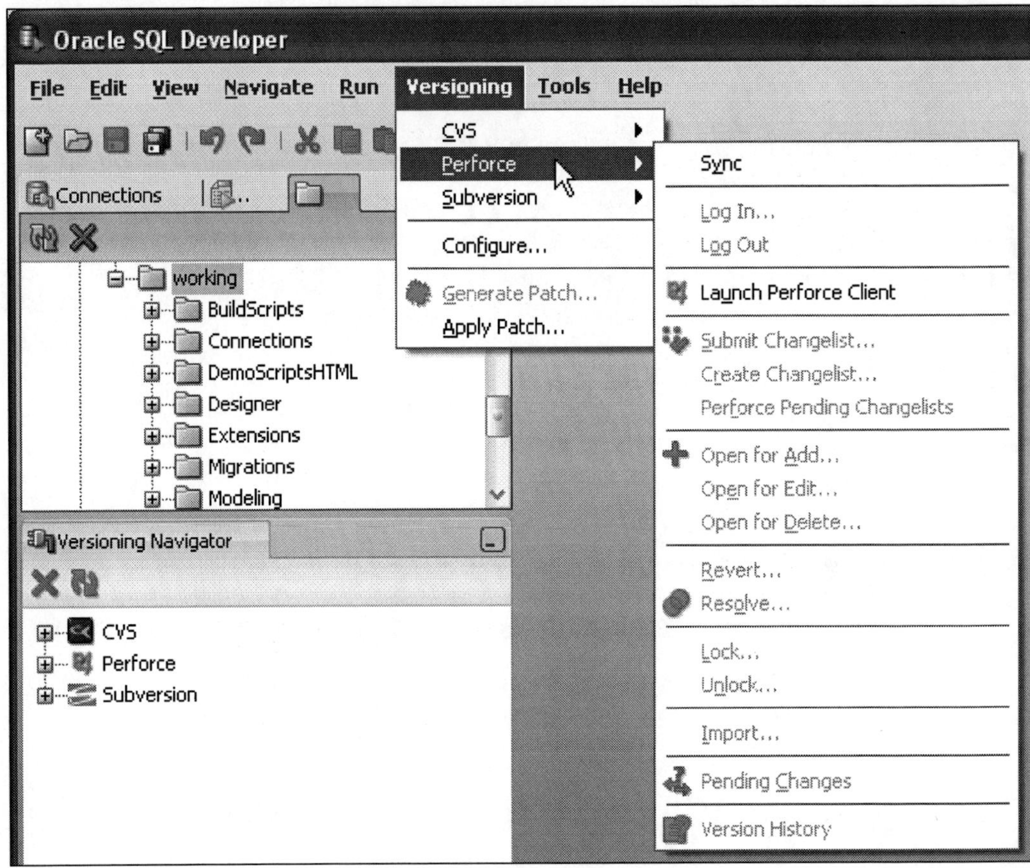

Getting started

Oracle SQL Developer can act as a client to your file system and your version control repository by providing a:

- File-browsing navigator that is independent of any version control management system
- Separate versioning navigator

Whether you are going to version your files or not, you can simply use SQL Developer to browse and edit files. While the two navigators are independent of each other, the **Files** navigator forms an integral part of version control management in SQL Developer, and so it is useful to start there.

Invoking the Files navigator

The **Files** and **Versioning** navigators are not displayed by default when you start the product. To invoke either, select the **View** menu:

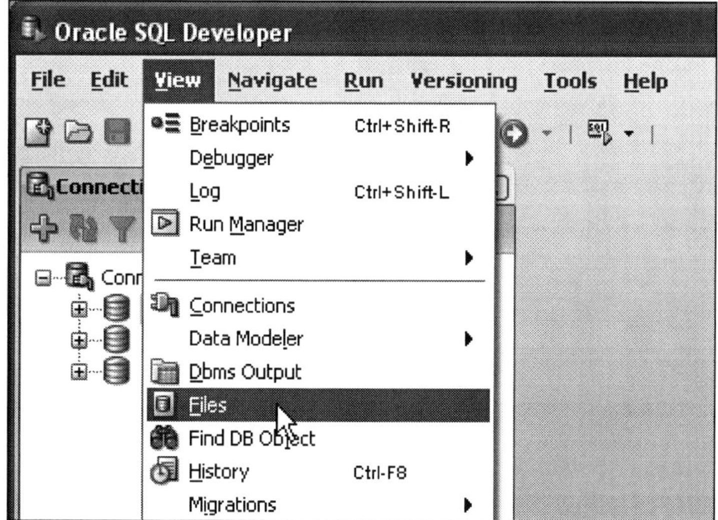

All navigators that are displayed when closing SQL Developer are opened again on start-up.

Browsing and editing files

The **Files** navigator allows you to browse all of the directories on your machine. It does not include any files on shared servers, which you may have mapped in your system. To open any recognized text file in SQL Developer, expand the **Files** navigator and double-click on the required file. SQL Developer recognizes files with SQL and PL/SQL extensions. It also recognizes files with tags, such as HTML and XML files.

You can open and edit the following file extensions in SQL Developer:

- `.html`
- `.xml`
- `.sql`
- `.plc, .pls, .pkb, .pkh`
- `.txt`

SQL Developer also keeps track of recently opened files and displays them in a separate directory. The **Recent Files** directory only displays `.sql`, `.pks`, `.pkb`, `.plc`, and `.pkc` files:

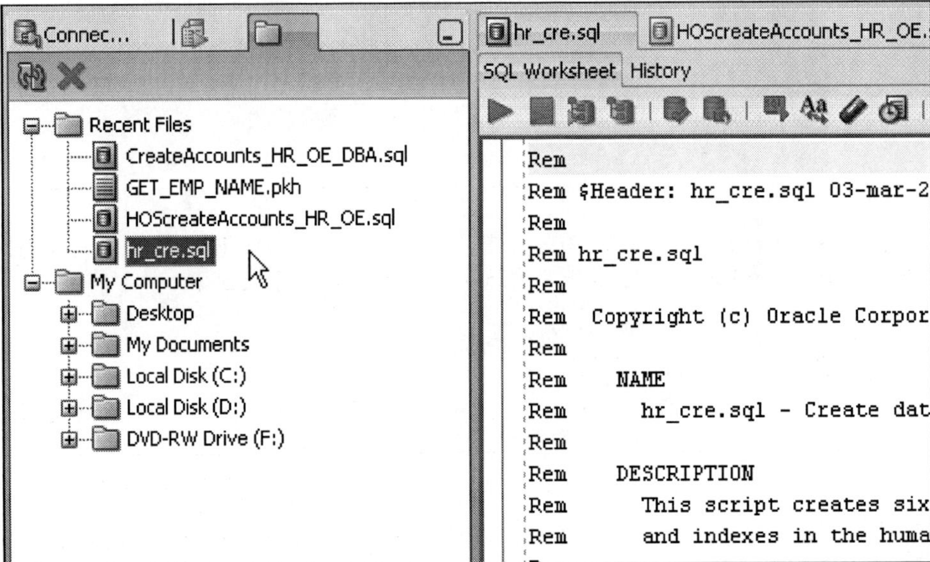

Reviewing the file editors

SQL Developer has two file editors. The SQL Worksheet works with all SQL files, and the PL/SQL code editor works with all PL/SQL files. The SQL Worksheet is displayed in the previous screenshot, and is easily recognizable by the **Run**, **Commit**, and **Rollback** buttons on the top left-hand side. These are initially unavailable until you select a connection, which then brings them into focus, making them available.

The PL/SQL editor is easily identifiable by the search field and the **Compile** button, as shown in the following screenshot:

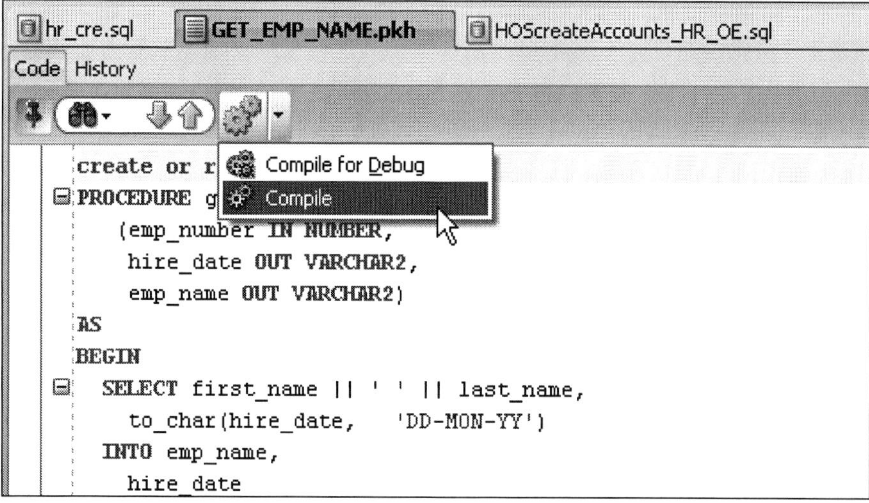

If you want to compile a PL/SQL file, you need to access a database connection by selecting the connection from the drop-down list on the right-hand side.

Editing other file types

You can also open and edit other file types using SQL Developer. An editor is still opened for these, allowing you to make updates and save the changes. For these files, there is no additional database connections drop-down list. SQL Developer color formats reserved words for all supported file types. In the example shown in the following screenshot, two files are open: an SQL and an XML file. In both cases, SQL Developer recognizes and formats any reserved words.

You can also see the differences between these two file types, with the file on the left displaying an **SQL Worksheet** and **History** tab together with the connections drop-down list. The file in the editor on the right has none of these:

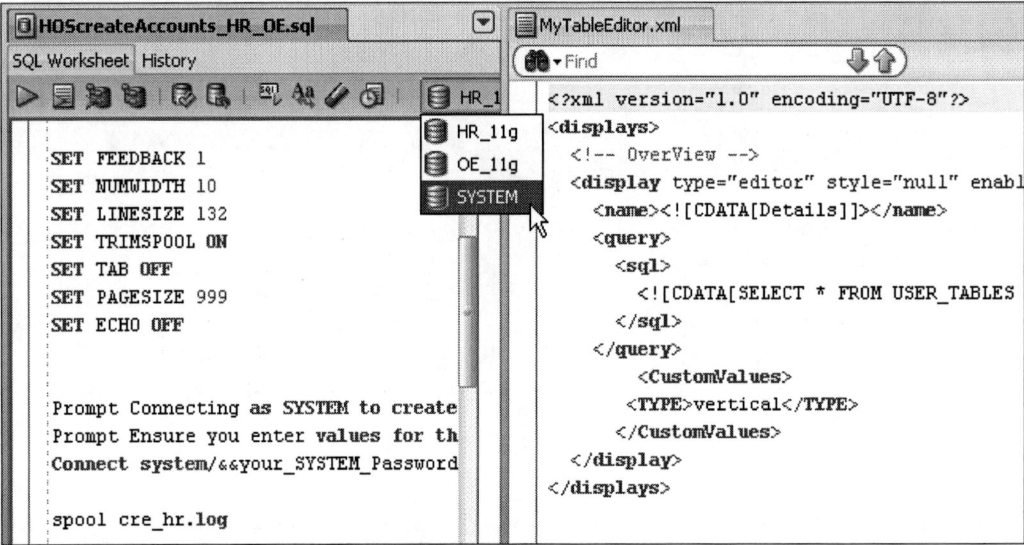

Working with the file history

The SQL Worksheet and PL/SQL file editors both have an editor and a **History** window. For files not under version control management, you can use the history management available for comparing the file on disc and the file opened. For files under version control, there is a history of file activity, and so you can select and review the individual files and make updates.

In the example shown in the following screenshot, the changes made to the file are clearly marked, together with different options for accepting or overriding the changes. The options available are:

- File options
    - Purge Local History
    - Restore from Revision
- Individual line edits
    - Replace Adjacent Difference
    - Insert after Adjacent Difference
    - Delete Difference

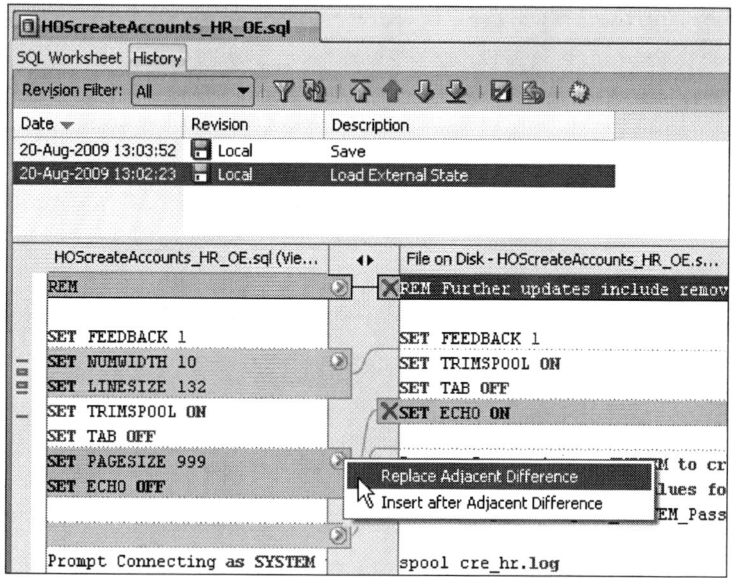

Introducing the Versioning Navigator

To open the Versioning Navigator, select **Team | Versioning Navigator** from the **View** menu. The **Versioning Navigator** opens below the **Files** navigator by default. While you can rearrange these to suit your needs, you will typically work with these together. The **Versioning Navigator** displays **Subversion** and if you added CVS or Perforce using the **Check for Updates** utility, they are displayed here too. You need only display the system you are working with. By hiding any others, you can reduce the menu options offered. To hide either of the default version control systems, select **Versioning | Configure...**.

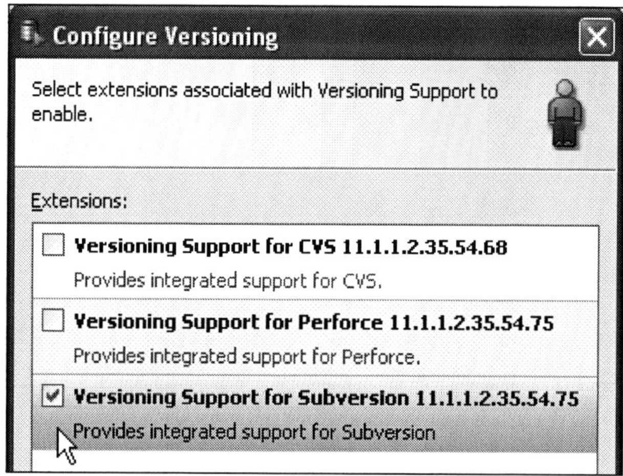

Managing general version control preferences

SQL Developer provides a set of preferences for controlling various aspects of version management. For example, for CVS, you can specify whether you need to separately install the **CVS Client** or want to use the client installed with SQL Developer. You can also specify the overlay system, used to indicate the versioning status. To change or review the versioning preferences, select **Versioning** in the **Preferences** dialog. A set of general Subversion versioning preferences is shown in the following screenshot:

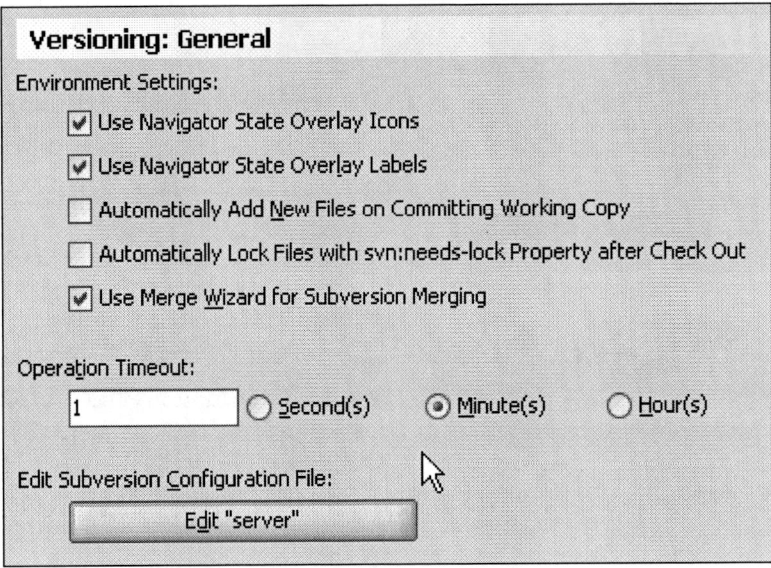

We will refer to other versioning preferences as required in the sections ahead.

Setting up the repository

Before you start versioning files, you need to have access to, or set up, a version repository. We'll then use SQL Developer as a client interface to the repository.

Working with the Subversion repository

When using Subversion, you can use SQL Developer to create the repository from within the product. To do this, select **Versioning | Create Local Repository…**. The process is straightforward as you provide the path and a connection name.

In most cases, if your team is working with Subversion, the repository will already be available and in use so you can just access the existing repository. If you do not yet have a repository, we recommend that you set this up outside of SQL Developer. This way, you can plan and lay out your repository as required, and then manage it independently from outside SQL Developer. Either way, you can access the repository and files using SQL Developer and other Subversion clients.

Creating a Subversion repository from within SQL Developer creates a single node. Using an external tool to create the repository means that you can create the branches and tags nodes in addition to the trunk.

Adding CVS repositories

SQL Developer allows you to access one or more CVS repositories locally or on a remote central server. You can create a new CVS repository using SQL Developer if you have installed external CVS client software. To determine whether you use external client software or internal CVS client installed with SQL Developer, select **Tools | Preferences** and then select **Versioning | CVS**.

Creating connections to a version repository

Select the versioning tool of your choice in the list displayed in the **Versioning Navigator** and invoke the context menu. Before you can start, you need to create a new connection to your version repository. Once created, it is useful to export any or all of the connections to an XML file. You can offer this to other team members or save it for the future. At any point, if you need to recreate the connections, you can import the connections from file.

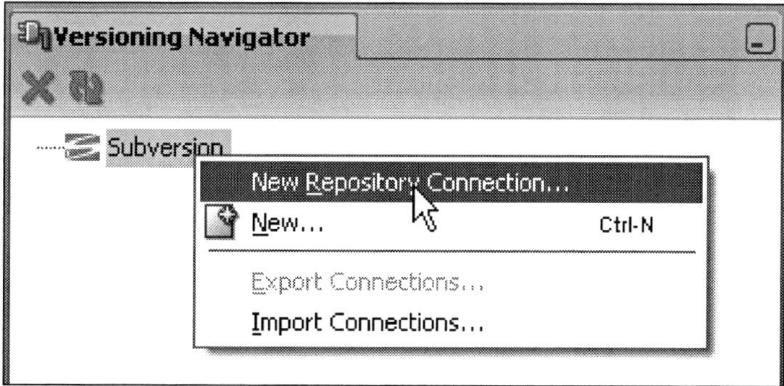

The **New...** menu option displayed in the context menu previously shown invokes the **New Gallery** dialog. This provides more generic options for creating new connections.

> **Exporting and importing connections**
>
> You can export and import versioning connections in the same way as you can export and import a regular database connection. Use the context menu options available for the version tool in the **Versioning Navigator**.

When creating the new connection, you need to provide the location of the repository, the connection name, and the username and password. In general, you will provide the URL for a central server. This URL could be:

- `http://` for access to the repository using a WebDav protocol
- `https://` for access using a WebDav protocol with SSL encryption
- `svn://` for access using a custom protocol to an svnserve Server
- `svn+ssh://` for access using a custom protocol to an svnserve Server using an SSH tunnel

For more details on these, and recommendations on the best configuration to use, refer to the Subversion Redbook (`http://svnbook.red-bean.com/`).

In the example shown in the following screenshot, the repository resides on the local machine. Therefore, so the URL provided is to a local file, using `file:///` .

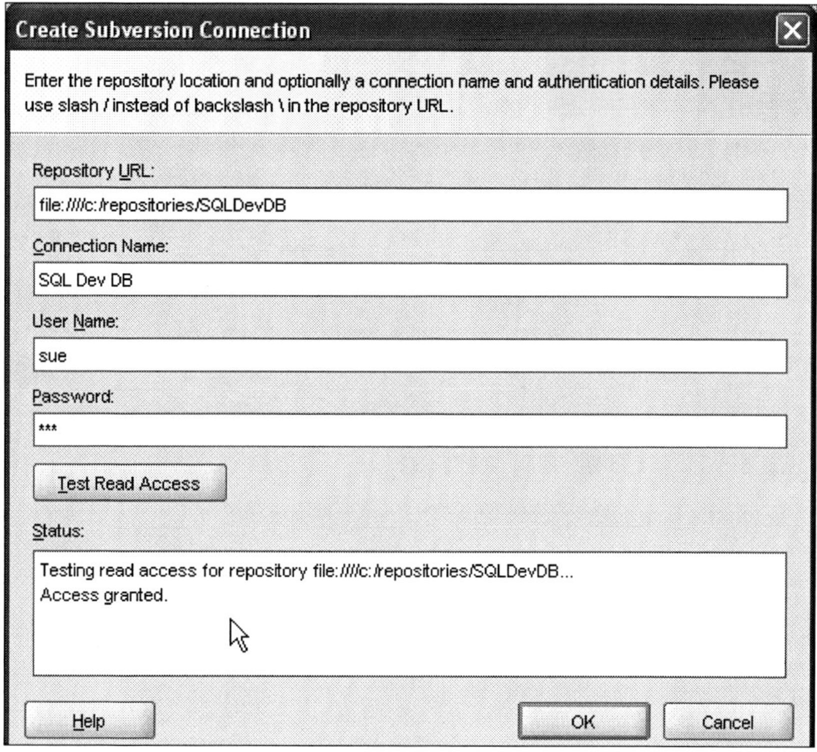

Browsing files in the repository

Once you have a connection to the repository, you can browse and review the contents. Files opened at this level are not editable, as you are viewing them from within the repository. However, you can still open them to verify if the file or contents are what you are looking for:

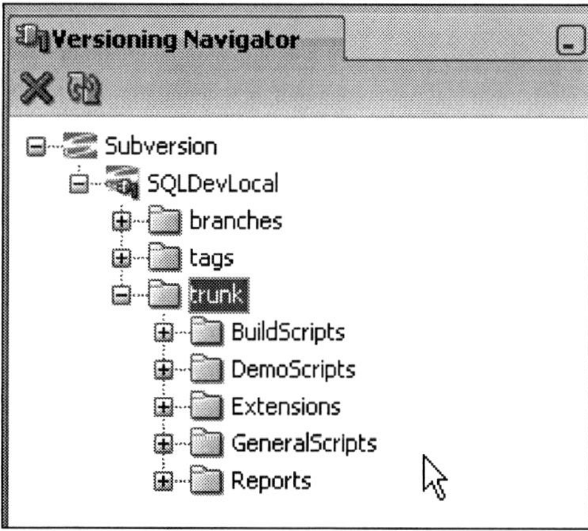

Working with files under version control

Source code control management differs from tool to tool, but in general, there are more similarities than differences. If you have more than one versioning extension installed, you'll see the different menus offered under the main **Versioning** menu. In all cases, the files are placed in a repository as the central point of truth. To work on and edit files, you need to first check them out. To make changes available for other users, the files should be checked back in. Where differences exist, these need to be reviewed and the files merged.

Of the tools used and supported by SQL Developer, Subversion is currently the more widely used, and so we will use Subversion for all of the examples that follow.

Placing files under version control

To start the process, you need to move any files you are working on into the repository. The repository is your point of truth. Therefore, all of the files that are not checked into the repository should be considered as working documents and can be discarded without affecting the contents of the repository.

For further details on the concepts about versioning files using Subversion, refer to Subversion's Red Book.

Importing files into the repository

You can quickly pull a selection of files and their directories into your Subversion repository using the **Import Files** menu option.

With the **Files** navigator active, select the main **Versioning** menu, and then use **Import Files** from the **Subversion** context menu:

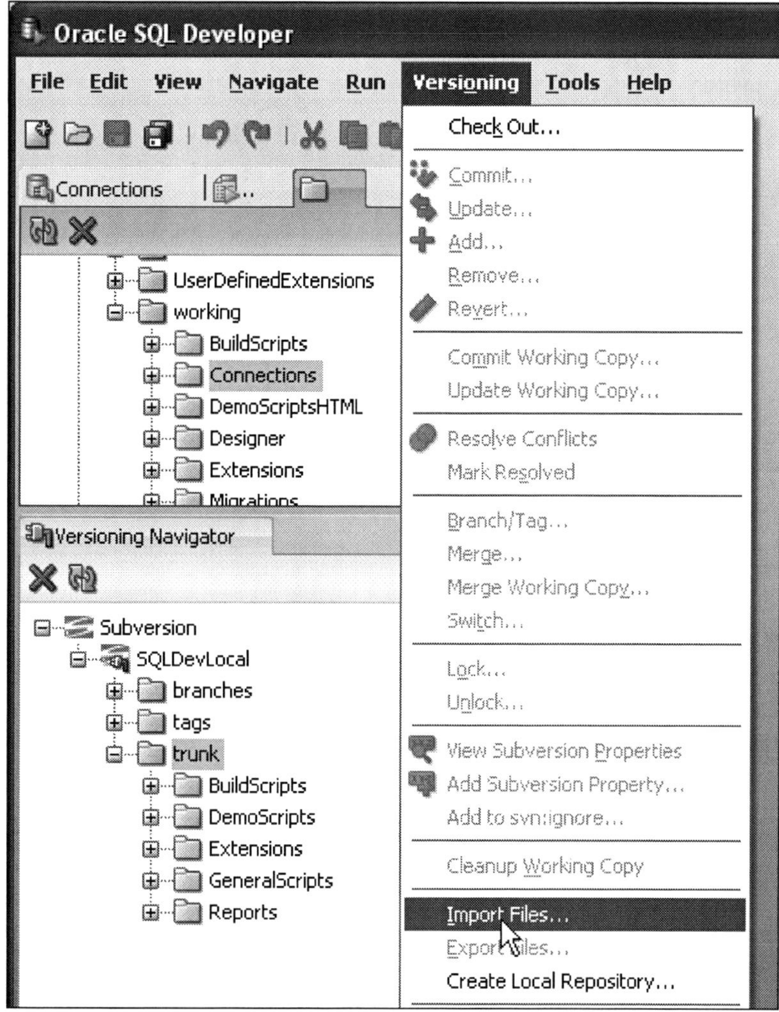

Importing files into the repository

The **Import Files** menu is only available when you have a directory selected in the **Files** navigator.

Once you have the **Import** dialog active, follow the directions for each of the panels. The general advice is that you have a main **trunk** directory for your primary development (often called the main line), and **branches** and **tags** directories for additional tag and branch copies.

Working with directories

In the example in the following screenshot, if you select **trunk** for the import, all of the files will be imported into the repository at the trunk level. You should create, or select, a directory under the trunk node, and import the files into that. This keeps the files more organized. You can either expand the trunk and navigate to the directory of your choice, or use the **Create New Remote Directory** button, marked on the right of the dialog (seen below), to add new directories in at this stage. Alternatively, you can plan the repository directory structure in the navigator, before you start the import, by adding directories to the high-level nodes as required. You then need only navigate to and select them in the import dialog.

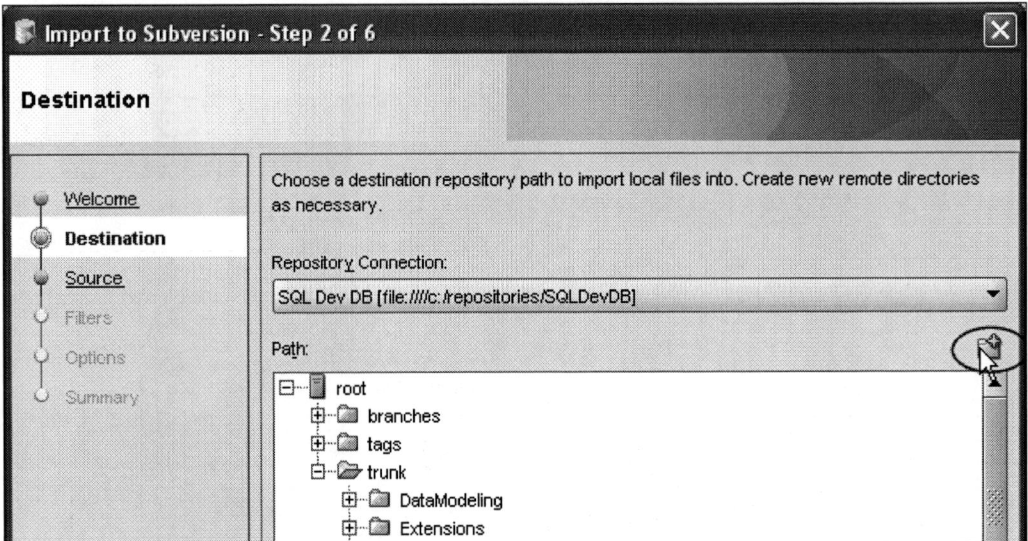

Once you have selected or created a new directory to store your files, you need to select the location of the files and directories you want to import. This is the source directory.

Performing a Check Out after import

Before you complete the import wizard, you are given two choices:

- **Do Not Recurse**—do you want to step through the sub-directories within the main directory that you have selected?
- **Perform Checkout**—do you want all of the files to be checked out once the import is complete?

We generally leave both of these deselected. In so doing, we get all of the files and additional subdirectories included on import, with none of the files checked out after the first import.

Refreshing the repository

Once you have completed an import of directories and files into the repository, refresh the **Versioning Navigator**. Do this by clicking the **Refresh** button in the **Versioning Navigator**. The new directories and files are now displayed in the repository.

Once you have refreshed the repository, you'll see the list of new directories and files. In the following screenshot, you can see the files in the file system and those now registered in the repository. These are now the point of truth so you can discard the initial working copy. From this point on, you should check the files out of the repository and work on those, before checking them back in.

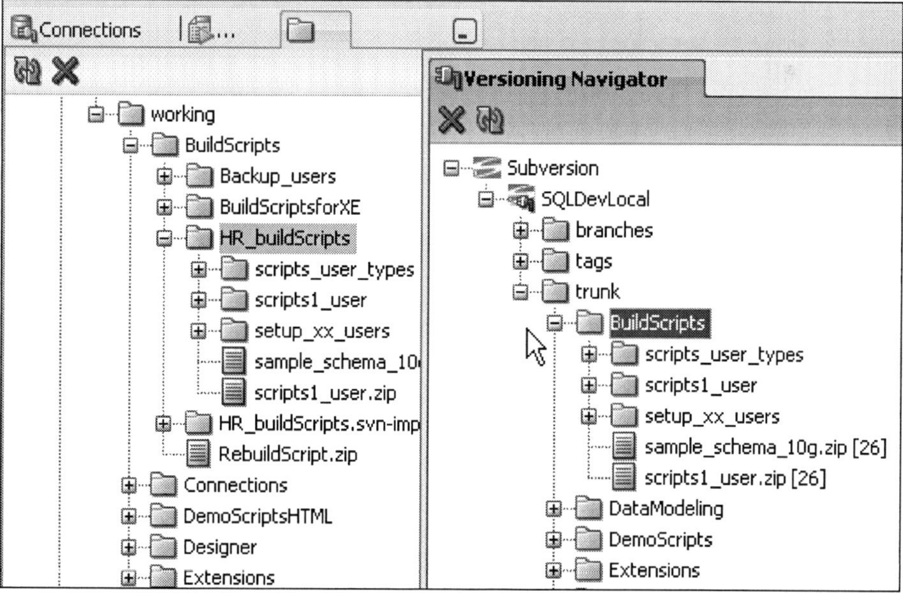

Understanding revision numbers

Subversion supports global revision numbers, which means that each revision applies to the complete tree. In the example in the previous screenshot, the DDL Scripts are newly imported into the repository. The repository itself is an active repository with a number of other directories checked in. The latest revision number of the repository is then applied to the new directory of files checked in. The revision numbers of working copies of files may differ, but each time you check files in, the version of the repository increases and the new files pick up the new revision number.

Checking out files

Although you can check out files as a final stage of the import process in SQL Developer, checking out files is an activity that you repeat, whereas importing the initial files into the repository is a one-off step. Once the files are in the repository, you will check out any files you want to work on, and then check the files back into the repository, and then merge the changes as required.

To check out the files, select the directory that contains the files you want to work with and invoke the context menu **Check Out...**.

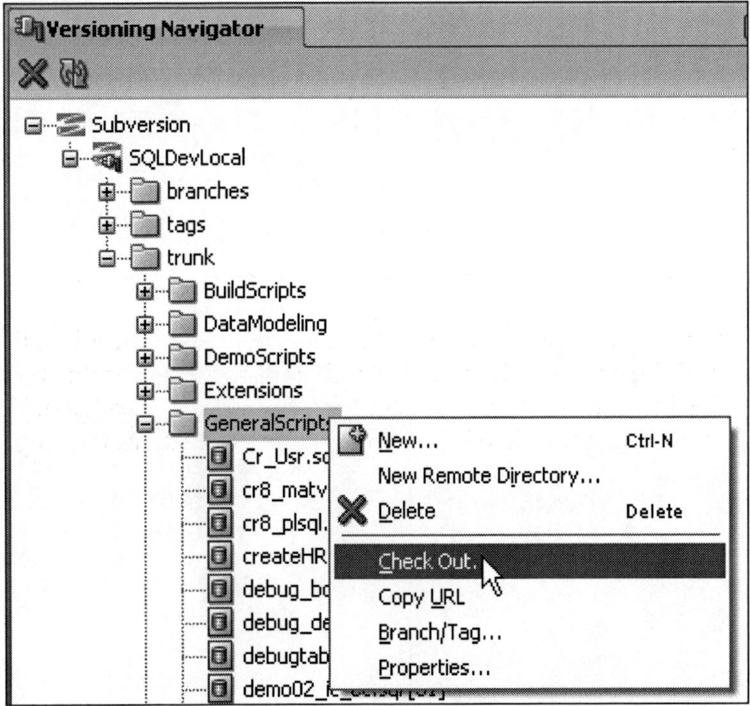

The files you are checking out will be working copies, so you need to create a "working copy" location. You can either create a new folder for this purpose before you start the checkout, or you can add a new folder using the **Check Out from Subversion** dialog.

Identifying checked out files

Once the files have been checked out, refresh the directory that now contains the new working copy. Visual indicators appear on the files, indicating the current state of the file.

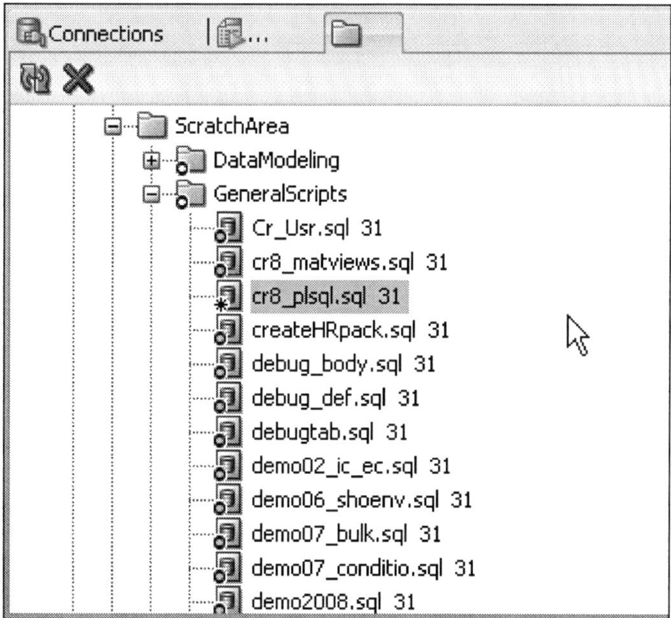

In the example in the previous screenshot, the files displayed in the SQL Developer **Files** navigator all indicate they have been checked out. Except for the third file in the list, all of the files indicate they have been checked out, but not updated. The * marks the single file that has been updated, but not yet checked back into the repository.

Tracking the working copy

Subversion keeps track of the state of these working copies in the `.svn` folder, which is added when you first check out the files. Details of the revision of the working copy and the timestamp are maintained. You can see the `.svn` folder in the file explorer, outside SQL Developer:

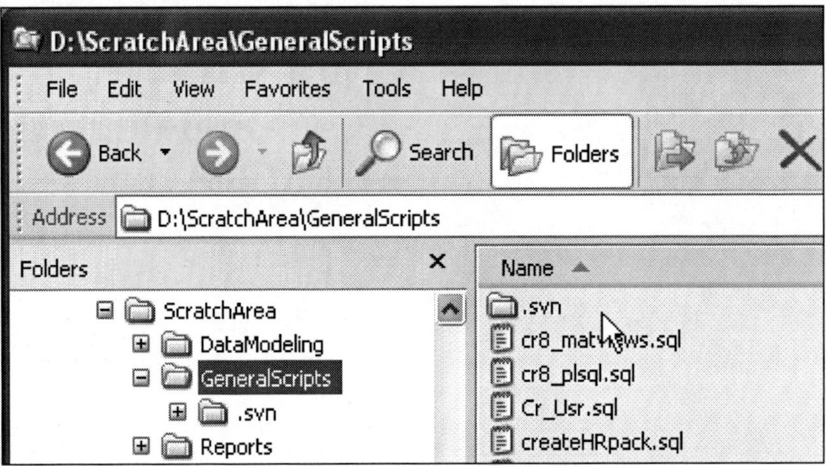

Saving files

Once you start editing files in your working copy directory, you can save them to maintain any changes you have made. This does not impact the files in the repository, but saves the changes to the local working copy. As illustrated in the example (in the screenshot above), you can visually keep track of files that have been changed and saved before they are committed back to the repository.

Pending changes preferences

As you edit and save files, keep track of all pending changes by displaying a **Pending Changes** window. To invoke this window, select **Versioning | Pending Changes** from either the context menu on the file itself, or from the main **Versioning** menu, with the file or the **Files** navigator selected.

This **Pending Changes** window lists the various files you are currently working on. It includes files that have been:

- Modified locally, these are listed under the **Outgoing** tab
- Added locally, but not yet added to source control, these are **Candidates**
- Modified or added at a remote location, these are listed as **Incoming**

Click on the **Comments** button to open the section, which is closed by default to save real estate.

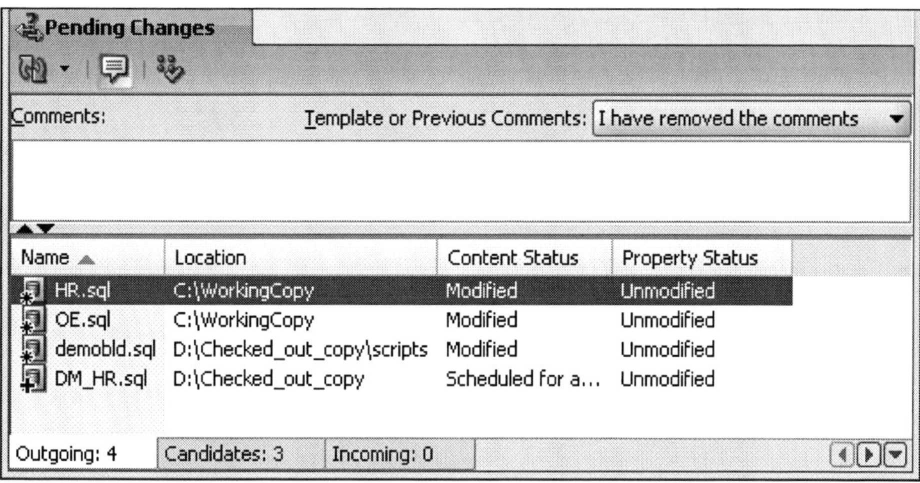

In the previous screenshot, the **Pending Changes** window has been undocked and displays a number of files. Some of the files have an icon indicating they have been saved. The last of the files was added from the **Candidates** list.

You can check in the files from this **Pending Changes** window, or from the Versioning menus available. SQL Developer offers a preference to use the detail in the **Pending Changes** window without invoking an additional **Commit Resources** dialog. In the example shown in the following screenshot, the additional **Commit Resources** dialog is displayed if the **Pending Changes** comment section is hidden. This choice allows the user to add check in comments at that stage:

Subversion: Version Tools
Pending Changes Window:
Use Outgoing Changes Commit Dialog:
Always
When Comments Hidden
Never
Incoming Changes Timer Interval:
15 Minute(s) Hour(s)
Merge Editor:
Merge Files Locally
Merge Files at Server

Checking files in

Once you start to work with and edit files, changes are only made available to other users after the files are checked back into the repository. You have a number of available options when working with these files, as shown in the **Versioning** context menu in the following screenshot:

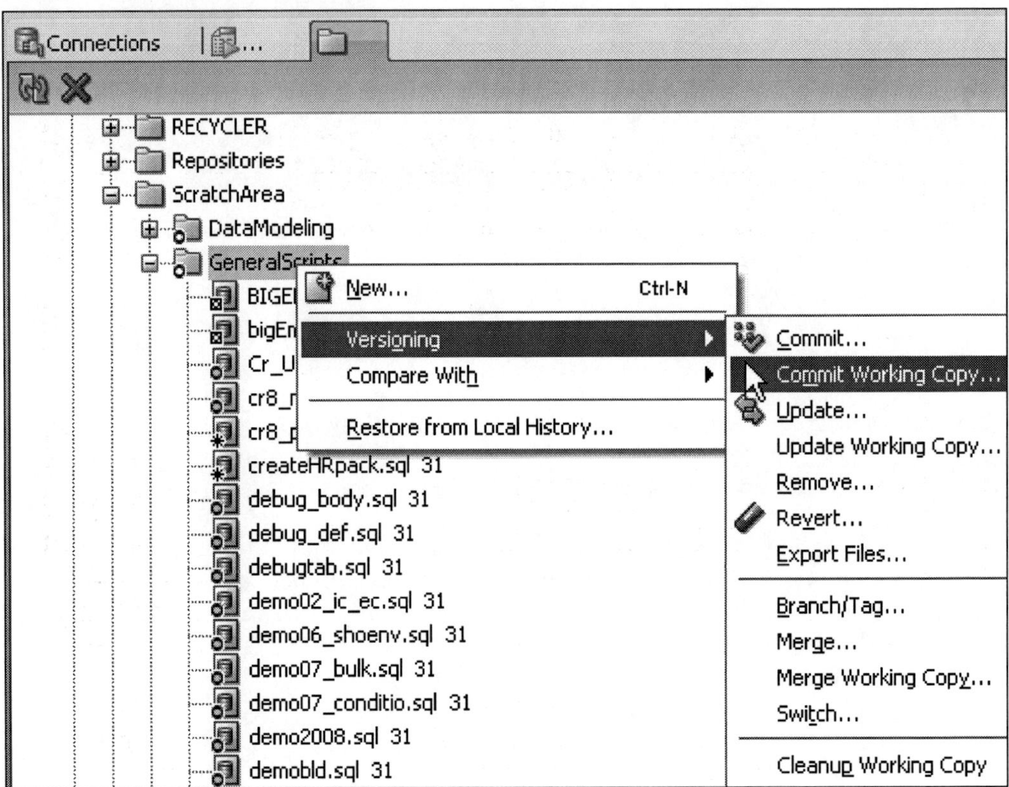

Updating the working copy

If you have checked out a directory of files that you and other team members are all working on, then it is easier to get updates to the files before you check your change back into the repository. In this case, you can pull any changes made and updated in the repository by selecting **Update...** from the **Versioning** context menu. If you want to update all of the changed files in your local working copy directory, then select **Update Working Copy...**. When updating files, you can select which revision you want to use to update the file.

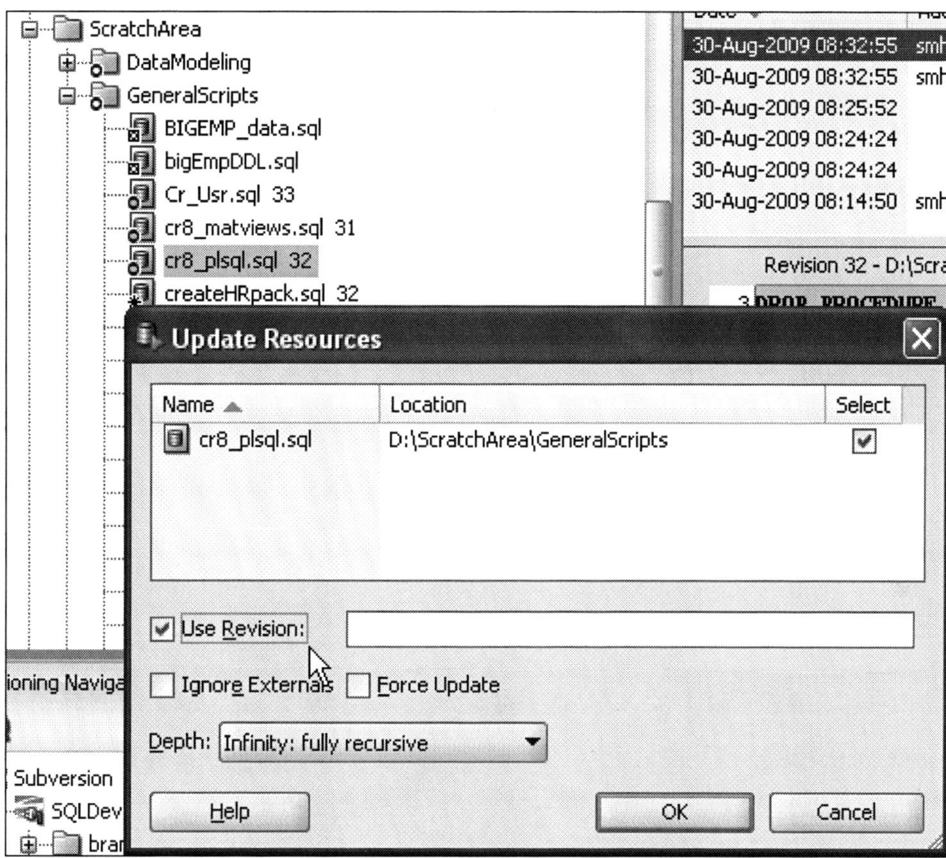

The example in the previous screenshot shows a file with its revision history displayed. As you step through the various revisions, you can see the changes made. You can update your working copy with a revision of your choice.

Reverting changes

If you have started working on a file, and don't want the changes made, you can just discard the working copy and start again since the repository does not keep a track of the checked out files. However, if you have a number of files updated in your directory and only need to go back to the original version of the current file, then use **Revert...** from the context menu. Reverting the changes overwrites the local file with the latest file in the repository, replacing any changes that you may have made.

Committing changes to the repository

You should commit your working copy changes to update the file or files in the repository. This saves your work and makes any updates available to other users. If you have a single file to commit, select **Commit...** from the context menu for that file. Alternatively, select **Versioning | Commit Working Copy...**, which commits all of the saved and as yet uncommitted files to the repository, updating the revision numbers for all to the latest repository revision number.

Versioning menu options are available on the main toolbar **Versioning** menu. They are also available in the **Versioning** context menu for the files or directories you are working on.

Comparing and merging code

Unless you have placed a lock out on the files you are working on, you may need to handle conflicts if the files have been updated since you checked them out. The **Subversion Merge Wizard** provides a selection of merge types, as shown in the following screenshot:

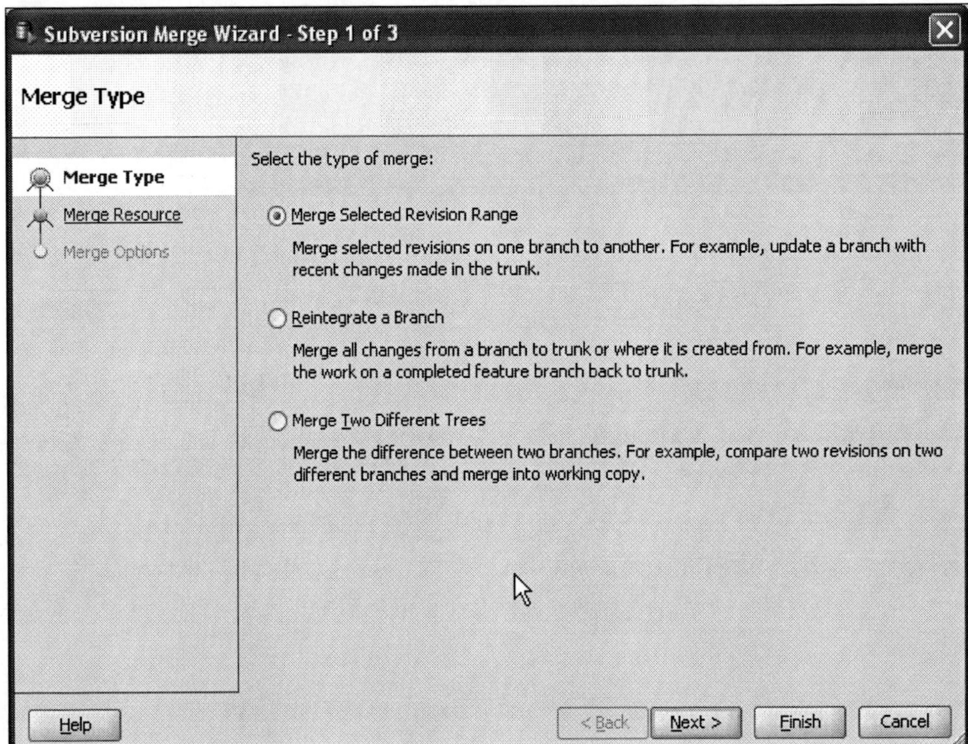

Once you have selected the type of merge and details of the merge, you have a choice of merge options which includes the ability to force the merge or to ignore the file ancestry.

Creating patches

Create a patch to collect the changes created between two files. You can then apply these changes to other files by applying the patch. To create a patch, open the file with the changes and select the **Generate Patch...** button:

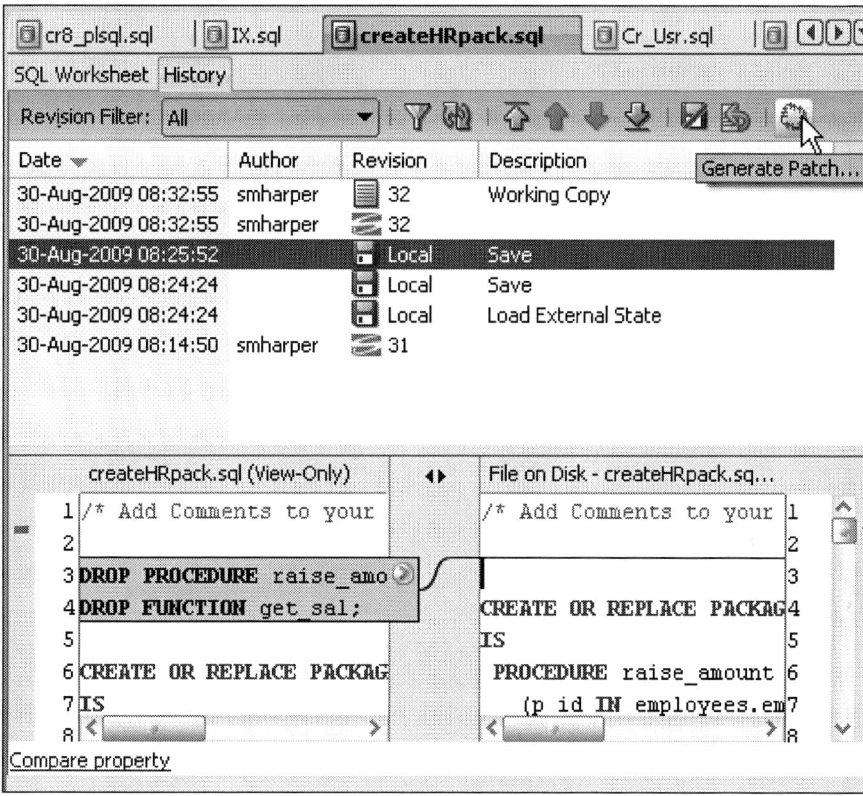

In the case of SQL Developer, the patch dialog that opens gives a choice of sending the patch to the clipboard, or opening it in the patch editor. This allows you to see the revisions and make updates as required:

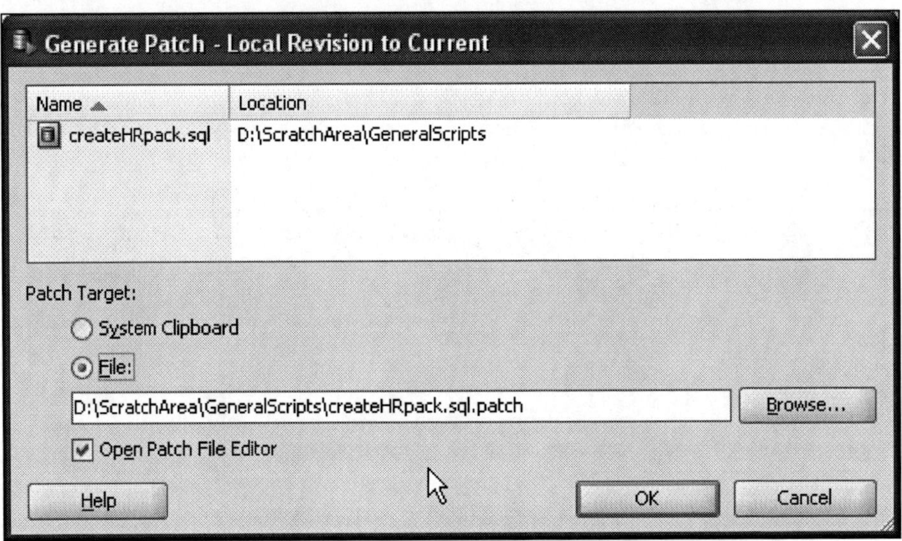

Once you have reviewed the patch, select **Apply Patch...** from the main **Versioning** menu. This opens a new patch preview dialog with a list of all of the changes made between the files. There is still an opportunity to select those changes you want applied.

Summary

In this chapter, we looked at the integration of SQL Developer and open source version control systems CVS and Subversion. All users who work with files on a regular basis should have some method of managing and maintaining them. Having a rigorous process in place together with an underlying version code tool, makes this task easier. SQL Developer provides integrated support, which means you can work easily with the version control system of your choice. It provides menu access to the repository and allows you to place files under version control, check out, edit, and check them back in. Without in-depth details on the full process of managing files under version control, this chapter provided an overview of how you can use SQL Developer as a client in this task.

In the next chapter, we'll look at the various utilities provided for moving or copying both the data structures and the instance data between schemas and databases. We'll introduce the schema copy, diff, and export wizards, and discuss the various related export and import utilities.

8

Importing, Exporting, and Working with Data

Working with one or more databases during development cycles, will invariably mean that developers need to replicate schemas between different databases, such as test and production, or they need to test data based on a subset of instance data. To do this, developers need to produce easily replicable scripts that copy and move data from one database instance to another, or from one schema to another.

"Data" means many things to people. Here, data is both the instance data (rows in a table) and metadata (object definitions, such as tables, stored in the Data Dictionary). In this chapter we look at the variety of options offered in SQL Developer, specifically we'll look at exporting instance data and metadata and at importing instance data. We'll show the different options available when copying instance and metadata from one schema to another and at comparing metadata between two schemas. We'll look at how to create and then use the scripts produced. The choices you make depend on the activity and the desired results.

Exporting data

In this section, we'll look at the various options and utilities provided by SQL Developer to export either instance data or metadata. The utilities range from copy and paste to wizard-driven export and import, and we'll progress from quick and easy to more involved.

Exporting instance data

Throughout SQL Developer, data of different types is displayed in data grids, whether you are querying the definitions of a table by clicking on the table in the **Connections** navigator, running a report, running a query from the SQL Worksheet, or selecting the **Data** tab for a table. All of these data grids have a set of standard context menus, which include exporting the data in the grid to various file formats. In the following example, the **Export Data** context menu has been invoked for the **EMPLOYEES** table's **Columns** display editor:

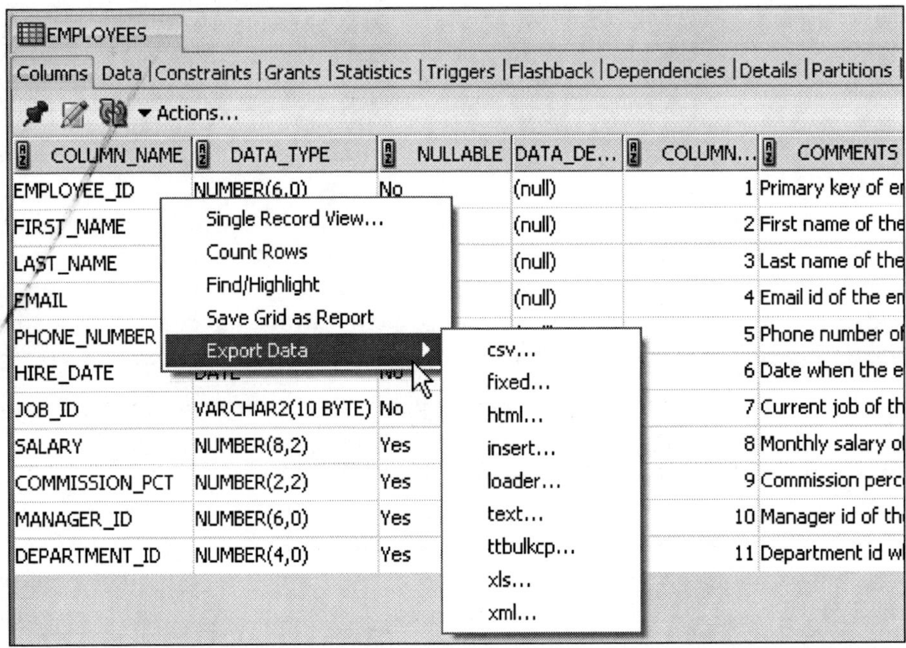

Another powerful method of exporting the data is to specify a query in the SQL Worksheet. Run the query using the **Run Statement** (*F9*) command. This returns the data in a grid and you'll have access to the same context menu as before.

The choice of file formats for exporting the data is:

- CSV—comma separated values
- Fixed—space delimited file
- HTML—HTML tagged text
- Insert—SQL DML commands
- Loader—SQL Loader file format
- Text—unstructured text

- Ttbulkcp—TimesTen Bulk Copy (this is only visible if the TimesTen is setup on your desktop)
- XLS— Microsoft Excel spreadsheet
- XML—XML tagged text

Exporting table data

To export the data for a specific table, select the table in the **Connections** navigator, and right-click to invoke the **Export Data** context menu. This displays the same **Export Data** menu shown on any data grid. The advantage of using the context menu in the navigator is that it pre-populates the **Table** name in the dialog.

For each of these formats, as seen in the following screenshot, you can elect to write the text to a:

- File, specifying the location
- Clipboard, and paste it to a location of choice

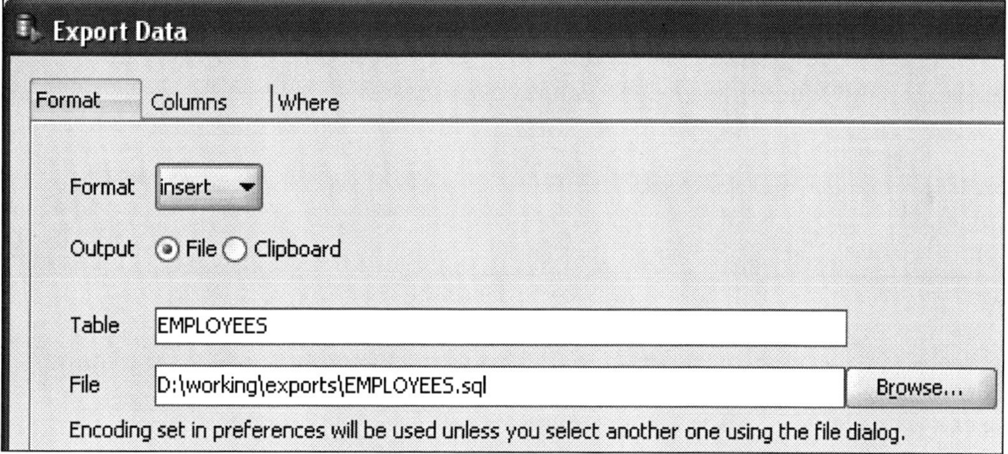

You can browse to find and set the file location, or you can set the default export location in the **Preferences** dialog. Select **Database** from the tree, and set the default location, as shown in the following screenshot:

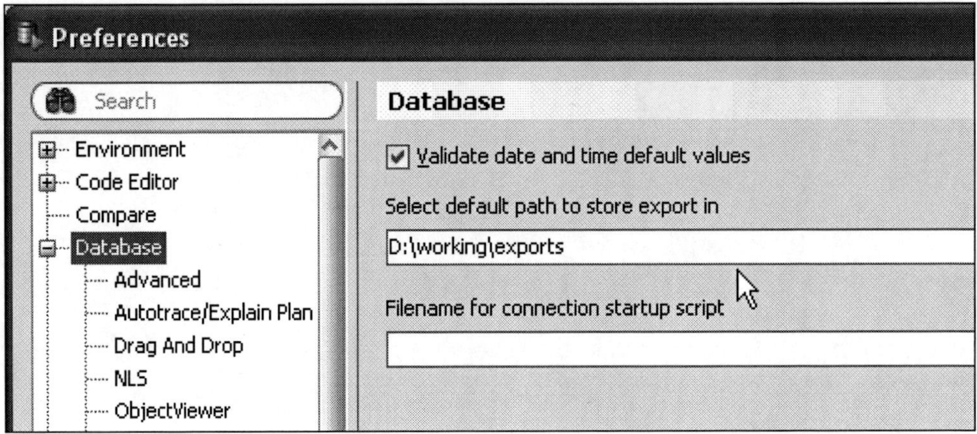

You can set a preference to handle file encoding on export. Select **Tools | Preferences,** select the **Environment** node in the tree, and set **File Encoding**. The export output is written out using the specified encoding. There is an additional **File Encoding** drop-down list on the **Export File Chooser** dialog. If selected, this overrides the preference set.

Setting up the export file

Whether you are invoking **Export Data**, for a particular table in the **Connections** navigator, or from the table's data grid, the default output includes all of the columns and data. This is also true if you have run one of the shipped SQL Developer reports. If you want to export any subset of data from any of these or the other data grids available, you can change the number of rows of data exported, or even the columns in the grid, using the **Export Data** dialog to restrict the export detail. The first choice is selecting the columns that you want to export:

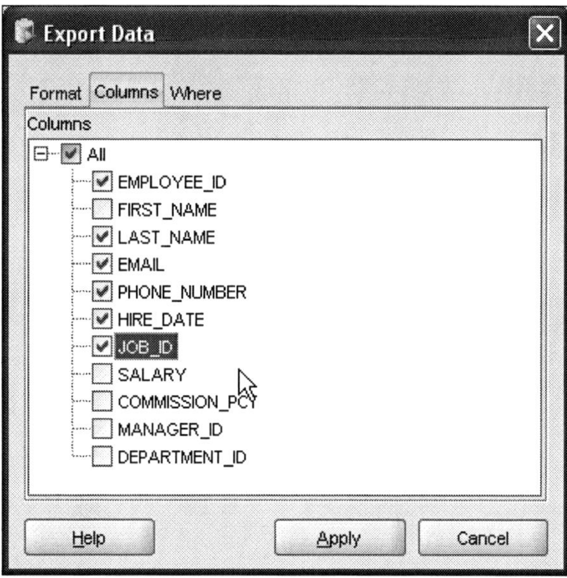

Once you have the columns selected, you can also restrict the data returned. Add the `WHERE CLAUSE` restriction criteria and click on **Go** to restrict the data returned.

> If you modify the number of rows returned by including the **Where clause**, the query is only re-run on clicking on **Go**, and not by clicking on **Apply**, which merely writes the data to file.

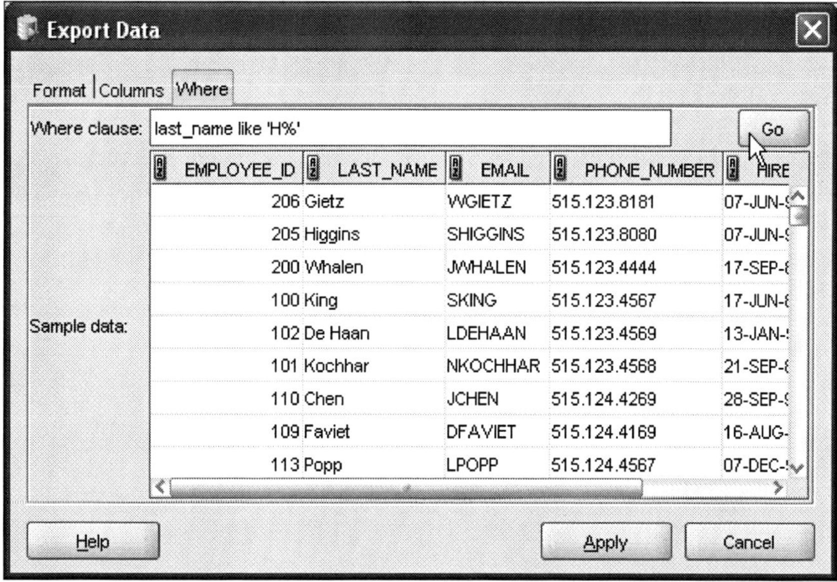

Instead of using the dialog, if you set up the query in the SQL Worksheet, you'll need to write the query to ensure it contains exactly the data that you want to export. Indeed, some file formats, such as XLS, have a maximum records file size. Therefore, you're advised to limit the data you want to export. Once the data is prepared and ready, you can simply invoke the context menu to export the data. Select the file format and location, and run the export.

Preparing the contents of data grid for export

You can sort, filter, and rearrange column order on data grids. If you make any changes to the data grids before exporting the data, the updated detail is reflected in the exported file.

Exporting SQL DML

Creating an SQL script file of insert commands is very useful when creating sets of test data. You can then modify and update the data at will and then re-run the script to restore the data to the initial state. To create the SQL DML commands, select **Export Data | insert** from the context menu.

If you export this format to clipboard, then open an SQL Worksheet and paste (*Ctrl+V*), you are then in an ideal position to run the script. Ensure you provided the correct table name in the **Export Data** dialog. If, for example, you write an SQL query and then invoke the **Export Data** dialog, the **Table** field is "table_export", so you'd need to update that field as needed.

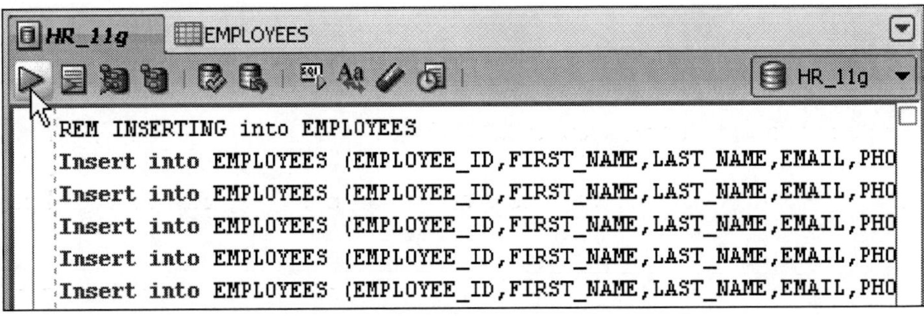

Exporting to HTML

You can export the data to HTML format. To create the HTML, select **Export Data | html** from the context menu. Once created, you can store the file on a central server and display it in a browser. This is very useful when you need to share data with other users, without providing any update permissions. The exported HTML file includes a basic search box, allowing users to further restrict the records displayed. In the following screenshot, the file shown is open in a browser:

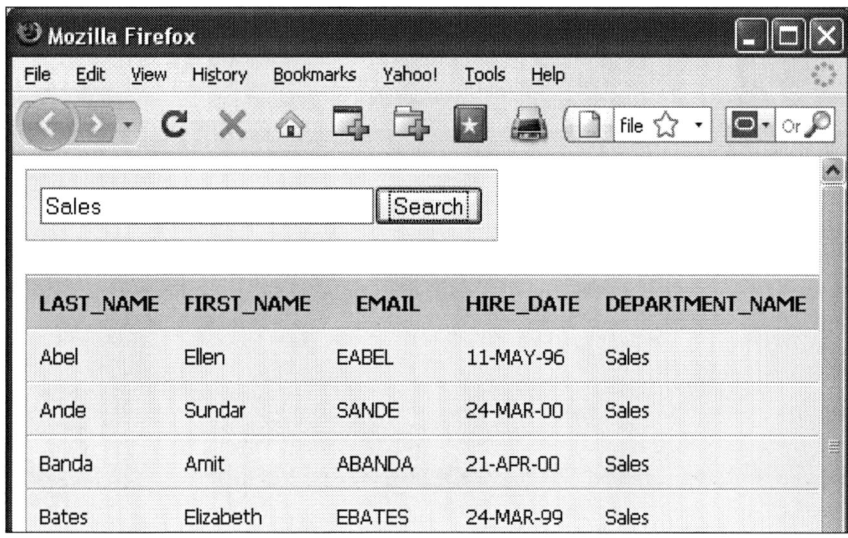

Supporting export for SQL*Loader

SQL Developer supports exporting data to an SQL*Loader file. Select **Export Data | loader** from the context menu to create the SQL*Loader file. Once created, you can use SQL*Loader to load the data into the Oracle database. The file format is set by SQL Developer, so you don't have the option to set parameters to control the Loader file format.

To create a working example, enter the following query into the SQL Worksheet:

```
select E.FIRST_NAME,
  E.EMAIL ,
  E.HIRE_DATE ,
  E.LAST_NAME,
  D.DEPARTMENT_NAME
from EMPLOYEES E,
  DEPARTMENTS D
where E.DEPARTMENT_ID = D.DEPARTMENT_ID;
```

- Click on the **Run Statement** button (or press the *F9* key)
- Right-click in the data grid and select the **Export Data | loader** option from the context menu
- Set the **Table** and **File** values as required
- Click on **Apply**

The default control file created in SQL Developer, based on the example that we have just seen, is structured as follows:

```
LOAD DATA
INFILE *
TRUNCATE
INTO TABLE "EMPLOYEES"
FIELDS TERMINATED BY '|'
TRAILING NULLCOLS (
FIRST_NAME,
EMAIL,
HIRE_DATE timestamp "DD-MON-RR",
LAST_NAME,
DEPARTMENT_NAME)
begindata
Whalen|Jennifer|JWHALEN|17-SEP-87|Administration
Hartstein|Michael|MHARTSTE|17-FEB-96|Marketing
Fay|Pat|PFAY|17-AUG-97|Marketing
```

Exporting to Microsoft Excel

SQL Developer supports the export of data to Microsoft Excel (XLS) format. This is one of the more popular export formats. The data, once in the Microsoft Excel spreadsheet, is easily used for graphs and statistical review. To create the Microsoft Excel file, select **Export Data | xls** from the context menu. In this instance, the **Table** field in the **Export Data** dialog is not available. You only need to provide a file name and make the columns and **Where clause** choices. The new file, when opened in Microsoft Excel, also includes the column headings.

It's important to be aware that there are limitations when working with large sets of data. There is a 65,536 row limit in Microsoft Excel, so SQL Developer writes the records to new worksheets when 65,000 is reached. In addition, working with an XLS file, SQL Developer loads all of the records into memory before writing. If the XLS file is significantly large, you can run out of memory. If this is an issue, then edit the `sqldeveloper.conf` file in the `<YourDirectory>\sqldeveloper\sqldeveloper\bin` directory and increase the heap size by increasing the default value set to `AddVMOption -Xmx1024M`.

Exporting to XML

The SQL Developer **Data Export** also supports export to XML. To create an XML file, based on the data in the grid, select **Export Data | xml** using the context menu. A single row of data, in this case from the **EMPLOYEES** table, exported to XML follows a structured format as follows:

```
<ROW>
  <COLUMN NAME="EMPLOYEE_ID"><![CDATA[100]]></COLUMN>
  <COLUMN NAME="FIRST_NAME"><![CDATA[Steven]]></COLUMN>
  <COLUMN NAME="LAST_NAME"><![CDATA[King]]></COLUMN>
  <COLUMN NAME="EMAIL"><![CDATA[SKING]]></COLUMN>
  <COLUMN NAME="PHONE_NUMBER"><![CDATA[515.123.4567]]></COLUMN>
  <COLUMN NAME="HIRE_DATE"><![CDATA[17-JUN-87]]></COLUMN>
  <COLUMN NAME="JOB_ID"><![CDATA[AD_PRES]]></COLUMN>
  <COLUMN NAME="SALARY"><![CDATA[24000]]></COLUMN>
  <COLUMN NAME="COMMISSION_PCT"><![CDATA[]]></COLUMN>
  <COLUMN NAME="MANAGER_ID"><![CDATA[]]></COLUMN>
  <COLUMN NAME="DEPARTMENT_ID"><![CDATA[90]]></COLUMN>
</ROW>
```

Exporting data to XML has great benefit in broader application development, since the structure of the XML file means that you can use this data in other applications. It may be more common to export the metadata for reuse than the instance data in this case.

Exporting DDL (Metadata)

One of the most basic tasks you can perform with SQL Developer, once you have created a connection, is to select a table in the **Connections** navigator. In earlier chapters, we discussed the various display editors that are invoked by this action. At this point, we're only interested in the SQL display editor. The SQL display editor for any object selected in the **Connections** navigator displays the SQL code required to recreate the object in question, the **Data Definition Language** (**DDL**). The SQL is derived from executing procedure calls to the package `DBMS_METADATA`. Once opened, you can simply select, copy, and paste the SQL text into the SQL Worksheet to run it or save it to a file to run later.

Exporting table DDL

If you're working with the default settings provided by SQL Developer, selecting the SQL display editor for a table reveals an involved `CREATE TABLE` statement, as shown in the following screenshot:

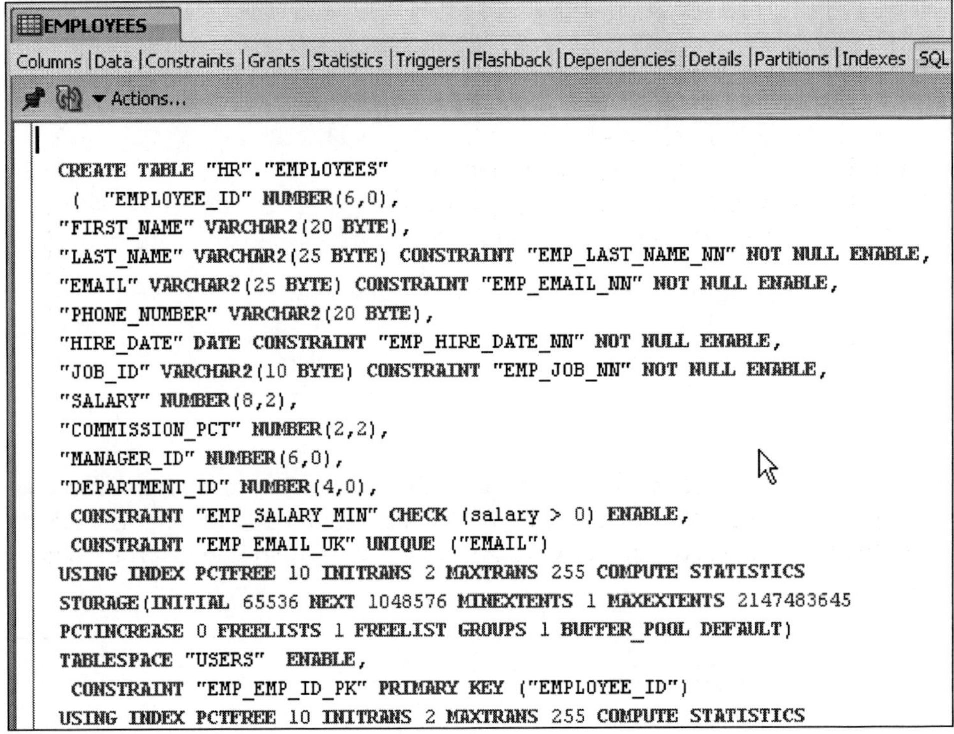

This is useful if you want to reproduce the exact `HR.EMPLOYEES` table, with all of its storage details, for your database. However, if you want to use the text to create this table in another schema or in another database, you need to strip away some of that extra detail. To do this, you can set preferences, by selecting the **Database** node in the **Tools | Preferences** dialog. Select **ObjectViewer** and change the settings. In the following screenshot, we have deselected the **Show Storage** and **Show Schema** properties:

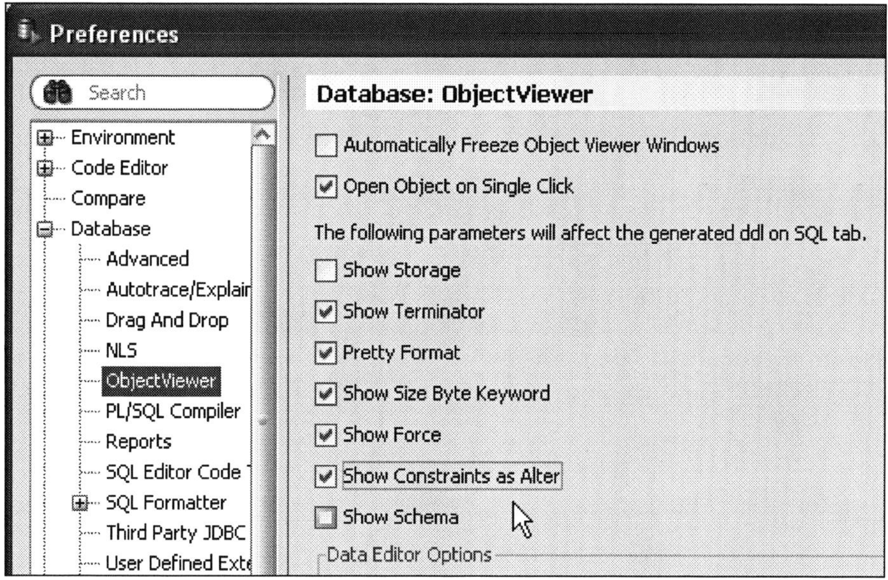

The parameter settings here are passed to the package `DBMS_METADATA`. By selecting the property **Show Constraints as Alter**, the inline constraints are also removed from the `CREATE TABLE` command. Compare the resulting DDL, shown in the following screenshot, with the results based on the default settings as shown earlier:

EMPLOYEES

Columns | Data | Constraints | Grants | Statistics | Triggers | Flashback | Dependencies | Details | Partitions | Indexes | SQL

Actions...

```
CREATE TABLE "EMPLOYEES"
 (  "EMPLOYEE_ID" NUMBER(6,0),
"FIRST_NAME" VARCHAR2(20 BYTE),
"LAST_NAME" VARCHAR2(25 BYTE) CONSTRAINT "EMP_LAST_NAME_NN" NOT NULL ENABLE,
"EMAIL" VARCHAR2(25 BYTE) CONSTRAINT "EMP_EMAIL_NN" NOT NULL ENABLE,
"PHONE_NUMBER" VARCHAR2(20 BYTE),
"HIRE_DATE" DATE CONSTRAINT "EMP_HIRE_DATE_NN" NOT NULL ENABLE,
"JOB_ID" VARCHAR2(10 BYTE) CONSTRAINT "EMP_JOB_NN" NOT NULL ENABLE,
"SALARY" NUMBER(8,2),
"COMMISSION_PCT" NUMBER(2,2),
"MANAGER_ID" NUMBER(6,0),
"DEPARTMENT_ID" NUMBER(4,0)
 ) ;
ALTER TABLE "EMPLOYEES" ADD CONSTRAINT "EMP_SALARY_MIN" CHECK (salary > 0) ENA
ALTER TABLE "EMPLOYEES" ADD CONSTRAINT "EMP_EMAIL_UK" UNIQUE ("EMAIL") ENABLE;
```

The deselected **Show Schema** setting removes the schema name from all of the `CREATE` commands, with the exception of the **column comments DDL**, where the schema is still retained. This is a known database issue.

Selecting multiple tables for DDL export

Selecting the SQL display editor is an easy way to get the DDL for a single table. Selecting **Export DDL** from the context menu in the **Connections** navigator provides the additional capability of generating DDL for one or more tables at a time. For the DDL export, select the table(s) and write the DDL to file, clipboard, or directly to the SQL Worksheet:

The structure of the DDL in the **Export DDL** menu is driven by the same preferences that shape the SQL in the SQL display editor: **Database | ObjectViewer**.

Using the Database Export wizard to export DDL and data

You can use the preceding utilities to set up and save the DDL or DML scripts. Generally, you'd use those for ad hoc statements to quickly create a table and populate it with data. There are occasions when you'll want a script that you can use repeatedly for many tables or objects. You can use the **Database Export** wizard to create a file that you might:

- Run on a regular basis
- Share across teams
- Ship as an initial setup script

Starting the export wizard

The **Database Export** follows a series of steps and choices, allowing you to choose the object types, the specific objects, and to select or restrict the data exported. Select **Tools | Database Export...** to invoke the wizard:

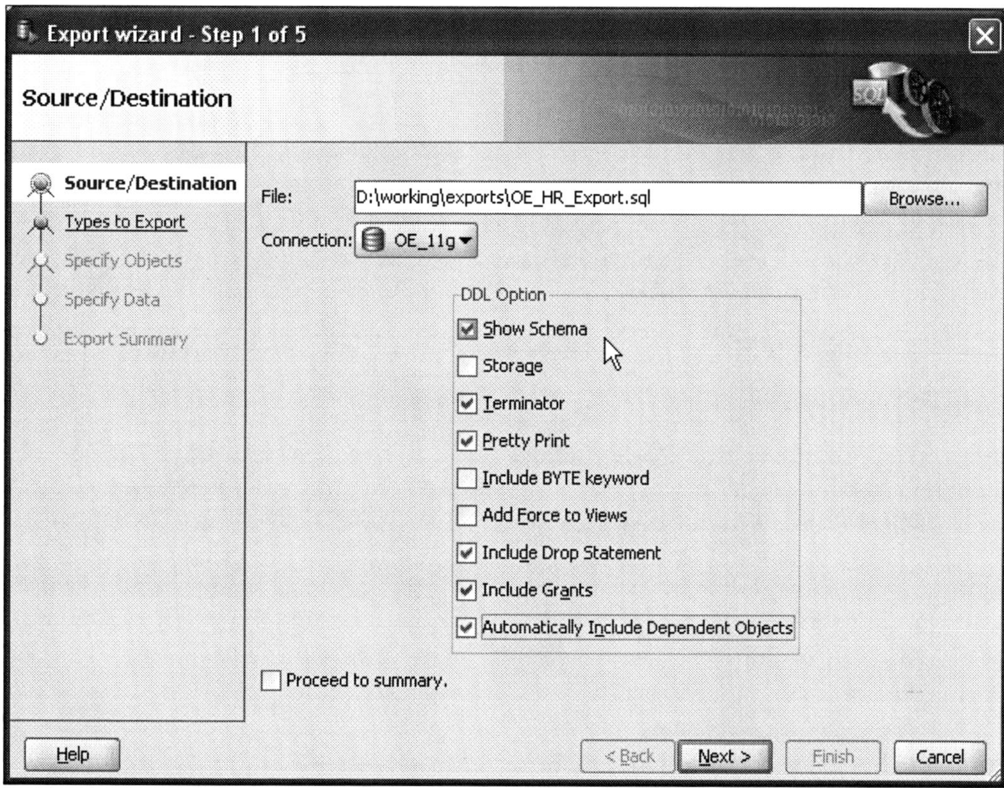

The outcome of the **Database Export** is a file containing DDL and possibly, DML statements. The DDL statements are almost all `CREATE` object statements, although you can also include `GRANT` statements, and the DML comprises `INSERT` statements. You can control the structure of the statements in the first stage by setting different options. Set the file location and the schema driving the export on this first page.

Controlling the default export location

Set the default export location in the **Preferences** dialog. Select **Database** from the tree and then set the default location.

The DDL is again derived from executing procedure calls to the `DBMS_METADATA` package. Most of the options set on this first page are parameters sent to this package. However, not all options are, such as the **Include Drop Statement**. In the preceding screenshot, the lowest three statements are *not* set by default.

By selecting **Include Drop Statements,** you can create a script that is useful in a test environment. By including the `DROP` commands, you can re-run the script repeatedly, by first dropping the tables, then creating them, and then inserting the data. Oracle supplies many similar scripts. `demobld.sql`, which creates the EMP and DEPT tables, is one such example.

Although many of the scripts run are for a single schema, you can also create scripts for a number of schemas by including the **Include Grants** option. The wizard reads and replicates the current object privileges in the schemas. If you are selecting objects from multiple schemas, you need to include **Show Schema** to ensure the appropriate schema prefixes each object created.

Selecting objects for generation

Once you have set the options driving the DDL, you need to select the objects for generation. By default, all of the objects are selected, including the **Data**. This means you can select **Proceed to Summary** and then **Finish**, and the DDL and DML for the full schema and data will be created. To restrict the choice of objects, deselect the **Toggle All** checkbox, which then gives you the option of selecting individual items by allowing you to just select only those object types you want to appear in the file. On the next page of the wizard, you select the specific, named items.

Including dependent objects

If you select **Automatically Include Dependent Objects** with the other DDL options, you only need to select tables on the **Object Types** page. The related constraints and triggers are then included. Left deselected means you need to select named tables, constraints, and triggers.

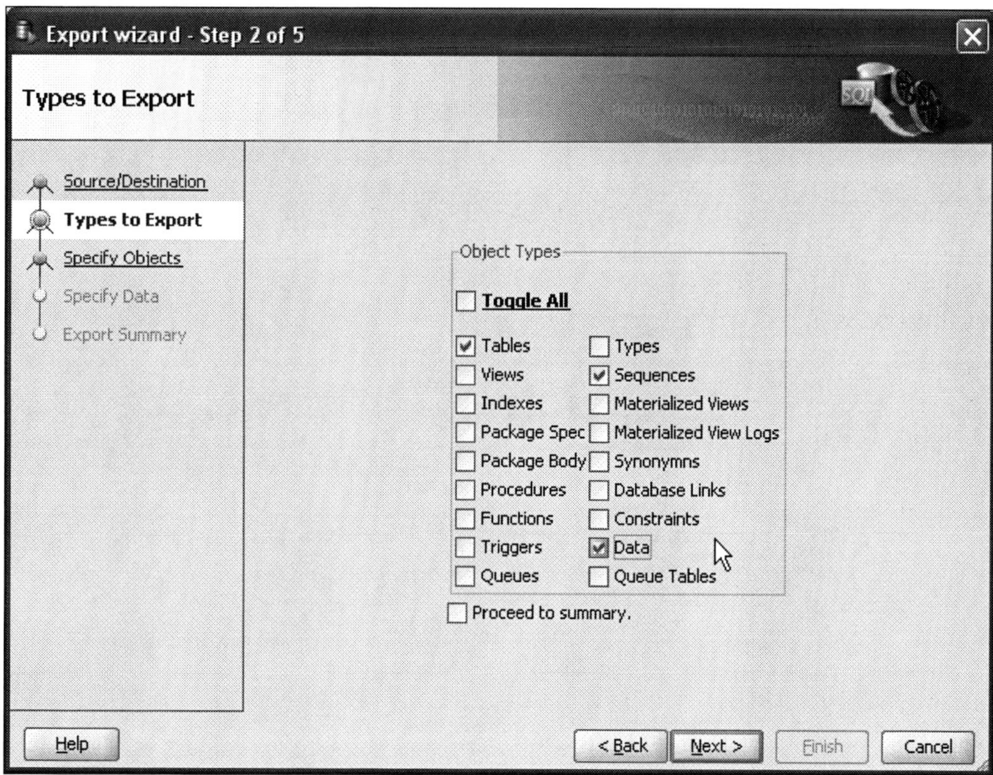

Select **Data**, as shown in the previous screenshot, to ensure that the DML for the selected tables is also created.

Specifying objects

The details in Step 3 of the wizard are driven by the choices made on the previous pages. The schema selected controls the objects you have access to, both in the schema itself and across other schemas. You need only select a starting schema, such as SCOTT, or another schema with very few privileges, to see how few tables are available.

The OE sample schema can query and therefore can produce the DDL for some of the HR tables. In the screenshot that follows, the four areas marked are:

1. A drop-down list of all available schemas. For each schema selected, the associated objects are displayed.
2. A drop-down list that displays the object *types* selected on the previous page. This helps reduce the list of objects displayed in area #3.
3. Objects belonging to the schema selected and are driven by the object types in the object list #2.

4. Move any required objects here to reduce the list to just those selected. If none are selected, then by default, the DDL for all objects is created.

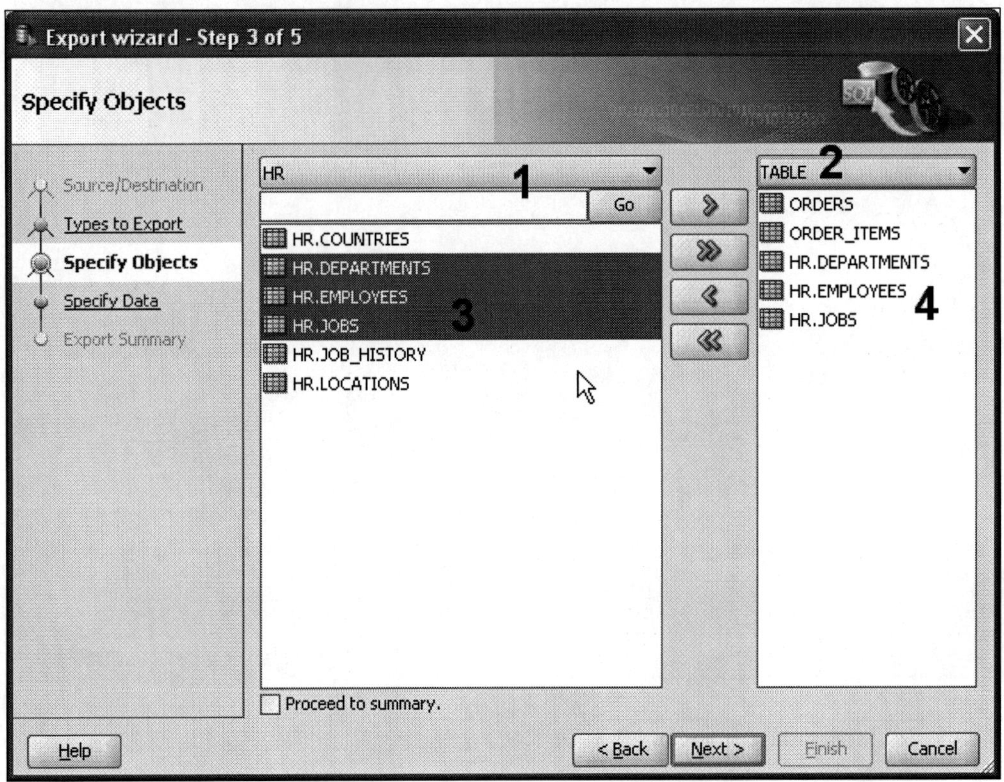

All objects are selected by default. Select **Proceed to summary**, or click on **Next** to move on. Shuttling a few objects restricts this list to the objects selected.

In the screenshot just shown, the OE sample schema is the driving connection. Therefore, the three tables added from the HR schema, reflect that schema detail.

Specifying data

Step 4 of the wizard is only available if you check the **Data** option when selecting **Types to Export**. Once again, all of the data is exported by default. To restrict the data exported, you need to shuttle the required tables to the right-hand panel and then add the restricting where clause. If you need to restrict the data for many tables, then select each table in turn, add the required `WHERE` clause. You must click on **Apply Filter** for each table, with the table selected, as you proceed through the list of tables. In the example shown below, only the `DEPARTMENTS` table has been selected and it also includes a restriction on the records:

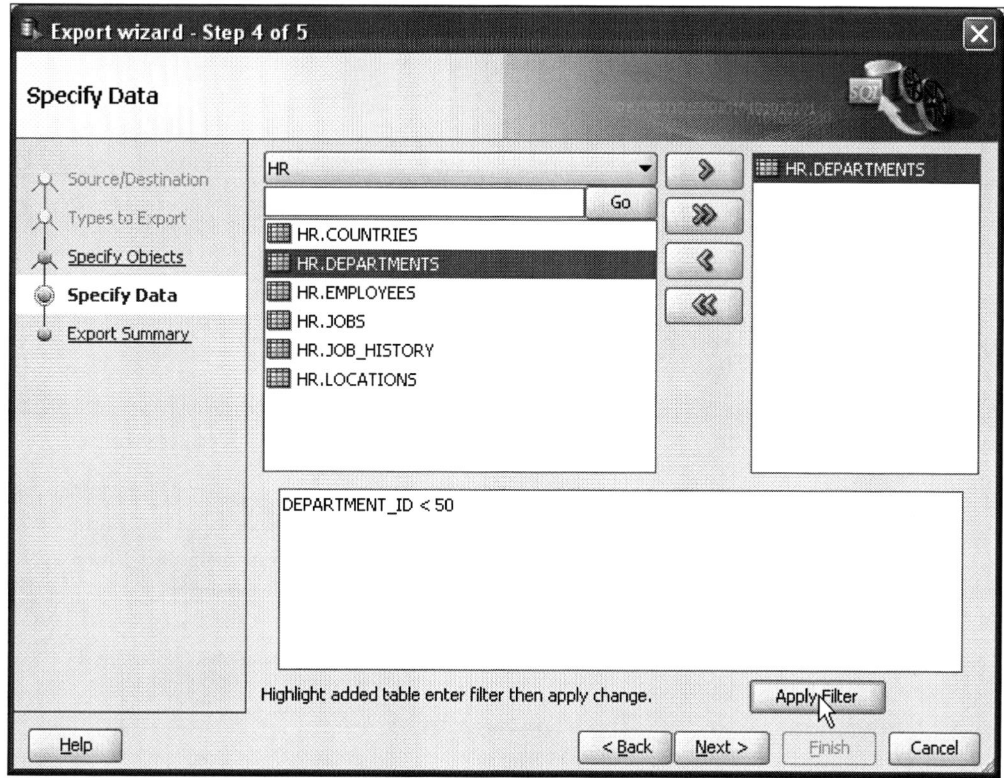

Once you have selected the object types, objects, and set any data restrictions, you can proceed to the summary. Details of all options set, the objects to be exported, and any data and restrictions are all listed. At this stage, you can review and verify that the correct information has been listed. Once you finish, the DDL and DML scripts are created and the file is automatically opened in the SQL Worksheet, ready for you to run against the required schema.

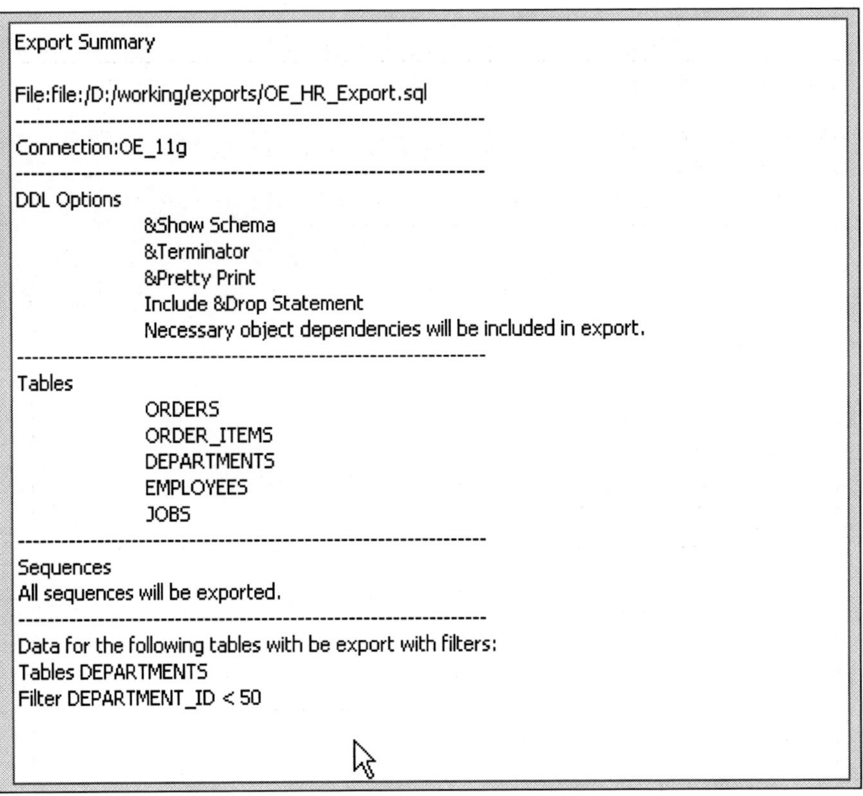

In the **Export Summary** example from the screenshot just shown, the summary includes information such as the details of the parameters set, the objects for each object type, and any tables for data export, with filters set restricting the records returned.

Running the script

Taking the example we have been working on in the wizard, the output is sent to the SQL Worksheet, as a single file that you can run. Notice that the start of the script includes a `DROP` statement for all objects to be created, in this case, tables and sequences. Once these have been dropped, the path is clear to create new objects, and then insert the data. The connections drop-down list on the right-hand side makes it easier to select alternate schema to run the script against:

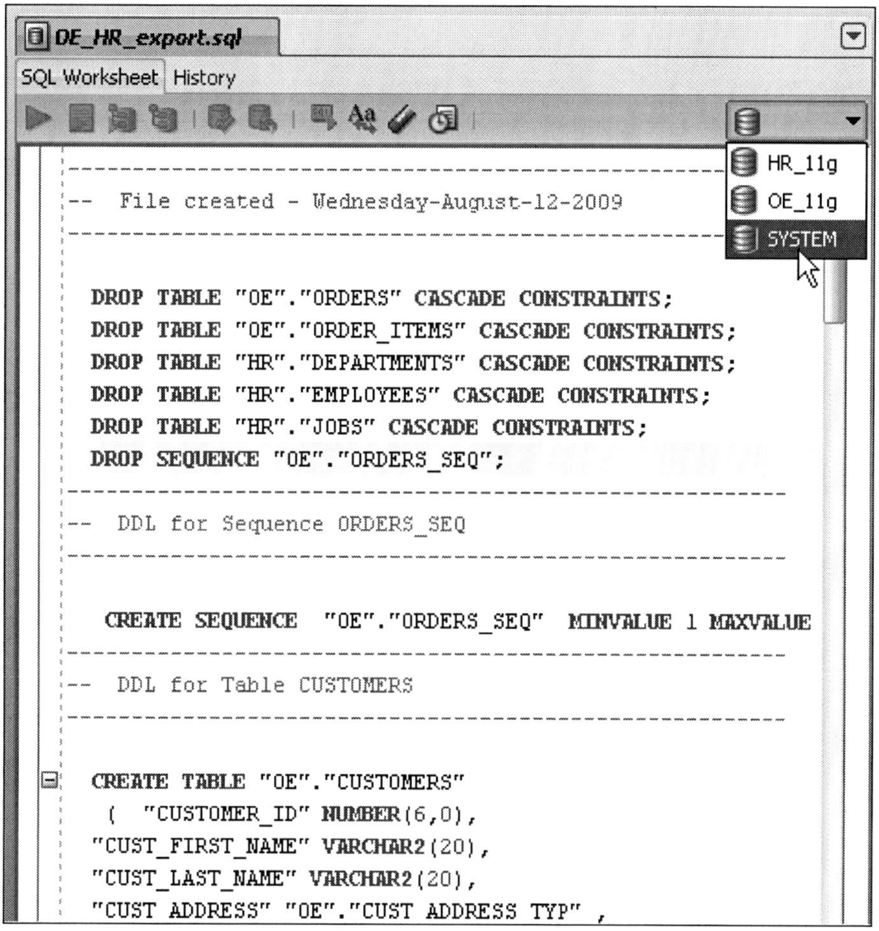

```
OE_HR_export.sql
SQL Worksheet | History
HR_11g
OE_11g
SYSTEM
--------------------------------------------------------
--  File created - Wednesday-August-12-2009
--------------------------------------------------------

  DROP TABLE "OE"."ORDERS" CASCADE CONSTRAINTS;
  DROP TABLE "OE"."ORDER_ITEMS" CASCADE CONSTRAINTS;
  DROP TABLE "HR"."DEPARTMENTS" CASCADE CONSTRAINTS;
  DROP TABLE "HR"."EMPLOYEES" CASCADE CONSTRAINTS;
  DROP TABLE "HR"."JOBS" CASCADE CONSTRAINTS;
  DROP SEQUENCE "OE"."ORDERS_SEQ";
--------------------------------------------------------
--  DDL for Sequence ORDERS_SEQ
--------------------------------------------------------

   CREATE SEQUENCE  "OE"."ORDERS_SEQ"  MINVALUE 1 MAXVALUE
--------------------------------------------------------
--  DDL for Table CUSTOMERS
--------------------------------------------------------

  CREATE TABLE "OE"."CUSTOMERS"
   (  "CUSTOMER_ID" NUMBER(6,0),
  "CUST_FIRST_NAME" VARCHAR2(20),
  "CUST_LAST_NAME" VARCHAR2(20),
  "CUST_ADDRESS" "OE"."CUST_ADDRESS_TYP" ,
```

Export full schema

On the initial screen in the **Export wizard**, set the required DDL options and select **Proceed to Summary**. Click on **Next** and **Finish**. All of the objects and data in the schema are exported.

Importing data

Using SQL Developer, you can also import data into tables. The most common approach is running a well-formed (syntactically correct) script file of `INSERT` statements. The **Import Data** wizard is available from the context menu of existing tables and on the context menu of the **Tables** node, where you can import data and create the table in a one-step operation. The import wizard allows you to import data from a delimited format file or a Microsoft Excel XLS file. In this section, we'll look at three of the supported SQL Developer **Data Export** file formats.

Importing data from SQL script files

When importing data into tables from a file, the structure of the file, whether it is SQL or XLS, determines how the import works. For an SQL script file of insert statements, you need only run the script from the SQL Worksheet, or open the file in the SQL Worksheet, and then run it against a particular schema to import the data.

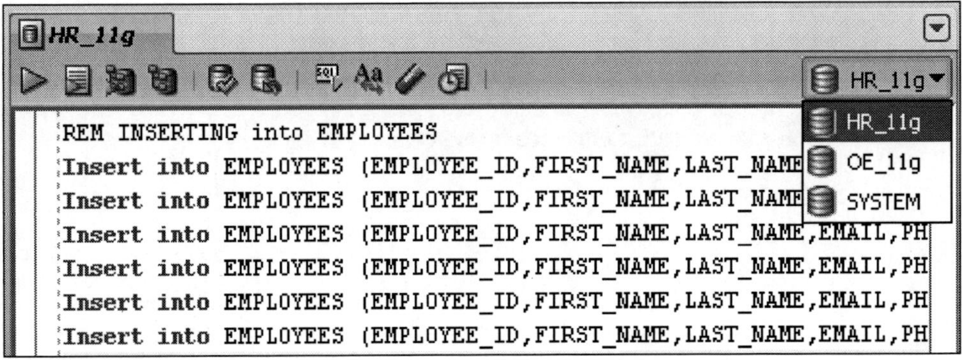

In the example in the screenshot just shown, the file is open in the worksheet. You can run this script against any schema with an `EMPLOYEES` table, assuming the columns match and any constraints are met. A typical use would be if you had run the DDL to create the table, and then run the DML to populate it.

Importing data from XLS and CSV files

SQL Developer provides you with the ability to import data from CSV and XLS files into a table. To import a spreadsheet of data into an existing table, select the table and select **Import Data** from the context menu, as shown in the following screenshot:

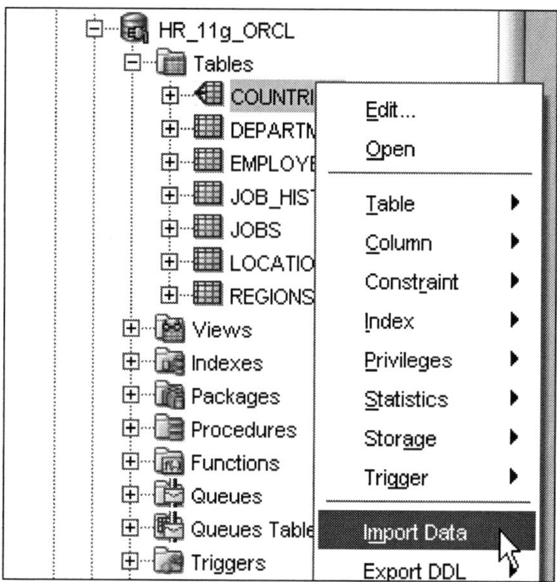

This invokes the **Import Data** wizard (shown in the following screenshot). If the **Import Data** wizard has recognized the file format, it will display the columns and data having opened the dialog. You can also review the SQL Query that produced the spreadsheet, if available.

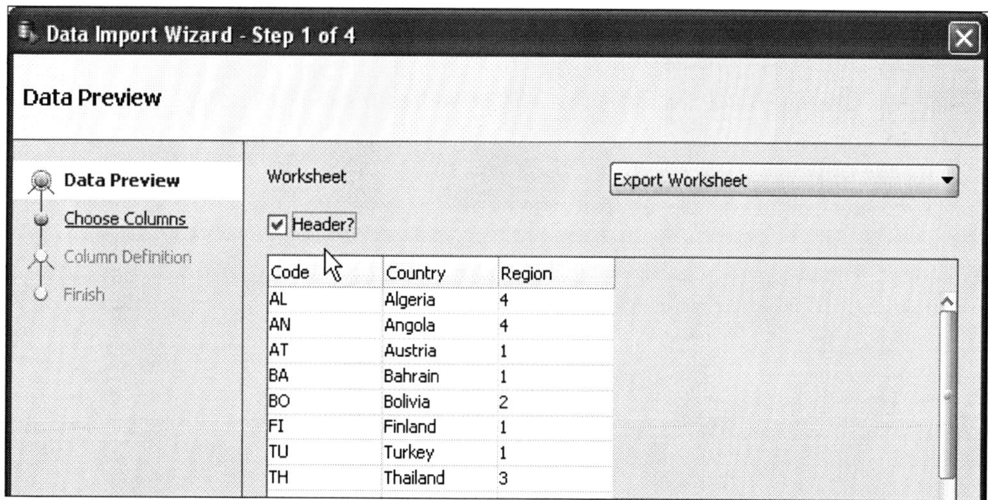

By stepping though the wizard, you can select the columns that you want to import and rearrange the order of those selected. The third page of the wizard is where you need to match the columns you've selected from the file with the columns in the table you have chosen to import into. The wizard tries to match the columns in the spreadsheet to those in the table, based on the column header. If this is not selected, or the column headers are not an exact match, then you need to select each column in turn as shown in the following screenshot:

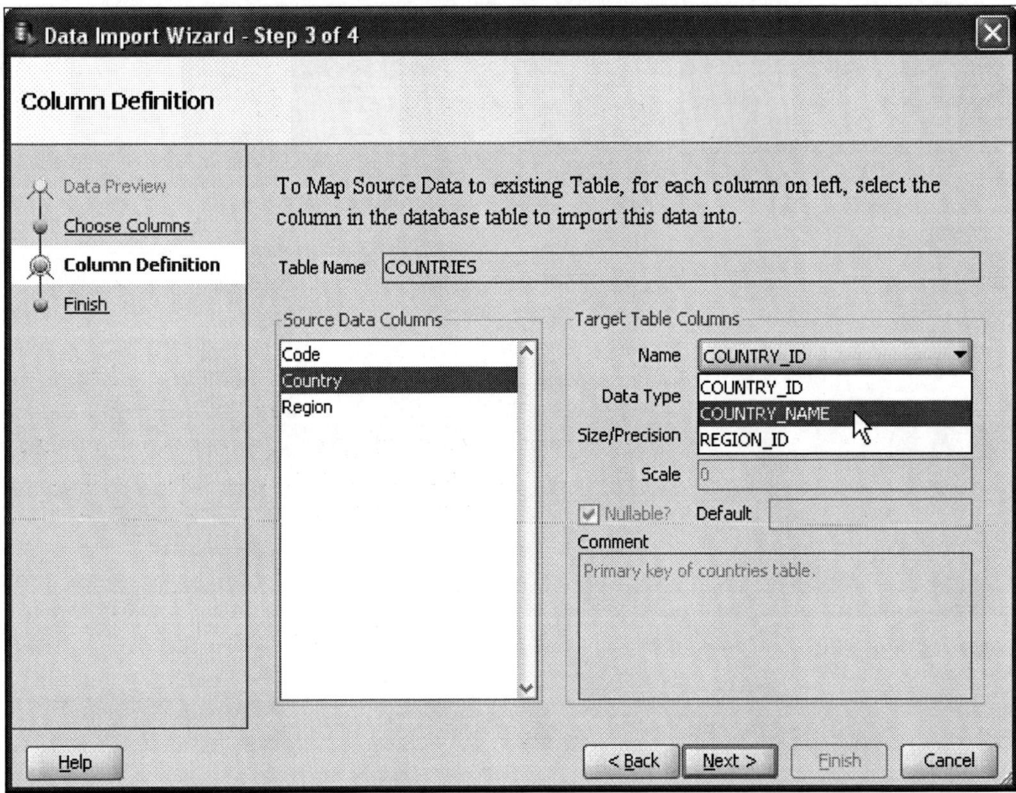

The last page of the wizard runs a verification test to ensure the data in the spreadsheet or chosen file can be imported into the table of choice. At this stage of the import, only a data mapping and matching is verified. If there are duplicate records in the table, or other data issues that cause constraints to fail or triggers to fire, this will only be encountered as you run the import.

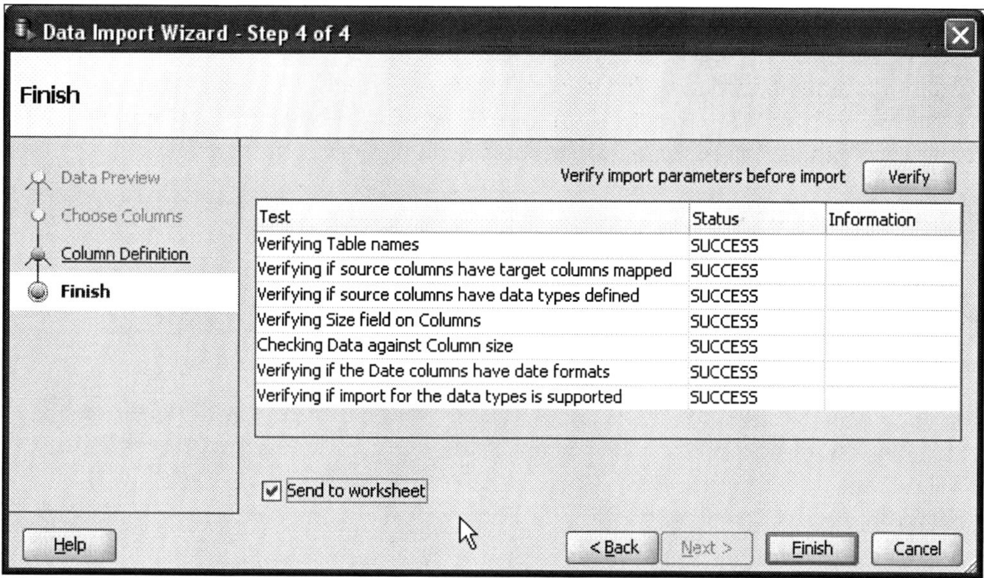

On the last page of the wizard (shown in the previous screenshot), you can elect to have the script sent to the SQL Worksheet. This passes the control back to you and you can run the script when you are ready. The advantage of this is you can save and run the script later. You can also track any errors that may result due to constraint validation or triggers firing or constraints. An example of the script and execution is shown in the following screenshot:

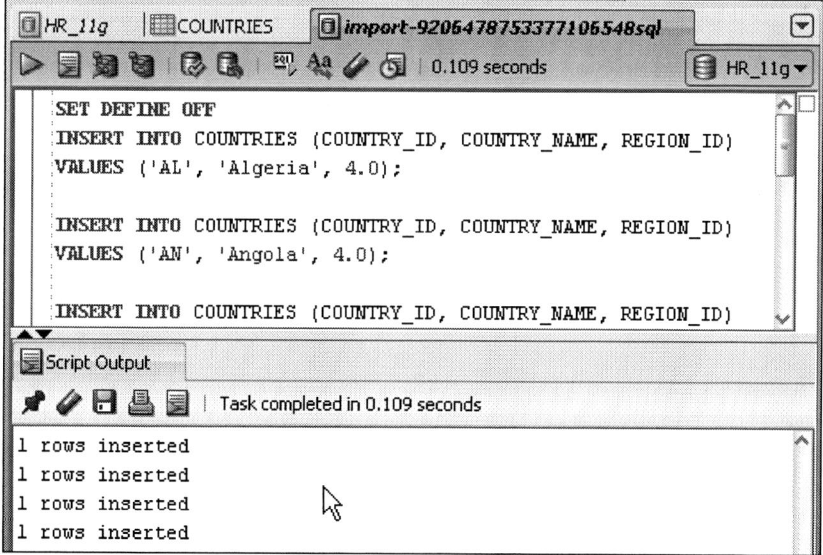

If you do not check this option, then the insert is handled by Java batch inserts. The preference **Database | Advanced | Sql Array Fetch Size** controls the size of the batch, with a bigger batch size providing faster performance. In this case, all of the rows in the batch may be rejected if there is an error. The bad file identifies the error and contains `INSERT` statements for the rows not inserted.

This **Import Data** wizard also supports the import of a CSV file. The only real difference here is that the first page does not provide you the choice of Worksheet or SQL Query.

Creating a table on XLS import

If you have a structured Microsoft Excel file, you can use SQL Developer to create a new database table, based on the details in the file. To invoke the **Import Data** wizard for this activity, you need to select the context menu at the *Table* level, as shown in the following screenshot:

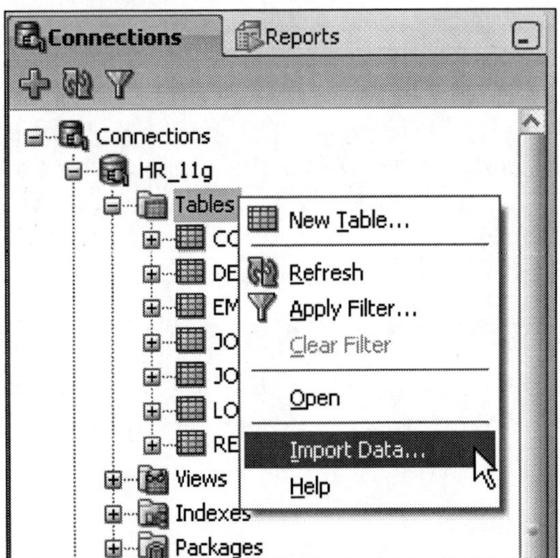

The **Import Data** wizard supports both XLS and CSV formats for creating a table. The initial page in the wizard displays the structure of the file and the data. As you step through the wizard, you'll see the same options as you do when you are importing from a spreadsheet into an existing table. In this case, selecting the columns required from the spreadsheet drives the number of columns that are created in the new table. Where the two **Import Data** wizard differ is the third page (seen in the following screenshot). In this case you need to specify the name of the new table. You can also edit the column details here, by changing the default columns names and data types, which are derived from any column headings in the spreadsheet file.

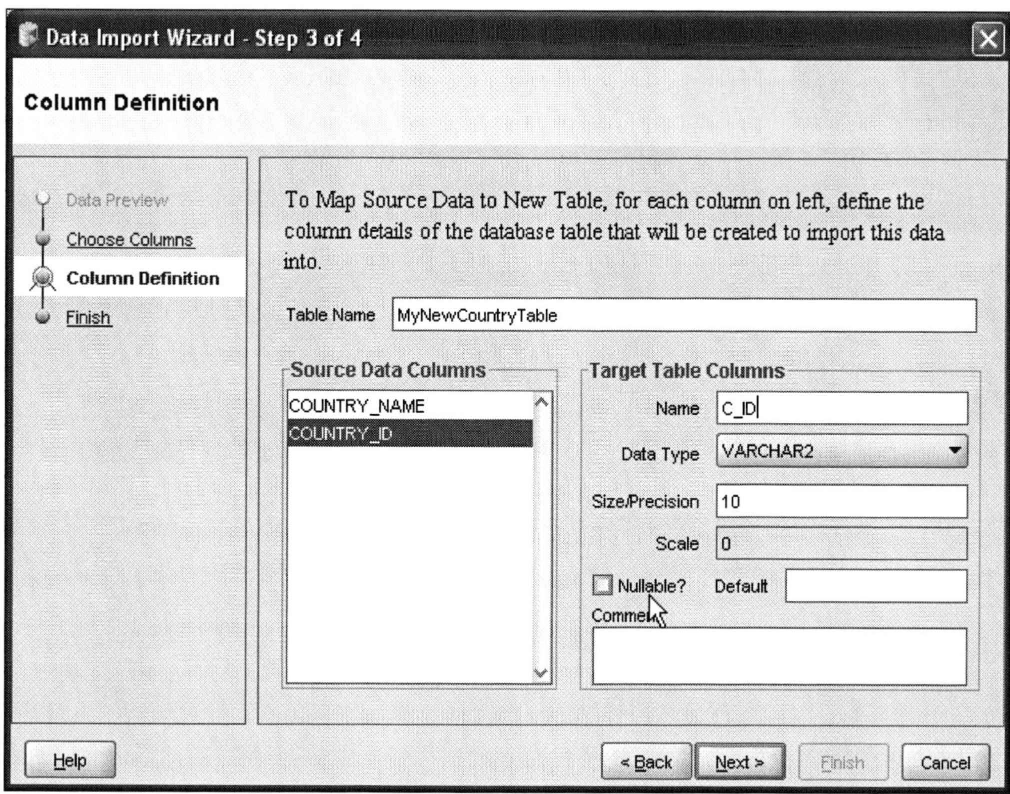

The wizard completes with a verification page, to ensure all of the data types and columns match for import. Once again, you have the choice on the final page of the wizard to send the detail to the SQL Worksheet, where you can run the script. Alternatively, the new table is created and the rows inserted when you click on **Finish**.

When working with a CSV, on the Data Preview page of the **Data Import Wizard**, you can select either the External Table or SQL *Loader options. The former selection creates an external table that provides read-access to the data in the file, while the latter creates a control file for loading the table with the data in the file using SQL*Loader. In the following screenshot, the selection in the Data Preview was External Table. Having provided a name for the new table, the wizard follows to the final verification screen:

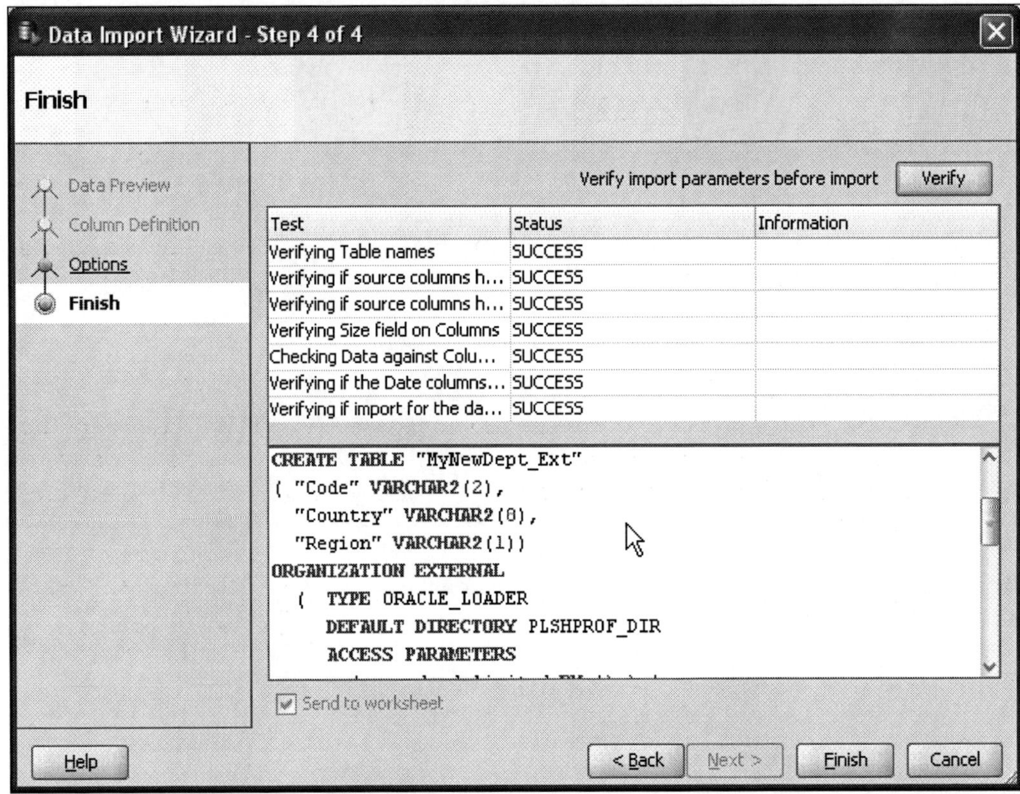

The detail for the external table and SQL*Loader table creation are automatically written to the SQL Worksheet.

Using the Database Copy wizard

SQL Developer provides the **Database Copy** wizard for quickly copying data from one schema to another. This mechanism is useful when the results do not need to be replicable or when the table contains large objects types, such as BLOB or CLOB. This wizard does not produce a script file, even in the background, which is run to perform the task. Instead, it copies the data from one table to another, whether within the same schema or between schemas, thus handling the LOB column copy too. All you need is to be able to connect to both schemas.

Comparing the database copy alternatives

The **Database Copy** wizard, available from the **Tools** menu, offers a choice of approaches when copying the data:

- **Create Objects**—creates new objects in the destination schema for the objects you have in the originating schema. If the objects already exist, those actions will fail. There are no `DROP` commands.
- **Truncate Objects**—truncates all of the existing tables in the destination schema, based on the detail in the source connection, and then copies the data from the source into the destination schema tables. In this case, all of the tables in the second schema are truncated. The wizard does not create any new tables in the destination schema, it just moves data to the tables that are already there.
- **Drop Objects**—creates `DROP` and `CREATE` scripts to drop all of the objects in the destination schema, based on the detail in the source connection, and then recreates the objects. In this case, all of the matching tables in the second schema are dropped. The wizard does not take into account any existing tables in the destination schema.

In addition to providing a quick and powerful method for loading data, the copy wizard also manages the required data definition. The first page of the wizard provides the ability to the specify how to manage the data definitions, which is important when copying to a database that may already contain the definitions of the tables being copied. Select the appropriate option, based on whether the table should simply be created, whether the existing data should be truncated, or whether the tables should be dropped and re-created.

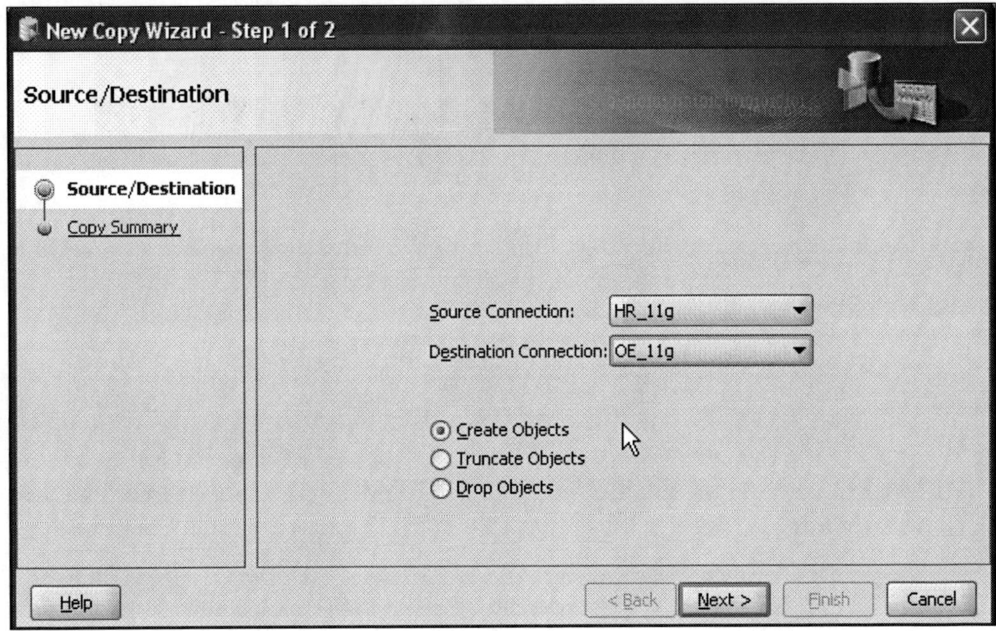

Consider the following scenarios that illustrate these options:

- **Create**—you have some test data and want to create a new schema. **Database Copy** is very useful for copying data from an existing schema to the new, empty schema.
- **Truncate**—you have one user with a set of "dirty data". You can truncate the data and then copy new, fresh data into the existing tables.
- **Drop**—you have a test scenario where the table structures have gotten out of alignment and you need to set them back to the group standard. Dropping the structures, before copying the fresh data into the structures using the **Database Copy**, is a clean route.

Running the Database Copy wizard

Invoke the **Database Copy** wizard from the main **Tools** menu and complete the initial schema detail as required. There are no further choices, as the wizard only considers the objects in the originating schema and produces a report of the actions which will take place.

> Before you start the **Database Copy** wizard, create a database connection for the source and destination schemas.

In the following screenshot, the **Create Objects** selection was made to copy the objects from the source to the destination schema. The wizard has prepared the scripts and actions which will be performed:

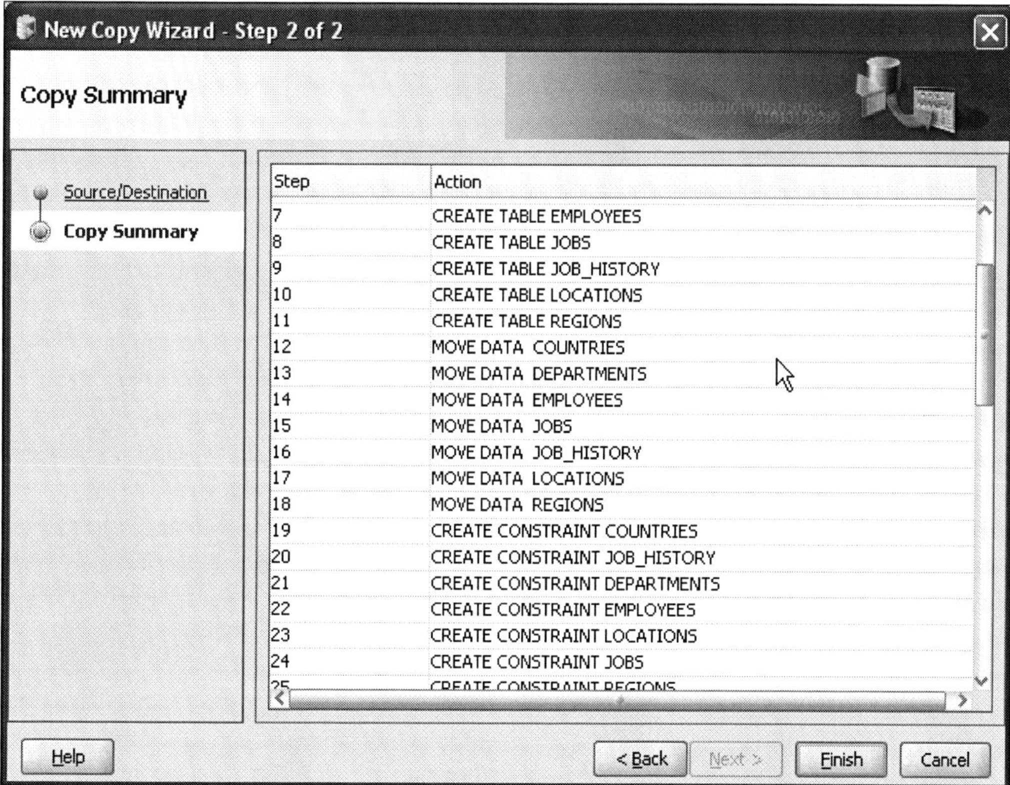

Click on **Finish** to complete the process. The results of the actions are displayed in SQL Developer as an output report file. This includes all failures, such as those that might occur if the secondary schema is not empty, which would then cause the `CREATE` statements to fail.

Comparing schemas

You can use the SQL Developer **Database Diff** wizard to compare the objects in two schemas, identify the differences and then selectively apply changes to the destination schema based on the results of the comparison. The **Database Diff** wizard is available from the main **Tools** menu. You need to have a connection to each of the schemas.

When using the **Database Diff** wizard, the order of the schemas you compare is key. The assumption is that the first schema is the point of truth. Therefore, the scripts are created assuming that it is the second schema to be updated.

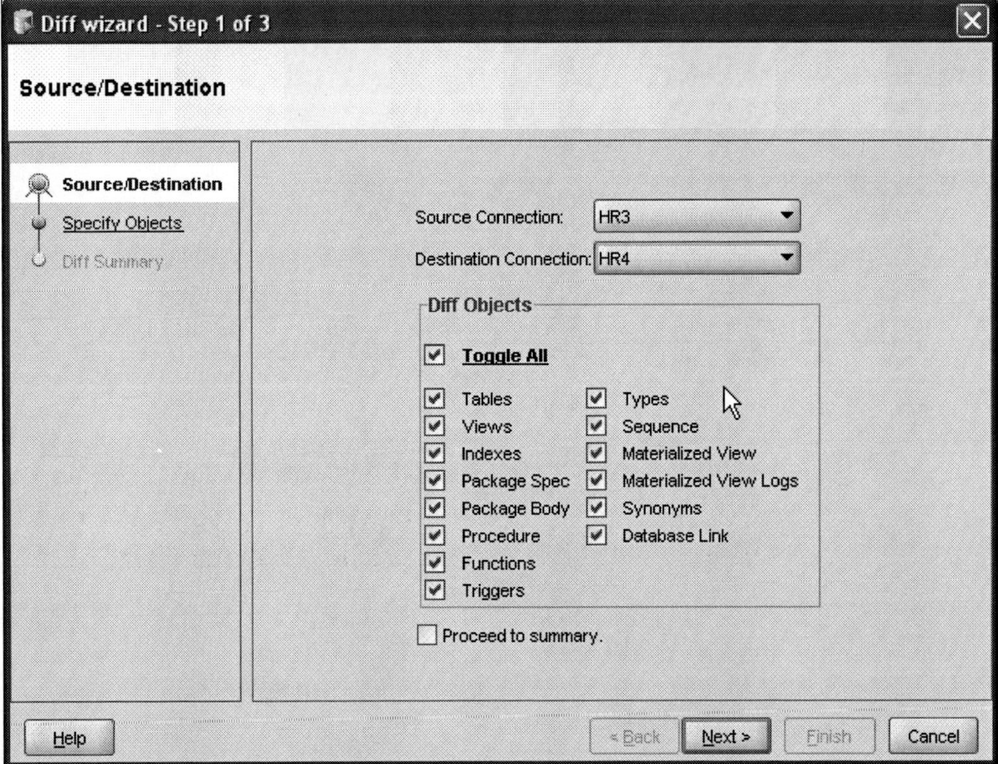

The wizard has the same options provided by the **Database Export** wizard when selecting objects. You can deselect the **Toggle All** option to select individual objects types for comparison. Once you have the schemas selected, and you have selected the object types, you can select the specific objects.

The final page of the **Database Diff** wizard is a summary of all objects that will be compared. Once you click on **Finish**, the differences are written to a report and displayed in the SQL Worksheet. The **Diff Report** displays the new and updated objects. It takes into account that it is the second schema which will be updated, should you choose to run the script. For each of the object difference, you can see the SQL by selecting the item in question, as shown in the following screenshot:

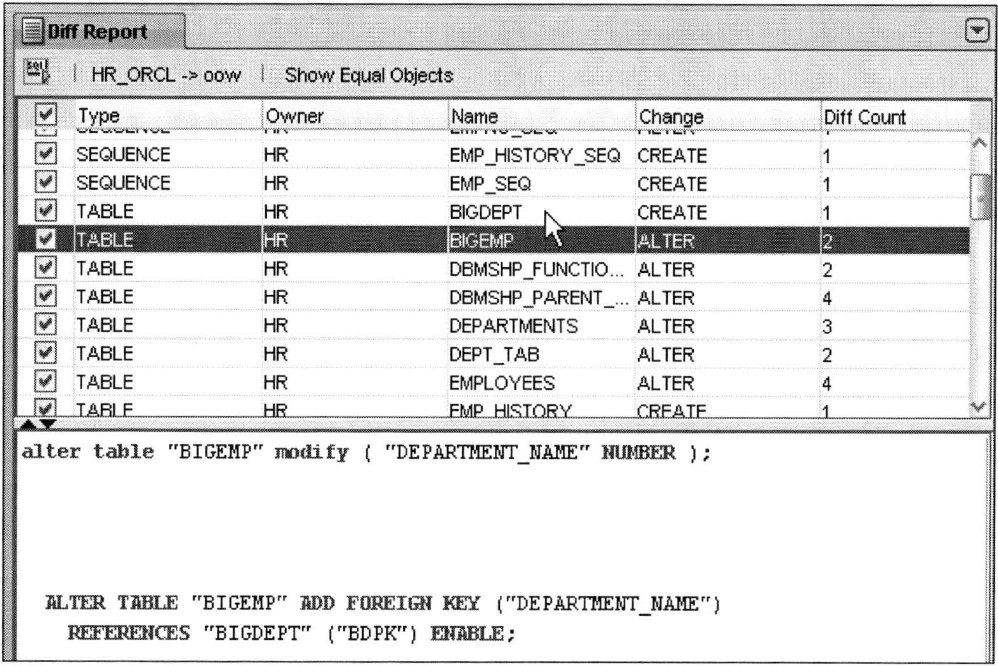

You can deselect all of the records displayed, and then include only those you want to run, by checking the items individually. Whether you select all, or choose individual statements, by selecting the SQL script button, the statements are all written to the SQL Worksheet, where you can run them for the required schema.

Summary

SQL Developer provides a number of quick and easy-to-use utilities to work with data, whether it's instance data in your tables or metadata that defines your schema. You can create DDL and DML to save and run at a later stage by using a context menu option or by running a step-by-step wizard. The Database Copy and Diff wizards provide additional resources to manage, compare, and update schema data. When working with and maintaining multiple schemas, or doing application development, each of these utilities plays a useful role.

In the next chapter, we'll revisit making database connections. Even though you have been using a connection throughout the book to this point, the options in the next chapter take connections a little further and discuss the alternatives and merits of the different connection types available.

9

Database Connections and JDBC Drivers

SQL Developer provides a variety of options when making database connections, by supporting connections to both Oracle and non-Oracle databases. For all of these connections, you'll need the required JDBC drivers. Within the Oracle connections, there are a variety of connection types (such as the TNS or LDAP connections) and authentication methods (such as the OS or Kerberos authentication).

In this chapter, we'll review the basic connection type used in the examples earlier in the book. We'll see how to add these additional Oracle connection types and review the connections for the supported authentication methods. We'll also look at how to add the required drivers and set up the connections for non-Oracle databases.

Working with Oracle connections

We'll start by reviewing the various Oracle connection types available. We'll then look at the authentication methods supported by SQL Developer.

Using alternative Oracle connection types

SQL Developer focuses on ease of use right from the start. With a mantra of "Download, unzip to install and you're ready to start", this intended ease of use means that you do not need any additional Oracle clients on your machine to connect to an Oracle database. However, in many Oracle environments, having an **Oracle Home** is standard, and therefore you can access the alias in a `tnsnames.ora` file.

To create any new connection, select **File | New... | Database Connection** or right-click on the **Connections** node and select **New Connection**. By now, you'll be familiar with the default settings on the connections dialog, shown in the following screenshot:

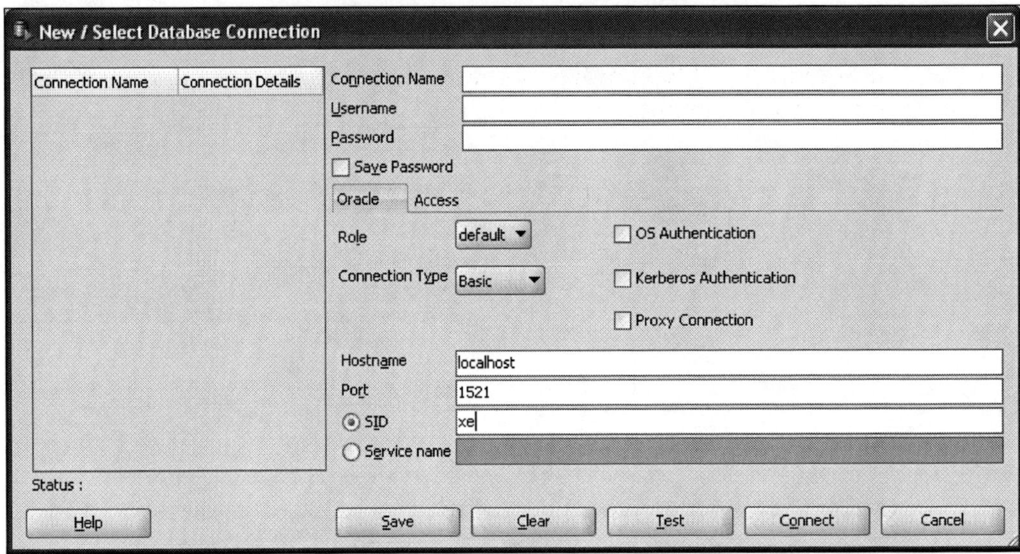

The databases listed in the default **Database Connection** dialog are Oracle and Microsoft Access. Access, displayed only for SQL Developer on Microsoft Windows, is available by default as it uses the JDBC-ODBC bridge and requires no additional drivers. For all other database support, you'll need to add the required drivers, which we'll discuss later in the chapter.

For the Oracle connections, the different options are in the **Connection Type** drop-down list. As you make each selection, the dialog and required input values change:

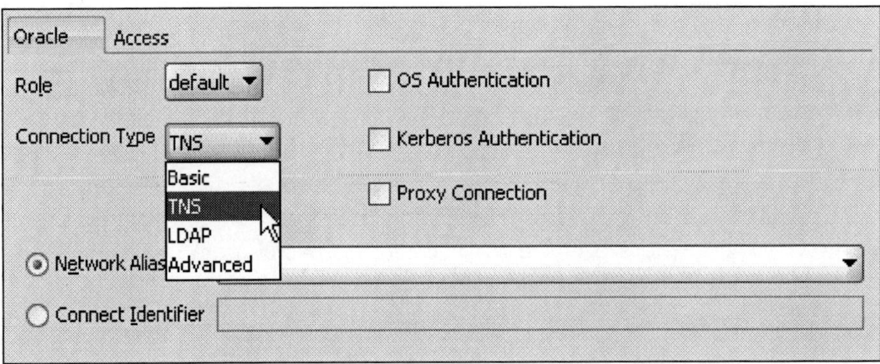

Reviewing the Basic connection

The default connection is the **Basic** connection and it uses a thin JDBC driver, shipped with SQL Developer, which allows you to connect to the Oracle Database without other Oracle clients on your machine. The default **SID** is set for XE, which is the default SID for Oracle Express Edition, the free Oracle 10g database. When using the **Basic** connection type, all you need to know is the location of your database, the port, and the SID or Service name.

> **Reminder**: Selecting the **Save Password** checkbox saves the password to an encrypted file. This makes it secure. However, a better level of security is not saving the password at all. That way, there is no file to be compromised.

> **Disable the Save Password option**
>
> To disable the checkbox to save the password, add the following entry to the `sqldeveloper.conf` file:
>
> `AddVMOption -Dsqldev.savepasswd=false`

Accessing the tnsnames.ora file

The **New Connection** dialog provides two options when you switch to the **TNS** connection type. These are a **Network Alias** drop-down list, which is read from your `tnsnames.ora` file, or the **Connect Identifier**:

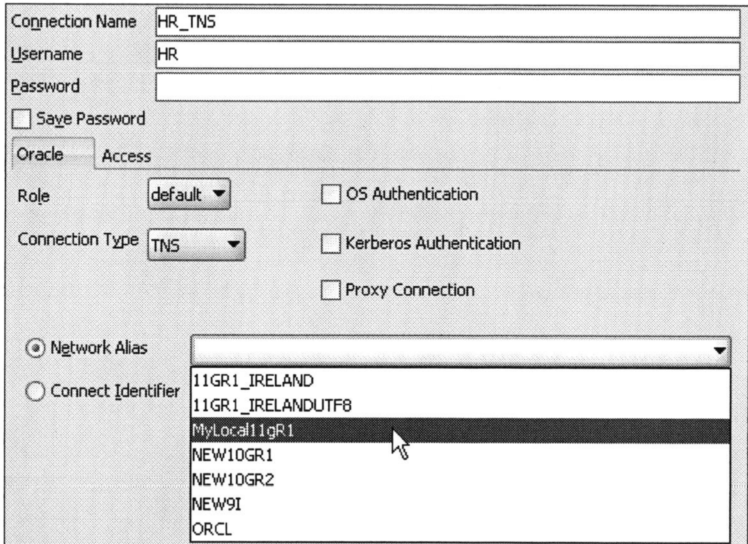

The `tnsnames.ora` file is, by default, defined in the `$ORACLE_HOME/network/admin` directory. However, you can set the `TNS_ADMIN` environment variable to specify an alternate location.

You may have multiple `tnsnames.ora` files setup on your machine. SQL Developer only reads one of these, searching for the file in the following order of priority:

1. `$HOME/.tnsnames.ora.`
2. `$TNS_ADMIN/tnsnames.ora.`
3. `/etc/tnsnames.ora` (for non-Microsoft Windows environments).
4. `$ORACLE_HOME/network/admin/tnsnames.ora.`
5. Registry Key accessing the correct TNS Names file.

If SQL Developer does not locate the required `tnsnames.ora` file, you can set the directory location using the `TNS_ADMIN` system environment variable.

In Microsoft Windows, you can create the `TNS_ADMIN` environment variable using the Control Panel. Select **System | Advanced | Environment Variables**, and add or update the value for the `TNS_ADMIN` variable.

Although not a recommended approach, you can also directly set the registry variable. To set the Registry Key, open the registry editor and find the entry `HKEY_LOCAL_MACHINE\SOFTWARE\ORACLE`. Locate or create the entry `TNS_ADMIN` and set it to the required path.

SQL Developer 2.1 has introduced a preference for specifying the directory location of the `tnsnames.ora` file. This setting overrides all of the settings above. The preference is the **Tnsnames Directory** setting in the **Database | Advanced** section of the **Tools | Preferences** dialog.

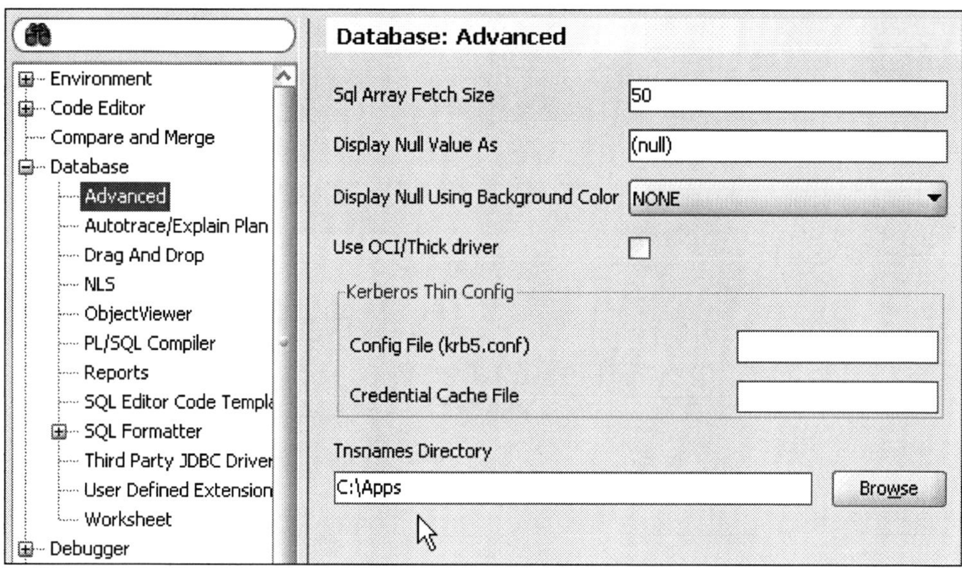

Accessing LDAP server details

SQL Developer provides LDAP authentication for accessing database service names in the **Oracle Internet Directory** (**OID**). **Lightweight Directory Access Protocol (LDAP)**, is an application protocol used to query and modify directory services. The OID is a directory service that stores and manages net service names in a central location. In order to use or access an LDAP server, you need to have the LDAP parameter set in the `sqlnet.ora` file:

```
NAMES.DIRECTORY_PATH=(LDAP)
```

The `ldap.ora` should have an entry such as seen in the following sample:

```
DIRECTORY_SERVERS= (localhost:389:636)
DEFAULT_ADMIN_CONTEXT = ""
DIRECTORY_SERVER_TYPE = OID
```

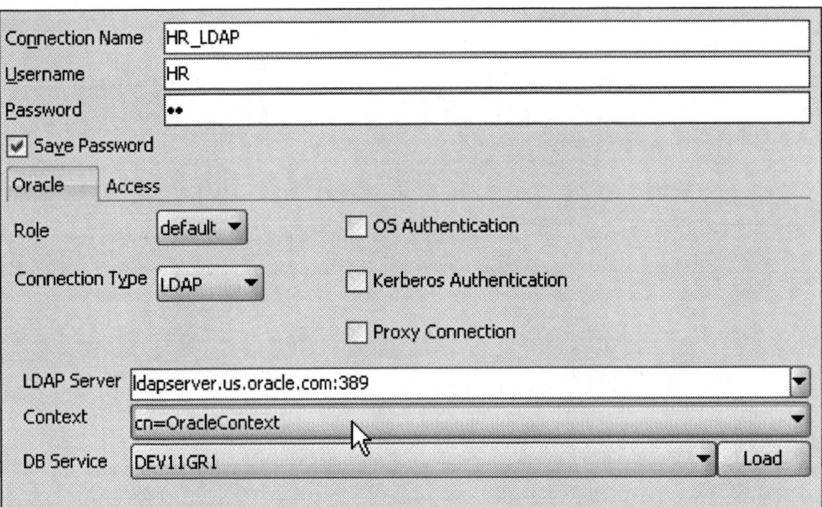

SQL Developer reads the `ldap.ora` file in the same way that it reads the `tnsnames.ora` file, and populates the **LDAP Server** drop-down list. Alternatively, you can type in the details for the LDAP server as shown in the previous screenshot. Once you have entered the LDAP server details, click on the **Load** button to populate the **Context** and **DB Service.**

Creating advanced connections with JDBC URLs

Instead of using the preconfigured connection types (that provide the appropriate drop-down lists based on information given), you can use the **Advanced** connection type, which connects directly to the database using Java. Selecting this provides an empty field where you can enter the full connection string and specify the driver type in the URL. The connect string can, for example, be `jdbc:oracle:thin:@localhost:1521:orcl`. In the following example, there is no **Username** and **Password** provided. Therefore, we can't use **Test** or **Connect** in the dialog (you can of course include these in the URL, and then test the connection). If you save and close the dialog, when you try to connect, you are prompted for the connection username and password and can then connect:

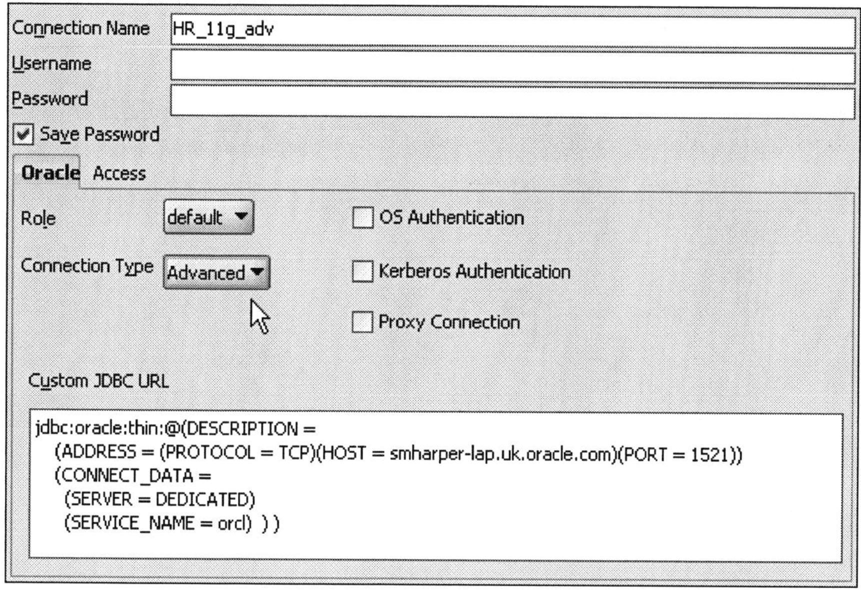

Connecting to Oracle TimesTen

You can connect to an Oracle TimesTen In-Memory Database using SQL Developer. The connection details are available through a separate tab, which only appears alongside the Oracle connections tab if you have TimesTen set up in your environment. The ability to work with the TimesTen In-Memory database is integrated into SQL Developer 1.5 and above. For more details on setting up Oracle TimesTen, refer to the documentation on the Oracle Technology Network `http://www.oracle.com/technology/products/timesten/`.

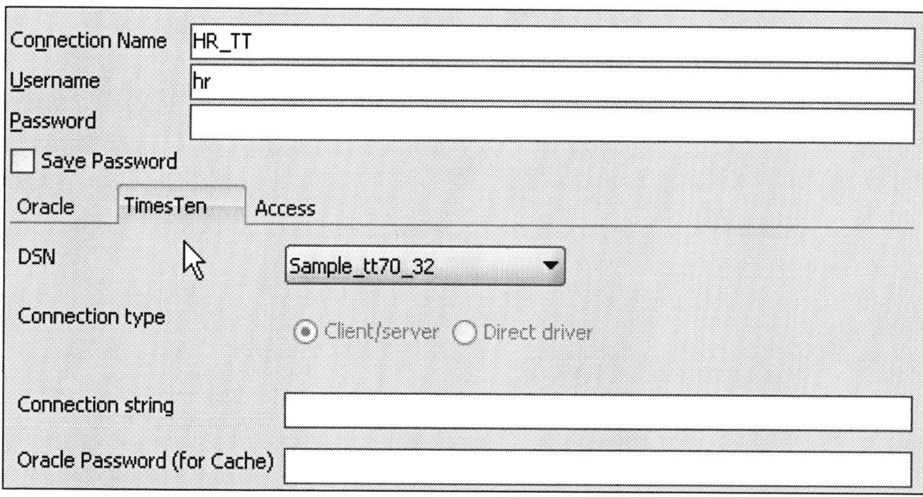

Once you have created a connection, you can connect to and work with the objects as you do for other database connections:

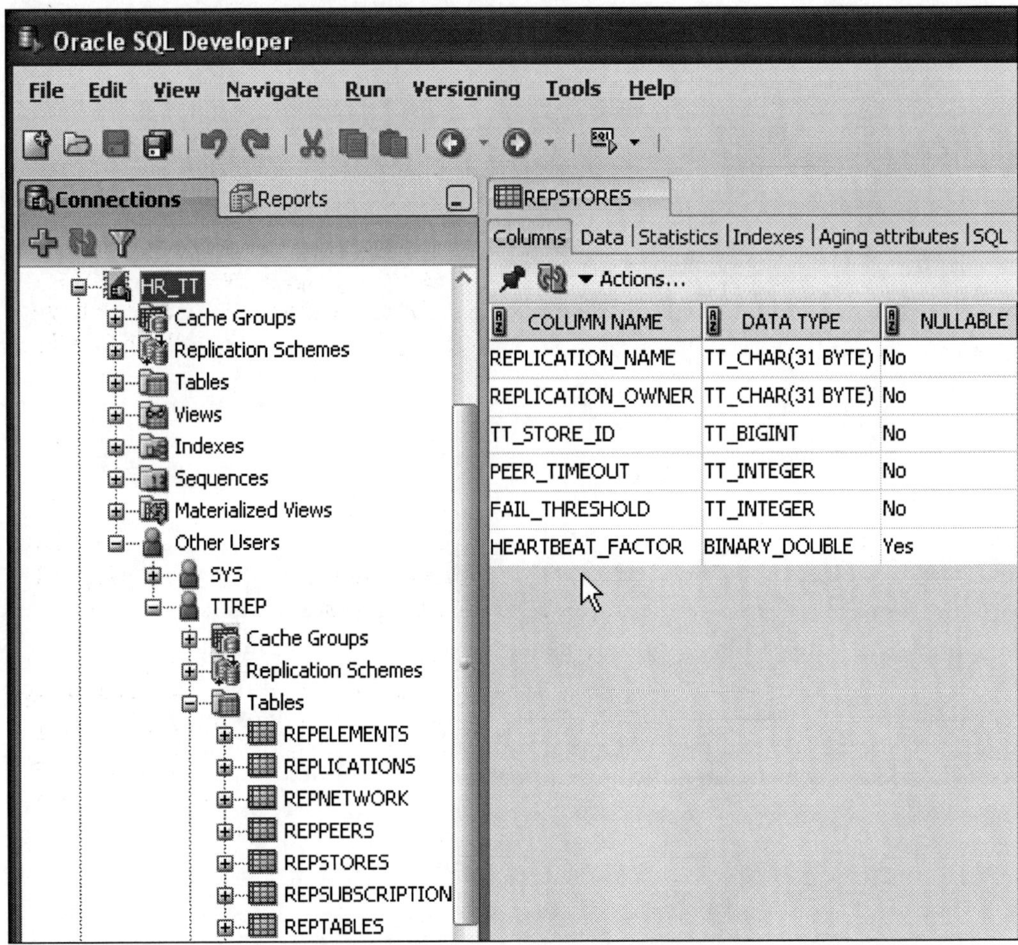

Reviewing JDBC drivers

We have now reviewed connections that seamlessly use either the thin or thick JDBC drivers. Before we look at further connections that use these or at when you should force the use of the thick driver, we'll provide a brief explanation of the two driver types mentioned, when you need additional client software and provide a few points to watch out for.

Oracle JDBC thin driver (Type IV driver)

The JDBC thin driver, also referred to as the Type IV driver, is platform independent, and as such does not need an Oracle client, **Oracle Call Interface** (**OCI**), or SQL*Net on the machine. This is the driver that SQL Developer uses by default and which you access when using the **Basic** connection type.

Oracle JDBC thick driver (Type II driver)

Installing Oracle Database, or many other Oracle tools, sets up an Oracle Home. In examples like this, you are likely to have a `tnsnames.ora` file in your environment, which you can use when connecting to the database using SQL Developer. In this case, you can generally use the 'thick' JDBC OCI (Type II) driver. If you do not have an Oracle Home and need to use the Type II driver, you'll need to install the Oracle Instant Client.

SQL Developers shipped drivers

SQL Developer 2.1 ships with the Oracle Database 11g JDBC driver, `ojdbc5.jar`. This same driver was also included in the SQL Developer 1.5.x releases. Prior to that SQL Developer 1.2 was shipped with the 10.2 driver, while Oracle SQL Developer 1.1 patch 3 and earlier releases were shipped with a 10.1 driver.

The Oracle JDBC drivers are certified for the respective currently supported databases. For example, the JDBC drivers shipped with Oracle Database 11g Release 1 are certified for Oracle Database 11g Release 1, Oracle Databases 10.2.x, 10.1.x, 9.2.x and 9.0.1. As SQL Developer is certified for Oracle Databases 9.2.0.1 and above, this driver is compatible for all of the current SQL Developer releases. These drivers are not certified for older, unsupported databases such as 8.0.x and 7.x.

Fixing connection errors

When installing Oracle JDBC drivers, the installer installs the JDBC drivers into the `$ORACLE_HOME/jdbc` directory. If you have an issue with the drivers, verify that you have the correct path in your CLASSPATH.

It is also important to ensure that your connections are compatible with the client. If not, you need to update your client installation. Updating your client is not related and does not affect your database or other Oracle software installations.

Using different authentication methods

In addition to providing a choice of connection types, you also have a choice of authentication methods. As a rule, users use the standard database authentication, enforced with username, password, roles, and privileges. With security being of such importance in almost all systems today, stronger authentication methods are necessary. In many applications working across multiple tiers, each tier is also required to provide authentication. Where these authentication methods exist, SQL Developer allows users to use these as part of the connection settings. It is not in the scope of this book to define or describe each of the authentication approaches in detail, but where possible, we provide some background.

OS Authentication

Used more often in the past, operating system (OS) Authentication is employed to avoid logging into both the operating system and then the database. When first introduced, users had a secure profile to connect to Unix, for example, and then immediately connected to the database using SQL*Plus. Using OS Authentication means the user is not required to provide the additional authentication. The database is aware of the OS connection, but does not need to manage the user passwords. The action is that you'd connect to the OS and then connect to the database in SQL*Plus using `connect /` or even `sqlplus /` at the command prompt.

Security risks

If you use OS Authentication in any system, once you have logged on to your system, anyone can access your database without further authorization. Therefore, this is a potential security risk and should be used cautiously.

To set up this environment in the database, you need to create a database user using the same details as the operating system user. First, you should find the OS username and then you need to create the user in the database. If you don't know the username then enter the following code in the SQL Worksheet.

```
SELECT UPPER(SYS_CONTEXT('USERENV','OS_USER'))
FROM DUAL;
```

You can use the **Create User...** dialog on the **Other Users** node for your SYSTEM connection, but it's as easy to enter the syntax in the SQL Worksheet:

```
CREATE USER "OPS$SMHARPER-LAP\SMHARPER" IDENTIFIED EXTERNALLY;
GRANT CREATE SESSION TO "OPS$SMHARPER-LAP\SMHARPER";
```

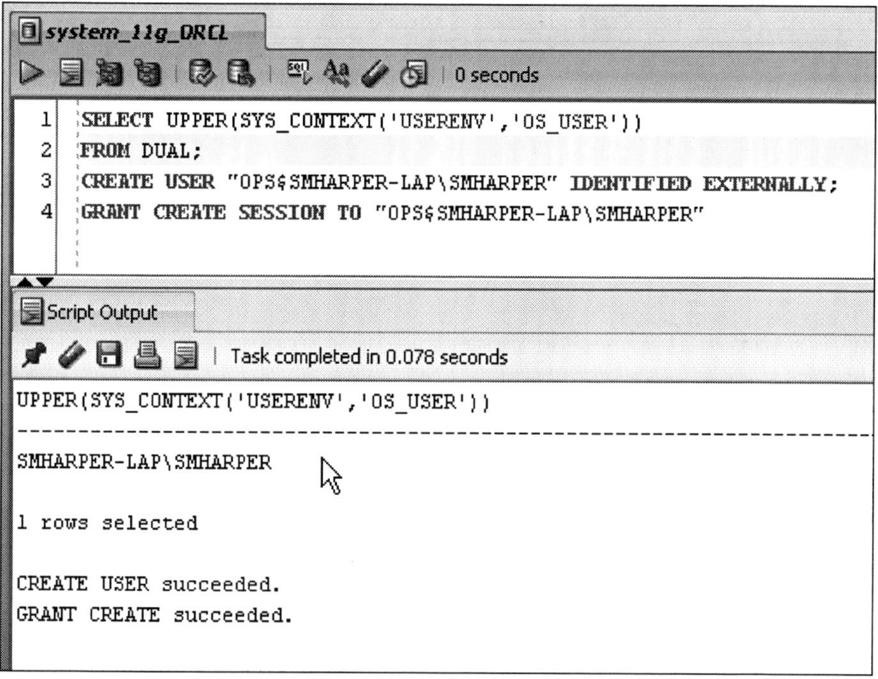

Setting the database environment variables

Notice the use of the `OPS$` variable in front of the username. The `OPS$` value is historical and can be changed or omitted by setting the database initialization parameter `OS_AUTHENT_PREFIX` that controls this value. In Microsoft Windows, the username also includes the machine name.

You can use OS Authentication when you connect to a database that is local to your machine. Therefore, you're connecting and authenticated on your machine and then connecting to your local database. You can use OS Authentication to connect to a remote database. To do this, you also need to set the `REMOTE_OS_AUTHENT = TRUE`.

Finally, in SQL Developer, the OS Authentication needs to use the thick OCI driver. So, if you use the OS Authentication with the **Basic** connection type, you must ensure that the thick OCI driver is used. To force the use of this driver, set the preference **Use OCI/Thick driver**, found in the **Database | Advanced Parameters**.

Creating a connection using OS Authentication

Once you have created the user in the database, have set the required database initialization parameters, and the OCI driver preference, you can create the new connection:

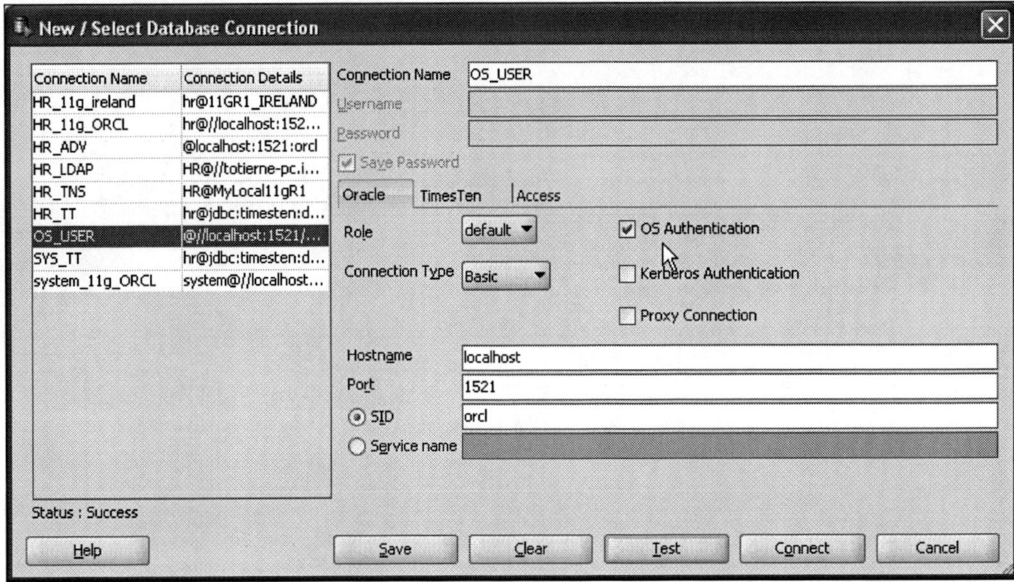

Without the OS Authentication selected, you are required to provide username and password. Once selected, you no longer require these values and so the fields are unavailable.

Using Proxy authentication

Typically used in a three-tier environment, proxy authentication allows one connection to act as a proxy for the next connection. This can eliminate the overhead of additional authentication between clients.

To illustrate this, we need to have two users, one will be the actual or destination database user and the second will be the proxy user. If we assume HR is the actual user in this example, we need to create an additional proxy to HR. We'll allow the new HR proxy to connect to the HR schema and details, without needing to know the HR schema password. To start, you need to create the new proxy user and grant the correct proxy authentication:

```
GRANT CONNECT, RESOURCE TO HR_PROXY IDENTIFIED BY ORACLE;
ALTER USER HR GRANT CONNECT THROUGH HR_PROXY;
```

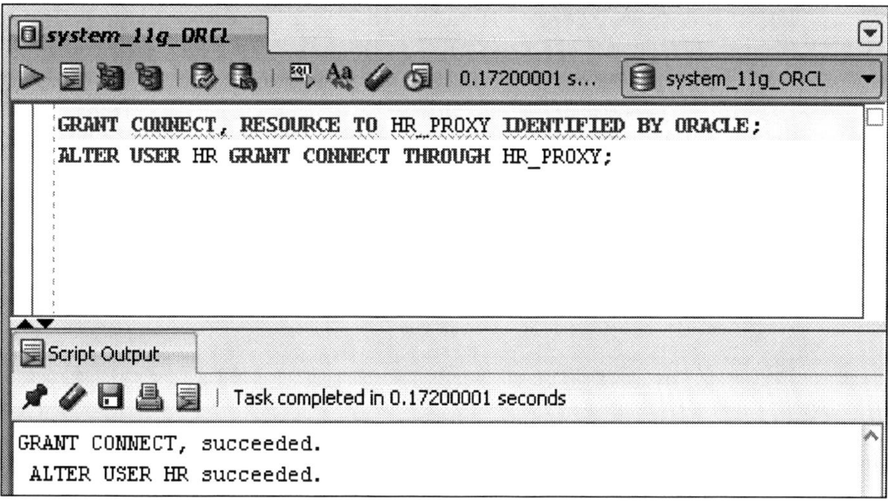

SQL Developer supports the ability to use:

- A single session with the connection
- Two sessions with the connection

In the first instance, we can use the proxy connection syntax, which is also available in a command line such as SQL*Plus, in the connection dialog. This syntax is `proxy_user_name[user_name]/proxy_user_password` and is illustrated in the following screenshot:

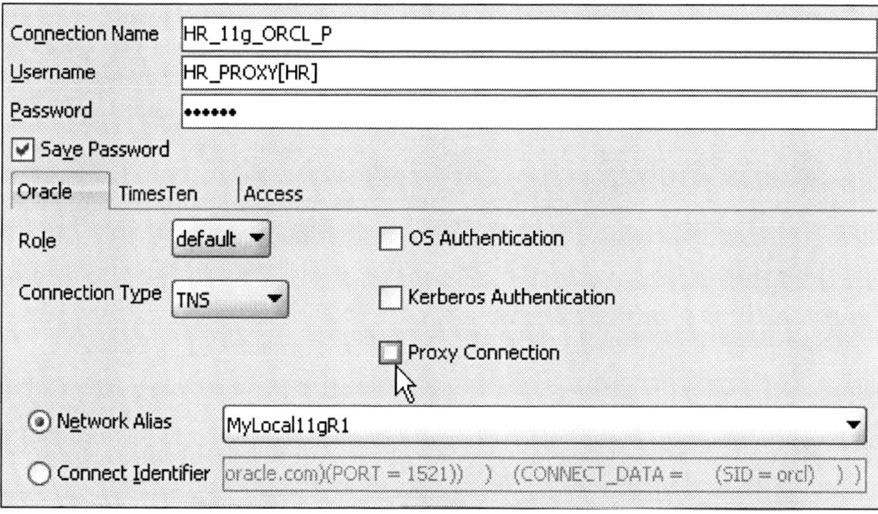

When doing this single session connection, do not select the **Proxy Connection** option in the dialog. Instead provide the proxy **Username** and **Password**, together with the destination user, HR.

You can also use two sessions with the connection. In this case, provide the proxy user and password in the connections dialog, and then click on the **Proxy Connection** checkbox. This action invokes a new dialog for the destination user:

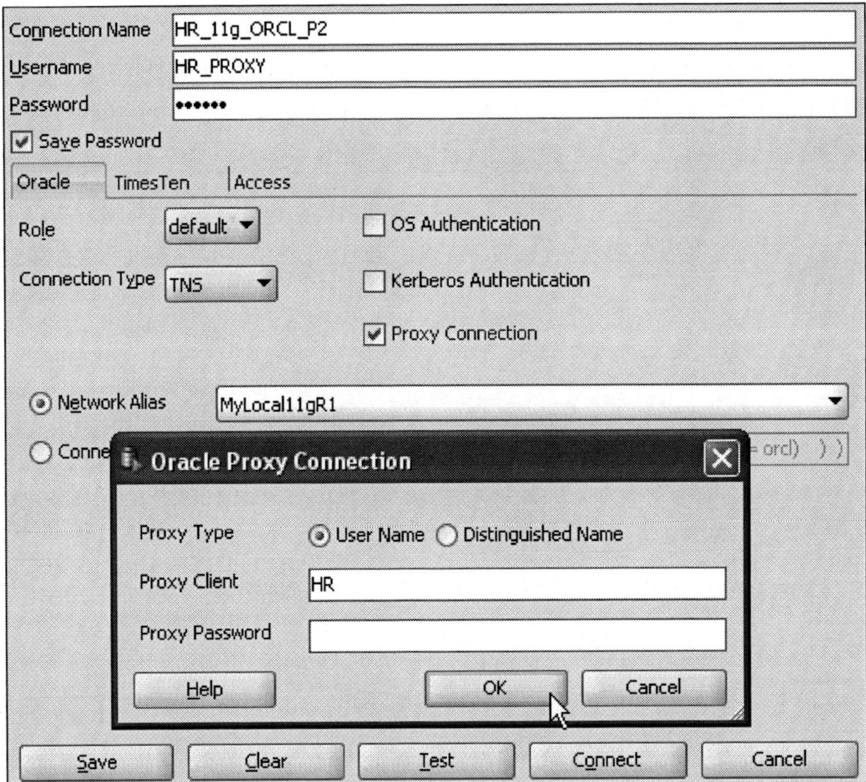

The screenshot displayed shows both the connection dialogs, with the **Proxy Connection** checkbox selected and the **Oracle Proxy Connection** dialog. Here, you need only supply the username, the password is optional. The optional password is driven by the way you create the proxy user as illustrated in the following two statements:

```
ALTER USER HR GRANT CONNECT THROUGH HR_PROXY AUTHENTICATED USING
PASSWORD;
ALTER USER HR GRANT CONNECT THROUGH HR_PROXY;
```

If you omit the authentication clause, then it is sufficient to use the name without the password.

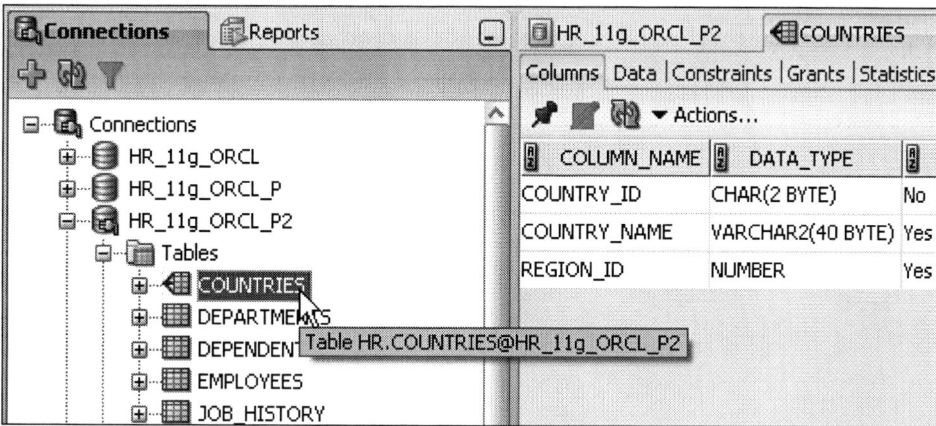

In the example displayed in the previous screenshot, the proxy user **HR_PROXY**, is connected to the user account HR, and can review objects in the HR schema.

Using Kerberos authentication

Kerberos is one of the strong authentication methods available for companies today to ensure identity security in a networked environment. It uses secret-key cryptography to store the username and password, and means that a client is required to prove its identity to the server and the server to the client. For more detail on Kerberos, refer to `http://web.mit.edu/kerberos/www/` and `http://www.kerberos.org`.

SQL Developer 1.5.3 introduced the ability to connect to the Oracle database using Kerberos authentication. It is beyond the scope of this book to provide the details on setting up and configuring a Kerberos server for authentication. However, that process is fully documented in the Oracle Advanced Security manual. For this section, we'll assume you have a Kerberos server setup.

Implementing Kerberos authentication in SQL Developer

SQL Developer provides support for Kerberos authentication using either the thin or the thick JDBC drivers. Once the Kerberos server is setup, you need to setup and access two files on the client, these are the Kerberos configuration file and the credential cache file. If you use the thick JDBC driver, you'll need to provide the location of these files in the `sqlnet.ora`, while for the thin driver, we'll set this up in SQL Developer.

We'll start by looking at the preferences that influence Kerberos authentication. In the **Database | Advanced Parameters**, selecting the **Use OCI/Thick driver** preference directs SQL Developer to use the thick driver, which in turn reads the `sqlnet.ora` file.

Kerberos authentication using the thin JDBC driver

The easier of the two to use and setup is the thin JDBC driver, which you do by using the **Preferences** dialog as follows:

1. Keep the **Use OCI/Thick driver** preference deselected.
2. Provide the path for the Kerberos configuration and credential cache files (seen below):

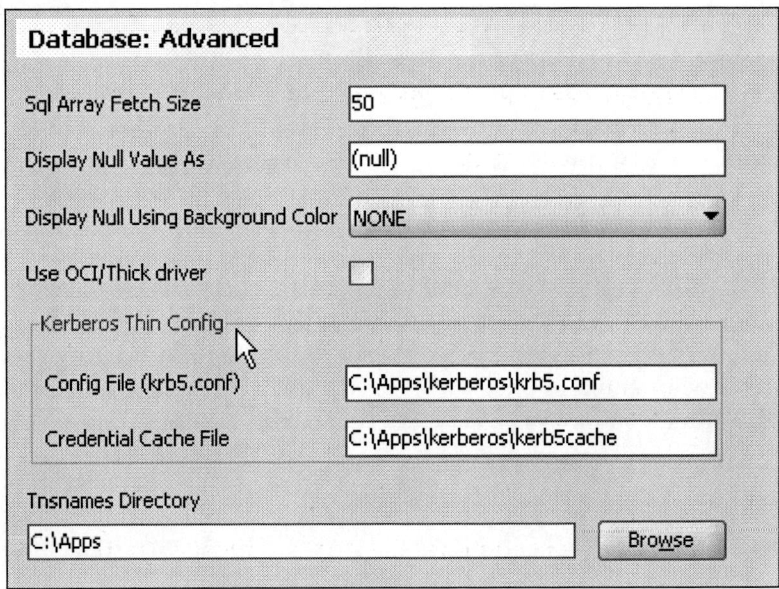

Once you have the preference set, you can create the connection. When using the thin driver, you'll need to provide a **Username** and **Password** in the connection dialog as shown in the following screenshot:

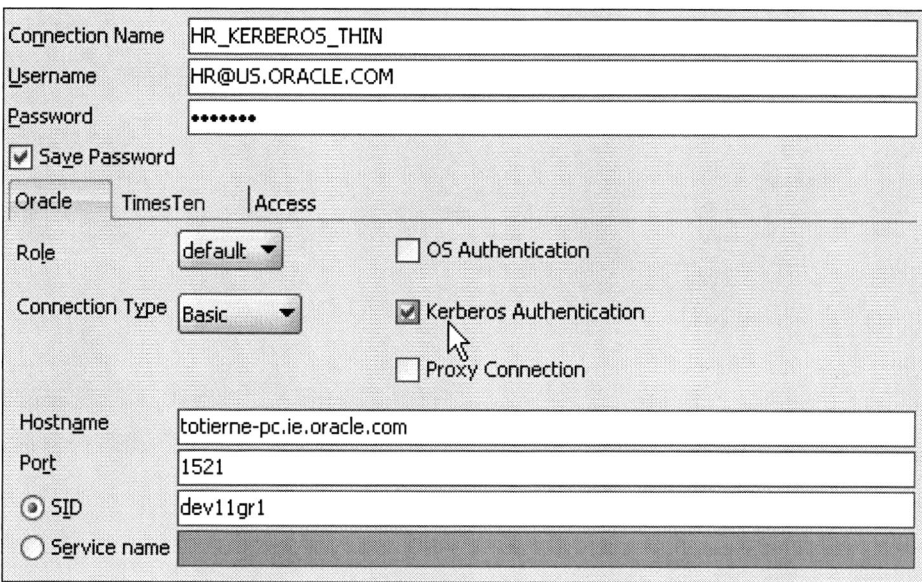

In the connection screenshot shown above, we have selected the **Kerberos Authentication** option, which in this case, due to the preferences that have been set, requires the username and password.

Kerberos authentication using the thick driver

If you want to use the thick driver, you'll need to follow a set of steps before you can use SQL Developer. The process is discussed, in full, in the Oracle Database Advanced Security Administrators Guide. A few salient points are mentioned here.

Set up the sqlnet.ora file

The `sqlnet.ora` file must include the path for the Kerberos configuration and the credential cache files, in additional to further parameters that define the service. You can edit the file manually, or use the Oracle Net Manager tool to set up the Kerberos5 Advanced Security option, which updates the file and adds the entries for you. An example of the entries in the `sqlnet.ora` is as follows:

```
SQLNET.KERBEROS5_KEYTAB = C:\Apps\kerberos\v5srvtab
SQLNET.KERBEROS5_REALMS = C:\Apps\kerberos\krb.realms
SQLNET.KERBEROS5_CC_NAME = C:\Apps\kerberos\krbcache
SQLNET.AUTHENTICATION_SERVICES= (KERBEROS5)
```

```
NAMES.DIRECTORY_PATH= (TNSNAMES, EZCONNECT)
SQLNET.KERBEROS5_CONF = C:\Apps\kerberos\krb5.conf
SQLNET.AUTHENTICATION_KERBEROS5_SERVICE = oratst
```

You'll need to create the client configuration `krb5.conf` file. Below is an example:

```
[libdefaults]
   default_realm = US.ORACLE.COM
[realms]
US.ORACLE.COM = {
       kdc = mymachine.us.oracle.com
                  }
[domain_realm]
     us.oracle.com = US.ORACLE.COM
```

Once you have the files set up, ensure the `TNS_ADMIN` environment variable includes the path for the Kerberos configuration and the credential cache files.

Setting up the user

The Kerberos administrator should set up the username and password in the Kerberos server, and you need to create an Oracle user that corresponds to the Kerberos user. In much the same way as we set up OS Authentication, the `OS_AUTHENT_PREFIX` drives part of the username defined, which if set to null, means you can omit a prefix when creating the Oracle user:

```
CREATE user "SUEHARPER@ORACLE.COM" identified externally;
```

Preparing the authentication ticket

Before you can use the Kerberos Authentication to connect to the database, you'll need to create an initial ticket, which identifies the user, who can then ask for additional service tickets. With Oracle, you need to run `okinit <username>` to create the ticket.

Connecting to Oracle using Kerberos, SQLNET, and SQL Developer

Once the setup is in place, you can connect to Oracle without a username or password, leaving the Kerberos server to verify the authentication.

In SQL Developer, select the **Database | Advanced Parameters** in the **Preferences** dialog, and select the **Use OCI/Thick Driver** preference. You are now ready to create a database connection in SQL Developer:

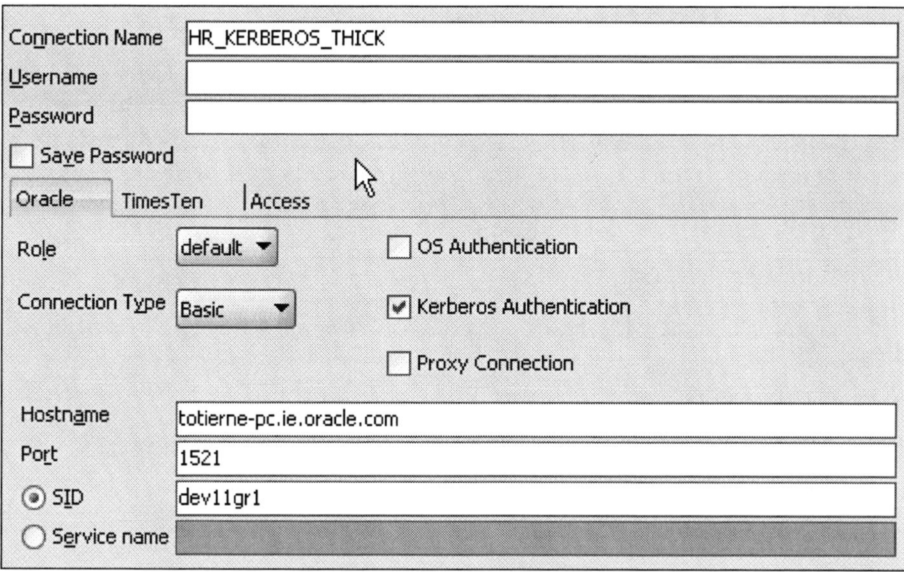

In the previous screenshot, the **Kerberos Authentication** is selected, which means that, due to the preferences just set, that the username and password can be omitted.

Using RADIUS authentication

If you have the Oracle Advanced Security option, you can also use RADIUS Authentication to connect. **Remote Authentication Dial In User Service** (**RADIUS**) is a networking protocol that provides strong authentication for users to connect over a network. When using Oracle SQL Developer you have no extra settings, as this method of authentication is transparent to the user. You enter the connection, as for basic or TNS connections, by supplying a username, password, and connection string. This detail goes to the Oracle database server, which, acting as the RADIUS client, passes the data from the Oracle client to the RADIUS server. The RADIUS server passes the data to the appropriate authentication server.

Creating non-Oracle database connections

SQL Developer allows you to connect to and browse a non-Oracle database. Primarily available for migrating from these databases to Oracle, the connections also allow you to use the SQL Worksheet for SQL queries. More detail on migrations and working with non-Oracle databases is described in the chapter on *Working with SQL Developer Migrations*. Here, we focus on setting up the environment.

Setting up JDBC drivers

In order to work with the non-Oracle databases supported by SQL Developer, with the exception of Microsoft Access, you need to install additional drivers. Even though these are freely available, they do require additional license consent, and as such are not shipped as part of SQL Developer. If you do not work with non-Oracle databases, there is no need for the additional drivers, and the extra connection tabs do not display in the **New Connection** dialog. There are two ways of installing these third-party database drivers:

- Using the **Check for Updates** utility, which includes walking through the license agreements required
- Manually downloading and adding the drivers

Using Check for Updates

The **Check for Updates** utility provides a quick way of adding the JTDS JDBC and MySQL drivers for connecting to the Microsoft SQL Server, Sybase, and MySQL databases. To run the **Check for Updates** utility, select **Help | Check for Updates**. This invokes the dialog to download and install the required drivers:

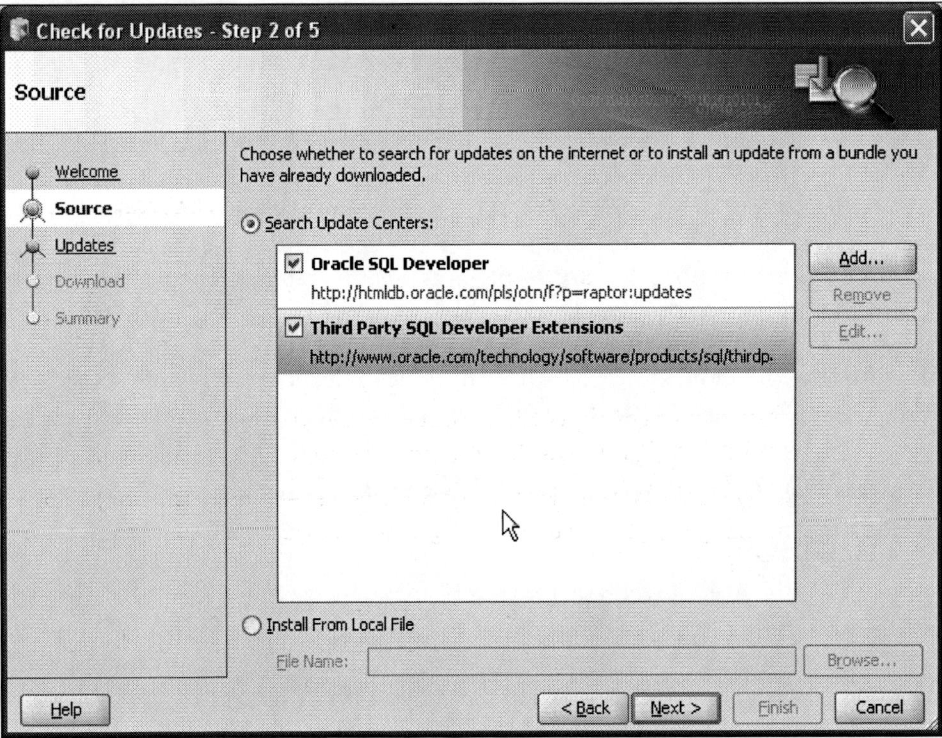

SQL Developer provides a selection of download centers. To access the third-party database drivers, select the **Third Party SQL Developer Extensions** option. This center includes other non-oracle extensions, so check only those that are required:

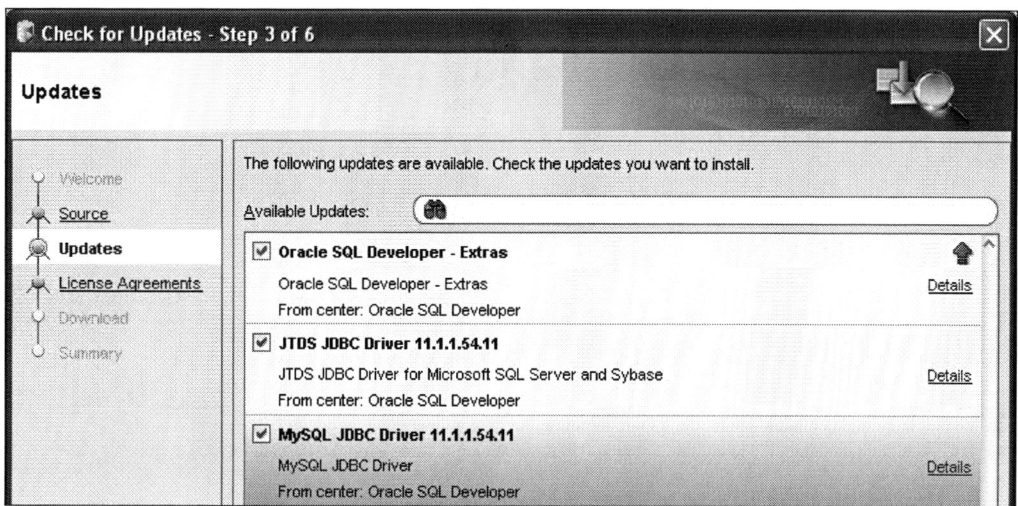

Once the **Check for Update** utility has run, restart SQL Developer. The new third-party drivers are listed in the **Preferences** dialog, under **Database | Extensions**.

Manually adding JDBC drivers

In order to connect to IBM DB2 and Teradata, you need to manually download and add drivers. You can use this approach for adding all of your drivers, including the drivers for Microsoft SQL Server, Sybase, and MySQL.

The first step is to download the drivers to a location of your choice. In each case, you need to unzip the files and point SQL Developer to the specified JAR file. The various drivers are available from the Internet as follows:

- MySQL—download the driver from `http://dev.mysql.com/downloads`. The required driver is the `mysql-connector-java-5.0.4-bin.jar`.
- Sybase Adaptive Server *and* Microsoft SQL Server—download the JTDS driver from `http://jtds.sourceforge.net/`. The required driver is the `jtds-1.2.jar`.
- DB2—download the drivers from IBM, `http://www-306.ibm.com/software/data/db2/express/additional-downloads.html`. You need to include both the `db2jcc.jar` and `db2jcc_license_cu.jar` files.

- Teradata—download the driver from `http://www.teradata.com/DownloadCenter/Topic9466-54-1.aspx`. You need to add both the `tdgssconfig.jar` and `terajdbc4.jar` files.
- Microsoft Access—no additional driver is required as SQL Developer uses the JDBC-ODBC bridge to make the connection. The Access tab only appears for SQL Developer installed on Microsoft Windows.

Once you have downloaded and unzipped the files, open the **Preferences** dialog and select the **Database | Third Party JDBC Drivers** node. In the following screenshot, the paths to the DB2 and Teradata JDBC drivers have been added:

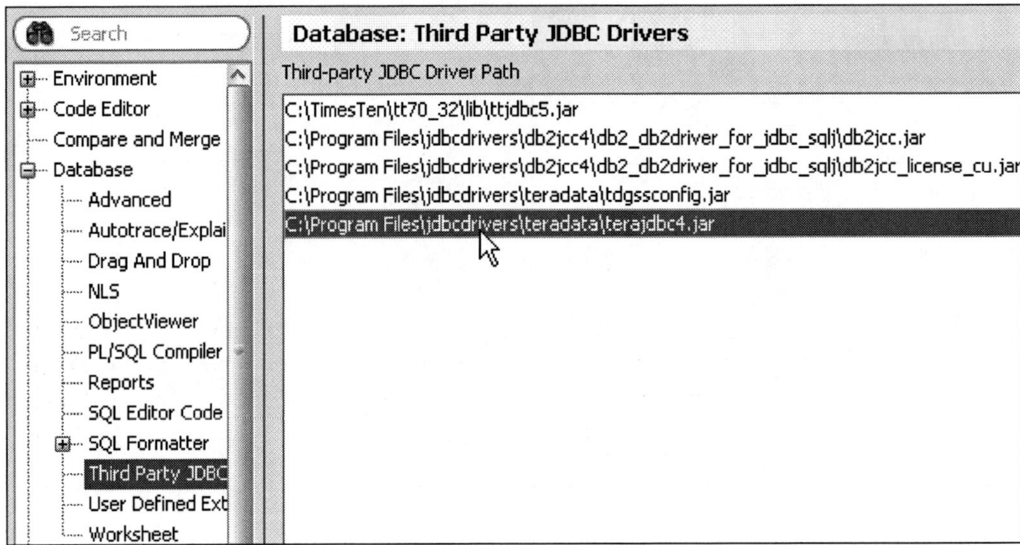

Whether you complete the process manually, or by using **Check for Updates**, you need to restart SQL Developer for the changes to take effect. Once done, the new non-Oracle database tabs appear in the **New Connection** dialog.

Creating connections to the third-party databases

Creating database connections to non-Oracle database uses the same dialog and process. Select the appropriate database tab and complete the details required. All connections require a connection name, username, and password. In this next section, we'll look at a few of the different connection dialogs available.

Connecting to IBM DB2

SQL Developer 2.1 includes support for IBM DB2 LUW 7, 8, and 9.

When setting up the driver for connecting to DB2, ensure that both the `db2jcc.jar` and `db2jcc_license_cu.jar` are included. Once the driver is in place, creating the connection is straightforward. You need only enter the machine hostname, port, and select the database name from the drop-down list, in addition to providing the usual connection name and password:

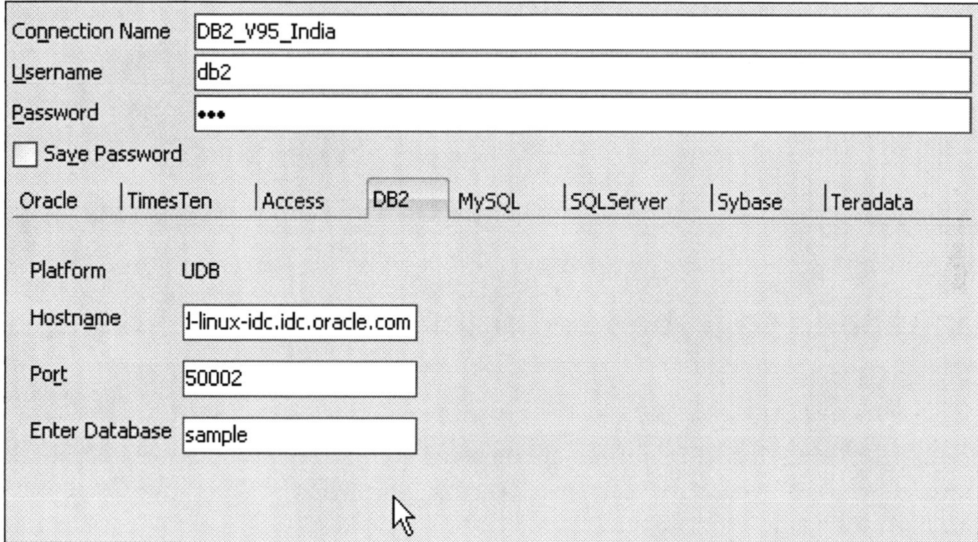

Microsoft Access

Not requiring any additional drivers, MS Access is always visible on Microsoft Windows in the set of connection tabs available. This is the most straightforward of the connection types, requiring only access to an Access `mdb` file.

Microsoft Access is only available on Microsoft Windows, so the connection tab does not appear on the Linux or Mac OS X platforms.

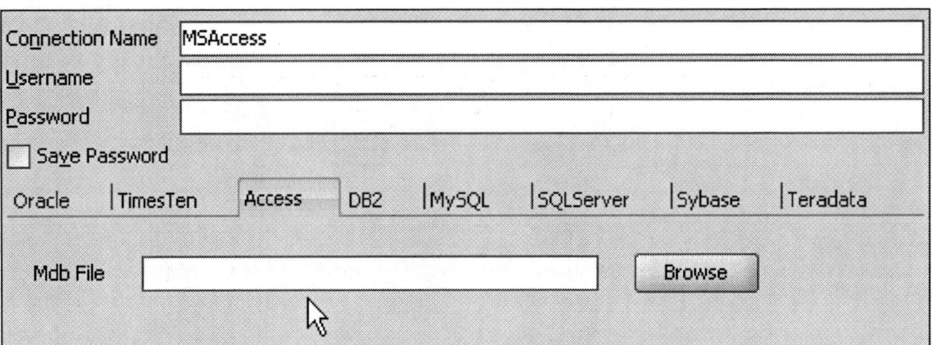

Connecting to Sybase Adaptive Server or Microsoft SQL Server

For connecting to either Sybase Adaptive Server or Microsoft SQL Server, you need the `jtds-1.2.jar`. Once set, you can create connections to the required databases. In both cases, you can specify the database location and then select **Retrieve database** to populate the drop-down list of available databases:

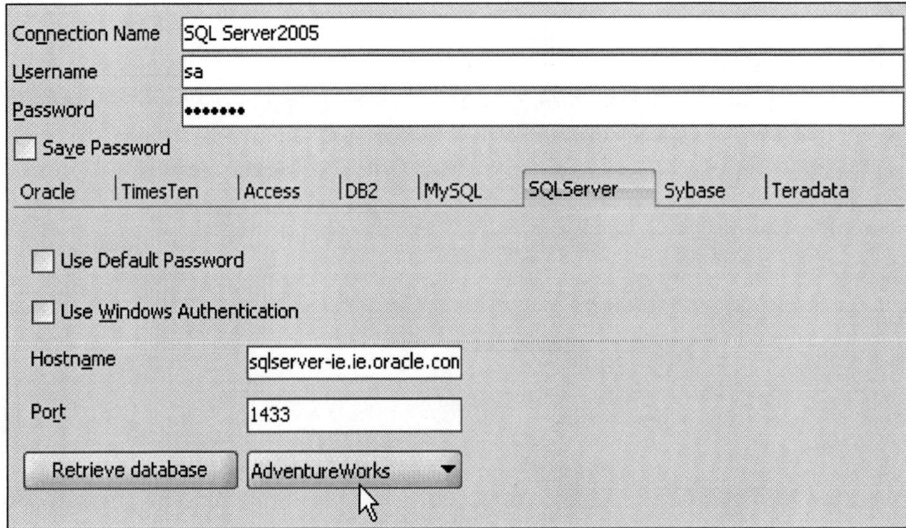

Connecting to MySQL

The **New Database Connection** dialog for MySQL includes the ability to handle Zero Dates. Setting up other properties is the same as for other databases:

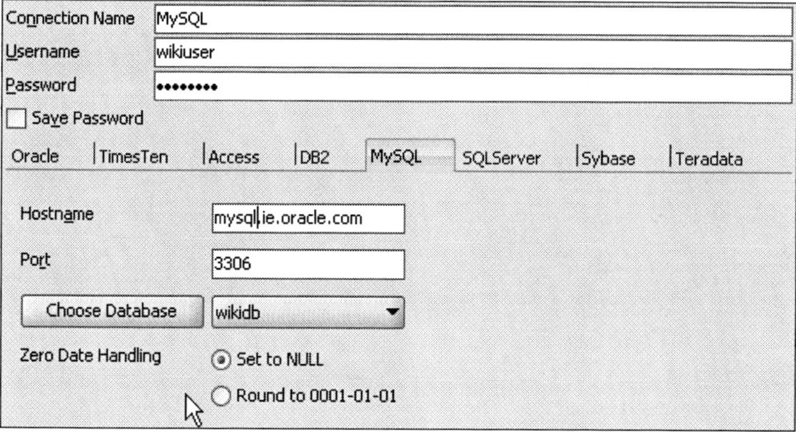

Organizing your connections

You can group your connections into folders to organize them. Prior to SQL Developer 1.5.0, the only way you had to categorize your connections was using a naming convention. In the following screenshot, you see the connection names we use often include the database version and location (for example, **OE_9i_IRELAND**):

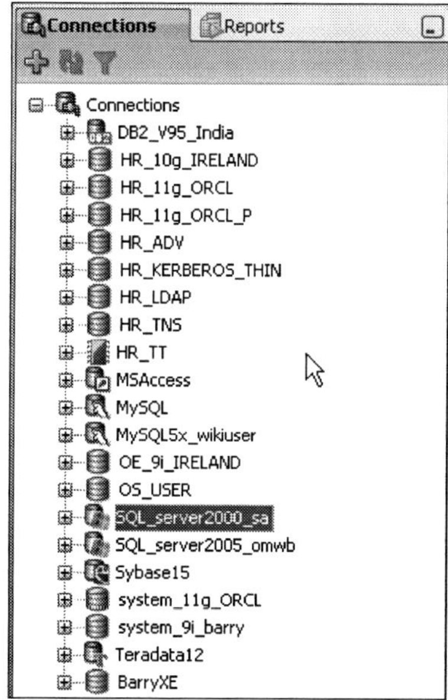

In addition to a useful naming convention, it is much easier to group these connections by categorizing them to suit your needs (for example, by location, user type, or database). We can take the same list of connections displayed in the previous screenshot and group them usefully using folders.

Creating folders

You can multi-select the connections created, and add them to a folder. In the next example, we have selected all Microsoft SQL Server connections and, using the context menu, selected **Add to Folder**. Initially, you need to create the folders. However, you can add to existing folders as you develop your folder structure.

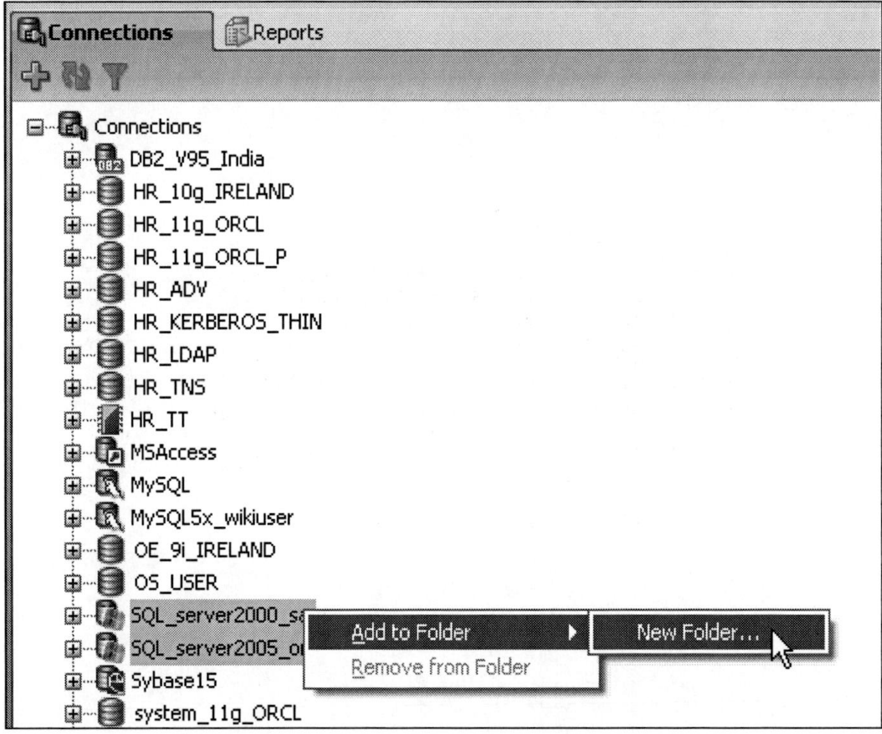

Working with folders

Folders are displayed alphabetically above all connections that are not in a folder. This list of folders is also displayed in the folder context menu, and so you can continue to add one or more connections to existing folders or create new. These folders are only displayed in the **Connections** navigator and are not used in any other connection drop-down list:

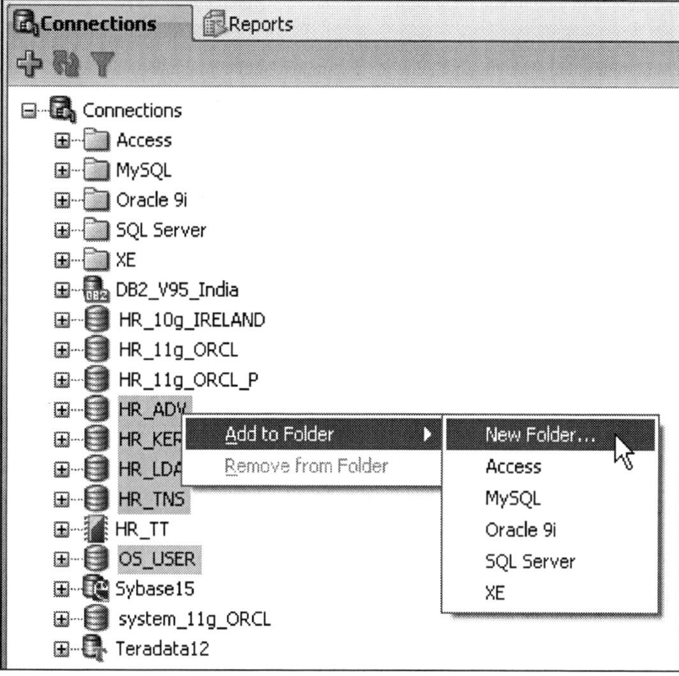

Managing folders

You can delete any folder you create by selecting **Remove Folder** from the context menu (shown in the following screenshot). This does not remove or delete any of the connections, just the folder.

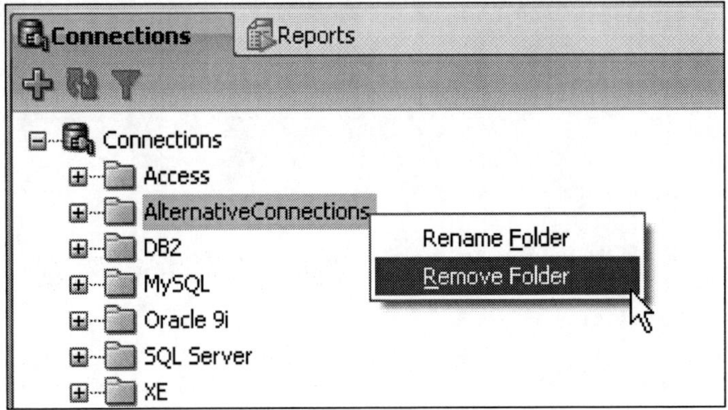

Exporting and importing connections

Once you have created your connections, it's useful to export them to an XML file that you can save and reuse. If you then install SQL Developer on another system, you can import these connections and all of the associated details. Starting with SQL Developer 2.1, any folders you create, either in SQL Developer 1.5.x or above, are reused.

When importing connections, you can select all or some of the connections in the XML file (seen in the following screenshot). If the connection already exists, you have the choice to overwrite or ignore the new connection import.

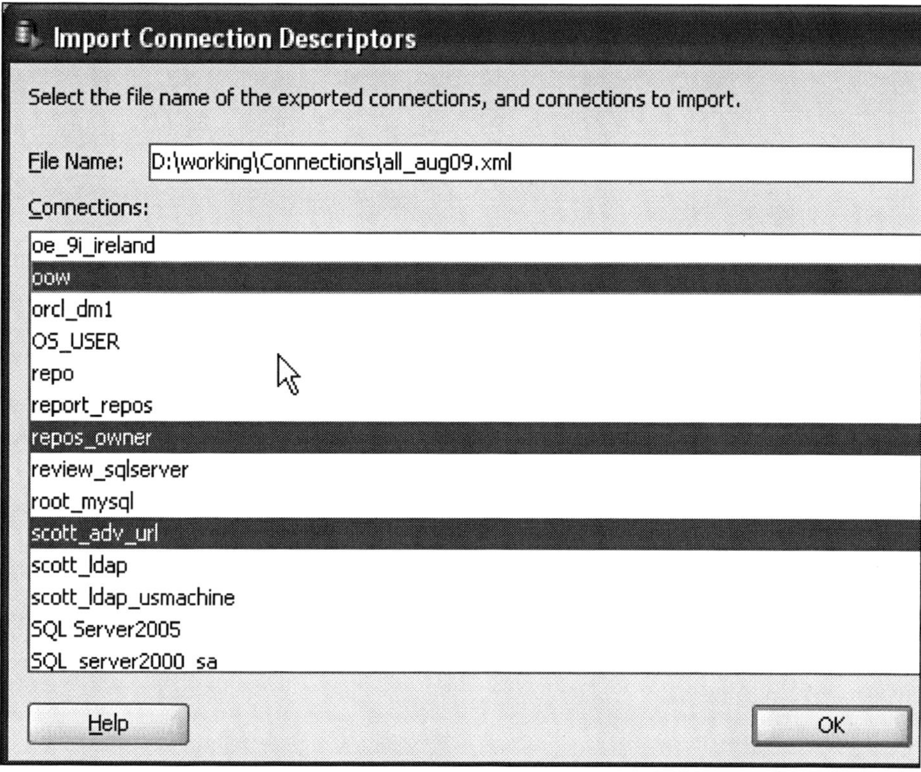

Connection names are case sensitive. When importing connections, you will only replace existing connections with an exact match.

Summary

SQL Developer is easy to install and use. Once you have unzipped the file and started the product, you can connect to your Oracle database without downloading or needing additional files. This easy connection uses the thin JDBC driver to make the connection. In addition to this, the product supports a wide variety of alternative connection and authentication types for Oracle and non-Oracle databases. In this chapter, we reviewed the SQL Developer support offered for Oracle database connections and authentication methods. We reviewed the various drivers required for non-Oracle databases and how to set them up. Finally, we looked at managing connections and folders.

In the next chapter, we'll look at database data modeling, and how to use SQL Developer Data Modeler to create and update entity relationship diagrams, as well as relational and physical data models.

10

Introducing SQL Developer Data Modeler

Oracle SQL Developer Data Modeler is available as an independent product, providing a focused data modeling tool for data architects and designers. There is also a Data Modeler Viewer extension to SQL Developer, which allows users to open previously created data models and to create read-only models of their database schemas. SQL Developer Data Modeler is a vast tool, supporting the design of logical Entity Relationship Diagrams, and relational models, with forward and reverse engineering capabilities between the two. It supports multi-dimensional, data flow, data type, and physical models, and allows files to be imported from a variety sources and exported to a variety of destinations. It allows users to set naming conventions and verify designs using a set of predefined design rules. Each of these topics is extensive, so in this chapter we'll review a few of the areas, illustrating how you can use them and highlight a few key features, using the independent, stand alone release of SQL Developer Data Modeler. We'll include a brief review of the integration points of the Data Modeler Viewer extension to SQL Developer. The product offers support for Oracle and non-Oracle Databases. In the interest of time and space, we have elected to only work with the Oracle database.

Oracle SQL Developer Data Modeler

SQL Developer Data Modeler provides users with a lightweight tool which provides application and database developers a quick and easy way of diagrammatically displaying their data structures, making changes, and submitting the new changes to update a schema. In this chapter, we will not attempt to teach data modeling (except to provide some generally accepted definitions). Instead, we will discuss how the product supports data modeling and a few of the features provided. There are a variety of books available on the subject, which describe and define modeling best practice.

Feature overview

The Data Modeler supports a number of graphical models and a selection of text-based models. The graphical models are:

- **Logical**—this is the entity relationship model or **Entity Relationship Diagram** (**ERD**), and comprises entities, attributes, and relationships.
- **Relational**—this is the schema or database model and is comprised of tables, columns, views, and constraints. In SQL Developer Data Modeler, these models are database independent, and need to be associated with the physical model to support database specific DDL.
- **Data Types**—this is the model that supports modeling SQL99 structured types and for viewing inheritance hierarchies. The data types modeled here are used in both the logical and relational models.
- **Multidimensional models**—these models support fact, dimension, and summary classifications for multi-dimensional models.
- **Data Flow**—these models support the definition of primitive, composite, and transformational tasks.

The following support these graphical models:

- **Domains**—these allow you to define and reuse a data type with optional constraints or allowable values. You can use domains in the Logical and Relational models.
- **Physical**—this model is associated with a relational model and defines the physical attributes for a specific database and version.
- **Business Information**—this allows you to model or document the business details that support a design.

Tying these graphical and textual models together are a variety of utilities, which include:

- Forward and reverse engineering between the Logical and Relational models
- Import from various databases
- Export, including DDL script generation, for various databases
- Design Rules for verifying standards and completeness
- Name templates, glossary, and abbreviation files for supporting naming standards

Integrated architecture

SQL Developer Data Modeler is made up of a number of layers, which have a tightly synchronized relationship. The Logical model is thought of as the core of the product, providing the starting point for any design, and feeding details into other models. The following diagram shows an illustration of how the models relate to each other:

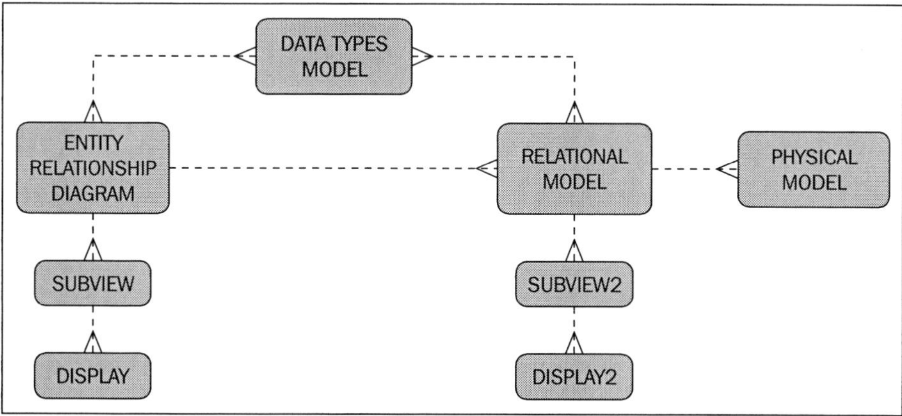

The logical ERD provides the basis for one or more relational models, and each of these feeds into one or more physical models, which are in turn used for the DDL generation. You can create separate data types models and use the defined data type in either the logical or relational models. Both relational and logical models can have multiple subviews created, and each subview can have many displays created.

Getting started

SQL Developer Data Modeler is an independent product, and with the exception of the Data Modeler Viewer extension to SQL Developer 2.1, is not packaged with other Oracle tools. You can download it and install it in a directory of your choice, with no impact on other tools. To install, simply unzip the file.

Installing and setting up the environment

Getting started with SQL Developer Data Modeler is straightforward. Follow the links from the Data Modeler site on OTN, `http://www.oracle.com/technology/products/database/datamodeler` to the download location. You are offered a choice of files to download:

- For Microsoft Windows, a ZIP file with or without the JRE included
- For the Mac OS X, a ZIP file without the JRE included
- For Linux, a ZIP file without the JRE included

For any of these ZIP files, extract the file contents and run the `datamodeler.exe`, which is in the top-level `/datamodeler` folder, or in the `/datamodeler/bin` folder. For Linux, use the `datamodeler.sh` executable.

If the file you choose does not include a JRE, you will be prompted on startup for the location of your installed JRE. The minimum supported release is JRE 1.6 update 6.0.

Oracle clients and JDBC drivers

If you are designing and building a model from scratch, or have access to the DDL script file for importing models, then you do not need to have access to a database. However, if you want to import from a database, you'll need to create a database connection. In this case, there is no need for an Oracle client in your development environment because you can use the thin JDBC Driver to connect to the database. SQL Developer Data Modeler also supports the TNS alias. Therefore, if you have access to a `tnsnames.ora` file, or have other Oracle software installed in your environment, you can access the `tnsnames` file to make the database connection if and when required.

Creating your first models

The Data Modeler browser starts with empty **Logical** and **Relational** models. This allows you to start a new design and build a model from scratch, whether a logical model with entities and attributes, or a relational model with tables and columns. The Data Modeler also supports metadata to be imported from a variety of sources, which include:

- Importing metadata from:
    - DDL scripts
    - Data dictionary
- Importing from other modeling tools:
    - Oracle Designer
    - CA Erwin 4.x
- Importing other formats:
    - VAR file
    - XMLA (Microsoft, Hyperion)

The context menu displaying the choices available is shown in the following screenshot:

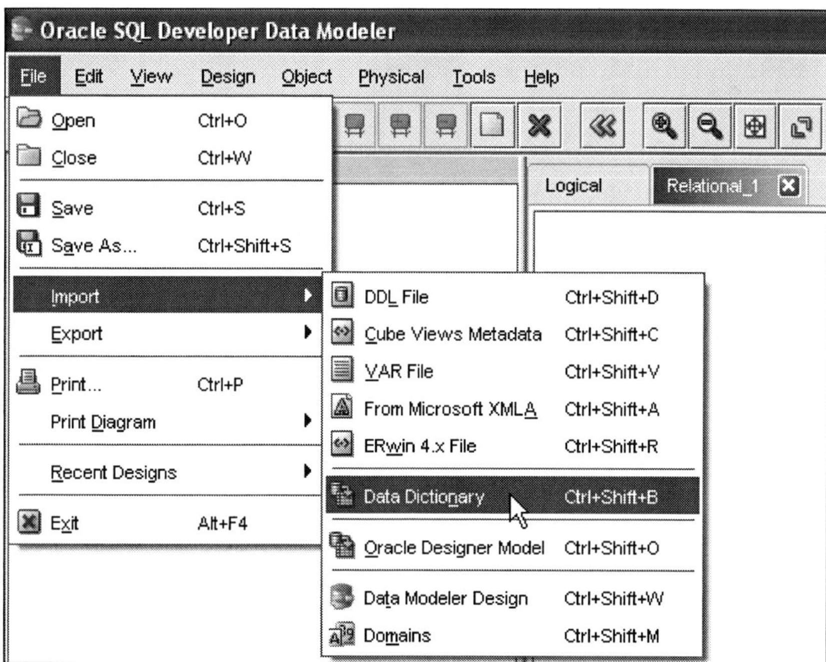

Once you have created and saved your models, you can open these or share them with colleagues. To open an existing model, use the menu:

- **File | Open**—browse to the location of the files, which then opens the full design with all of the saved models
- **File | Recent Designs**—opens the full design, with all of the saved models, with no need to first search for the location
- **File | Import | Data Modeler Design**—more granular, offering a choice of models saved in a set of models

Recent diagrams

Use **File | Recent Diagrams** to display a list of all diagrams you have recently worked on and saved. Using this approach saves you from needing to browse to the location of the stored files.

Importing from the Data Dictionary

There are many ways to start using the tool by just starting to draw any one of the model types mentioned. Later in the chapter, we'll start with an ERD and work our way down to the DDL scripts. In this first section, we'll import the details from an existing schema. It's a useful place to start, as the process quickly creates a model you can investigate and then use to learn more about the tool. This may also be one of the most frequently used features in the tool, allowing anyone to quickly see a model of the data structures that underpin their database-based application.

In the screenshot shown earlier, we highlighted the **File | Import | Data Dictionary** option. Using this allows you to import from Oracle 9*i*, Oracle 10*g*, Oracle Database 11*g*, Microsoft SQL Server 2000 and 2005, and IBM DB2 LUW Versions 7 and 8.

Creating a database connection

Before you can import from any database, you need to create a database connection for each database you'll connect to. Once created, you'll see all of the schemas in the database and the objects you have access to.

Access the **New Database Connection** dialog from the **File | Import** wizard (seen in the following screenshot). If you have no connections, click on **Add** to create a new connection.

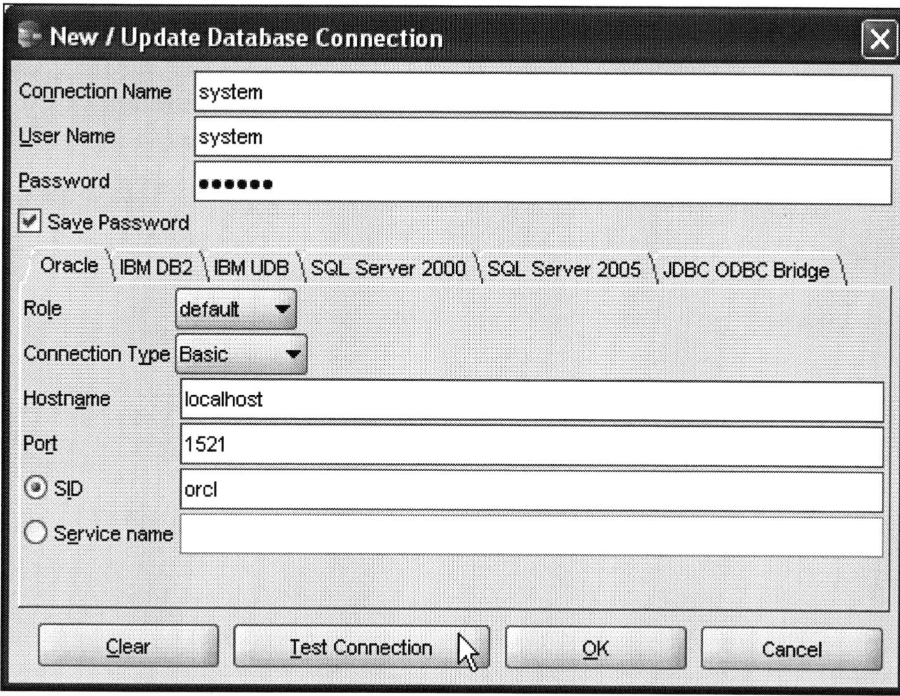

For a **Basic** connection, you need to provide the **Hostname** of the database server, the **Port**, and **SID**. The connection dialog also supports TNS alias and the advanced JDBC URL.

Before you can add connections for non-Oracle databases, you need to add the required JDBC drivers. To add these drivers, use **Tools | General Options | Third Party JDBC Drivers**.

Using the import wizard

Once you have a connection created, select the connection and continue using the dialog by clicking on **Next**. You can select more than one schema during import. In the example below, we have selected two schemas, which results in three diagrams, one central model with all of the imported tables and views, and two *subviews*. When importing, a separate subview is created for each schema you select and all of the imported objects are displayed in that schema (this is not the only role for subviews, and we'll expand on that later in the chapter).

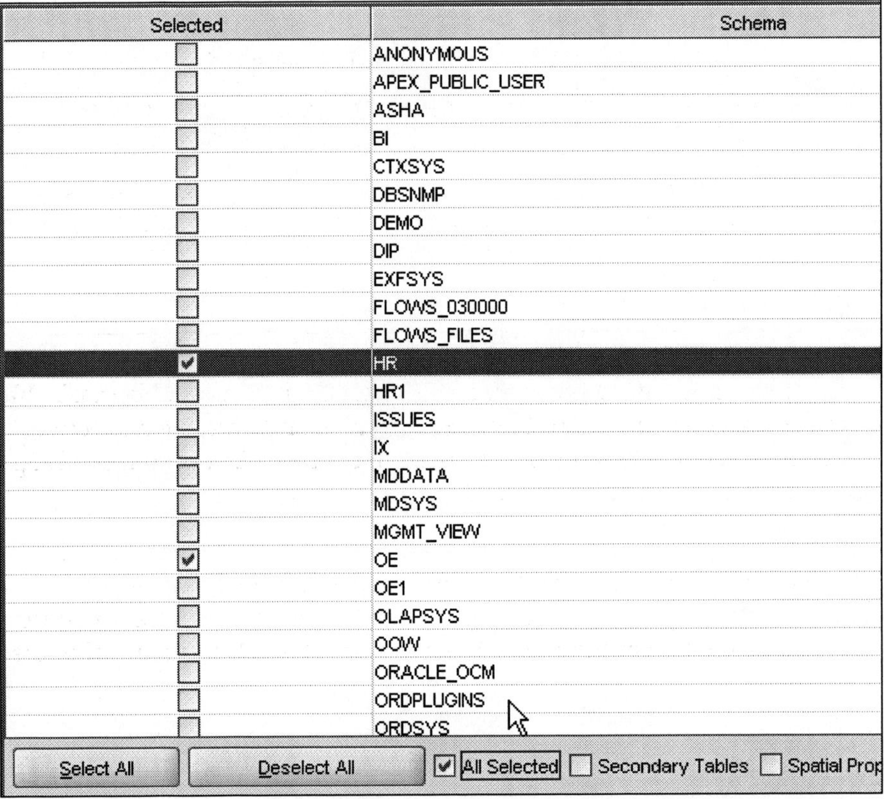

In the **Import Wizard** displayed, there is a set of checkboxes and buttons below the listed schemas. By selecting **All Selected**, the screens that follow will have all instances of all objects automatically selected. Depending on what you are planning to import, it is often easier to keep that deselected and then use the **Select All** button on each object type tab:

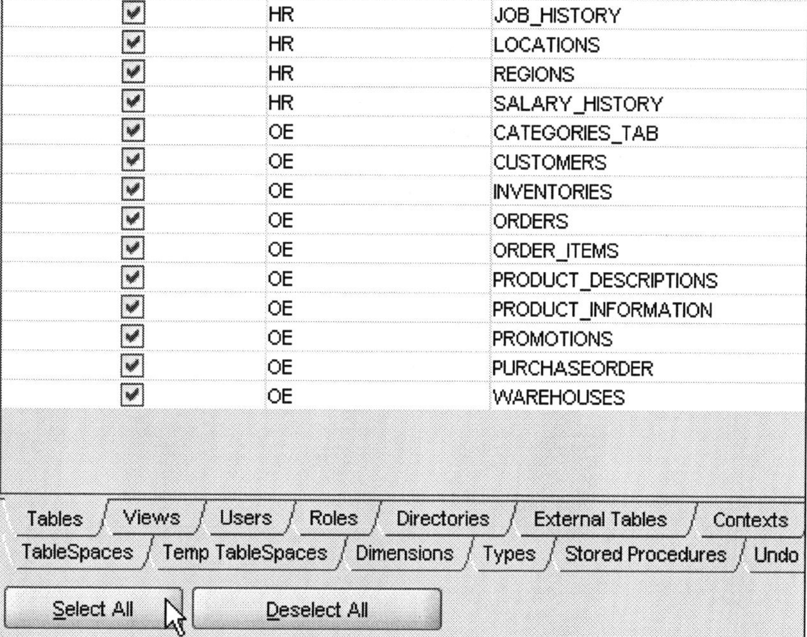

Once you have selected the schemas, you can select the individual objects. **Tables** and **Views** are placed on the central Relational model and onto the respective subviews for each schema. All other objects, such as **Roles**, **Users**, and **TableSpaces**, are maintained in the Physical model listed in the object browser.

A summary of objects to be imported is displayed and you are offered the choice of the model destination. The default destination is **Relational_1.** The choice given here is needed for second or any subsequent imports. For these you need to decide whether you'll want to merge the objects into an existing model or create a new model.

To create the initial model, complete the dialog and select **Finish**. Each time you import a set of database objects, a log file of the completed activity is created, which tallys the number of statements and errors. It is worth saving the log files to use for troubleshooting later.

[Importing multiple schemas from the **Data Dictionary** creates a central Relational model and a subview for each of the schemas imported.]

Reviewing the results

Once the import is complete, the main Relational diagram opens:

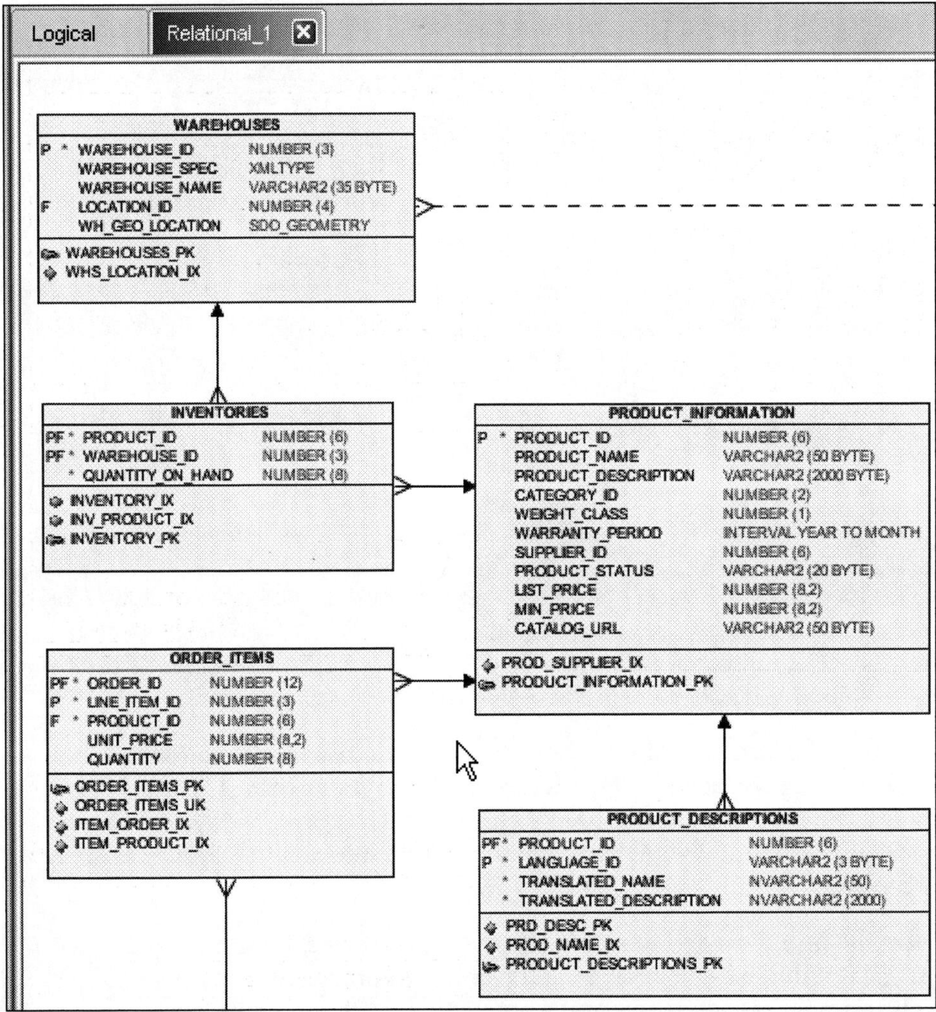

The previous screenshot shows a few of the tables imported into the Relational model. To see the initial subviews created for each schema created, expand the **Relational Models** node and then the **SubViews** node. Right-click on one of the schema subviews listed and select **Show Diagram**.

In the following screenshot, we have opened the **HR** subview and are preparing to open the **OE** subview:

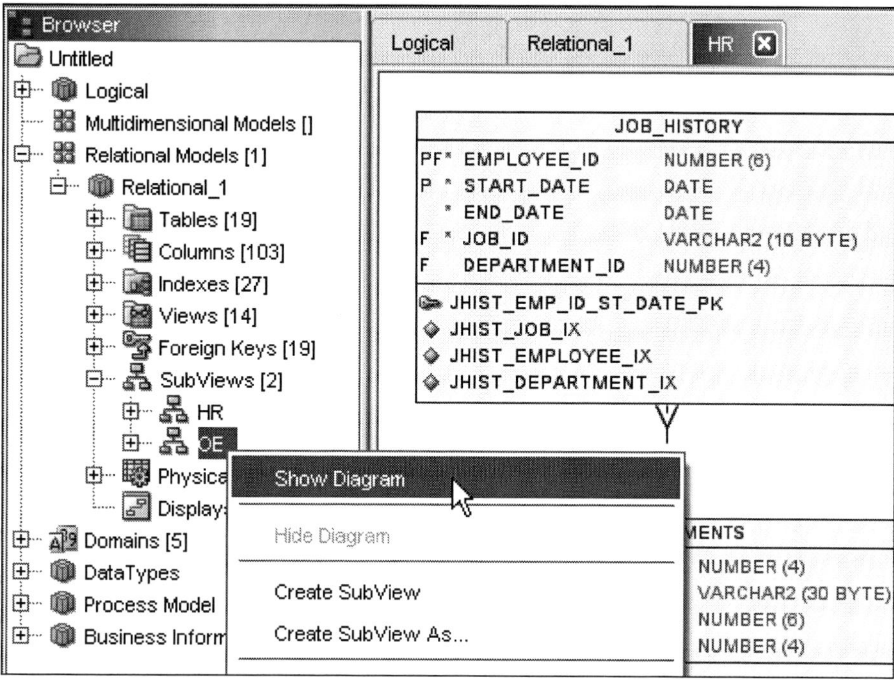

Saving designs

As you work, it is wise to save the design you are working on. It is prudent, in case something goes wrong, and necessary if you are going to close and reopen the tool later. Initially, a design is untitled. You can change this by saving the design. Once saved, the new name appears in the browser, and a set of folders and XML files are saved on your file system:

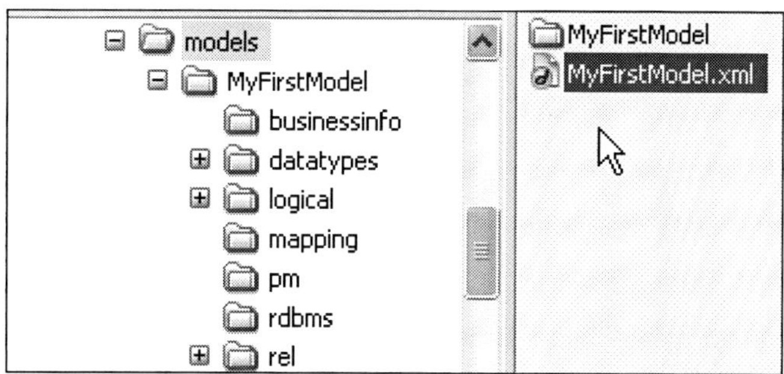

When you save a design, a folder and a file of the same name are created. The previous screenshot shows Windows Explorer with a folder of a saved design. Here, the top-level folder is called `MyFirstModel`, as is the top-level XML file. It is this top-level file that you select when opening a design. All of the files are XML and can be read. Do not edit these as doing so can corrupt your design.

Working with diagrams and their components

You can waste away many hours laying out the elements on a diagram. Therefore, this aspect of modeling can be time consuming. However, a model serves as documentation and a communication device. Therefore, taking the time to make sure it is well annotated and clearly designed is important. Most of the controls for the models are on the context menu, allowing you to modify individual aspects of the diagram. The context menu changes depending on whether you have an object or line selected, or you're just clicking in the open space. You can also set general defaults using **Tools | General Options | Diagram**. In this section, we'll look at the various options available when working with the diagrams.

Formatting the elements

Before moving a relationship line, entity, or table, you can dramatically change the impact and readability of a large diagram just by changing the colors. This is readily demonstrated when importing from two or more schemas. Using the previous example where we imported from two schemas, open one of the subviews and select all of the tables. With the objects selected, invoke the **Format Object** dialog using the context menu:

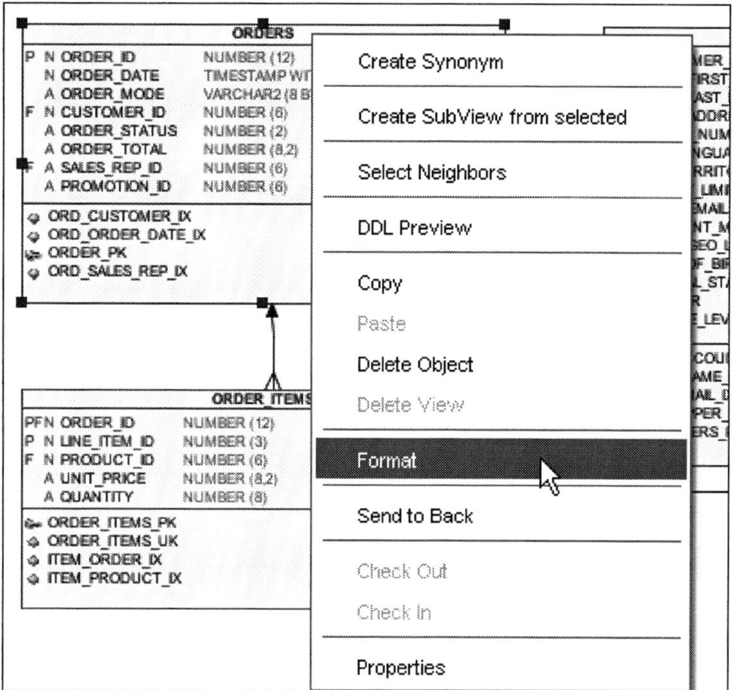

If this is the first time you are adjusting the colors, the dialog does not display any colors as you open it. The colors used in the diagram are the default settings. Deselect **Use Default Color** and click on the **Background** and **Border Color** items to select and set the new color. When you are done, click on **OK** and note the changes applied to the subview. Switch to the main relational model to review the impact there. The color applied to the subview is also applied to the main model as shown. This is very useful when illustrating how tables in different schemas relate to each other. For example, take the HR and OE sample schema, all of the tables related to human resources are maintained in the HR schema, while those related to the order entry system are maintained in the OE schema. You may well have applications designed around the HR schema and others tied to the OE schema, but some may involve both. In the following relational model, the OE tables are now colored green, so we're able to identify them, but we can also see where the schemas link. We can see that a CUSTOMER may deal with one EMPLOYEE and has many ORDERS:

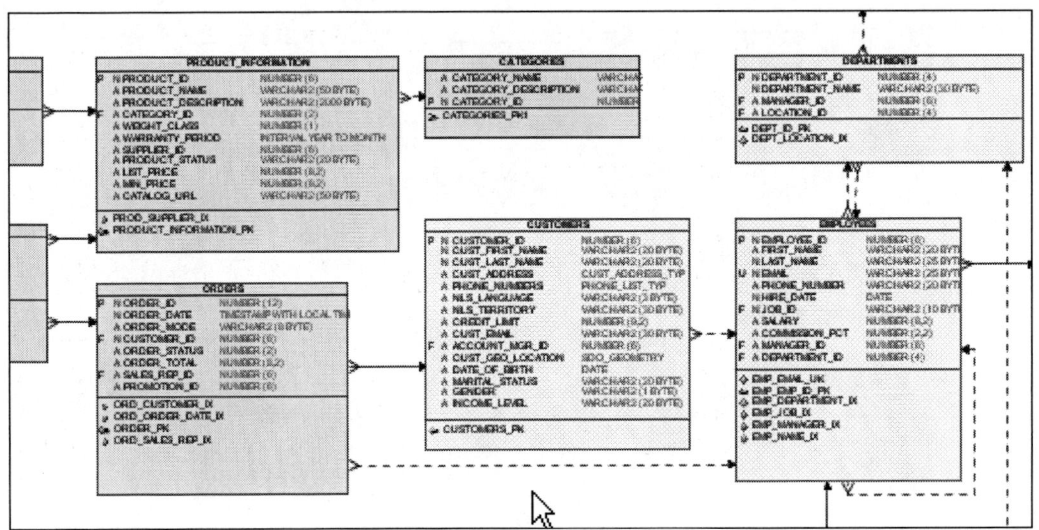

Selecting all of the tables in a model

Select any table and click on **Select Neighbors** from the context menu. Select **All Zones**, to select all of the tables. Use this instead of *Ctrl+A*, which selects all tables *and* all lines.

Changing the default format settings

Instead of changing individual items or even a set of items, you can change the default color for each of the element types displayed on a diagram. The **Tools | General Options | Diagram | Format** provides the ability to control the color of each of the elements displayed such as tables, views, and entities:

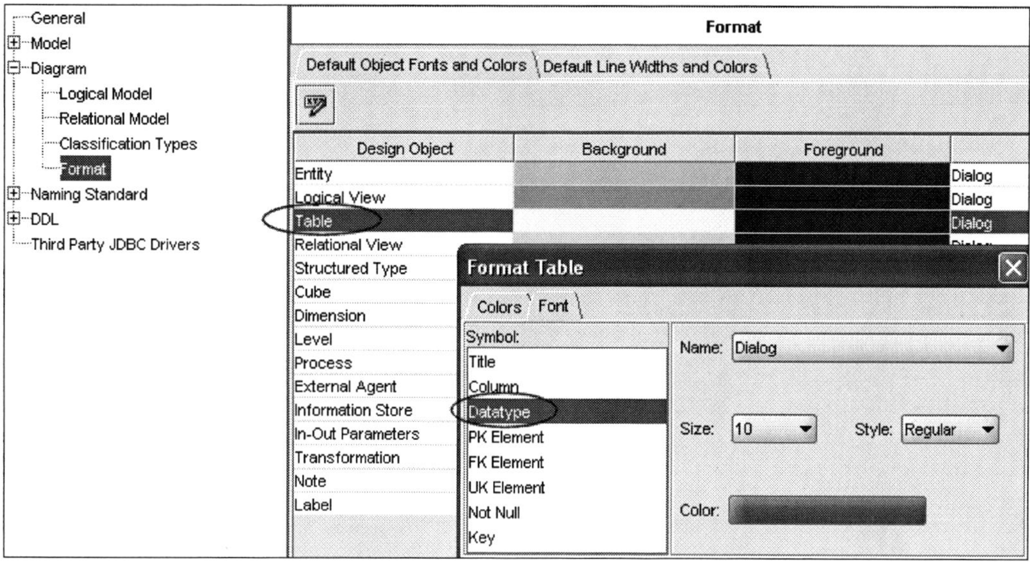

To edit any of the elements in the dialog, double-click on the object, or select the object and the edit icon. This allows you to adjust the color of the item and to format the font. You can use the font color to highlight mandatory, Unique, or Foreign Keys.

Setting general diagram properties

Use the same **Tools | General Options | Diagram** to set model properties, which include:

- Displaying the grid
- Controlling the background color of the diagram
- Controlling the **Auto Route** feature which is *on* by default

Set display properties for certain items on each of the models, including the control of:

- The diagram notation for the logical model, which supports the Barker and Bachman notations
- The display of the relationship names for either the logical or relational models
- The flow names for process models

For example, to display the relationship names on an Entity Relationship Diagram (as seen below), check the display property on the **Tools | General Options | Model | Logical**, and ensure that the Relation Cardinality properties for the relationships are also set.

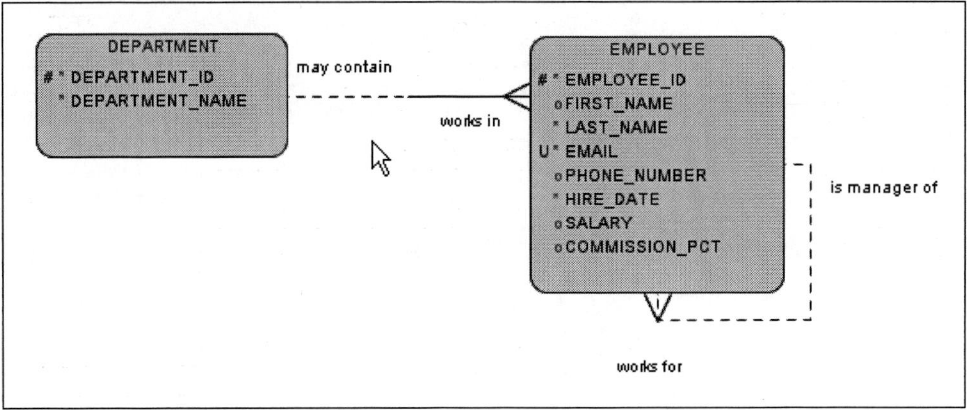

Creating subviews and displays

Adding subviews and displays offers you alternative ways of laying out elements on a diagram and for working with subsets of items. You can create multiple subviews and displays for either logical or relational models, and remove them as easily, without impacting the main models.

Adding subviews to your design

You have already encountered a subview by importing from a number of schemas in the data dictionary. Subviews are not only a reflection of the different schemas in a design, but they can also represent any subset of elements in the design, allowing you to work with a smaller, more manageable set of elements.

You can create a subview from the object browser by selecting:

- The **SubViews** node and using the **New SubView** context menu. In this case, you have a new empty diagram that you can populate by dragging tables or entities (depending on the subview in question) onto the page.
- Any of the model tabs and then selecting the **Create SubView** menu. This creates a new and empty subview.
- An element or elements on an existing model and using the **Create SubView from selected** context menu on the diagram. In this case, the new subview will contain the tables or entities you selected:

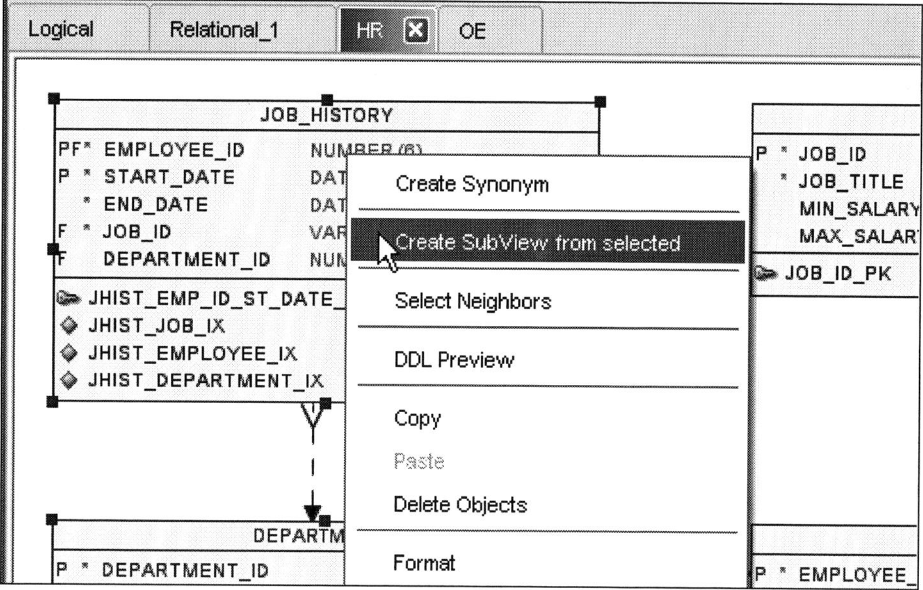

The layout of the subview is not linked to the main model in any way. What *is* linked is how you format the items on the subview and any structural changes you make to the objects. You can continue to add new items to the subview by dragging them onto the surface from the object browser. When deleting items from the subview, you should choose whether the item is deleted:

- From the view (**Delete View**)
- From the complete design (**Delete Object**)

Adding displays

A display is an alternative view of a diagram, whether a main model or a subview, and is linked directly to that model. If you delete the model, the display is also deleted. Any items that you add or remove from displays are also automatically added or removed from the main model they are linked to.

To create a new display, select the tab of any model and select **Create Display** from the context menu. The new display created is, initially, a replica of the model you selected in both layout and items available. All additional displays are listed at the bottom of the model. In the following example, the **HR** subview has two displays created, as highlighted at the bottom of the screenshot, the main **HR** display and the new **Display_1**. The **Create Display** context menu is also illustrated:

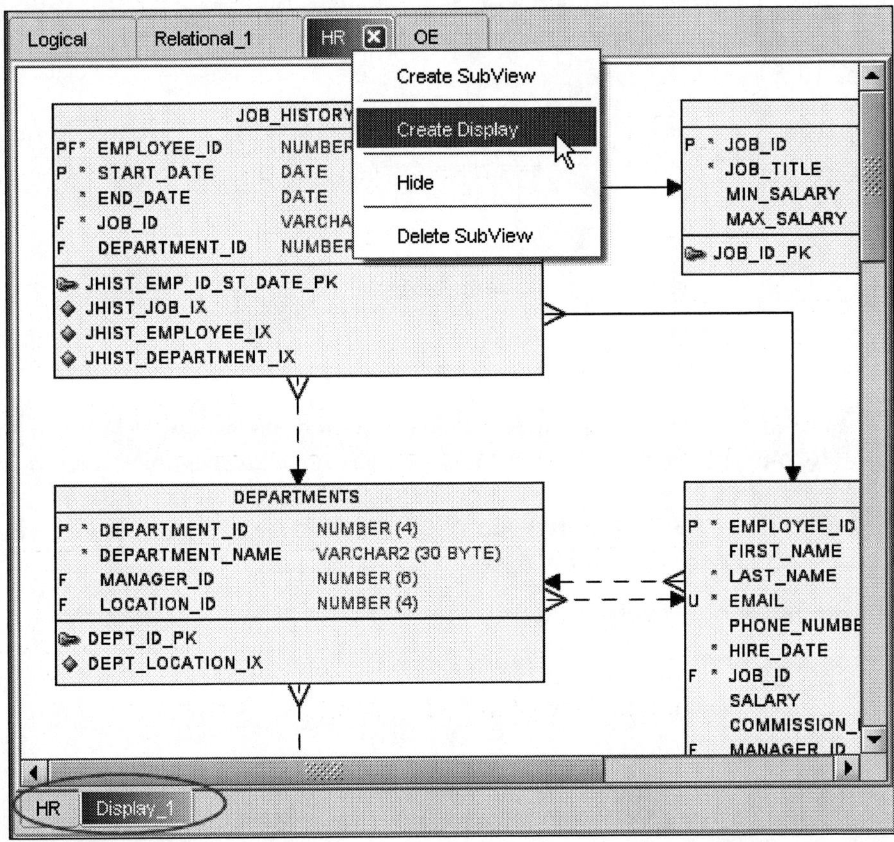

Use the new display to change the layout of the model and to adjust the level of detail displayed on the diagram.

A second display of the same model is useful when you want to show more or less detail on a model. You can, for example, create a display which only displays the entity or table names. Right-click in the space on a diagram and select **View Details | Names Only**. We'll discuss how to layout the diagram elements later in the section.

Creating a composite view

If you create a number of subviews, create a new diagram showing the composite models of each of these on a single layout. This serves as a useful reminder of the number of subviews or models you have by having a thumbnail of the various layouts. Alternatively, you can add a composite view of one subview and place it on another.

To create a composite view, select the model in the browser and drag it onto the diagram surface. You can drag any model onto any other diagram surface, except its own:

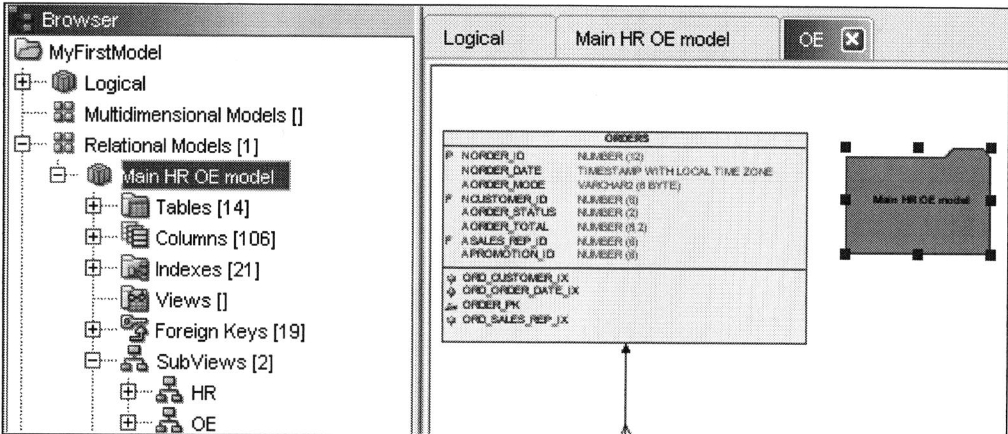

Once you have the composite folder displayed on the diagram, display the composite model within that folder by selecting **Composite View** from the context menu. If the model you want to view has a selection of displays, then you can also select the display you want to see within that composite.

The following screenshot shows the, subview, displaying the composite models of the HR subview, the main logical model, and both displays of the logical model:

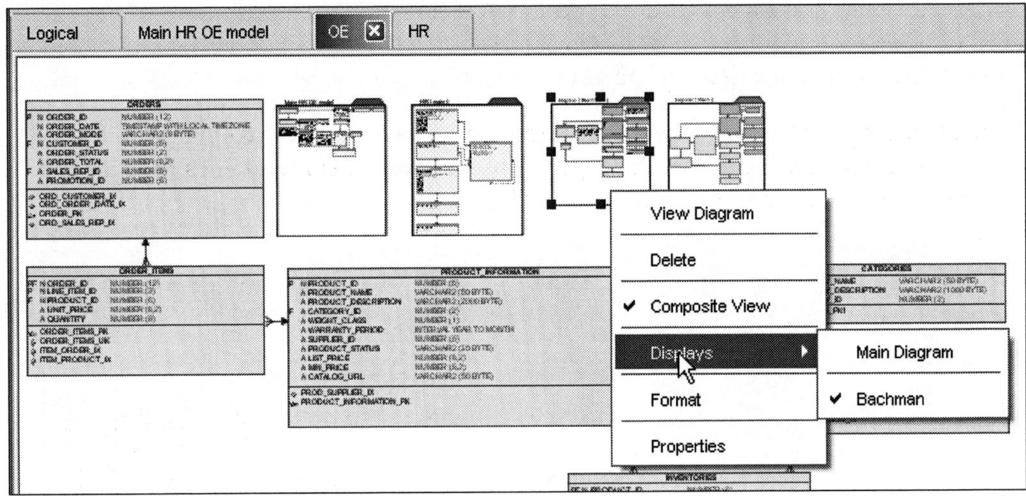

Controlling the layout

When working with a large number of items in a model, it's important to keep the layout organized. A variety of tools to help with the process are explained in the following sections.

Adjusting the level of detail displayed

Change the amount of detail displayed in a table (or entity) using the **View Details** menu. It is invoked with a right-click on the white space of any diagram. The **View Details** menu has options for displaying:

- All Details
- Names Only
- Columns
- Datatype
- Keys

Adjusting the width and height across the model

If you have a large diagram and want to see how tables or entities relate to each other, you can create a more compact model using a display, without impacting the main model. This can be done by setting the details to display the name only and then resizing and repositioning the objects.

In the following screenshot, we have set the model to display only the name of the tables. Create a more compact diagram by resizing one of the tables to a more fitting set of dimensions, select the rest, and then resize them all to the same width and height:

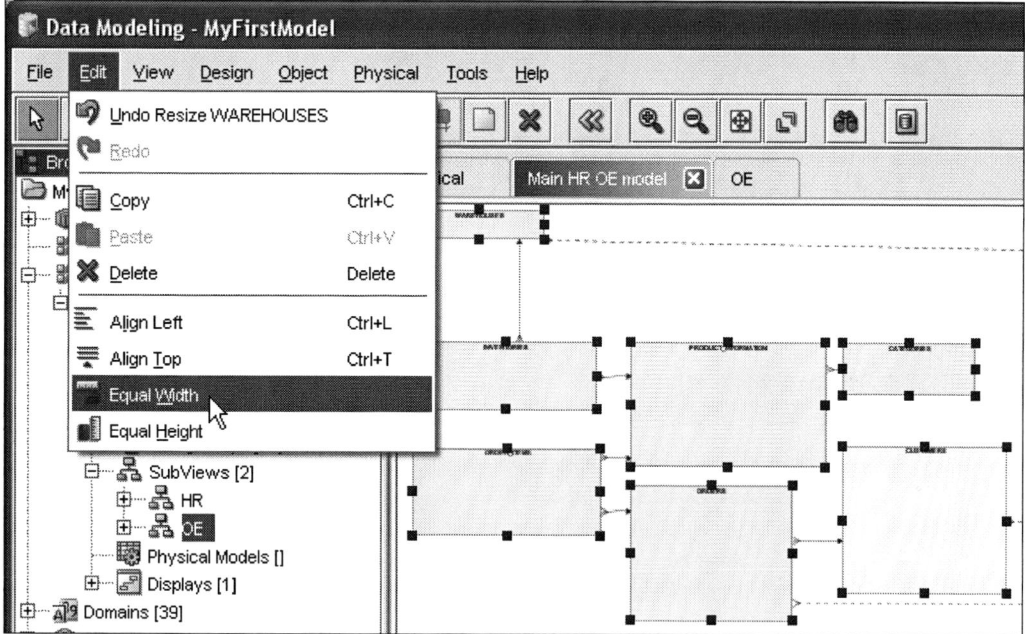

Controlling alignment

Once you have positioned the items, align them to complete the model. Use the **Edit** menu with the required items for top and left alignment as shown in the following screenshot:

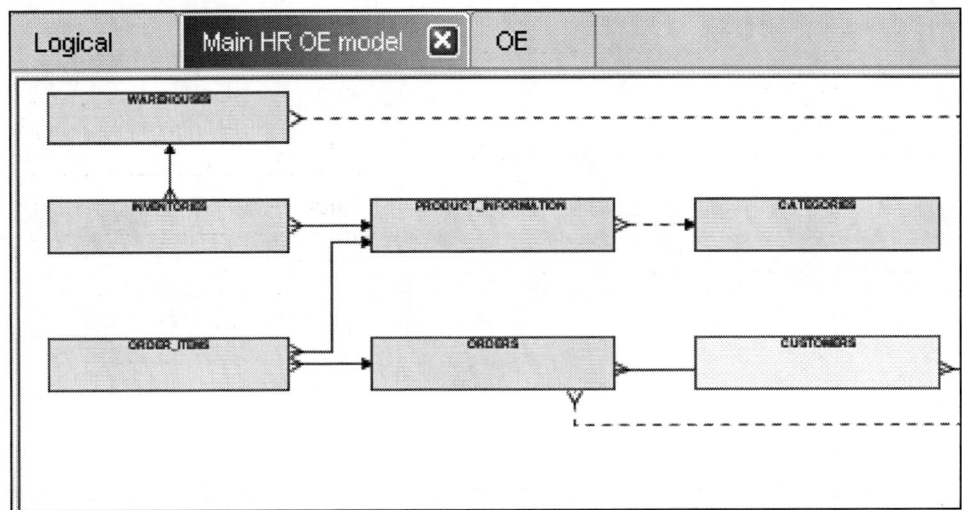

Resizing and alignment

The first item you select is the one that drives the position for left or top alignment, and the item that controls the width and height of all subsequent items selected.

Working with lines

A clear layout is fundamental to a clear diagram. This includes ensuring that lines do not cross or lie underneath tables. SQL Developer Data Modeler has an **Auto Route** feature that is *on* by default (seen in the following screenshot). This prevents you from manually moving any of the relationship lines yourself.

Take manual control of the lines by using a right-click on the white space of the diagram and deselecting **Auto Route**. You can also set the **Auto Route** option to *off*, by default, using the **Tools | General Options | Diagram** setting.

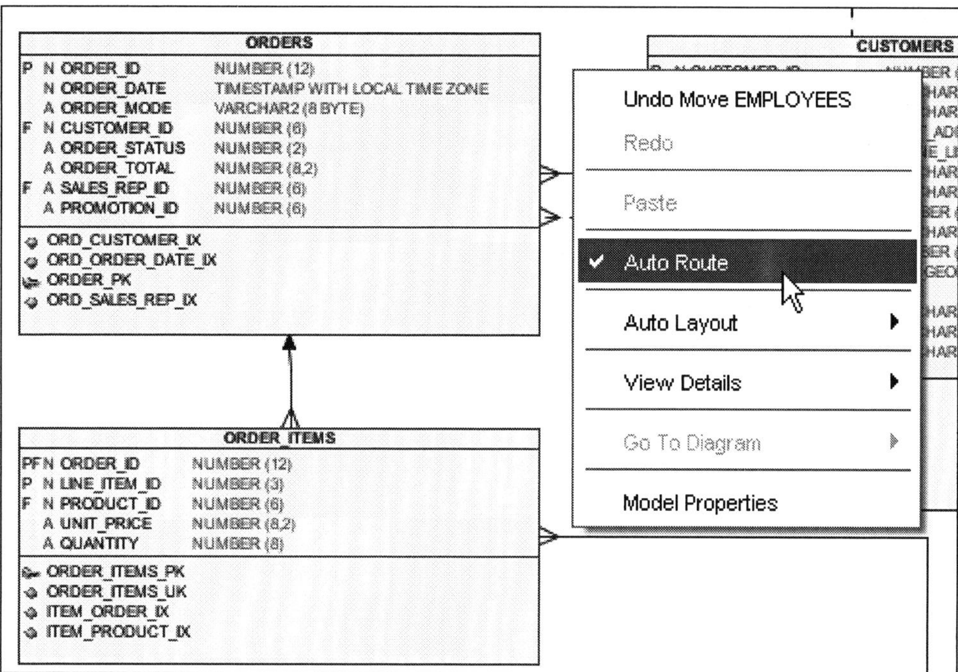

Once you have control of the lines, you can select any relationship line and use the context menu to:

- Add Elbow—to reroute a line around other shapes
- Remove Elbow
- Straighten Lines

Managing lines with elbows

For lines that have elbows (angles), you can select any point on the line to move them and change the shape. Moving the line also moves the end points of the line. You cannot select and move the end points themselves. You can also select any of the elbows to change the angles within the lines:

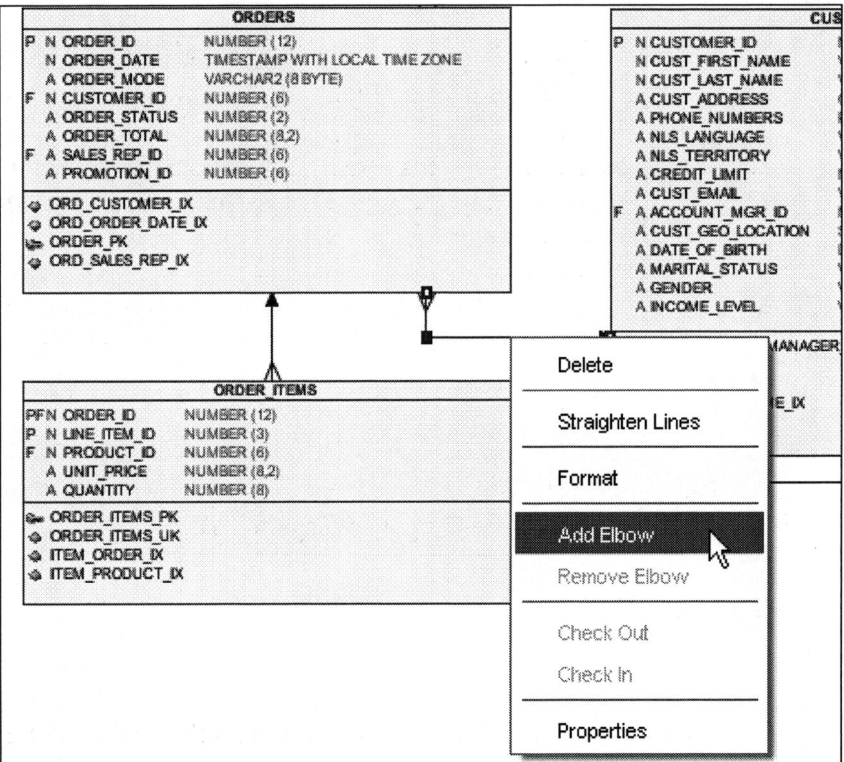

Managing straight lines

Diagrams are neater if there are fewer lines crossing and more straight lines. Where possible, remove the elbows and straighten lines. There is an option to straighten lines by removing all elbows on the lines. **Straighten Lines** will create a horizontal straight line between two tables or entities next to each other, and a diagonal line between elements that are not adjacent. You can only move the endpoints on a straight line and not the entire line.

Moving a straight line

To select and move a straight line, add an elbow. Then, without bending the line, you can select and position it where you choose to without needing to move both endpoints.

Analysis, design, and generation

Some developers like to have a clear separation between the logical analysis and physical design of an application system. SQL Developer Data Modeler supports this separation of tasks and also supports the synchronization of metadata between these. This means you can start new application development with a logical model, without needing to think about the physical implementation details. Once you have completed the analysis, you can then transform the entities to tables and work on the physical implementation. SQL Developer Data Modeler also allows you to work on the relational model with its tables, views, and constraints, without needing to consider the physical detail. Without the physical detail, you can create a relational model that is database agnostic. Then, for a single relational model, you can create multiple physical implementations and generate the different DDL for each of these.

In this section, we'll start with a logical model, transform this to a relational model, and then look at the physical details before generating the DDL.

Flow of work

While some believe that the only way to start data modeling is with conceptual analysis, others believe that this extra layer of work is not necessary. Therefore, they skip any high-level conceptual analysis and start by building the data model. SQL Developer Data Modeler supports these alternatives and provides the option to synchronize these models.

Starting with analysis (top down)

This is often considered to be the most traditional approach to database design and generation, and falls into the waterfall approach of strategy, analysis, design, and generation. The mindset behind this approach is that the more work you do up front, the better. Early changes to the design are less costly than they are likely to be later on. Liken this to building a house. If you plan to change the position of the bathroom while the house is still in the drawing and architectural phase, it's much less costly than planning to move it once the building work has begun. The further down the line that changes are requested, the more costly the decision.

The flow of work in this approach is to build the logical model, set any standards and build the glossary, and then transform or forward engineer it to the relational model. Once you have the relational model, review and make any adjustments as required. At this stage, you can add extra columns, rename columns or tables, and add constraints. Once the relational model is sound, you can create the additional physical detail required. Generate the DDL and review the scripts when the relational and physical models are complete.

Importing existing models (bottom up)

If you already have an application built, the database will be in place. Being able to visualize the model allows you to view and extend the mode or migrate the details to a new database. Starting with the schema supports migrating to new environments or upgrading applications. In the current climate, consolidating applications is important. Therefore, being able to review the models for these existing applications means you can make decisions before embarking on updates.

Building the relational model

Some teams want to model their databases, but feel the ERD is an unnecessary layer. Therefore, they start by building a schema model. At this level, you are building tables, columns, and constraints. You can start by importing tables from an existing database and then augment them by adding new tables and modifying the tables imported. This is a valid approach to modeling, but does mean that you are already thinking about implementation details while starting to design.

Logical models

A logical ERD is made up of entities and attributes. You can identify unique identifiers and relationships between entities. You are not tied down to the implementation details at this point, and can therefore create a many-to-many relationship or supertypes (if they support the business requirement). In essence, you are using the ERD to capture the business needs:

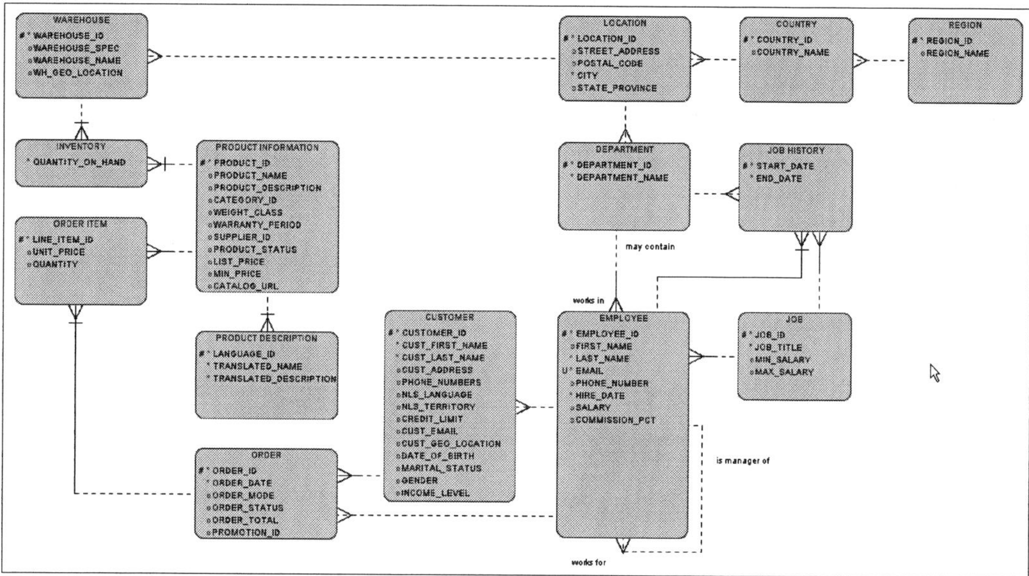

Creating an ERD

Select the **Logical** node in the object browser and select **Show** from the context menu to create or open a blank page for your logical model.

To start creating the model, use the set of buttons on the toolbar (shown in the following screenshot). The button is "sticky" by default. This means you can draw an entity, which invokes the property dialog, and then on closing the dialog, you are immediately ready to draw the next entity, without needing to select the button again.

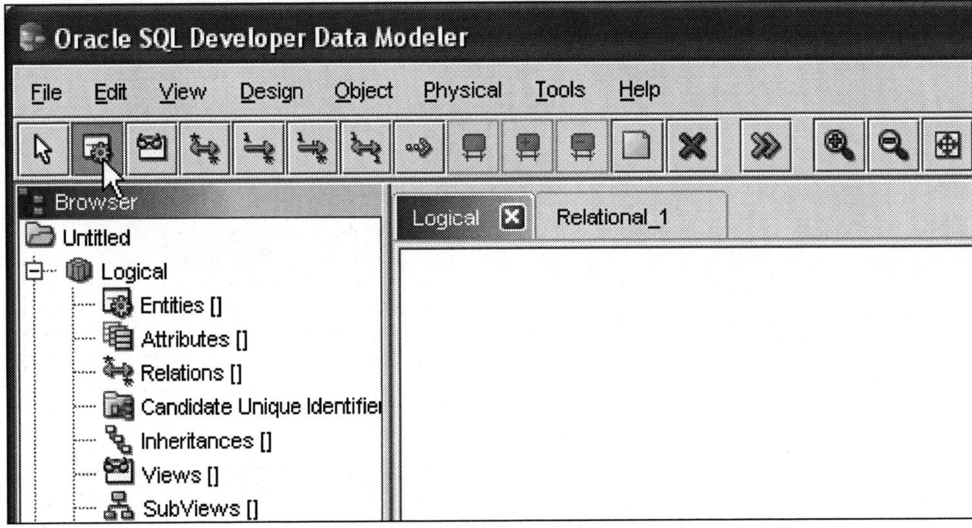

Creating entities

As soon as you have drawn the shape, the **Entity Properties** dialog is invoked, allowing you to populate the details.

You can provide a broad spectrum of details for each entity, including documentation details, such as change request details and comments.

General entity properties include adding synonyms and abbreviations. Synonyms are for documentation purposes and can be part of your glossary. They are not database synonyms.

Singular entity names and plural table names

Typically, entity names are singular and table names are the plural. Some products allow you to set this plural value under the entity properties, and the plural value is then used when engineering to create the table. You can use the **Preferred Abbreviation** field for this purpose in SQL Developer Data Modeler. If you want to use the preferred abbreviation, you will also need to set the **Use preferred abbreviation** in the forward engineering **General Options** dialog.

Adding attributes

Once you have entered the main detail for the entity, you can add the required attributes. In the image that follows, you can see the basic requirements for each attribute, such as setting the data types and the unique identifier properties. To add further detail to each attribute, click on the **Properties** button or double-click on the attribute.

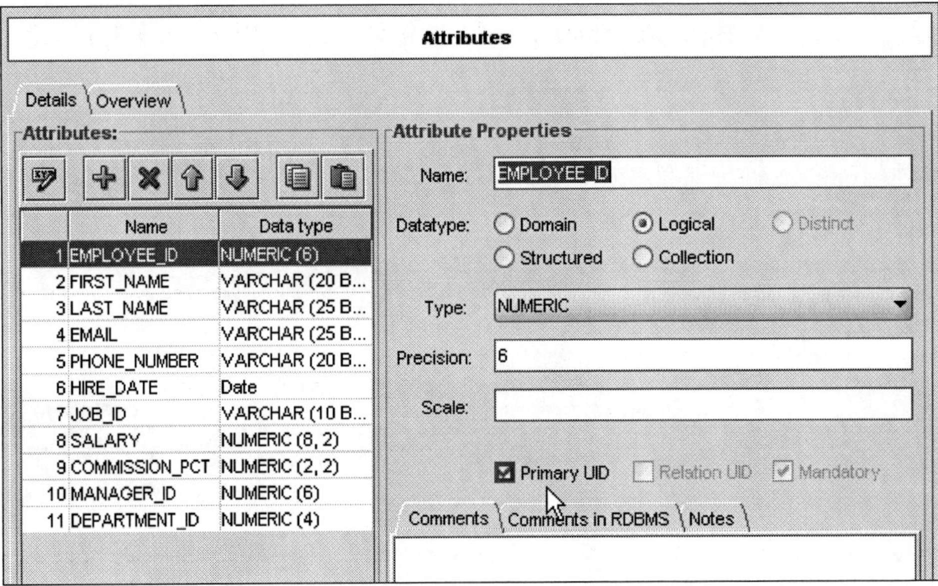

Working with relationships

The **Entity Properties** dialog includes a **Relationships** node with a list of all available relationships. Double-click on the name of the relationship to drill down to the detail. The **Cardinality** detail is useful to review (seen in the following screenshot). If you reverse engineer the details from a relational model, the name on the source and target are blank. Completing this detail and displaying it on the model is very useful for later documentation when using the model as a discussion point.

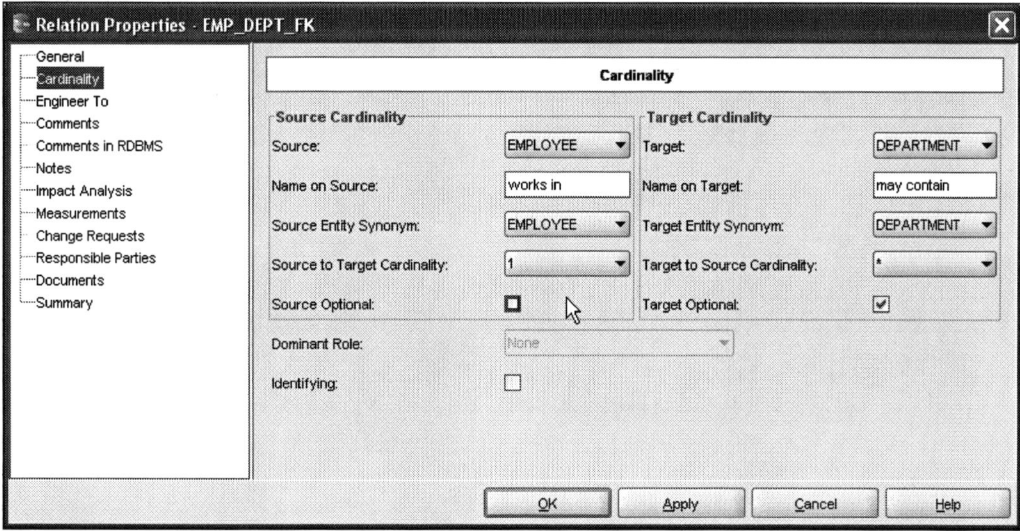

In the earlier section on syntax, we mentioned the Cardinality, Optional, and Identifying properties on the diagram. These are all set on this dialog.

You can invoke the same dialog by selecting the relationship in the diagram and invoking the Properties dialog.

To display the relationship names on the model, use the **Tools | General Options** menu and select **Diagram | Logical Model** to set the display property **Show Source/Target Name**.

Creating arcs

To create an arc, you need to select both relationships in the arc and the associated entity. This will bring the arc buttons into focus on the drawing toolbar.

Supporting alternate notations

SQL Developer Data Modeler supports two notations for the ERD (the Barker and Bachman notations), and allows you to switch between them. To set the default notation used, select **Tools | General Options | Diagram | Logical Model**. We prefer to keep to one notation, as there are subtle visual and semantic differences between them.

For example, in the Barker notation, you do not include the Foreign Key columns at this stage of the analysis, but for the Bachman notation you do. In SQL Developer Data Modeler, this is supported by not including the Foreign Key columns in the diagram model, but by including the detail in the definitions.

In the following example, we have created a Logical model, displaying the detail, and using the Bachman notation. Notice that the constraints are displayed in the model:

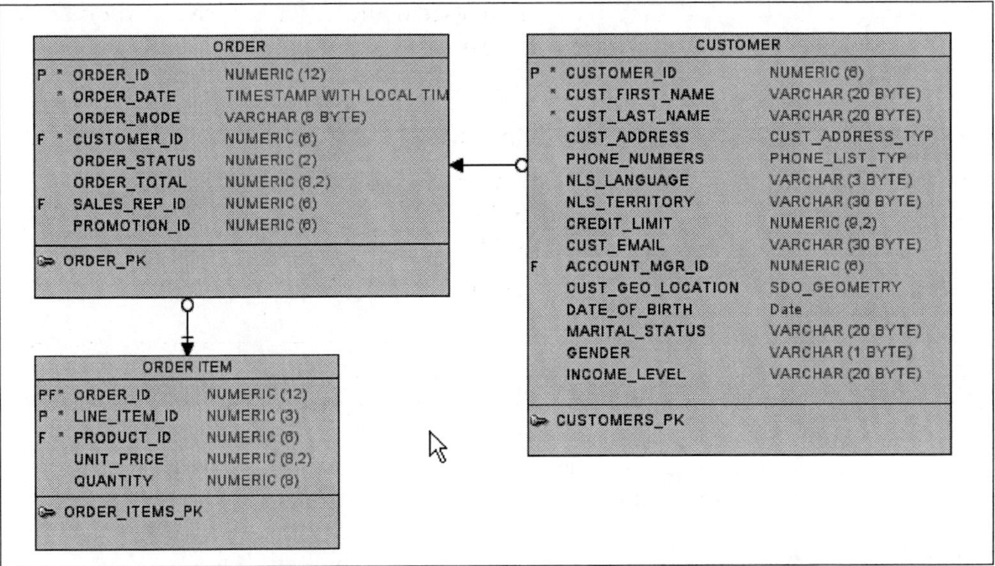

In the following example, we have taken the same model and used the Barker notation. Here, only the attributes are listed in each entity:

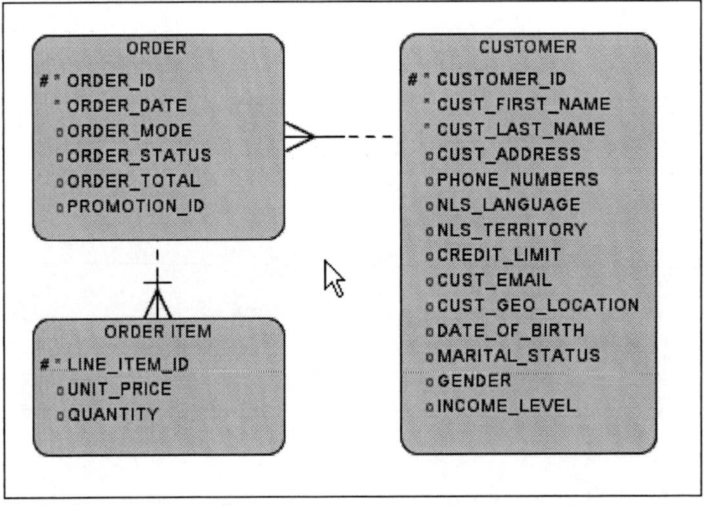

Using the Barker notation as shown in the following screenshot, the various elements of the ERD are as follows:

- Mandatory items are designated with a * and are generally at the top of the list. It is advised that mandatory items are listed first as these will then be first in the table after forward engineering.
- Primary Keys are designated with a #.
- Optional items are designated with a ○.
- Optional relationships use a dashed line to represent MAY HAVE. In the example shown, "Each department MAY HAVE one or more employees". Mandatory relationships use a solid line and represent MUST HAVE. In the example shown, "Each employee MUST work in a department".

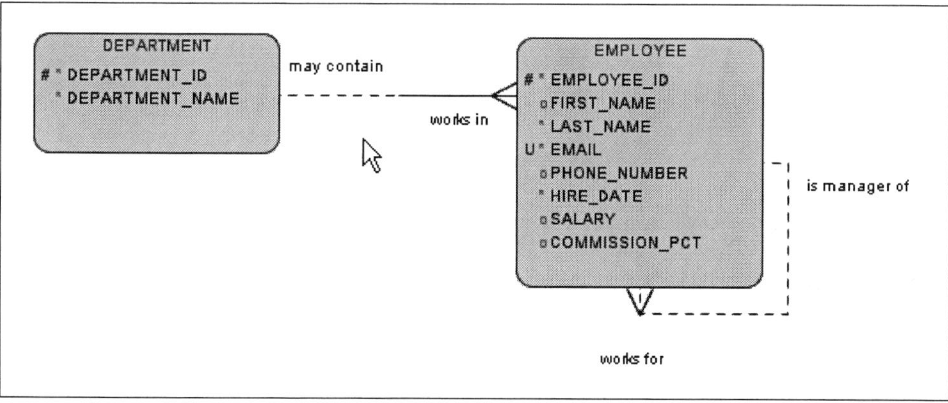

In both the Barker and Bachman notations seen earlier, an identifying relationship in the relationship between the **ORDER** and **ORDER_ITEM** entities is barred, indicating that the Foreign Key forms part of the Primary Key.

Supporting subtypes and supertypes

Consider the scenario where you want to define a CUSTOMER entity. You also find that you have special kinds of customers and think they may need to be handled differently in the design. You may start out by creating separate entities, but quickly come to realize that the special type of customer is still a customer. In this case, you can model a customer entity, which will be the supertype, and then create a subtype for your special customers. Create the first customer entity as normal. When you create the second entity, set the supertype property to CUSTOMER. By setting this, you create the subtype. In the following screenshot, the supertype is the **CUSTOMER** entity, with **PREMIER** customers as a separate subtype. The general entity properties allow you to set the forward engineering options:

- Single Table
- Table per child
- Table for each entity

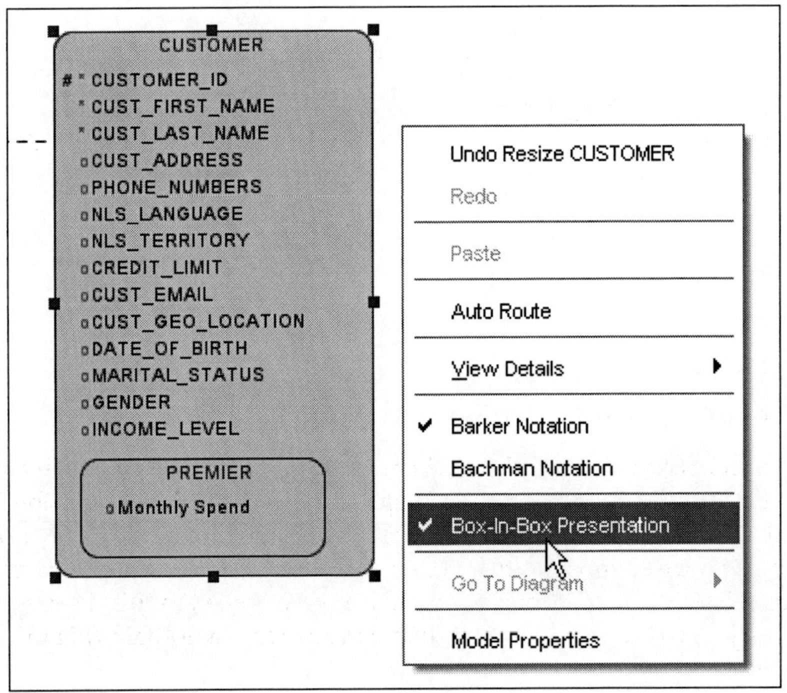

Once you have these previously created you can decide the notation you prefer. In the previous screenshot, we have selected the **Box-in-Box Presentation** notation. If you deselect this option, the subtypes are shown linked to the supertype with a red line.

Creating constraints, domains, and setting default values

A domain is a defined data type, which may have associated valid values. By defining domains, you can reuse these throughout the model, providing consistency to the model. For example, you can create a Yes/No domain and set the data type and associate valid values to Yes and No. Once created, you can associate it with all columns or entities that use Yes/No values. Domains need not have associated valid values. Instead, you can just set the data type and then apply the domain to columns or entities. You can work with domains and default values independent of the ERD or Relational models. If you set these at the attribute level and then forward engineer, the detail is carried forward to the tables and columns. However, these can easily be added directly to the columns.

Working with domains

When setting data types for attributes or columns, you have a choice of categories, such as:

- Domains
- Logical
- Distinct
- Structured
- Collection

The most common of these is the Logical type, where you can set the type and scale for the data type. When working with a large number of entities and attributes, using domains is more efficient as any changes made to the domains are propagated through to all of the columns or attributes that use them. SQL Developer Data Modeler provides a default domains file. All domains added to this file are available for all designs you work on. Alternatively, you can create a domains file to use with specific designs.

Creating domains

Select **Tools | Domains Administration** and create your own new domain by clicking on **Add**. This action adds a new domain to the default domains file. When adding domains, provide the name and logical type details and add the details such as size and precision. You can also remove or modify domains using this dialog (shown in the following screenshot). The changes made here are maintained separately from your design. Therefore, you can enforce standards across designs.

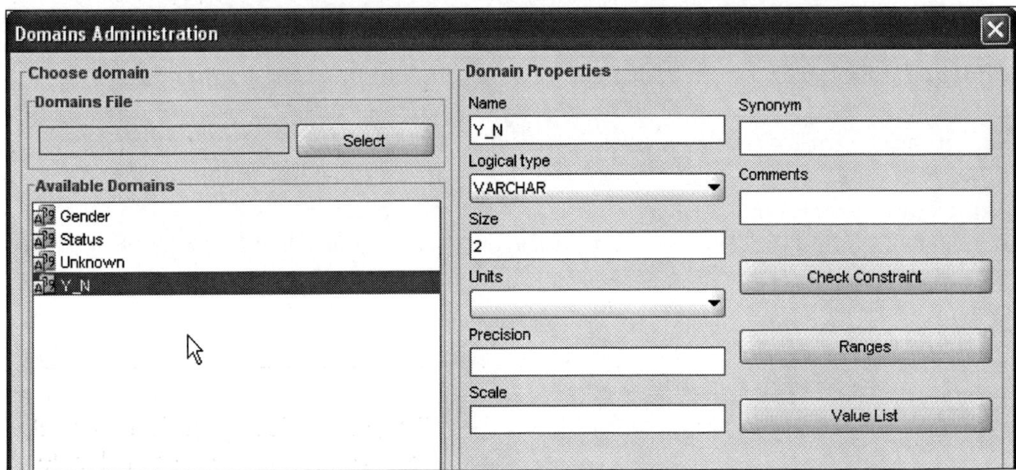

You can create a separate domains file that is associated with your design by clicking on the **Select** button in the **Domains Administration** dialog. This action allows you to create or open a separate domains file. Once created, add new domains to the file as previously described. To use these domains in a design, select **File | Import | Domains**. When you save the design, these domains are then saved with the design.

Using domains to implement check constraints

Domains offer more than just providing standard data types. They can also contain valid values and thus allow you to use the domain to:

- Implement a check constraint
- Enforce a range of values
- Provide a set of valid values

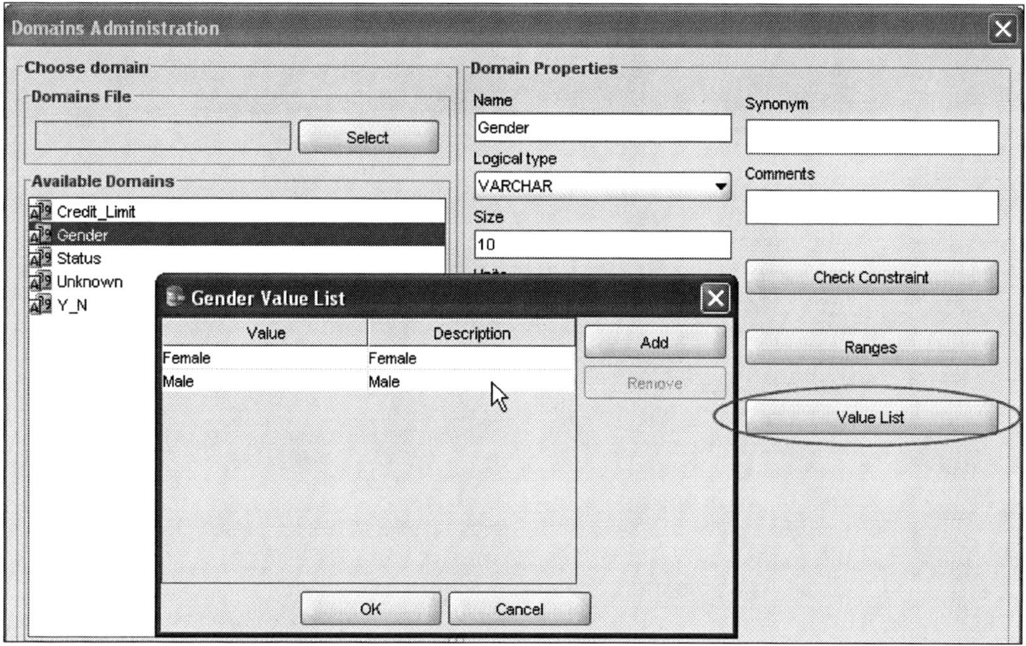

In the previous screenshot, we have added a value list. When adding check constraints to domains, you can add constraints specific to a database version, or you can elect to create a generic constraint which will be applied to any database you choose.

Assigning domain valid values to an attribute or column

Add the domain value to the attribute or column when setting the data type property. Double-click on the table or entity to invoke the Properties dialog, and then select the **Columns** or **Attributes** node to set the properties. If there are valid values or constraints associated with the domain, they will be picked up during the forward engineering, or when generating the DDL scripts.

The earlier **GENDER** example produces the following DDL:

```
DDL Preview
CREATE TABLE CUSTOMERS
    (
     CUSTOMER_ID NUMBER (6)  NOT NULL ,
     CUST_FIRST_NAME VARCHAR2 (20 BYTE)  NOT NULL ,
     CUST_LAST_NAME VARCHAR2 (20 BYTE)  NOT NULL ,
     CUST_ADDRESS CUST_ADDRESS_TYP ,
     PHONE_NUMBERS PHONE_LIST_TYP ,
     NLS_LANGUAGE VARCHAR2 (3 BYTE) ,
     NLS_TERRITORY VARCHAR2 (30 BYTE) ,
     CREDIT_LIMIT NUMBER (9,2) ,
     CUST_EMAIL VARCHAR2 (30 BYTE) ,
     ACCOUNT_MGR_ID NUMBER (6) ,
     CUST_GEO_LOCATION MDSYS.SDO_GEOMETRY ,
     DATE_OF_BIRTH DATE ,
     MARITAL_STATUS VARCHAR2 (20) DEFAULT 'Married' ,
     GENDER VARCHAR2 (10) CHECK ( GENDER IN ('Female' , 'Male' ))
     INCOME_LEVEL VARCHAR2 (20 BYTE)
```

Setting valid values at attribute or column level

Set valid values, or define check constraints for individual attributes or columns using the **Entity Property** dialog. Double-click on the attribute in question to invoke the dialog:

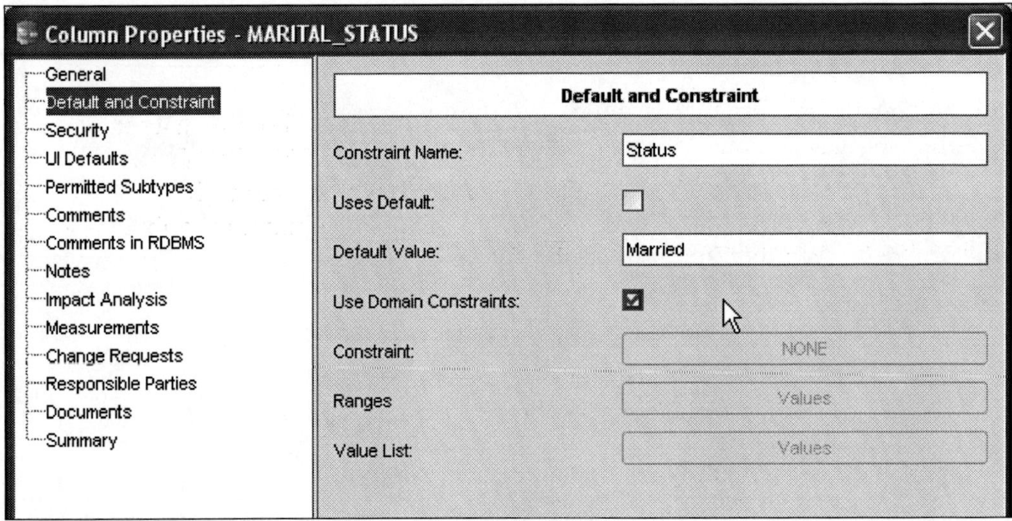

In the previous example, we named the constraint and selected **Use Domain Constraints**. This enforces a named check constraint in the DDL. By omitting the **Constraint Name**, the resulting DDL contains an inline constraint.

If you want to override the valid values or constraint at this level, deselect the **Use Domain Constraints** options and select the options you require, as illustrated for the **GENDER** column in the following screenshot:

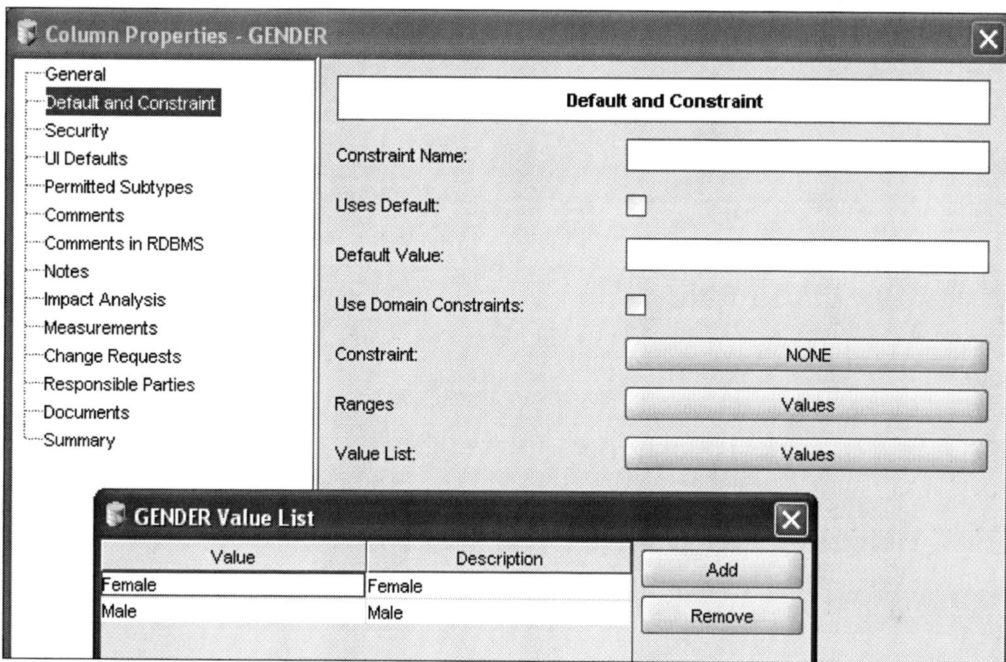

In this example, we created two domains, Status and Gender, both with a set of valid values and assigned these to the MARITAL_STATUS and GENDER columns of the CUSTOMERS table. For the MARITAL_STATUS column, we set the **Constraint Name** to **Status** and set a default value. For the GENDER column, we only set the data type to the domain. The resulting DDL is as follows:

```
CREATE TABLE CUSTOMERS
    (
     CUSTOMER_ID NUMBER (6)  NOT NULL ,
     CUST_FIRST_NAME VARCHAR2 (20 BYTE)  NOT NULL ,
     CUST_LAST_NAME VARCHAR2 (20 BYTE)  NOT NULL ,
     CUST_ADDRESS CUST_ADDRESS_TYP ,
     PHONE_NUMBERS PHONE_LIST_TYP ,
     NLS_LANGUAGE VARCHAR2 (3 BYTE) ,
     NLS_TERRITORY VARCHAR2 (30 BYTE) ,
```

```
        CREDIT_LIMIT NUMBER (9,2) ,
        CUST_EMAIL VARCHAR2 (30 BYTE) ,
        ACCOUNT_MGR_ID NUMBER (6) ,
        CUST_GEO_LOCATION MDSYS.SDO_GEOMETRY ,
        DATE_OF_BIRTH DATE ,
        MARITAL_STATUS VARCHAR2 (20) DEFAULT 'Married' ,
        GENDER VARCHAR2 (10) CHECK(GENDER IN ('Female','Male')) ,
        INCOME_LEVEL VARCHAR2 (20 BYTE)
    )
;

ALTER TABLE CUSTOMERS
    ADD CONSTRAINT Status
    CHECK (MARITAL_STATUS IN ('Divorced','Married','Single'))
;
```

Adding a default value

Using the same column properties dialog discussed above, you can set the default value for a database column. To set the default value, select the **Default and Constraint** property in the tree. In the earlier example for MARITAL_STATUS, not only is there a check constraint, we also set the default value for the column.

Introducing forward and reverse engineering

SQL Developer Data Modeler supports forward and reverse engineering. These transformation tools support:

- Forward engineering from an ERD to a new or existing relational model
- Reverse engineering from a relational model to a new or existing ERD

When engineering to an existing model, you can elect whether to include or exclude changes made in the different models.

Forward engineering

SQL Developer Data Modeler supports multiple relational models for each logical model. Whether you are starting with a logical model, or the logical model is derived from an existing relational model, you can forward engineer to a new relational model. Create an empty relational model by selecting **New Relational Model** from the **Relational Models** context menu in the object browser. This automatically opens a new blank relational model. Open the **Logical** model and select the **Engineer to Relational Model** button (»). Once the dialog opens, you can use the drop-down list of relational models to determine which model you want to update or create:

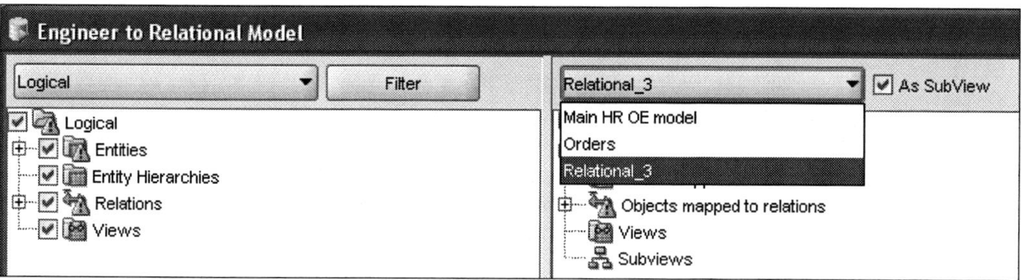

General engineering dialog features

In the following screenshot, we have elected to engineer from an existing relational model to an existing logical model, as both models have been updated. Here are details about the updates:

- In the Relational model, the **CUSTOMERS** table has changes, the **ORDER_ITEMS** table has been removed, and the **PRODUCTS** table has been added.
- In the Logical model, the **REGION** entity has been removed, so it appears as if the relational model has a new **REGIONS** table that needs to be added, together with the relation between **COUNTRIES** and **REGIONS**.

The different icons indicate the different updates made. The alert icon () indicates that there are some differences in the items between the two models, and the () and () icons indicate dropped or new items respectively:

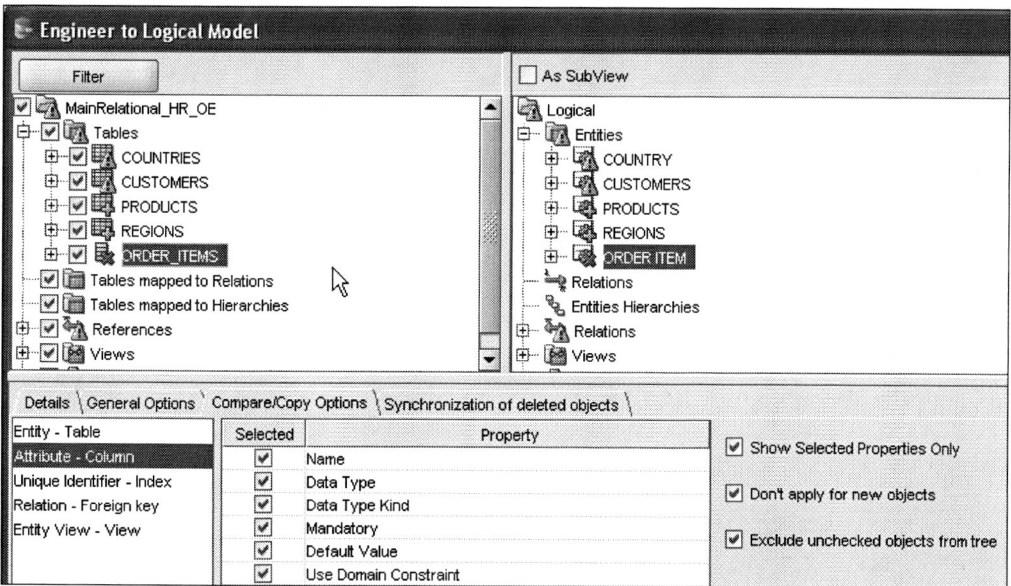

In the previous example, only some of the items are displayed in the tree. If you are updating large models, it's easier to use the filter to display only the new, modified, or deleted items. Alternatively, you can deselect the items you don't want to appear, and then click on the **Update Tree** button (not shown in the image) to refresh the tree.

When engineering, you can elect to reduce the extent of properties that are engineered. Still referring to the previous dialog, notice that there is a list of properties for the **Attribute - Column** selection. You can deselect the properties that you don't want engineered, and then refresh the view of the dialog by selecting **Show Selected Properties Only**.

Maintaining the model layout

When forward or reverse engineering against an existing model, you can choose to use the layout from the driving model to update the existing model layout, or to include the updated items without updating the layout of the existing model. To maintain the existing layout when engineering, select the **General Options** tab in the engineer dialog and ensure that **Engineer Coordinates** is selected. Both of the options have their advantages. If you spend time on laying out a model, it can be very useful to have that work carried through to the newly engineered model. However, if you have updated the layout of the logical and relational models separately, then it could be frustrating to have all your effort overwritten with the new layout.

The default value of the **Engineer Coordinates** property is checked, meaning that by default, the layout of the driving model is used for creating or updating the engineered model.

Reverse engineering models

This is the reverse action of the previously described forward engineering option. In this case, you use a relational model to create or update a logical model. If you already have a model, the decisions you need to make revolve around layout, and adding, deleting or updating items. Reverse engineering relational to logical models is very useful when you are doing a "bottom up design". In other words, you have imported the table definitions from an existing script or data dictionary. Once the relational model has been created and refined, reverse engineer the model to create a logical Entity Relationship Diagram.

Creating relational models

The relational model is made up of tables and views with their columns and relationships. The details for these items is listed in the object browser under the **Relational Models** node. These are also the only details that are displayed on the diagram as shown in the following screenshot. Details such as tablespaces, triggers, or any physical properties are listed in the physical model.

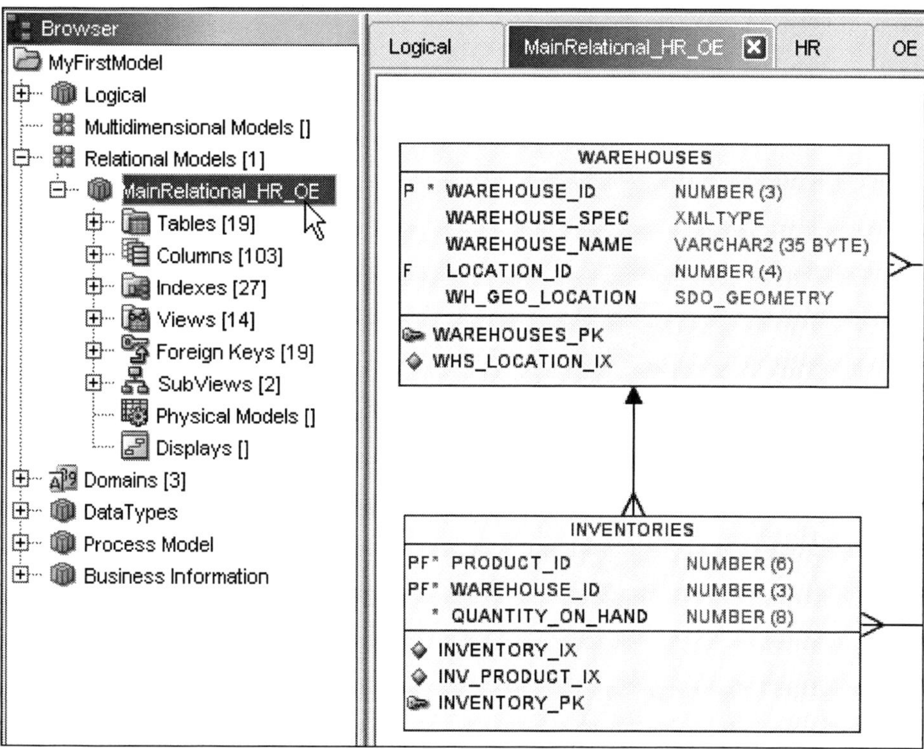

Working with the relational model

You can create a relational model by forward engineering the detail from the logical model. Alternatively, you can import the details from an existing schema or schemas in the data dictionary. Working with the relational model can therefore entail adding tables and Foreign Key constraints, or amending existing models. However, it is quite possible that you'd start with a blank page and create a relational model from scratch.

Creating a table and adding columns

The **Table Properties** dialog is not dissimilar to that of the **Entity Properties** dialog. Once you have set the general properties and added any column detail, you can build the constraints. When adding columns, you need to specify the data types, and should consider using domains where possible. If not already set through forward engineering, you can add the column default values and set check constraints by adding them directly or using the domain for this purpose. Creating constraints and setting domains is done in the same way as was discussed earlier for attributes.

Including Foreign Key constraints

Foreign Key relationships are easily built using the diagram and drawing in the lines. Click on the **New FK Relation** button and click in the parent table. Next, click on the child table. In the following screenshot, we have selected the **JOBS** table as the parent. Notice that there is no **JOB_ID** Foreign Key column in the **JOB_HISTORY** table. This is added automatically by the Data Modeler:

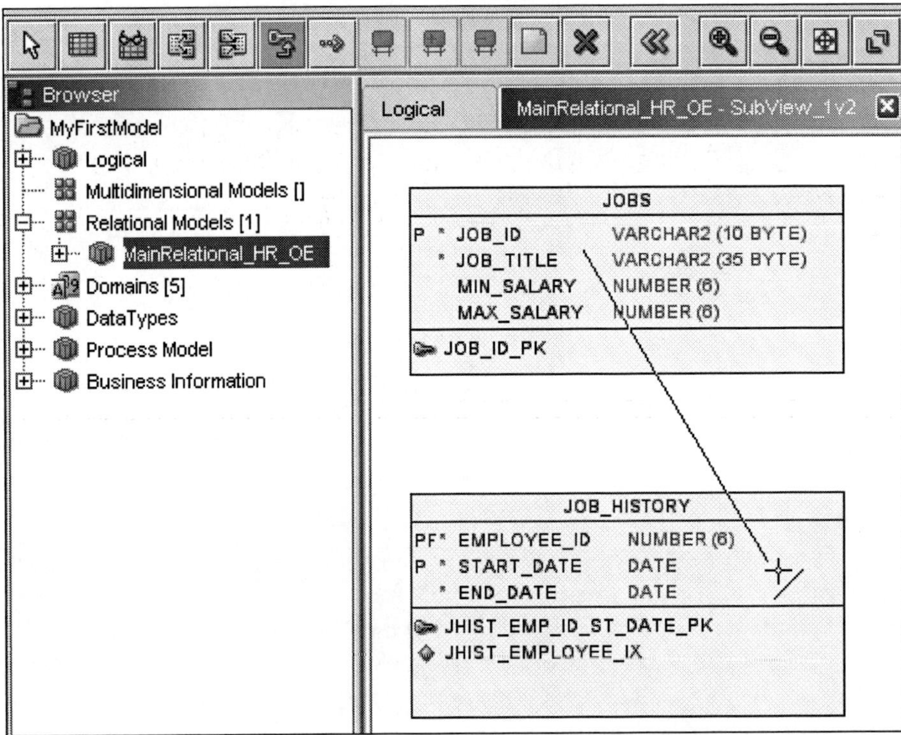

If you want to use your own column, you can change the referenced column. Double-click on the Foreign Key relationship and select **Associated Columns**. Select the new column from the **Child Column** drop-down list. If you change the column from the automatically generated column, by default you are prompted to delete the added column.

To delete a Foreign Key relationship, select the line on the diagram and use the keyboard to select *Delete*. If you use the diagram to delete a relationship and the Foreign Key column was generated, you'll be prompted as shown in the following screenshot:

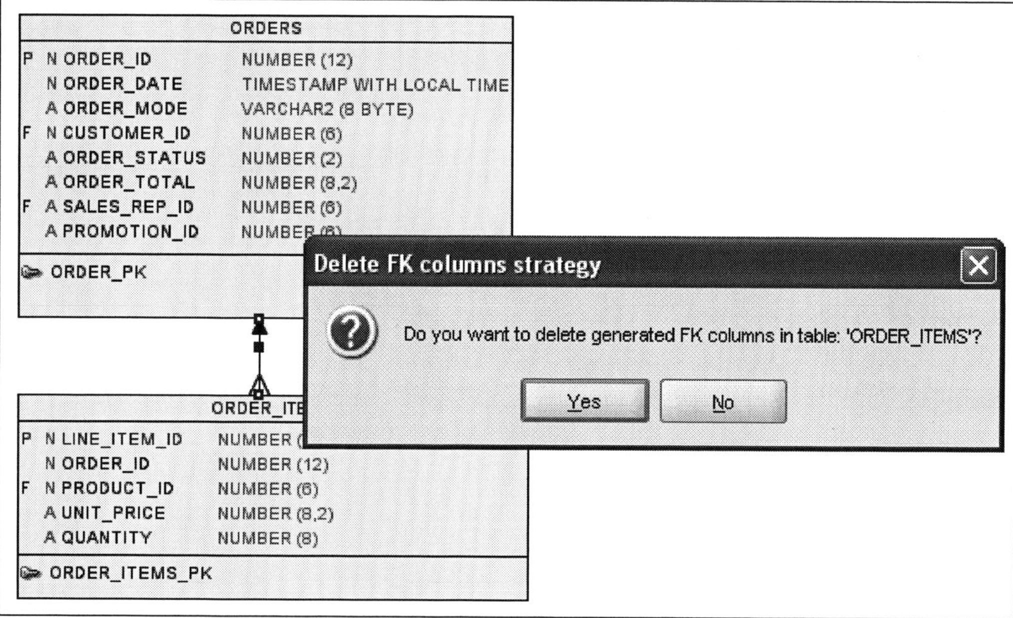

To control the behavior when deleting Foreign Keys, select the **Tools | General Options** menu, then select **Model | Relational** and select the required **Delete FK columns Strategy**:

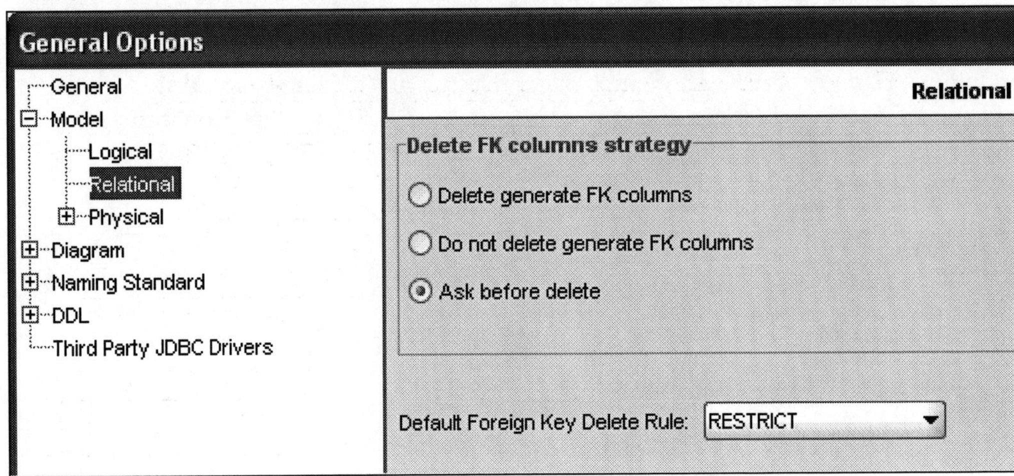

Setting naming standards templates

SQL Developer Data Modeler provides a number of different features that support creating, enforcing, and verifying naming standards. This is an extensive topic. Therefore, we will just look at the naming standard templates, which you can define for the relational model. This is especially useful if you are importing an existing model where the standards used do not confirm to your industry or company standards, and you want to run a set of standard templates across your entire model or a selection of objects within the model.

To review or update the default templates, open the **Tools | General Options** dialog and select the **Naming Standard | Templates**, as shown in the following screenshot:

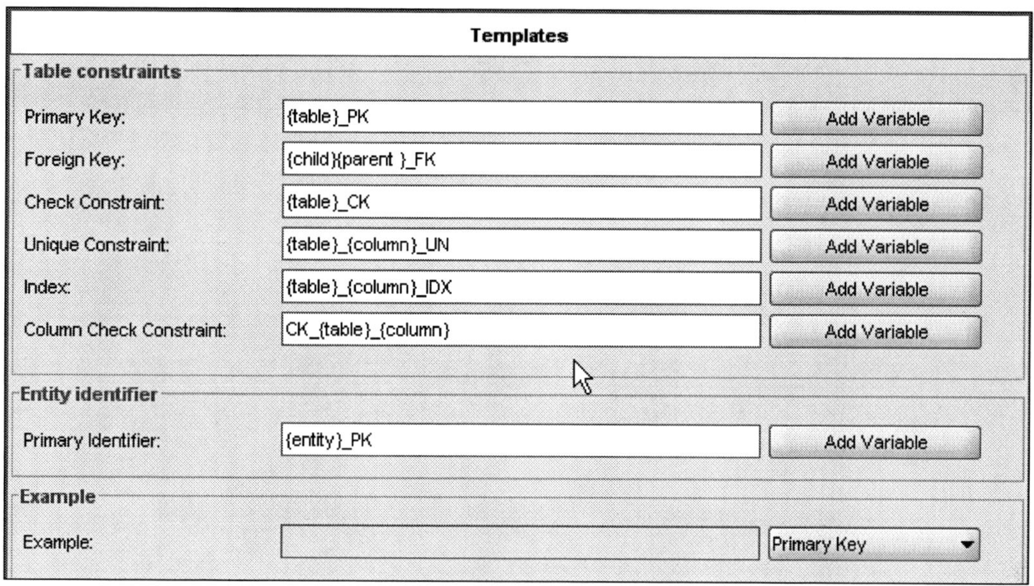

At any point, templates can be applied to a relational model, to ensure that all keys, indexes, and constraints are named according to the predefined set of standards. They are also used when adding new Foreign Keys or forward engineering the relational model from the logical model.

In the previous example shown, the Primary Key template is **{table}_PK**. This will be the naming convention used when creating any Primary Key constraint, and this is the convention which will be applied to all existing Primary Key constraints if you apply the standards to your model.

> Naming Standard Templates are not validation rules. If you apply the templates and then continue to add and modify the model, there are no further checks, unless you reapply the templates.

Applying the templates to the model

Each table dialog has a **Naming Rules** button for applying the template detail. You can select the items the rules are applied to, which include:

- Primary and Foreign Keys
- Check and Unique Constraints
- Indexes
- Column Check Constraints

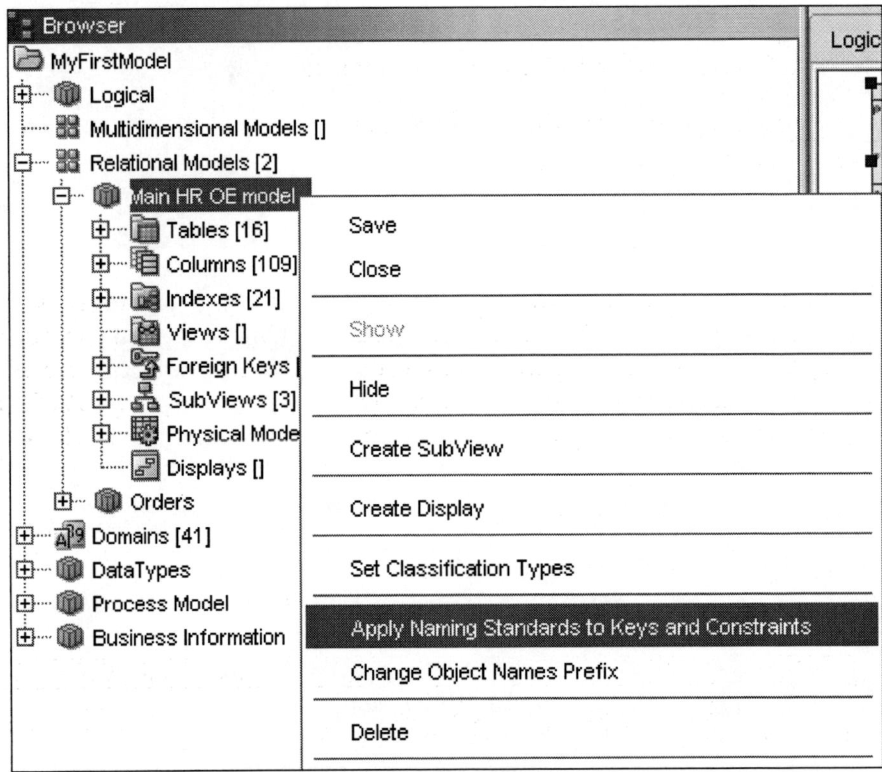

Updating the object names prefix

Often, when working on models, you might prefix all of the tables with the name or a code associated with the application. The **Change Object Names Prefix**, also in the menu displayed above, allows you to add a new prefix to all your tables, columns, views, or indexes, or to replace a current prefix with something new.

Building the physical model

The physical model is the source for the DDL scripts, and therefore contains much more detail than is available on the diagram. If you start from the logical model and engineer forward to the relational model, you'll need to start building the physical model from scratch. It will initially only be populated with the details in the relational model. If you are working from an existing database model, then importing the schema also imports the physical model.

SQL Developer Data Modeler supports multiple physical models for each relational model. This is useful if you want to build different DDL scripts for different databases (whether Oracle and non-Oracle), or Test, Development, and Production databases all in Oracle. In the next section, we'll look at:

- Importing a schema from the data dictionary
- Creating a new physical model

Importing a schema from the data dictionary

Importing from a database connection imports objects such as tables, columns, and views, and places them on the relational model diagram. You can also import physical properties such as tablespaces, roles, and directories. These details are listed under the physical node in the object browser. The **Data Dictionary Import Wizard** lets you select the objects and object types you can import, as shown in the following screenshot:

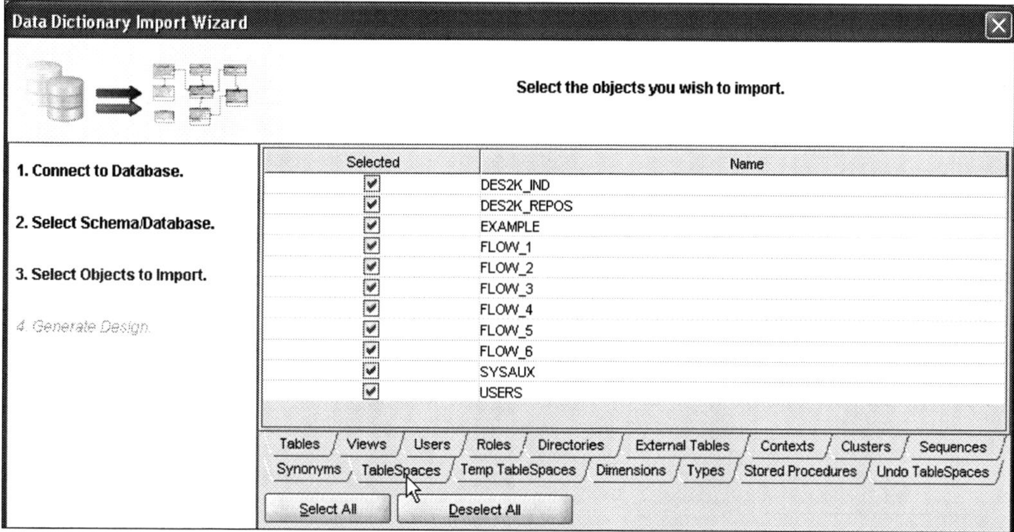

Creating a new physical model

If you have no physical model and want to create one, expand the relational model and select the **Physical Models** node. Right-click and select **Open**. This opens the **Database Sites** dialog. Select the database you want to add the physical details for and click on **OK**:

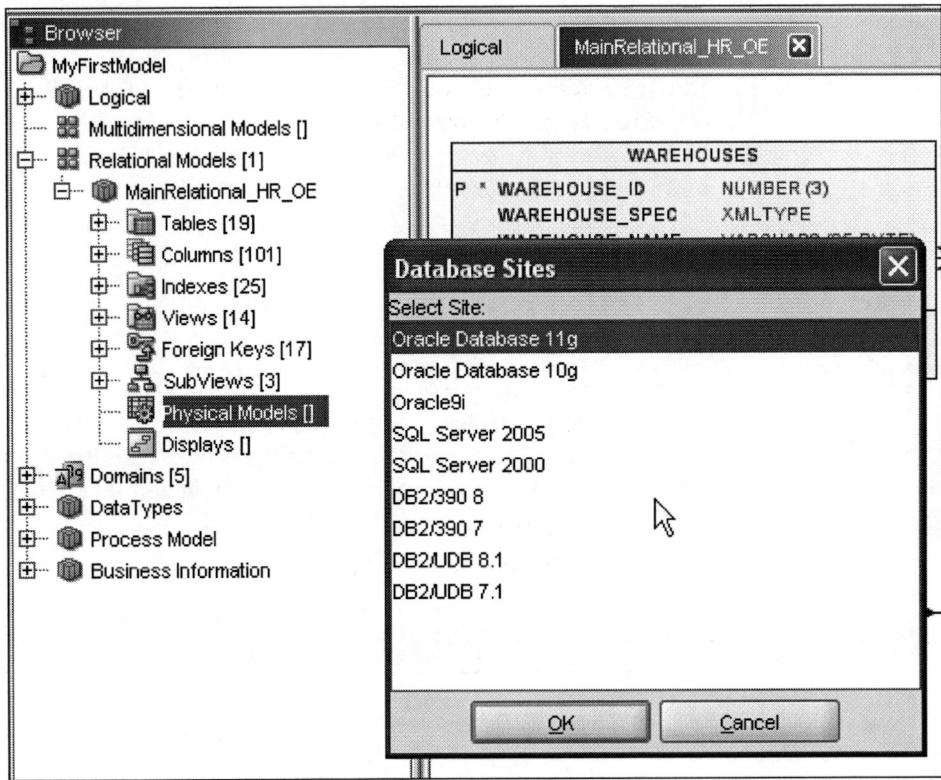

The **Physical Models** node now includes the database selected and all of the nodes to support defining additional physical detail. In the following screenshot, the **Stored Procedures** node is expanded, displaying four procedures:

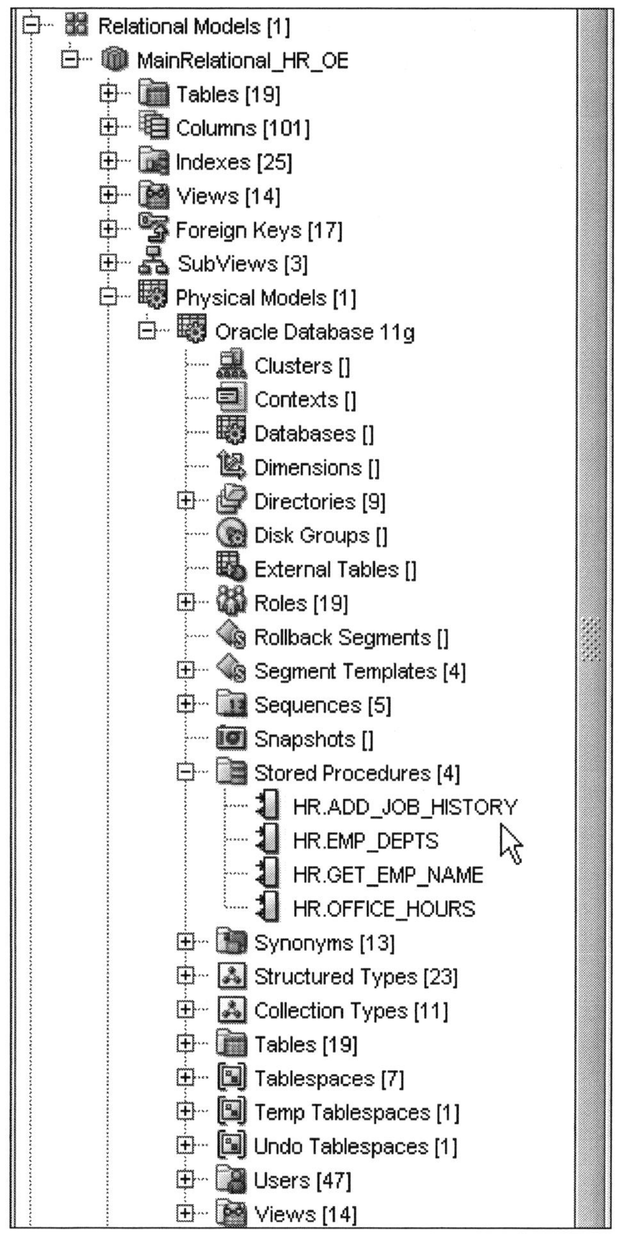
Relational Models [1]
MainRelational_HR_OE
Tables [19]
Columns [101]
Indexes [25]
Views [14]
Foreign Keys [17]
SubViews [3]
Physical Models [1]
Oracle Database 11g
Clusters []
Contexts []
Databases []
Dimensions []
Directories [9]
Disk Groups []
External Tables []
Roles [19]
Rollback Segments []
Segment Templates [4]
Sequences [5]
Snapshots []
Stored Procedures [4]
HR.ADD_JOB_HISTORY
HR.EMP_DEPTS
HR.GET_EMP_NAME
HR.OFFICE_HOURS
Synonyms [13]
Structured Types [23]
Collection Types [11]
Tables [19]
Tablespaces [7]
Temp Tablespaces [1]
Undo Tablespaces [1]
Users [47]
Views [14]

Adding new database sites

The Data Modeler allows you to create multiple physical models for the same relational model. For example, you can define physical properties for a Test, Development, and Production database. In this case, you have the same set of tables defined, but the physical tablespace properties may differ considerably. Before you can do this, you need to update the list of Database Sites. The default list of sites displays the various database and version alternatives that SQL Developer Data Modeler supports. To add alternative sites, select **RDBMS Site Administration** and add the new site name and database type:

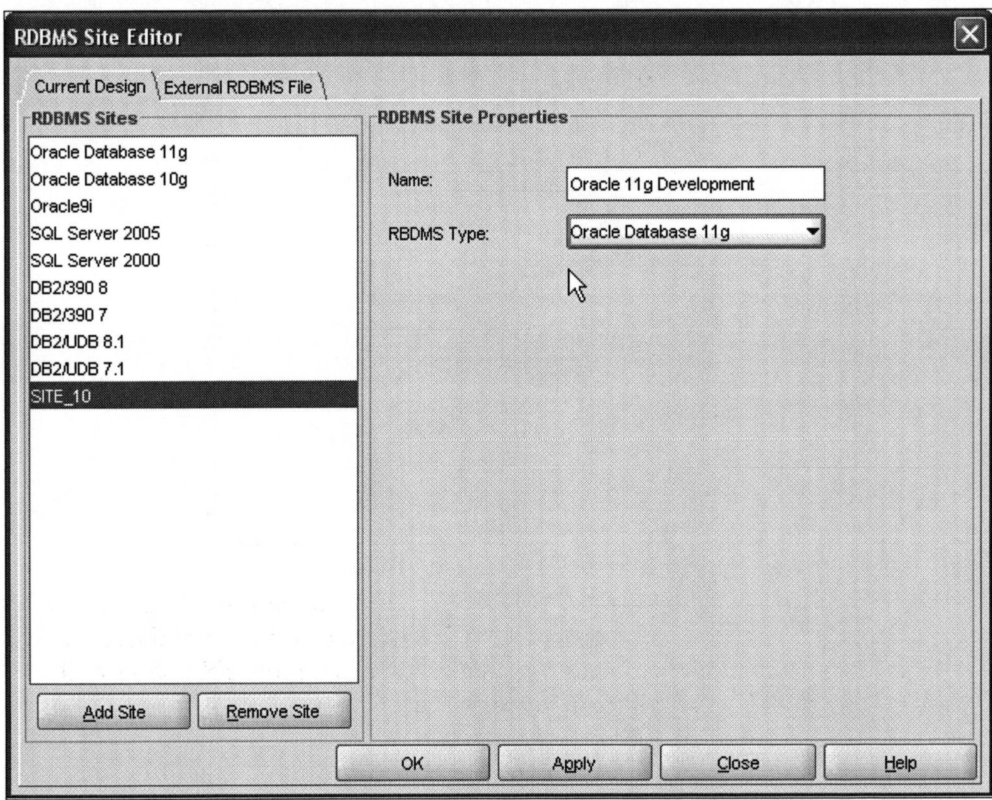

Once you have added the new site(s), you can return to the **Physical Models** node and open more physical sites. In the following example, we have opened three Oracle database sites and one SQL Server site:

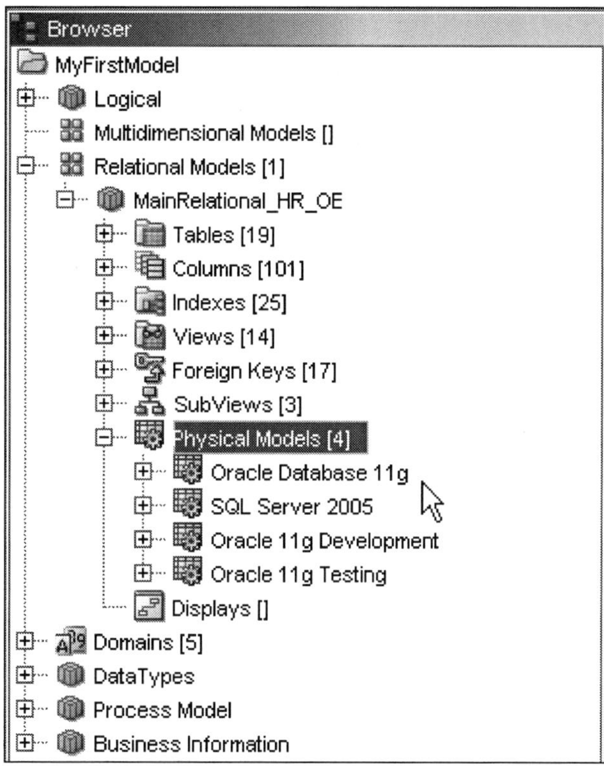

Once you have the physical model specified, you can add all of the details for the physical properties. It is here you can add (or review if you imported from a database) details such as triggers and sequences. You can define tablespaces and associate them with tables and indexes as required.

Reviewing physical properties

To invoke the Properties dialog for any of the objects in the physical model, double-click on the item, or right-click and select **Properties**. In the following example, we have selected the table properties for the **CUSTOMERS** table:

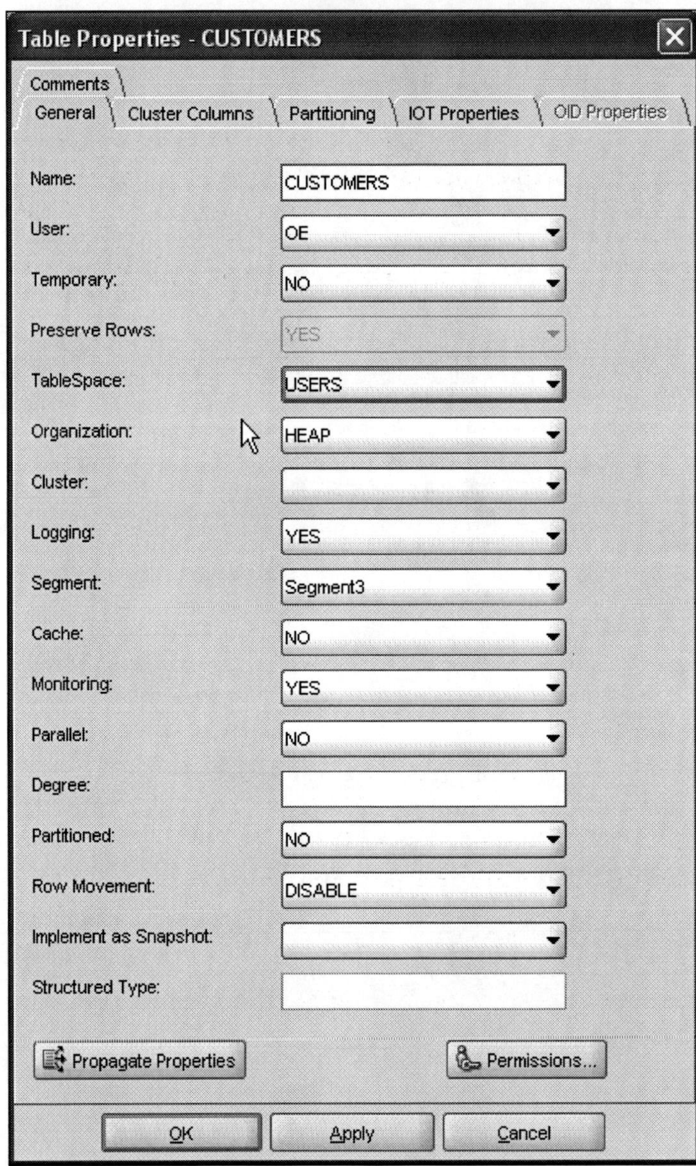

Notice that the dialog differs from the table properties dialog in the relational model. Here, you can add properties such as partition details, the schema name, and tablespace. By adding the schema name here, you can generate the DDL for a number of schemas, each with its own tables. By omitting database-specific details, such as the schema name and tablespace details, you can generate a more generic script.

Propagate properties

All physical model dialogs have a **Propagate Properties** button, as shown in the previous screenshot. This allows you to set a property for one object, such as the max value in a sequence or the tablespace for a table, and then propagate that property to a selection of other objects in that type. In this example, we have set the **TableSpace** to **USERS** for the **CUSTOMERS** table. By selecting the **Propagate Properties** button, we can select the properties we want to propagate, and the tables (or objects) we want to propagate them to:

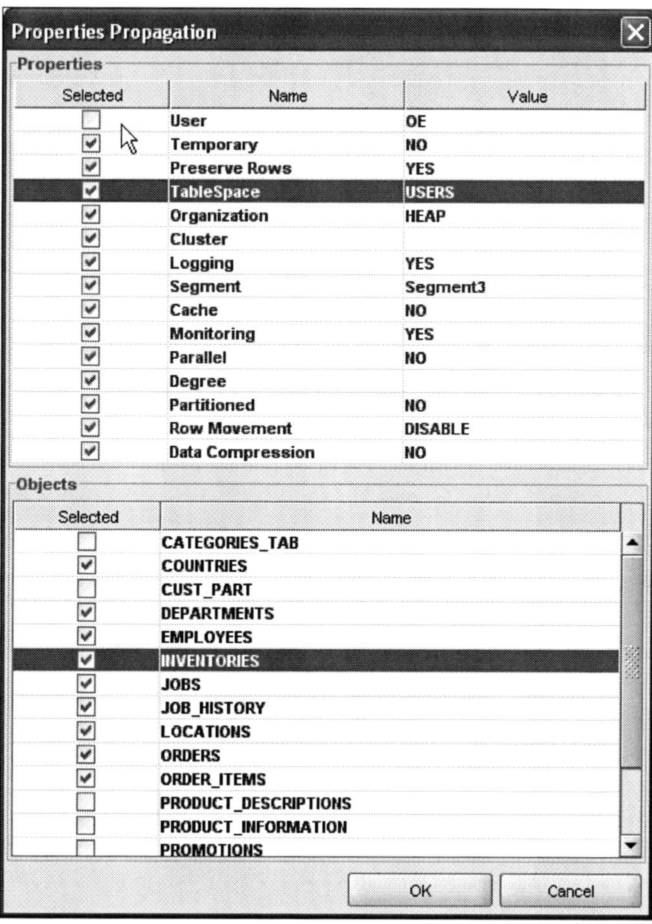

We have deselected the **User** property as we do not want this to be propagated to all of the selected tables.

Generating the DDL

All of the preceding work culminates in producing the DDL scripts to create or update a schema design. Invoke the DDL Generation dialog using **File | Export**, and then select the model of your choice. You can also click on the **Generate DDL** button in the toolbar to invoke the **DDL File Editor** dialog.

With the correct database selected, click on **Generate** to invoke the **DDL Generation Options** dialog:

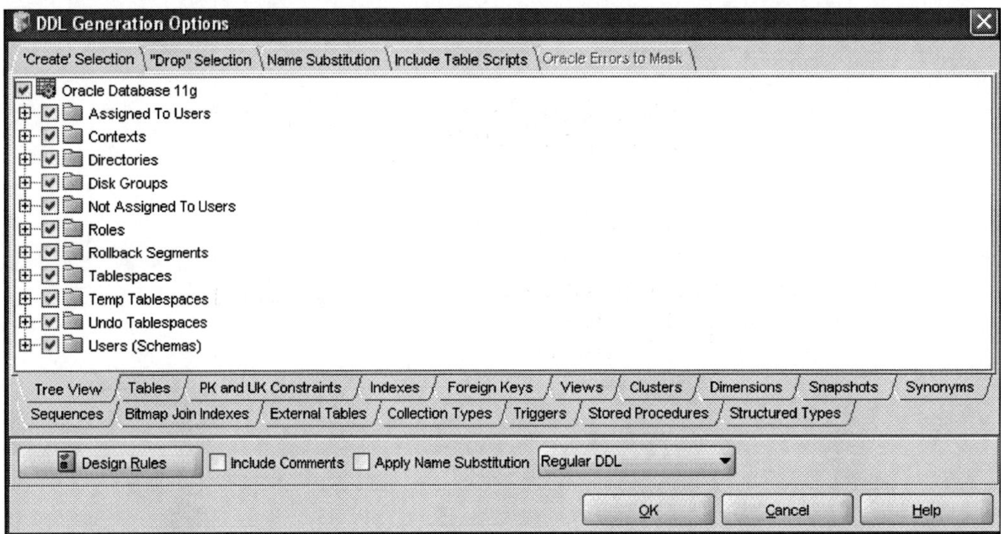

By default, all of the objects are marked for generation, so you can work through the lower tabs and remove any items you don't want in the DDL.

Use the **Tree View** tab to generate the DDL for a specific schema or for any of the objects not assigned to users (seen in the following screenshot). For example, if you have associated various objects with the HR schema in the physical model, then you can generate all of the DDL for the HR schema. To generate schema-specific DDL, select the **Assigned To Users** node in the tree and expand the required user, in the case, **HR**.

The top set of tabs drives additional text within the scripts. We mentioned naming standard templates and resetting object prefixes earlier; here we have another opportunity of switching the names, either for certain object names, or to switch out a prefix and replace it:

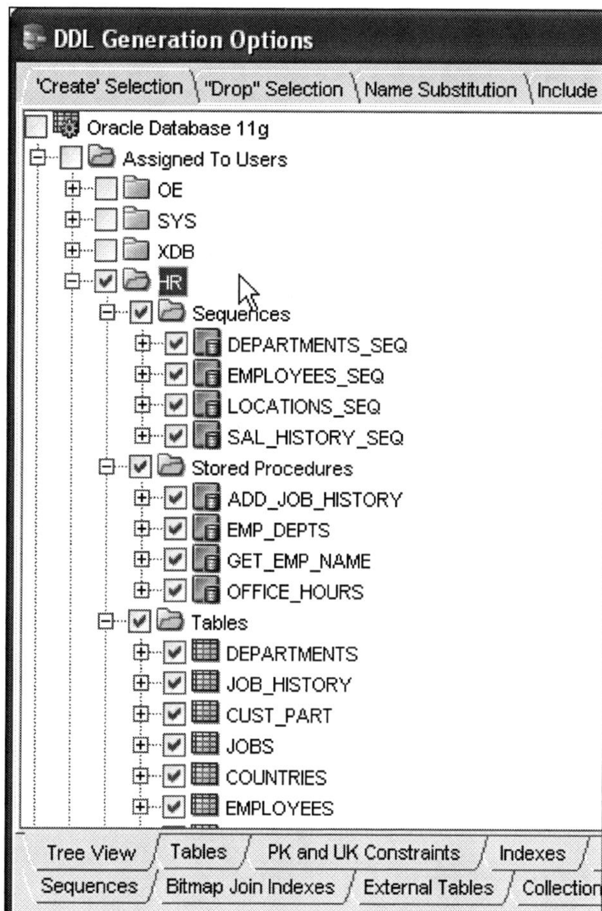

Reviewing and applying Design Rules

Before you consider the objects you want to generate, it's worth ensuring that you have a sound model. SQL Developer Data Modeler provides a lengthy list of **Design Rules** which you can run at any time, and which will help find missing items and incorrectly named objects. You can invoke the Design Rules dialog from the DDL Generation dialog, to verify that the model is in order before producing the DDL scripts. Alternatively, you can access them from the **Tools | Design Rules** menu.

When rules are violated, they're flagged as a **Warning** (shown in blue) or as an **Error** (shown in red). You can navigate from an error to the point of the issue in the model by double-clicking on the error record:

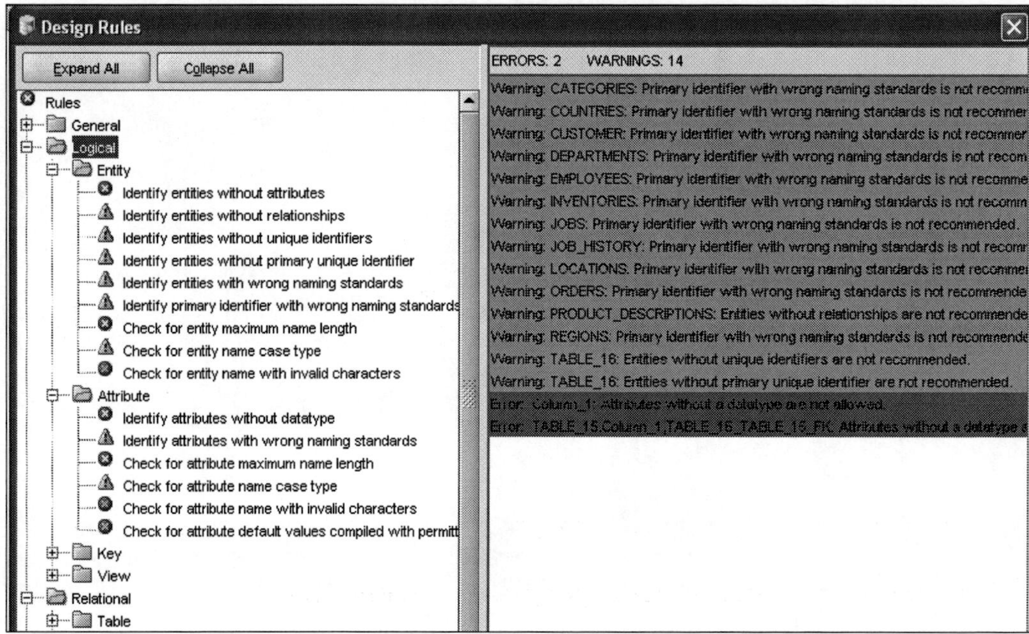

Most Design Rules are not updateable and you can't add your own. However, you can influence some of them, such as the maximum length of a table name. To see a few items that you can set, which influence the Design Rules, invoke the property dialog for your model. The **Naming Options** node provides a few default settings for the Design Rules, such as setting the maximum length of the table name.

Generating the DDL script

Once you have verified the Design Rules and made any additional updates to the model, you can generate the DDL. You have a choice of a standard DDL script, an interactive script, which will require input from the user when run, and a command-line script.

The DDL is sent to a single file and will need to be saved and run in SQL Developer or SQL*Plus at a later stage.

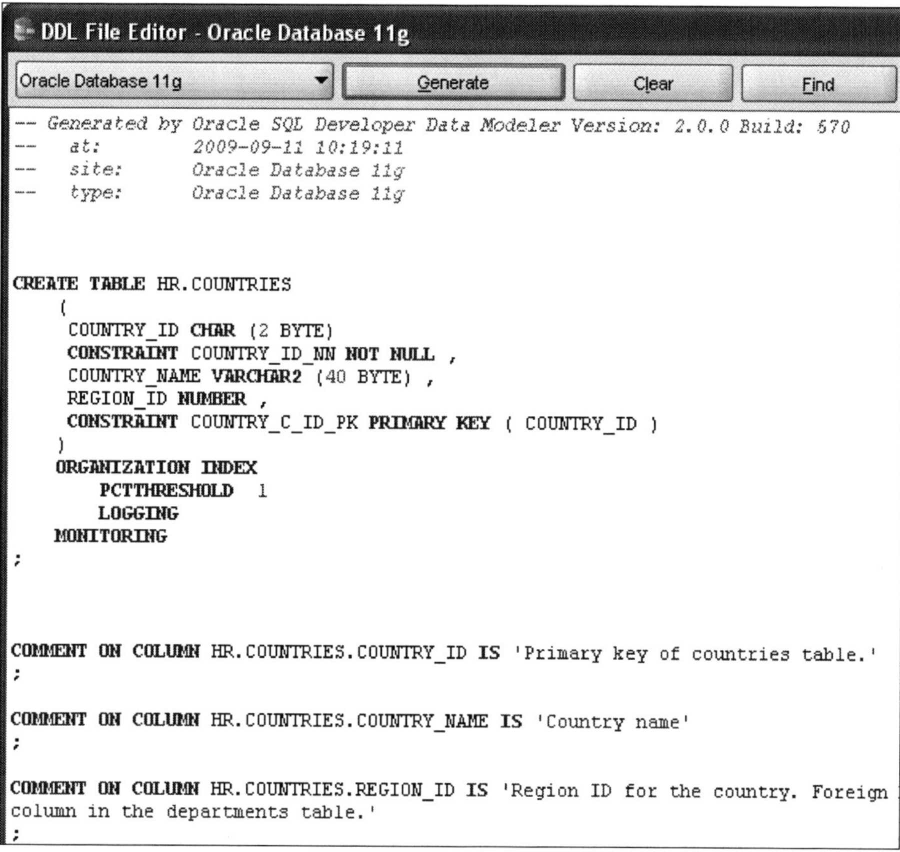

Updating an existing schema

The Data Modeler supports the creation of DDL scripts for creating new database objects as discussed. Invariably, users want to update schemas, and so often want to produce `ALTER`... and not `CREATE`... DDL scripts. Two different scenarios need to be addressed:

- You import and create a relational model based on a schema in the data dictionary. You update the model and want to update the database schema using DDL `ALTER` scripts.
- You have a relational model design, and the database schema is modified independently of the design, you need to see the differences between the two and want to create the DDL to update the database.

In both examples, you need to open the design you want to compare, and connect to the database to import the objects you want to compare against the design. The initial step is to import the objects using **File | Import | Data Dictionary**. Follow the import dialog as you would for a normal import, until you reach the summary page. Here, you have a choice of whether to import the object into an existing model or to create a new model. If you are comparing, then you should import to the existing model. You also need to determine the point of truth, is it the design or the data dictionary? Depending on the decision, you may need to swap the target model:

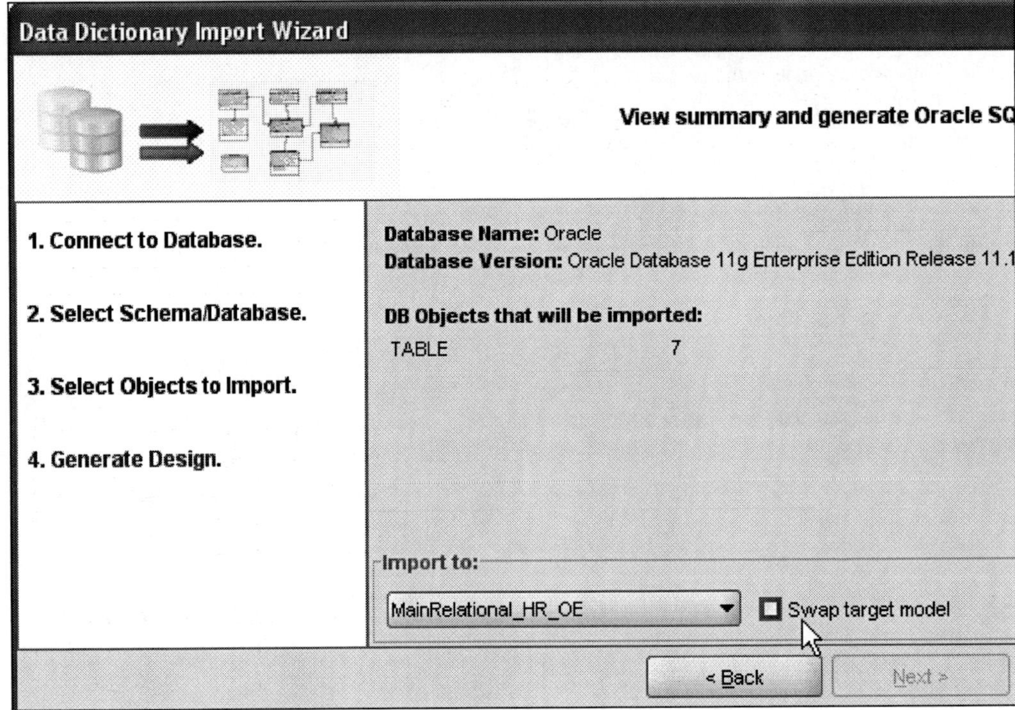

Importing into an existing model, invokes the **Compare Models** dialog. In the example that follows, we have imported the HR tables into the existing **HR_OE** relational model design, assuming the database is the point of truth. We had deleted a few columns and Foreign Key constraints associated with the **JOB_HISTORY** table from the design. In the following **Compare Models** dialog, the database import detail is shown on the left-hand side, with the relational model detail on the right-hand side. In order to update the model with the detail from the database, you need to check the required values on the left-hand side and click on the **Merge** button:

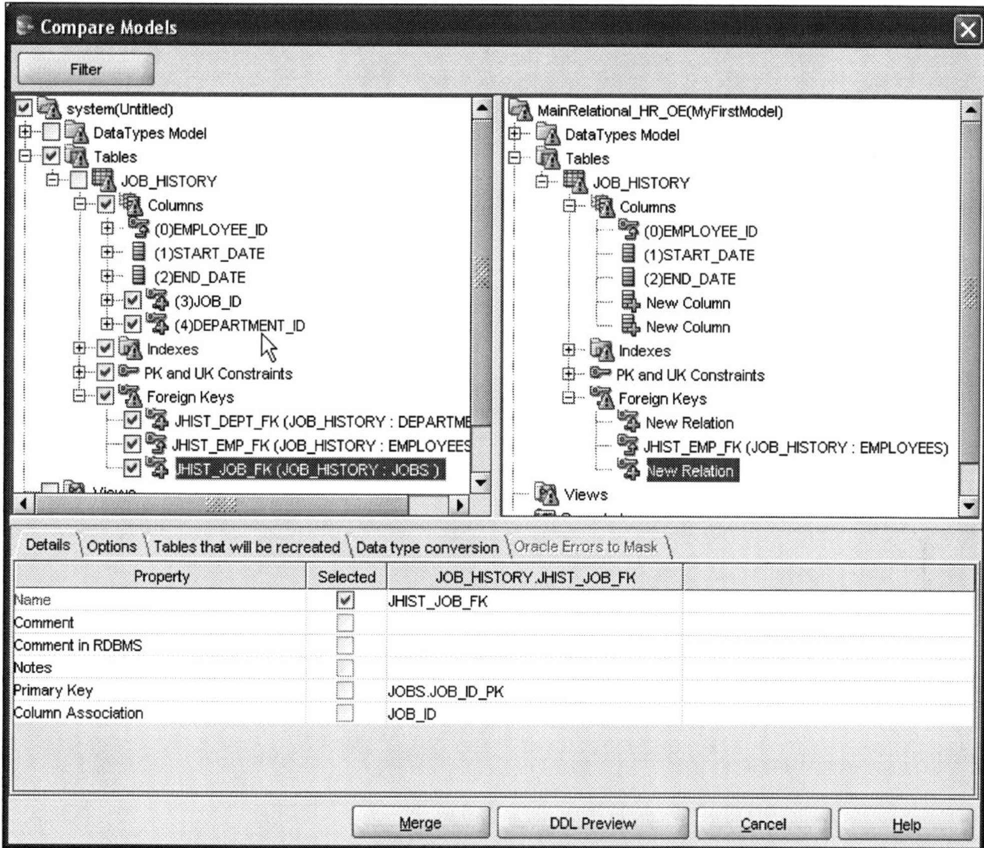

If you want to use the model as the point of truth to update the database, then you must select the **Swap target model** option on the import dialog. This ensures that the relational design is on the left-hand side and is the driving force for the changes. In that case, you can click the **DDL Preview** button to see the DDL `ALTER` commands.

Integration with Oracle SQL Developer

SQL Developer 2.1 includes the Data Modeler Viewer extension. This viewer provides users with the option of opening existing SQL Developer Data Modeler diagrams or creating models based on the database connection. To open the Data Modeler in SQL Developer, select **Tools | Data Modeler**. This opens the **Logical** and **Relational** model tabs. Once open, you can open any data model created in the Data Modeler. To review the details of the model in the navigator, select **View | Data Modeler | Browser**.

You can open any Data Modeler model in SQL Developer 2.1 by selecting **File | Open Data Modeler Design**. Once you have the model and the **Data Modeler** browser open, you can browse and review all of the model properties. The model and properties are all read-only:

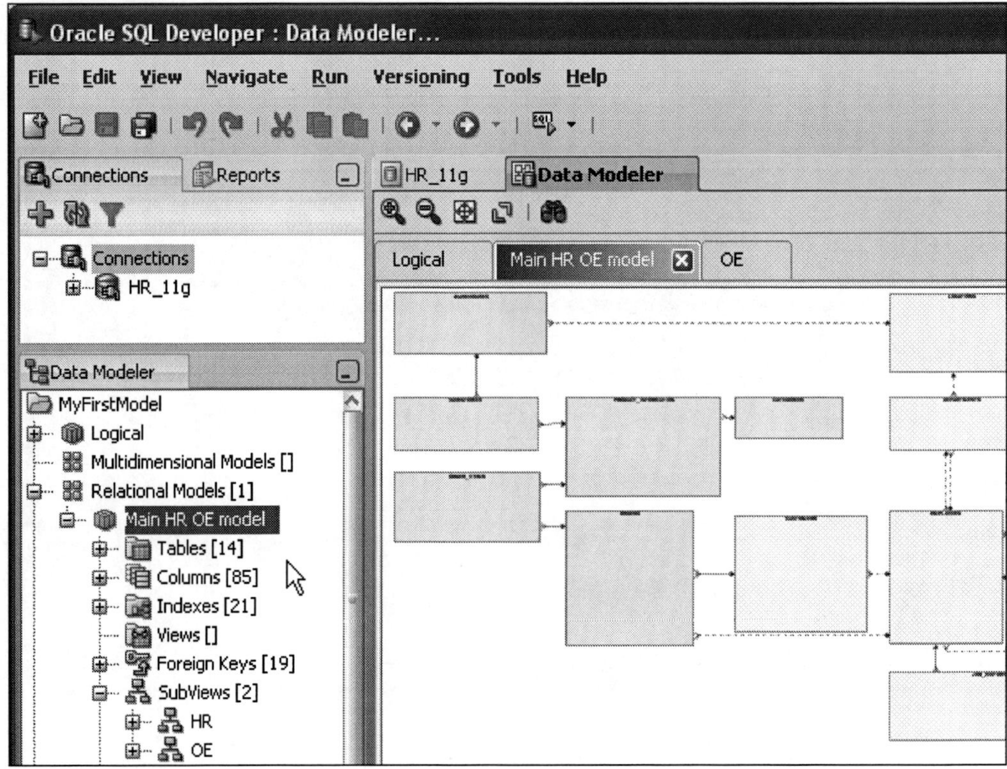

Creating a new model

The Data Modeler Viewer extension to SQL Developer also allows you to create models of the tables, views, and constraints in the database connections you have access to. To create a new model, expand the database connection in the **Connections** navigator, and then select the tables you want to include on a diagram. Drag the selection on the relational model (as seen in the following screenshot). You can't save the model, but you can move the objects on the diagram to change the default layout.

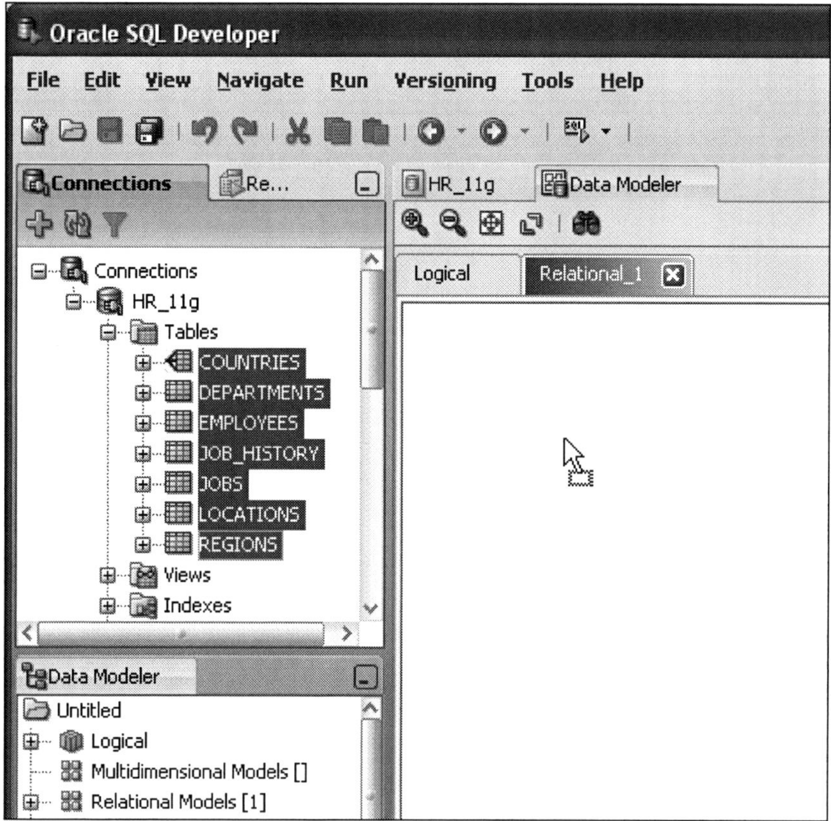

Creating and running reports

An important aspect of building a data model is to run reports against the designs, to ascertain if there are:

- Tables without columns
- Entities without attributes
- Columns or attributes without data types set

SQL Developer and the SQL Developer Data Modeler work together to support this functionality. You can use the Data Modeler to create and save the design to the reporting repository, and then use SQL Developer to run the shipped reports against the saved design.

Setting up the reporting schema

Before you can export any designs to the reporting schema, you need to create a user which will own the tables in the reporting repository. The repository is made up of 42 tables, with columns and associated indexes. You can use either the SQL Worksheet, or the **Create User** context menu on **Other Users,** to create a repository owner. Grant the user `CONNECT` and `RESOURCE` privileges.

Starting in SQL Developer Data Modeler, create and refine your data model designs. Once they are ready, select **Files | Export | To Reporting Schema**. This action invokes the **Export to Reporting Schema** dialog:

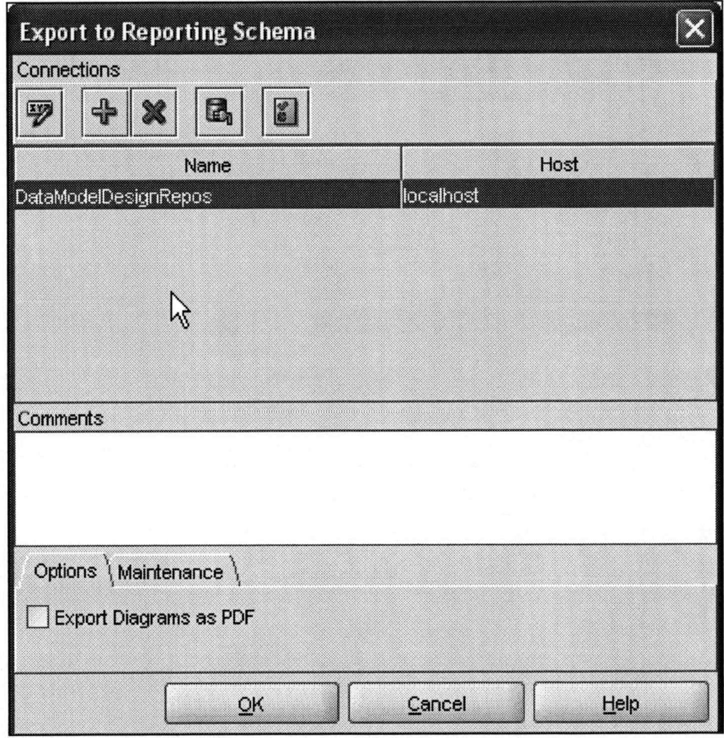

The first time you export your design, you'll need to create a connection to the new repository schema. Click on the **Add** button to invoke the **New Database Connection** dialog. The repository is built in an Oracle database, so the connection details here are for an Oracle connection. Once you have created the connection you can reuse it on subsequent exports. Select the new connection, and click on **OK**. The first time you perform the export, the tables for the repository are created in the repository schema. Subsequent exports write new records to the tables.

Having exported the design, open SQL Developer and select the **View | Reports** tab. Expand the **Data Modeler Reports** node. There are two categories of reports available, as shown in the following screenshot. These are **Design Content** and **Design Rules**:

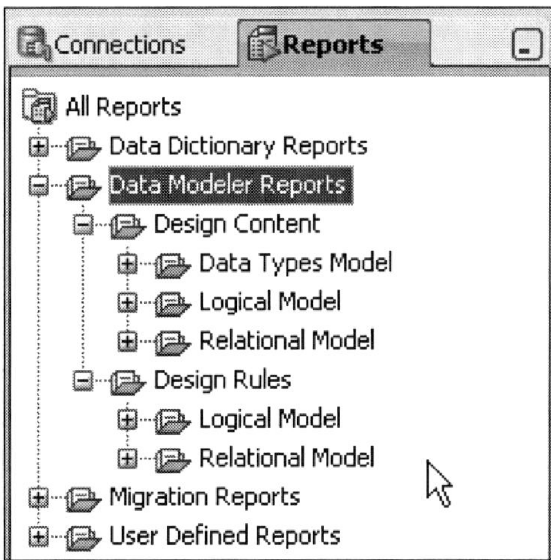

By default, the latest report for each design is displayed in the report. In order to see all exports of the design, enter **FALSE** in the **Enter Bind Values** dialog when running the report, and then click on **Apply**:

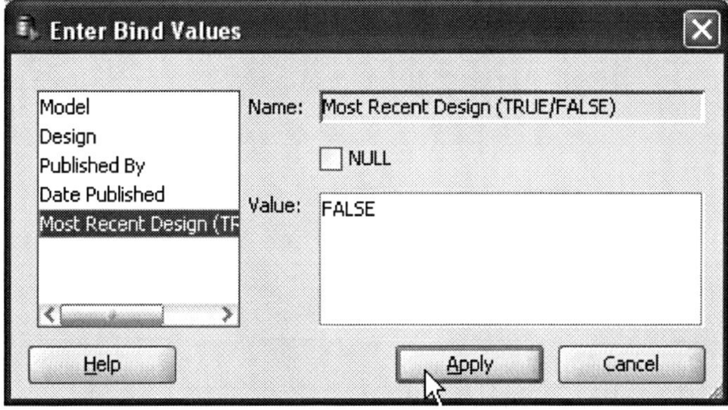

Use the reports to verify the completeness of your design, or create additional reports to extract further detail about your models. In the following screenshot, we have run the **Design Rules | Relational Model | Columns** report to determine which columns have no data type set. The report also provides the tables these columns belong to:

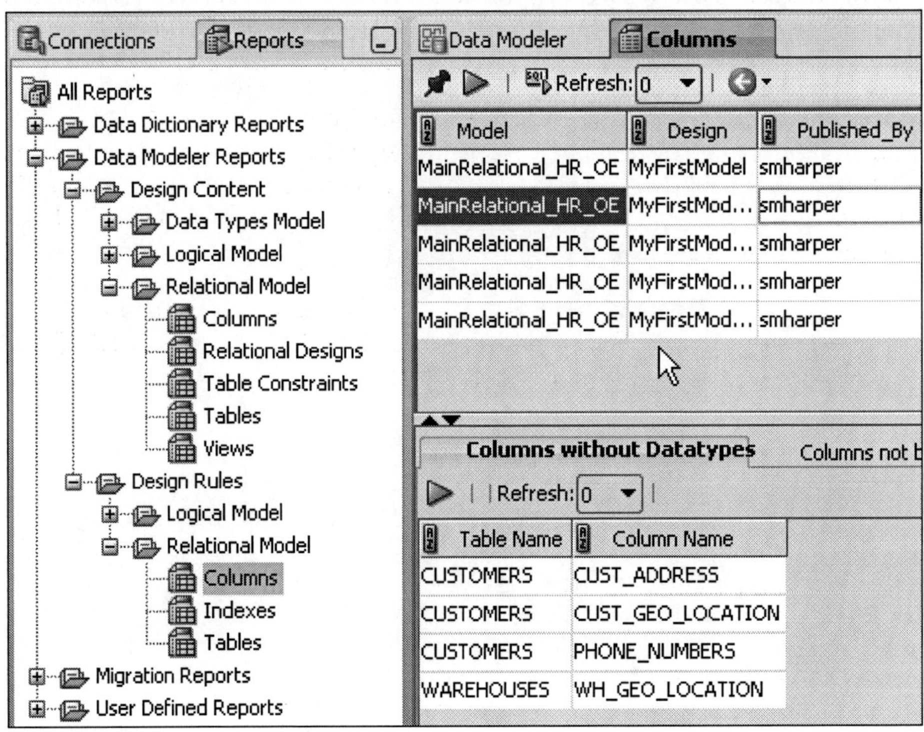

Summary

In this chapter, you have had an insight into the features offered by SQL Developer Data Modeler. The Data Modeler provides a number of graphical and textual modeling tools for Logical, Relational, and Multidimensional models. We looked at how to create Logical and Relational models, and how you can import models form the data dictionary or create models from scratch. We looked at forward and reverse engineering, how to build a physical model, and generate the DDL.

The subject of data modeling is vast, and this chapter only introduced some of the many and varied features available in SQL Developer Data Modeler. Whether you are a data architect, or updating an existing design, you can use SQL Developer Data Modeler for building full Entity Relationship Diagram or update schema models and generate the DDL scripts.

In the next chapter, we'll discuss SQL Developer's extensible framework, and look at how you can create user-defined extensions, using XML with embedded SQL and PL/SQL to add features to your SQL Developer environment.

11 Extending SQL Developer

Oracle SQL Developer is written using a Java framework. Provided by Oracle JDeveloper, this underlying integrated development environment is commonly referred to as the JDeveloper IDE, or more recently the **Fusion Client Platform** (**FCP**). The framework provides the underlying structure onto which both Oracle JDeveloper and Oracle SQL Developer developers add their features. This framework is extensible and is available to development engineers and end users to add functionality. The nature of these extensions can range from including a single XML report to adding complex Java extensions bundled as JAR files. In this chapter, we'll look at the range of the support available for adding XML extensions, a task that is easily within the reach of any database developer with SQL and PL/SQL skills. While it is considered beyond the scope of the book to include information on building a Java extension, we will discuss working with existing Java extensions.

Introducing extensibility

Extensibility, in terms of software development, means that the software can have components added without impacting, or having to change, the underlying code. Moreover, the underlying code provides 'hooks' within the infrastructure specifically designed for the addition of new components, thus allowing developers to add new or alternative capabilities not provided by the product.

Extensibility in SQL Developer

The FCP is designed to allow users to build Java extensions that can be added into either JDeveloper or SQL Developer. You can build large complex features using Java. The Migrations and Versioning support within SQL Developer are examples of this, and there are external customers building Java extensions.

SQL Developer provides an additional infrastructure with code 'hooks' for adding in items using only XML with embedded SQL and PL/SQL. The extra item types you can add are:

- Display editors
- Context menus
- Reports
- Navigator nodes

We will review these XML extension types and consider various examples to illustrate them.

Who builds extensions?

With the ability to support both XML and Java extensions, there is the opportunity to support different extension-building audiences. XML extensions are more typically used by developers well versed in SQL and PL/SQL. These are database developers and DBAs who use tools and command-line interfaces to access the database. The extensions they build are often shared within a team or the company. Java extensions are more often developed by development teams in Oracle, Oracle Partners, and other Java literate developers and engineers. **Oracle TimesTen** and the **Versioning Navigator** are Oracle-developed Java extensions, built by different teams, and are shipped as part of SQL Developer. Java bundled extensions, which could be a combination of XML and Java, lend themselves to be viable as commercial entities. There are a few public Java-based user-defined extensions, some are commercial and some are freely available.

Why extend?

Software products do not always provide the full functionality you need in your development environment. Being able to add a few additional components to those already provided means you can augment your environment with features that are specific to your needs. With SQL Developer extensions, you only need one person in the team to create the extension(s), which can then be shared, and so create an enhanced, yet company standard tool. The kind of missing functionality might be that grey area between being developer and DBA. For example, while the product is geared at database developers, many of us do have access to our own sandbox databases and want to use SQL Developer to maintain and view tablespaces. SQL Developer does not provide many DBA focused utilities, so this is an area rich in extensibility opportunities.

SQL Developer XML extension types

In this next section, the extensions described focus on XML extensions and can be added by anyone who has a good grasp of SQL and PL/SQL. Although the documents we create are written in XML, they conform to a set of **XML Schema Definition** (**XSD**) standards, which you can think of as templates. For all extensions added, whether you create Java extensions bundled as JAR files, or XML extensions and add them individually or bundled as JAR files, you need to restart SQL Developer for the additions to take effect. In this next section, we'll look at the different types of XML extensions you can create in SQL Developer. We'll start with the easiest, progressing to the more complex.

Adding an XML extension

Regardless of the XML extension you are adding, you add the files to SQL Developer in the same way. They are either as individual files or bundled as JAR files. When adding a single file or a few files, it's easy to add them individually.

To add a single XML file as an extension, select **Tools | Preferences**, expand **Database | User Defined Extensions**, and click on **Add.** Add the extension details and restart SQL Developer.

If you have a large number of files, then it's easier to bundle them in JAR files and add the files. This is more efficient, however, you need a certain level of Java knowledge to create the JAR file, and so we'll add them individually. We will show you how to add Java extensions later.

Sharing user-defined reports

The most straightforward of all extensions to create is the shared reports extension. Once you have created a set of your own reports, use the context menu to export them to an XML file. You can export reports at any level in the **User Defined Reports** section. You can either select:

- The top-level **Users Defined Reports**—this exports all sub-folders and reports
- Any subfolder—this exports all sub-folders, if there are nested folders, and reports
- Any report—this exports the selected report only

Regardless of the level you select, invoke the context menu and select **Export** (as shown in the following screenshot). Provide a report name and the file location.

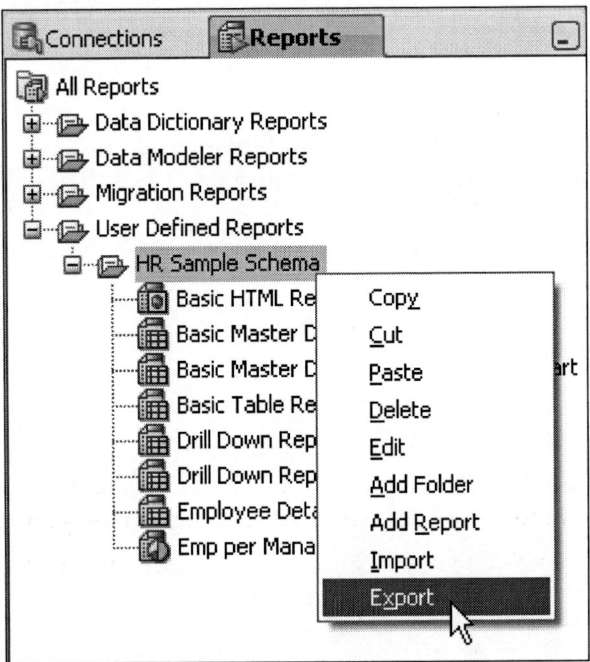

When creating reports, SQL Developer creates the XML file in the correct format. Therefore, in order to create the XML file for shared reports, you only need to worry about creating the initial reports, using the **Create Report** dialog for assistance. Once you have exported the reports to an XML file, and you can create one or many files, move them to a central file or web server to be made available for more general use.

To include the shared reports, open the **Database | User Defined Extensions** preference and click on **Add Row**. Select **REPORT** from the drop-down list for the extension type, and browse to locate the XML file, as shown in the following screenshot:

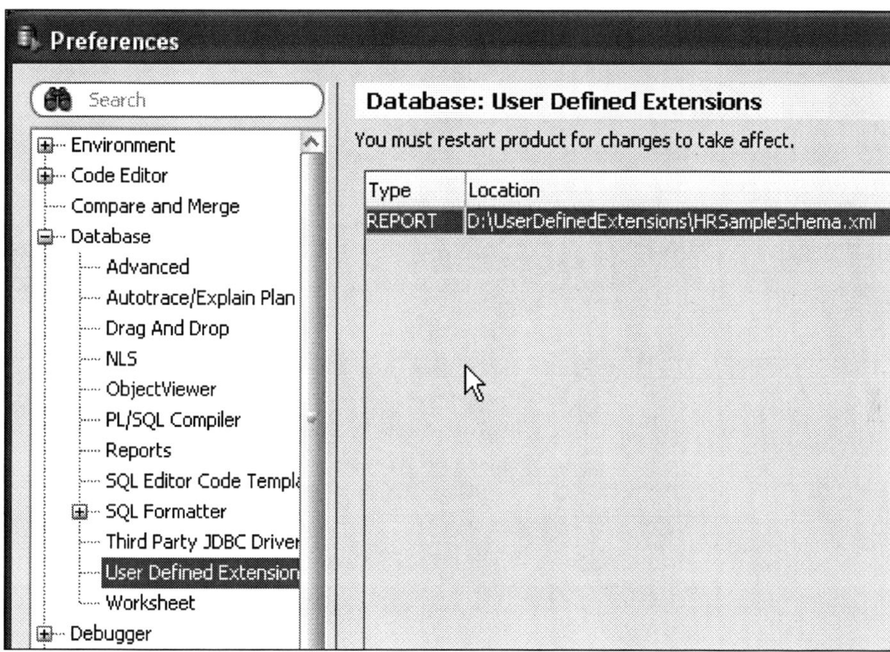

By sharing reports, you can:

- Save time and resources by having only one or a few team members create the reports and then share them with the group
- Use the best skills for the job, by using those developers with the most knowledge of the data dictionary or of the application you are working with
- Use those best skilled at writing well tuned SQL queries that others can take advantage of

Save shared reports on a web server

You can save the report's XML file on a web server. If the file is stored on a web server, use the full URL for the location of the file in the **User Defined Extensions** settings.

Once the new file location has been added, restart SQL Developer. A new **Shared Reports** folder now displays in the **Reports** navigator (as shown in the following screenshot). These reports, like those in the **Data Dictionary Reports** node, are not updateable. To review or edit the SQL, you can copy and paste them into a new report in the **User Defined Reports** node, or run the report and copy the SQL to the SQL Worksheet once run.

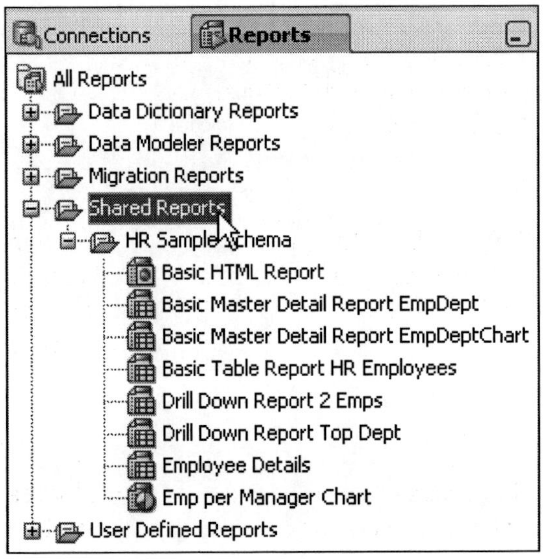

Another advantage of shared reports is that the next time you re-start SQL Developer, you pick up any updates to the existing reports or new reports added to the centrally stored file.

Adding display editors

Adding display editors is a little more involved than adding shared reports, because you need to create the XML file yourself. You invoke a set of display editors each time you click on an object in the **Connections** navigator. The set of view display editors is highlighted in the following screenshot:

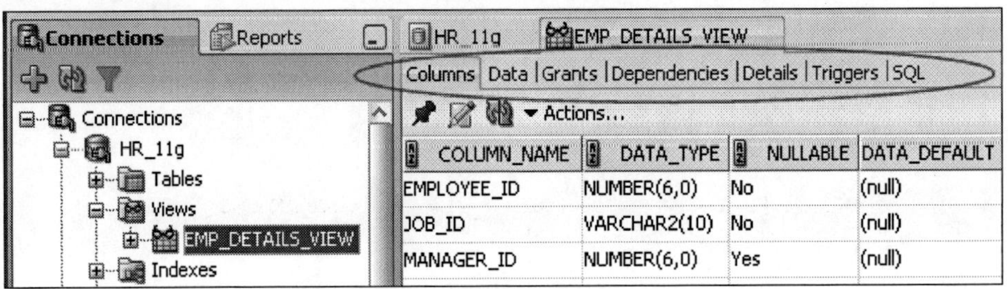

The contents of these display editors are the results of queries run against the data dictionary. For example, to get the kind of detail in the **Triggers** or **Columns** display editors shown in the previous screenshot, you can write queries against the **USER_TRIGGERS** or **USER_TAB_COLUMNS** dictionary views. For more detail, you need to write more complex queries, possibly joining many dictionary views.

Examples of display editors

The list of examples is potentially long, and we offer a few here only to give you an idea of the kind of content you can add. Naturally, any additional displays you add will depend on your areas of focus.

Include subpartitions

If you work with partitioned tables, then prior to SQL Developer 2.1, you only see the partitions display editor when you select a partitioned table with no additional subpartition information. You can add a user-defined extension to display the subpartitions details. SQL Developer 2.1 now includes subpartitions as detail records in a new permanent master-detail partitions display editor.

Use restricted queries

You can create editors that focus on a feature, for example, by creating display editors that display only the disabled constraints or triggers of a certain status.

Add display editors for new navigator nodes

If you create a new node in the **Connections** navigator, such as adding a Tablespaces, Dimensions, or a new Projects node, then you need to add the full set of display editors that define the objects you have listed.

Building the XML file for a display editor

Taking the idea of adding a subpartitions display, consider the following piece of code:

```
<displays>
  <!-- OverView -->
  <display type="editor" style="null" enable="true"
           class="Oracle#SUBPARTITION" objectType="TABLE">
    <name><![CDATA[Subpartitions]]></name>
    <query>
      <sql>
        <![CDATA[Select * FROM USER_TAB_SUBPARTITIONS WHERE
                TABLE_NAME = :TABLE_NAME]]>
```

```
        </sql>
      </query>
          <CustomValues>
          <TYPE>horizontal</TYPE>
          </CustomValues>
    </display>
  </displays>
```

By saving this code to an XML file, and then hooking that file into SQL Developer, you add another display editor to the set already defined for tables.

The structure for each display editor you add is the same. The first `CDATA` entry highlighted above is for the title, displayed in the display editor tab. The second `CDATA` entry highlighted is the SQL query, which provides the content. The results of the new display editor are shown in the upcoming screenshot. Notice that the new editor is added at the end, after the SQL editor. Notice too that in the example, the table name is unnecessarily included in the list. Here, we have used a simple "`Select * FROM` ..." query. Even for a simple query, just by specifying the columns in the select statement means that you can control the columns that display and avoid the unnecessary additional columns, in this case the table name.

The example we have included is basic and is sufficient to add in additional display editors. If you are familiar with XML, then you'll want to see the XSD. The **XSD,** or **XML Schema Definition,** provides the syntax and structure of the way the elements should be defined in the XML file.

The structure of the display editor conforms to an XSD called `displays.xsd`. The `displays.xsd` includes a `query.xsd`. These are included in the code bundle of the book, available at the Packt web site.

The SQL query you include in the XML file can be as simple as `SELECT * FROM <a data dictionary view>`, or a more complex query, joining multiple dictionary views. A sample SQL query to create the following partitioned table is included in the code bundle.

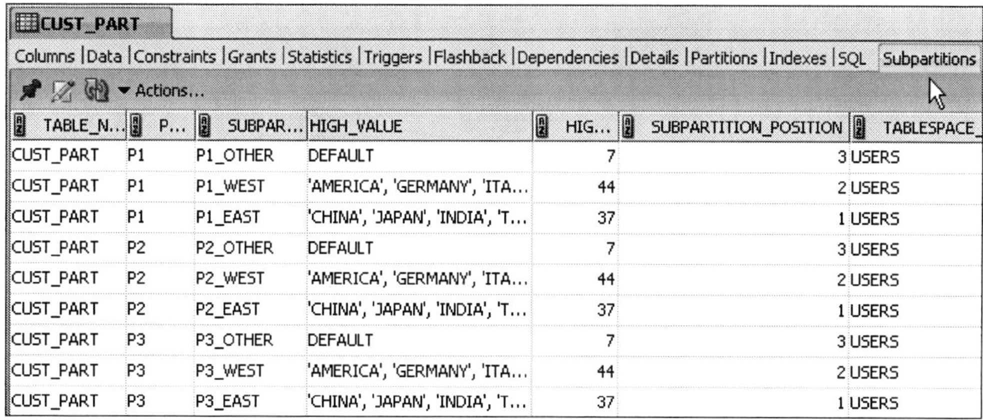

CUST_PART

Columns | Data | Constraints | Grants | Statistics | Triggers | Flashback | Dependencies | Details | Partitions | Indexes | SQL | Subpartitions

TABLE_N...	P...	SUBPAR...	HIGH_VALUE	HIG...	SUBPARTITION_POSITION	TABLESPACE_
CUST_PART	P1	P1_OTHER	DEFAULT	7	3	USERS
CUST_PART	P1	P1_WEST	'AMERICA', 'GERMANY', 'ITA...	44	2	USERS
CUST_PART	P1	P1_EAST	'CHINA', 'JAPAN', 'INDIA', 'T...	37	1	USERS
CUST_PART	P2	P2_OTHER	DEFAULT	7	3	USERS
CUST_PART	P2	P2_WEST	'AMERICA', 'GERMANY', 'ITA...	44	2	USERS
CUST_PART	P2	P2_EAST	'CHINA', 'JAPAN', 'INDIA', 'T...	37	1	USERS
CUST_PART	P3	P3_OTHER	DEFAULT	7	3	USERS
CUST_PART	P3	P3_WEST	'AMERICA', 'GERMANY', 'ITA...	44	2	USERS
CUST_PART	P3	P3_EAST	'CHINA', 'JAPAN', 'INDIA', 'T...	37	1	USERS

Once you have created the XML file, save it to the file or web server location of your choice, and open the **User Defined Extensions** preference. Click on **Add Row,** select **EDITOR** from the drop-down list for the extension type, and browse to locate the XML file as shown in the following screenshot:

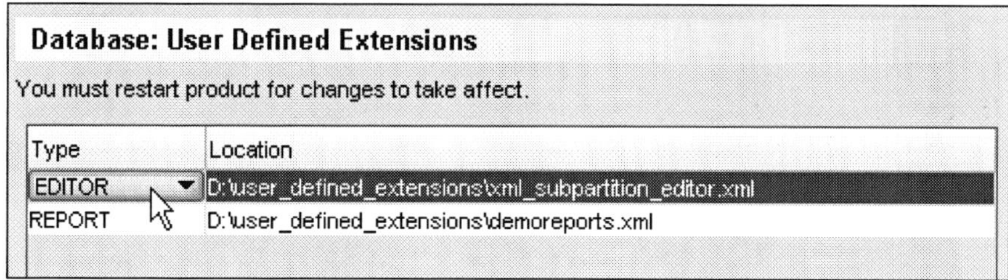

Group display editor topics into a single file

Instead of creating multiple, individual XML files for each display editor, add all of the code for the display editors for a single object into one file. For example, create an `ExtraTableEditor.xml` file with all of the additional table related display editors.

Working with context menus

Throughout SQL Developer, a right-click on the mouse invokes a context sensitive menu. The menus in the **Connections** navigator are all DDL commands which provide actions such as dropping, adding, and setting privileges. For example, if you select a table and invoke the context menu, you can drill down to the **Drop** menu as shown:

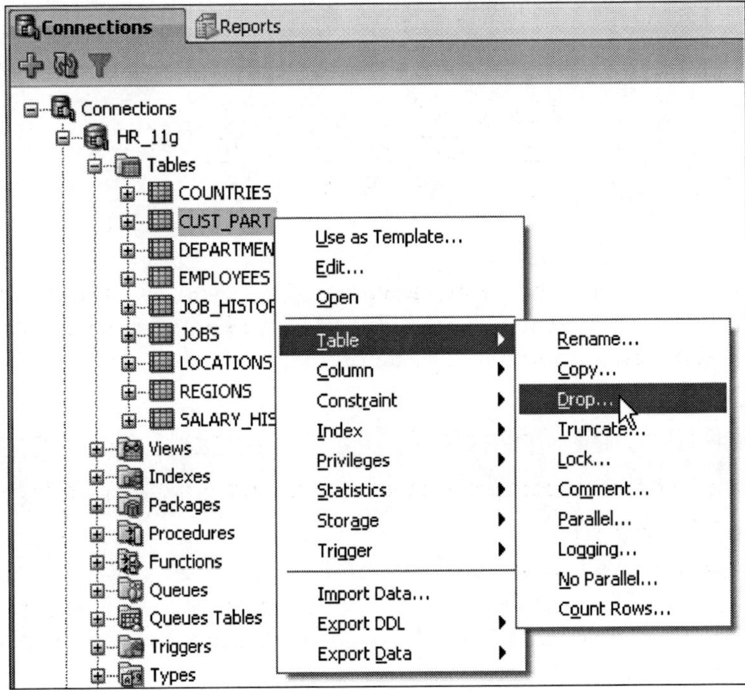

Selecting the menu item invokes the dialog with two tabs. The pieces that are consistent for each of these context menu dialogs are the three buttons, **Help**, **Apply**, **Cancel**, and the two tabs, **Prompts** and **SQL**. The initial **Prompts** panel also displays the context you are in, the schema name, displayed as the **Owner**, and the selected object name. In the example in the following screenshot, we have selected a table, and so the **Name** displayed is that table name:

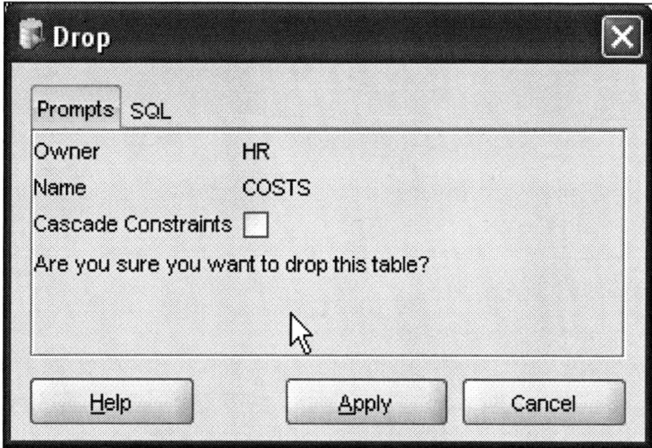

You can add these extra context menus at various levels in the **Connections** navigator tree such as at the connection, object node or instance level, so the name displayed depends on the node you have selected.

Adding a context menu to the connections menus

You can add the option to compile the schema currently selected. Consider the following piece of code:

```
<?xml version="1.0" encoding="UTF-8"?>
<items xmlns:xsi="http://www.w3.org/2001/XMLSchema-instance"
                  xsi:noNamespaceSchemaLocation="dialogs.xsd">
  <item type="CONNECTION" reload="true">
   <title>Compile Schema</title>
   <prompt type="confirm">
     <label>Confirm to compile all in the schema.</label>
   </prompt>
   <sql>
      <![CDATA[BEGIN DBMS_UTILITY.COMPILE_SCHEMA
          (:OBJECT_OWNER); END;]]>
     </sql>
   <help>Compiles all the objects in the schema. </help>
  </item>
</items>
```

This adds a new context menu when you right-click on the connection. It invokes a dialog with two tabs, the first with all of the details of the action about to take place, and the second displays your SQL or, in this case, PL/SQL code. You can include help text and a confirmation dialog to follow the action.

As before, if you are familiar with XML, there is an XSD file to assist with the development of the XML file structure.

The structure of the context menu conforms to an XSD called `dialogs.xsd`. This is included in the code bundle available at the Packt web site.

Passing parameters

In the previous example, we only passed a single parameter: the object owner name. You can create context menus and provide empty fields, checkboxes, or drop-down lists, which allow the user to have more control over the SQL executed. In the **Drop** table example illustrated at the start of this section, the checkbox allows the user to include the **Cascade Constraints** option. To provide the user with a fixed list of values, add the static list options after the `<title>`Compile Schema`</title>`. The code is shown below:

```
<prompt>
  <label>Compile All </label>
  <value><![CDATA[STATIC:TRUE:FALSE]]></value>
</prompt>
```

Once you start passing in additional parameters, you can use them in the SQL as follows:

```
<sql>
    <![CDATA[BEGIN
      DBMS_UTILITY.COMPILE_SCHEMA('#OBJECT_OWNER#', #0#);
      END;]]>
</sql>
```

Here, the parameter is referred to by the value `#0#`. You can pass a number of additional values to the SQL statement, referencing each in turn by using the values `#0#`, `#1#`, `#2#`, and so on.

The result of our code is shown in the following screenshot, including the drop-down list. Notice that we do not need to code for the **Owner** or the **Name** values displayed. These are exposed in the dialog through the extensions framework. If you do not see them, no connection has been made.

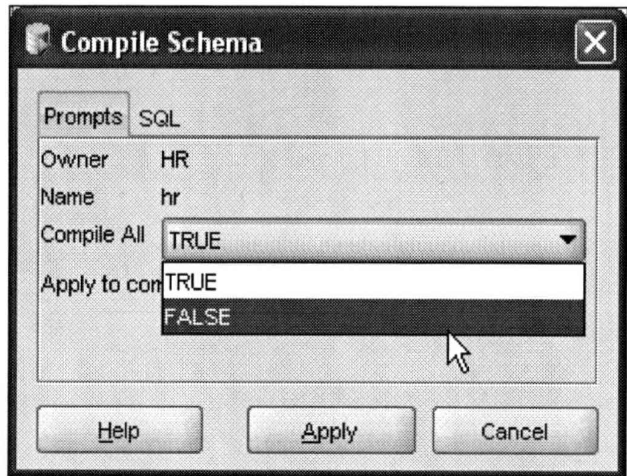

Creating a utility using context menus

The extent of what the context menu does is up to you. You can create a simple menu to drop or rename an object, or you can create more complex menus. You don't need to limit yourself to a single command either (whether basic or complex). Instead, you can bundle a set of commands to create a small utility, like the **Normalize** menu, provided by SQL Developer.

The context menu is available off **Columns | Normalize** when you select a table.

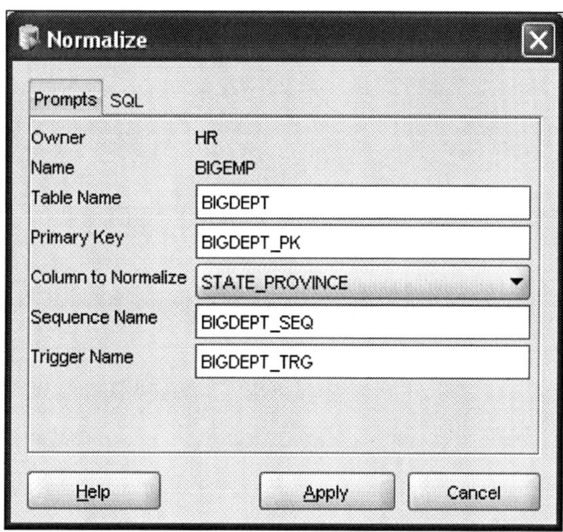

In the dialog previously displayed, you can see that the code requires four free form values to be added, and one selected from a drop-down list.

This little utility is very useful if you have imported a spreadsheet to create a new table populated with that data. Invariably, there are redundancies and the table is better suited to be split into two or more. You manually need to create a new table and move the duplicate values to the new table, populating a Primary Key automatically while you do so. Then you need to create a Foreign Key constraint to link the two tables. This utility does all of the steps, wrapped in PL/SQL.

In the code shown in the following screenshot, you can see a subset of the code, displaying the steps that you need to follow when doing the process manually:

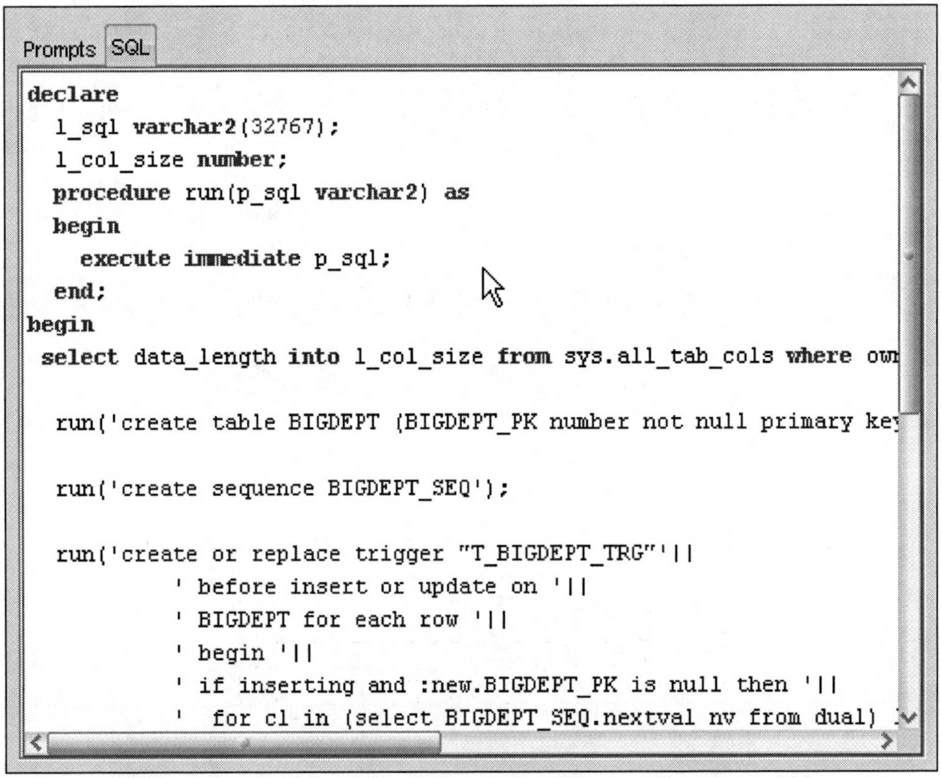

Prompts SQL

```
declare
  l_sql varchar2(32767);
  l_col_size number;
  procedure run(p_sql varchar2) as
  begin
    execute immediate p_sql;
  end;
begin
 select data_length into l_col_size from sys.all_tab_cols where own

  run('create table BIGDEPT (BIGDEPT_PK number not null primary key

  run('create sequence BIGDEPT_SEQ');

  run('create or replace trigger "T_BIGDEPT_TRG"'||
           ' before insert or update on '||
           ' BIGDEPT for each row '||
           ' begin '||
           ' if inserting and :new.BIGDEPT_PK is null then '||
           '  for c1 in (select BIGDEPT_SEQ.nextval nv from dual) 
```

Including the user-defined extension for context menus

In the same way as you have done for the previous examples, once you have created the XML file, save it to the file or web server location of your choice and open the **User Defined Extensions** preference. Click on **Add Row** and select **ACTION** from the drop-down list for the extension type, and browse to locate the XML file as shown in the following screenshot:

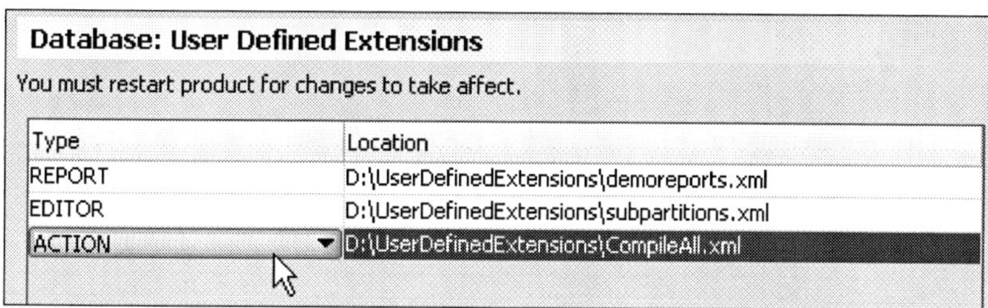

In this case, the code adds an extra menu item in the **Connections** context menu:

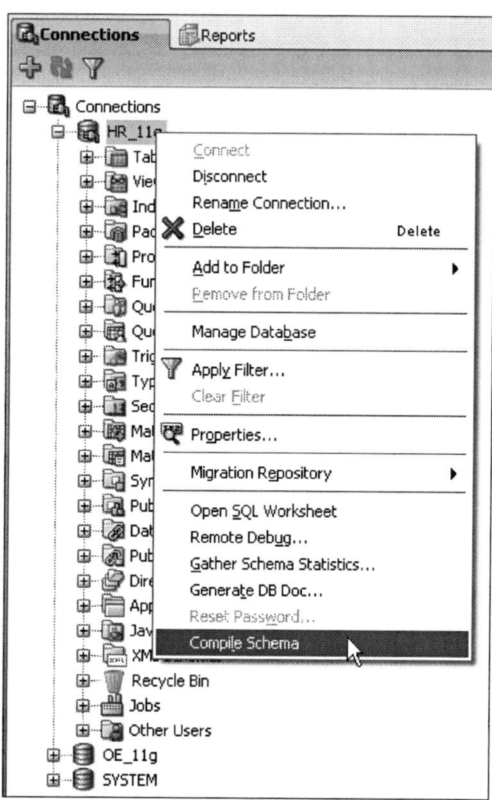

When adding context menus in the **Connections** navigator, you can add individual menus, or a menu with a number of submenus. There are many such menus in SQL Developer, such as the **Column** context menu with its set of sub-menus. To include a collection of context menus for one node, add all of the pieces of XML code into the same file:

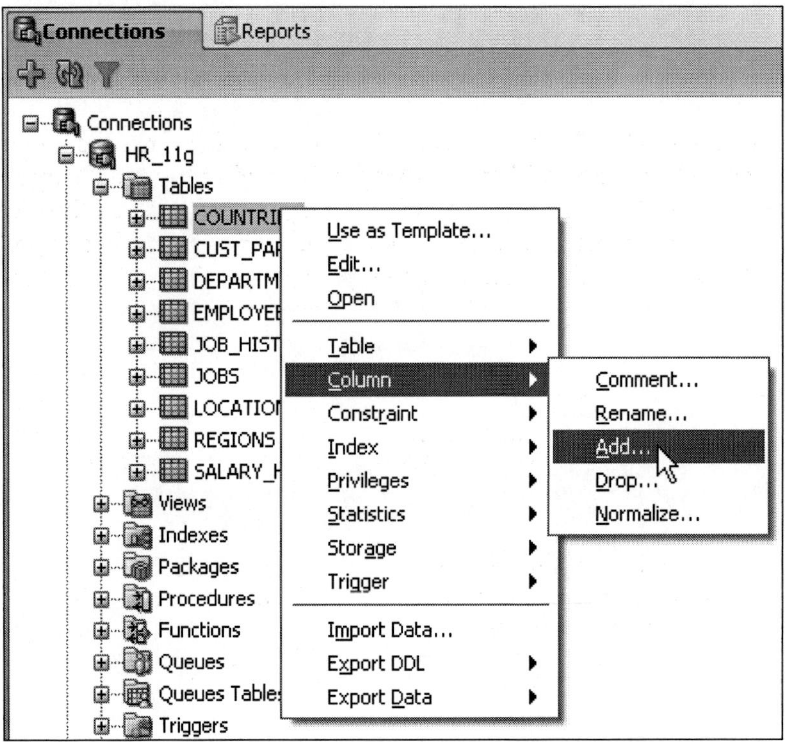

Adding new nodes to the Connections navigator

The last of the XML user-defined extension types available in SQL Developer is the Navigator. The name is a little misleading because the "Navigator" user-defined type allows you to add a new node into the list of currently available nodes in the **Connections** navigator. Currently, these nodes are predominantly made up of data dictionary objects types such as Tables, Views, and Indexes. The list includes the Application Express node that allows you to browse the detail of your Oracle Application Express applications. In this case, you are browsing the metadata that defines the application.

You can add nodes for database objects not yet supported in the navigator, such as tablespaces, or you can add new nodes to browse external application metadata stored in database repositories, for example, you can create an Oracle Designer node, to query the Oracle Designer Workareas. Alternatively, you can add a node to query instance data in applications.

Including user-defined extensions for a navigator node

Adding extra nodes to the **Connections** navigator is a little more involved than for the preceding examples. You still create a single file, and in the same way as you have done for each of the previous examples, once you have created the file, save it to the file or web server location and open the **User Defined Extensions** preference. Click on **Add Row,** and in this instance you should select **NAVIGATOR** from the drop list for the extension type, and browse to locate the XML file.

To investigate this example, we'll break up the file and code into sections and then build it up in phases. You can start by creating the skeleton, adding it into SQL Developer, and restarting the product. Then, you only need to refresh the navigator by restarting SQL Developer after any additional changes to the XML file.

> **Updating the navigator extension**
>
> You will not be able to save changes to the XML file while SQL Developer is still open. Include the XML skeleton and then close and reopen SQL Developer. Close SQL Developer each time you want to update and save the XML.

In the following screenshot, a number of additional nodes have been added. The new nodes are added above the shipped nodes, which are sorted by typical usage priority:

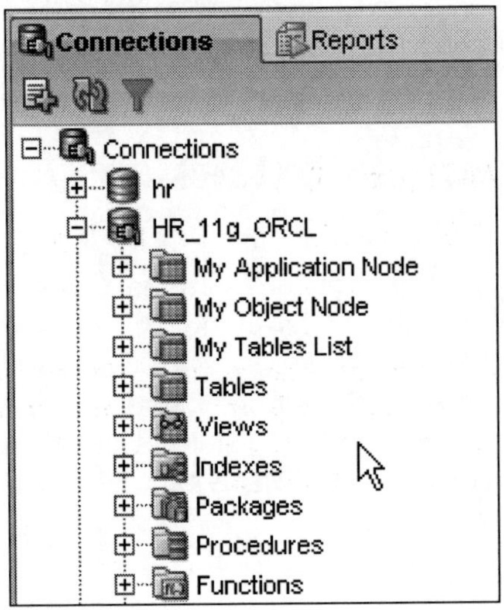

Adding a new tree to the navigator

The structure that you generally want to replicate in the tree is a top-level node, for example, **Tables**, and then to display the list of tables. Below, we have the columns that are associated with each of those tables. Using that example, we have the following structure:

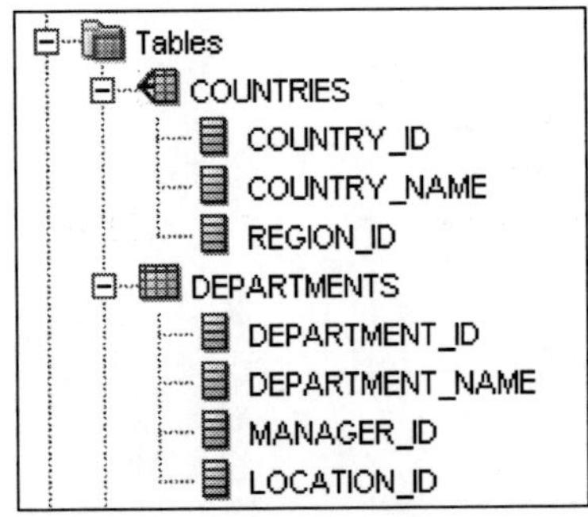

Extrapolating from the structure above, which you know, call the Tables node *Level 1*, the actual table listing *Level 2*, and the columns *Level 3*:

Tables (*Level 1*)
 COUNTRIES (*Level 2*)
  COUNTRY_ID (*Level 3*)
  COUNTRY_NAME (*Level 3*)

Once again, there is an XSD file to assist with the development of the XML file structure.

> The structure of the navigator node conforms to an XSD called `navigator.xsd`. The `navigator.xsd` also calls the `query.xsd`. These files are included in the code bundle available at the Packt web site.

To add a new top-level folder, consider the following code:

```
<?xml version="1.0" encoding="windows-1252" ?>
<navigator RESOURCE_FILE="oracle.dbtools.raptor.navigator.
OracleNavigatorResource"
  xmlns:xsi="http://www.w3.org/2001/XMLSchema-instance"
  xsi:noNamespaceSchemaLocation="navigator.xsd">
  <objectType connType="Oracle" id="MyApplication"
    weight="50.0" includesSyns="true">
    <folder> <!-- level1 -->
      <icon RSKEY="TABLE_FOLDER_ICON" />
      <label RSKEY="My Application Node" />
      <queries> <!-- level2 -->
            <query minversion="8">
        <sql constrained="true"><![CDATA[]]></sql>
        </query>
      </queries>
    </folder>
  </objectType>
</navigator>
```

The only piece you are really interested in changing is the `label`, which is the name of the new **Connections** navigator node that you are creating. The other value you can change when creating your own copy of this file, is the `id`. It is a good idea to keep this `id` as descriptive as you can.

There is currently no query listed in the CDATA section. Therefore, if you add this code and open SQL Developer you'll only get the new node, there is no tree of objects below the node, and so no detail of any interest at this stage. To list the elements under that first node, you need an initial query. The example we use here is trivial, to illustrate the concept, and does not take into account other objects you might want listed or any privileges.

In addition to including an SQL query to populate the list, you also need to add in a <columns> section. This references the columns in the query. Notice that the query below includes an alias, which is referenced in the <columns> section. The following code listing is just that portion of the full file above which lies between the <queries>...</queries> tags:

```
<queries> <!-- level2 -->
   <query minversion="8">
    <sql constrained="true">
    <![CDATA[SELECT TABLE_NAME NAME FROM TABS]]></sql>
  </query>
  <columns>
    <column filterable="true" sortable="true" id="NAME">
      <colName><![CDATA[name]]></colName>
    </column>
   </columns>
</queries>
```

Once again, you have an id field, in this case id="NAME". It is a good idea to keep these id values meaningful, as they can be used as bind variables for future sub-nodes, or to link to the display editors.

To finish off that node, you still need to add the icon detail. Add this detail into the file below the </folder> tag as follows:

```
<node> <!-- level2 details -->
  <icon RSKEY="OracleIcons.TABLE" />
</node>
```

In this example, we are referencing the icons shipped as part of SQL Developer. The icons are available in the \sqldeveloper\sqldeveloper\extensions folder in the oracle.sqldeveloper.jar file. If you browse this file, you can see the images are in the folder structure /oracle/dbtools/raptor/images/ which you can reference, as follows:

```
<icon RSKEY=" /oracle/dbtools/raptor/images/snippets.png" />
```

Instead of using the shipped SQL Developer icons, you can create your own set in a JAR file, and add these as a Java extension.

The output of what we have achieved until now is shown below. Notice that there is a list of tables, based on that SQL query, but we don't have any columns, which would complete this node in the navigator:

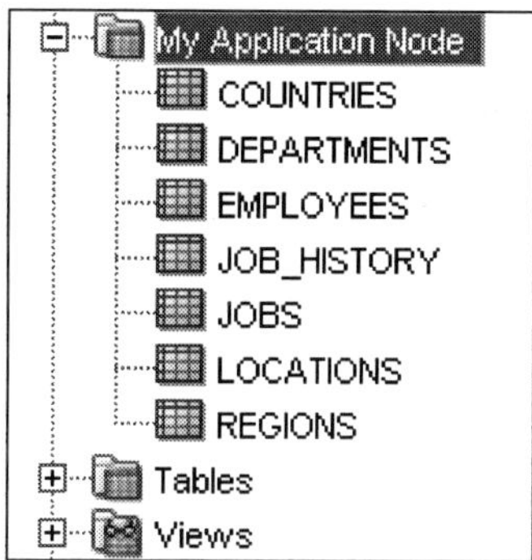

To complete the node, you need to add in the third-level query. The structure here is as before, using the same queries and columns tags as shown:

```
<queries>
  <query>
    <sql> </sql>
  </query>
  <columns>
  </columns>
</queries>
```

This third level is included in the second level's `<node>` details. With the extra code as follows:

```
<node> <!-- level2 details -->
  <icon RSKEY="OracleIcons.TABLE" />
  <childType id="Level3"> <!-- Level3 -->
  <icon RSKEY="OracleIcons.COLUMN" />
  <queries>
     <query>
      <sql> SELECT COLUMN_NAME FROM USER_TAB_COLUMNS
              WHERE TABLE_NAME = :PARENT_NAME
      </sql>
    </query>
    <columns>
      <column filterable="true" sortable="true" id="NAME">
      <colName><![CDATA[column_name]]></colName>
      </column>
```

```
        </columns>
          </queries>
      </childType>
    </node>
```

Notice how this SQL now includes the bind variable to ensure that you only get the required detail records. In this case, we have not used an alias in the query, so we need to ensure that the full column name is referenced in the `<column>` section.

The addition to this `<node>` detail results in the output shown in the following screenshot:

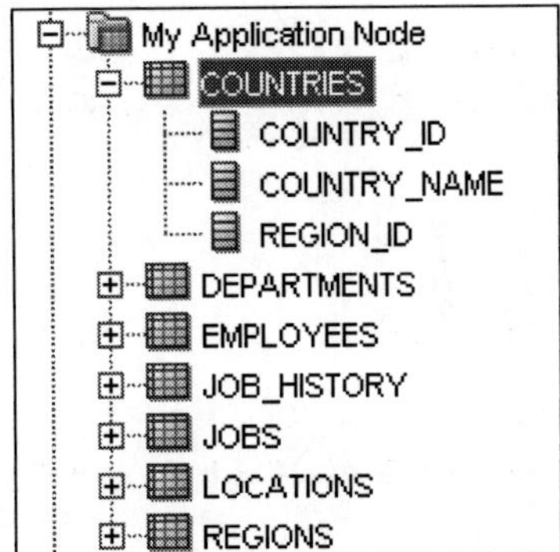

You have now reached the point where you can return to the start of this chapter and add all of the display editors and the context menus for each of the nodes, as required.

Adding multiple nodes

You can add as many nodes to the **Connections** navigator as you need. These new nodes all appear at the top of the list, above the predefined nodes. You can't control the order of the full navigator, but you can control the order that these new nodes appear in, by changing the weight value. In the example we used, the value was `weight="50.0"`, so setting `weight="30.0"` would appear above this, and `weight="80.0"` below.

If you have lots of XML files, instead of adding the individual files using the **Database | User Defined Extensions** preference, you can create a folder called `userextensions` in the `\ sqldeveloper\ sqldeveloper\` folder and add the files there. When you restart SQL Developer the extensions are available.

Reviewing an example

Using the details given, we'll expand that to add a new extension to SQL Developer. The following example is designed to show you how to bring all of the pieces together. As before, we use the most basic SQL code to illustrate the point and it serves only as a starting point.

Adding support for dimensions

In this example, we add a Dimensions node, with sub-node, a context menu and some display editors. The sample schema we will use in this illustration is the Sales History (SH) schema, as it has a selection of dimensions defined. To follow the example, create a database connection for the SH schema.

Adding a dimensions navigator

We'll start by creating a new node for **Dimensions**, and ensure we have the first, second, and third level defined in the single XML file as shown in the following code:

```
<?xml version="1.0" encoding="windows-1252" ?>
<navigator RESOURCE_FILE="oracle.dbtools.raptor.navigator.
OracleNavigatorResource"
  xmlns:xsi="http://www.w3.org/2001/XMLSchema-instance"
  xsi:noNamespaceSchemaLocation="navigator.xsd">
  <objectType connType="Oracle" id="DIMENSION" weight="100.0"
    includesSyns="true">
<folder>
  <icon RSKEY="TABLE_FOLDER_ICON"/>
       <label RSKEY="Dimensions"/>
    <queries>
        <query minversion="8">
          <sql constrained="true">
            <![CDATA[SELECT DIMENSION_NAME FROM USER_DIMENSIONS]]>
          </sql>
        </query>
        <columns>
          <column filterable="true" sortable="true" id="NAME">
              <colName>
                <![CDATA[dimension_name]]>
              </colName>
          </column>
        </columns>
    </queries>
</folder>
    <node>
```

```
        <icon RSKEY="OracleIcons.TABLE" />
          <childType id="Level3">
            <icon RSKEY="OracleIcons.COLUMN" />
            <queries>
              <query>
                <sql>SELECT LEVEL_NAME FROM USER_DIM_LEVELS
                           WHERE DIMENSION_NAME = :PARENT_NAME
                </sql>
              </query>
              <columns>
                <column filterable="true" sortable="true" id="NAME">
                <colName><![CDATA[level_name]]></colName>
                </column>
              </columns>
            </queries>
          </childType>
        </node>
      </objectType>
    </navigator>
```

The resulting output is as shown in the following screenshot:

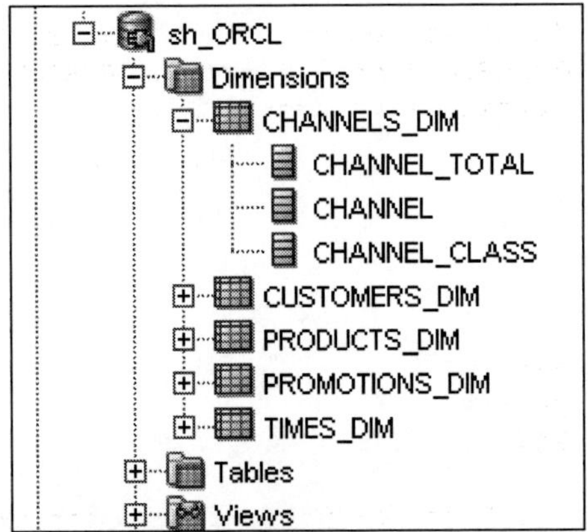

Adding dimension display editors

Once you have the new node in place, you need to add a set of display editors, so that when you click on a dimension or level, you see relevant details.

You can create individual XML files and link each one in turn, or you can add all of the details into a single file. In the following example, we have only included the code for the first two displays. The full listing is included in the code bundle. However, you can see how additional displays are added into the same file. In this example, notice how the bind parameter is called `:NAME`. This matches the ID in the navigator file.

```
<?xml version="1.0" encoding="UTF-8"?>
<displays>
  <!-- OverView -->
  <display type="editor" style="null" enable="true"
    class="Oracle#DIMENSION" objectType="DIMENSION">
    <name><![CDATA[Attributes]]></name>
    <query>
      <sql>
        <![CDATA[SELECT ATTRIBUTE_NAME, COLUMN_NAME, INFERRED,
           LEVEL_NAME  FROM USER_DIM_ATTRIBUTES
           WHERE UPPER(DIMENSION_NAME) = UPPER(:NAME)]]>
      </sql>
    </query>
        <CustomValues>
        <TYPE>horizontal</TYPE>
      </CustomValues>
  </display>
  <display type="editor" style="null" enable="true"
    class="Oracle#DIMENSION" objectType="DIMENSION">
    <name><![CDATA[Details]]></name>
    <query>
      <sql>
        <![CDATA[SELECT * FROM USER_DIMENSIONS
           WHERE UPPER(DIMENSION_NAME) =UPPER(:NAME)]]>
      </sql>
    </query>
        <CustomValues>
        <TYPE>vertical</TYPE>
       </CustomValues>
  </display>
  <display type="editor" style="null" enable="true"
    class="Oracle#DIMENSION" objectType="DIMENSION">
    <name><![CDATA[Levels]]></name>
    <query>
      <sql>
        <![CDATA[SELECT LEVEL_NAME, NUM_COLUMNS, DETAILOBJ_OWNER,
           DETAILOBJ_NAME FROM  USER_DIM_LEVELS
           WHERE UPPER(DIMENSION_NAME) =UPPER(:NAME)]]>
      </sql>
```

```
        </query>
            <CustomValues>
            <TYPE>horizontal</TYPE>
          </CustomValues>
    </display>
  </displays>
```

Associating the display editor with the navigator

By creating well-defined IDs in the navigator file, you can easily identify the bind values required in the display editor files.

Adding context menus

To complete the new node, you should add a few context menus. These can be as numerous and as complex as you need (for example, to create, drop, or rename objects). Here we have added two context menus.

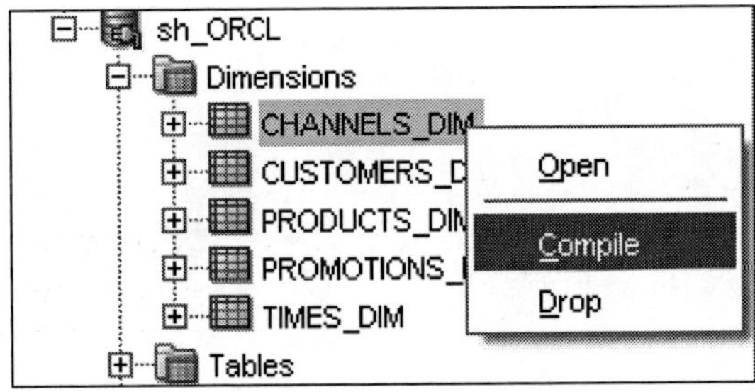

The sample of code for these context menus is as follows:

```
<?xml version="1.0" encoding="UTF-8"?>
<items xmlns:xsi="http://www.w3.org/2001/XMLSchema-instance"
                  xsi:noNamespaceSchemaLocation="dialogs.xsd">
  <item type="DIMENSION" reload="true" >
    <title>Compile</title>
    <prompt type="confirm">
      <label><![CDATA[Are you sure you want to compile this
              Dimension?]]></label>
    </prompt>
    <sql>
      <![CDATA[ALTER DIMENSION #DIMENSIONNAME# COMPILE]]>
    </sql>
    <help>Compiles the selected dimension.</help>
    <confirmation>
      <title>Confirmation</title>
```

```
      <prompt>Dimension #DIMENSIONNAME# has been compiled.</prompt>
    </confirmation>
  </item>
  <item type="DIMENSION" reload="true" >
    <title>Drop</title>
    <prompt type="confirm">
      <label><![CDATA[Are you sure you want to drop this
              Dimension?]]></label>
    </prompt>
    <sql>
      <![CDATA[DROP DIMENSION #DIMENSIONNAME#]]>
    </sql>
    <help>Drops the selected dimension.</help>
    <confirmation>
      <title>Confirmation</title>
      <prompt>Dimension #DIMENSIONNAME# has been dropped.</prompt>
    </confirmation>
  </item>
</items>
```

Working with extensions

Whether you create your own extensions or use SQL Developer out of the box, you are taking advantage of the product's extensibility when you use the features. In this section, we'll consider the additional external extensions available and how you can work with them.

Controlling existing extensions

You can add or remove Java extensions using the **Extensions** preferences. Oracle TimesTen, Migrations, and the version control support are all extensions designed and shipped with the product. You can see these extensions listed in the **Extensions** node.

Adding in new Java extensions

You can add in new Java extensions using the **Check for Updates** facility. There are a number of options:

- Check for Updates—Use the Update Center
- Check for Updates—Install from Local File

In the first instance, developers outside of Oracle, who have created a Java extension, can approach Oracle to have these included in the **Check for Updates** facility. If you want to use these extensions, then invoke the wizard and select **Search Update Centers** and include the **Third Party SQL Developer Extensions**. The third party database drivers are also included in this selection.

If you have a Java extension internally, you can also add a link to your own update center by selecting **Add** and then providing the URL of the location of your file:

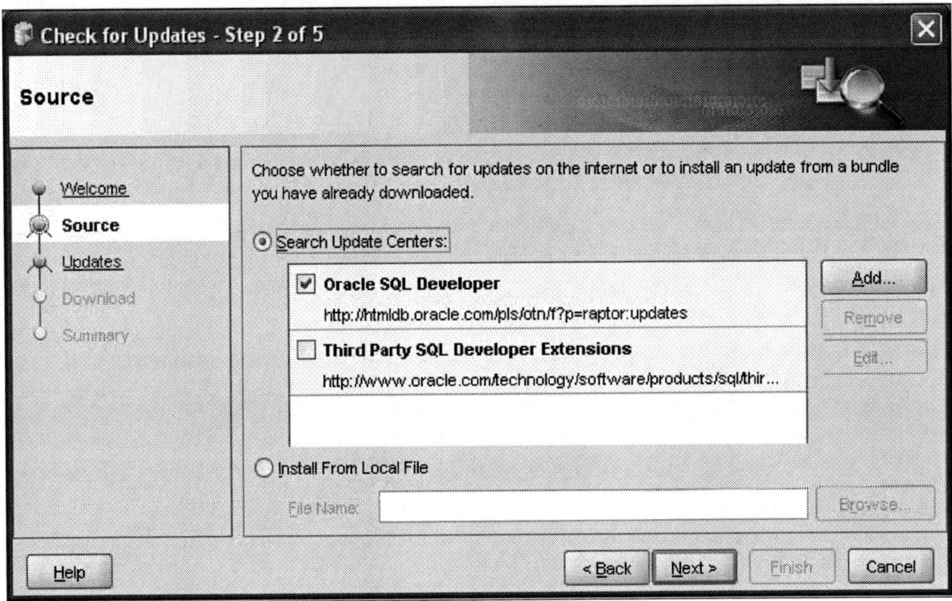

Using the **Check for Updates** wizard, you can install Java extensions that you or someone else has developed and provided you with the file. For example, your own icon image bundle. Here, select **Install From Local File** and browse to locate the zipped bundle.

All of your additional Java extensions are listed together with the shipped extensions in **Preferences | Extensions.** In the following screenshot, the **JTDS JDBC Driver** is one that was added using the **Check for Updates** facility:

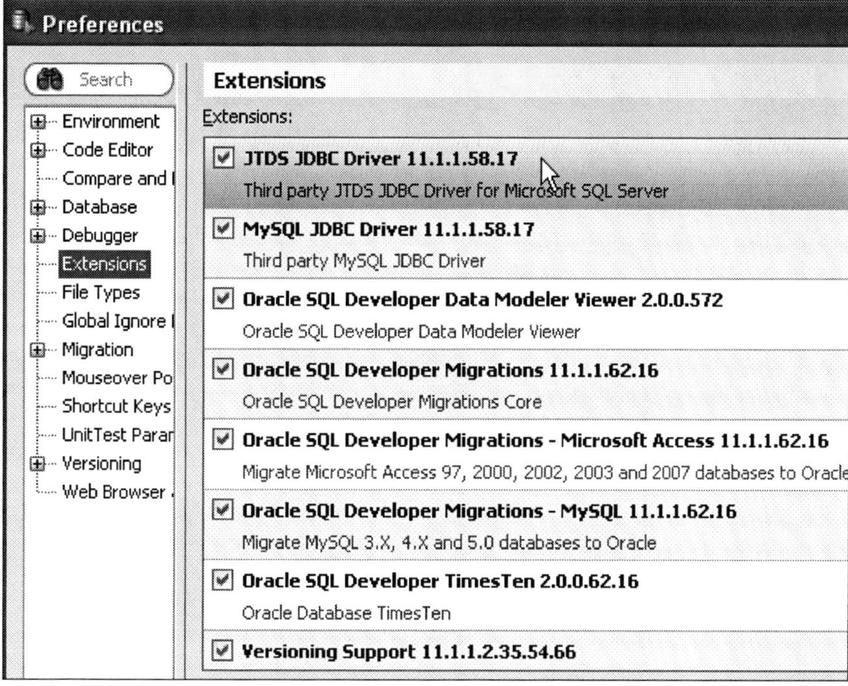

Removing extensions

No matter whether these are shipped extensions or ones that you have added using **Check for Updates**, you can remove any of them by deselecting the extension in the list and restarting SQL Developer.

Delete the link to the XML file to remove any of the XML extensions you create, and include in the **User Defined Extensions** preference.

> Whether you are adding or removing extension, whether Java or XML, you need to restart SQL Developer for the changes to take effect.

Sharing extensions

The real advantage of the extensible environment is that you only need a few members in the team to create the extensions, whether they are Java or XML, and then share these among the group. To share extensions, you can store them on a shared file server or on a hosted web server. In either case, any changes made to the XML files will be reflected in your product the next time you start it.

Summary

In this chapter, we reviewed the ability to extend SQL Developer by adding XML-structured, user-defined extensions. The structure of SQL Developer means that you can also take advantage of any Java-developed extensions available. User-defined extensions give you the flexibility of adding in small or larger utilities to augment the tool's capabilities. Sharing extensions within a team means that you can use the new functionality without having to define it yourself.

In the next chapter, we'll look at the integration of SQL Developer and Oracle Application Express. This is an example of where another team within Oracle took advantage of the extensibility and created a new node in the **Connections** navigator, much as we have discussed in this chapter.

12
Working with Application Express

SQL Developer provides an access point to Oracle Application Express for browsing, monitoring, and managing your applications. Using SQL Developer, you can browse and review application data in the same way that you browse and review any other schema data using the **Connections** navigator. SQL Developer also provides administrative utilities, such as being able to rename or deploy applications. Also, by using the PL/SQL coding and SQL tuning capabilities, you can test and tune pieces of code to enhance the performance of the application. In this chapter, we will show you how to connect to Application Express, browse your applications, review some of the administration utilities, and use the SQL Worksheet to refactor PL/SQL code.

Setting the scene

To derive benefit from this chapter, you should have an Application Express environment set up. If you are already a regular user of Application Express, you can follow these examples using your own applications. In this case, you can skip the section on *Setting up in Application Express*, which is about creating a workspace and schema for the examples that follow. Alternatively, you can follow the preparation setup steps provided next to create an example that you can delete later.

If you are new to Application Express, you can still take advantage of the combination of the two tools and the details in this chapter. Before you start, it is recommended that you visit the **Getting Started** section on `http://apex.oracle.com` (`http://www.oracle.com/technology/products/database/application_express/html/getting_started.html`). The site provides a number of useful links to help you get Application Express set up and to familiarize yourself with the environment.

To follow the examples we use in this chapter you need access to:

- Create a new workspace and schema in Application Express. This action also creates the default sample application we refer to. The database schema created is the one that we connect to using SQL Developer.
- Create an Application Express user. This is the user that we use to connect to Application Express to edit and update the sample applications.
- Import and use one of the packaged applications available for download from the Application Express site, `http://apex.oracle.com/i/index.html`, or from the Oracle Technology Network.

We provide the details on how to do this in the next section.

Setting up in Application Express

For most of this chapter we'll work in SQL Developer. There are sections that require you to work in Application Express, like this first one, where you set up your Application Express environment.

Creating a workspace and database schema

Invoke Application Express using the administrator login and select **Manage Workspaces**. You can either invoke the **Manage Workspaces** page and select **Create Workspace**, or access the **Create Workspace** pages from the front panel as shown in the following screenshot:

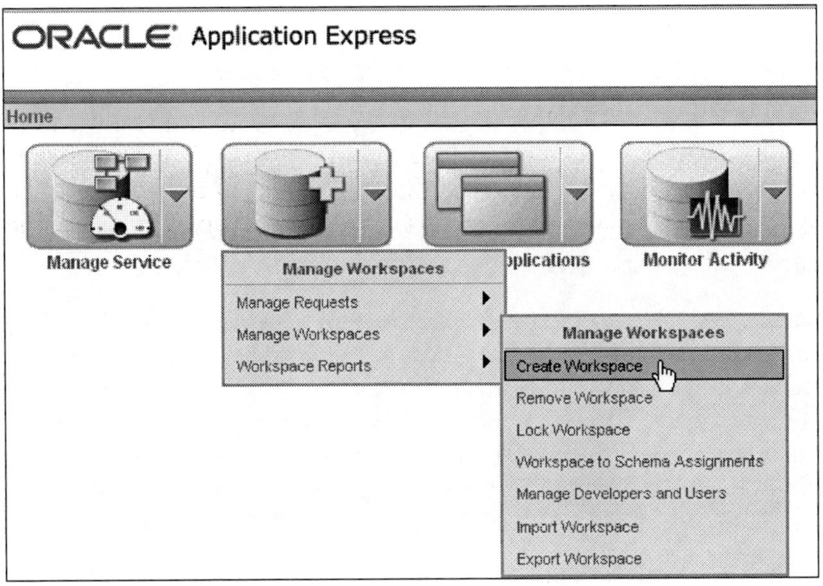

The wizard guides you through the steps of creating the workspace and schema. Creating a new workspace also creates the default sample application for the schema associated with the workspace. It is this schema and application that we use in the examples that follow.

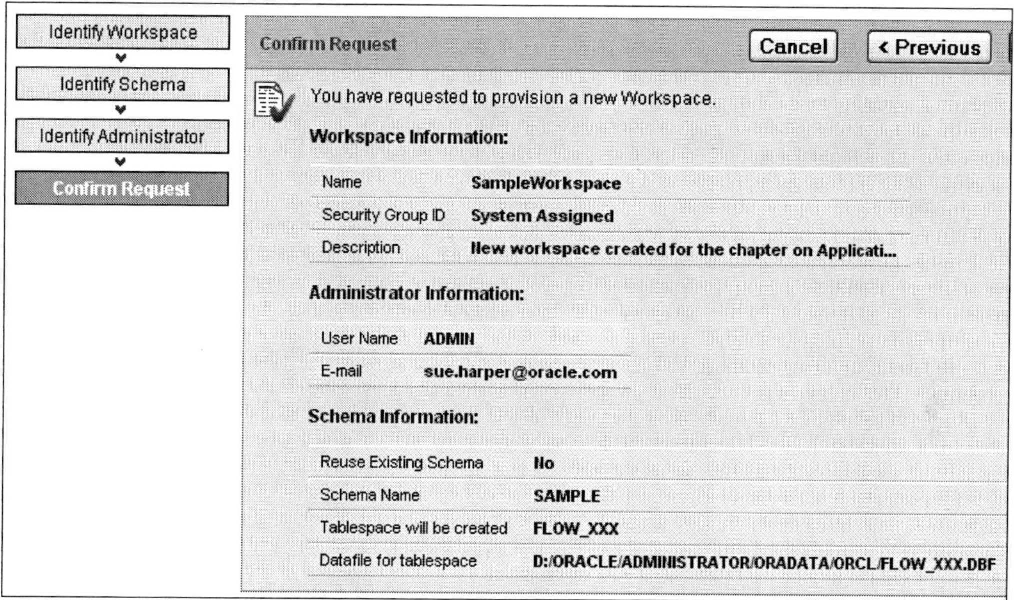

In the example shown in the previous screenshot, we created a workspace called **SampleWorkspace** and a new database schema called **SAMPLE**.

Creating an Application Express user

You can, at this point, use SQL Developer to connect to the database schema and view the details of the sample application created. However, later in the chapter, we'll return to Application Express to edit an application, and for that you'll also need an Application Express user who can access the workspace, modify, and run the application.

To create an Application Express user and associate it with one or more workspaces, use the **Manage Developers and Users** page, accessed from the main **Manage Workspaces** page as shown in the following screenshot:

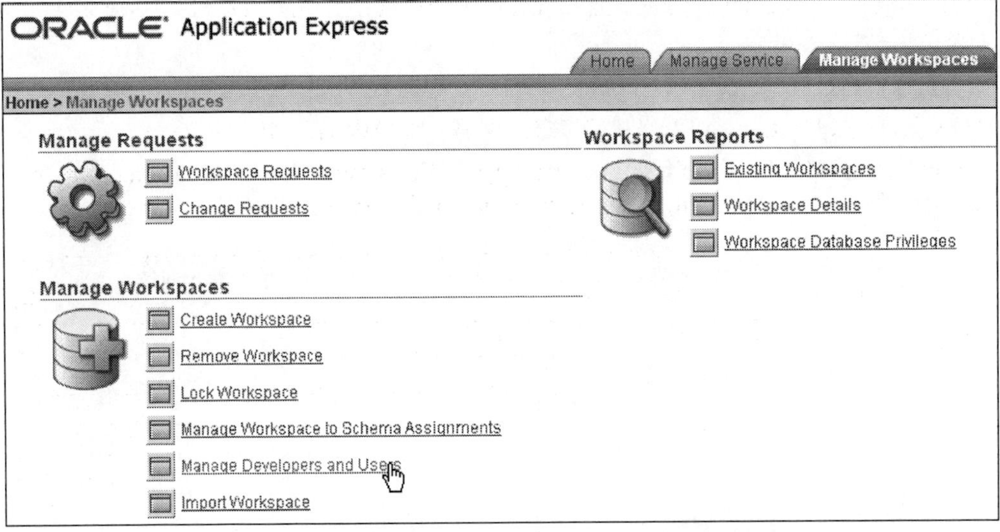

Click on the **Create** button to invoke the **Create/Edit User** screen and add your new user details to this. In the following screenshot, we show part of the page with the initial details populated. Use this user to connect to Application Express and edit the applications in the workspace.

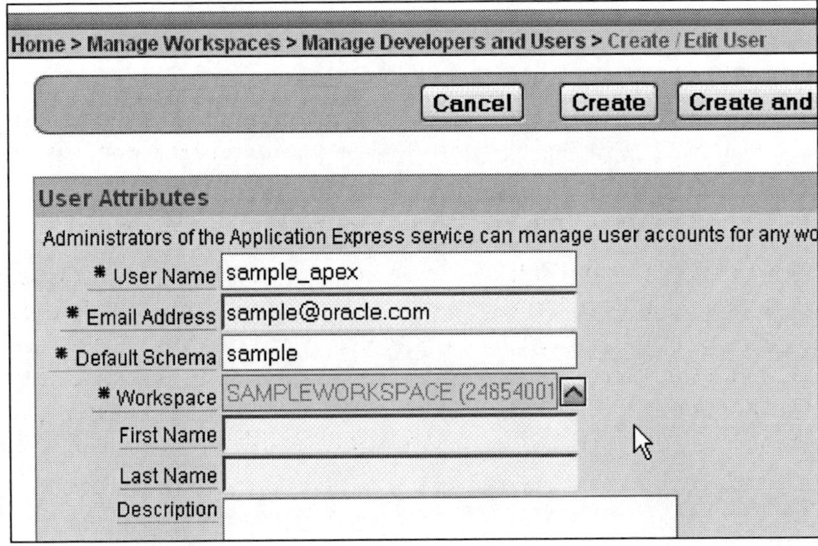

Browsing applications in SQL Developer

The rest of the chapter is about working with, and accessing applications from within, SQL Developer. So unless otherwise directed, assume the instructions refer to working in SQL Developer. The section starts with creating a connection and browsing applications.

Creating a connection in SQL Developer

To view both the schema objects and the applications owned by the schema, create a new database connection in SQL Developer for the Application Express schema:

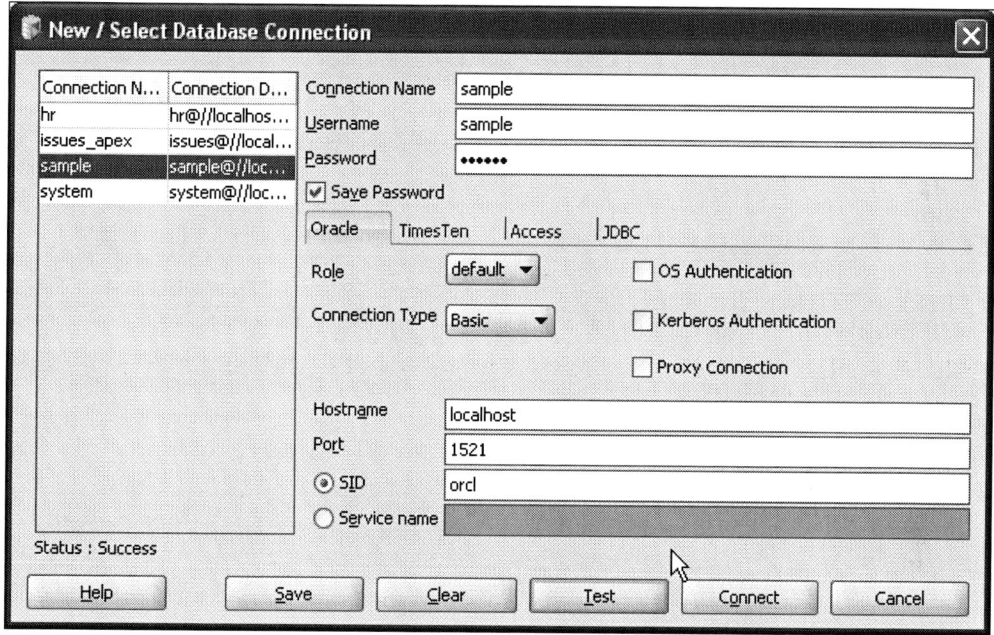

Browsing and working with schema objects

In addition to viewing the applications, you can use SQL Developer's **Connections** navigator to review schema objects such as tables, views, and indexes, in the same way as you have browsed, created, and updated any other database schema objects. Application Express provides an **SQL Workshop** (similar to SQL Developer's **SQL Worksheet**) for creating, editing, and updating database objects. You may prefer to use SQL Developer for these activities when working with Application Express.

The following screenshot shows the tables used in the sample application. SQL Developer provides easy access to browse and query these tables and the data they hold.

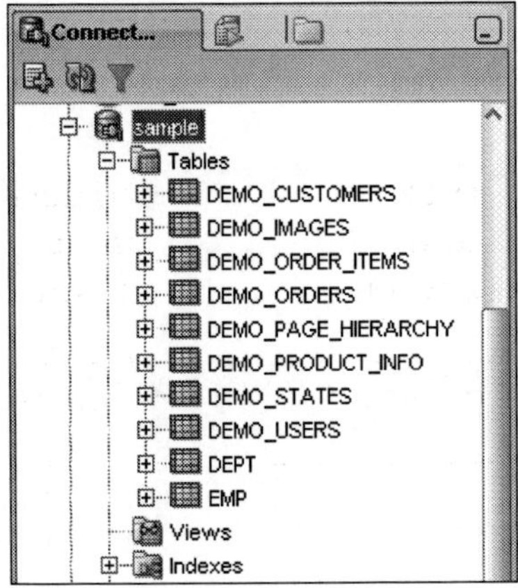

Browsing the applications

Expand the **Application Express** node in the **Connections** navigator and select the **Sample Application**. As you select the application, a selection of display editor tabs reveals the application details, including **Pages**, **LOVs**, and **Items**. This top-level set of display editors includes the scripts to install, deinstall, and upgrade your applications. The following screenshot shows an example of the **Deinstall** script for an application called **Timesheets**:

sample | Timesheets, 1.0 (114) | hr_apex

Application | Pages | LOVs | Lists | Templates | Breadcrumbs | Tabs | Nav Bar | Items | Comp. | Procs. | Auth | Install | Upgrade | Deinstall | SQL

Actions...

```
DROP TABLE "EBA_TIME_TIMECODES"
cascade constraints
/
DROP TABLE  "EBA_TIME_TIMESHEET"
  cascade constraints
/
DROP TABLE "EBA_TIME_ADMINISTRATORS"
  cascade constraints
/
DROP PACKAGE "EBA_TIME"
/
begin
    wwv_flow_api.create_or_remove_file(
        p_location => 'WORKSPACE',
        p_name     => 'eba_timesheets.png',
        p_mode     => 'REMOVE',
        p_type     => 'IMAGE');
end;
/
```

There is also an **SQL** display editor, just as there is for other objects in the **Connections** navigator. In this case, it contains the full SQL script of the application.

Using SQL Developer, not only can you review the details of your application quickly and easily by clicking through the display editor tabs, but you can also compare these details across applications as shown in the following screenshot. When comparing you can:

- Select the detail you want to focus on, such as the **Pages** or **Tabs** display editors, and then click down through the list of applications in the **Connections** navigator, seeing the details of each as you go.
- Use the **Freeze View** pin to freeze one application and then open the next. By tiling the applications, you can compare values across applications.

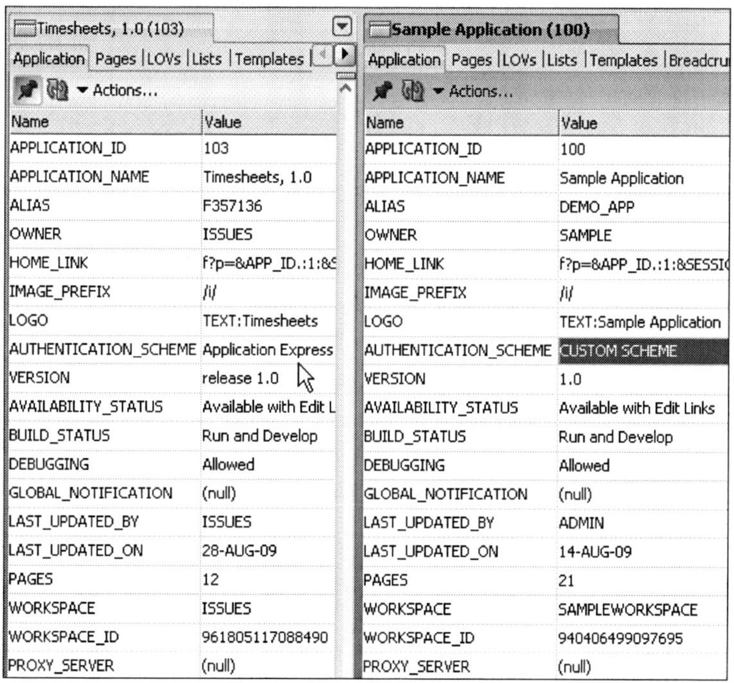

Drilling down into lists of values

Some of the display editor tabs have a set of detail records for each of the master records returned. The **List of Values** (**LOV**) display editor is one of these. You'll notice that each **LOV TYPE** is either **Static** or **Dynamic.** The detail records for these are displayed in either a **Query** or **Static Values** report. In the following example, the **CATEGORIES** list of values, in the sample application, is selected and the list of static values is displayed in the **Static Values** report:

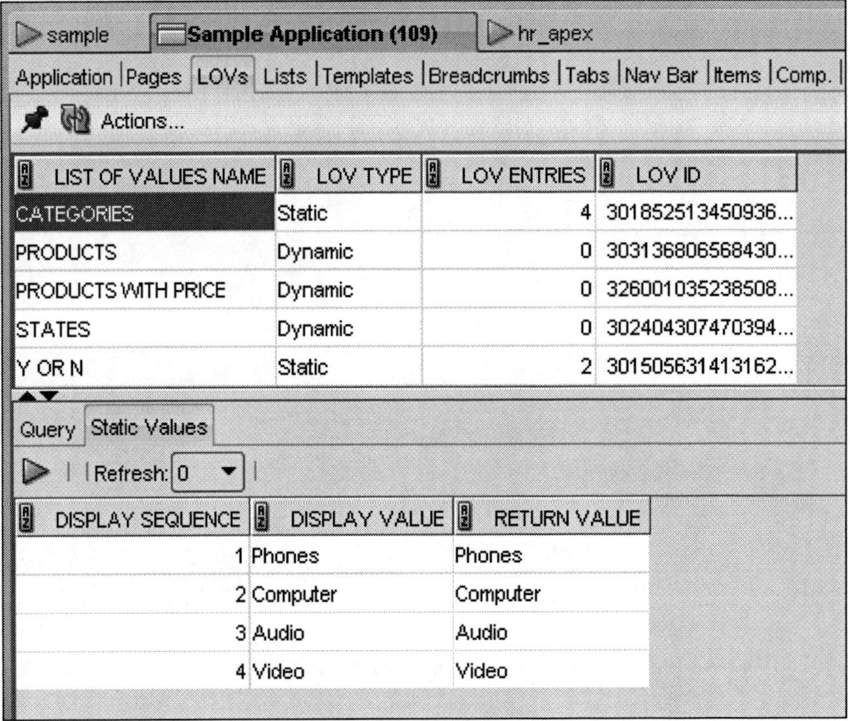

You can't use SQL Developer to update these values, but you can use it to quickly review and decide if there are incorrect or missing values, and then use Application Express to update the values.

Focusing on pages

Each of the pages displayed in the **Pages** display editor is also listed in the **Connections** navigator under the application node. Each page has its own set of display editors describing the page and providing detail on aspects of the page, including items, regions, and buttons.

If you select each page in the **Connections** navigator in turn, and review the resulting page detail, you'll see that the high-level page summary changes, detailing the number of buttons, items, and regions defined for each page. To get more details about each of these objects, select the appropriate display editor. In the following screenshot, the **Buttons** display editor shows the details for the buttons on the **Add/Modify Products** page:

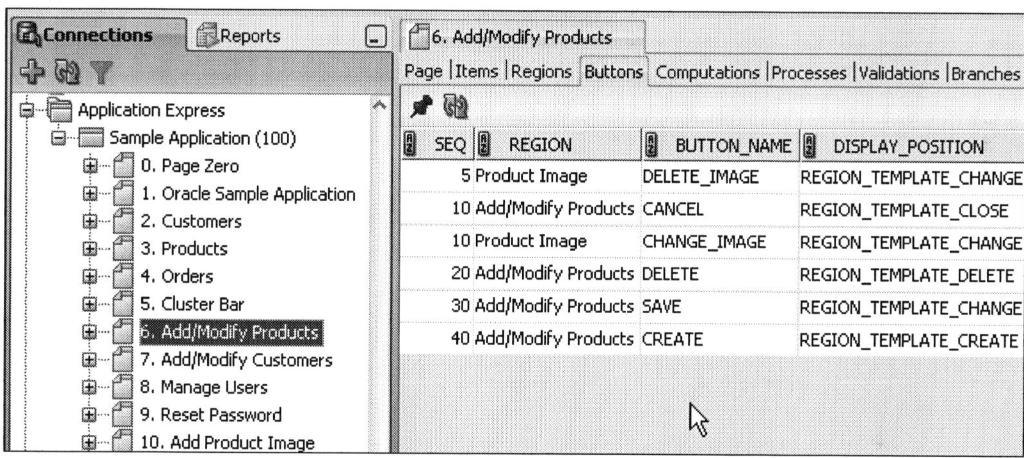

Mapping objects in SQL Developer to Application Express

While reviewing your application in SQL Developer, you may want to make modifications to some of the objects in Application Express. Consider again the example shown in the screenshot above, where a list of buttons is displayed. You can also look back at the previous example where a set of LOV static values was shown. Each of these is an object defined in Application Express and you need to know where to find each object in order to update it. Invoke your Application Express environment, and edit the **Add/Modify Products** page.

Notice that each grouping on the Application Express page has a matching area in SQL Developer:

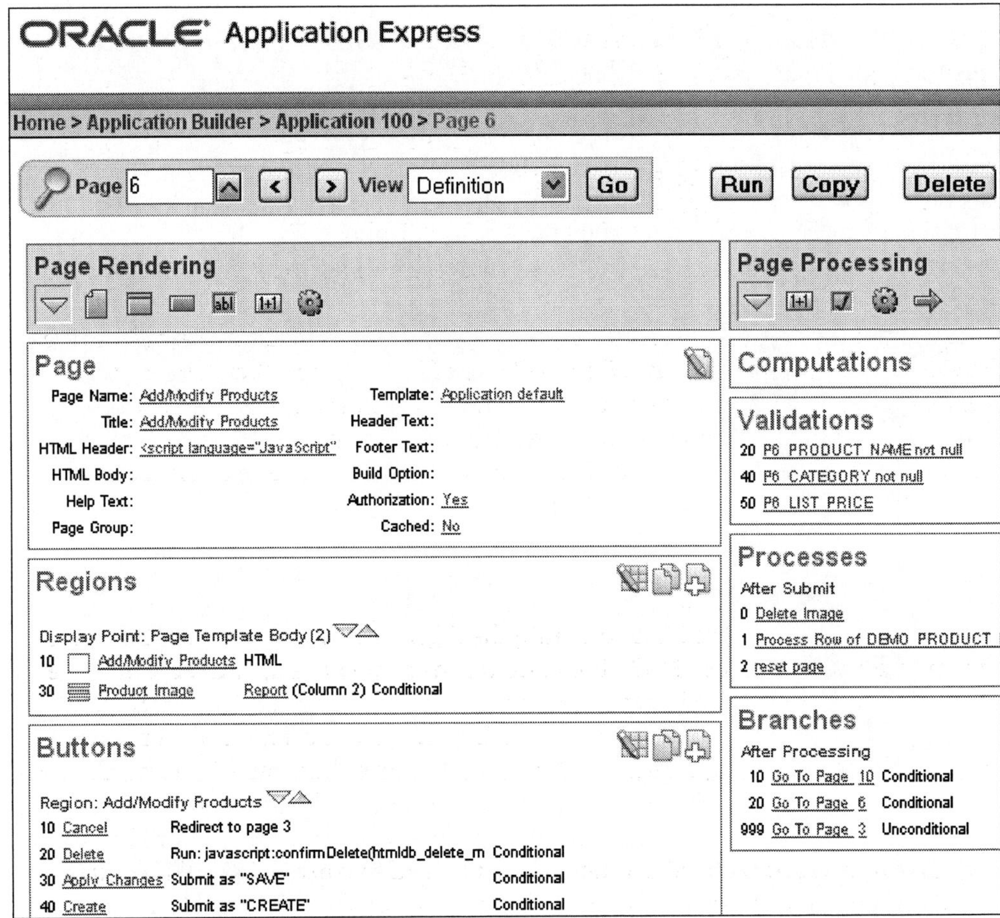

Use Application Express to update any objects in the application, and then refresh the view in SQL Developer.

Tuning SQL and PL/SQL code using SQL Developer

Not only can you use SQL Developer to review the details about the objects you create in Application Express, you can also use it to see the source code. Consider the **Regions** display editor for Page 1, **1. Oracle Sample Application**, as shown in the following screenshot:

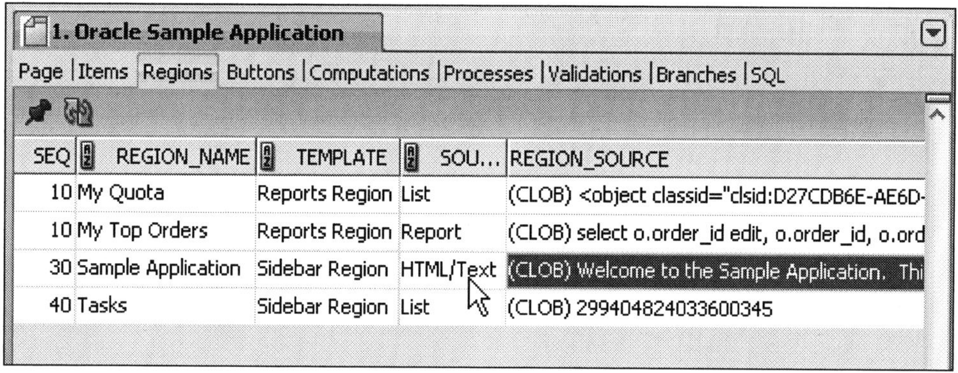

The regions on this page are derived from different source types. For example, the **Sample Application** region has a **Source Type** of **HTML/Text**. You can copy and paste this into a text editor, or even an HTML editor, and refine the text, before pasting it back into the application, using Application Express. It becomes more interesting when this region source is SQL or PL/SQL, because you can use SQL Developer to review, test, and even tune the code.

Working with Region Source SQL

You can select and copy the SQL code into the SQL Worksheet, and then tune it as you would any other piece of SQL code. Using the same Page 1, **1. Oracle Sample Application** in the example in the previous screenshot, select the **Region Source** for the region **My Top Orders.** This is an SQL query. To select the code, click to highlight the value. *Ctrl+C* copies the code, and you can then paste it, using *Ctrl+V*, into the SQL Worksheet. Alternatively, double-click in the field to expose the edit button, which, when clicked in turn, invokes a new window displaying the full text. Now you can use *Ctrl+A* to select the text and *Ctrl+C* to copy it. Cancel the window and the use *Ctrl+V* to paste the code into the SQL Worksheet. You need to remove the word **CLOB**, which precedes the text.

Once you have completed the copy and paste, you'll have the SQL in the SQL Worksheet, and you can run it just as you would any other SQL. Often, the Application Express SQL includes bind variables, as this example does. In this case, use the, **Run Statement** *(F9)*, to be prompted for the bind values.

Tuning with Explain Plan

Once you have the SQL code in the SQL Worksheet, you can execute the **Explain Plan** (*F6*) to review the code. The following screenshot displays the code and the plan details:

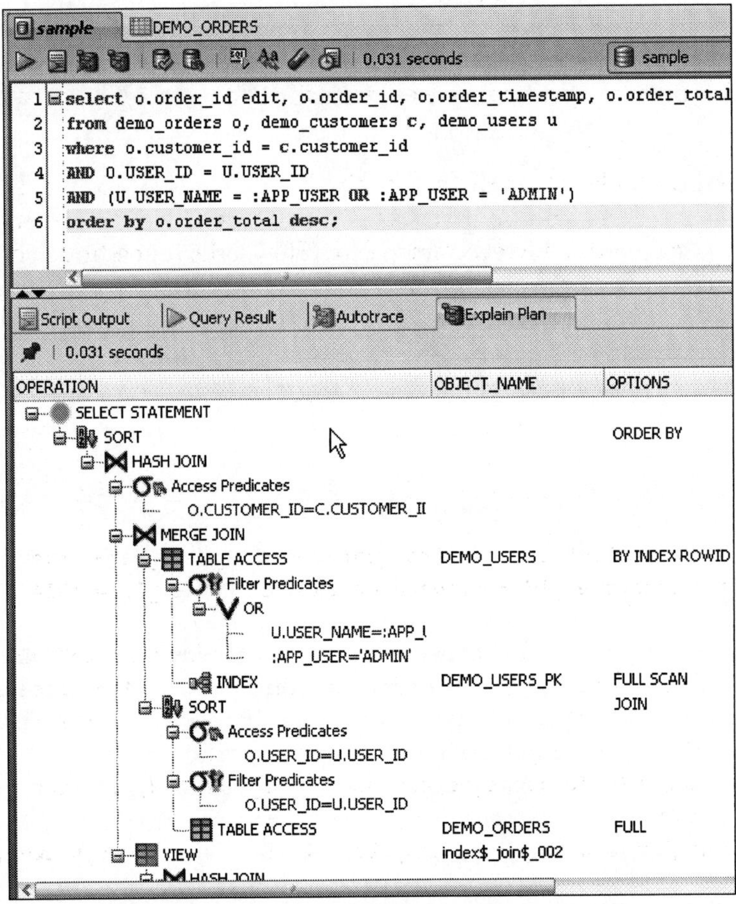

It is beyond the scope of this book to delve into tuning code using the results. However, SQL Developer does provide an extensive list of **Optimizer Hints** in the **Snippets** dialog, which you can drag into the query. Once you have added the **Optimizer Hints**, you can re-run the plan and compare the differences. Adding in **Optimizer Hints** is not a solution for tuning SQL, and it is recommended that you read some of the documentation on tuning and writing queries available online. If you have updated the SQL query, you need to return to Application Express and edit and replace the query.

Working with PL/SQL code

While the SQL queries in Application Express applications may be straightforward, developers sometimes create anonymous blocks when adding PL/SQL code. Certainly, tuning SQL is important to an application, but reducing the calls to anonymous blocks in any application is also very important. Anonymous blocks are compiled at run time, thus placing unnecessary overhead on the application. If you can identify and replace anonymous blocks with compiled procedures, you can significantly improve the performance of an application since the application calls compiled code.

Consider Page 14, **14. Place Order**. Once again there is a piece of SQL code, as can be determined by the `select` command. Notice too that there is PL/SQL code in the **Order Header** region. To work with the PL/SQL code, first edit, select, and then copy the PL/SQL block to the SQL Worksheet, as previously described for the SQL query. The PL/SQL code now pasted into the SQL Worksheet is shown in the following screenshot:

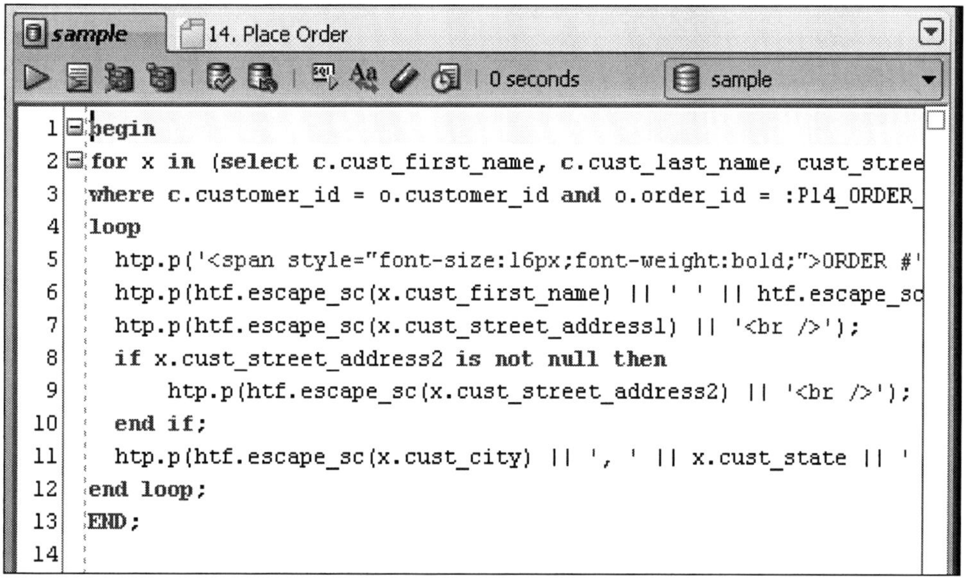

```
begin
for x in (select c.cust_first_name, c.cust_last_name, cust_stree
where c.customer_id = o.customer_id and o.order_id = :P14_ORDER_
loop
  htp.p('<span style="font-size:16px;font-weight:bold;">ORDER #'
  htp.p(htf.escape_sc(x.cust_first_name) || ' ' || htf.escape_sc
  htp.p(htf.escape_sc(x.cust_street_address1) || '<br />');
  if x.cust_street_address2 is not null then
      htp.p(htf.escape_sc(x.cust_street_address2) || '<br />');
  end if;
  htp.p(htf.escape_sc(x.cust_city) || ', ' || x.cust_state || '
end loop;
END;
```

This is an anonymous block. SQL Developer provides the facility to refactor to PL/SQL code and extract a procedure. To create a PL/SQL procedure from the anonymous block, select the full PL/SQL text, and use the context menu to invoke the **Refactoring** menu. Click on **Extract Procedure...** to invoke the **New Procedure** dialog. You need to provide a name and ensure that the procedure is stored as shown in the following example:

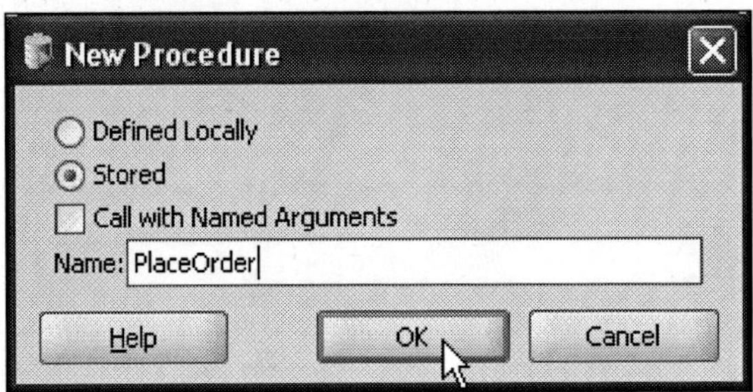

You can edit the code in the **Confirm Running SQL** dialog. Some anonymous blocks expect a bind variable, and so when you refactor the code and extract a procedure, you'll need to take this into account. We prefer to review the code in the PL/SQL Code Editor. To do this, accept the default code. This is now available for later review.

Once you have refactored the code, you can browse this code in the **Connections** navigator. To see the new procedures, expand the **Procedures** node and, using the previous example, reveal the new stored procedure, named `PlaceOrder`. Notice that the Application Express bind variable has been replaced by a declared variable, and that the refactored code includes the required input parameter, as shown in the following screenshot:

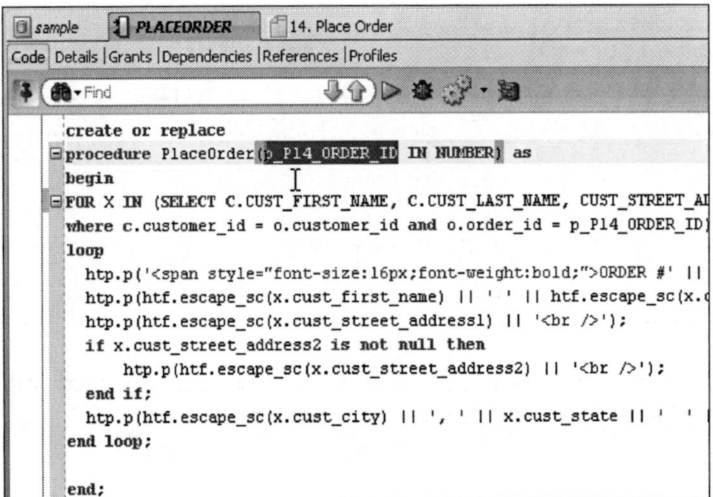

Replacing the anonymous block in Application Express

Once you have refactored the code in SQL Developer, you can replace the anonymous block in the Application Express environment. Return to Application Express, using the Application Express user created earlier, and edit **Page 14.** The following example shows the **Regions** area in Application Express, with the **Order Header PL/SQL** region selected:

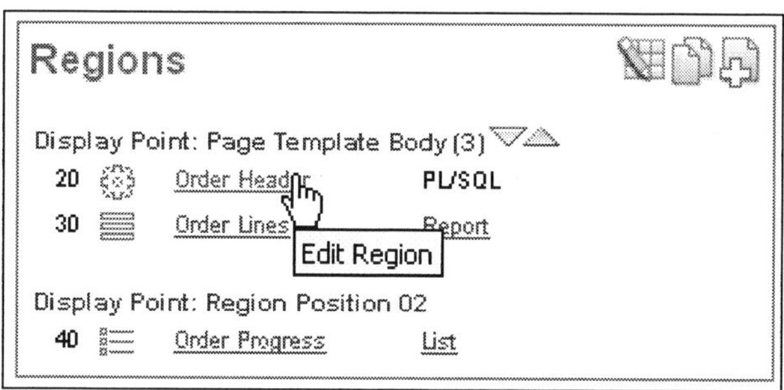

Replace the region source with **placeorder (:P14_ORDER_ID);** and select **Apply Changes.** To verify the code has been correctly handled, run the application, and place a new order for an existing customer. If you have replaced the code correctly, there are no errors when you add the order.

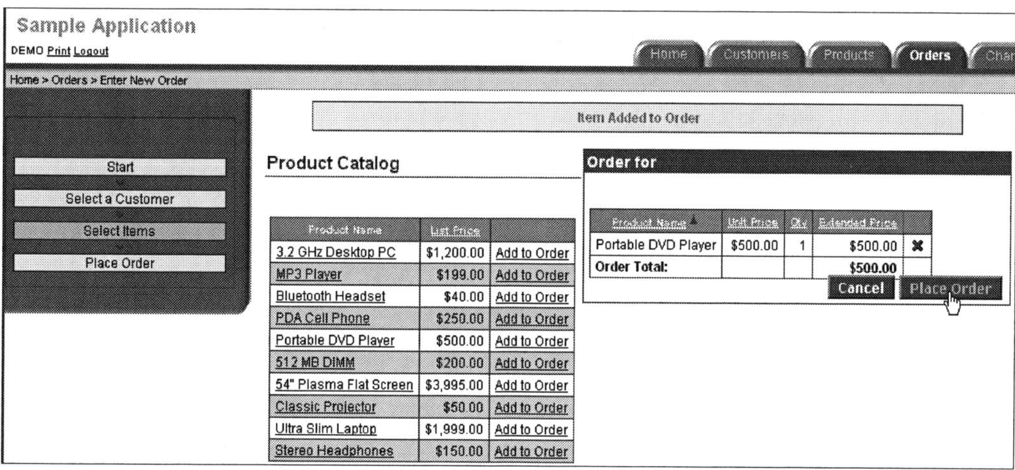

In SQL Developer, if you review the updates, you'll see that the anonymous PL/SQL block is now replaced with a call to a compiled procedure.

Improve performance of Application Express applications

Use SQL Developer to refactor any anonymous PL/SQL blocks and replace these with calls to compiled procedures.

To learn more about compiling and debugging PL/SQL, refer to *Working with PL/SQL*, the chapter focusing on those topics.

Managing applications in SQL Developer

SQL Developer also provides the capabilities for managing applications by offering a variety of administrative utilities. In this next section, we look at importing, modifying, and deploying applications.

Importing applications

The Application Express home page, `http://apex.oracle.com`, has a link to a long list of packaged applications. These are ready-built and functional applications that you can download, import, run, review, and also edit. They are useful as starter applications and provide examples of code and techniques.

To learn more about importing applications, download and unzip one of the packaged applications, or you can follow the steps by importing one of your own applications. To import a new application, select the **Application Express** node in the **Connections** navigator, and click on **Import Application** using the context menu. You need to select an SQL install script to import. Once you have the file, you can set the import options as shown in the following screenshot:

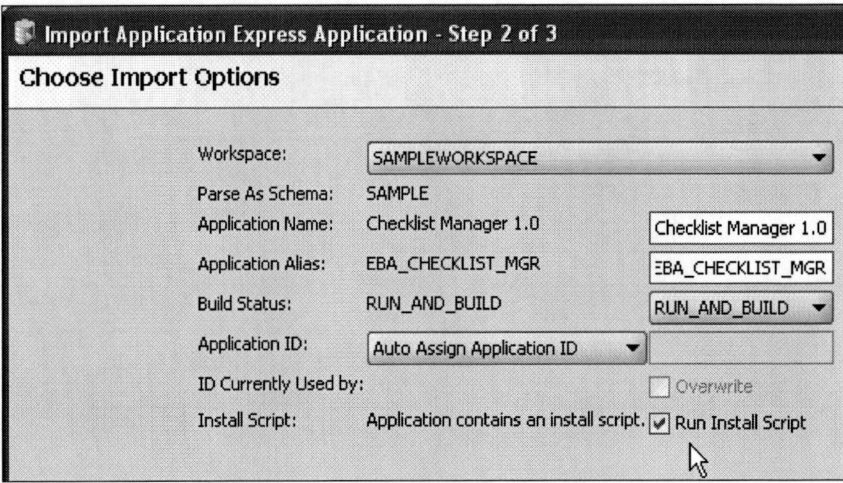

You can select the workspace this application is imported into. You can also change:

- The name and alias of the application.
- The application ID. Although this is automatically assigned by default, you can control this.

Be sure to select the **Run Install Script** checkbox, to install the application into your chosen workspace.

Download and install a packed application

You can download and install a selection of packaged applications from `http://www.oracle.com/technology/products/database/application_express/packaged_apps/packaged_apps.html`.

Modifying applications

You can change the name and alias of an application using the **Modify Application** context menu:

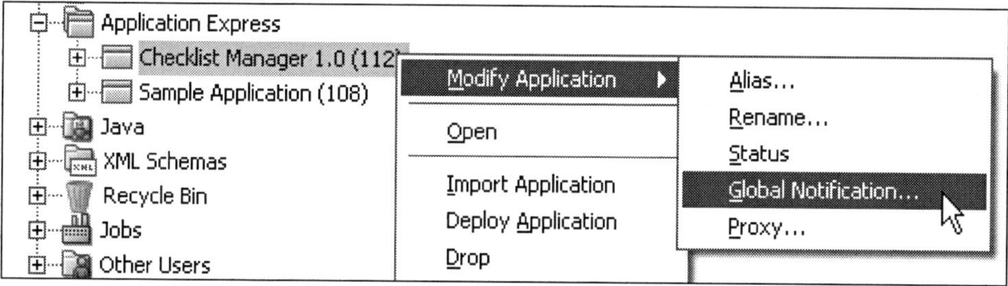

In addition, this menu offers additional options such as being able to send out a global notification. The **Modify Application** menu is displayed in the previous screenshot with the **Global Notification...** option selected. Once selected, you should supply the message you want to send to the users:

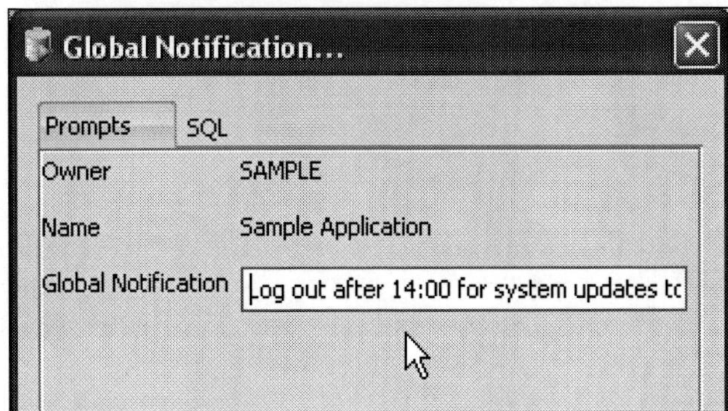

When created, a global notification appears on all pages of an application and is visible for all of the users who start up or are accessing the application, as is shown below for the sample application:

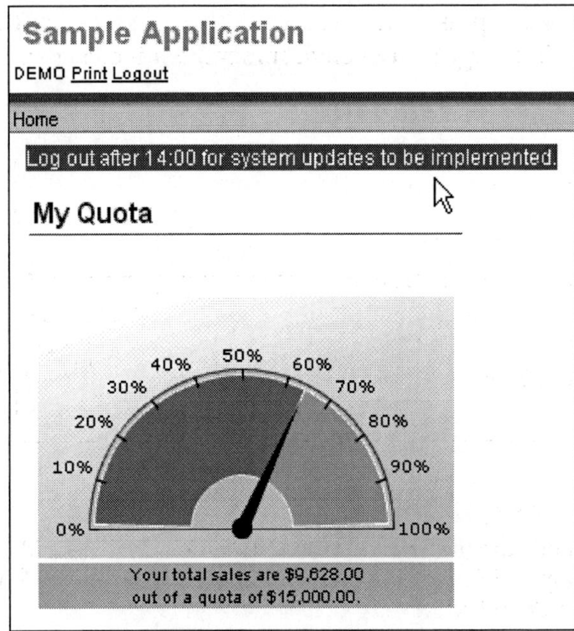

You can also set the status of the application, which is useful when you need to do maintenance on the application and have a few users accessing the application simultaneously. The choice of status options are:

- Available
- Available_w_edit_link
- Developers only
- Not available

Deploying applications

This facility allows you to deploy a completed application to another schema from outside of Application Express. This is useful when you are working on an application in a "sandbox" environment and you want to move it, say to test or production schemas. When deploying an application to another schema, this new schema must have access to a workspace in Application Express.

Controlling services

SQL Developer offers users the ability to start and stop the embedded PL/SQL gateway for Application Express (shown in the following screenshot). You may not have access to do this in a large shared environment, but it can be useful in a test setup.

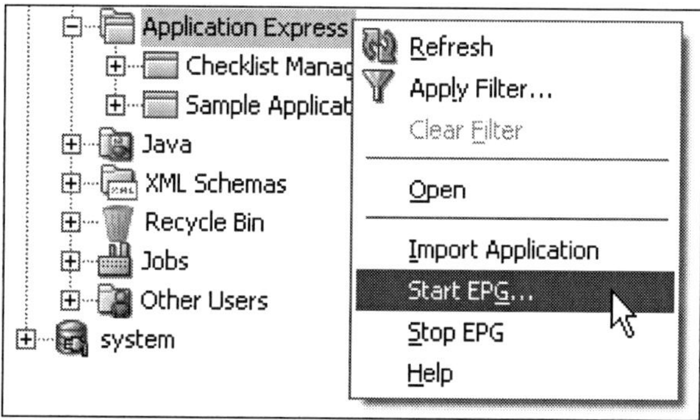

Start and stop the embedded PL/SQL gateway

Start and stop the embedded PL/SQL gateway from within SQL Developer. Select the **Application Express** node in the **Connections** navigator and select **Start EPG** or **Stop EPG**.

Reporting on applications using SQL Developer

SQL Developer includes a set of Application Express shipped reports. You can find these under the **Data Dictionary Reports**. Most of these reports, such as the **Applications** and **Pages** reports, provide the same detail as is available in the **Connections** navigator as described earlier, using a slightly different layout.

The reports also include a **Workspace** report, which is a Master/Detail report on the different aspects of a workspace. This report provides details on the different applications in the various workspaces a schema has access to, and the applications in each respective workspace. The details shown in the following screenshot reveals that this schema has access to a number of workspaces, and that the packaged application workspace includes a number of applications:

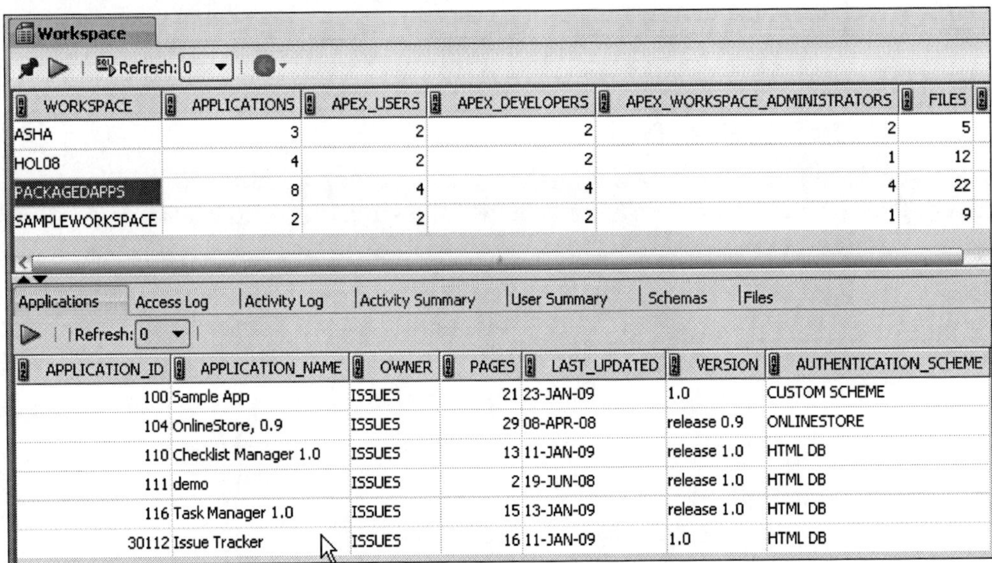

Summary

In this chapter, we reviewed the many aspects of using SQL Developer and Application Express together to provide a strengthened working environment. By supporting Oracle Application Express, SQL Developer offers additional support to an Application Express developer who is working with, and managing, a large number of applications, or who writes a lot of extra SQL and PL/SQL code to support the applications.

The next and final chapter is about working with non-Oracle databases, and migrating database objects and data to Oracle. We'll show the tight integration of SQL Developer and the migration features in working with, and browsing, non-Oracle databases, and then using the migration utilities.

13
Working with SQL Developer Migrations

Oracle SQL Developer Migrations is an integrated feature of Oracle SQL Developer, for migrating from some of the popular non-Oracle databases to Oracle. It provides users with a basic migration wizard (for small, less complex migrations) and an interactive migration alternative, where the stages of the migration are separated, allowing users to make changes to the objects and code at each stage. SQL Developer Migrations supports the migration of most database objects, depending on the database in question (including procedures, functions, and the data in the tables), to Oracle. In this chapter, we'll look at preparing the SQL Developer environment, preparing the required Oracle database repository, and the steps involved in the migration process.

Migrating a database requires careful planning and preparation. In this chapter, we'll review the tool support for a migration, while not discussing the additional work required when planning and preparing for a migration. We will not list the reasons for migrating from one database to another, or the advantages of one database over another. We'll make the assumption that these decisions have been made.

Introducing SQL Developer Migrations

Oracle SQL Developer's Migrations feature supports the conversion of tables, views, triggers, stored procedures, and other objects from non-Oracle (third-party) databases to the Oracle database equivalents. Once the objects are converted to Oracle, the data can be copied from the source to the target database. The extent of what is converted depends on the third-party database in question. For example, not all migrations support the migration of procedures and functions.

An overview of the migration process

SQL Developer offers users a choice when converting from a third-party database to Oracle, by offering a:

- Quick migration wizard
- Interactive migration

For both approaches, SQL Developer Migrations provides a phased approach to migrate from a third-party database to Oracle. Initially, the tool queries the source database, and the captured metadata is written to an Oracle repository. The next phase is a conversion of the objects to Oracle metadata. Once converted, the Oracle metadata is used to generate the DDL for execution in the target database. The final phase is to copy the data from the source database to the target database.

If you use the migration wizard, the entire process flows from start to completion with no chance to make adjustments before completion. This is typically used for smaller, less complex migrations. If you use the interactive approach, you can make adjustments (such as deleting or updating objects) after each phase has completed. We'll look at the details of these phases later in the chapter.

Offline or online migration choices

The quick migration wizard requires a direct connection to the database being migrated, while the interactive migration allows you to make a direct connection to the source database, or to migrate from files. There may be a multitude of reasons for not wanting to directly access the database, and so using files as the source can be very useful. Using files as a source means:

- You have a point in time when the files are created. If the source database is still actively in use, you know the point in time when the objects are migrated.
- You don't need to grant additional database access to the source database to users working on the migration.

The interactive migration follows the same approach for a direct or offline migration, with the exception of how you start off the migration and load the data at the end.

Supported third-party databases

SQL Developer Migrations supports browsing and migrating from the following databases:

- IBM DB2 LUW—7, 8, and 9
- Microsoft Access—97, 2000, 2002, 2003 and 2007
- Microsoft SQL Server—7, 2000, and 2005
- MySQL—3, 4 and 5
- Sybase Adaptive Server—12 and 15
- Teradata 12

Setting up your environment

There are a few one-off setup steps that you need to complete before you can use Oracle SQL Developer to browse or migrate from other databases. Before you can create a connection to a database like MySQL, you need to set up the required database driver for the database. Once you have the drivers installed, you can create the database connections, as you do for an Oracle connection. If you plan to migrate to Oracle, you'll also need to set up a migrations repository. In this section, we'll review the options available for setting up the additional database drivers, creating the database connections, and managing the migrations repository.

Setting up the JDBC drivers

Due to additional licensing requirements, Oracle SQL Developer does not ship the JDBC drivers needed to connect to IBM DB2, Microsoft SQL Server, MySQL, Sybase, and Teradata. To connect to any of these databases, whether for browsing or migration purposes, you need to download additional drivers and set up SQL Developer to access the drivers. This setup is not required for Microsoft Access, as it uses the JDBC/ODBC bridge. For a detailed explanation on downloading and setting up the required third-party drivers, please refer to the earlier chapter on *Database Connections and JDBC Drivers.*

Once you have set up the drivers, the connection dialog changes to include the additional tabs for those database drivers you have added, as shown in the following screenshot:

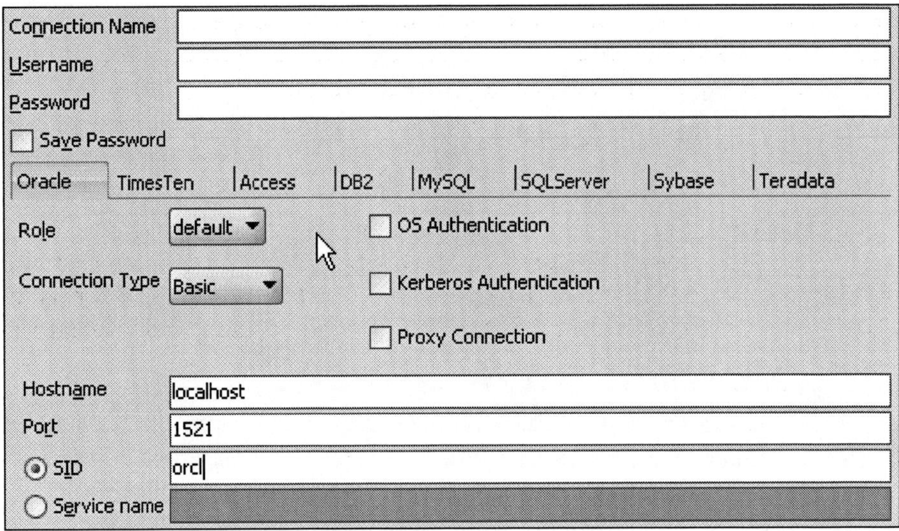

Creating third-party connections

You are ready to create the connections. Each of the connection tabs requires slightly different details. In the following example, shown for SQL Server, once you have entered the **Hostname** and **Port**, click on **Retrieve database** to connect to and access the list of available databases:

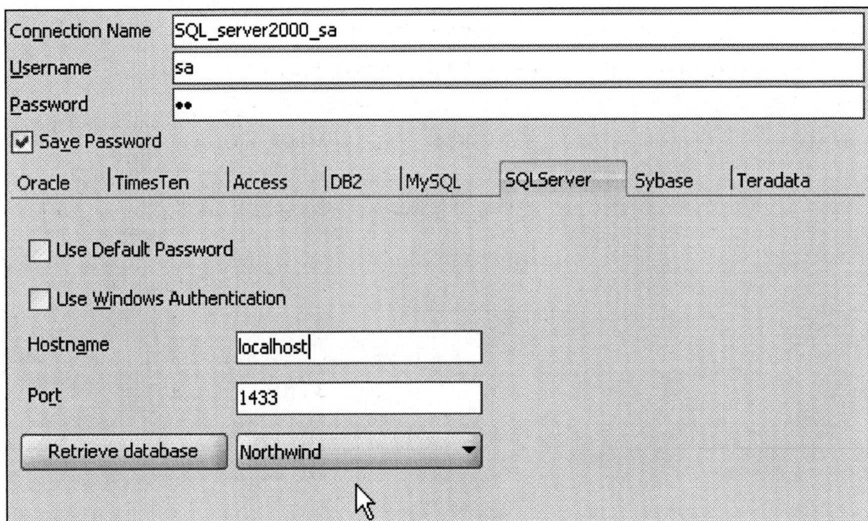

By contrast, the Microsoft Access connection only requires the MDB file access. Setting up connections for the supported third-party databases is discussed in the chapter on *Database Connections and JDBC Drivers*.

For each database, create the connection, optionally save the password, and test the connection. The **Save** and **Connect** buttons both save the created connection, while **Connect** also closes the dialog and makes the connection.

Accessing non-Oracle databases

You can browse any of the non-Oracle databases in the same way you can browse any Oracle database connection. The features available differ, depending on the database you connect to. You can browse the objects and their details, and review data. The context menus for these objects are migration-specific and do not support any DDL.

Browsing database objects

In the example that follows, we created a database connection to Microsoft SQL Server, as shown in the previous screenshot, using the Microsoft SQL Server Northwind sample database.

Select and expand the database connection. Expand the **Tables** node and select a table in the list. Details for **Columns**, **Keys** (for Primary and Foreign Keys), **Indexes**, **Constraints**, and **Triggers** are all displayed. There is also a **Data** display editor for browsing the instance data:

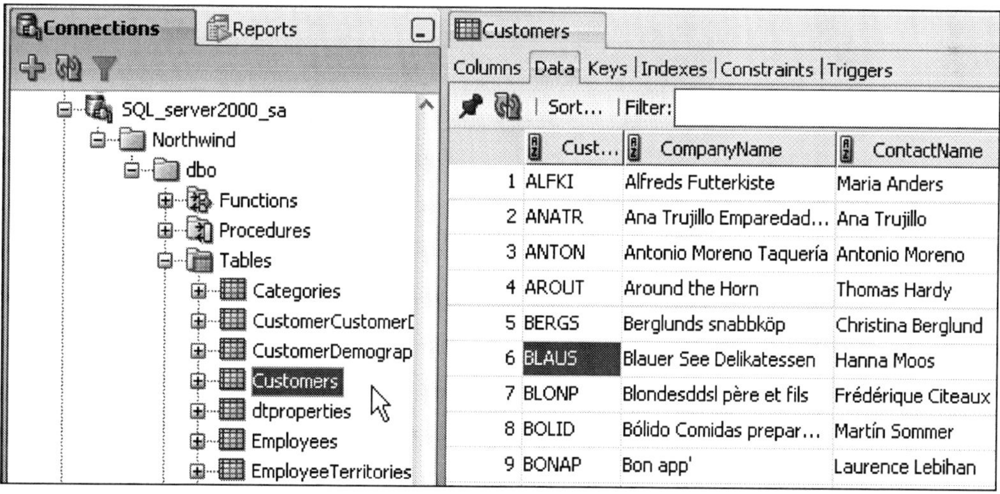

This level of detail differs for each database type. For example, when connecting to MySQL, the set of display editors is column, index information, and constraints. All third-party connections display the data in the tables, and some support the ability to export the data to various formats. The main difference between the non-Oracle database connections and the Oracle connections is that these are read-only views of the database objects *and* data, while the Oracle connections provide context menus for executing DDL and DML.

Using the SQL Worksheet

The primary focus for supporting non-Oracle databases is for migrating the database objects and data to Oracle. If you want to update data, or create and update database objects in other databases, you'll need to use ANSI standard SQL in the SQL Worksheet. For example, the following Transact-SQL (T-SQL) example to create a table for Microsoft SQL Server is valid:

```
CREATE TABLE JOBS
  (
    JOB_ID    SMALLINT IDENTITY(1,1) PRIMARY KEY CLUSTERED,
    JOB_DESC  VARCHAR(50) NOT NULL DEFAULT 'NEW POSITION',
    MIN_LVL   TINYINT NOT NULL CHECK (MIN_LVL >= 10),
    MAX_LVL   TINYINT NOT NULL CHECK (MAX_LVL <= 250)
  )
```

You can also write and execute ad hoc queries. In the next example, we have written a basic query and executed it, both as a script and a statement. The latter sends the query result to a data grid:

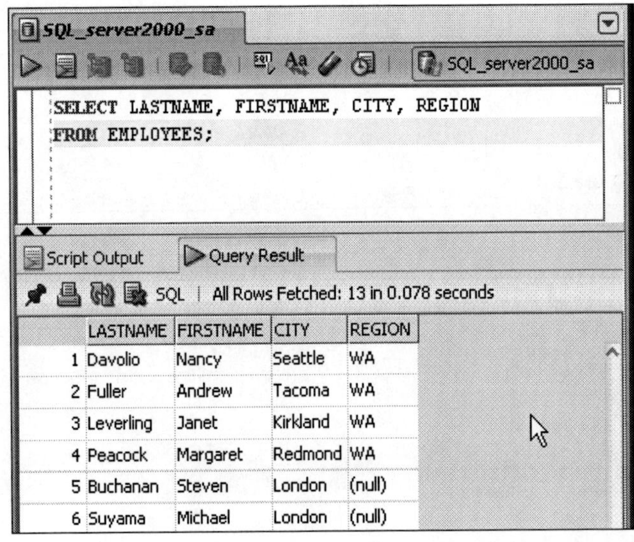

Formatting options are also available for SQL Worksheet users, while Oracle-specific functionality, such as Explain Plan and Autotrace, are not. The **Rollback** and **Commit** buttons are also not available. Therefore, you need to explicitly commit any transactions you execute. It's important to note that SQL Server is always in autocommit mode.

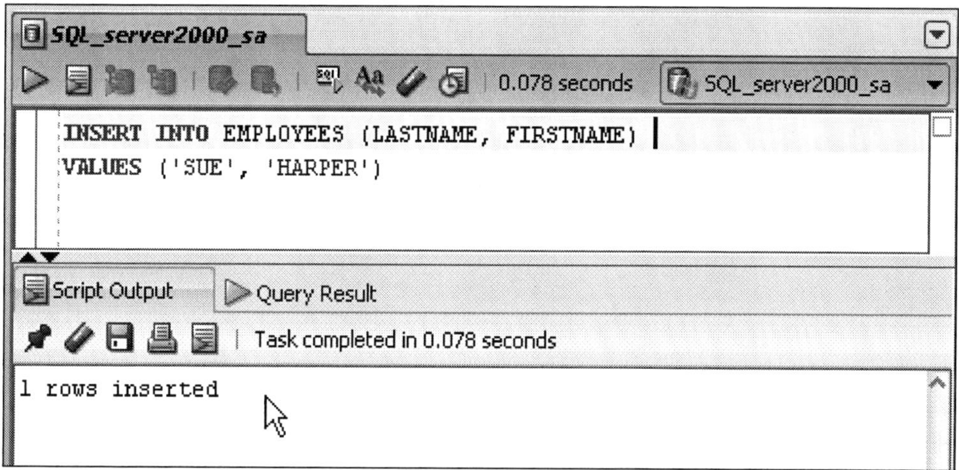

Managing the repository

SQL Developer Migrations uses a database repository to collect, store, and transform the metadata during the migration process. The repository is only used during the migration process, which once complete can be discarded.

Setting up the repository owner:

Using either the SQL Worksheet or the **Create User...** context menu for **Other Users**, create a new Oracle database user with the role and system privileges:

- Resource
- Create Session
- Create View

Once you have the new user set up, create a new database connection for that user.

Creating the repository

Using the main **Tools | Migration** menu, you can manage all aspects of your repository, including creating, truncating, and deleting. Initially select **Create Repository...**:

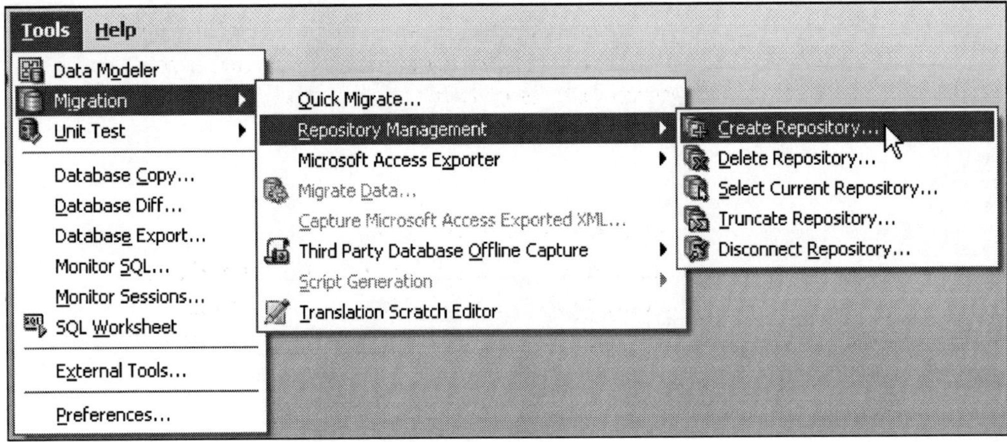

This builds an Oracle database repository with:

- 37 tables, with required Primary Keys, indexes, and triggers
- 9 views
- 4 packages

Creating the repository is not a long process, with the progress tracked in a pop-up dialog that displays the current activity.

Associating a repository with a user

At any stage, to connect to a previously created repository, select **Associate Migration Repository** from the context menu for the connection to the repository owner. This **Associate Migration Repository** menu option performs a number of activities, such as:

- Associating the user to an existing repository set up for that user
- Updating a repository created in an earlier release of SQL Developer
- Creating a new repository for the user if one does not yet exist

If you have a number of migration repositories, you can also select and set the current repository, by using **Select Current Repository...**.

As soon as you have a user connected or associated with the repository, then two new windows open. These windows are:

- Captured Models
- Converted Models

If the windows do not open, you can open them manually from the **View** menu. These windows will display a list of the captured or converted models you have previously worked with, unless you delete or truncate the repository between migrations.

Planning database connections

Before you can start the migration, you should set up two additional database connections, one for the source database and one for the target database. The connections are no different from connections you have created previously, but you should give some thought to the database schemas you are going to use.

Setting up the source database connection

The database you are migrating from is known as the source database. You need to create a connection to that database. SQL Developer Migrations uses "Least Privilege Migration". This means any user can migrate database objects and data to an Oracle database. However, the migration only reads and migrates those objects you have access to, depending on your privilege level.

Create a database connection as described in the chapter on *Database Connections and JDBC Drivers*, using a schema that owns the objects you want to migrate.

Setting up the target database connection

When migrating to Oracle, you need to create a database connection to a schema that will hold the new database objects. This can be an existing or a new schema. If you use an existing schema, you should be sure that no conflicts would arise due to the objects already in the schema. If you create a new schema, you need to ensure the schema has the following privileges:

- Resource
- Create session
- Create view

Moreover, if you're doing a multi-schema migration, this is the main Oracle schema that is used to create the additional target schemas, and so it needs the following additional privileges:

- Create user
- Alter any trigger

We recommend setting up source and target database connections before you start the migration.

Migrating

You are now almost ready to start the migration. The last step is to decide on the approach you'll use for the migration. For a quick review, prototype, or when migrating a small, straightforward database, the **Quick Migrate** option is ideal. Alternatively, you can use a more interactive approach and step through each phase of the migration. We'll review both approaches in the next section.

Using Quick Migrate

Quick Migrate is a wizard-driven dialog that follows 6 steps:

1. You can start the **Quick Migrate** from two areas, either from the main **Tools | Migration** menu, or from the context menu of the source database connection you are planning to migrate (seen in the following screenshot). Either action invokes the same **Quick Migrate** dialog. If you start the wizard from the context menu of the source database connection, the first page of the wizard will be already populated with the source database connection.

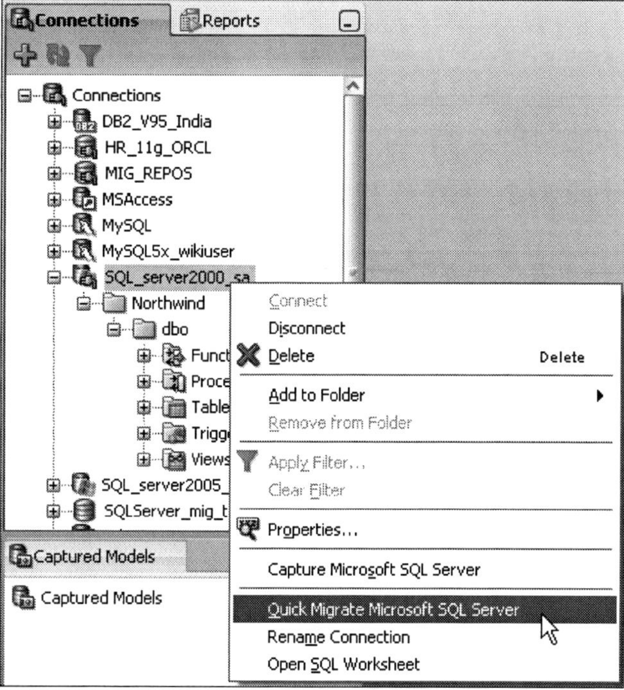

2. The next step is to select the **Target Connection**. As you can see in the following screenshot, this step reminds you of the required privileges and offers the opportunity of setting up a new target Oracle database connection, if you do not already have one created:

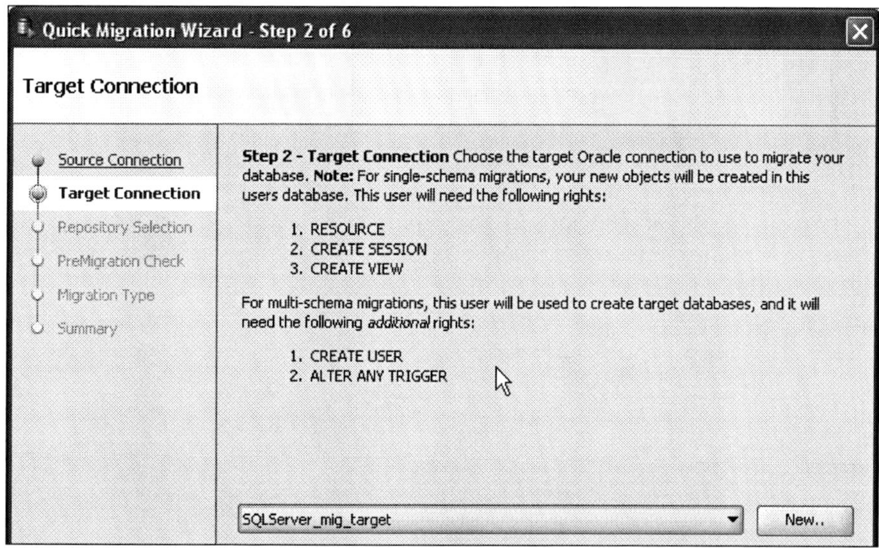

Create Source and Target Connections before starting

If you start the **Quick Migrate** without having connections to the source database or to the schema in the target database, you can create these new connections from within the dialog. We recommend setting up all of the connections you'll need before starting the process.

3. Select the repository you plan to use during the migration. If you only have one repository, this will be in the drop-down list. If you have more than one repository, then the repository that you last associated with your repository user will appear first here. At this stage, if you have no repository, the dialog is a little different, looking more like the screenshot shown for Step 2. You have the option of creating a repository here. This repository is created at the start of the migration and you can have it removed on completion.
4. This is the pre-migration step and gives you the opportunity to check that all of the required privileges and connections are valid. If you are not working on a multi-schema migration, and have not assigned the additional privileges, you get a privilege warning as shown below. This does not affect a single user migration.

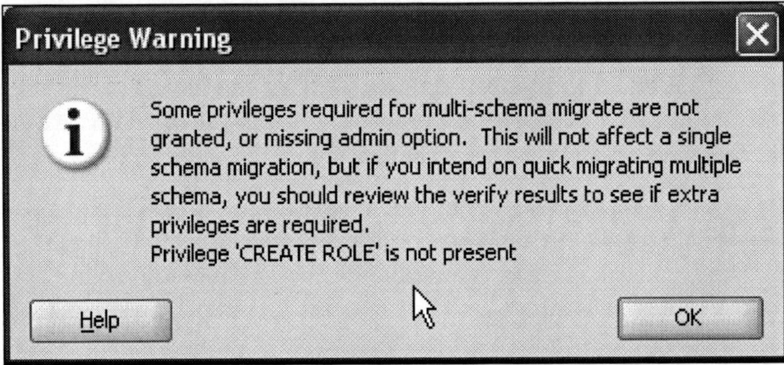

The result of the checks should be a success status for all but the multi-schema privilege test, which fails for single schema settings, which is OK:

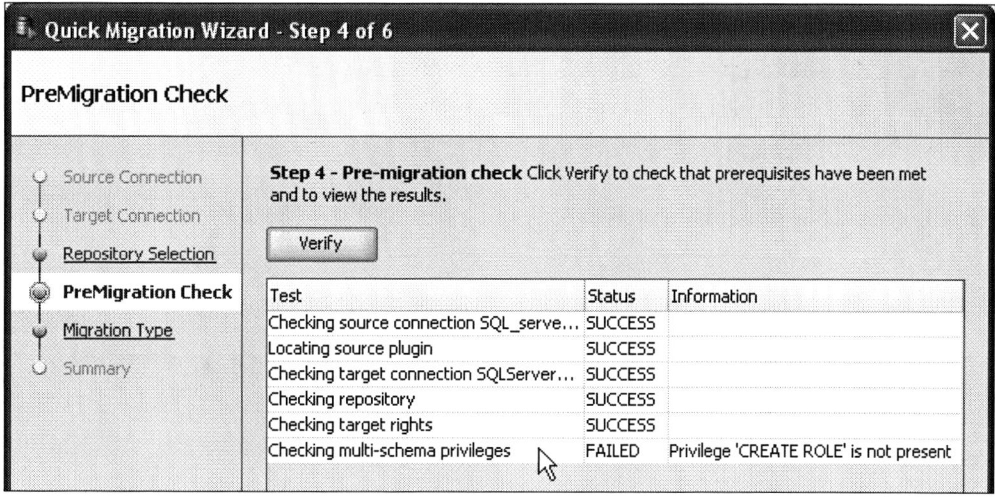

5. In Step 5, you can select the type of migration as follows:
    - Migrate tables only
    - Migrate tables and data
    - Migrate everything

   These are self-explanatory, except possibly for the last option where "everything" includes the additional structures in the schema including the procedural code, which is translated to PL/SQL in Oracle.

6. This is a summary of the source and target connections, the repository you are using, and the type of migration you're about to use:

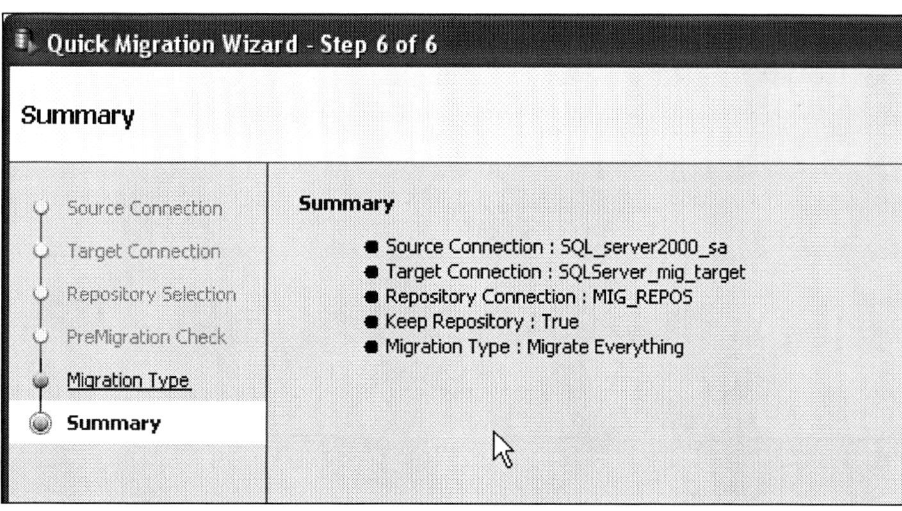

The migration

This follows the five phases mentioned earlier in the chapter:

1. **Capture**—write the metadata to the repository
2. **Convert**—convert the metadata to Oracle metadata
3. **Generate**—generate the DDL scripts based on the metadata
4. **Build**—execute the scripts to create the new objects in the target schema
5. **Data Move**—copy the data from the source to the target database

Once the process is complete, you can review the steps in a tabbed window. The following images show three points of the migration.

The first screenshot of the migration is towards the end of the first phase. You can see the types and tallies of the objects being migrated. Notice that you can elect to automatically close the dialog on completion. This is true for many of the migration dialogs. For the **Quick Migrate** wizard, we recommend leaving this deselected. That way you can review all of the phases of the migration when the wizard completes them before the dialog closes.

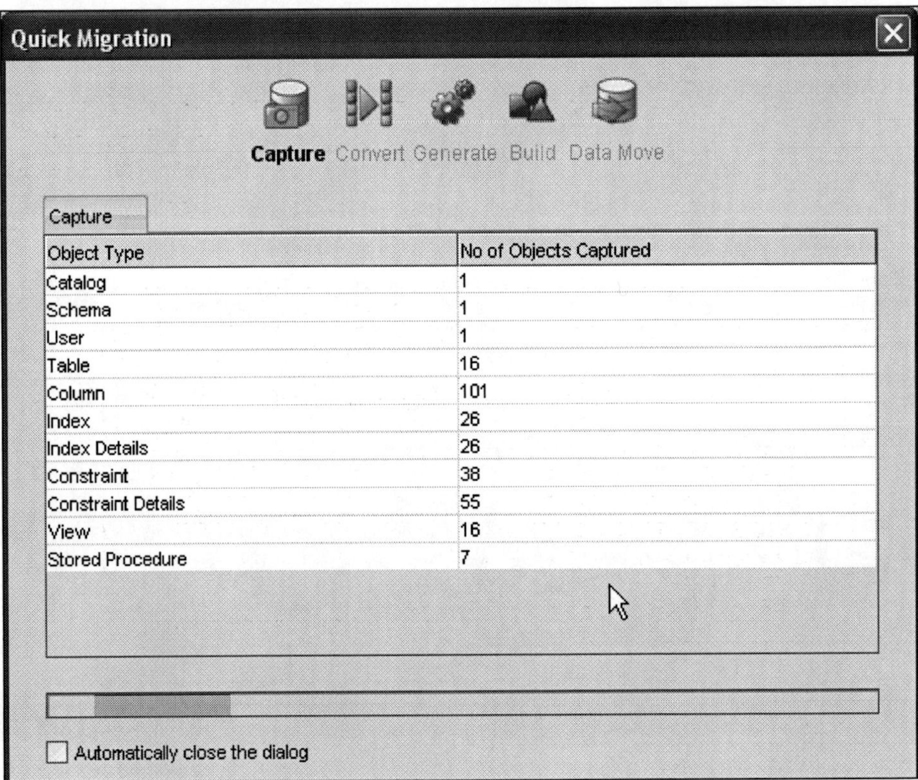

Object Type	No of Objects Captured
Catalog	1
Schema	1
User	1
Table	16
Column	101
Index	26
Index Details	26
Constraint	38
Constraint Details	55
View	16
Stored Procedure	7

> If at any point the migration appears to have completed, check the icons at the top of the window. These icons indicate the progress of the migration and should all be highlighted if the migration has finished successfully.

The tail end of the **Convert** phase is shown in the following screenshot. Here you see that the **Capture** icon now has color and there is also a **Capture** tab, indicating that phase is now complete.

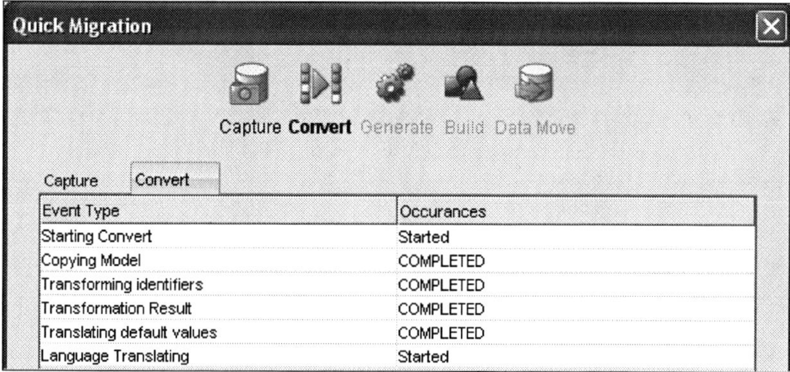

The next screenshot shows the final stage of the migration where the data is being moved to the target database. You can see that the other phases are all complete, and their tabs are now ready for review. Significant too is that the data is not moved to the tables sequentially, but instead by using threads, so that much of the data is moved at the same time.

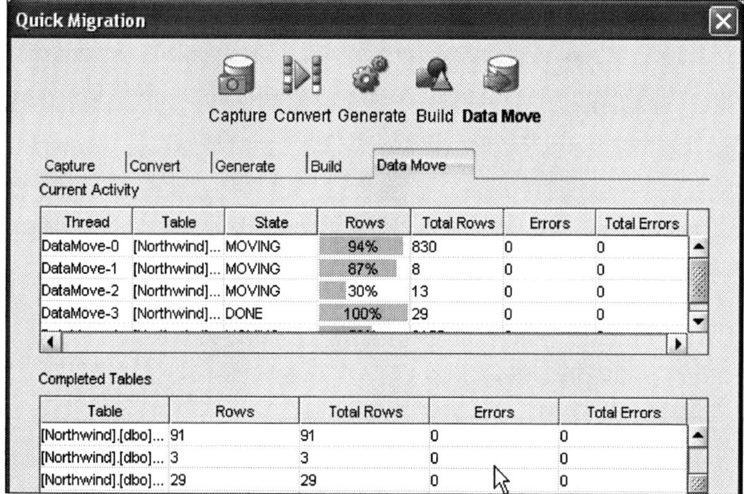

Data Move is a misnomer. The data is copied from the source to the target database. None of the artifacts or data in the source database are affected in any way by the migration.

Verifying the results

Once the migration is complete, all that remains for you to do is to verify the data. You can expand your connection and review the objects and data created by browsing these as you would in any other Oracle connection that you have made.

The **Captured** and **Converted** metadata is still in your repository and so you can return to metadata that resulted from the Quick Migrate and make some fine-grained adjustments. In the next section, we'll review the individual steps of the migration. Therefore, you can return to metadata that resulted from the Quick Migrate and make some fine-grained adjustments.

Delving into a complex migration

The **Quick Migrate** option is very useful if you are migrating a small database with little or no complex procedural code. It is acceptable to take the migrated results as they are presented, or make any modifications once the migration has completed. However, in general, the chances of this are rare, and the Quick Migrate is used to get an idea of the outcome of the complete migration. Instead of performing the Quick Migrate, you can perform an interactive migration, wherein you can initiate each step in the phases described in the Quick Migrate. You can delete, update, and modify the objects before moving on to the next phase. You can also migrate individual or selections of objects. In this section, we'll describe the process.

Preparing for the migration

There is no difference when preparing for an interactive migration to the preparation work for a Quick Migrate. As before, you need a:

- Connection to the source database
- Schema with the appropriate privileges in the target database
- Connection to the schema in the target database
- Repository owner in the target database
- Migration repository associated with the repository owner

Offline versus online migration

Earlier, we mentioned that the interactive migration could connect directly to the target database for an online migration, or read files for an offline migration. The interactive migration follows the same approach for a direct or offline migration, with the exception of how you begin the migration and load the data at the end.

In the examples that follow, we will use a combination of Microsoft SQL Server and Sybase to illustrate the points of each of the five phases of the migration.

Capturing the model

Select the connection to the source database, invoke the context menu, and select the capture option. This is dependent on the database type in the connection. For example, the context menu option is **Capture Sybase** or **Capture Microsoft SQL Server**. If you do not have a migration repository set up, or no user associated with a migration repository, then you'll get a warning telling you to connect to the migration repository before you can start.

The dialog for capturing the metadata from the source database is the same for both an online and offline capture. It runs through and captures the details for all of the object types. Notice in the dialog displayed in the following screenshot, that you can:

- Elect to run the capture in the background
- Have the dialog close automatically when the migration has completed

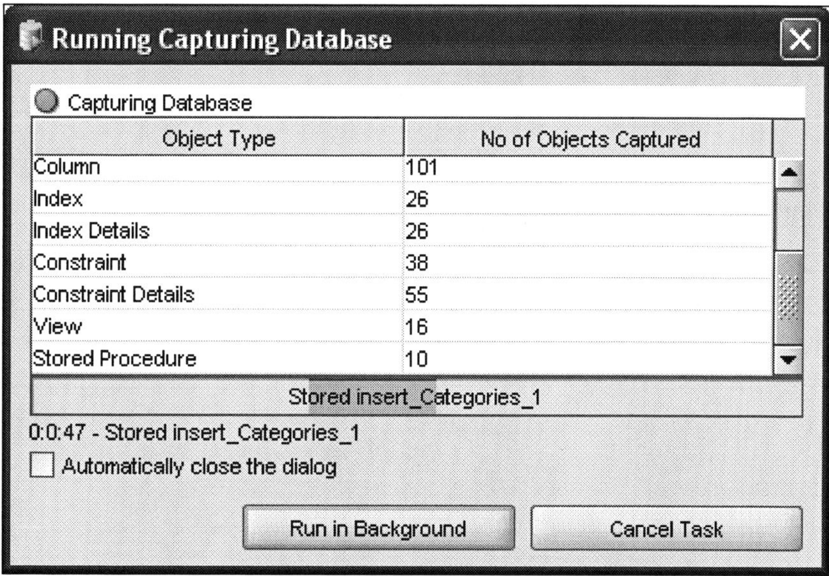

Using background tasks

Run the capture and convert tasks in the background to free you to continue with other tasks using SQL Developer during the migration process.

Reviewing the captured model

Once you have completed the capture, select the model in the **Captured Models** window. If you have previously run the capture and are using the same repository, this window may have a list of captured models. You can identify the migration you have just completed, using the name of the connection and the date. A summary report is displayed when you select the captured model.

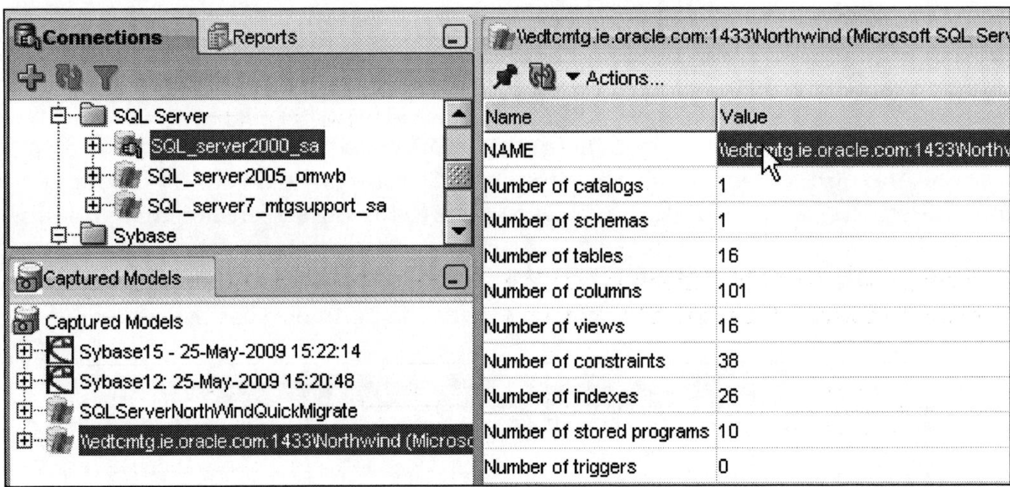

You can browse the metadata at this point, expand the nodes, and review the objects that have been migrated. You will observe that:

- There is no data tab for table, as we're only migrating the definitions of the objects at this point
- The data types will match the source database, as they are not yet in the Oracle format you might be familiar with
- The procedural code is still in line with the code of the source database and is not yet converted to the Oracle PL/SQL code

Updating the model

There are context menus at all levels in the **Captured Models** window, which allow you to rename elements, update, or delete them. We prefer to rename the captured model at this point, to make the name more manageable to work with, and also more easily recognizable.

Converting objects at a more granular level

Instead of selecting the connection for the migration, expand the source database connection, select a node, and invoke the context menu. For example, if you select the **Tables** node and open the context menu, you have the choice of:

- Capturing the tables
- Capturing the tables into an existing model
- Quick migrate

On expanding the **Tables** node, you'll see that you can do the same. This level of granularity allows you to capture individual tables into models, offering a much finer level of control during the migration.

Converting the model

Once you have made all of the modifications to the captured model metadata, you are ready to convert these to an Oracle model.

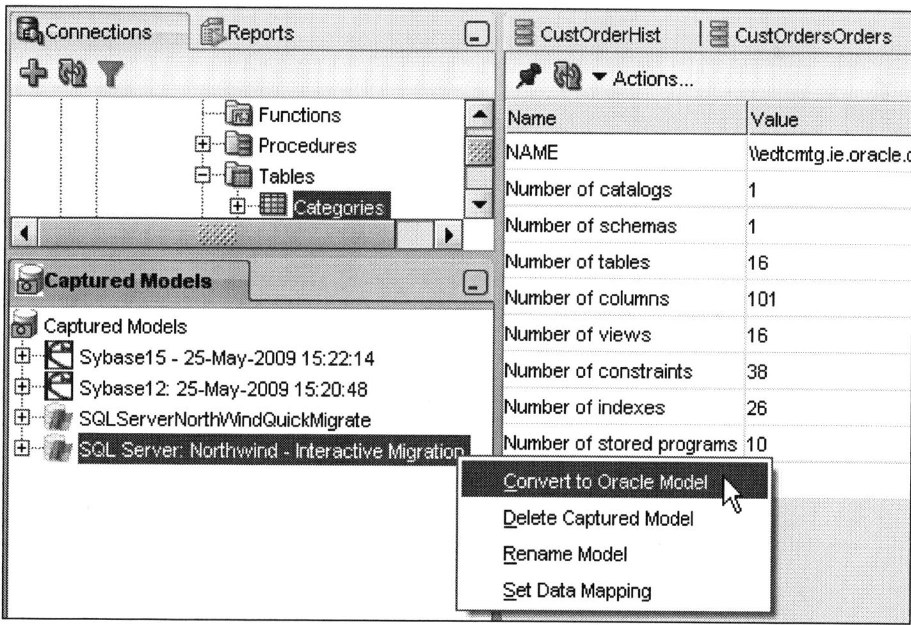

In the same way as there are different levels of granularity when capturing the details, you can also convert to Oracle at different levels. In the previous screenshot, we have selected the top level for the conversion.

Setting the conversion data mapping

Before the conversion starts, you are presented with a dialog where you can set the data mapping for the source and target data types. For example, the default mapping for a SQL Server **TINYINT** is **NUMBER (3, 0)** in Oracle. You can modify these mappings, or add new mappings, if the data types you are converting do not yet exist in the list:

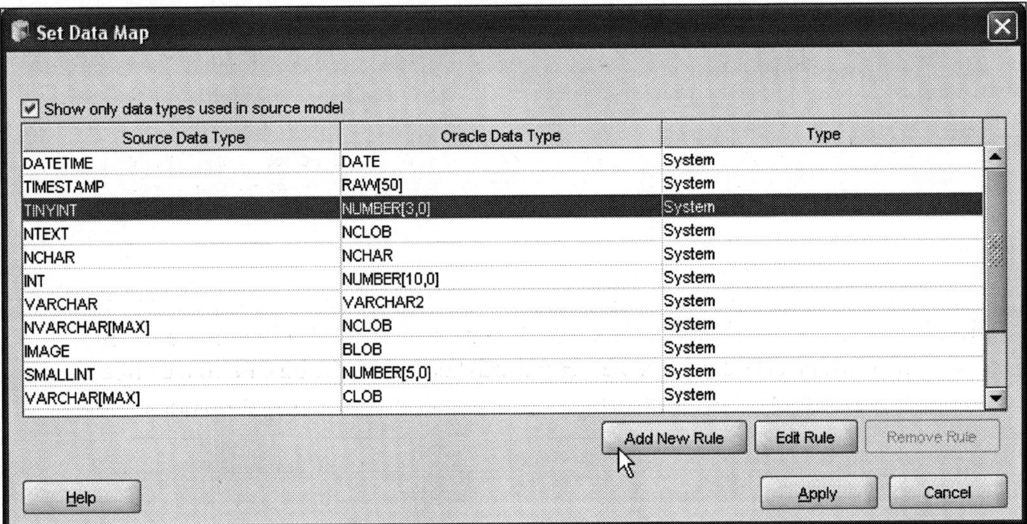

You can elect to run the conversion activity in the background and have the dialog closed on completion. Once the conversion is complete, you can review the captured model in **Captured Models** window.

Select the converted model to display the summary details of the migration. At this stage, you can delete, rename, and generally update the model before progressing.

Reviewing the logs

When running a migration, the details of any issues or information are tracked in the **Migration Log** window. If you don't see a log window, select **View | Log** to display it. Many entries are informative, while others show errors. The images that follow show the Microsoft SQL Server log and the Sybase migration log.

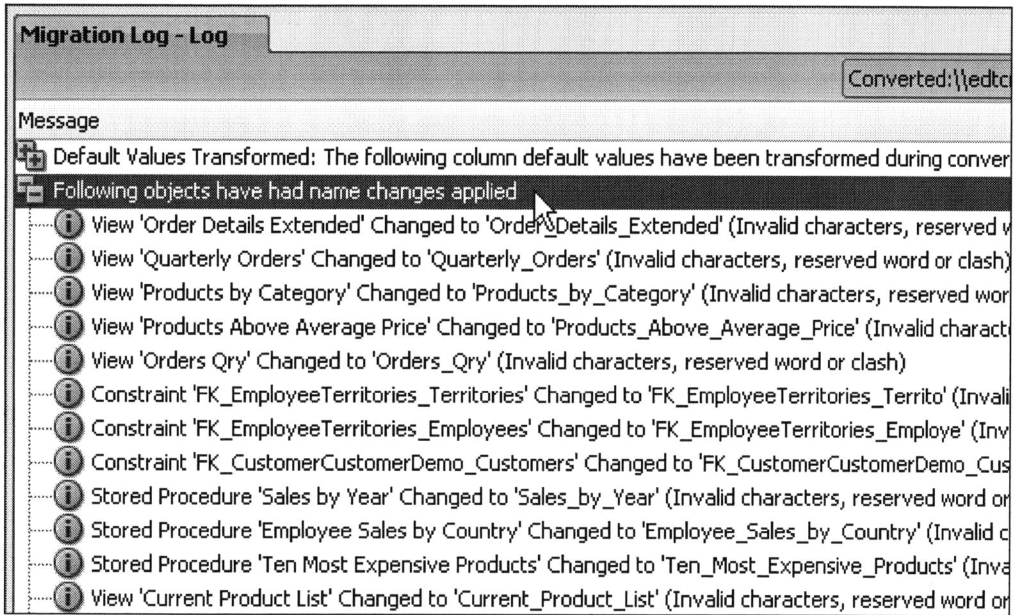

In the log displayed in the previous screenshot, we have expanded the second item which has gathered together a collection of changes with a similar theme. Here, the names of the converted objects have been modified. It might be due to duplicate names that would result from names being shortened during the conversion to comply with Oracle naming standards, or there may be other characters, which are not a match to Oracle naming standards. In these cases, the name changes are for information purposes, and no error exists. You may still want to adjust some of the names to comply with your company or project standards.

This is a good opportunity to review the changed names, and to make additional modifications to the objects, before the DDL scripts are prepared.

In the Sybase example that follows, there are the same name change warnings as we've just described. In addition to these, in this example, we have illustrated some errors that have been highlighted in the translated code:

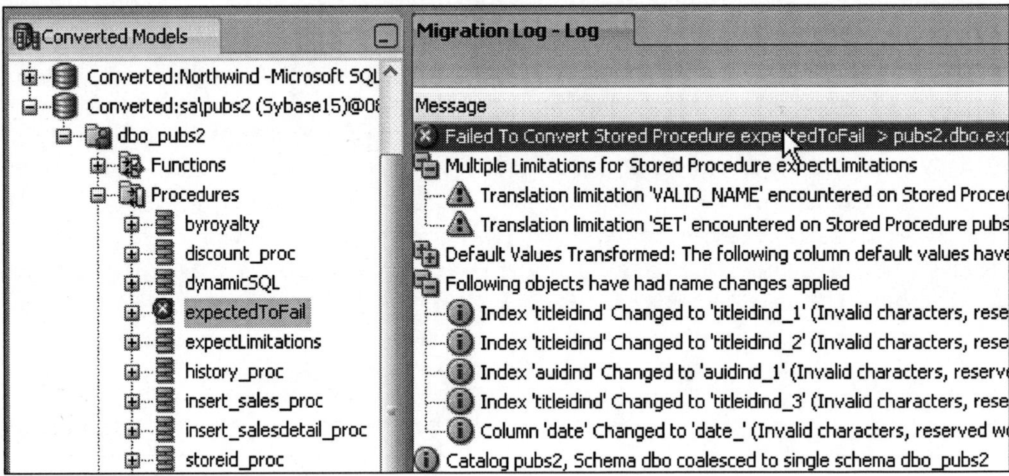

Where errors or failures are listed in the log, double-click on the error. The converted model expands to link you to the object in the model where the error was found.

If you now double-click on the object in the **Converted Models** tree, the object definition opens up for editing.

At this point, you can review the issues and make any changes you need. If you're working with converted PL/SQL code, you can make changes but can't, at this point, compile them as they're not associated with any schema. However, there are changes that can be made to the code before you generate the scripts. Using the log window to identify the problem code, select and copy the code, and then paste it into the **Translation Scratch Editor**, which you can invoke from the main **Migration** menu (this is described in the next section). The more changes you make at this stage, the better it will be for the next phase. Once the DDL scripts have run, you'll be able to review the code and compile it against your Oracle schema. However, you'll be able to change the values where naming conventions are not suitable for Oracle, and make these changes before the DDL scripts are created.

Translating procedural code

While all of the objects are migrated from the source to the target database, the procedural languages between the databases differ. Therefore, you do need to review the translated code and make adjustments as needed. In the interactive examples shown, we've illustrated that the migration log tracks the expected errors that you encounter. Once you have migrated the objects, you can use the **Translation Scratch Editor** to translate and work with individual pieces of code. SQL Developer supports the translation of the following sources to PL/SQL code:

- DB2 SQL
- Microsoft SQL Server T-SQL
- Microsoft Access SQL
- Sybase T-SQL

To translate a piece of code, invoke the **Translation Scratch Editor** from the main **Migration** menu. Paste the piece of code you want to translate into the left-hand side window. If there are errors that you can see at this point, you can edit the source code before translating it. Otherwise, select the translation type you want to execute from the drop-down menu, and then click on the **Generate** ( ) button:

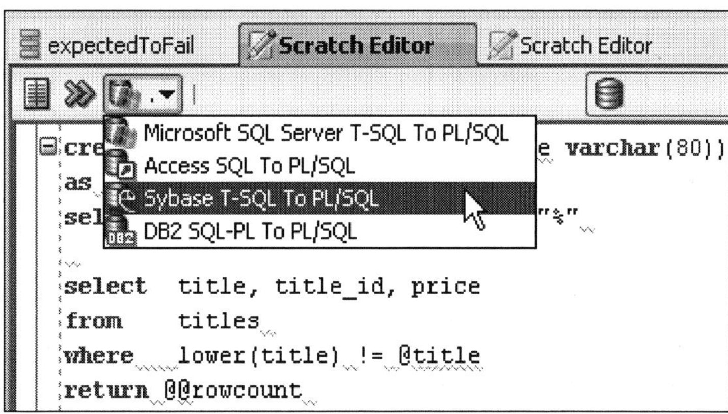

Review the translated PL/SQL code. During the translation, the editor adds comments to the code where there are issues that need to be addressed. If you want to match the T-SQL to the translated PL/SQL, the easiest way is to use the **Translation Diff Editor**:

The **Translation Diff Editor** provides a match of the various pieces of code and what they have become after being translated.

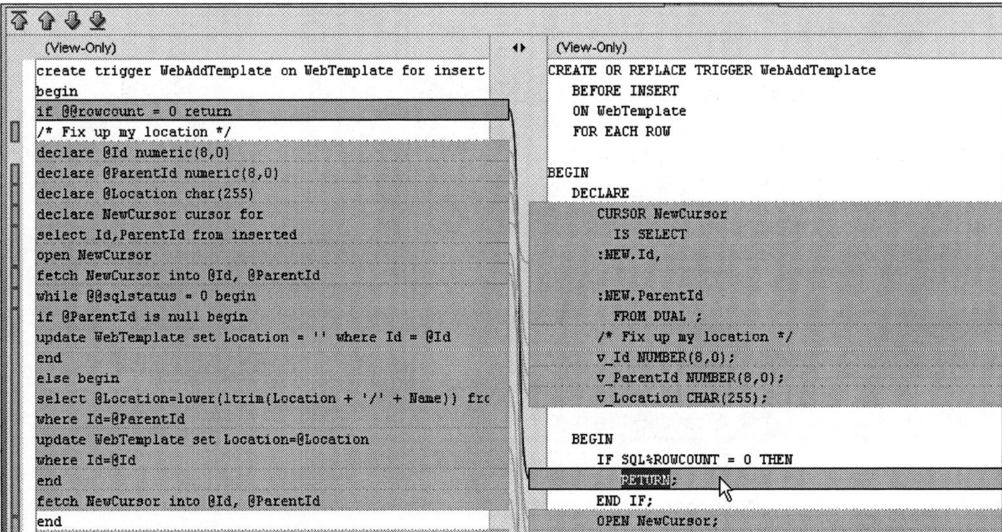

In the previous screenshot, a piece of PL/SQL code is selected and the matching code in the T-SQL is highlighted. In conjunction with the Translation Scratch Editor, you can now edit and compile the PL/SQL to complete your migration.

Generating the scripts

Once you have made the changes and updated the converted model, you are ready to generate the scripts that are executed against the target schema. You may have changed the name of the captured and converted models, but the DDL script creates the new target schema based on details the source schema. We recommend you review this name before you generate the DDL.

In the example that follows, the default name created for the Northwind sample model is shown. To change that name, select the main folder in the converted model and invoke the context menu. Select **Rename Schema** and change this to a more appropriate name for your target database:

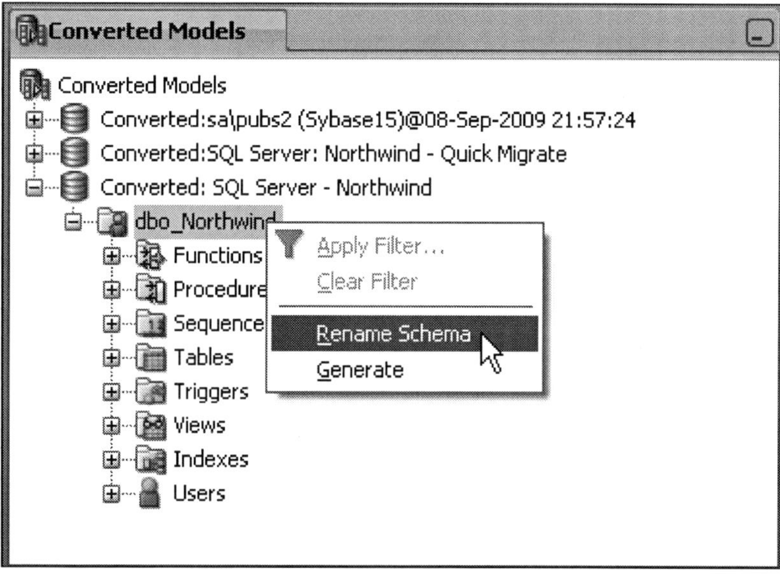

Once you're happy with all of the changes you have made, select **Generate** from the context menu. Close the dialog to reveal the full script. In the example that follows, we have highlighted the **Create User** statement. This is the schema name that you may have changed:

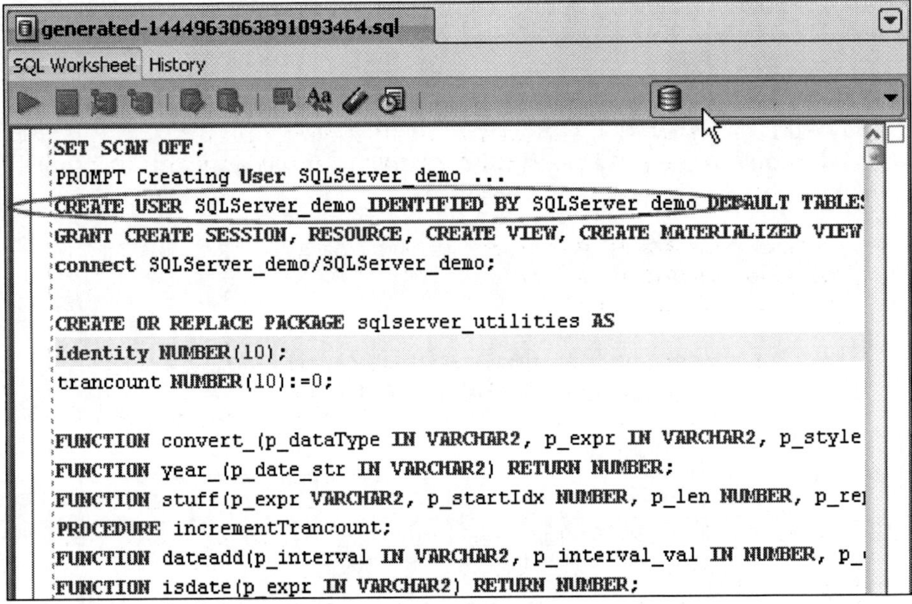

Executing the script

You are now ready to execute the script. Using the drop-down list on the right-hand side (also highlighted in the following screenshot), select a privileged user to execute the script. This user needs to be able to create a user and grant the privileges displayed at the start of the script. Once the new schema has been created, the script switches to the new user and the remaining items are created in the new schema.

In the following screenshot, you can see the script and the output as a result of running it:

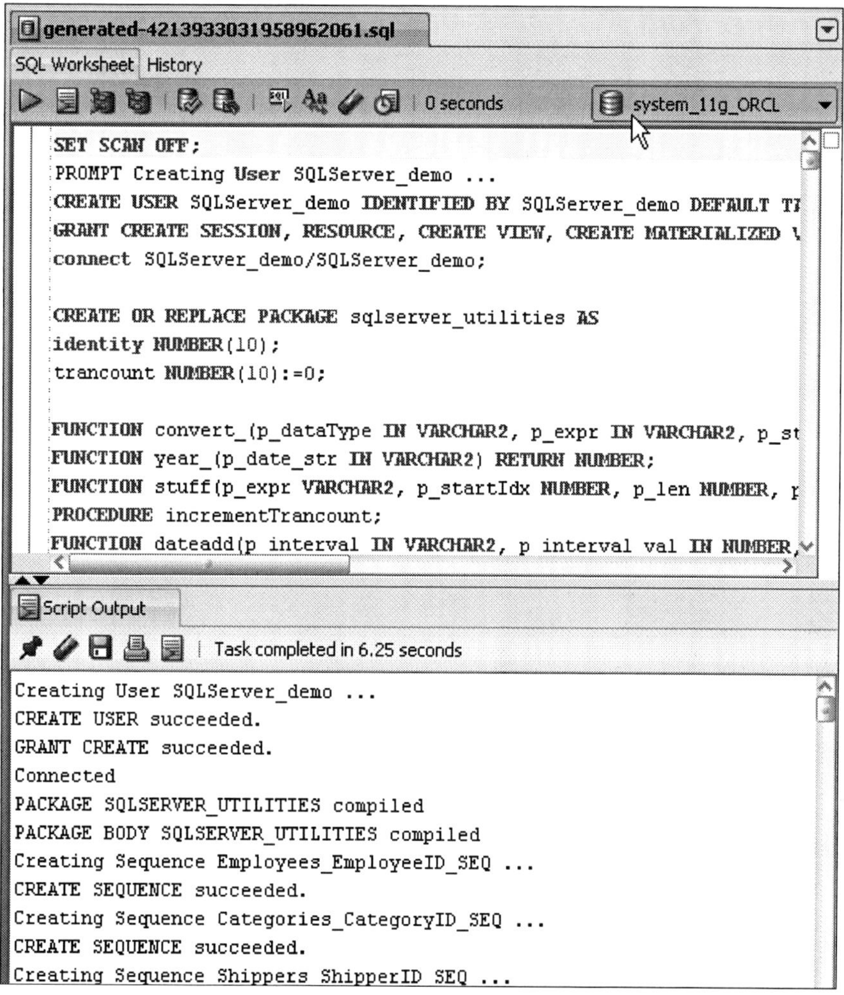

Renaming the schema

Take note of the schema name for the converted model. Passwords in Oracle Database 11g are case sensitive, if your script is run with the password in uppercase letters, that might catch you.

To review the new database object in your new schema, create a new Oracle database connection and browse the details. You may find there are PL/SQL compilation errors, but you should already be aware of most of these from the **Migration Log** details.

Populating the target tables with data

You are now ready to move the data to the target tables. Return to the **Converted Models** window, and using the correct converted model, select **Move Data** from the context menu:

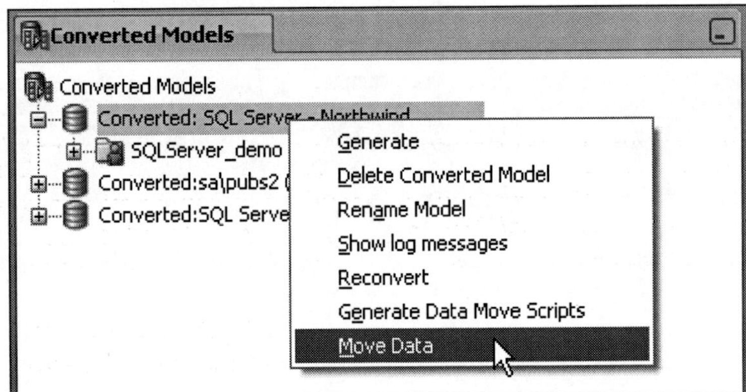

Before the data is moved, you need to select the source and target connections. Be sure to select the correct schemas, and then start the move.

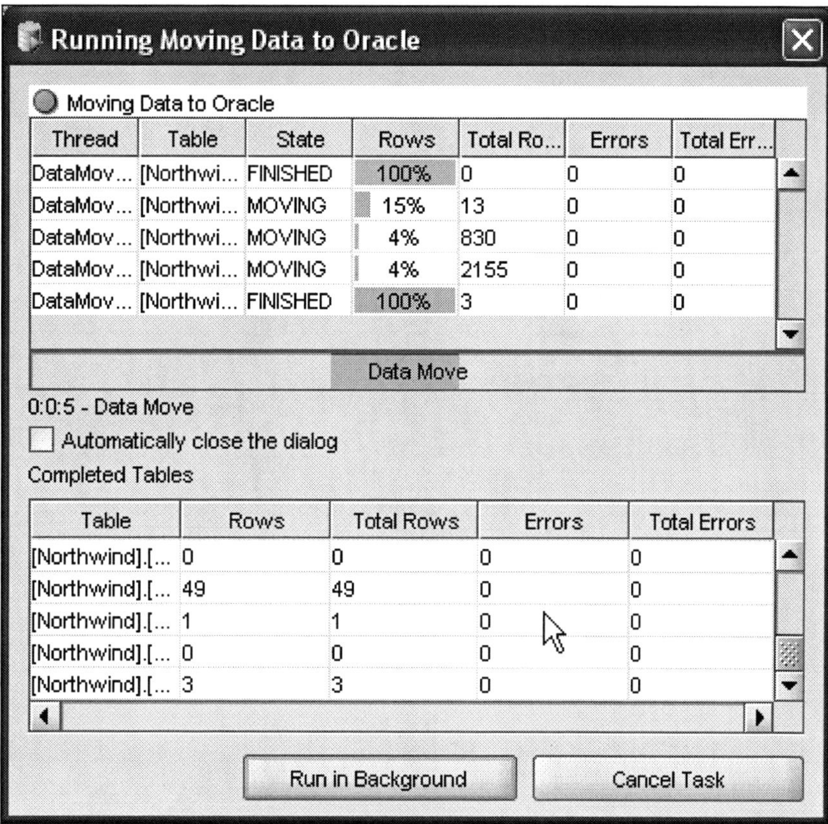

Once again, you can see in the previous screenshot that the data is moved to a number of tables simultaneously, improving the performance of the activity.

Complete the migration by reviewing the new target schema and the data moved.

Offline migrations

There is no real difference in the process between the online and offline capture, except the menu that you use to start the process:

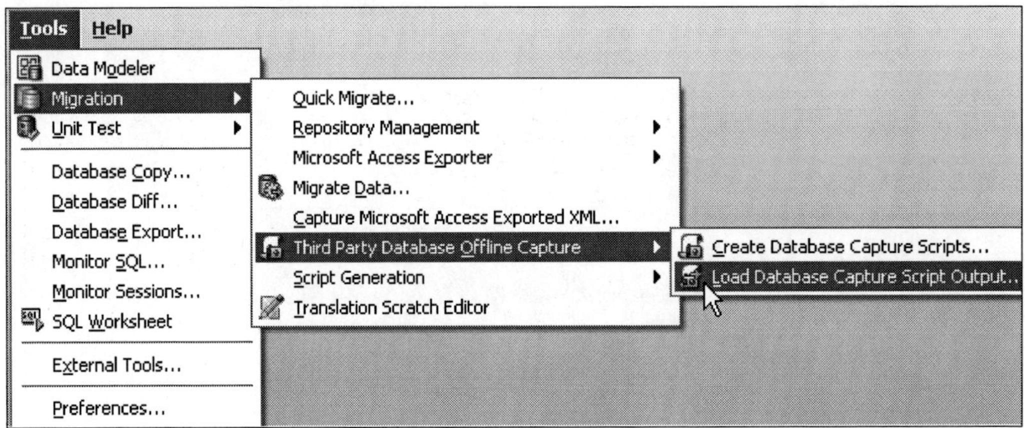

For SQL Server and Sybase you need to supply an `.ocp` file. Once you have completed the offline capture, you can move on to the conversion and script generation phases, as you did for the online interactive migration.

The remaining phases are the same until you reach the **Data Move**. At this stage, you have a choice. You can either connect to the source database to migrate the data, or you could use SQL Loader to do an offline data move.

Additional migration activities

The bulk of the full migration process is what happens before and after the actual physical migration occurs. The decision to change databases is based on many factors, and then the planning occurs. You need to determine how much time the move will take, as well as the housekeeping that might need to be done before you move. Knowing the number of objects to be moved and the complexity of the procedural code are just two examples. There are various reports and calculations that you should work through to determine the length and complexity of the move planned.

Once the migration is complete, you can run reports to determine the points of success and failure, so you can work on completing the exercise.

Migration reports

Once you have completed your migration, you can review the output of the various phases by reviewing reports that are run against the repository owner.

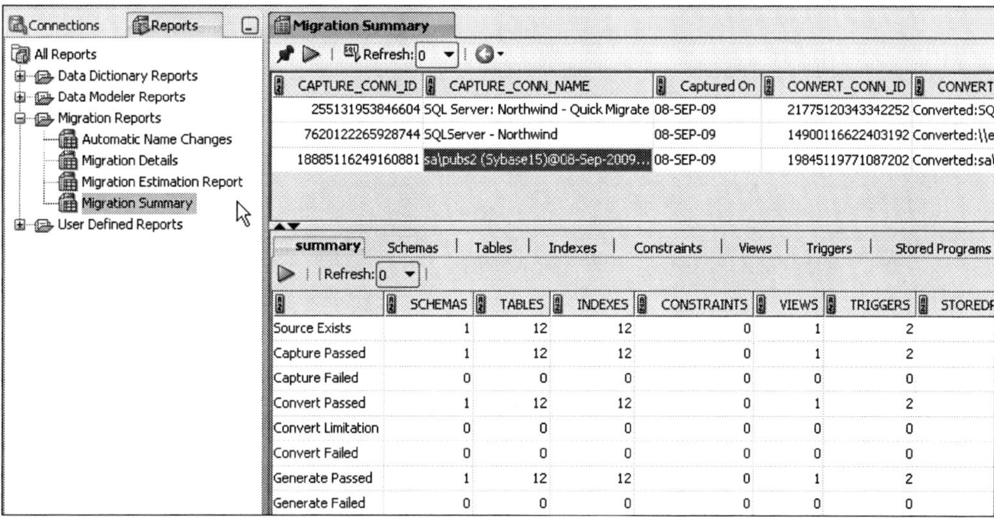

Migration reports are a useful addition to the migration process. These reports:

- Help you determine the size of the project by outlining the number of objects you have
- Show the number of objects that failed to migrate, and in doing so help determine what and how much needs to be handled manually
- Display the automatic changes made to names

SQL Developer provides three reports that detail the success and failure points of the migration. An example of one of these reports is displayed in the previous screenshot. The set of reports also includes a **Migration Estimation Report**.

Summary

In this chapter, we showed you how to prepare a migration repository, set up the database drivers, and create connections to non-Oracle databases. We discussed the two approaches that you can use when migrating database schemas to Oracle. For further information on preparing for a database migration, refer to the Migration Technology Center on the Oracle Technology Network.

Index

D

E

F

G

H

I

J

K

P

Q

R

S

X

About Packt Publishing

Packt, pronounced 'packed', published its first book "*Mastering phpMyAdmin for Effective MySQL Management*" in April 2004 and subsequently continued to specialize in publishing highly focused books on specific technologies and solutions.

Our books and publications share the experiences of your fellow IT professionals in adapting and customizing today's systems, applications, and frameworks. Our solution based books give you the knowledge and power to customize the software and technologies you're using to get the job done. Packt books are more specific and less general than the IT books you have seen in the past. Our unique business model allows us to bring you more focused information, giving you more of what you need to know, and less of what you don't.

Packt is a modern, yet unique publishing company, which focuses on producing quality, cutting-edge books for communities of developers, administrators, and newbies alike. For more information, please visit our website: `www.packtpub.com`.

Writing for Packt

We welcome all inquiries from people who are interested in authoring. Book proposals should be sent to `author@packtpub.com`. If your book idea is still at an early stage and you would like to discuss it first before writing a formal book proposal, contact us; one of our commissioning editors will get in touch with you.

We're not just looking for published authors; if you have strong technical skills but no writing experience, our experienced editors can help you develop a writing career, or simply get some additional reward for your expertise.

Processing XML documents with Oracle JDeveloper 11g

ISBN: 978-1-847196-66-8 Paperback: 384 pages

Creating, validating, and transforming XML documents with Oracle's IDE

1. Will get the reader developing applications for processing XML in JDeveloper 11g quickly and easily
2. Self-contained chapters provide thorough, comprehensive instructions on how to use JDeveloper to create, validate, parse, transform, and compare XML documents.
3. The only title to cover XML processing in Oracle JDeveloper 11g, this book includes information on the Oracle XDK 11g APIs.

Oracle Essbase 9 Implementation Guide

ISBN: 978-1-847196-86-6 Paperback: 444 pages

Develop high-performance multidimensional analytic OLAP solutions with Oracle Essbase

1. Build multidimensional Essbase database cubes and develop analytical Essbase applications
2. Step-by-step instructions with expert tips from installation to implementation
3. Can be used to learn any version of Essbase starting from 4.x to 11.x
4. For beginners as well as experienced professionals; no Essbase experience required

Please check **www.PacktPub.com** for information on our titles

Made in the USA
Lexington, KY
09 March 2010